BIRDER'S CONSERVATION HANDBOOK

BIRDER'S CONSERVATION HANDBOOK

100 North American Birds at Risk

—ᴼᴼᴼ—

JEFFREY V. WELLS

PRINCETON UNIVERSITY PRESS

Princeton and Oxford

Copyright © 2007 by Princeton University Press
Published by Princeton University Press, 41 William Street, Princeton, New Jersey 08540
In the United Kingdom: Princeton University Press, 3 Market Place, Woodstock, Oxfordshire OX20 1SY

Library of Congress Cataloging-in-Publication Data

Wells, Jeffrey V. (Jeffrey Vance), 1964–
Birder's conservation handbook : 100 North American birds at risk / Jeffrey V. Wells.
p.   cm.
Includes bibliographical references and index.
ISBN 978-0-691-12322-6 (cloth : alk. paper)
ISBN 978-0-691-12323-3 (pbk. : alk. paper)
1. Birds—Conservation—North America.   2. Rare birds—North America.
I. Title.
QL676.57.N7W45 2007
598.168097—dc22   2007017248

British Library Cataloging-in-Publication Data is available

This book has been composed in Goudy text and Gill Sans for display

Printed on acid-free paper. ∞

pup.princeton.edu

Printed in the United States of America

1   3   5   7   9   10   8   6   4   2

Princeton University Press is committed to preserving ancient forests and natural resources. We elected to print *Birder's Conservation
Handbook* on 30% post consumer recycled paper, processed chlorine
free. As a result, for this printing, we have saved:

28 Trees (40' tall and 6-8" diameter)
11,804 Gallons of Wastewater
4,747 Kilowatt Hours of Electricity
1,301 Pounds of Solid Waste
2,556 Pounds of Greenhouse Gases

Princeton University Press made this paper choice because our
printer, Thomson-Shore, Inc., is a member of Green Press Initiative,
a nonprofit program dedicated to supporting authors, publishers, and
suppliers in their efforts to reduce their use of fiber obtained from
endangered forests.

For more information, visit www.greenpressinitiative.org

Research for the Book Was Made Possible through the
Generous Financial Support of

ELLSWORTH KELLY FOUNDATION

Boreal Songbird Initiative
Conserving the Boreal Forest for Our Songbirds
www.borealbirds.org
1904 Third Avenue, Suite 305
Seattle, WA 98101
Tel: (206) 956-9040

Canadian Boreal Initiative
Canada's Boreal is Ours—Share the Commitment
www.borealcanada.ca
249 McLeod Street
Ottawa, ON
Canada
K2P 1A1
Tel: (613) 230-4739

Commission for Environmental Cooperation
Three Countries Working Together to Protect Our Shared Environment
www.cec.org
393, rue St-Jacques Ouest
Bureau 200
Montréal, QC
Canada
H2Y 1N9
Tel: (514) 350-4300

Cornell Lab of Ornithology
Interpreting and conserving the earth's biological diversity through research,
education, and citizen science focused on birds
www.birds.cornell.edu
159 Sapsucker Woods Road
Ithaca, NY 14850
Tel: (800) 843-BIRD

Defenders of Wildlife
*Dedicated to the protection of all native wild animals
and plants in their natural communities*
www.defenders.org
1130 17th Street NW
Washington, DC 20036
Tel: (800) 385-9712

The Nature Conservancy
Saving the Last Great Places on Earth
www.nature.org
4245 North Fairfax Drive, Suite 100
Arlington, VA 22203
Tel: (703) 841-5300

U.S. Fish and Wildlife Service
Conserving the Nature of America
www.fws.gov
1849 C Street, NW
Washington, DC 20240
Tel: (800) 344-WILD

U.S. Bureau of Land Management
www.blm.gov
Office of Public Affairs
1849 C Street NW, Room 406-LS
Washington, DC 20240
Tel: (202) 452-5125

U.S. Environmental Protection Agency
35 Years of Protecting Human Health and the Environment
www.epa.gov
Ariel Rios Building
1200 Pennsylvania Avenue NW
Washington, DC 20460
Tel: (202) 272-0167

Contents

Foreword

Consider the tools all of us have at our fingertips these days to help us become more knowledgeable birders. Thousands of books, audio guides from every corner of the planet, plus a burgeoning number of websites, listservs, and chatrooms. At any level of skill or experience, we can find answers to any question about bird identification, bird biology, bird sounds, and birding locations. But until now, a conspicuous gap has existed in these resources: what about bird conservation?

North American birders have become increasingly concerned about the status of some of our most familiar species, and the time was ripe for an easy-to-use but definitive guide to the conservation status of our most vulnerable birds. My colleague and long-time birding compatriot Jeff Wells has filled the void with the creation of this book. Birders and biologists alike will find here a resource that highlights the most threatened bird species in North America, and outlines what we must do to secure their populations.

During the years that Jeff worked at the Cornell Lab of Ornithology I frequently stopped by his office to discuss conservation issues. He has long been "plugged in" to the latest status reports, and has made a successful career out of analyzing conservation priorities based on real data. His desk was always piled high with journals, bird biographies, journal articles, government reports, management guidelines, and books on threatened species, not to mention data tables of his own creation. Throughout his period as Director of Bird Conservation for National Audubon, and now as Senior Scientist for the Boreal Songbird Initiative, Wells has been engaged in detective work that always is as thorough and scholarly as his conversations are lively.

Now all his painstaking efforts (and even some of that lively conversation) are pulled together in one place. In *The Birder's Conservation Handbook* we find Wells' holistic look at how policies, conservation projects, and protection efforts—many of them designed to accomplish narrow initial purposes—are helping conserve whole ecosystems and even human health, as well as the birds. Take, for example, the efforts to curb acid rain originally designed to reduce impacts on aquatic life in lakes and ponds. Wells highlights how these are benefiting the Wood Thrush, a species in which today's low reproductive rates appear to be indirectly caused by acid rain. Likewise, policies that reduce reliance on fossil fuels responsible for global warming can have positive implications for species as diverse as Piping Plovers (affected by severe storms and tides), Bald Eagles (affected by mercury poison from coal-fired power plants), and Cerulean Warblers (affected by mountaintop removal for coal extraction).

It is important to acknowledge that besides being a first rate scholar, Jeff Wells also is an extraordinary birder. I saw and learned from his most impressive skills during our nine consecutive years together as "Sapsuckers" (the Cornell Lab's World Series of Birding team, which included two first-place finishes during that period). Watching him pick out the song of a Bay-breasted Warbler from a moving vehicle on a gravel road, amidst a dizzying spring chorus, was one of the most amazing feats I ever witnessed in birding, but to Jeff this was business as usual. Conversation in the long car rides back from Cape May, New Jersey, to Ithaca, New York often turned to the potential for the 40 to 60 million North American birders to help define and push bird conservation in the twenty-first century. Jeff was a key player in our creating eBird and the Great Backyard Bird Count, now among the largest continent-wide bird population surveys.

Engaging birders of all skill levels has always been one of Jeff's most far-reaching goals, and *The Birder's Conservation Handbook* was born out of his commitment to this mission. This book belongs on the shelf right next to your field guides, and you should use it the same way. Browse it over breakfast, consult it often as a reference, and dog-ear its key passages. Unlike some of the other conservation classics (Greenway's *Extinct and Vanishing Birds of the World*, Leopold's *A Sand County Almanac*, and Carson's *Silent Spring* come to mind), this book is purposely created to be portable. Not intended to sit under glass in the den, this book was made to end up with coffee stains on it just like your favorite bird guide.

This book gives everyone who cares about birds some real, practical information on how we can make a difference as individuals in keeping our common birds common and our rarest birds from disappearing. Ranging from the obvious (contribute to conservation organizations and land trusts) to the subtle (use energy-efficient light bulbs), Wells's tips serve as a "best-practices guide" for the birder-citizen. And, speaking of citizens, Wells encourages everyone to take seriously today's abundant opportunity to become a "citizen scientist." Participation in meaningful data-collection projects has never been easier (thanks to the Internet), and the information gathered through these projects will help scientists and conservation planners set priorities throughout the rest of this century.

Having a copy of this book on hand empowers you to understand birds and the myriad challenges they face. Following the tips contained here, you will know that you are making a difference in keeping all our birds for future generations of birders to appreciate.

John W. Fitzpatrick, PhD
Executive Director, Cornell Lab of Ornithology
Past-President, American Ornithologists' Union

Acknowledgments

It would have been impossible for me to complete the research for the book without the financial support of the project sponsors: Ellsworth Kelly Foundation, Boreal Songbird Initiative, Canadian Boreal Initiative, Commission for Environmental Cooperation, Cornell Lab of Ornithology, Defenders of Wildlife, The Nature Conservancy, U.S. Fish and Wildlife Service, U.S. Environmental Protection Agency, and the U.S. Bureau of Land Management. I especially wish to thank the Ellsworth Kelly Foundation and its director, Jack Shear, for the foundation's large lead gift that provided the core financial support that moved the project from dream to reality. The Commission for Environmental Cooperation, as one of the first agencies to commit to the project, paved the way for further agency support. I especially wish to thank Jürgen Hoth for his leadership in his former role there. Marilyn Heiman of the Boreal Songbird Initiative became one of the most enthusiastic supporters and encouragers of the book and made many key connections that brought other organizations on board. She also was very understanding as I toiled to finish the final stages of the book while working as the senior scientist for the Boreal Songbird Initiative. Many others played key roles in supporting the book including Claire Cassell, Gaby Chavarria, Kevin Killcullen, Eric Lawton, Terry Ritchey, Valerie Dorian, John Meagher, and Kathleen Kutschenreuter. Great assistance in navigating what sometimes seemed like endless mazes of paperwork and forms was ably and cheerfully provided by a number of people, including especially Gwen Ames, Molly Brewton, Cindy Marquis, and Carol Pyhtila at Cornell, Jill Silvey and Melinda Ritacco at the Bureau of Land Management, Randy Rutan at the Fish and Wildlife Service, and Karen Schmidt at the Commission for Environmental Cooperation.

I was fortunate to be able to enlist the help of two excellent young biologists in the time-consuming task of compiling information for various parts of the book. Matt Medler worked tirelessly to provide supporting information for many of the species accounts and Julie Hart compiled the appendices and Breeding Bird Survey information in the latter stages of the project.

The book greatly benefited from the comments of many reviewers. I especially need to single out the many U.S. Fish and Wildlife Service (USFWS) biologists and other employees who gave freely of their time and expertise to provide comments, edits, and sometimes new information, for most of the 100 species accounts within the book. Soliciting and organizing comments from the many people with expertise within the various branches of the USFWS was possible only through the gracious goodwill and patience of stellar USFWS staff, especially Claire Cassell, Kevin Killcullen, Susan Jewell, and Cyndi Perry.

To those of you who provided comments, let me extend my heartfelt gratitude for your help. While in the end, any errors or omissions are my own responsibility, I hope I have incorporated the suggestions and improvements you each provided in a manner that is responsible to the facts and to conservation. People who reviewed earlier drafts of one or more chapters or species accounts and/or provided background information included Kelly Acton, George Allen, Greg Balogh, Mike Bender, Gregory Breese, Karem Boyla, Stuart Butchart, Eric Carey, Matt Carlson, Claire Cassel, Gaby Chavarria, Ralph Costa, Ian Davidson, Pat Deibert, James Dubovsky, Chris Elphick, Suzanne Fellows, John Fitzpatrick, Jessie Grantham, Hector Gomez de Silva, Michael Green, Nancy Green, Kevin Hannah, David Haskell, David Haukos, Kevin Kardynal, Bradford Keitt, Marilyn Heiman, Keith Hobson, Jürgen Hoth, Bill Howe, Chuck Hunter, Alan Hutchinson, Susan Jewell, Stephanie Jones, Jim Kelly, Patty Kelly, Dave Krueper, Richard Lanctot, Steve Matsuoka, Matt Medler, David Mehlman, Timothy Merritt, Lane Nothman, Stefanie Scheetz, John Stanton, Bernie Tershy, David Rabon, Gregory Risdahl, Bruce Robertson, Ken Rosenberg, Bob Russell, Paul Salaman, Sue Thomas, Jim Thrailkill, John Trapp, Craig Watson, David Wega, Allison Wells, Tony White, Cathy Wilkinson, Shaye Wolf, Sarah Wren, and Dawn Zattau.

I am especially pleased and proud of the maps in this book. For that I must give grateful kudos to Dimitri Karetnikov and Shane Kelley of Princeton University Press for turning my rough, hand-drawn creations into crisp, clear representations of the full breeding and wintering ranges of the birds covered in the book.

Thanks to artists George Dremeaux, Dan

Lane, Shawneen Finnegan, John Fitzpatrick, Michael O'Brien, John Sill, Sophie Webb, Mimi Hoppe Wolf, and Louise Zemaitis. All shared their talents to provide exceptional illustrations for the species accounts in the book and all dealt graciously with my timelines and comments. I especially wish to thank Louise Zemaitis of Swallowtail Studios who unselfishly served as a sort of bird artist promoter by providing me with names and contact information for many artists.

The bulk of the first draft of the book was created in a wonderful office overlooking Sapsucker Woods at the Cornell Lab of Ornithology. I often kept my door closed, not because I loathed the company of my colleagues but rather because I found them to be such enjoyable and knowledgeable people that the temptation to engage in extended conversation was omnipresent. Still, I found respite from my writing with many colleagues at my morning tea and at lunch. Ken Rosenberg and Eduardo Iñigo-Elias, who inhabited adjoining offices from which I could often hear phone calls and conversations over the dividers, were always ready to let me vent frustrations and bounce ideas off. Ken was always ready to lend a book, fill me in on the latest Partners in Flight plans, or discuss the identity of a high-flying hawk that we could see from the window. More than once, Eduardo opened up his apparently limitless Rolodex of contacts to help me track down a person or some kind of information. My teammates on Cornell's World Series of Birding team, Ken, John Fitzpatrick, Steve Kelling, and Kevin McGowan, were among those at the Lab who provided willing ears to discuss various ideas and issues.

The last stages of the book were completed after a move from Ithaca to Maine. I was fortunate to find a wonderful office overlooking the Kennebec River within weeks of arrival in Maine thanks to Will Sugg of the Environmental Policy Institute who opened his office suite to me. The relatively quick transition meant the book project was only minimally delayed. Will was always ready to hear the latest news about bird conservation, family, or the family car and introduced me to a who's-who of people working on Maine environmental issues.

I want to thank Robert Kirk, my editor at Princeton University Press, for his commitment to the conceptual idea from the start, his straightforwardness and professionalism throughout, and most importantly for his good humor.

For lighting the spark and fanning the flame of interest in the birds and the natural world that has enriched my life beyond belief, I thank Nanny, Mom and Dad, and Inez.

Finally let me thank my family, Allison and Evan. My wife, Allison, supported me in the beginning when I took a leap of faith to devote myself full time to this book project for nearly two years, she buoyed me with her encouragement and spurred me on in the intervening years, and she focused her discerning editorial eye on what sometimes must have seemed like endless drafts. My son, Evan, who was about eight months old when I started the book, was in many ways the inspiration for its creation. Again and again as he experiences the world he lets me see why conservation is so important.

Scope and Purpose

In the fall of 2002, as National Bird Conservation Director for the National Audubon Society, I developed a website providing information about the 201 North American bird species of highest conservation concern that made up the Audubon WatchList. While gathering the data for that site, I found myself time and again wanting to reach to my bookshelf for the quick-and-easy book that pulled together the salient facts about a species' status, distribution, and population changes. That book did not yet exist, I knew, from my years as a conservation professional. Creating the Audubon WatchList website highlighted to me the need for such a reference—a book not only to provide the facts about birds of conservation concern but to do so in such a way as to inspire people to action.

I know first hand that cries of alarm too often fall on deaf ears; despite best intentions, people can hear only so much bad news before they become desensitized to it or so overwhelmed that they feel inadequate to do anything to help. I wanted to provide a book that presents the facts but that also offers hope, encouragement, and inspiration for those who want to take action to protect our birds and our environment.

It may come as a surprise to hear that North America is in the midst of a renaissance in bird conservation. The number of initiatives focused on various aspects of bird conservation has blossomed at an unprecedented rate in the last decade to include coalitions focused on conservation of songbirds, shorebirds, and waterbirds, in addition to the more traditional waterfowl and upland game bird conservation groups. All of this activity, and the parallel birth of other types of conservation work across the hemisphere, is exciting and gives me hope that my son and future generations will indeed be able to see for themselves the beauty and ecological significance of what today are some of the most critically endangered species. This is news that I wanted to share, especially since among the good work are countless examples of projects and actions initiated by ordinary people—people who are protecting birds and their habitats based on passion, not profession. Unfortunately, most of these wonderful examples are scattered across a dizzying array of documents and websites and often are placed in the context of some large environmental initiative that doesn't describe all of the species benefiting from the work.

I hope that by my highlighting these actions, you will be encouraged to get involved, perhaps with one of the projects described in this book or perhaps by starting a new project. Above all, remember that anyone can make a difference for bird conservation. It is my hope that among the readers of this book will be some of the great conservationists of the future, whose work will lower the number of species that need to be included in the next edition.

WHAT ARE NORTH AMERICA'S BIRDS OF HIGHEST CONSERVATION CONCERN?

Sadly, including every species of conservation concern in a handbook intended for a broad audience is not feasible—there are just too many North American birds that fit into that category. To keep the book and what I hope is a strong and urgent conservation message from becoming overwhelming, I limited the number of species to 100—a manageable, memorable number. I hope that doing so has resulted in a book that is easy to use by anyone interested in learning about the major issues causing bird population declines and what's being done to reverse those trends.

Now, why these 100 species? For the last decade I have been engaged with colleagues in research to help develop lists of bird species that should be given highest priority for conservation. There are a number of different ways in which lists can be and have been developed. There's the IUCN (International Union for the Conservation of Nature) Red List, the USFWS (U.S. Fish and Wildlife Service) Birds of Conservation Concern list, the USFWS endangered and threatened species list, the Partners in Flight WatchList, the Audubon Watchlist, the American Bird Conservancy Greenlist, the North American Waterbird Conservation Plan list, and the U.S. Shorebird Conservation Plan list. Then there are countless state and provincial wildlife agency lists that all spotlight bird species of conservation concern. These are all important lists, each based on factors that are most relevant to the organization's reason for developing the list—which is to say, each list reflects the conservation mission and priorities of the entity creating the list. As a result, collectively, more than 500 bird species occur on one or more of these lists!

Although the total number combined is high, my colleagues and I have found in our research that virtually all of the lists agree on the species that are of greatest conservation concern. Many are painfully obvious because their population sizes have reached critical lows—birds like California Condor, Whooping Crane, and Kirtland's Warbler. Some are more obvious to the professional ornithologist but less so to the lay birder—species like Buff-breasted Sandpiper, Bicknell's Thrush, and Saltmarsh Sharp-tailed Sparrow, most biologists know, are important to include because they have limited ranges and small populations. There are about 80 species in these more obvious categories. Choosing the remaining 20 to include was more difficult.

While writing this book, I was lobbied by many groups and individuals to include species they considered a priority in their own work. There are several criteria I used to determine the remaining species to include. First, I did not include a species if it had only a small portion of its total global range within the U.S. and Canada and was secure in the remainder of its range, unless there was very clear evidence that the population in North America was distinct enough that it might eventually be elevated to species status. Second, I did not include species for which the information on population declines came from only a portion of the range, was unclear, or was contradictory. A final criterion I used was not to include species with a decline of less than 50% over the last 50 years unless they also had a relatively small population size, had a small total range, or were considered to have significant threats.

In the end, the final 20 are all species of high priority that appear on one or more existing lists and most are showing steep population declines. Weight was given such that these remaining species represented a range of ecosystems, conservation issues, geographic areas, and bird families. While I have limited the number of species included in this book to 100, I have included in Appendix I a table showing which species occur on which of the various major lists. I invite you to delve more deeply into the background of each of these lists and to read some of the academic papers published on the science of conservation priority-setting.

SPECIES ACCOUNTS

Each species account provides information about the species, including status and distribution, ecology, threats, and conservation action and needs. Each species is illustrated, and there is a map for each species showing its entire range (not ending arbitrarily at the Mexican border, as is typical of field guides). But the bulk of each account is composed of text relating directly to the species' conservation.

Status and Distribution

Information on the limits of the species' distribution, including breeding and wintering ranges, is provided to complement a map illustrating the same. Whenever possible, specific protected areas or other locations known or thought to be important to the species are mentioned, along with the number of individuals of the species at the site, based on the most recent surveys, if available. In many cases, where such information was lacking or very limited, locations mentioned are those where the species is known to have been recorded but the overall importance of the site to the species may be uncertain. In some other cases (especially for species on their wintering ranges in the Caribbean and South or Central America), locations mentioned are where the species should occur based on known distribution and habitat, and are described as such in the species account. This section concludes with a summary of the most recent available trend information and population estimates.

Ecology

This section provides a brief summary of habitat use, ecology, and life history information about the species. It is not meant to be exhaustive but to provide a basic overview that sometimes also helps explain why the species may be vulnerable.

Threats

I have described threats considered of greatest significance or potential significance and quantified the significance of threats whenever possible. For example, I provide estimates of the amount of specific habitat already lost and/or predicted to be lost over a particular time period for some species.

Threats that are likely to affect only a small portion of the range or that have a comparatively small impact on a species total population are not discussed.

Conservation Action

This section provides a synthesis of some of the activities that I believe are particularly important or novel and that have benefited the species. Many of the conservation actions I describe are not focused specifically on the bird species that are benefiting from the activity but instead were originally developed to benefit other species, resources, or issues. In many cases, these benefits may be easily and inexpensively broadened and enhanced if the particular needs of priority species are considered early in the process. This allows projects to develop a wider base of public support because there are clearly articulated benefits to multiple resources. My account of conservation initiatives for each species is not meant to be exhaustive but to show important examples and unique models. I encourage readers to learn more by following up on the references and website links to projects mentioned.

Conservation Needs

This section provides a list of specific recommendations for conservation actions and activities that will help increase populations of the species, increase protections for the species, and increase knowledge about the species. These recommendations are synthesized from available resources but ultimately reflect my own interpretations and opinions.

References

To make the species accounts easy to read for those unfamiliar with standard scientific writing, I have departed slightly from tradition in how I present references to the source materials, from which the facts are drawn. I place a numbered series in superscript at the end of each section that refers to the numbered citations within this section. Rather than list them alphabetically, the citations appear in the order that the facts are presented within each section. I recognize that scientists reading this will find this system awkward and less precise but I feel that it is worth the

trade-off to make the material more easily read by the broadest audience.

RESEARCH, WRITING, REFERENCES, AND REVIEW

The research, writing, and editing of the book was largely completed over a period of 35 months, from April 2003 until March 2006. I tried hard to ensure that I included the most up-to-date information available in published sources, in reports, and on websites from credible organizations and government agencies. Species accounts were reviewed by a multitude of experts who often had access to recent but unpublished survey data.

When checking information on distribution, ecology, and life history, I always started with *The Birds of North America* (BNA), the most up-to-date resource for such data. Completed between 1992 and 2002, BNA is a monumental, 28-volume series that provides an immensity of facts about 720 North American breeding bird species. Each account was written by one or more experts in some aspect of the species' biology. The BNA accounts are excellent, but many, depending on the author's interest and expertise, lack conservation-related information. Species accounts also typically have little relevant information about important threats and conservation activities benefiting the species.

Other sources important to research for this book included BirdLife International's *Threatened Birds of the World*, *American Bird Conservancy Guide to the 500 Most Important Bird Areas in the United States*, *Terrestrial Ecoregions of North America*, *Precious Heritage: The Status of Biodiversity in the United States*, *Áreas de Importancia Para La Conservación de las Aves en México*, Wetland International's *Waterbird Population Estimates*, *Neotropical Birds: Ecology and Conservation*, and *Biogeographical Profiles of Shorebird Migration in Midcontinental North America*. I also made frequent use of Audubon's Important Bird Area (IBA) information from published Important Bird Area books (including those from California, New York, Panama, and Washington) as well as unpublished IBA manuscripts (Florida) and web-accessible IBA databases (most available via Audubon's website at www.audubon.org).

Species accounts were reviewed by more than 50 experts from many institutions. A full list of reviewers appears in the acknowledgments. Without the expertise of my fellow professionals, the book simply would not be complete. I especially wish to thank the dozens of biologists from the U.S. Fish and Wildlife Service who devoted considerable time in reviewing the species accounts and gave freely of their expertise and their data in order to make the accounts as up-to-date as possible. They have done a great service to users of this book. In the end, of course, all errors or omissions are mine, and all views expressed herein are mine and do not reflect the position of any agency, institution, or other individual.

I hope that you find this book useful and the conservation examples inspiring and a source of hope for you and your family. Good birding to you!

Birds as Indicators

Many people think of the concept of using birds as environmental indicators as a new idea. But the most ancient human cultures were the first to use birds and other wildlife to track changes in their world. Our ancestors had to be exceptionally observant of nature to survive. The signals that they read from birds gave them clues about changes in food availability and seasonality. A drop in numbers of grouse in one area might have indicated to them that hunting pressure had become too great or that the habitat had grown too thick. An intentionally set fire might be in order. A concentration of Ospreys and Bald Eagles on the river in June would be cause for celebration. It meant that the migratory fish had returned to spawn and, like the birds, human families would soon also be feasting. The early arrival of fall migrant ducks and geese would warn that cold weather was on its way and that winter preparations should begin.

All of us today use birds as indicators in our own lives in subtle ways that we might not even recognize. Millions of Americans eagerly await the spring return of robins, swallows, or waterfowl that tells us that warmer weather is on the way. In the Northwest Territories of Canada, the return of gulls in the spring is a sign of open water somewhere in the area. And after enduring almost constant darkness and 30-below (°F) temperatures, any sign of spring there is joyfully received. Backyard bird enthusiasts are quick to share with their bird-feeding friends the news that they have seen fewer or more of their favorite birds. And often they wonder if the lack of some particular bird is related to the new construction across the street, the weather, or something else. In recent years, more and more people in northern regions of the U.S. report seeing larger numbers of American Robins in the winter. "Is it a sign of the impact of global warming?" they often ask. For my father-in-law, it wasn't summer until he was again awakened every morning by the harsh mewing of a Gray Catbird outside his window. Since the new house went in next door, he tells me that he doesn't hear it anymore, and he's pretty sure he knows why.

Today, in North America and elsewhere in the world, we don't think of the signals that birds are sending as vital to our survival in the same way that they were to our ancestors. But the truth is, they may be. Birds continue to serve as indicators for many environmental problems that affect us and our families. In recent history, birds provided the first or most visible indication of wider environmental problems in case after case.

- Unsustainability of unregulated commercial hunting was first demonstrated by the decline and eventual extinction of Passenger Pigeon, Great Auk, and Eskimo Curlew and later by declines in Wild Turkeys, American Golden-Plovers, Atlantic Puffins, Herring Gulls, Common Terns, Snowy Egrets, Great Egrets, and many other species.

- Pesticide contamination (especially DDT) impacts were shown by declines in Ospreys, Peregrine Falcons, Brown Pelicans, and Bald Eagles and, more recently, die-offs of waterfowl, shorebirds, and waders from agricultural runoff.

- Declines in water quality were signaled by mercury contamination in loons and scaup and, in Europe, declines in dippers and wagtails.

- Declines in air quality were signaled by acid rain effects on thrushes in Europe and potential impacts on Wood Thrushes in northeastern North America as well as from mercury contamination in Common Mergansers, Common Loons, Bald Eagles, and Bicknell's Thrushes.

- Loss of special or unique habitats was shown by major declines in Marbled Murrelets, California Gnatcatchers, Ivory-billed Woodpeckers, and many others. Some have conjectured that this is probably what caused the extinction of Bachman's Warbler as it may have been a specialist in cane habitats of the southeastern U.S.

- The ecological impact of widespread predator poisoning and persecution was demonstrated in the mortality of California Condors, and declines in Ferruginous Hawk and Mountain Plover (reliant on prairie dog towns). In much of eastern North America the total extirpation of top mammalian predators has contributed to massive deer populations that browse forests so heavily that there is no understory habitat for songbirds.

- The impacts of poor and unsustainable forestry practices certainly were signaled by the near extinction of the Ivory-billed Woodpecker and by declines of the Red-cockaded Woodpecker, Brown-headed Nuthatch, Spotted Owl, and others.

- An understanding of the many ways in which habitat fragmentation can impact wildlife was demonstrated in forest songbirds from studies in eastern North America. Much of this work was stimulated by the discovery that certain birds, often long-distance migrants, had disappeared from isolated woodlots in the mid-Atlantic states of the U.S.

- Declines in Piping Plovers, Least Terns, and other coastal beach and inland sand-bar nesters were a clear signal that beaches, dunes, and other coastal ecosystems were being heavily impacted by home development, pollution, and recreational overuse and that inland river systems were damaged as a result of the building of dams and flood-control projects.

- The impact on ecosystems from the loss of habitat from agriculture was demonstrated by the extinction of the Heath Hen, the near extinction of Attwater's Prairie-Chicken and Whooping Crane, and, more recently, massive declines in grassland and shrub-land birds, including Henslow's Sparrow, Lesser Prairie-Chicken, Greater Prairie-Chicken, Gunnison Sage-Grouse, Greater Sage-Grouse, and Northern Bobwhite, as well as declines in prairie nesting waterfowl like the Northern Pintail.

- Changes in marine ecosystems as a result of fishing practices that are unsustainable and/or that cause high mortality of incidentally captured wildlife species have been signaled by birds in locations around the world. Here in North America, examples include the decline in Red Knots from overharvest of horseshoe crabs in Delaware Bay, declines in Elegant Terns and Brown Pelicans in southern California attributable to overfishing of anchovy, and declines in various albatross species when they are incidentally hooked and drowned in the practice of long-line fisheries.

- The effects of oil spills and oil pollution have been demonstrated most vividly in alcids, penguins, and other waterbirds. For example, even nine years after the Exxon Valdez oil spill in Prince William Sound, Alaska, populations of cormorants, Pigeon Guillemots, and certain duck species had not fully recovered because populations of the fish that they forage on had not recovered.

- Birds have proved to be excellent indicators of the spread of new diseases introduced through human-mediated enterprises, including West Nile virus and the House Finch eye disease.

- The varied and often unexpected effects of global warming have been shown by studies of birds to include changes in timing of migration and egg laying, sudden drops in prey populations, decoupling of life-history events among component members of ecological communities, and others.

Because birds are such effective bellwethers, some nations have officially adopted the idea of using them as indicators. In Great Britain, for example, the government publishes an annual summary of 15 "headline" indicators of quality of life, one of which is based on population trends of breeding birds. A number of nonprofit bird conservation organizations also regularly publish "state of the birds" reports. In the U.S., Audubon published such a report in 2004.

One of the primary reasons that birds are excellent species to use to monitor changes in our environment is that they are the most well-known and easily studied group of organisms on earth. They are conspicuous, often brightly colored and aesthetically appealing to the human eye, with loud songs and other vocalizations, and they live everywhere that people live. Countless books have been published on them, covering everything from identification to art. We may not always know what they are telling us, but the clues birds provide can give scientists a starting point to understanding the complex ecological webs that are impacted by our activities.

One of the finest opportunities available for any of us to contribute to conservation is by participating in monitoring birds through organized surveys—a concept embodied by the term "citizen science." There are now dozens, perhaps even hundreds, of opportunities for everyone from the beginning birder to the expert to volunteer to count birds and submit the counts for use in monitoring bird populations and studying various aspects of their biology. Some citizen science programs are national or international in scope—projects like the Christmas Bird Count, Breeding Bird Survey, Great Backyard Bird Count, Project Feederwatch, International Shorebird Survey, eBird, Bird Studies Canada's Important Bird Areas online monitoring program, North American Birds, Marshbird Monitoring Program, and Hawk Migration Association hawk counts. Others are regional or local—projects like the various state or provincial loon counts and owl surveys, National Wildlife Refuge surveys, state and provincial checklist programs like those ongoing in the Northwest Territories, Quebec, Wisconsin, and Montana, and state and provincial breeding bird atlases, to name just a few.

I encourage anyone reading this book, whether amateur or professional, casually interested or avid birder, to make an effort to participate in at least one citizen science project. It is only by having thousands of people collectively reporting their observations from across North America that we will be able to both monitor the changes in bird populations and more fully grasp the intricacies of their ecology. Birds are great indicators if we will only listen to what they are telling us. And by becoming a citizen scientist you not only help the birds but learn more about them yourself. So, if you are not yet a citizen scientist then you should get involved. If you are, get someone else involved. Below I've included contact information for a few of the larger citizen science projects but there are literally hundreds of projects from the local to international scales. Contact your local environmental organizations or do an Internet search to find out about state and local citizen science programs.

BREEDING BIRD SURVEY
Website: www.pwrc.usgs.gov/bbs/participate/

CHRISTMAS BIRD COUNT
National Audubon Society
Audubon Science Office
545 Almshouse Road
Ivyland, PA 18974
Phone: 215-355-9588
Email: citizenscience@audubon.org
Website: www.audubon.org

EBIRD
Email: eBird@cornell.edu
Website: www.ebird.org

GREAT BACKYARD BIRD COUNT
Cornell Lab of Ornithology
159 Sapsucker Woods Road
Ithaca, NY 14850
Phone: 800-843-2473 (toll free in U.S.) or
607-254-2473 if calling internationally
Email: cornellbirds@cornell.edu
Website: www.birdsource.org/gbbc/
OR
National Audubon Society
Audubon Science Office
545 Almshouse Road
Ivyland, PA 18974
Phone: 215-355-9588
Email: citizenscience@audubon.org
Website: www.birdsource.org/gbbc/

THE INTERNATIONAL SHOREBIRD SURVEYS
Manomet Center for Conservation Sciences
PO Box 1770
Manomet, MA 02345
Phone: 508-224-6521
Email: bharrington@manomet.org
Website: www.manomet.org

NOCTURNAL OWL MONITORING PROGRAM (CANADA)
Bird Studies Canada
PO Box 160
115 Front Road
Port Rowan , ON, Canada N0E 1M0
Phone: 1-888-448-2473 (toll free in Canada)
Email: dbadzinski@bsc-eoc.org
Website: http://www.bsc-eoc.org/national/
nationalowls.html

NORTH AMERICAN BIRDS
American Birding Association
4945 N 30th Street, Suite 200
Colorado Springs, CO 80919
Phone: 800-850-2473 or 719-578-9703
Website: www.americanbirding.org

PROJECT FEEDERWATCH

In the U.S.:
Cornell Lab of Ornithology
159 Sapsucker Woods Road
Ithaca, NY 14850
Phone: 800-843-2473 (toll free)
Email: feederwatch@cornell.edu
Website: www.birds.cornell.edu/pfw/
In Canada:
Bird Studies Canada
PO Box 160
115 Front Road
Port Rowan, ON, Canada N0E 1M0
Phone: 888-448-2473 (toll free)

Email: pfw@bsc-eoc.org
Website: www.bsc-eoc.org/national/
pfw.html

PROJECT NEST WATCH

Bird Studies Canada
PO Box 160
115 Front Road
Port Rowan, ON, Canada N0E 1M0
Phone: 888-448-2473 (toll free)
Email: generalinfo@bsc-eoc.org
Website:
www.bsc-eoc.org/national/nestwatch.html

The State of North American Bird Populations

A good friend who is not a biologist or birder once said to me upon hearing that there were debates about bird declines, "How can birds not have declined? So much of their habitat has been replaced with buildings, factories, and farmland?" I think his point is a good one to consider. The numbers of birds and other animals thriving in North America's grasslands, forests, wetlands, and oceans before European arrival and expansion is beyond comprehension. Imagine 3 billion Passenger Pigeons, 100,000 Eskimo Curlews, 5 million Short-tailed Albatross, 65 million bison, and 33 million green sea turtles! For most species, we don't have even rough estimates of their former abundance. We can only look at changes in the amount of the habitats they require, and when we do, the statistics are more than a little sobering.[1–5]

A study by the Nature Conservancy and the Association for Biodiversity Information in 2000 reported that 58% of the area in the lower 48 states no longer supports natural vegetation. They also found that 57% of all ecological communities in the U.S. are imperiled or vulnerable. Research by the World Wildlife Fund in 1999 found that 67 of 76 ecoregions in the 48 contiguous U.S. states were in critical, endangered, or vulnerable condition.[6,7]

These numbers are daunting and hard to fully grasp. It helps to look at some familiar habitats. Let's start with the deciduous and mixed forests of eastern North America. Many of these forests still ring with the sounds of Red-eyed Vireos and American Redstarts each spring and summer. In 1600, approximately 70% of the eastern U.S. was covered with forest. Today, that number stands at 40%. Put in context, the estimated 140 million Red-eyed Vireos alive today doesn't sound so huge—imagine about 245 million! Or how about those fragrant pine forests of the southern U.S., where many of us have ventured for our life Red-cockaded Woodpecker or Bachman's Sparrow? It is almost stupefying to realize that southern pine forests once covered 60–90 million acres but now occupy only 3 million acres. It is equally difficult to imagine the number of the now-endangered Red-cockaded Woodpecker that inhabited such vast forests—was it hundreds of thousands or millions?[4,7,8,9,10]

Especially sad to consider is the decline of the cathedral-like bottomland forests and cypress swamps of the southeastern U.S. that echoed with the double-raps of Ivory-billed Woodpeckers, the screeches of Carolina Parakeets, and the buzzy songs of the Bachman's Warbler. The loss and degradation of the habitats that these birds relied upon has been estimated at more than 90%. These species are gone now, though some people, myself included, continue to hope that indisputable evidence of undiscovered populations of Bachman's Warbler and Ivory-billed Woodpecker still living out their lives in some remote southern swamp will someday be obtained.[7–9,12,13]

The pioneering days of American agriculture in the latter half of the 19th century transformed the midwestern U.S. into the nation's "bread basket" but turned our native grasslands to dying memories. The original 167 million acres of tallgrass prairie was reduced by 97% to about 5.3 million acres. Remnants of tallgrass prairie habitat in southern Iowa and northern Missouri are now restricted to 20 sites, each less than 20 acres in size. Today's population of Henslow's Sparrow is thought to number about 80,000 and falling in the remaining habitat; the historic population was certainly in the millions. And tallgrass prairie wasn't the only grassland habitat that was lost. The total loss of prairies in the U.S. and Canada (including tallgrass, mixed-grass, and short-grass prairies) is estimated at 79%. Symbols of the prairie like the Greater Prairie-Chicken and Lesser Prairie-Chicken have dropped to perilously low levels despite once being superabundant. The eastern subspecies of the Greater Prairie-Chicken, the Heath Hen, became extinct in 1932, and the Attwater's Prairie-Chicken population of the Texas and Louisiana coastal prairies dropped from a million birds historically to a mere 42 individuals in 1996.[7,11–16]

Moving farther west, consider the sagebrush habitats that were the backdrop of so many cowboy movies. Millions of acres of sagebrush have been destroyed for croplands, and on millions more, sagebrush has been systematically removed to make way for cattle production. Less than 10% of the 84 million acres of the Great Basin Shrub Steppe ecoregion remains as intact habitat. Greater Sage-Grouse have dropped from historic highs of 1.1 million or more to, by one estimate, just 142,000 today, and the Gunnison Sage-Grouse now numbers fewer than 5,000.[7,9,17]

In the western U.S., water has always been at a premium, whether for drinking water, cattle watering, agriculture, power production, or industrial uses. As a result, an estimated 95% of habitat along western rivers and streams (not to mention the aquatic habitat itself) has been lost or degraded in the last 100 years. Suffering the brunt of this destruction are species like Bell's Vireo, especially Least Bell's Vireo, and western populations of Black Rail, Yellow-billed Cuckoo, and Willow Flycatcher. All of these species have declined dramatically in the western U.S., some from populations that once had to have numbered in the millions.[8]

Along the Pacific Coast, the forests of massive trees awed the early explorers. It didn't take long, though, before the economic opportunities of cutting down and sawing up the trees became apparent. Since prelogging days, about 96% of the original coastal forest from Canada's Vancouver Island to Oregon has been removed, and more than 95% of the northern California Redwood forests are now gone. The best known casualty of these changes has been the Marbled Murrelet. Current estimates put its total population (including those in Alaska) at about a half-million birds. The original population certainly had been in the millions.[7,18]

Of course, some species of birds have increased as a result of the massive habitat changes that have occurred in North America since historical times. Species that thrive in urban environments are the most obvious examples. Introduced species like Rock Pigeons, European Starlings, and House Sparrows marched steadily across the continent after their release on American shores. Native species like American Crow, Black Vulture, Yellow Warbler, American Robin, House Wren, Tufted Titmouse, Red-bellied Woodpecker, and Northern Cardinal have seemingly done well, the latter three species increasing their range northward in the eastern U.S. over the last 50 years. It is impossible to know, though, how many Northern Cardinal, Red-bellied Woodpecker, and Tufted Titmouse once inhabited the millions of acres of southern bottomland forest that no longer exist. Many grassland species showed an initial range extension into the northeastern U.S. following the conversion of forests into hayfields. Henslow's Sparrows bred as far east as New Hampshire, and Sedge Wrens and Loggerhead Shrikes nested regularly throughout New England. Except for occasional rare occurrences, all three species are now gone from the region and most of their original native grassland habitat has now also been destroyed. In Illinois, where only 2,500 acres of the original 21 million acres of tallgrass prairie remain, Horned Larks, which can do well in open tilled land, increased from an estimated 1.5 million in 1907 to 4.5 million by 1958. But again, we have no way to know how many Horned Larks were around when grazing bison, fires, and unimaginably huge prairie dog towns provided millions of acres of the kind of sparsely vegetated habitat that they prefer. It is fortunate that some bird species, like those mentioned above, were able to adapt to the habitat changes of the last 200 years. Sadly, though, an overwhelming number of bird species have not adapted and are now of conservation concern.[4,8,9,14,19,20–23]

LISTS, LISTS, LISTS

Many species have been identified as being of conservation concern through various formal lists created by different agencies and organizations. Let's consider a few of these lists. The most well known is the list of Endangered or Threatened species given protections under the U.S. Endangered Species Act. As of 2006 there were 92 species, subspecies, or populations of birds on the list. Eighteen birds on this list (20%) are now considered extinct or likely extinct, or exist only in captivity. While more than half of the birds protected under the Endangered Species Act list are from Hawaii or islands of the Pacific, a surprising 43 occur in the continental U.S. and Alaska. That may not sound like much to worry about when you consider the 700 or so species that breed in the U.S.. But consider two things: First, only a few species have been given sufficient resources that their numbers have increased to levels that would warrant removal from the list; most species on the list have continued to decline, and many island-inhabiting birds on the list have already gone extinct. We will never again hear the haunting song of the Kaua'i o'o echoing from the high-elevation rainforest of the island of Kaua'i—the last known survivor sang futilely for a mate until 1987 and then the species disappeared from the earth forever. This happened despite the fact that the species had been listed as Endangered since 1967. Second, because listing under the Endangered Species Act is a policy process, not a scientific process, a great many species do not appear on the list that are in fact endangered or threatened. The Endangered Species Act has been amazingly successful when resources have been applied through it to restoring endangered and threatened species. There is no doubt that it is one of the most significant pieces of legislation ever enacted in the U.S. and remains vitally important to protecting many endangered bird species within the changing political context in which it must operate, but it has never included all endangered and threatened birds under its protective umbrella.[24,25]

Perhaps the most widely accepted, scientifically derived list of globally endangered and threatened birds is that of the International Union for the Conservation of Nature (IUCN). Administered for IUCN by BirdLife International, the list, which is better known as the Red List, contains only those species that meet one or more of a number of strict criteria. For example, species that have shown a well documented decline of 80% or more in the last 10 years are included as Critically Endangered. Those that have declined by more than 50% in the last 10 years are considered Endangered. Species whose entire population consists of fewer than 250 adults are listed as Critically Endangered as well, and there are a number of other similar, very specific and data-driven criteria for listing. In the continental U.S. and Alaska, there were 36 species that appeared on the IUCN Red List in 2000 and 16 (44%) of these were not listed under the U.S. Endangered Species Act.[25]

There are a number of other lists of birds of conservation concern published by different groups, each using a slightly different methodology to prioritize species. For example, National Audubon released an Audubon WatchList in 2002 that included 160 species (17% of total avifauna) from the continental U.S. and Alaska, plus an additional 41 species from Hawaii and Puerto Rico. The American Bird Conservancy's Green List, published in 2003, contained 187 species (20% of total avifauna) from the continental U.S. and Alaska, plus an additional 33 species from Hawaii. In 2002, the U.S. Fish and Wildlife Service released its Birds of Conservation Concern list, which included 131 species at the national level (12% of total avifauna including Hawaii and Pacific Islands) and 275 species at both national and regional levels (26% of total avifauna including Hawaii and Pacific Islands). The 2004 Partners in Flight National Watch List included 100 species (22%) of 448 landbird species found in the continental U.S., Alaska, and Canada. The U.S. Shorebird Conservation Plan in 2000 rated 44 (88%) of 50 regularly occurring shorebird species as being of conservation concern. The 2002 North American Waterbird Conservation Plan rated 106 (71%) of 150 waterbirds as of conservation concern (including those species for which there was sufficient information and including species from parts of the Pacific, the Caribbean, Mexico, and Central America). Taken together, the various lists of birds of conservation concern in North America include more than 500 species.[9,26–30]

BENCHMARKS

All of these lists can leave even the most initiated among us feeling dazed. Without some past benchmark, how can one go about assessing what these numbers mean? It seems a reasonable goal at least to ensure that there are no further human-induced extinctions. The best research into background global extinction rates for bird species over geological time periods (millions of years) has estimated that one species has gone extinct about every 100 years worldwide. Since about the year 1500, that rate has greatly changed. In the last 500 years since humans have come to dominate the planet, the extinction rate has skyrocketed to an average of about 30 per 100 years (151 bird species are considered to have become extinct since 1500). Put another way, this equates to the loss of a bird species about every three years. Since 1900, the rate has nearly doubled to the loss of a species every two years (61 species since 1900). All of these facts indicate an ecological system far out of balance with historical extinction rates.[25,31,32]

Further, if we make the assumption that a *long-term* declining abundance trend signals a species becoming at greater risk of eventual extinction (the smaller the population, the higher the probability of extinction), then one can also argue that we should be concerned if more than a handful of species exhibit continuing, long-term declines in abundance. Of course, we expect populations of birds to go up and down from year to year through births, deaths, emigration, and immigration. In years with large outbreaks of spruce budworms in the boreal forest of Canada and Alaska, for example, Tennessee, Cape May, and Bay-breasted warblers can vastly increase in numbers as they are able to raise large broods to fledging by feeding them on superabundant budworm larvae. Harsh winter weather can kill large numbers of Carolina Wrens and Eastern Bluebirds so that their populations plummet. From one year to the next, we would expect on average that about half of the species in North America would increase and half decrease.[32–37]

But over long enough time periods, declining species must increase again. If they don't, they eventually will become extinct. Without human-caused problems or a major catastrophe like a meteor strike, we would expect that only a few bird species would continue to become fewer, year after year, decade after decade. In fact, the number of bird species in North America that have shown long-term declining trends is more than a handful of species. Of the 424 species that occur on enough Breeding Bird Survey routes to estimate trends, more than 100 showed statistically significant declines from 1966 to 2003. At least 35 of these species had declined by 50% or more in the 37 years since the survey began. Especially troubling are the 70–90% long-term declines of species like the Cerulean Warbler, Henslow's Sparrow, Pinyon Jay, Lesser Yellowlegs, Sprague's Pipit, and Rusty Blackbird.[38]

A closer examination of Breeding Bird Survey population trends (1966–2003) indicates some broader problems. For example, more birds of grassland habitats are in decline than those from other habitats—68% are showing significant declines as compared to 28% overall. Along with Henslow's Sparrow and Sprague's Pipit, the list of declining species includes Baird's Sparrow, Greater Prairie-Chicken, and Long-billed Curlew. Birds that breed in shrub–scrub habitats are also showing higher-than-expected numbers of declining species (36%), and the list includes Brewer's Sparrow, Bell's Vireo, Golden-winged Warbler, and Painted Bunting. As a group, forest-breeding species are not showing disproportionate numbers of declining species, but 31 of the 131 species adequately surveyed are showing statistically significant declines, including Cerulean Warbler, Olive-sided Flycatcher, Rufous Hummingbird, "Blue" Grouse, Wood Thrush, Canada Warbler, and Prothonotary Warbler.[38]

THE SPECIAL CASE OF HAWAII

To birders, Hawaii represents the exotic, birds found nowhere else in the world, with names like I'iwi, Elapaio, and Po'o-uli, frequenting the hot, humid, rain-drenched forests on the upper slopes of mountains rising from the blue waters of the Pacific. Although it is part of the United States, geographically the Hawaiian archipelago is unique, located as it is more than 2,000 miles from the closest continents. With more than 9,000 endemic plant and animals species, ecologically, too, Hawaii is vastly different from any other part of the U.S. The species that evolved there over millions of years from the occasional off-course migrants that stumbled upon the islands are or were unlike anything else found on Earth. Sadly, Hawaii has also come to be known as the land of extinction.

More than any other part of the U.S., Hawaii and the tropical Pacific embodies the harshest lessons of conservation. An astounding array of thrushes, honeycreepers, and finches that took millennia to evolve in the luxurious forests of these isolated islands, were reduced to only a handful of species in less than 250 years. Since 1778, when the first Europeans arrived in Hawaii, at least 29 species have become extinct or are likely extinct; an additional 28 species are endangered or threatened. Several birds have become extinct just in the last 25 years. They include both the Kaua'i o'o and Kama'o, two forest thrushes endemic to Kaua'i that were last detected in 1987 and 1993 respectively. The Po'o-uli, a strikingly plumaged honeycreeper first discovered in 1973, was reduced to a single individual within 30 years. The last known bird died in captivity in 2004. There may be no other place on earth where so many of today's ornithologists have witnessed, in their own lifetimes, the extinction of so many species they themselves have studied and observed.

The factors that have led to Hawaii's enormous conservation crisis read like a textbook litany of the causes of endangerment and extinction the world over: habitat loss and degradation, invasive species and disease, and uncontrolled hunting. The problems for the birds of Hawaii started 1,500 years ago when the first humans arrived there. Needing food to survive, these Polynesians brought about the extinction of a host of flightless rails and waterfowl that had evolved on the islands in the absence of predators. The Polynesians also destroyed most of the drier lowland forest for agriculture and building materials before the arrival of Europeans, relegating birds and other animals that required such habitat either to marginal, higher elevation forests or to extinction. Fossil evidence suggests that at least 60 bird species became extinct after Polynesians colonized Hawaii.

Polynesians had already imported some nonnative, invasive species, the most notable being the pig. But the invasive species problem was taken to a new level after the arrival of Europeans. Sailors saw islands as places to establish food storehouses so that fresh meat could be obtained in the midst of long voyages. On island after island across the world's seas, goats, cows, pigs, donkeys, horses, rabbits, and occasionally other creatures, were released with the hope that they would survive and multiply. On many of the Hawaiian Islands, these nonnative animals flourished. Just as flightless birds had evolved in the absence of major predators, so too had plants evolved without any major herbivores to select for thorns and spines and nasty sap that would deter things that would eat them. The plants were a defenseless smorgasbord to these nonnative invaders, and the forests, as well as the many species that relied upon them, quickly suffered because of it.

Other nonnative species arrived by mistake. Mosquitoes were thought to have been first introduced in the early 1800s when sailors newly arrived from Mexico dumped the remaining water from the bottom of their barrels into a stream before filling them with freshwater. The old water, which they had picked up in Mexico, apparently contained mosquito larvae. Unfortunately for many Hawaiian birds, mosquitoes were the carriers of new diseases to which the birds had no resistance. Like the Polynesians of the Hawaiian Islands who were decimated by measles and other diseases brought in with the European sailors, the birds too began quickly disappearing from avian pox and avian malaria. On some islands it happened amazingly fast. Ornithologists of the late 1800s reported time and again that within a few years native birds went from being abundant to nonexistent in forests that were largely intact. Eventually, the last stronghold of many native Hawaiian birds was in the marginal habitat of the upper-elevation forests where the temperatures were too low for mosquitoes to survive.

Today, a complex dynamic has arisen among the scores of nonnative species that have been introduced, one that threatens to cascade into an extinction free-fall. Much of the lower-elevation habitats are dominated by nonnative plants (more than 4,600 have been introduced to Hawaii) with entire communities of nonnative birds, mammals, and insects. Populations of feral hogs, sheep, cattle, and goats that come into higher-elevation native forest eat the native plants and disturb the soil, providing a foothold for aggressive nonnative plants to invade and displace the native plants. The invading mammals also often leave muddy pools in their wake that provide perfect breeding habitat for mosquitoes, therefore enabling the mosquitoes to move into regions that were once mosquito-free. In addition, mosquito varieties that can withstand cooler temperatures are now creeping higher and higher into mountain forests. It may be these cascading dynamics that account for the rapid disappearance of birds like the Po'o-uli and others just in the last few decades.

Conservationists and scientists are working feverishly to find and implement solutions to Hawaii's extinction crisis. Miles of fencing have been put in place to keep feral mammals out of preserves. In other areas, hunts have been established to control populations of wild pigs, and trapping is undertaken to control introduced rats and mongoose—major predators of the eggs and young of birds. The Nature Conservancy, Hawaii Audubon, the U.S. Fish and Wildlife Service, and the State of Hawaii are among many groups that have been very active in establishing more protected areas and trying to slow the rate of fragmentation and loss of habitat. Captive breeding programs established in Hawaii and staffed by the San Diego Zoo have shown success in raising birds in captivity and releasing them back into the wild to augment local populations. But it is clear that Hawaii's remaining native avifauna is in a race for its life. Without continued financial and political support of conservation activities in Hawaii, more species will lose their frantic race for survival.

Since a full discussion of the conservation of the birds of Hawaii would require a book of its own, I have focused in this book on the birds of North America. Fortunately, a number of books and other material have been published that highlight the conservation issues in Hawaii, including *Evolution, Ecology, Conservation, and Management of Hawaiian Birds: A Vanishing Avifauna*, edited by J. M. Scott, S. Conant, and C. van Riper, an excellent chapter on Hawaii in *The Condor's Shadow* by David Wilcove, *The Birds of Hawaii and the Tropical Pacific* by Doug Pratt, Phillip Bruner, and Delwyn

Berrett, and *Birdwatcher's Guide to Hawaii* by Rick Soehren.

CONCERN VERSUS RESPONSIBILITY

Given that there are more than 500 bird species in North America considered of conservation concern by one group or another, and given that we have limited resources to carry out conservation work, conservationists must decide which species will receive the benefit of those limited resources. Generally, precedence is given first to those species that are most in danger of becoming extinct.

But as groups started coming together to work on bird conservation problems, an interesting issue came to light. An organization focusing on bird conservation in Ontario, for example, has little opportunity to help most of North America's most globally endangered species. California Condors, Whooping Cranes, and Marbled Murrelets are not part of Ontario's avifauna. Yes, there are a few globally endangered and threatened species that occur regularly enough in Ontario that the efforts of an organization focused on the province could contribute to the overall well being of the species, but most of North America's most endangered birds don't occur within the province. Contrast this with an agency working on bird conservation in California that might be focused on Snowy Plovers, Spotted Owls, California Condors, Marbled Murrelets, California Gnatcatchers, Xantus's Murrelets, Tricolored Blackbirds, Bell's Vireos, and more. Does this mean that an Ontario group has little to do? Hardly.

California has an extremely wide range of habitats and an unfortunate history of massive habitat conversion and loss, both factors that account for the large number of endangered and threatened species that occur there. Ontario, on the other hand, has an equally important responsibility. The northern two-thirds of Ontario is part of the largest remaining wilderness habitat left in the Western Hemisphere—North America's boreal forest region. At 1.5 billion acres, the boreal, stretching from Alaska to Newfoundland, is 12 times the size of California and is estimated to support over 3 billion birds, including more than 50% of the populations of nearly 100 species. While conservationists in places like California are struggling to hold on to species for which there is immediate concern for their survival, people in places like Ontario are charged with the awesome

long-term responsibility of ensuring that this last, great reservoir of bird habitat—North America's bird nursery—does not become lost and degraded like those in most of the rest of the world.[39]

While I have used California and Ontario as examples at opposite ends of a spectrum, the point is that conservationists tend to focus on rarity because that is where there is most immediate need—without action, a species may be lost forever once it reaches perilously low numbers. But without long-term planning, more and more species will edge closer and closer to this fate. Long-term planning forces us to correctly think about places of abundant bird life—the remaining still-intact large expanses of habitat like the boreal forest in the North and the Amazon basin in the South, the wetlands that still harbor massive numbers of shorebirds during migration, and the island nesting colonies that still have tens, or even hundreds, of thousands of seabirds. These are the last great conservation opportunities of our generation—places where we still have the chance to save intact ecosystems and full complements of species woven together in ways unchanged for thousands of years.

BAD NEWS—GOOD NEWS

While the overall health of bird populations (and by extension, our overall environment) is clearly at a substandard level, we are fortunate in North America that we do have large numbers of people interested in making things better. For people committed to restoring and protecting bird populations and the habitats upon which they depend, there are an almost infinite number of ways to get involved. The species accounts in this book are full of opportunities to make a difference, as is the chapter on the state of bird conservation.

In my own view, the recent weakening of governmental environmental policies in the U.S. will certainly result in further declines of many of the birds of highest conservation concern—something I see as a squandering of the natural resources that are a birthright of our children. But the ability of government leaders to weaken such policies is a result of a failing among those of us concerned about the health of birds and our environment. Concerned citizens need to speak out for the values they care about both individually and through organizations that share those values.

For the Labrador Duck, the Carolina Parakeet, and the Passenger Pigeon, it is too late. My Great-Grandfather Reed could have taken his young daughter Beatrice to see Martha, the last Passenger Pigeon, before it died at the Cincinnati Zoo in 1914. My Grandmother Beatrice could have taken her young son (my father) down to Louisiana in 1944 to see the last known breeding pair of Ivory-billed Woodpeckers. But my dad would never have the chance to take me to see these birds. Nor would he have the opportunity to take me to see the last documented Bachman's Warbler that sang from a swamp in South Carolina in 1962 or the last known Eskimo Curlew that chased grasshoppers in the grass on Galveston Island, Texas, that same year—two years before I was born.

My own son also will never see these creatures (except, let's hope, maybe an Ivory-billed Woodpecker), but he has learned to identify a Bald Eagle when we see one perched along the river near our house in Maine. Bald Eagles are now quite common in many parts of North America because of the legacy of positive environmental policies like the Endangered Species Act, the Clean Water Act, and the Clean Air Act, and from the legacy of government agencies like the Environmental Protection Agency and the U.S. Fish and Wildlife Service, among others. My son *will* see a California Condor soaring over the massive redwoods of Big Sur, California. He will see Whooping Cranes dancing in a marsh on the Texas coast. He will see Brown Pelicans diving for fish off a Florida beach. But will there be a Florida Scrub-Jay like the one he saw when he was four months old—a bird from a dwindling population being overtaken by development along Florida's east coast—still living in the sugar-sand oak thickets of Florida so that he can show one to his own daughter or son?

The success at restoring populations of Bald Eagle, Brown Pelican, California Condor, and Whooping Crane shows us that it is possible to improve the health of bird populations. But people—regular people like you and me—need to get involved, speak up, buy recycled, save energy, take a child birding, vote for candidates who care about the kind of home we will leave to our children and future generations. Start a project to save a piece of habitat, restore a grassland, or reduce levels of harmful chemicals in your watersheds. Do whatever you can so that all of our children will have healthy air to breath, clean water to drink, and the opportunity to see the birds that are our heritage.

REFERENCES

1. Blockstein, D.E. 2002. Passenger Pigeon (*Ectopistes migratorius*). In *The Birds of North America*, No. 611 (A. Poole and F. Gill, eds.). The Birds of North America, Inc., Philadelphia, PA.

2. Gill, R.E., Jr., P. Canevari, and E.H. Iverson. 1998. Eskimo Curlew (*Numenius borealis*). In *The Birds of North America*, No. 347 (A. Poole and F. Gill, eds.). The Birds of North America, Inc., Philadelphia, PA.

3. Fadely, J. 1999. Short-tailed Albatross: Back from the Brink. *Endangered Species Bulletin* 24(2):8–9.

4. Wilcove, D.S. 1999. *The Condor's Shadow: The Loss and Recovery of Wildlife in America*. Random House, New York, NY. 339 pp.

5. Jackson, J.B.C., et al. 2001. Historical Overfishing and the Recent Collapse of Coastal Ecosystems. *Science* 293:629–637.

6. Stein, B.A., L.S. Kutner, and J.S. Adams. 2000. *Precious Heritage: The Status of Biodiversity in the United States*. Oxford University Press, New York, NY. 399 pp.

7. Ricketts, T.H., E. Dinerstein, D.M. Olson, C.J. Loucks et al. 1999. *Terrestrial Ecoregions of North America: A Conservation Assessment*. Island Press, Washington, DC. 485 pp.

8. Askins, R.A. 2000. Restoring North America's Birds: Lessons from Landscape Ecology. Yale University Press, New Haven, CT. 320 pp.

9. Rich, T. D., C. Beardmore, H. Berlanga, P. Blancher, M. Bradstreet, G. Butcher, D. Demarest, E. Dunn, C. Hunter, E. Iñigo-Elias, J. Kennedy, A. Martell, A. Panjabi, D. Pashley, K. Rosenberg, C. Rustay, S. Wendt, and T. Will. 2004. *Partners in Flight North American Landbird Conservation Plan*. Cornell Lab of Ornithology, Ithaca, NY.

10. Jackson, J.A. 1994. Red-cockaded Woodpecker (*Picoides borealis*). In *The Birds of North America*, No. 85 (A. Poole and F. Gill, eds.). The Academy of Natural Sciences, Philadelphia, PA, and the American Ornithologists' Union, Washington, DC.

11. White, R.P., S. Murray, and M. Rohweder. 2000. *Pilot Analysis of Grassland Ecosystems*. World Resources Institute, Baltimore, MD. http://www.wri.org/wr2000.

12. Vickery, P.D., P.L. Tubaro, J.M. Cardoso da Silva, B.G. Peterjohn, J.R. Herkert, and R.B. Cavalcanti. 1999. Conservation of Grassland Birds in the Western Hemisphere. Pages 2–26 in *Ecology and Conservation of Grassland Birds in the Western Hemisphere* (P.D. Vickery and J.R. Herkert, eds.). Studies in Avian Biology No. 19, Cooper Ornithological Society, Camarillo, CA.

13. Gauthier, D.A., A. Lafon, T. Tombs, J. Hoth,

and E. Wilken. 2003. *Grasslands: Toward a North American Conservation Strategy.* Canadian Plains Research Center, University of Regina, Regina, SK, and Commission for Environmental Cooperation, Montreal, QC, Canada. 99 pp.

14. Herkert, J.R., P.D. Vickery, and D.E. Kroodsma. 2002. Henslow's Sparrow (*Ammodramus henslowii*). In *The Birds of North America*, No. 672 (A. Poole and F. Gill, eds.). The Birds of North America, Inc., Philadelphia, PA.

15. Schroeder, M.A. and Robb, L.A. 1993. Greater Prairie-Chicken (*Tympanuchus cupido*). In *The Birds of North America*, No. 36 (A. Poole and F. Gill, eds.). The Academy of Natural Sciences, Philadelphia, PA, and the American Ornithologists' Union, Washington, DC.

16. Giesen, K.M. 1998. Lesser Prairie-Chicken (*Tympanuchus pallidicinctus*). In *The Birds of North America*, No. 364 (A. Poole and F. Gill, eds.). The Birds of North America, Inc., Philadelphia, PA.

17. Schroeder, M.A., J.R. Young, and C.E. Braun. 1999. Sage Grouse (*Centrocercus urophasianus*). In *The Birds of North America*, No. 425 (A. Poole and F. Gill, eds.). The Birds of North America, Inc., Philadelphia, PA.

18. Nelson, S.K. 1997. Marbled Murrelet (*Brachyramphus marmoratus*). In *The Birds of North America*, No. 276 (A. Poole and F. Gill, eds.). The Academy of Natural Sciences, Philadelphia, PA, and the American Ornithologists' Union, Washington, DC.

19. Grubb, T.C., Jr. and V. V. Pravosudov. 1994. Tufted Titmouse (*Parus bicolor*). In *The Birds of North America*, No. 86 (A. Poole and F. Gill, eds.). The Academy of Natural Sciences, Philadelphia, PA, and the American Ornithologists' Union, Washington, DC.

20. Shackelford, C.E., R. E. Brown, and R. N. Conner. 2000. Red-bellied Woodpecker (*Melanerpes carolinus*). In *The Birds of North America*, No. 500 (A. Poole and F. Gill, eds.). The Birds of North America, Inc., Philadelphia, PA.

21. Halkin, S. L., and S. U. Linville. 1999. Northern Cardinal (*Cardinalis cardinalis*). In *The Birds of North America*, No. 440 (A. Poole and F. Gill, eds.). The Birds of North America, Inc., Philadelphia, PA.

22. Yosef, R. 1996. Loggerhead Shrike (*Lanius ludovicianus*). In *The Birds of North America*, No. 231 (A. Poole and F. Gill, eds.). The Academy of Natural Sciences, Philadelphia, PA, and the American Ornithologists' Union, Washington, DC.

23. Herkert, J.R., D. E. Kroodsma, and J. P. Gibbs. 2001. Sedge Wren (*Cistothorus platensis*). In *The Birds of North America*, No. 582 (A. Poole and F. Gill, eds.). The Birds of North America, Inc., Philadelphia, PA.

24. U.S. Fish and Wildlife Service. 2006. *Species Information Threatened and Endangered Animals and Plants.* http://www.fws.gov/endangered/wildlife.html (accessed 15 February 2006).

25. BirdLife International. 2000. *Threatened Birds of the World.* Lynx Editions and BirdLife International, Barcelona, Spain, and Cambridge, UK.

26. National Audubon Society. 2002. *Audubon WatchList 2002.* http://www.audubon.org/bird/watchlist/index.html (accessed 10 March 2006).

27. Chipley, R.M., G.H. Fenwick, M.J. Parr, and D.N. Pashley. 2003. *The American Bird Conservancy Guide to the 500 Most Important Bird Areas in the United States.* Random House, New York, NY.

28. U.S. Fish and Wildlife Service. 2002. *Birds of Conservation Concern 2002.* Division of Migratory Bird Management, Arlington, VA. 99 pp. http://migratorybirds.fws.gov/reports/bcc2002.pdf.

29. Brown, S., C. Hickey, and B. Harrington, eds. 2000. *The U.S. Shorebird Conservation Plan.* Manomet Center for Conservation Sciences, Manomet, MA.

30. Kushlan, J.A., M.J. Steinkamp, K.C. Parsons, J. Capp, M. Acosta Cruz, M. Coulter, I. Davidson, L. Dickson, N. Edelson, R. Elliot, R.M. Erwin, S. Hatch, S. Kress, R. Milko, S. Miller, K. Mills, R. Paul, R. Phillips, J.E. Saliva, B. Sydeman, J. Trapp, J. Wheeler, and K. Wohl. 2002. *Waterbird Conservation for the Americas: The North American Waterbird Conservation Plan*, Version 1. Waterbird Conservation for the Americas, Washington, DC. 78 pp.

31. Crosby, M.J., A.J. Stattersfield, N.J. Collar, and C.J. Bibby. 1994. Predicting Avian Extinction Rates. *Biodiversity Letters* 2:182–185.

32. BirdLife International. 2004. *State of the World's Birds 2004: Indicators for Our Changing World.* BirdLife International, Cambridge, UK.

33. Rimmer, C.C., and K. P. McFarland. 1998. Tennessee Warbler (*Vermivora peregrina*). In *The Birds of North America*, No. 350 (A. Poole and F. Gill, eds.). The Birds of North America, Inc., Philadelphia, PA.

34. Baltz, M. E., and S. C. Latta. 1998. Cape May Warbler (*Dendroica tigrina*). In *The Birds of North America*, No. 332 (A. Poole and F. Gill, eds.). The Birds of North America, Inc., Philadelphia, PA.

35. Williams, J. M. 1996. Bay-breasted Warbler (*Dendroica castanea*). In *The Birds of North America*, No. 206 (A. Poole and F. Gill, eds.). The Academy of Natural Sciences, Philadelphia, PA, and the American Ornithologists' Union, Washington, DC.

36. Haggerty, T. M., and E. S. Morton. 1995. Carolina Wren (*Thryothorus ludovicianus*). In *The Birds of North America*, No. 188 (A. Poole and F. Gill, eds.). The

Academy of Natural Sciences, Philadelphia, PA, and the American Ornithologists' Union, Washington, DC.

37. Gowaty, P. A., and J. H. Plissner. 1998. Eastern Bluebird (*Sialia sialis*). In *The Birds of North America*, No. 381 (A. Poole and F. Gill, eds.). The Birds of North America, Inc., Philadelphia, PA.

38. Sauer, J.R., J. E. Hines, and J. Fallon. 2003. *The North American Breeding Bird Survey, Results and Analysis 1966–2002*, Version 2003.1. USGS Patuxent Wildlife Research Center, Laurel, MD.

39. Blancher, P., and J.V. Wells. 2005. *The Boreal Forest Region: North America's Bird Nursery*. Canadian Boreal Initiative, Boreal Songbird Initiative, Bird Studies Canada, Ottawa, ON, Seattle, WA, and Port Rowan, ON. 10 pp.

Major Conservation Issues Affecting North America's Birds

At different times in my own personal growth as a conservationist, I, like most people who are aware of our connection to the natural world, have felt that so many bad things were happening to the environment that whatever I could do to make a difference was futile. But as I learned more about the major conservation issues impacting our lives, families, and economy, I became empowered by a new realization.

What I hadn't been able to see before was that the major conservation issues of our day are not separate, isolated problems, but are intimately related. These interconnections mean that any action we take to impact one of these issues will also benefit many others. Maintaining large unfragmented forest wilderness areas prevents or slows the spread of invasive species, slows global warming, provides clean drinking water and lowers flooding risks, protects plant and animal populations, and provides sustainable economic benefits to communities. Decreasing consumption of electricity and gas decreases global warming pollution, prevents loss and degradation of habitat for birds like Cerulean Warbler and Greater Sage-Grouse, and reduces the poisoning of Common Loons and Bicknell's Thrushes from mercury contamination that results from dirty-burning power plants. We can help save our birds through a myriad of actions once we understand the issues impacting them. Many solutions can be easily incorporated into our daily lives.

This chapter summarizes the major conservation issues impacting birds and provides the background for readers to make their own decisions about ways in which they can take action to save our birds. I have provided examples and statistics, mainly for the U.S., with some also from Canada. However, I have not attempted to be exhaustive, as each topic could easily be the subject of an entire book. In fact, many of these topics are already the subjects of numerous books.

Typically, the earth's major conservation issues are put in four categories: habitat loss and degradation, invasive species and disease, overexploitation, and pollution. To these we must now add the formidable but not insurmountable issue of global warming as well as the issue of incidental mortality caused by fishing and collisions with buildings, towers, and other human-made structures.

GLOBAL WARMING

By now most people have personally felt or seen the changes brought about by the accelerated rise in global temperatures. From the increase in the number and severity of hurricanes to the hotter summers to the drier or wetter climates (depending on geographic region), most of us have already experienced the impact of a century of burning massive amounts of gas, oil, and coal. Unlike most of the other major bird conservation issues discussed here, the known effects of global warming on birds are only beginning to be understood, yet the impacts are already being felt. And projections show that global warming could overwhelm all of the other issues in the severity and speed of its impact on birds, wildlife, and habitat, and ultimately, of course, humans.[1–6]

Already, spring arrival dates of many migratory birds are 10–12 days earlier than they were in the early 1900s. Short-distance migrants like Yellow-rumped Warblers and Ruby-crowned Kinglets have shown the most advance in arrival dates, some by as much as 2 weeks. On the other hand, long-distance migrants, such as the Cerulean Warbler and Olive-sided Flycatcher, have seen only a 3- to 4-day advance in arrival time. Short-distance migrants and resident birds have also begun nesting earlier. In Great Britain, many species have shown an advance in onset of egg laying, some by as much as 18 days. In North America, the question has been thoroughly studied in only a single species, the Tree Swallow, which was shown to have advanced its egg-laying date an average of 9 days between 1959 and 1991.[7–12]

In a recent review published in the illustrious journal *Nature*, Terry Root and others found that in over 694 species of plants and animals examined, there had been an average advance of 5.1 days per decade (over the last 50 years) in spring life history events. These events ranged from leafout in trees to flowering times to egg-laying dates in amphibians to insect emergence. The earlier nesting dates of birds are the result of their adaptation to these advances in various other biological events. For example, when insects emerge sooner, birds must lay eggs sooner if they are to raise their young when the caterpillars and other insects that they feed their young are at maximum abundance. For residents and short-distance migrants this is possible because they are able to effectively track the climatic changes that are occurring with global warming in the more northerly climes where they winter. But long-distance migrant birds that winter in the tropics are at a disadvantage because they do not use climactic cues to begin spring migration but rather rely on seasonal changes in daylight. As a result, these birds may not arrive on the breeding grounds soon enough to ensure that the hatching of their young coincides with the abundant insect food supply that is required to raise them. In the Pied Flycatcher of Europe, the one species in which this phenomenon has been effectively studied, the birds arrive from their African wintering grounds too late, so that the unfortunate young hatch after the peak of insect abundance, resulting in lowered reproductive output and natural selection favoring those individuals that start nesting earlier.[9,10,13]

The potential future impacts of this unraveling of ecological webs as a result of global warming became especially alarming to consider in 2004 when there was a major collapse of Great Britain's North Sea sand eel population as a result of increased sea temperatures. Sand eels are the major food supply for most of the region's seabirds. With this sudden loss, massive numbers of birds were not able to raise a single young. The more than 170,000 breeding pairs of murres, 24,000 pairs of Artic Terns, and 16,700 pairs of Black-legged Kittiwakes in the Shetland Islands produced almost no young in 2004 because of this drop in food supply, the result of global warming.[14,15]

Recent modeling work has shown that the likely changes in the distributions and abundance of birds under currently forecast climate change scenarios could be catastrophic. Research published in 2004 projected that 78 species will decrease in abundance in the eastern U.S. by at least 25 percent. Under some modeled scenarios, certain species are predicted to disappear from the U.S. altogether as breeding species as their ranges shift northward into Canada. This includes White-throated Sparrow, Clay-colored Sparrow,

Yellow-bellied Sapsucker, Blackburnian Warbler, and Mourning Warbler.[4,16]

While we already have seen the changes caused by other problems, those that we are likely to see as a result of global warming pollution will make the others seem insignificant. A modeling study published in the journal *Nature* in 2004 found that 15–37% of 1,103 species considered will likely become extinct at current expected rates of climate change. Further, the study showed that in most regions the projected extinction rates from global climate change were far greater than those even from habitat loss and degradation.[6]

HABITAT LOSS AND DEGRADATION

With today's rapidly changing world and dramatically increasing human population, there is no doubt that habitat loss and degradation continues to be the current overriding cause of declines of birds, other wildlife, and plants. Habitat loss also contributes to a host of human health and economic problems. A 1998 study by David Wilcove and associates found that habitat loss and degradation was the greatest current threat to biodiversity in the U.S., affecting over 80% of imperiled bird species. At the global level, BirdLife International reported in 2000 and 2004 that habitat loss and degradation was the overriding problem for over 80 percent of the world's endangered and threatened birds.[17–19]

Agriculture

There are, of course, many types of habitat loss and degradation, and their contribution to the problem has varied over time and from one region to another. In general, at both the global level and within North America, conversion of land for agriculture has been the greatest cause of endangerment. The amount of wildlife habitat lost to agriculture in the U.S. and Canada is staggering— 290 million acres of grasslands, for example, and 100 million-plus acres of wetlands. Although much of the losses in the U.S. and southern Canada occurred 50–150 years ago, in some regions the problems continue. From 1982 to 1997, 1.1 million acres of native prairie were lost in South Dakota alone. Between 1991 and 1996, 1.4 million acres of Canada's native grassland were lost. In the U.S., the 2002 Farm Bill provided incentives for further conversion of native prairie to cropland (especially for wheat production) and worked against the smaller conservation provisions of the bill that encouraged farmers to set aside acreage for conservation.[17-25]

In large portions of the western U.S., overgrazing or lack of proper grazing rotations has left millions of acres in a degraded condition. Approximately 7 million livestock (mostly cattle) graze on 268 million acres of federal lands across 16 western states. An estimated 20 percent of endangered and threatened bird species in the U.S. were found to be significantly negatively affected by livestock grazing.[17,26]

Agricultural intensification has further eliminated even marginally ecologically productive agricultural habitats in many regions. In much of the northeastern U.S., hayfields are now planted with new fast-growing grass varieties that allow hay to be cut so early and so many times a season that virtually all grassland birds attempting to nest in the fields—species like Bobolinks, Eastern Meadowlarks, Grasshopper Sparrows, and Savannah Sparrows—have their nests destroyed and have no reproductive output. In the western Great Plains, farmers are now cultivating new crops that are not planted until later in the season when some bird species—the Mountain Plover, for example—have already begun incubating eggs. The nests are often destroyed by the planting activity. Birds that renest find themselves in a sea of tall crop plants later in the season and will likely abandon their nests.[27-29]

Commercial Development

For many of the most threatened and endangered species and those with limited ranges, habitat loss from development for homes, retail stores, factories, and offices is the greatest threat to their continued survival. Thirty-three percent of the endangered and threatened bird species of the U.S. were found to be harmed by land conversion for commercial development. According to a U.S. Environmental Protection Agency report, 25 million acres of land in the U.S. were developed for commercial uses between 1982 and 1997, bringing the total amount of developed acreage to 98 million acres. In many regions the amount of land consumed greatly exceeds the population growth rate. For example, in Los Angeles, California the human population grew by 46% from 1970 to 1990, but the area of developed land increased by

300%. Similarly, during the same time period in the Chicago area, the population grew by 4% while developed land grew by 45%. In a few areas, the human population actually decreased while the amount of land consumed continued to rise. Cleveland, Ohio, lost 11% of its population but saw a 33% increase in developed land. Florida Scrub-Jay, Golden-cheeked Warbler, and California Gnatcatcher are among the species that are rapidly losing their limited remaining habitat to commercial development.[17,30,31]

Forestry

At the global level, unsustainable or incompatible forestry practices are the most pervasive threat to threatened species, impacting 31% of all threatened species. In the U.S., 18% of endangered and threatened species studied by Wilcove and associates were harmed by logging practices, including plantation forestry. And while we may think that major loss of habitat to incompatible logging in North America is all in the past, there are many parts of North America where the problem continues. In the southeastern U.S., approximately 2 million acres of forest are clearcut annually and another 3.3 million acres are logged using other methods. Between 1987 and 1997, over 100 new chip mills were built across the southeastern U.S., bringing the total number of pulp and chip mills in the region to over 250. A U.S. Forest Service report in 2001 predicted that logging rates in the southeastern U.S. would increase to 8 million acres per year by 2040. The same report noted that pine plantations now occupied 32 million acres of the region (15% of all southeastern forests) while 38 million acres of natural pine forests had disappeared between 1953 and 1999. The report projected that pine plantations will occupy about 52 million acres by 2040, making up 25% of all southeastern forests. Sadly, for Red-cockaded Woodpecker, Brown-headed Nuthatch, Bachman's Sparrow, and many other wildlife species, these pine plantations are largely uninhabitable. Eastern U.S. lowland hardwood forests are also showing continuing declines from 60 million acres in 1963 to 45 million acres in 2002. Cerulean Warblers are one of the most obvious victims.[17,18,32,33]

In the western U.S., 25% of ponderosa pine forests (10 million acres) were lost between 1963 and 2002. During the same time period, hemlock–sitka spruce forests declined by 30% (11 million acres) and lodgepole pine by 20% (5 million acres). In many western forests, long-term fire suppression has caused great degradation of habitat so that huge areas are unsuitable for certain species.[26,34]

In the boreal forests of Canada, 2.5 million acres of forest are cut every year and more than 60% of the commercially viable southern boreal forest has already been allocated to timber companies. Since 1975 over 60 million acres of forest has been logged in Canada. Some of the leases of logging rights on publicly owned land are massive—61 million acres to Louisiana Pacific and 54 million acres to Abitibi Consolidated, for example. In 1987 and 1988, the province of Alberta sold logging rights to two Japanese firms for forest tracts covering 15% (24.7 million acres) of the province. The provincial government of Ontario in 1994 began actively pushing for a 50% increase in logging rates for aspen and birch and had achieved a 12% increase by 1997.[26,35,36]

An additional issue related to forestry is the increasingly shorter rotation of cutting cycles within forests managed for the paper industry. In many parts of Maine and the Maritime Provinces of Canada, forest stands are not allowed to grow beyond 60 years before they are harvested again. Without appropriate consideration of the amount and configuration of different forest ages across the broad landscape, many bird species will show significant regional declines.[27,28]

To be sure we must also recognize that forestry can be used as an important management tool to create habitats that benefit certain species. In areas where habitat patches are so small, fragmented, and disconnected from other patches that it is unlikely that natural disturbance (storms, wind, fire, etc.) can operate, then forestry may be the only viable option for maintaining habitat conditions to support populations of certain species in the landscape. On private lands managed as industrial forest there may be opportunities for small changes in forestry management practices that provide increased and improved habitat for birds of conservation concern within the recognized financial limitations of the landowner. But, as always, forestry management decisions on public lands as related to birds and other wildlife and their habitats should be considered in a landscape context that takes into account the expected changes in amounts of different habitat types and ages (early successional/mature) on private and public lands. If the amount of a certain habitat type is expected to fall below a desired landscape level threshold because of changes on private lands, then public land managers may have an opportunity to manage their lands to maintain the desired amount and configuration of such habitat through prescribed fire, compatible forestry, or other means. Or they may decide that there is a need for more acreage of mature forest, which will require a slowing of rates of logging. One thing, though, that should not be forgotten in considering the issue of using forestry as a management tool is what a friend coined the "nonequal trading principle." He pointed out that while converting a mature forest to an early successional state can be done quickly and easily through logging, it will take decades for the logged habitat to revert back to a mature forest habitat. In other words, mature forest habitat can be swapped almost immediately for early successional habitat but early successional habitat cannot be swapped for mature forest habitat.[27,28,37–42]

Changes in Fire Regimes

Every summer, newspaper headlines trumpet stories about massive wildfires "destroying" thousands of acres of habitat. The truth of the matter is that fires are and always have been a key shaper of habitats and wildlife communities across many parts of North America. Rather than "destroy" habitat, fire often renews it and maintains it. But fires are understandably not welcomed by people whose homes are situated in or near natural areas that are prone to burning. Therefore, as more and more people build homes near natural areas and habitat becomes fragmented and surrounded by residential areas, the immediate suppression of unplanned fires in those habitats becomes the norm. The Wilcove analysis found that 8% of the endangered and threatened birds of the U.S. were harmed by changes in fire regimes.[17]

Many of the ecosystems of the birds of conservation concern highlighted in this book are degraded by changes in fire regimes, especially from our decades of active fire suppression policies. Without regular fires, the scrub habitat that Florida Scrub-Jay populations rely upon for food and cover grows too thick. Populations in patches without fire eventually die out. Pine habitats in many parts of the U.S. are fire-adapted. Without regular fires, many bird species of the southern longleaf pine and pine savannah habitats—species like Bachman's Sparrow, Brown-headed Nuthatch, Henslow's Sparrow, and Red-cockaded Woodpecker—dwindle as understory bushes and trees grow too thick. In northern Michigan, the reliance of Kirtland's Warbler on young jack pine forests that naturally result from fires is well known. In the western U.S., ponderosa pine, pinyon pine, and lodge-pole pine forests have historically been shaped by fire, though the historic frequency of fires is very different for each forest type. For example, the lodge-pole pine forests of Yellowstone National Park have burned approximately every 200–300 years. Ponderosa and pinyon pine habitats are adapted to much more frequent fires.[22,26,28,43–47]

Grasslands and shrub–scrub habitats are also often adapted to frequent fires that allow the succession of plants and animals, including birds, to use the habitat as it cycles from being very open and bare immediately after a fire to becoming thicker and more covered with grasses, flowering plants, and shrubs over the ensuing years until another fire occurs. In many forests, the legacy of our years of successful fire suppression has resulted in forests that are so full of fuel that when fires do occur, they burn hotter and can actually destroy or damage the normally fire-adapted trees. In some grasslands and shrub–scrub habitats there has been an opposite problem. Overgrazing has lowered the amount of burnable fuel so much that fires have become rare or else burn so lightly that they do not maintain the habitat. In other cases, too frequent fires have allowed invasive species to take hold or have altered the plant communities in ways that preclude the survival of the full complement of native species. Species like Greater Sage-Grouse and Brewer's Sparrow are among those impacted by changes in fire ecology within western sage-brush ecosystems.[22,26,28,48–55]

Virtually all terrestrial ecosystems have been influenced and shaped by fire over the ages. The changing fire regimes of the last 100 years in North America have impacted many species. It is clear that with increasing fragmentation of habitats and encroachment of residential areas into natural areas, it will be increasingly difficult to maintain fire-adapted bird habitat without strong recognition of its vital role and proactive use of it as a management tool.

Water Use and Development

The use of water is the third highest factor causing habitat destruction and degradation that impacts endangered and threatened birds in the U.S., according to the Wilcove analysis—22% of the species considered. Not surprisingly, for other aquatic wildlife species, the number is much higher. More than 40% of North American freshwater fish species are endangered or threatened; 51% of crayfish species are at risk, as are 67% of freshwater mussel species. Sadly, the rate of extinction of freshwater fish species in the U.S. has doubled in the last century. According to a 1992 report by the National Research Council, there are now over 2.5 million dams in the U.S. Another study found that only a single river system in the lower 48 U.S. states was not significantly impacted by dams. Most aquatic ecosystems have been profoundly changed from altered flow regimes, by decreases in the amount of flow as water is diverted for agriculture or for drinking water, and by the massive flood-control projects on major river systems like the Mississippi. Changes to the Mississippi River system have resulted in the loss of 1.2 million acres of wetlands along the Louisiana coast at its mouth. In Canada, large hydropower projects developed in the 1970s and 1980s have flooded massive areas, especially in parts of the eastern boreal forest region. For example, five reservoirs established in the La Grande River region of central Quebec flooded 2.8 million acres of terrestrial habitat.[17,56–59]

The list of bird species impacted by water use and development is long and varied. It includes traditional "wetland" birds like Brant, Mottled Duck, American Black Duck, Black Rail, Yellow Rail, Whooping Crane, and Snowy and Piping plovers. It also includes many songbirds that rely on habitats along river edges or flooded woodlands like Bell's Vireo, Prothonotary Warbler, Cerulean Warbler, and Rusty Blackbird.

Oil, Gas, and Mining

It is difficult to assess the overall impact to bird populations of activities related to oil and gas extraction and the various forms of mining. The impacts range from direct loss of habitat from the building of infrastructure (buildings, roads, pipelines) and extracting soil and minerals to the secondary effects of habitat fragmentation, increased human activity and disturbance, heavy metal runoff, spills, and other pollution. The Wilcove study found that 11% of all endangered and threatened species in the U.S., but only 3% of endangered and threatened birds, were harmed by oil, gas, and mining activities.[17]

There is no doubt that massive amounts of habitat have been lost or degraded from these activities, but there has been no clear accounting of the losses. There are more than a million gas and oil wells across North America, with over 200,000 in Texas alone. Over 500 million acres of public land in the U.S. are available for oil and gas leasing, including over 200 million acres in the western U.S. We can expect that impacts will grow, since the U.S. is the top consumer of energy (including from oil, coal, and natural gas) in the world. The number of drilling permits approved for public lands by the Bureau of Land Management grew from 1,803 in 1999 to 6,399 in 2004. A 1996 report estimated that 6,000–11,000 new oil and gas wells would be developed in southwestern Wyoming by 2016, and in the Powder River Basin of Wyoming and Montana over 65,000 additional wells are being considered for development. A study in 2004 estimated that a minimum of over 120 million acres of habitat in the western U.S. were impacted by oil and gas well pads, pipelines, and roads. In Canada, a record 22,800 oil and gas wells were drilled in 2004 and the number of new wells drilled annually is projected to continue increasing.[60-65]

In Canada, the source nation for the majority of U.S. oil and gas imports, major new initiatives are underway for the building of natural gas pipelines. This includes an 800-mile-long pipeline through the Mackenzie Valley of the Northwest Territories to provide fuel for extraction of oil from the Alberta oil sands deposits of northern Alberta. Already one study in the region has documented the conversion of over 350,000 acres of habitat, mostly for oil and gas development in a section of northeastern Alberta. These oil sand deposits are estimated to hold oil reserves second only to those of Saudi Arabia in size. But the mined sand requires burning the equivalent of a barrel of oil for every four barrels that can be "cooked" out. The oil sand deposits underlay an area of about 35 million acres. One of the largest existing oil sand mining operations already occupies 32,000 acres. An analysis in 2006 by Global Forest Watch Canada estimated the current industrial footprint from oil and gas extraction activities throughout Canada's boreal region at 114 million acres.[66-72]

So-called "hardrock mining" can be divided into fuel (coal) and nonfuel mineral mining. In 2003, according to the USGS Minerals Yearbook, there were 14,721 nonfuel mineral mines in the U.S. The number of coal mines in the U.S. in 2000 was tallied at 1453. In addition, the U.S. General Accounting Office reports that there are an estimated 560,000 abandoned mines of all sorts on federal lands in the U.S. While we don't know how many acres are impacted overall from these activities, at least one study has measured recent environmental impacts from coal mining in one region, the southern Appalachians. In a mountainous region encompassing parts of West Virginia, Virginia, Tennessee, and Kentucky—an area that supports the highest densities of Cerulean Warblers on earth—the federal government reported that 816,000 acres have been or will be lost or degraded by mountaintop removal mining. Some 1,200 miles of streams were filled in within the region between 1992 and 2002.[73-75]

What are some of the species discussed in this book that are likely to be impacted by oil and gas development and mining? Along with the previously mentioned Cerulean Warbler and Greater Sage-Grouse the list includes Steller's Eider, Spectacled Eider, Brant, Lesser Prairie-Chicken, Greater Prairie-Chicken, Yellow-billed Loon, American Golden-Plover, Pacific Golden-Plover, Whimbrel, and Buff-breasted Sandpiper.

NONNATIVE SPECIES AND DISEASE

Wilcove and associates found that 69% of endangered and threatened bird species were affected by nonnative species and that 37% were impacted by disease. These were the threat categories impacting the most species after habitat loss and degradation. A similar study using slightly different methodologies found that nonnative species ranked second after habitat loss as the factor impacting the most endangered and threatened species (all taxa considered). One-third of the 201 species on the Audubon WatchList are threatened by introduced, nonnative species and disease.[17,76,77]

It is shocking to most people when they learn that 17% of all plant species in Canada and the U.S. are now nonnative species—over 3,700 species! In some areas, the statistics are even more staggering. For example, 32% of the plant species of both New York State and Massachusetts are nonnative species.[26]

There are many examples of how invasive nonnative plants have destroyed large amounts of bird habitat. Along many rivers in the southwestern U.S., riparian habitat for species like Willow Flycatcher and Yellow-billed Cuckoo has been replaced by introduced and fast-spreading saltcedar. In Bosque del Apache National Wildlife Refuge, an estimated 6,000 acres of riparian habitat has been infested by saltcedar, and a million acres of the southwest U.S. are now occupied by the species. At Aransas National Wildlife Refuge along the Texas Coast, an estimated 55,000 acres have been lost or degraded by the introduced Chinese tallow tree. Across the U.S. and southern Canada, but especially in the northeast U.S., purple loosestrife is estimated to overtake over 400,000 acres of wetlands every year. In south Florida, melaleuca, an Australian tree introduced to Florida in the early 1900s, is now estimated to infest 500,000 acres of habitat and is consuming 10–50 acres more every day. Kudzu, a fast-growing Japanese vine, is now estimated to cover 7 million acres of land in the southeast U.S. Perhaps the king of all exotic invaders is cheatgrass, which is now estimated to be established on an astounding 20–100 million acres, rendering vast amounts of sagebrush and grassland habitats in the western U.S. virtually uninhabitable for many native birds, including species of high conservation concern like Greater Sage-Grouse.[64,77–81]

Introduced insects are also having an impact. Balsam wooly adelgid is destroying high-elevation habitat in the Appalachians that supports isolated southern populations of Red-breasted Nuthatch and Golden-crowned Kinglet. The hemlock wooly adelgid is ravaging hemlock stands and spreading at a rate of 20–30 kilometers per year in the mid-Atlantic states—destroying habitat for Blackburnian Warbler, Black-throated Green Warbler, and Acadian Flycatcher, among others.[28,82–84]

Of introduced nonnative mammals, perhaps the worst offender is the cat. Free-ranging cats are estimated to kill at least 200 million birds a year. For those of us who are cat lovers (our two cats are indoor only), this is a sad and difficult realization, but it highlights how little we understand the workings of the natural world around us. Despite the knowledge of the overwhelming toll that cats take on local native bird and small mammal populations, some people have begun trying to establish feral cat colonies, often in parks or other natural areas. Such efforts place the life of the nonnative cat higher than those of our native warblers, sparrows, and other songbirds that are killed throughout the year by these skilled predators.[85,86]

The impacts of introduced cat and rat populations on island nesting seabirds is especially disturbing. On many islands, entire populations of seabirds have been wiped out from cats and rats that kill virtually all young birds and burrow-nesting adults and eat all the eggs. On Natividad Island off the coast of Mexico's Baja California, the mortality from cats was estimated at more than 1,000 birds per month in 1997. For the Black-vented Shearwater that has 95% of its entire dwindling population attempting to nest on Natividad, such heavy mortality leads down a path toward extinction.[87]

I have included disease within this section because it is usually newly introduced diseases, to which species have not been previously exposed, that are usually the greatest threat to bird populations. The most widely known example in today's world is the West Nile Virus. Although the total impact of West Nile on birds is unknown, it is clear that certain species have seen high mortality. Hundreds of thousands, perhaps millions, of American Crows must have died from the disease and likely many millions of other birds have as well since its inadvertent introduction into the U.S. in 1999. West Nile has been detected in individuals of at least 220 North American bird species according to the USGS National Wildlife Health Center. While species that have very large populations, like American Crows (total population estimated at 31 million), will likely evolve resistance to the disease, species with small populations are potentially at high risk. This is because there is less genetic variability in smaller populations, so that there may not be any individuals that can survive and pass on resistance. That's why a vaccine was developed that allows captive birds to be inoculated, and why all California Condors that had been released into the wild were recaptured and inoculated. But for certain species, capturing them for inoculation is probably impossible. Species like Whooping Crane and Gunnison Sage-Grouse, with populations numbering in the hundreds or low thousands, could be particularly vulnerable to West Nile or other disease outbreaks.[88–92]

In contrast, avian influenza (avian flu) is probably not of major concern for bird conservation as many strains occur naturally in many bird populations so that most probably already have resistance. Strains dangerous to humans have arisen from captive poultry flocks, which provide the ideal (from the disease's standpoint) conditions for the spread and evolution of new strains of avian influenza. Such conditions—large numbers of animals in very close proximity to each other where they share the same food, air, and water—are rarely encountered in wild bird populations. Even in flocking species and colonially nesting species, the disease-breeding conditions under which many poultry are maintained are virtually never replicated.

Other diseases do not directly kill birds but cause impacts by destroying or changing their habitat. In eastern North America the introduced chestnut blight disease virtually eliminated the American chestnut from deciduous forests and relegated it to a living extinction. Trees continue to send up new sprouts, which quickly become infected themselves and die back. Chestnut trees were once a dominant tree in many eastern forests but were essentially gone by the 1950s. Similarly, the introduced butternut canker disease is estimated to have wiped out 77% of butternut trees in the southeast U.S. and Dutch elm disease continues to spread. Sudden oak death syndrome, inadvertently introduced into California in 1995, has already killed at least 100,000 oak trees in coastal California. The impact of the loss of such large numbers of important habitat components of forest ecosystems on birds and other wildlife has never been quantified but certainly must be dramatic.[93–96]

OVEREXPLOITATION

While the Wilcove study found that overexploitation was a factor impacting 33% of endangered and threatened U.S. birds, the threat from overexploitation within the U.S. is generally a fact of history rather than a current threat. However, a number of species that occur in the U.S. are targets of the caged bird trade, or in a few cases, of unsustainable hunting, when they migrate south of the U.S. A good example is the Painted Bunting, which is captured by the tens of thousands in Mexico and Cuba for sale in the caged bird trade. At the global level, overexploitation does remain a major threat (30% of globally threatened bird species), especially in undeveloped countries, for many species of birds, including parrots, pigeons, and pheasants.[17,18,97]

POLLUTION

The impacts of various forms of pollution on birds are diverse and significant. At the global level, BirdLife International reports that 187 globally threatened birds are threatened by pollution, while Wilcove and associates found that 22% of U.S. endangered and threatened birds were affected by pollution.[17,18]

Between 300 and 500 million tons of hazardous waste are produced annually across the globe. The number of synthetic chemicals in production on earth is estimated at 50,000–100,000. Human activities have doubled the annual release of nitrogen into the environment and tripled that of phosphorus.[98]

More than two million tons of pesticides are used across the world every year, 20% of that total in the U.S. alone. Agricultural pesticides alone are estimated to kill a minimum of 67 million birds annually in the U.S. Many migrant birds are the victims of pesticide poisoning outside of North America where there is often little or no regulatory oversight of pesticide use or other pollutants. During the winter of 1995–96 researchers documented the deaths of over 5,000 Swainson's Hawks from the spraying of an insecticide on the Argentinean wintering grounds.[99–101]

The U.S. Environmental Protection Agency estimated that 200 million tons of air pollutants were emitted into the atmosphere in the U.S. in 1997. While significant drops in the amount of sulfur dioxide emitted from industrial sources have been achieved in the U.S. and Canada in recent decades, there is still enough coming down to damage thousands of lakes, streams, and ponds across the eastern U.S. and Canada. Among many ways in which acid rain can impact birds is through the depletion of calcium in the soil so that less is available to female birds for egg production, causing reductions in reproductive success. A study by researchers at the Cornell Lab of Ornithology in 2002 found that in areas with high levels of acid rain, Wood Thrushes showed lowered probabilities of breeding—a result that may be linked to decreases in calcium availability in such regions.[102–106]

Mercury is another pollutant that is emitted in harmful quantities into the air from industrial sources, especially coal-fired power plants and incinerators. Despite reductions in the amount of mercury released from industrial sources over the last twenty years, research published in 2005 showed that mercury contamination from these sources continues to harm fish, wildlife, and people in northeastern North America. Mercury levels were above the U.S. EPA suggested threshold in 42% of water bodies sampled for yellow perch and 15% sampled for brook trout within the region. Ten popular game fish species had average mercury levels across northeastern North America that exceeded the EPA criterion. In much of the region, human health advisories recommend that pregnant women and young children not eat any fish taken from freshwater lakes and rivers. Perhaps not surprisingly, species that eat fish, like Common Loon and Bald Eagle, were found to be among birds with the highest mercury levels. More shocking was the discovery that even many forest songbirds are now exhibiting unusually high levels of mercury in their bodies. Bicknell's Thrush, a high-elevation forest specialist restricted to northeastern North America, was found to have the highest levels among the species of high-elevation songbirds.[107]

INCIDENTAL MORTALITY

Many human activities result in the direct, but unintentional, mortality of birds. All of us have probably been in a vehicle that has hit a bird or heard the concussive thud of a bird striking a window in a home or workplace. And many of us have listened to the radio, watched television, talked on a cell phone, and eaten fish captured on longlines or gill nets—all activities that indirectly kill birds. While very large numbers of birds are killed each year from these sources, it is important to realize that the impacts of habitat loss and degradation, nonnative species and disease, and pollution (and eventually global warming) are many times greater, certainly involving losses of hundreds of millions or even billions of birds when considered annually. Certainly anything that can be done to reduce the numbers of birds killed through incidental mortality is important. But if birders focus more of their attention on these issues and neglect those that are really causing the declines then we will ultimately lose the battle to protect our birds, our habitats, and, by extension, the health and welfare of our families.

In a few cases though, particular forms of incidental mortality can be among the most significant factors impacting some bird species. A good example is the impact of fishery practices on certain long-lived seabirds. An estimated 300,000 seabirds (some put the number at over a million) are killed annually across the world's oceans when accidentally snagged on the more than one billion longline hooks that are set each year in the open ocean. Albatrosses, in particular, have been hard hit by such activity. As many as 19,000 Black-footed Albatross and 15,000 Laysan Albatross are estimated to be killed annually when they are inadvertently hooked as they go after bait on longlines and subsequently drown on the submerged lines. Thousands of seabirds are also drowned each year in gill nets and other types of fishing apparatus. Over 3,000 Marbled Murrelets were killed in 1995 in nearshore waters from Alaska south to Washington in gillnetting operations.[108–112]

Other sources of incidental mortality and their estimates of mortality include collisions with windows (550 million), collisions with cars and trucks (80 million), collisions with electric transmission lines (130 million), collisions with communication towers (4.5 million), and collisions with wind power facilities (currently estimated in the tens of thousands). In almost all cases (except perhaps for vehicle collisions), significant work is ongoing to find ways to reduce mortality from all these sources. Solutions include turning off lights on tall buildings during migration, placing nonreflective surfaces on windows, changing types of warning lights on communication towers, building towers with no or fewer supporting guywires, and developing guidelines for placement of towers and wind turbines away from major bird migration corridors and concentration points.[113,114]

HUNTING

In North America, unsustainable hunting as a factor contributing to bird declines is a thing of the past, except perhaps in a few local regions. Many birders are also avid hunters, including of game birds, and hunters and hunting-related environmental groups are among the most active and successful conservationists. According to the U.S. Fish and Wildlife Service, annual mortality of birds from hunting in the U.S. is between 100 and 150 million, including from waterfowl, rails, grouse, pheasant, and doves. The majority of birds taken, though, are Mourning Doves and Ring-necked Pheasant. The former species continues to be one of the most abundant birds in North America and the latter is an abundant but introduced species from its native range in Asia. The question of whether hunting can exacerbate declines in certain cases where species are already declining from other causes is one that is often hotly debated, unfortunately, often because of political rather than biological reasons. It is clear that in some cases relief of hunting pressure for a particular species, in a particular part of the range, or during an important period in the life history cycle of a species, is warranted. But also clear is the fact that hunting alone is not a major conservation issue for most bird species in the U.S. and Canada.[115,116]

REFERENCES

1. Webster, P.J., G.J. Holland, J.A. Curry, and H.R. Chang. 2005. Changes in Tropical Cyclone Number, Duration, and Intensity in a Warming Environment. *Science* 309:1844–1846.

2. United States Global Change Research Program (USGCRP). 2000. *Climate Change Impacts on the United States: The Potential Consequences of Climate Variability and Change*. Cambridge University Press, Cambridge, UK. 154 pp.

3. Root, T.L., and S.H. Schneider. 2002. Climate Change: Overview and Implications for Wildlife. In *Wildlife Responses to Climate Change: North American Case Studies* (S.H. Schneider and T.L. Root, eds.). Island Press, Covelo, CA.

4. Price, J., and P. Glick. 2002. *The Birdwatcher's Guide to Global Warming*. National Wildlife Federation and American Bird Conservancy, Reston VA, and The Plains, VA. 32 pp.

5. Glick, P. 2005. *The Waterfowler's Guide to Global Warming*. National Wildlife Federation, Washington, DC. 37 pp.

6. Ferreira de Siqueira, M., A. Grainger, L. Hannah, L. Hughes, B. Huntley, A.S. Van Jarrsveld, G.F. Midgley, L. Miles, M.A. Ortega-Huerta, A.T. Peterson, O.L. Phillips, and S.E. Williams. 2004. Extinction Risk from Climate Change. *Nature* 427:145–148.

7. Butler, C. J. 2003. The Disproportionate Effect of Global Warming on the Arrival Dates of Short-distance Migratory Birds in North America. *Ibis* 145:484–495.

8. Mills, A.M. 2005. Changes in the Timing of Spring and Autumn Migration in North American Migrant Passerines During a Period of Global Warming. *Ibis* 147: 259–269.

9. Root, T.L., J.T. Price, K.R. Hall, S.H. Schneider, C. Rosenzweig, and A. Pounds. 2003. 'Fingerprints' of Global Warming on Wildlife Animals and Plants. *Nature* 421:57–60.

10. Crick, H.Q.P. 2004. The Impact of Climate Change on Birds. *Ibis* 146:48–56.

11. Leech, D. 2002. The Effect of Climate Change on Birds. British Trust for Ornithology. http://www.bto.org/research/advice/ecc/eccsection62.htm (accessed 28 January 2005).

12. Dunn, P.O., and D.W. Winkler. 1999. Climate Change Has Affected the Breeding Date of Tree Swallow Throughout North America. *Proceedings of the Royal Society of London* 226:2487–2490.

13. Both, C., and M.E. Visser. 2001. Adjustment to Climate Change Is Constrained by Arrival Date in a Long-distance Migrant Bird. *Nature* 411:296–298.

14. BirdLife International. 2005. *Seabirds in the North Sea: Victims of Climate Change?* http://www.birdlife.org/news/features/2005/01/north_sea_seabirds.html (accessed 23 February 2006).

15. BBC. 2005. Seabird Colonies in Scotland Have Suffered One of the Worst Breeding Seasons on Record, Experts Have Warned. http://news.bbc.co.uk/2/hi/uk_news/scotland/4201880.stm (accessed 7 September 2005).

16. Mathews, S.N., R.J. O'Connor, L.R. Iverson, and A.M. Prasad. 2004. *Atlas of Climate Change Effects in 150 Bird Species of the Eastern United States*. Gen. Tech. Rep. NE-318. U.S. Department of Agriculture, Forest Service, Northeastern Research Station, Newton Square, PA. 340 pp.

17. Wilcove, D.S., D. Rothstein, J. Dubow, A. Phillips, and E. Losos. 2000. Leading Threats to U.S. Biodiversity: What's Threatening Imperiled Species? In *Precious Heritage: The Status of Biodiversity in the United States* (B. Stein et al., eds.). Oxford University Press, Oxford, UK.

18. BirdLife International. 2000. *Threatened Birds of the World*. Lynx Editions and BirdLife International, Barcelona, Spain, and Cambridge, UK.

19. BirdLife International. 2004. *State of the World's Birds 2004: Indicators for Our Changing World*. BirdLife International, Cambridge, UK.

20. White, R.P., S. Murray, and M. Rohweder. 2000. *Pilot Analysis of Grassland Ecosystems*. World Resources Institute, Baltimore, MD. http://www.wri.org/wr2000.

21. Dahl, Thomas E. 1990. *Wetlands Losses in the United States 1780's to 1980's*. U.S. Department of the Interior, Fish and Wildlife Service, Washington, DC. Jamestown, ND: Northern Prairie Wildlife Research Center Home Page. http://www.npwrc.usgs.gov/resource/othrdata/wetloss/wetloss.htm (Version 16JUL97).

22. Stein, B.A., L.S. Kutner, and J.S. Adams. 2000. *Precious Heritage: The Status of Biodiversity in the United States*. Oxford University Press, New York, NY. 399 pp.

23. Delta Waterfowl Foundation. 2003. *The Great American Plowout Threatens Duck Production*. http://www.deltawaterfowl.org/home/archive/2003/030818_plowout.html (accessed 28 January 2004).

24. Vickery, P.D., P.L. Tubaro, J.M. Cardoso da Silva, B.G. Peterjohn, J.R. Herkert, and R.B. Cavalcanti. 1999. Conservation of Grassland Birds in the Western Hemisphere. Pages 2–26 in *Ecology and Conservation of Grassland Birds in the Western Hemisphere* (P.D. Vickery and J.R. Herkert, eds.). Studies in Avian Biology No. 19, Cooper Ornithological Society, Camarillo, CA.

25. Statistics Canada. 1997. *1996 Census of Agriculture*. Ottawa, ON, Canada.

26. Ricketts, T.H., E. Dinerstein, D.M. Olson, C.J. Loucks, et al. 1999. *Terrestrial Ecoregions of North America: A Conservation Assessment*. Island Press, Washington, DC. 485 pp.

27. Rosenberg, K.V., and J.V. Wells. 2005. Conservation Priorities for Terrestrial Birds in the Northeastern United States. Pages 236–253 in *Bird Conservation Implementation and Integration in the Americas*. Proceedings of the 3rd International Partners in Flight Conference, 2002 March 20–24; Asilomar, CA, Volume 1 (C.J. Ralph and T.D. Rich, eds.). USDA Forest Service, Gen. Tech. Rep. PSW-GTR-191, Albany, CA.

28. Askins, R.A. 2000. *Restoring North America's Birds: Lessons from Landscape Ecology*. Yale University Press, New Haven, CT. 320 pp.

29. Knopf, F.L. 1996. Mountain Plover (*Charadrius montanus*). In *The Birds of North America*, No. 211 (A. Poole and F. Gill, eds.). The Academy of Natural Sciences, Philadelphia, PA, and the American Ornithologists' Union, Washington, DC.

30. U.S. Environmental Protection Agency. 2003. *Draft Report on the Environment*. http://www.epa.gov/indicators/roe/html/roeExec2.htm (accessed 28 March 2005).

31. Tregoning. H.1999. Why Smart Growth Matters. Pages 22–24 in *Smart Growth Conference Proceedings 1999* (A. Heaphy and G. Cox, eds.). Audubon Society of New York State, Albany, NY.

32. Luom, J.R. 1997. Whittling Dixie. *Audubon* Nov./Dec: 40–45, 97–100.

33. Wear, D. N. and J.G. Greis, eds. 2002. *Southern Forest Resource Assessment*. Gen. Tech. Rep. SRS-53. U.S. Department of Agriculture, Forest Service, Southern Research Station, Asheville, NC. 635 pp.

34. H. John Heinz III Center for Science, Economics and the Environment. 2003. *The State of the Nation's Ecosystems*. http://www.heinzctr.org/ecosystems/report.html (accessed 30 March 2005).

35. Lee, P., D. Aksenov, L. Laestadius, R. Nogueron, and W. Smith. 2003. *Canada's Large Intact Forest Landscapes*. Global Forest Watch Canada, Edmonton, AB. 84 pp.

36. ForestEthics. Undated. *Bring Down the Boreal: How U.S. Consumption of Forest Products is Destroying Canada's Endangered Northern Forests*. ForestEthics, San Francisco, CA. 25 pp.

37. Hamel, P., K.V. Rosenberg, and D.A. Buehler. 2005. Is Management for Golden-winged Warblers and Cerulean Warblers Compatible? Pages 322–331 in *Bird Conservation Implementation and Integration in the Americas*. Proceedings of the 3rd International Partners in Flight Conference, 2002 March 20–24, Asilomar, CA, Volume 1 (C.J. Ralph and T.D. Rich, eds.). USDA Forest Service, Gen. Tech. Rep. PSW-GTR-191, Albany, CA.

38. Sallabanks, R., and E.B.Arnett. 2005. Accommodating Birds in Managed Forests of North America: A Review of Bird–Forestry Relationships. Pages 345–372 in *Bird Conservation Implementation and Integration in the Americas*. Proceedings of the 3rd International Partners in Flight Conference, 2002 March 20–24; Asilomar, CA, Volume 1 (C.J. Ralph and T.D. Rich, eds.). USDA Forest Service, Gen. Tech. Rep. PSW-GTR-191, Albany, CA.

39. Baker, J.C., and W.C. Hunter. 2002. Effects of Forest Management on Terrestrial Ecosystems. Pages 91–112 in *Southern Forest Resource Assessment* (D.N. Wear and J.G. Greis, eds.). Gen. Tech. Rep. SRS-53, U.S. Department of Agriculture, Forest Service, Southern Research Station, Asheville, NC.

40. Thompson, F.R. III, J.R. Probst, and M.G. Raphael. 1995. Impacts of Silviculture: Overview and Management Recommendations. Pages 201–219 in *Ecology and Management of Neotropical Migratory Birds* (T.E. Martin and D.M. Finch, eds.). Oxford University Press, New York, NY.

41. Hejl, S.J., R.L. Hutto, C.R. Preston, and D.M. Finch. 1995. Effects of Silvicultural Treatments in the Rocky Mountains. Pages 220–244 in *Ecology and Management of Neotropical Migratory Birds* (T.E. Martin and D.M. Finch, eds.). Oxford University Press, New York, NY.

42. Dickson, J.G., F.R Thompson III, R.N. Conner, and K.E. Franzreb. 1995. Silviculture in Central and Southeastern Oak-Pine Forests. Pages 245–266 in *Ecology and Management of Neotropical Migratory Birds* (T.E. Martin and D.M. Finch, eds.). Oxford University Press, New York, NY.

43. Jackson, J.A. 1994. Red-cockaded Woodpecker (*Picoides borealis*). In *The Birds of North America*, No. 85 (A. Poole and F. Gill, eds.). The Academy of Natural Sciences, Philadelphia, PA, and the American Ornithologists' Union, Washington, DC.

44. Dunning, J.B. 1993. Bachman's Sparrow (*Aimophila aestivalis*). In *The Birds of North America*, No. 38 (A. Poole, P. Stettenheim, and F. Gill, eds.). The Academy of Natural Sciences, Philadelphia, PA, and the American Ornithologists' Union, Washington, DC.

45. Withgott, J.H., and K.G. Smith 1998. Brown-headed Nuthatch (*Sitta pusilla*). In *The Birds of North America*, No. 349 (A. Poole and F. Gill, eds.). The Birds of North America, Inc., Philadelphia, PA.

46. Herkert, J.R., P.D. Vickery, and D.E. Kroodsma. 2002. Henslow's Sparrow (*Ammodramus henslowii*). In *The Birds of North America*, No. 672 (A. Poole and F. Gill, eds.). The Birds of North America, Inc., Philadelphia, PA.

47. Mayfield, H.F. 1992. Kirtland's Warbler (*Dendroica kirtlandii*). In *The Birds of North America*, No. 19 (A. Poole, P.Stettenheim, and F. Gill, eds.). The Academy of Natural Sciences, Philadelphia, PA, and the American Ornithologists' Union, Washington, DC.

48. Vickery, P.D., M.L. Hunter, Jr., and J.V. Wells. 1999. Effects of Fire and Herbicide Treatment on Habitat Selection in Grassland Birds in Southern Maine. Pages 149–159 in *Ecology and Conservation of Grassland Birds in the Western Hemisphere* (P.D. Vickery and J.R. Herkert, eds.). Studies in Avian Biology No. 19, Cooper Ornithological Society, Camarillo, CA.

49. Winter, M. 1999. Relationship of Fire History to Territory Size, Breeding Density, and Habitat of Baird's Sparrow in North Dakota. Pages 171–177 In *Ecology and Conservation of Grassland Birds in the Western Hemisphere* (P.D. Vickery and J.R. Herkert, eds.). Studies in Avian Biology No. 19, Cooper Ornithological Society, Camarillo, CA.

50. Shriver, W.G., P.D. Vickery, and D.W. Perkins. 1999. The Effects of Summer Burns on Breeding Florida Grasshopper and Bachman's Sparrow. Pages 144–148 in *Ecology and Conservation of Grassland Birds in the Western Hemisphere* (P.D. Vickery and J.R. Herkert, eds.). Studies in Avian Biology No. 19, Cooper Ornithological Society, Camarillo, CA.

51. Vickery, P.D., B. Zuckerberg, A.L. Jones, W.G. Shriver, and A.P. Weik. 2005. Influence of Fire and Other Anthropogenic Practices on Grassland and Shrubland Birds in New England. Pages 1087–1089 in *Bird Conservation Implementation and Integration in the Americas*. Proceedings of the 3rd International Partners in Flight Conference, 2002 March 20–24, Asilomar, CA, Volume 1 (C.J. Ralph and T.D. Rich, eds.). USDA Forest Service, Gen. Tech. Rep. PSW-GTR-191, Albany, CA.

52. Bock, C.E., and W.M. Block. 2005. Response of Birds to Fire in the American Southwest. Pages 1093–1099 in *Bird Conservation Implementation and Integration in the Americas*. Proceedings of the 3rd International Partners in Flight Conference, 2002 March 20–24, Asilomar, CA, Volume 1 (C.J. Ralph and T.D. Rich, eds.). USDA Forest Service, Gen. Tech. Rep. PSW-GTR-191, Albany, CA.

53. Saab, V.A., N.B. Kotliar, and W.M. Block. 2005. Relationships of Fire Ecology and Avian Communities in North America. Pages 1083–1085 in *Bird Conservation Implementation and Integration in the Americas*. Proceedings of the 3rd International Partners in Flight Conference, 2002 March 20–24, Asilomar, CA, Volume 1 (C.J. Ralph and T.D. Rich, eds.). USDA Forest Service, Gen. Tech. Rep. PSW-GTR-191, Albany, CA.

54. Schroeder, M.A., J.R. Young, and C.E. Braun. 1999. Sage Grouse (*Centrocercus urophasianus*). In *The Birds of North America*, No. 425 (A. Poole and F. Gill, eds.). The Birds of North America, Inc., Philadelphia, PA.

55. Rotenberry, J.T., M. A. Patten, and K. L. Preston. 1999. Brewer's Sparrow (*Spizella breweri*). In *The Birds of North America*, No. 390 (A. Poole and F. Gill, eds.). The Birds of North America, Inc., Philadelphia, PA.

56. National Research Council. *Restoration of Aquatic Ecosystems: Science, Technology, and Public Policy*. National Academy Press, Washington, DC, 1992.

57. Dynesius, M., and C. Nilsson. 1994. Fragmentation and Flow Regulation of River Systems in the Northern Third of the World. *Science* 266:753–761.

58. Penland, S. 2005. Taming the River to Let in the Sea. *Natural History*, Feb. 2005:42–47.

59. Gauthier, J, and Y. Aubry. 1996. *The Breeding Birds of Quebec*. Province of Quebec Society for the Protection of Birds and Canadian Wildlife Service, Environment Canada, Quebec Region, Montreal, QC. 1302 pp.

60. American Petroleum Institute. No date. *Exploring for Gas and Oil: Where Does the U.S. Produce Oil and Natural Gas?* http://api-ec.api.org/policy/index (accessed 1 March 2006).

61. Horwitt, D., C. Campbell, S. Gray, J. Mata-Fink, S. Myers, and J. Houlihan. 2006. *Big Access, Little Energy—The Oil and Gas Industry's Hold on Western Lands*. Environmental Working Group, Washington, D.C. http://www.ewg.org/oil_and_gas/execsumm.php (accessed 2 March 2006).

62. United States Government Accountability Office. 2005. *Oil and Gas Development: Increased Permitting Activity Has Lessened BLM's Ability to Meet Its Environmental Protection Responsibilities.* GAO-05-418. http://www.gao.gov/new.items/d05418.pdf.

63. Debevoise, N., and C. Rawlins (eds.). 1996. *The Red Desert Blues: The Industrialization of Southwest Wyoming.* Wyoming Outdoor Council, Lincoln, WY.

64. Connelly, J. W., S. T. Knick, M. A. Schroeder, and S. J. Stiver. 2004. Conservation Assessment of Greater Sage-Grouse and Sagebrush Habitats. Unpublished report. Western Association of Fish and Wildlife Agencies, Cheyenne, WY.

65. Canadian Association of Petroleum Producers. 2005. *CAPP Releases 2004 Petroleum Reserves Estimate.* http://www.capp.ca (accessed 1 March 2006).

66. Mackenzie Wild. No date. *Mackenzie Gas Project.* http://mackenziewild.ca/gas-project/index.html (acceseed 2 March 2006).

67. Sierra Club of Canada. 2005. *Mackenzie Valley Pipeline and Alberta Oil Sands.* http://www.sierraclub.ca/national/programs/atmosphere-energy/energy-on-slaught/campaign.shtml?x=307 (accessed 2 March 2006).

68. Schultz, C., and S. Hazell. 2005. *Migratory Birds and IBAs: Technical Review of Mackenzie Gas Project EIS.* Nature Canada, Ottawa, ON. http://www.cnf.ca/parks/mgp.html.

69. Schneider, R. R., J. B. Stelfox, S. Boutin, and S. Wasel. 2003. Managing the Cumulative Impacts of Land Uses in the Western Canadian Sedimentary Basin: A Modeling Approach. *Conservation Ecology* 7(1): 8. http://www.consecol.org/vol7/iss1/art8.

70. Government of Alberta. 2004. *Oil Sands.* http://www.energy.gov.ab.ca/89.asp (accessed 2 March 2006).

71. Woynillowicz, D., C. Severson-Baker, and M. Raynolds. 2005. *Oil Sands Fever: The Environmental Implications of Canada's Oil Sands Rush.* Pembina Institute, Drayton Valley, AB. 86 pp.

72. Anielski, M.,and S. Wilson. 2005. *Counting Canada's Natural Capital: Assessing the Real Value of Canada's Boreal Ecosystems.* Canadian Boreal Initiative, Ottawa, and Pembina Institute, Drayton Valley, AB. 78 pp.

73. USGS. 2003. *USGS Minerals Yearbook.* http://minerals.usgs.gov/minerals/pubs/myb.html.

74. General Accounting Office.1996. *Federal Land Management: Information on Efforts to Inventory Abandoned Hard Rock Mines.* http://www.gao.gov/archive/1996/rc96030.pdf

75. EPA. 2005. *Mountaintop Mining/Valley Fills in Appalachia: Final Programmatic Environmental Impact Statement.* http://www.epa.gov/region3/mtntop/index.htm.

76. Flather, C.H., L.A. Joyce, and C.A. Bloomgarden. 1994. *Species Endangerment Patterns in the United States.* USDA Forest Service General Technical Report RM-241. U.S. Department of Agriculture, Forest Service, Rocky Mountain Forest and Range Experiment Station, Fort Collins, CO.

77. Audubon. No date. *Cooling the Hot Spots: Protecting America's Birds, Wildlife, and Natural Heritage.* http://www.audubon.org/campaign/invasives/index.shtm (accessed 6 March, 2006).

78. Federal Interagency Committee for the Management of Noxious and Exotic Weeds. No date. https://www.denix.osd.mil/denix/Public/ES-Programs/Conservation/Invasive/contents.html (accessed 6 March 2006).

79. Pimental, D., L. Lach, R. Zuniga, and D. Morrison. 2000. Environmental and Economic Costs of Nonindigenous Species in the United States. *BioScience* 50:53–65.

80. Thomposon, D.G., R.L. Stuckey, and E.B. Thompson. 1987. *Spread, Impact, and Control of Purple Loosestrife* (Lythrum salicaria) *in North American Wetlands.* U.S. Fish and Wildlife Service, Washington, DC.

81. Carpenter, A.T., and T. A. Murray. No date. *Elemental Stewardship Abstract for* Bromus tectorum L. The Nature Conservancy, Arlington, VA. http://tncweeds.ucdavis.edu/esadocs/documnts/bromtec.pdf.

82. Foster, D.R. 1999. Hemlock's Future in the Context of Its History: An Ecological Perspective. Page 15 in *Proceedings: Symposium on Sustainable Management of Hemlock Ecosystems in Eastern North America* (K. A. McManus, K. S. Shields, and D. R. Souto, eds.). General Technical Report NE-267, U.S. Department of Agriculture Forest Service Northeastern Research Station, Newtown Square, PA. http://www.fs.fed.us/na/morgantown/hemlock_proceedings/hemlock_proceedings_index.html.

83. Tingley, M.W., D. A. Orwig,, R. Field, and G. Motzkin. 2002. Avian Response to Removal of a Forest Dominant: Consequences of Hemlock Woolly Adelgid Infestations. *Journal of Biogeography* 29:1505–1516.

84. Evans, R.A. 2004. Hemlock Woolly Adelgid and the Disintegration of Eastern Hemlock Ecosystems. *ParkScience* 22:53–56.

85. American Bird Conservancy. No date. Cats Indoors! The Campaign for Safer Birds and Cats. http://www.abcbirds.org/cats/.

86. Chipley, R.M., G.H. Fenwick, M.J. Parr, and

D.N. Pashley. 2003. *The American Bird Conservancy Guide to the 500 Most Important Bird Areas in the United States.* Random House, NY.

87. Keitt, B.S., B.R. Tershy, & D.A. Croll. 2000. Black-vented Shearwater (*Puffinus opisthomelas*). In *The Birds of North America*, No. 521 (A. Poole and F. Gill, eds.). The Academy of Natural Sciences, Philadelphia, PA, and The American Ornithologists' Union, Washington, DC.

88. National Audubon Society. 2005. Effects on Wildlife [from West Nile]. http://www.audubon.org/bird/wnv/pdf/effects_on_wildlife.pdf (accessed 6 March 2006).

89. Yaremych S.A., R.E. Warner, P.C. Mankin, J.D. Brawn, A. Raim, and R. Novak. West Nile Virus and High Death Rate in American Crows. *Emerging Infectious Diseases* 2004 Apr. http://www.cdc.gov/ncidod/EID/vol10no4/03-0499.htm.

90. Caffrey, C., S.C.R. Smith, and T.J. Weston. 2005. West Nile Virus Devastates an American Crow Population. *Condor* 107: 128–132.

91. Naugle, D. E., C.L. Aldridge, B.L. Walker, T.E. Cornish, B.J. Moynahan, M.J. Holloran, K. Brown, G.D. Johnson, E.T.Schmidtmann, R.T. Mayer, C.Y. Kato, M.R. Matchett, T.J. Christiansen, W.E. Cook, T. Creekmore, R.D. Falise, E. Thomas Rinkes, and M.S. Boyce. 2004. West Nile Virus: Pending Crisis for Greater Sagegrouse. *Ecology Letters* 7: 704–713.

92. Komar O, M.B. Robbins, K. Klenk, B.J. Blitvich, N.L. Marlenee, K.L. Burkhalter, et al. 2003. West Nile Virus Transmission in Resident Birds, Dominican Republic. *Emerging Infectious Diseases* 2003 Oct. http://www.cdc.gov/ncidod/EID/vol9no10/03-0222.htm.

93. Anagnostakis, S.L. 1987. Chestnut Blight: The Classical Problem of an Introduced Pathogen. *Mycologia* 79: 23–37.

94. Nuss, D.L.1992. Biological Control of Chestnut Blight: An Example of Virus-mediated Attenuation of Fungal Pathogenesis. *Microbiology Reviews* 56: 561–576.

95. Schlarbaum, S. E., F. Hebard, P. C. Spaine, and J. C. Kamalay. 1997. Three American Tragedies: Chestnut Blight, Butternut Canker, and Dutch Elm Disease. Pages 45–54 in *Proc. Exotic Pest of Eastern Forests, 8–10 April 1997, Nashville, TN.*

96. The Nature Conservancy. 2005. Gallery of Pests: Recently Introduced Pathogen—Sudden Oak Death Syndrome—*Phytophthora ramorum* Werres et al. http://tncweeds.ucdavis.edu/products/gallery/phyra1.html (accessed 6 March 2006).

97. Inigo-Elias, E. E., K. V. Rosenberg, and J.V. Wells. 2002. The Danger of Beauty. *Birdscope* 16:1, 14.

98. Worldwatch Institute. 2003. *State of the World 2003.* W.W. Norton & Company, New York, NY. 241 pp.

99. Kiely, T., D. Donaldson, and A. Grube. 2004. *Pesticides Industry Sales and Usage: 2000 and 2001 Market Estimates.* U.S. Environmental Protection Agency Washington, DC. http://www.epa.gov/oppbead1/pestsales/.

100. Pimentel, D., H. Acquay, M. Biltonen, P. Rice, M. Silva, J. Nelson, V. Lipner, S. Giordano, A. Horowitz, and M. D'Amore. 1992. Environmental and Economic Costs of Pesticide Use. *Bioscience* 42:750–760.

101. Goldstein, M.I., T. E. Lacher, B. Woodbridge, M. J. Bechard, S. B. Canavelli, M. E. Zaccagnini, G. P. Cobb, E. J. Scollon, R. Tribolet, and M. J. Hopper. 1999. Monocrotophos-induced Mass Mortality of Swainson's Hawks in Argentina, 1995–96. *Ecotoxicology* 8:201–214.

102. U.S. Environmental Protection Agency. 1998. *National Air Quality and Emissions Trend Report, 1997.* U.S. Environmental Protection Agency, Research Triangle Park, NC.

103. Geological Survey. 2000. *Atmospheric Deposition Program of the U.S. Geological Survey,* USGS Fact Sheet FS–112–00. http://bqs.usgs.gov/acidrain/.

104. Environment Canada. 2004. *Canadian Acid Deposition Science Assessment 2004.* http://www.msc-smc.ec.gc.ca/saib/acid/acid_e.html.

105. White, J.C. (ed.). 2003. *Acid Rain: Are the Problems Solved?* American Fisheries Society, Bethesda, MD. 250 pp.

106. Hames, R.S., K. V. Rosenberg, J. D. Lowe, S. E. Barker, and A. A. Dhondt. 2002. Adverse Effects of Acid Rain on the Distribution of the Wood Thrush *Hylocichla mustelina* in North America. *Proceedings of the National Academy of Sciences* 99:11235–11240.

107. Evers, D.C., and T.A. Clair (eds.). 2005. Biogeographical Patterns of Environmental Mercury in Northeastern North America. *Ecotoxicology* 14.

108. BirdLife International. No date. *BirdLife International Global Seabird Programme.* http://www.birdlife.org/action/science/species/seabirds/seabird_calling_card.pdf.

109. Montevicchi, W.A. 2002. Interactions Between Fisheries and Seabirds. Pages 527–557 in *Biology of Marine Birds* (E.A. Schreiber and J. Burger, eds.). CRC Press, Boca Raton, FL.

110. Cousins, K., P. Dalzell, and E.L. Gilman. 2001. Managing Pelagic Longline–Albatross Interactions in the North Pacific Ocean. *Marine Ornithology* 28(2): 159–174.

111. Nelson, S.K. 1997. Marbled Murrelet (*Brachyramphus marmoratus*). in *The Birds of North America*, No. 276 (A. Poole and F. Gill, eds.). The Academy of Natur-

al Sciences, Philadelphia, PA, and The American Ornithologists' Union, Washington, DC.

112. Manville, A.M., II. 2005. Seabird and Waterbird Bycatch in Fishing Gear: Next Steps in Dealing with a Problem. Pages 1071–1082 in *Bird Conservation Implementation and Integration in the Americas*. Proceedings of the 3rd International Partners in Flight Conference, 2002 March 20–24, Asilomar, CA, Volume 1 (C.J. Ralph and T.D. Rich, eds.). USDA Forest Service, Gen. Tech. Rep. PSW-GTR-191, Albany, CA.

113. Erickson, W.P., G.D. Johnson, and D.P. Young, Jr. 2005. A Summary and Comparison of Bird Mortality from Anthropogenic Causes with an Emphasis on Collisions. Pages 1029–1042 in *Bird Conservation Implementation and Integration in the Americas*. Proceedings of the 3rd International Partners in Flight Conference, 2002 March 20–24, Asilomar, CA, Volume 1 (C.J. Ralph and T.D. Rich, eds.). USDA Forest Service, Gen. Tech. Rep. PSW-GTR-191, Albany, CA.

114. Manville, A.M., II. 2005. Bird Strikes and Electrocutions at Power Lines, Communication Towers, and Wind Turbines: State of the Art and State of the Science—Next Steps Toward Mitigation. Pages 1051–1064 in *Bird Conservation Implementation and Integration in the Americas*. Proceedings of the 3rd International Partners in Flight Conference, 2002 March 20–24, Asilomar, CA, Volume 1 (C.J. Ralph and T.D. Rich, eds.). USDA Forest Service, Gen. Tech. Rep. PSW-GTR-191, Albany, CA.

115. Banks, R.C. 1979. *Human Related Mortality of Birds in the United States*. Special Scientific Report—Wildlife No. 215:1–16, National Fish and Wildlife Lab, Fish and Wildlife Service, U.S. Department of the Interior. GPO 848–972.

116. U.S. Fish and Wildlife Service. 2005. *Migratory Bird Harvest Information, 2004: Preliminary Estimates*. U.S. Department of the Interior, Washington, DC.

The State of Bird Conservation in North America and Beyond

By the time this book has been released, the news of the apparent rediscovery of the Ivory-billed Woodpecker will have long become public. The debate over the species' continued existence may or may not be quelled, but the event will have sharpened the focus on preserving and restoring segments of the once-vast bottomland hardwood forests of the Mississippi Valley. As a participant in the first search teams to have descended on the cypress cathedrals of southeastern Arkansas where the initial sightings were reported in the spring of 2004, I thought a lot about the strengths and weaknesses of past bird conservation efforts. While sitting on a log surrounded by the muddy waters of the flooded swamp for 10 hours each day, I was often struck by the fact that the 500-year-old cypress that I was leaning against had once felt the feet of Ivory-billed Woodpeckers on its bark. I could imagine hearing the screeches of Carolina Parakeets as flocks darted over the tree tops. And, amid the buzzy songs of the early spring migrating Northern Parula warblers, there was a vague anticipation that I might hear one that was a bit different—a Bachman's Warbler, perhaps?

The lack of understanding or concern about the interdependence of people and the environment that resulted in the extinction or near extinction of at least six North American bird species spawned a revolutionary grassroots movement in the late 1800s and first half of the 1900s that brought the idea of conservation into the American consciousness. One of the most well-known embodiments of this movement was the various Audubon societies that sprang up initially to combat the excesses of commercial hunting. In those days, it was not uncommon to see feathers, bird heads, whole birds, or even an entire nest site complete with adult birds, nest, and eggs poised in death atop ladies' hats. Many bird species were also relentlessly hunted to be sold for food in markets. The hunting and harvesting of Passenger Pigeons in the late 1800s was as horrifying as it was efficient. Adult birds were blasted from the skies and young were knocked from the nests with long poles or forced to jump from the nests because of fires set under the breeding colonies. Hundreds of thousands of Passenger Pigeons were killed,

packed in barrels, and shipped quickly by train to major cities for sale in bustling food markets. The last Passenger Pigeon the earth would ever see died in a Cincinnati zoo in 1914.

In reaction to these excesses, Audubon societies and other pioneers of the first U.S. conservation movement carried out education, outreach, and advocacy work that led to a series of new laws and government initiatives that reflected the increasing understanding of the natural world and a resultant shift in values toward stewardship of natural resources. America's early conservation proponents helped bring about the establishment of national and state parks, beginning with Yellowstone National Park in 1872 and New York's famed Adirondack and Catskill parks in 1885. The Lacey Act, passed in 1900, effectively prohibited interstate transport of wildlife taken in violation of state law, which curbed much of the excessive commercial hunting of wildlife. National Wildlife Refuges were born in 1903 with Theodore Roosevelt's well-known decree protecting Florida's Pelican Island. The Migratory Bird Treaty Act was passed in 1916. State fish and game agencies began to form in the late 1800s and early 1900s. All of this activity and new-found public support for a conservation ethic was highly successful in eventually eliminating the overharvesting of wildlife by commercial hunting through the passage of a number of state and federal laws and the hiring of game wardens to enforce the new laws. Bird species that had been hardest hit by the excesses of commercial hunting began to respond over the first half of the 1900s from these positive changes. Terns began nesting again on coastal islands. Gulls returned to the coast of Maine after near obliteration. Populations of egrets and herons that had been decimated for their plumes began the road to recovery.

It wasn't until the mid-20th century that the next crisis in conservation began rearing its ugly head—pesticides and pollution. Chemicals had been touted as the great technological savior for agriculture and human health as the U.S. moved into its post-World War II years. The use of pesticides quickly became widespread and indiscriminate—after all, as the old adage goes, if a little is good then a lot must be better. And, as in the introduction of many new technologies, the broader issues and impacts are never obvious at the start. Few, if any, realized the harmful effects that pesticides can have on human health and wildlife. An acquaintance who had spent his life working in the agricultural production of blueberries in Maine recounted to me how as a young man he had spread DDT on the fields by taking handfuls of the chemical dust and throwing it into the wind so it would float over the fields. Neither he nor his fellow workers used any protection for their hands, face, or eyes, and tossed the poison for hours until the fields were covered.

The public snapped to attention in 1962, when Rachel Carson published her book *Silent Spring*. It carefully laid out the issue and the facts around the nation's virtually unregulated use of pesticides and their many negative effects on humans and the environment. The second wave of the U.S. conservation movement that came at this time may have been a result of the larger 1960s movement that caused many people to look critically at the credibility of large institutions, whether governments or corporations. Whatever the reason, *Silent Spring* resonated with the American public, and a set of new groundbreaking public policy initiatives and new organizations protecting the environment came into being. The Environmental Protection Agency was created in 1970. The Clean Air Act was amended in 1970 (from a weaker 1967 law) to become a significant force for environmental protection. The Federal Environmental Pesticide Control Act was signed into law by President Nixon in 1972, and a few months later DDT was banned from sale in the U.S. The Clean Water Act was also passed in 1972. The Endangered Species Act was signed into law in 1973. Many environmental organizations were formed during this period as well, by citizens who wanted to ensure that the values that they cherished—clean air and water, healthy children, and intact ecosystems—remained part of the nation's legacy. The Nature Conservancy was formed in 1950, World Wildlife Fund in 1961, the Environmental Defense Fund (now Environmental Defense) in 1967, and the Natural Resources Defense Council in 1970, to name a few.

Now as we move into the 21st century, some authors have stirred debate by writing about what they describe as the "death of environmentalism." Indeed, the issues that we are now dealing with are so complex and the technological age within

which we are imbedded has overwhelmed us with such a flood of information that the concept of conservation seems to have lost its resonance with the broad segment of the U.S. public. And, although bird enthusiasts in the U.S. are estimated to number into the tens of millions (perhaps as high as 70 million), they are only now starting to unite into a potent force to support policies and programs that benefit the birds they love and the habitats upon which the birds depend.

But in bird conservation, a quiet third revolution is brewing. Over the last two decades, professionals from government agencies, not-for-profit organizations, and a few for-profit corporations have begun forming coalitions to plan and implement conservation activities. One of the first and best-organized of these is made up of supporters of waterfowl conservation who put forth a North American Waterfowl Management Plan in 1986 and were instrumental in passing the North American Wetland Conservation Act in 1989, which essentially provided the necessary funding to carry out many elements of the plan. As much as $4.5 billon has been invested, and 15.7 million acres of wetland habitat have been preserved, restored, or enhanced through the work of the multitude of partners involved in implementing the North American Waterfowl Management Plan.

Following that successful model, other coalitions were created. Partners in Flight, a coalition focused on conservation of landbirds, was started in 1990 and published a North American Landbird Conservation Plan in 2004. The U.S. Shorebird Plan Council formed in 1998 and published its U.S. Shorebird Conservation Plan in 2000. A coalition called Waterbird Conservation for the Americas that focuses on colonial nesting birds and nonwaterfowl wetland species was launched in 1998; the group published its North American Waterbird Conservation Plan in 2002. The North American Grouse Partnership was formed in 1999.

These coalitions include thousands of partners, many of them among the largest conservation agencies and organizations. At the national level, key U.S. federal agencies involved in these efforts have included the Fish and Wildlife Service, the Bureau of Land Management, the Environmental Protection Agency, and the Forest Service. As for implementation of on-the-ground conservation activities, the most involved U.S. governmental partners are state fish and wildlife agencies from across the country. At virtually all stages of the conservation process, from organizing and planning to fundraising and implementing, more state agency staff have been involved than from any other source. State agencies, with the help of their association, the Association of Fish and Wildlife Agencies (formerly International Association of Fish and Wildlife Agencies), have been the driving force that have made much of this new, quiet renaissance of bird conservation begin to unfold. In particular, the group spearheaded the Teaming with Wildlife coalition that has brought together over 5,000 agencies and organizations to successfully lobby Congress for increasing funding for state agency-administered wildlife conservation programs.

While state and federal government agencies have provided much of the infrastructure and funding to drive these new bird conservation engines, it is the not-for-profit conservation organizations that have been the catalyst to get the engine started. Groups like the Nature Conservancy and Ducks Unlimited were and continue to be major players in the success of the North American Waterfowl Management Plan and carry over that interest and involvement into all the other bird conservation initiatives. The American Bird Conservancy, Bird Studies Canada, Cornell Lab of Ornithology, National Audubon Society, Point Reyes Bird Observatory, and Rocky Mountain Bird Observatory are among many U.S. nonprofit organizations that moved forward the Partners in Flight agenda. These and other organizations, like the Manomet Center for Conservation Sciences, the Western Hemisphere Shorebird Reserve Network, Wetlands International, and BirdLife International, remain highly involved in the shorebird and waterbird coalitions.

While bird-focused conservation organizations have begun to ramp up their efforts to tackle many pressing conservation problems, other groups and policies focused on broader issues that impact our environment are, thankfully, having major impacts on bird conservation as well. Throughout the species accounts in this book, you will find many examples of initiatives and organizations that sometimes are the biggest players in bird conservation, often without even realizing it themselves. During the time in which this book was being researched and written, I talked to many people from a myriad of organizations who were surprised and delighted to hear that their efforts were benefiting bird conservation. Indeed, the problems that impact birds are the same problems that impact human health, the economy, plants, insects, mammals, fish, reptiles, amphibians, and everything else on Earth.

Within the U.S. federal governmental realm, the U.S. Fish and Wildlife Service, though one of the most important agencies to wildlife conservation, is no longer the only agency that is recognized as a major force in bird and wildlife conservation. We know now that the Environmental Protection Agency, the Bureau of Land Management, the Forest Service, the Department of Defense, the Natural Resources Conservation Service, the National Oceanic and Atmospheric Administration, the Department of State, and even the Department of Transportation, Department of Commerce, and the Federal Aviation Administration all have a major impact on bird conservation through the public land they manage, their policies, and the projects that they undertake. Many of these agencies now have specific bird conservation programs underway.

Interestingly, similar recognition of the importance of broad-based nonprofit organizations to bird conservation has been rather slow in coming. Defenders of Wildlife, National Wildlife Federation, and the Canadian Nature Federation (now Nature Canada) are well known for policy-related activism on behalf of wildlife, but only more recently has there been recognition that all play a vital role in bird conservation. Important nonprofit organizations like the Natural Resources Defense Council, Sierra Club, ForestEthics, Rainforest Action Network, and Greenpeace are rarely thought of as key members of the bird conservation movement. Yet groups like these often play a critical role in protecting bird habitats in ways that traditional bird conservation groups do not. And I doubt any but a few conservationists have considered how crucial a role nongovernmental organizations such as the American Red Cross, the American Association of Retired Persons, or the U.S. Chamber of Commerce (in my opinion, now an explicitly anti-environmental group) could and should have in conservation.

From my own perspective, the next exciting step in moving this third great conservation movement forward here in the U.S. and beyond will involve integration. We need to integrate values of the public into policies at the federal, state, and local levels in ways that increase resources and conservation activities to benefit children's health, the economy, and, of course, our birds, other wildlife, and habitats. We need to integrate the goals of existing initiatives, policies, and organizations to increase the efficiency of the resources already committed and the actions already underway. We need to integrate economic and health issues with conservation issues to speed recognition of the fact that all are interconnected. And, finally, we need to integrate the needs and activities of multiple nations that together share responsibility for conserving birds and all of our natural resources.

Integration has begun, but it will need to increase to an unprecedented level in the next decades if we are to tackle the challenges before us in the 21st century. Organizations like the North American Commission for Environmental Cooperation have led the way in integrating the conservation issues and needs of Canada, Mexico, and the U.S. through a whole host of programs and initiatives, including many focused on bird conservation. The North American Bird Conservation Initiative (NABCI) was formed in 1999 in response to the need for better integration across bird conservation initiatives, government agencies, and nations. The administrative structure of NABCI was carefully assembled to include state and federal government agencies, nonprofit organizations, and representatives from Canada, the U.S., and Mexico. The U.S. Neotropical Migratory Bird Act, signed into law in 2000, has provided an effective tool not only to fund and recognize the interconnectedness of the nations of the Western Hemisphere in protecting birds, but also to increase the efficiency of conservation efforts by integrating the work of multiple and diverse partners.

An example of integration in the nonprofit sector is the work of the Boreal Songbird Network. The Network is composed of both traditionally bird-centric conservation groups (National Audubon, Ducks Unlimited, American Bird Conservancy) and traditionally non-bird-centric groups (Defenders of Wildlife, National Wildlife Federation, Natural Resources Defense Council). It focuses the best strengths of each organization on contributing to the goal of the conservation of boreal birds and their boreal forest and wetland habitats. The Boreal Songbird Network, in turn, is part of a broader affiliation of nonprofits in Canada and U.S. that are also working toward boreal forest conservation as part of their own organizational missions. These organizations include Bird Studies Canada, the Canadian Boreal Initiative, the Canadian Parks and Wilderness Society, ForestEthics, Greenpeace, Nature Canada, the Rainforest Action Network, the Sierra Club, and the World Wildlife Fund.

Another opportunity that those in the U.S. bird conservation community have only begun to seize is the multitude of local grassroots and municipal organizations that together make up a significant force in conservation. The massive land trust movement that has swept across the U.S. in recent decades is one of the most exciting examples at the grassroots level. There are now more than 1,500 land trusts in the U.S. (and many beginning in other countries as well), each working to preserve important habitat within their communities. A 2004 survey by the Land Trust Alliance found that local and regional land trusts in the U.S. had protected more than 9.3 million acres of land in addition to 25 million acres protected by national land trusts. Many of these land trusts would be excited to start focusing their efforts in ways that would contribute to specific bird conservation goals, but most are unaware of the priorities for bird habitat protection in their areas. Municipal and county governments can also provide excellent opportunities for leadership in policy-related bird conservation initiatives. For example, mayors and city councils of many cities across the U.S. have agreed to implement energy-conservation policies in their own jurisdictions to counter the insidious effects of global warming pollution. Others have worked to increase use of recycled paper in offices to reduce logging pressure on bird habitat, or to turn off lights in tall buildings at night to decrease the numbers of birds killed during migration. This kind of leadership not only has a direct and positive conservation impact, but also demonstrates to the community and to political leaders at state and federal levels the degree of public support for conservation policies. Governmental leadership on conservation waxes and wanes at national levels from year to year and administration to administration, but there is always the opportunity for each of us to provide leadership within our own states, communities, and organizations.

I have focused largely on conservation in the U.S. because the U.S., through its government, its economy, and its ravenous consumption of goods and natural resources, has an overriding impact and influence on North American bird conservation. But we must also recognize that within each of our partner nations in North America—Canada and Mexico—and our multitude of partner nations in the Caribbean, Central America, and South America, there are many conservation activities underway through a growing number of governmental and nonprofit organizations. Like the U.S., each of these nations also has its own conservation history, sometimes similar to that in the U.S. but more often than not, vastly different. Because most of the birds profiled in this book rely on many countries for their survival, I have in the species accounts often highlighted conservation activities for those species in several different countries. I have also asked several of my colleagues to write short summaries of the current bird conservation initiatives ongoing in other countries or regions. These summaries are meant to give a broad sense of the exciting bird conservation efforts now underway across the Western Hemisphere.

GET INVOLVED

I urge all the readers of this book to get involved and become a part of the renaissance of bird conservation. This book is full of examples, ideas, and models of ways all of us can help birds. And remember that when you do good things for birds you are also doing good things for children's health, the economy, and the wildlife and habitat we value and enjoy. Get involved and make this third North American conservation movement the most significant legacy of our generation.

MEXICO
*by Eduardo E. Iñigo Elias, Coordinator,
Neotropical Bird Conservation Program,
Cornell Lab of Ornithology*

The history of bird conservation in Mexico is old, extraordinarily rich, and complex. It is rich in successes but also has several tragic chapters, including the extinction of the Guadalupe Caracara in the 1900s, the almost total loss of the wetlands in the Valley of Mexico, and the decimation of the country's cloud forests. Mexico is among the top twenty nations of the world with the richest avian diversity. Mexico's avifauna includes an estimated 1,074 species, of which 103 are endemics. Sadly, four species are already extinct and 48 are globally threatened. In 2001, the Mexican government

recognized 355 bird species (or 33% of the total avifauna of the country) as nationally threatened due to direct or indirect activities of humans.

Mexico also represents the primary wintering and migration grounds for 158 species classified as Neotropical–Nearctic migrants, including 41 species with more than 50% of their North American breeding range within Mexico. This latter group includes 17 species currently on the Partners in Flight (PIF) WatchList in the U.S. The PIF WatchList also includes an additional 29 nonmigratory species with large breeding ranges in Mexico, bringing the total to 30% of the U.S. PIF WatchList that breed primarily within Mexico.

In the pre-Hispanic cultures, birds were used and protected for several reasons. Resident and migratory birds such as waterfowl and shorebirds were harvested primarily as a food source. Bird parts such as feathers, nails, and bills had several uses, from personal ornaments, fabrics, and artistic frames using colorful bird feathers to precious currency. Birds such as the Golden Eagle were also admired, protected, and used by the early Mexicans. In fact, in 1325 the Golden Eagle was used by ancient Mexicans as a symbol for the foundation of Tenochtitlan (known today as Mexico City), and is still today officially used as the national symbol for Mexico. Other birds, such as the Resplendent Quetzal and the Scarlet Macaw, were highly admired, protected, and used by a select group of Mexicans for religious or magic ceremonies. There is also evidence that some parrot species were kept as pets in Mesoamerican cultures. During the peak of the pre-Hispanic cultures, particularly among Aztecs (1300–1519), emperors ordered the protection of birds and their habitats and established some protected areas such as Chapultepec (meaning Grasshopper Hill in the Nahuatl language) to secure water for the city and habitat for wildlife. They also kept large zoos with collections of live bird specimens.

The years 1521 to 1940 after the encounter of the Mexican and Spanish cultures (also known as the Conquest of Mexico) was a period of dramatic change for Mexico's environment, including its native peoples. Beginning in the 1800s, large biological expeditions were undertaken, the first systematic ornithological collections were established, and scientific illustrations describing the Mexican avifauna were initiated. In 1868, the Mexican Society of Natural History was created and began publishing the journal *Naturaleza*, where many national and international ornithologists first described much of the natural history and taxonomy of Mexican birds. Among the most influential was Rafael Montes de Oca who published several papers in this journal in 1874 on the natural history of Mexican hummingbirds.

During this period many ecosystems and bird populations in Mexico also suffered severe degradation. In the early 1900s the Guadalupe Caracara became extinct due to habitat destruction by introduction of exotic species such as goats to Guadalupe Island. Given the high rate of species loss, deforestation, and the severe alteration of natural springs and watersheds, the Mexican government established in 1917 the first protected areas. Some of these, like the "Desierto de los Leones" National Park, continue to protect important watersheds and provide recreational areas for inhabitants of Mexico City as well as important pine, pine-oak, and spruce habitat for species like the threatened Strickland's Woodpecker and many wintering birds from the U.S. and Canada. Another milestone in Mexican bird conservation came in 1936 when Mexico and the USA signed the provisions of the convention between the United States and the United Mexican States for the protection of migratory birds and game mammals, including the Migratory Bird Conventions and the Convention on Nature Protection and Wildlife Preservation in the Western Hemisphere.

In the early 1940s, Mexican president Lazaro Cardenas established the first environmental political agenda in the country, establishing more parks and protecting more habitat for avian species. Mexico's national system of protected areas now includes about 154 federal designated sites with differing levels of protection. Thanks to the vision of Dr. Enrique Beltrán, the Mexican Section of the International Committee for the Protection of Birds (ICBP) was established in 1944. This committee fostered important studies in natural history and management of birds and worked to protect species and their habitats across Mexico. The group also initiated environmental education activities to attract the general public to participate in bird watching and conservation activities. In 1951 Mexico established the first Hunting Federal Law, which regulated the taking of resident and migratory game bird species.

The Society for the Study and Conservation of Birds in Mexico (CIPAMEX) was established in 1947 and led by Dr. Beltrán. The influence of CIPAMEX on Mexican ornithology and bird conservation has been substantial and CIPAMEX continues to be Mexico's largest organization made up of bird watchers and ornithologist. In the early 1970s and 1980s, Mexican research institutions across the country (Universidad Nacional Autónoma de Mexico, Instituto de Ecologia A.C., Universidad Autonoma de Nuevo Leon, etc.) dramatically increased the number of young ornithologists and studies in biology, systematics, ecology, and conservation of Mexican birds.

In 1982 Mexico signed the Convention on Wetlands (RAMSAR), an intergovernmental treaty that provides the framework for national action and international cooperation for the conservation and wise use of wetlands and their resources. This commitment to wetland conservation by the Mexican government was furthered in 1986 when the environmental ministers of Canada, Mexico, and the USA signed the first North American Waterfowl Management Plan. The plan provided a framework for maintaining and restoring an adequate habitat base to ensure perpetuation of populations of North American waterfowl and other migratory bird species. A further agreement signed by the three countries in 1988 provided for expanded cooperative efforts in Mexico to conserve wetlands for migratory birds that spend the winter there. In 1991 Mexico also joined the Convention on International Trade in Endangered Species of Wild Flora and Fauna (CITES) to protect Mexican species from the international trade, particularly parrots.

In 1996, Mexican ornithologists from CIPAMEX in partnership with BirdLife International, the National Commission for the Knowledge and Use of Biodiversity (CONABIO), and many other organizations, initiated the development of the Important Bird Areas program (or AICAS in Spanish). The great momentum provided by the AICA project fed perfectly into a nascent North American-wide conservation movement spearheaded by the Commission for Environmental Cooperation (CEC). In 1998, the CEC hosted a meeting in Puebla, Mexico of nearly 120 leading conservationists from Canada, Mexico, and the United States to launch the North American Bird Conservation Initiative (NABCI). This initiative has established, for the first time in history, a forum for the integration of conservation priorities, plans, and on-the-ground actions across the three countries of North America. For Mexico,

NABCI has brought increased recognition of the importance of its varied habitats for migratory and resident bird species to a broader constituency of conservationists in the U.S. and Canada. In turn, this recognition is expected to build more financial and human resources from within the country and outside of Mexico to on-the-ground conservation projects to protect more populations and bird habitat in Mexico. International donors have invested $25 million dollars of the Global Environmental Facility (GEF) funds and matched by the Mexican federal government with an additional $50 million dollars for protected areas management through the National Commission of Protected Areas (CONANP). Other similar projects such as the Mesoamerican Biological Corridor of the GEF-CONABIO-CONANP have invested $11 million in GEF funds and $10 million from the Mexican government. On top of these two efforts several million dollars has been invested by international conservation groups such as Conservation International, World Wildlife Fund, Ducks Unlimited, the Nature Conservancy, the Wildlife Conservation Society, among others, to protect bird habitats.

Multiple conservation projects are underway throughout Mexico, many involving innovative partnerships between nonprofit organizations, government agencies, and community organizations. A promising avenue for conservation has been the development of agreements with local ejidos, a type of community land-ownership cooperative, in which a nonprofit organization purchases development or logging rights for an important habitat and in return the ejido leaves the habitat intact for birds and other wildlife. Examples of this are the conservation efforts by Pronatura North West, CONABIO, and the El Palmito Forestry Ejido in Sinaloa to protect the habitat of the microendemic Tufted Jay. Other projects are focusing on helping local communities develop sustainable natural resource extraction and carefully managed ecotourism businesses to increase long-term economic benefits to local communities from maintaining ecological reserves.

However, there are many challenges and increasing needs for conservation in Mexico with its high rate of development but with rich biodiversity and large number of birds. Mexico is fortunate to now have a cadre of conservation groups from Mexican and international nonprofits, academic and research institutions, and government agen-

cies. Many experienced Mexican nonprofit conservation institutions include Pronatura, Fondo Mexicano para la Conservación de la Naturaleza, Grupo Ecológico Sierra Gorda, Amigos de Sian Ka'an, Instituto de Ecologia, and Pro Esteros. These groups, working closely with Mexican government agencies such as CONABIO, the National Commission for Natural Protected Areas (CONANP), and the Wildlife Office (DGVS) are the greatest hope for the protection and conservation of Mexico's vast natural heritage.

CANADA
by Sarah Wren, Conservation Biologist,
Nature Canada

Canada's size and longitudinal/latitudinal extent on a map are a first clue to the diversity of bird habitats that it harbors. This ranges from breeding colonies of Ivory Gulls sheltered on mountains surrounded by ice fields on the high Arctic's Ellesmere Island, to Lake Erie's Pelee Island which is further south than many northern U.S. states and is home to a variety of birds considered southern specialities in Canada. In between, it includes vast prairie, temperate and boreal forest, tundra, and seemingly unending ocean and freshwater shoreline.

Canada is a country of vast areas of habitat that, in many ways, make it a prime "bird nursery" for the hemisphere—for example, nearly half of all of North American bird species (including waterfowl, waterbirds, shorebirds, and landbirds) rely on Canada's boreal forest region. Canada has a high stewardship responsibility for these species. And, because a high percentage of the birds that breed in Canada migrate south for the winter—sometimes as far south as Tierra del Fuego and beyond—we are intrinsically linked in conservation to countries to the south of us that play host to "our birds," often for longer periods than they are in Canada.

The roots of bird conservation in Canada are deep. Canada has an established community of amateur naturalist groups (dating back to 1879) that have long observed birds and monitored their populations. The federal authority responsible for bird conservation, the Canadian Wildlife Service, had its genesis in 1947. In many cases, bird conservation initiatives in Canada were borne out of the same factors that drove the push for stronger conservation in the United States: historical pressures from the overharvest of species, and more recent concerns about vanishing habitat for populations. Two multilateral initiatives to address the former and the latter—the Migratory Birds Convention Act and the North American Waterfowl Management Plan—have likely resulted in as many positive on-the-ground and policy changes for birds in Canada as in the U.S.

Canada is also home to one of the world's most ambitious conservation initiatives to protect the long-term ecological integrity of Canada's Boreal Forest—the largest intact forest ecosystem remaining in North America. Led by the Canadian Boreal Initiative, an unusual alliance of conservation organizations, First Nations and resource companies developed a broad conservation outline for the region called the Boreal Conservation Framework. The approach couples long-term economic development and broad conservation goals for the entire region. Its specific recommendations include the establishment of a network of large interconnected protected areas covering at least half of Canada's 1.3 billion acre boreal region and the use of cutting-edge sustainable development practices, such as Forest Stewardship Council's certification, in the remaining areas.

Today, naturalists, the federal government, NGOs, academic institutions, and industry organizations participate in and often collaborate on many facets of bird conservation in Canada, including surveys and censuses, citizen science initiatives like the Breeding Bird Survey that underpin many management decisions, programs of applied research, and campaigns to educate the public about the importance of bird conservation. But despite this healthy level of integration, much work remains to be done. Conservation initiatives and partnerships must continue to extend beyond the boundaries of Canada and North America, to ensure that effective conservation actions are in place for migrant birds across their entire ranges. There's also more work that needs to be done in Canada, including collecting information on birds that have a high proportion of their breeding range in Canada, but for which we don't yet have sufficient population information to make effective conservation decisions. And, while Canada is a country rich in nature, more needs to be done to ensure that Canadians understand and value this natural heritage, including bird populations. With a better appreciation of birds and their habitats,

and the challenges they face, conserving birds will become a priority for Canadians.

LATIN AMERICA AND THE CARIBBEAN
by Ian Davidson, Director BirdLife International America's Division, Quito, Ecuador

While looking out across the intertidal mudflats of southern Tierra del Fuego, a group of Argentinean, Brazilian, Canadian, Chilean, and U.S. scientists, conservationists, and members of the nearby community of Rio Grande City applauded the designation of this critical site for Hudsonian Godwits and Red Knots as the first Western Hemisphere Shorebird Reserve Network in Latin America. Held in 1991, this quiet event was an important turning point in bird conservation in the Americas. It represented the first time southern and northern interests came together outside of North America to recognize, embrace, and celebrate the joint responsibility of citizens throughout the Americas to conserve migratory birds.

The Americas are aptly named the "bird continents." Toucans, hoatzins, macaws, rheas, screamers, ovenbirds, and hummingbirds represent but a few of the well-known, charismatic "New World" species. While North American birds comprise less than 20% of the known 4,300 species found throughout the Americas, each year more than 340 species undertake substantial migrations to the Neotropical region.

With the exception of the Caribbean and parts of Central America, the Neotropical region still retains a significant extent of its original habitat. However, the forests, grasslands, wetlands, and marine areas face increasing pressure from growing human populations, intensive and extensive agricultural production, and urban and rural development. Combined, these pressures are impacting resident and migratory species alike. The World Conservation Union estimates that over 7 percent of all the Americas bird species are globally threatened, with a majority occurring in Latin American and the Caribbean.

The first organized bird conservation efforts were initiated by the Argentinean-based Asociacion Ornitologica del Plata (now Aves Argentinas) in the 1920s. Today, capable and growing Latin American groups like Armonia, the Belize Audubon Society, the Bahamas National Trust, Calidres, Guyra Paraguay, Jocotoco, ProAves

Colombia, SalvaNATURA, and the Society for the Conservation and study of Caribbean Birds, to mention a few, are dedicating their efforts to finding local solutions to bird and biodiversity conservation.

At the regional level, BirdLife International's Important Bird Areas (IBA) program aims to identify, characterize, and strengthen the conservation of priority areas that support endangered and endemic species but also sites that host large concentrations of birds. The Ecuadorian government was the first country in Latin America to legally recognize IBAs as priority areas for biodiversity conservation. Other hemisphere-wide bird conservation initiatives include the Partners in Flight program that successfully united groups working toward the conservation of Neotropical migrants, primarily in Central America. Others include Ducks Unlimited's waterfowl program, and the American Bird Conservancy's efforts to conserve globally threatened species. Broader ecosystem initiatives are also being supported by Conservation International, the World Wildlife Fund, the Nature Conservancy, the Global Environmental Facility, the Moore and MacArthur Foundations, and US AID, to mention a few.

At their annual meeting in 2001, the Presidents of the Americas recommended support for an Americas-wide migratory bird conservation initiative. During the Neotropical Ornithological Congress held in Chile in 2003, the USFWS convened a parallel meeting of government stakeholders and reached an agreement for the creation of the Western Hemisphere Migratory Species Initiative, whose mission it is to contribute to the conservation of migratory species of the Western Hemisphere by strengthening cooperation among nations, international agreements, and civil society, and by expanding constituencies and political support. It is hoped that this umbrella initiative will serve as the basis for bringing together a wide range of stakeholders involved in bird conservation throughout the Americas.

While international agreements are vital and important tools for stimulating broad level support, bird conservation also depends on concrete action at the site level. The Iwokrama project in the Guyanese rainforests is one of many heart-lifting examples where governments, indigenous communities, private industry, and scientists are successfully collaborating to find ways in which humans can coexist with nature in globally important habitats for resident and migratory species.

What You Can Do

PROTECT THE LAST OF THE LARGE

From the global to the local scale, there are still opportunities to protect the remaining large, intact ecosystems, regions, or habitat patches. At the global scale, the largest remaining intact ecosystem in North America is the boreal forest that encompasses 1.5 billion acres stretching from Alaska across northern Canada to Newfoundland. Other large, mostly intact ecosystems in North America include portions of the Arctic, the Northern Pacific Coastal Forests of Alaska, and the Sonoran Desert of Arizona and northwestern Mexico. While all of these regions are still relatively ecologically intact today, all are facing unprecedented threats. The fate of the boreal forest, for example, will be sealed in the next 15–20 years because during that time span most of the land will have become allocated to either industrial uses or protected areas. As I write this, single leases for logging rights for tracts of Canadian boreal forest as large as tens of millions of acres are being bought up by global companies while the second largest oil deposit in the world (35 million acres) is just beginning to be developed in northern Alberta. Clearly, we will need to act immediately if we are to maintain any of these large functioning ecosystems. Some recent work has concluded that we should be striving to protect 50% of remaining habitat to preserve ecosystem functions, including the full complement of bird and wildlife populations, and to serve as an ecological benchmark against which to assess impacts in regions that are targeted for industrial uses. These last great places are among the last opportunities for the human race to conserve the functioning ecological systems that are essential to keeping the planet—our life blood—in balance.[1–7]

Each of us can contribute to the protection of Earth's largest remaining intact ecosystems even by actions as simple as using recycled paper towels and tissue paper, installing energy efficient bulbs, writing letters to companies and politicians urging adoption of sustainable practices and conservation-minded regulations, and providing financial support of the organizations working to protect these areas. But we should also be thinking about ways to get involved in protecting the largest remaining habitat patches left in our own states and communities. In most parts of North America, organizations like the Nature Conservancy and World Wildlife Fund have completed conservation plans and assessments using state-of-the-art geographic information system technology and with the input of hundreds of experts that identify large habitat blocks as targets for conservation. A search on the Internet or a call to a local conservation organization should help you discover the priority sites in your area. In your own community, you can work with a local land trust or municipal government to ensure that the largest undeveloped habitat patches are protected.[2,8]

SAVE AND RESTORE THE REMNANTS OF THE RARE

Most parts of North America have already seen widespread habitat loss, fragmentation, and degradation. Some ecosystems and the species that rely on them are in critical condition, with only small fragments of native habitat still holding on. In North America, the most highly threatened ecoregions identified in a World Wildlife Fund report included the Florida sand pine scrub, the native pine forests of the southeastern U.S., the Central tall grasslands, Pacific coastal forests from California to British Columbia, California coastal sage and chaparral, California Sierra Nevada forests, and the mixed forest habitat of the Appalachians and Piedmont. To these we could easily add the San Francisco Bay wetlands, eastern native sandplain grasslands, and others. In these areas, conservation work is often underway to save the last few pieces of habitat to serve as islands from which to begin restoration of surrounding degraded habitat. Restoration can include everything from replanting native plants to carrying out controlled burns to removing dams to eliminating nonnative species.[2]

There are restoration and habitat management opportunities for projects in or near virtually every community led, not only by traditional conservation organizations and agencies, but sometimes also by civic groups like Rotary clubs or corporate service organizations. In many areas, nature centers and land trusts have volunteer workdays to remove invasive species or plant native grasses, shrubs, and trees.

PRESS FOR POLICIES THAT MAKE THINGS BETTER

At all levels of government there are a multitude of policies involving funding, regulations, incentives, and other mechanisms that can improve or worsen conditions for birds, wildlife, and the habitats upon which they depend. Nonprofit organizations (see appendix) that share your values for conservation will inform you of the policies that are having the greatest impact and will suggest ways for you to influence the adoption of those policies.

Along with direct funding for the acquisition, management, and restoration of critical habitat, there are many opportunities for governmental policies to lessen the effects of global warming, habitat loss, pollutants, invasive species, and incidental mortality among other issues. Those of us who care about birds should work hard to ensure that our elected leaders enact conservation-friendly policies.

In addition, there are policies within our workplaces (including both for-profit and nonprofit organizations) and homes that we can implement or support to make a difference. This could be everything from purchasing recycled office paper and tissue paper to participating in recycling programs to contributing financial or human resources to a local conservation project.

TEACH AT EVERY OPPORTUNITY

Unless you're a hermit, you will have countless opportunities to teach people about birds and conservation. This is especially true if you are not shy about using your binoculars and telescope in public places. People are curious creatures and will go out of their way to find out what you are looking at. When they do, use it as a chance to engage them in the wonder, beauty, and mystery of birds and the natural world. Because we are fairly bold about birdwatching in public, my wife, Allison, and I have met hundreds of people who were eager to see what we were seeing and hear more about birds and conservation.

If you are a skilled birder, volunteer to lead at least one bird walk a year—more if you have the time and interest—for beginning birders in your area, whether through an Audubon chapter, nature center, park, university, school, church, synagogue, or workplace. You will be amazed at how many people are intrigued by the idea of learning about birds.

It is especially important to foster children's curiosity in birds and the natural world. If you have kids yourself, find ways to make nature a fun, exciting, family experience that they will treasure forever. Our three-year-old loves to imitate the sounds of the Mourning Doves in the spring, fill the bird feeders, and hike the woods looking for feathers and bugs. He was greatly intrigued when we took him to see the captive owls in a bird rehabilitation and education facility. All of these activities are especially meaningful to him because they are a part of our family activity, a legacy that I am sure he will pass on to his own kids. Even if you don't have kids or grandkids of your own, you can encourage curiosity about nature in nieces, nephews, and friends. We've often had families with kids approach us when we were looking through our telescope at a bird and the kids are so excited to get a chance to look through a telescope themselves that they can hardly contain themselves.

Ask just about any professional ornithologist or conservation biologist how they got interested and you will almost always hear a wonderful story about a parent, grandparent, or other adult who sparked and nurtured their interest in nature. My grandmother was an especially important influence as she made everything in the natural world seem exciting and magical. Later, my mother and father encouraged my interest and then introduced me to a woman in our church who was the president of the local nature club. Inez, a busy woman involved in countless organizations and taking care of an ailing spouse, took the time to invite an awkward junior-high-school kid on regular birding trips. Those were times of explosive learning and excitement that propelled me to become an ornithologist.

BE A CITIZEN SCIENTIST

Voting isn't the only way to be a good citizen—counting birds counts, too! Join the hundreds of thousands of people across North America who participate in one or more (sometimes many more) citizen science projects to monitor bird populations or study a biological question about birds. Beginners can start with projects like the Great Backyard Bird Count or Project FeederWatch or, with the help of an experienced birder, take part in the Christmas Bird Count or assist with the Breeding Bird Survey. There are dozens of citizen science project opportunities for participation. Many projects even provide training in bird identification, banding, and other biological research techniques. Do a quick Internet search, call your local nature center, or contact a national or state conservation or bird research organization to find out about citizen projects you can be a part of.

HOW TO HELP SAVE BIRDS—
A Few Good Ideas

- Take your kids, grandkids, nieces, nephews, or friends birding and make it fun!

- Give a presentation on birds and bird conservation at a local library or school.

- Write a letter to the editor about a pressing bird conservation issue.

- Start a bird festival.

- Buy a Duck Stamp every year, even if you don't intend to go hunting. The money supports projects to purchase and enhance wetland habitats.

- Volunteer for a workday at a local preserve or refuge to restore habitat or eradicate invasive species.

- Advocate for land acquisition funds for important habitat.

- Recruit and organize volunteers for projects at natural areas, refuges, parks, preserves, and protected areas.

- Use energy-efficient lightbulbs and appliances and turn the lights off when you can.

- Drive a hybrid or low-emission vehicle that gets good gas mileage. Carpool or use public transportation.

- Recycle and use only recycled paper products.

- Decrease use of pesticides at home by finding less harmful alternatives.

- Support federal, state, county, and municipal government agencies and programs that benefit birds, wildlife, and habitats. Contact agency offices or nonprofit conservation organizations to find specific opportunities to help.

- Become involved with monitoring bird populations through citizen science.

- Work with local land managers of parks, preserves, refuges, and land trust properties to support efforts to protect, restore, and enhance habitats for birds. They will be glad to hear from you!

- Join and financially support nonprofit conservation organizations involved in conservation work that benefits birds and the habitats upon which they depend.

- Let your elected representatives know that you support policies that benefit birds, wildlife, and habitat and that you vote! You will be surprised at the impact your phone call or letter can have.

- Promote and vote for political candidates who support environmentally friendly policies that are good for families and the economy.

REFERENCES

1. Blancher, P., and J.V. Wells. 2005. *The Boreal Forest Region: North America's Bird Nursery.* Canadian Boreal Initiative, Boreal Songbird Initiative, Bird Studies Canada, Ottawa, ON, Seattle, WA, and Port Rowan, ON. 10 pp.

2. Ricketts, T.H., E. Dinerstein, D.M. Olson, C.J. Loucks, et al. 1999. *Terrestrial Ecoregions of North America: A Conservation Assessment.* Island Press, Washington, DC. 485 pp.

3. Lee, P., D. Aksenov, L. Laestadius, R. Nogueron, and W. Smith. 2003. *Canada's Large Intact Forest Landscapes.* Global Forest Watch Canada, Edmonton, AB. 84 pp.

4. ForestEthics. Undated. *Bring Down the Boreal: How U.S. Consumption of Forest Products is Destroying Canada's Endangered Northern Forests.* ForestEthics, San Francisco, CA. 25 pp.

5. Government of Alberta. 2004. *Oil Sands.* http://www.energy.gov.ab.ca/89.asp (accessed 2 March 2006).

6. Woynillowicz, D., C. Severson-Baker, M. Raynolds. 2005. *Oil Sands Fever: The Environmental Implications of Canada's Oil Sands Rush.* Pembina Institute, Drayton Valley, AB. 86 pp.

7. Schmiegelow, F.K.A., S.G. Cumming, S. Harrison, S. Leroux, K. Lisgo, R. Noss, and B. Olsen. In Review. A Reverse-matrix Model for Conservation of the World's Remaining Intact Areas. *Ecology and Society.*

8. Stein, B.A., L.S. Kutner, and J.S. Adams. 2000. *Precious Heritage: The Status of Biodiversity in the United States.* Oxford University Press, New York, NY. 399 pp.

Species Accounts

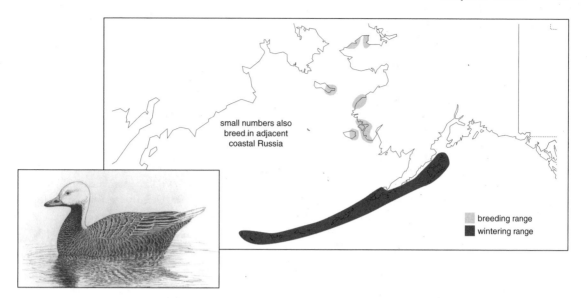

small numbers also
breed in adjacent
coastal Russia

breeding range
wintering range

EMPEROR GOOSE (*Chen canagica*)

One of the rarest geese in North America, the Emperor Goose is seldom found south of its primarily Alaskan breeding and wintering range where it has declined by at least 50% since 1964.

STATUS AND DISTRIBUTION

Breeds in arctic and subarctic coastal salt marshes, primarily in western Alaska but with some in northeast Russia. Most of the population breeds in Alaska's Yukon-Kuskokwim Delta. The Yukon Delta National Wildlife Refuge is one of the most important breeding areas for the species. Virtually the entire population winters in Alaska's Aleutian Islands National Wildlife Refuge, though small numbers and individuals occasionally make their way as far south as Washington, Oregon, and California. The population was estimated at 139,000 in 1964 but there were no surveys after that until 1981 when the USFWS began completing annual spring flight surveys. These surveys indicated a drop in the population to about 42,000 in 1986 but a subsequent rise to approximately 68,000 in 1993. The three-year average from 1996 to 1998 was 59,000 individuals and the 2006 spring surveys estimated 76,000 individuals.[1-4]

ECOLOGY

Breeds in coastal saltmarsh delta habitat where it nests on the ground. While staging, birds occur in intertidal mudflats and in winter they occur in rocky intertidal habitat.[1]

THREATS

The reasons for population decline are not well understood but subsistence hunting may have contributed to the declines as native peoples traditionally harvest birds in the spring and summer. Oil pollution on the wintering grounds may also be affecting overwinter survival but little is known about winter ecology of the species. Loss of habitat from sea level rise and other habitat changes as a result of global warming may become the most difficult and pervasive threat.[1]

CONSERVATION ACTION

A Yukon Delta Goose Management plan was developed that provided voluntary restrictions on Emperor Goose subsistence hunting levels, but level of compliance with the plan is unknown. The Pacific Flyway management plan calls for closing all hunting when population falls below three-year running average of 60,000, but closure has not been enforceable. Most of the breeding and wintering habitat for the species is already within National Wildlife Refuges.[1]

CONSERVATION NEEDS

- Slow production of global warming pollution.
- Continue to decrease subsistence hunting levels.
- Complete further studies designed to elucidate the major factors contributing to population declines.
- Decrease oil pollution on wintering intertidal feeding areas.

References

1. Petersen, M.R, J.A. Schmutz, and R.F. Rockwell. 1994. Emperor Goose (*Chen canagica*). In *Birds of North America*, No. 97 (A. Poole and F. Gill, eds.). The Academy of Natural Sciences, Philadelphia, PA, and the American Ornithologists' Union, Washington, DC.

2. BirdLife International. 2000. *Threatened Birds of the World*. Lynx Editions and BirdLife International, Barcelona, Spain, and Cambridge, UK.

3. U.S. Fish and Wildlife Service. 1998. *North American Waterfowl Management Plan—1998 Update*. U.S. Department of the Interior, Washington, DC.

4. U.S. Fish and Wildlife Service. 2006. *Waterfowl Population Status, 2006*. U.S. Department of the Interior, Washington, DC. 61 pp.

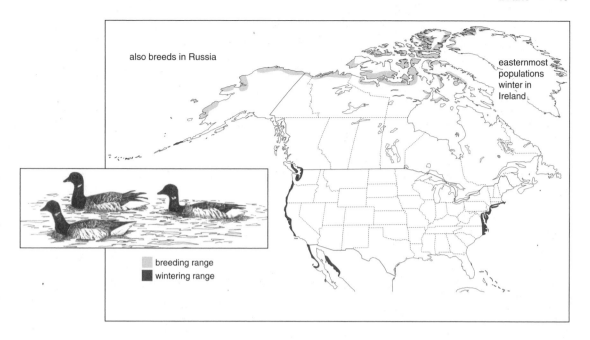

also breeds in Russia

easternmost populations winter in Ireland

breeding range
wintering range

BRANT (*Branta bernicla*)

A small Arctic breeding goose that winters in temperate regions of North America, Europe, and Asia, the Brant is unusually reliant on a particular plant food and has suffered severe declines when this food source has been unavailable.

STATUS AND DISTRIBUTION

Breeds across the world's Arctic regions. In North America breeding populations occur from northwest Greenland to Alaska. Within this breeding range there are four populations, which each winter in different areas. Birds from northwest Greenland and the eastern high Arctic (light-bellied form) winter in Ireland. Birds breeding in the eastern Canadian low Arctic (light-bellied form) winter along the U.S. Atlantic coast. The population from the western high Arctic (gray-bellied form) winters in Washington's Puget Sound. The fourth population (black-bellied form) breeds from the central Arctic to Alaska and eastern Siberia and winters along the Pacific Coast of North America but with the majority in the Mexican states of Baja California, Sonora, and Sinaloa and in California.

Important Canadian breeding sites include the Foxe Basin Islands Important Bird Area (IBA) in Nunavut, which harbors at least 15% of the breeding population of the form wintering along the U.S. Atlantic coast. Also in Nunavut, the Queen Maud Gulf IBA harbors at least 5% of breeding population of the black-bellied form and Great Plain of the Koukdjuak IBA on Baffin Island at least 1% of the breeding population that winters on the U.S. Atlantic coast. In Canada's Northwest Territories, both the Banks Island Migratory Bird Sanctuary IBA and the Anderson River Delta IBA support 2% of the breeding population of the black-bellied form. Important breeding sites for the species in Alaska include the Yukon-Kuskokwim National Wildlife Refuge (NWR) in western Alaska and the Prudhoe Bay area in northern Alaska.

Akimiski Island in western James Bay, Canada is an important fall and spring staging area, supporting as much as 3% of the population wintering along the U.S. Atlantic coast. Important staging and molting areas for Brant in Alaska include the Teshekpuk Lake Special Areas on the National Petroleum Reserve, where up to 32,000 birds occur, and Izembek Lagoon NWR, which hosts the majority of the world population of the black-bellied form every fall (over 125,000 counted in October 2002).

On average, about 70% of the population of Brant wintering on the U.S. Atlantic coast is found in New Jersey, another 20% in New York, and 7–8% in Virginia, with smaller numbers north to New England and south to Florida. Important wintering areas for the species here include New Jersey's Forsythe NWR and New York's Jamaica Bay Complex IBA, Great South Bay IBA, and Shinnecock Bay IBA.

Virtually the entire population of the gray-bellied form of the Brant winters in Puget Sound, Washington.

The majority of the population of the black-bellied form of the Brant winters in Mexico's Baja California and along the coasts of Sonora and Sinoloa. Important wintering areas here include Bahía San Quintín, Laguna Ojo Liebre, Laguna San Ignacio, and Bahia Magdalena.

Historically populations showed major decrease in the 1930s when eelgrass, their major winter food supply, declined from disease. Populations rebounded following that event but numbers of all three forms of Brant wintering in North America have shown declines since the 1960s when monitoring was started using midwinter aerial surveys and ground counts. More than 50% of Brant wintering along the U.S. Atlantic coast died of starvation in the severe winter of 1976–77 when feeding areas were frozen over, reaching a population low of approximately 45,000 birds. But numbers have increased at approximately 4% per year since 1982, with 2006 surveys tallying 146,600 individuals. The population of the gray-bellied form wintering in Puget Sound, Washington has decreased since the 1960s but was stable at approximately 11,000 birds during the 1990s; 2006 surveys estimated 9,500 individuals. The population of the black-bellied form wintering along the Pacific coast of North America also declined from a high of approximately 160,000 in the 1960s to about 120,000 in the 1990s. Much of this decline is thought to be attributable to a major decrease in numbers of birds nesting in the Yukon-Kuskokwim Delta. Since 1997 numbers have declined by 2% per year, with 133,900 counted in midwinter aerial surveys in 2006.[1–8]

ECOLOGY

The low Arctic population breeds in saltmarsh habitats within 1 km of coastal tidal areas. In high Arctic populations a portion of the breeding range can occur as much as 30 km from coast and in a variety of open habitats, but these birds often nest on small islands in ponds, lakes, or rivers where they are protected from mammalian predators. During molt, flocks of Brant are often found along the shores of inland lakes or sometimes intertidal areas within the Arctic. Preferred wintering and staging areas are shallow coastal estuaries typically with extensive eelgrass beds where the birds feed. Eelgrass is the preferred food of Brant during winter and migration and an extensive disease-caused die-off of eelgrass in the 1930s caused a major decline in Brant populations. Since then, many Brant have adapted to feeding on human-made shortgrass habitats like lawns and golf courses, though hundreds of Brant died from ingesting the pesticide Diazinon on golf courses on Long Island before it was banned in the U.S. in the late 1980s.[1]

THREATS

The species' tendency to concentrate in relatively small areas during breeding, migration, and winter places it at risk from severe weather events, accidents, disease, and other problems. This was demonstrated during the 1970s when severe weather conditions in the Atlantic coast wintering range caused the loss of half of the population. Similarly, the species' reliance on eelgrass continues to make it vulnerable to any factors that cause a decline in the health of the estuarine ecosystems where it occurs. In some areas certain practices of near-shore fisheries (oyster and crab fisheries), like dredging and the dumping of empty oyster shells, can degrade eelgrass habitat, causing a decline in the food supply for Brant.

Mortality from sport and subsistence hunting has historically been one of the major factors regulating population size, especially since in this species a higher proportion of adults versus juveniles are taken by hunters. The take of Brant from spring and summer subsistence hunting in Alaska was estimated at approximately 10,000 birds in 1994 and in Quebec at 6,400 during the 1970s. Sport hunters on the U.S. Atlantic coast took an average of 26,500 birds per year over the 23 years when the season was open from 1962 to 1993. Between 1994 and 2002, estimated sport hunting take averaged 16,600 per year. On the Pacific coast, annual take was estimated at approximately 8,000 birds in the 1980s, with at least 50% taken in Mexico.

Other potential threats identified on the breeding grounds and molting areas include habitat degradation from expansion of human settlements and disturbance from oil and gas exploration and extraction activities, including disturbance from aircraft flyovers. In 2004, a plan was announced to open for oil and gas leases the 8.8-million-acre Northwest Planning Area of the National Petroleum Reserve–Alaska, which includes several important molting and staging areas as well as some breeding habitat for the Pacific wintering Brant population. Loss of habitat from sea level rise and other habitat changes as a result of global warming may become the most difficult and pervasive threat.[1–11]

CONSERVATION ACTION

North American Brant populations are managed cooperatively between the U.S., Canada, and Mexico with management boards that set hunting regulations for the species depending on the status of populations. Hunting seasons are to be closed for Atlantic wintering population when numbers fall below 100,000 and for Pacific wintering population when numbers fall below 120,000. The hunting season was closed on the Atlantic wintering population for eight years between 1970 and 1980 because numbers were below 120,000. Season length and bag limits are reviewed annually in light of population estimates and are modified if necessary to ensure healthy populations. A hunt management plan for the Atlantic wintering population in effect since 1992 establishes increasing bag limits and season lengths for each 25,000 increase in population.

The North American Waterfowl Management Plan 1998 Update set population objectives of 124,000 for the Atlantic wintering population and 185,000 for the Pacific wintering population. The objective for the Atlantic wintering population has been met or exceeded in recent years but the Pacific wintering population has not met the objective for decades.

Many of the breeding areas in the Canadian Arctic are within protected areas and much of the Yukon-Kuskokwim Delta population breeds within the Yukon-Kuskokwim National Wildlife Refuge. To better manage the level of subsistence hunting mortality on Brant and other birds the USFWS negotiated an amendment of the Migratory Bird Treaty with Canada and Mexico in 1999 to allow the USFWS to develop and implement spring and summer subsistence harvest regulations that were disallowed by the original treaty. Following this, the USFWS convened an Alaska Migratory Bird Co-management Council with representation from Native Migratory Bird Working Group, and

the Alaska Department of Fish and Game and developed proposed harvest regulations for 2003.

The National Petroleum Reserve–Alaska contains important molting and staging areas as well as breeding habitat for the Pacific wintering Brant population. Certain areas had been established within the Reserve to protect important wildlife habitat. For example, the Teshekpuk Lake Special Area was established in 1977 within the northeast section of the Reserve with no oil and gas wells or support structures permitted within the Special Area. Audubon Alaska has advocated for a "Wildlife Habitat Alternative" plan for protecting biological hotspots within the Northwest Planning Area of the National Petroleum Reserve when the area is opened for oil and gas leasing as a way to ensure healthy populations of Brant and other wildlife species.

Laguna San Ignacio, an important wintering area for Brant in Mexico's Vizcaino Biosphere Reserve, was spared from environmentally damaging development in 2000 when the Mitsubishi Corporation announced it had abandoned its plans for a massive salt evaporation industrial plant at the site thanks to worldwide pressure from environmentally conscious citizens.

The Atlantic Coast Joint Venture (ACJV) has been very active in protecting wintering habitat for the species through a multitude of land acquisition and habitat restoration projects involving more than $230 million in grants and matching funds and nearly 300,000 acres of habitat. Many of these ACJV-funded projects are within important wintering areas for Brant along the Atlantic coast.[1,3,9,10,12]

CONSERVATION NEEDS

- Slow production of global warming pollution.
- Continue efforts to protect and enhance wintering habitat and ensure ecosystem function in coastal estuaries of the Pacific and Atlantic coasts of North America that provide essential habitat for Brant populations.
- Continue to decrease sport hunting pressure on Pacific-wintering Brant populations.
- Continue to decrease subsistence hunting pressure on Brant breeding populations in Alaska through efforts of Alaska Migratory Bird Co-management Council.
- Ensure that oil and gas exploration and extraction activity within portions of the Na-

tional Petroleum Reserve that provide key molting, staging, and nesting habitat for Brant does not adversely impact habitat, productivity, and survival of Brant.

- Study migration, staging, and wintering ecology of Brant to determine limiting factors and importance of fisheries and oil pollutants to survival of wintering birds.
- Continue funding for surveys designed to detect changes in abundance and distribution of the species.

References

1. Reed, A., D.H. Ward, D.V. Derksen, and J.S. Sedinger. 1998. Brant (*Branta bernicla*). *The Birds of North America*, No. 337 (A. Poole and F. Gill, eds.). The Academy of Natural Sciences, Philadelphia, PA, and the American Ornithologists' Union, Washington, DC.

2. Bird Studies Canada. 2003. *Important Bird Areas of Canada*. http://www.bsc-eoc.org/iba/IBAsites.html (accessed 14 April 2003)

3. International Brant Monitoring Project. 2003. *The International Brant Monitoring Project*. http:www .sd69.bc.ca/~brant/ (accessed 14 April 2003).

4. New Jersey Division of Fish and Wildlife. 2003. *Ecology and Research on Atlantic Brant*. www.state.nj.us/ dep/fgw/brant02/main.htm (accessed 14 April 2003).

5. Walsh, J., V. Elia, R. Kane, and T. Halliwell. 1999. *Birds of New Jersey*. New Jersey Audubon Society, Bernardsville, NJ.

6. Wells, J.V. 1998. *Important Bird Areas of New York State*. National Audubon Society, Albany, NY. 243 pp.

7. Washington Department of Fish and Wildlife. 2002. *Marine Goose Research Takes Biologists Above Arctic Circle*. www.wa.gov/wdfw/do/nov02/nov0502b.htm (accessed 14 April 2003).

8. U.S. Fish and Wildlife Service. 2006. *Waterfowl Population Status, 2006*. U.S. Department of the Interior, Washington, DC. 61 pp.

9. Atlantic Flyway Council. 2002. *Atlantic Brant Management Plan*. U.S. Fish and Wildlife Service, U.S. Department of the Interior, Washington, DC. 37 pp.

10. Audubon Alaska. 2002. *Alaska's Western Arctic: A Summary and Synthesis of Resources*. Audubon Alaska, Anchorage, AK. 240 pp. plus 49 maps.

11. BLM. 2003. Northwest National Petroleum Reserve–Alaska: draft integrated activity plan/environmental impact statement. Anchorage, AK.

12. BLM. 1998. Northeast National Petroleum Reserve–Alaska: final integrated activity plan/environmental impact statement. Anchorage, AK.

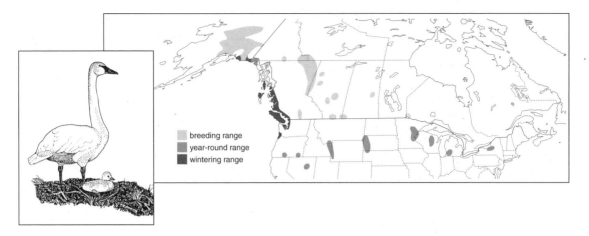

breeding range
year-round range
wintering range

TRUMPETER SWAN (*Cygnus buccinator*)

These large and beautiful birds were reduced to fewer than 100 individuals in the continental U.S. and several thousand in Canada and Alaska by the early 1900s. Protection and management efforts that started in the 1930s had increased the total population to over 34,000 by 2005.

STATUS AND DISTRIBUTION

Once bred across large part of sub-Arctic Canada and U.S., though exact limits of historical range, especially eastern and southern limits, seem to be a matter of conjecture. By the early 1900s the species had been extirpated from all of its former breeding range in the contiguous U.S. except for a small area encompassing the corners of Idaho, Montana, and Wyoming (tristate area) and by 1935 this population numbered only 69 individuals. Aerial waterfowl surveys in the 1950s discovered extant breeding populations in Alaska and western Canada that numbered in the low thousands. Birds breeding in Alaska winter in south coastal British Columbia and coastal Washington, while those breeding in western Canada winter largely in the tristate area. Those breeding in the tristate area remain there throughout the winter. Intensive efforts to protect habitat, reduce hunting mortality and human disturbance, and provide supplemental food began in the 1930s. Efforts to reestablish populations through translocations and reintroductions of captive-bred birds began in the 1930s but have increased since the 1980s. All of these efforts have succeeded in expanding the current breeding range of Trumpeter Swan beyond the 1950s range to include New York, Ontario,

Ohio, Michigan, Minnesota, Iowa, Illinois, Wisconsin, Nebraska, South Dakota, Saskatchewan, Manitoba, Oregon, and Nevada. These reintroduced birds show variability in migration patterns but most move only short distances to ice-free water bodies near breeding areas. Several projects were initiated beginning in 1997 that attempted to teach Trumpeter Swans to migrate by training them to follow an ultralight aircraft that flew the migration route but so far birds have not learned to repeat the migration on their own. Some birds from Wisconsin's breeding population that have been tracked using satellite transmitters move south to winter in southern Illinois and return in spring and two birds that followed an ultralight over 600 miles from Ontario to Indiana did return to Ontario. Trumpeter Swan ranges have been divided into three administrative segments for research and management: the Pacific Coast population (birds breeding primarily west of the Rocky Mountains), the Rocky Mountain population (birds breeding within the Rocky Mountains), and the Interior population (reintroduced populations breeding east of the Rocky Mountains).

Important breeding sites for the species in Alaska include the Bristol Bay area in western Alaska, the Copper River Delta, which hosts up to 800 breeding birds, and the West Fork of the Gulkana River, which is thought to support 30% of the world population of Trumpeter Swans. Important breeding sites in the tristate area include Red Rock Lakes National Wildlife Refuge (NWR) and the Centennial Valley in Montana and Yellowstone National Park in Wyoming. Virtually the entire the Rocky Mountain population of Trumpeter Swans winters in the tristate area.

Important Canadian breeding sites include the Nisultin River Delta Important Bird Area (IBA), Yukon Territory, which hosted 10–12 breeding pairs in 1997, and the Grande Prairie—Trumpeter Swan IBA in Alberta, which regularly supports 10 breeding pairs and up to 300 migrants. In Canada's Yukon Territory important spring staging areas include the M'Clintock Bay to Lewes River Marsh IBA, which is thought to support as many as 6,000 birds, and Tagish Narrows IBA, which regularly harbors as many as 1,000 birds. Chehalis River Estuary IBA, British Columbia is an important wintering site, with 2% of the Pacific Coast population wintering there.

Since surveys were started in 1968, the total number of free-ranging Trumpeter Swans (including reintroduced birds) has increased from 2,847 birds to 34,803 in 2005. This includes 24,928 in the Pacific Coast population, 5,228 in the Rocky Mountain population, and 4,647 in the Interior population.[1–10]

ECOLOGY

Breeds in freshwater marshes and at the edges of ponds and lakes, often constructing nests on tops of muskrat lodges. Rocky Mountain and Interior populations winter in ice-free rivers, ponds, and lakes usually near nesting areas. The Pacific Coast population uses open freshwater but also brackish estuaries, especially along the coast of southern British Columbia.[1]

THREATS

Historic decline is almost completely attributable to years of unregulated hunting pressure for subsistence and for market exports. Thousands of Trumpeter Swan skins were purchased and shipped to Europe by the famous Hudson Bay Company through the late 1800s. The current major threat or potential limiting factor for Trumpeter Swan populations is the loss and degradation of wetland habitats, though most populations have increased substantially since the early 1900s. Breeding areas in Alaska and western Canada seem relatively secure, though recreational use of certain important breeding areas like the Gulkana River has dramatically increased in recent years with unknown effect. Increasing urbanization in wintering areas of the Pacific Coast population may eventually cause a decrease in the amount and quality of available habitat. Collisions with power lines, lead poisoning, illegal shooting, and unintentional killing by hunters seeking Tundra Swans have been major sources of mortality. Loss of habitat from sea level rise and drying of boreal wetlands as a result of global warming may become the most difficult and pervasive threat.[1]

CONSERVATION ACTION

The restoration of Trumpeter Swan populations in North America has often been cited as one of the world's great conservation success stories. Beginning in the 1930s habitat was purchased for remaining birds in the tristate region in what is known as the Red Rock Lake NWR. There, Trumpeter Swans were protected from hunting, disturbance, and other sources of mortality, and given supplemental food during the winter. Other efforts started in the 1930s and 1940s included programs to reduce hunting mortality and efforts at captive breeding, translocations, and reintroductions. Between the late 1930s and the 1960s reintroductions by the USFWS from birds originating at Red Rock Lakes established new populations in Oregon, Nevada, and South Dakota on USFWS refuges. Cooperative efforts between USFWS, state wildlife agencies, zoos, and private conservation organizations were redoubled in the 1980s to a larger portion of the Trumpeter Swan historic range. Many of these programs used eggs taken from wild birds breeding in Alaska that were then hatched in incubators and carefully reared in captivity until their release. Such programs involved hundreds of released birds and have now established growing breeding groups of Trumpeter Swans in at least ten states and provinces with an estimated total wild population in 2006 of 4,647 birds. Controversy exists as to whether introductions in some parts of eastern North America are within the historic range of the species.

While reintroduction efforts will undoubtedly continue, more efforts toward increasing the amount and quality of available wetland wintering habitat are needed, especially for birds of the Pacific Coast population wintering in increasingly urbanized regions of southern British Columbia, and for birds of the Rocky Mountain population with its restricted winter range. Swans have been successfully reintroduced into some portions of their former range but most have remained as essentially nonmigratory, disjunct flocks. To be considered successful, traditional migratory behavior must be reestablished in these groups while quality winter habitat is secured in locations within the historic winter range.

A broad community of conservation organizations, industry, and First Nations have collaboratively developed a Boreal Forest Conservation Framework that provides a set of recommendations for a new national conservation approach in Canada's boreal region, including the western Canadian breeding range of Trumpeter Swan. One of the key recommendations is that a series of large, interconnected protected areas be established that cover at least 50% of the boreal region.[1,3,4,6,7,10,11]

CONSERVATION NEEDS

- Slow production of global warming pollution.
- Continue efforts to protect and enhance wintering habitat and ensure ecosystem function in coastal estuaries of the Pacific Coast of North America that provide essential habitat for Trumpeter Swan populations.
- Within the Trumpeter Swan's Canadian boreal breeding range, increase the number of large, protected areas and ensure adoption of sustainable development practices in areas that are developed.
- Continue efforts to protect and enhance breeding and wintering habitat and ensure ecosystem function in freshwater wetland habitats used by Rocky Mountain and Interior populations of Trumpeter Swans.
- Continue efforts to decrease the amount of lead shot and lead sinkers in wetland habitats to decrease mortality from lead poisoning in Trumpeter Swans.
- Continue hunter education efforts to decrease accidental hunting mortality of Trumpeter Swans.
- Continue funding for surveys designed to detect changes in abundance and distribution of the species.

References

1. Mitchell, C.D. 1994. Trumpeter Swan (*Cygnus buccinator*). In *The Birds of North America*, No. 105 (A. Poole and F. Gill, eds.). The Academy of Natural Sciences, Philadelphia, PA, and the American Ornithologists' Union, Washington, DC.

2. USFWS. 2003. Endangered and Threatened Wildlife and Plants: 90-Day Finding for a Petition to List the Tri-state Area Flock of Trumpeter Swans as Threatened. *Federal Register*, Vol. 68, No. 28: 4221–4228.

3. Lumsden, H.G. 1999. *The Trumpeter Swan Restoration Program in Ontario—1999.* http://www.bconnex.net/~smorel/trumpet/trumpeter1999.html (accessed 17 April 2003).

4. Maryland Department of Natural Resources. 1998. *Trumpeter Swan Migration Experiment in Maryland Status Report—December 1998.* http://www.dnr.state.md.us/wildlife/tswan.html (accessed 17 April 2003).

5. Wisconsin Department of Natural Resources. 2000. *Satellite Transmitters Successful in Tracking Wisconsin Trumpeter Swan Migrations.* http://www.dnr.state.wi.us/org/caer/ce/news/on/2000/ON000321.htm (accessed 17 April 2003).

6. Dubovsky, J.A., and J.E. Cornely. 2002. *An Assessment of Information Pertaining to the Status of Trumpeter Swans* (Cygnus buccinator). USFWS, Migratory Birds and State Programs, Region 6.

7. Conant, B., J.I. Hodges, D.J. Groves, and J.G. King. 1995. *1995 Census of Trumpeter Swans on Alaskan Nesting Habitats.* USFWS, Juneau, AK.

8. Christensen, H.H., L. Mastrantonio, J.C. Gordon, and B.T. Bormann. 2000. *Alaska's Copper River: Humankind in a Changing World.* General Technical Report PNW-GTR-480. USDA, Forest Service, Pacific Northwest Research Station, Portland, OR.

9. Bird Studies Canada. 2003. *Important Bird Areas of Canada.* http://www.bsc-eoc.org/iba/IBAsites.html (accessed 17 April 2003).

10. Moser, T.J. 2006. *The 2005 North American Trumpeter Swan Survey.* USFWS, Division of Migratory Bird Management, Denver, CO.

11. Canadian Boreal Initiative. 2003. *The Boreal Forest at Risk: A Progress Report.* Canadian Boreal Initiative, Ottawa, ON.

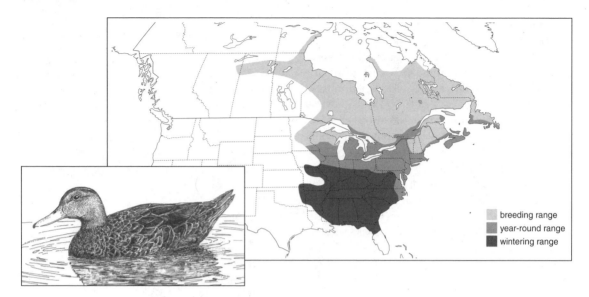

AMERICAN BLACK DUCK (*Anas rubripes*)

One of only two living waterfowl species limited to eastern North America, the American Black Duck occurs from the saltmarshes of the Atlantic coast to the freshwater ponds of Canada's eastern boreal forest.

STATUS AND DISTRIBUTION

Endemic to eastern North America, with a breeding range that extends from eastern Canada south into the northeastern U.S. High breeding densities occur in southern Quebec, New Brunswick, and Maine. Important breeding areas for the species include Canada's Northeast James Bay Important Bird Area (IBA), Maine's Moosehorn National Wildlife Refuge (NWR) and Rachel Carson NWR, and New York's Wertheim NWR. An estimated 52% of the total population of American Black Duck breeds within Canada's boreal forest.

In winter, the southern part of the breeding range remains occupied but birds move south as far as the northern portions of the Gulf states, with relatively high numbers along the Atlantic coast, St. Lawrence estuary, Great Lakes, and Mississippi River drainage. Important wintering areas include Quebec's Baie des Escoumins et Grandes-Bergeronnes IBA, North Carolina's Mattamuskeet NWR and Pea Island NWR, and New Jersey's Forsythe NWR.

Breeding Bird Survey (BBS) analysis shows a nonsignificant decline of approximately 46% (1.6% per year) from 1966 to 2005 rangewide (though there are no BBS routes in the northern portions of the Canadian breeding range).

An analysis of Christmas Bird Count (CBC) data shows a significant decline of 3.3% per year from 1959 to 1988, with highest abundances in Maine, Massachusetts, New Jersey, North Carolina, Connecticut, and Ohio. In addition, maps generated from CBC data also show areas of high wintering abundance along the St. Lawrence, and in Nova Scotia, southern Missouri, and northern Mississippi.

The Canadian Wildlife Service through its Black Duck Joint Venture project has conducted helicopter surveys in southern Quebec and the Maritimes to monitor the species' breeding status since 1990. Analysis of surveys for southern Quebec shows that the number of breeding pairs there has more than doubled since the mid-1990s. The species' total population was estimated at over 396,000 individuals in 2002.[1–11]

ECOLOGY

Within its rather large eastern Canadian and U.S. breeding range, occurs in small wetlands within the extensive matrix of boreal and mixed forest. In coastal areas, it breeds in saltmarsh habitats, and winters along salt and brackish coastline, feeding in intertidal mudflats.[1]

THREATS

On breeding and wintering grounds, loss of habitat from drainage and filling of wetlands for development, degradation of wetlands from pesticides, pollution, acid rain, and invasive plants, human-caused disturbance during nesting, and competition and hybridization with Mallards are the major threats. Loss of habitat from sea level rise and other habitat changes as a result of global warming may become the most difficult and pervasive threat.[1]

CONSERVATION ACTION

The North American Waterfowl Management Plan 1998 Update established a goal of increasing the midwinter survey index to 385,000 from the 1990s level of 285,000. The species has been highlighted as one of concern by the Black Duck Joint Venture, which has funded numerous studies to understand the relative importance of various factors in regulation of the species' abundance. Tightened harvest quotas have substantially decreased the number of birds taken by hunters in the U.S. and Canada since before 1989. In the U.S., the Fish and Wildlife Service has continued to purchase and manage habitat in many areas that support important wintering, migratory stopover, and breeding populations of American Black Ducks. For example, at Montezuma National Wildlife Refuge more than 1,000 acres of wetlands have been purchased and restored to provide stopover habitat for waterfowl, including the more than 10,000 American Black Ducks that use the refuge during fall migration. The Atlantic Coast Joint Venture (ACJV) has been very active in protecting habitat for the species through a multitude of land acquisition and habitat restoration projects involving more than $230 million in grants and matching funds and nearly 300,000 acres of habitat. Many of these ACJV-funded projects are within important wintering and breeding areas for American Black Duck, including a $1.3 million project protecting 2,200 acres in Maine's Merrymeeting Bay. The ACJV has also funded invasive species control projects, including a 25-state initiative to decrease the impact of the invasive purple loosestrife on wetland habitat through biological control agents.

A broad community of conservation organizations, industry, and First Nations have collaboratively developed a Boreal Forest Conservation Framework that provides a set of recommendations for a new national conservation approach in Canada's boreal region, including the eastern Canadian breeding range of American Black Duck. One of the key recommendations is that a series of large, interconnected, protected areas be established that cover at least 50% of the boreal region. The Canadian Parks and Wilderness Society has an active campaign to increase the number of protected areas throughout Canada, including Quebec, where large numbers of American Black Ducks breed.

The Boreal Songbird Initiative has spearheaded work by a network of U.S. conservation groups to increase awareness of the boreal wilderness and the threats it faces. For example, the National Wildlife Federation and the National Audubon Society both have conducted letter-writing campaigns asking large retail catalog companies to use recycled paper rather than paper made from trees harvested from virgin boreal forest.[1,6,11–16]

CONSERVATION NEEDS

- Slow production of global warming pollution.
- Increase acreage of wetland habitat within the range of the American Black Duck that is managed to attain conditions beneficial to the species.
- Within the American Black Duck's Canadian boreal breeding range, increase the number of large, protected areas and ensure the adoption of sustainable development practices in areas that are developed.
- Decrease the acreage of wetland habitat degraded by invasive species, pesticides, acid rain, and other pollutants.
- Discourage the release of captive-reared Mallards within the core breeding range of American Black Ducks to prevent continuing introgression of Mallard genes into the American Black Duck genome.
- Increase research on mortality factors, impact of human-caused disturbance on nesting success, nutrient dynamics, and energetics.

References

1. Longcore, J.R., D. G. McAuley, G. R. Hepp, and J. M. Rhymer. 2000. American Black Duck (*Anas rubripes*). In *The Birds of North America*, No. 481 (A.

Poole and F. Gill, eds.). The Birds of North America, Inc., Philadelphia, PA.

2. Bird Studies Canada. 2003. *Important Bird Areas of Canada.* http://www.bsc-eoc.org/iba/IBAsites.html (accessed 14 April 2003).

3. Audubon North Carolina. No date. *North Carolina's Important Bird Areas.* http://www.ncaudubon .org/IBA1.htm (accessed April 2004).

4. Chipley, R.M., G.H. Fenwick, M.J. Parr, and D.N. Pashley. 2003. *The American Bird Conservancy Guide to the 500 Most Important Bird Areas in the United States.* Random House, New York, NY.

5. Wells, J.V. 1998. *Important Bird Areas of New York State.* National Audubon Society, Albany, NY. 243 pp.

6. Blancher, P., and J. Wells. 2005. *The Boreal Forest Region: North America's Bird Nursery.* Canadian Boreal Initiative, Ottawa, ON, and Boreal Songbird Initiative, Seattle, WA.

7. Sauer, J. R., J. E. Hines, and J. Fallon. 2005. *The North American Breeding Bird Survey, Results and Analysis 1966–2005*, Version 6.2.2006. USGS Patuxent Wildlife Research Center, Laurel, MD.

8. Sauer, J. R., S. Schwartz, and B. Hoover. 1996. *The Christmas Bird Count Home Page*, Version 95.1. Patuxent Wildlife Research Center, Laurel, MD.

9. Bordage, D., C. Lepage, and S. Orichefsky. 2003. *2003 Black Duck Joint Venture Helicopter Survey—Québec.* Canadian Wildlife Service report, Québec Region, Environment Canada, Sainte-Foy, QC.

10. Lepage, C. and D. Bordage. 2003. *Black Duck Joint Venture (BDJV).* Environment Canada, Canadian Wildlife Service, Québec Region. http://www.qc.ec.gc .ca/faune/sauvagine/html/bdjv.html.

11. Delany, S., and D. Scott. 2002. *Waterbird Population Estimates*, 3rd ed. Wetlands International Global Series No. 12, Wageningen, The Netherlands.

12. U.S. Fish and Wildlife Service. 1998. *North American Waterfowl Management Plan—1998 Update.* U.S. Department of the Interior, Washington, DC.

13. Atlantic Coast Joint Venture. 2004. *Atlantic Coast Joint Venture.* http://www.acjv.org/ (accessed 2004).

14. Canadian Boreal Initiative. 2005. *The Boreal in the Balance: Securing the Future of Canada's Boreal Forest Region.* Canadian Boreal Initiative, Ottawa, ON.

15. Canadian Parks and Wilderness Society. 2005. Canadian Parks and Wilderness Society website: http:// www.cpaws.org.

16. Boreal Songbird Initiative. 2005. Boreal Songbird Initiative website: http://www.borealbirds.org.

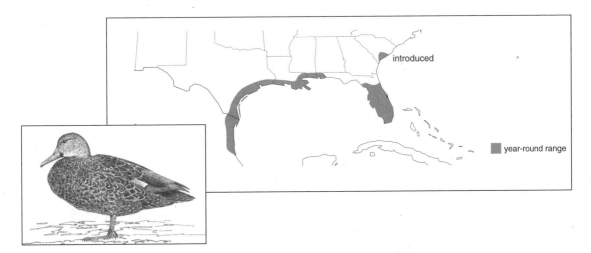

introduced

year-round range

MOTTLED DUCK (*Anas fulvigula*)

A characteristic dabbling duck of south-central Florida and the Gulf Coast, the Mottled Duck is threatened by major loss and degradation of its wetland habitat and by hybridization with introduced Mallards.

STATUS AND DISTRIBUTION

Confined to the southeastern U.S. and adjacent northeastern Mexico. Naturally occurring population extends from south-central Florida west along the Gulf Coast to Texas and the Mexican state of Tamaulipas. A gap in the distribution extends across the panhandle of Florida to eastern coastal Mississippi. An introduced population now occurs in coastal South Carolina. The species is nonmigratory within this range though there are extralimital records from as far south as Veracruz, Mexico and north to Wisconsin, Virginia, and New Jersey. High densities occur in the coastal marshes of Louisiana, including the Atchafalaya Delta, southeast Texas, and in Lake Okeechobee and St. John's River areas of south-central Florida. Important sites for the species on the upper Texas coast include the Anahuac National Wildlife Refuge (NWR), McFaddin and Texas Point NWRs, and the J.D. Murphree Wildlife Management Area owned by Texas Parks and Wildlife. Important sites for the species in Louisiana include Sabine NWR, Lacassine NWR, and Cameron Prairie NWR. Important sites in Florida include Loxahatchee NWR, Kissimmee Prairie Preserve State Park, and the Lake Apoka Restoration Area. In Mexico, the species is resident at the Laguna Madre Important Bird Area (IBA) in coastal Tamaulipas and, although no information is available about its current level of abundance, historically it was considered common in this region of coastal Mexico.

Breeding Bird Survey analysis shows a nonsignificant decline of approximately 76% (3.8% per year) from 1966 to 2004 rangewide. Florida surveys (1985 to present) indicate relatively stable densities and Texas surveys from 1985 to 1993 show a decrease then a subsequent increase back to early survey densities. However, surveys of Mottled Duck numbers on USFWS refuges in Texas indicate an 88% decline over the past 20 years. Unfortunately, all current surveys are carried out over only a portion of the species range, even in Florida and Texas, so that it is unknown how reflective they may be of overall population trends. The population of Mottled Ducks was estimated to average about 480,000 individuals from 1970 to 1979 and 170,000 in 2002. Population objectives in the North American Waterfowl Management Plan are 646,000, obviously much higher than current numbers.[1-10]

ECOLOGY

Within its restricted range, occurs in small prairie wetlands, freshwater marshes, drainage ditches, rice fields, and brackish ponds. Use of wetlands and subsequent breeding success is affected by water levels and in drought years large numbers of birds may move to more permanent wetlands.[1]

THREATS

Loss of habitat from drainage and filling of wetlands for agriculture and development is major problem, especially in Florida. For example, Florida is estimated to have lost 9.1 million acres of wetland habitats since European settlement. In Louisiana and Texas coastal wetlands are being lost to erosion and subsequent saltwater intrusion. From the 1950s to the 1990s, Louisiana lost nearly 900,000 acres of coastal wetland and Texas an estimated 210,687 acres. Competition and hybridization with introduced Mallards is a major threat. Already an estimated 5% of all of Florida's Mottled Ducks exhibit Mallard characteristics from hybridization. In Mexico, the Laguna Madre IBA is not currently part of the protected area system, and hunting has historically been a major activity in the area. Loss of habitat from sea level rise and other habitat changes as a result of global warming may become the most difficult and pervasive threat.[1,4,10–12]

CONSERVATION ACTION

The Florida Fish and Wildlife Conservation Commission released a Mottled Duck Conservation Plan in 1999. The plan calls for maintaining Mottled Duck densities in the state at or near current densities as determined by aerial surveys, continuing conservative hunting regulations, decreasing hybridization with feral Mallards through education programs to prevent further releases of Mallards, and developing recommendations for management of private grazing lands and agricultural lands that is beneficial to Mottled Ducks and compatible with other land use. The MacArthur Agro-Ecology Research Center, managed by Archbold Biological Station, is carrying out research on the compatibility of cattle grazing and wildlife management.

The Kissimmee Prairie Ecosystem Project had acquired at least 47,300 acres by 1999 and was working to restore dry prairie and central Florida wetlands, including through the elimination of an extensive ditch and dike system over these acres.

Coastal wetland habitat restoration efforts within the range of the Mottled Duck should be beneficial to the species, though there are no known habitat initiatives focused on the species. For example, the National Marine Fisheries Service and the Louisiana Department of Natural Resources initiated the $6.4 million Black Bayou Hydrologic Restoration Project to restore coastal marsh habitat and slow the loss of wetlands within this 25,530-acre wetland located in Louisiana's Cameron and Calcasieu parishes. Another example is the Texas Prairie Wetlands Project that was created by U.S. Fish and Wildlife Service, Texas Parks and Wildlife Department, USDA's Natural Resources Conservation Service, and Ducks Unlimited to provide technical assistance and financial incentives to private landowners for improving or restoring wetland habitats along the Gulf Coast. Through 2001, 299,000 acres of wetland projects in Texas had been completed or were under construction for more than 40 landowners.[2,6,7,13]

CONSERVATION NEEDS

- Slow production of global warming pollution.
- Increase the acreage of wetland habitat within the range of the Mottled Duck that is managed to attain conditions beneficial to the species.
- Decrease the acreage of wetland habitat degraded by erosion, pollution, invasive species, pesticides, and other factors.
- Discourage the release of farm-reared Mallards within the breeding range of Mottled Ducks and remove established Mallard populations to prevent continuing introgression of Mallard genes into the Mottled Duck genome.
- Implement a rangewide survey designed to assess overall population status and trends.

References

1. Moorman, T.E., and P.N. Gray. 1994. Mottled Duck (*Anas fulvigula*). In *The Birds of North America*, No. 81 (A. Poole and F. Gill, eds.). The Academy of Natural Sciences, Philadelphia, PA, and the American Ornithologists' Union, Washington, DC.

2. Pranty, B. 2002. The Important Bird Areas of Florida. Unpublished manuscript downloaded from website 9 April 2003. http://www.audubon.org/bird/iba/florida/

3. Benítez, H., C. Arizmendi, and L. Marquez. 1999. *Base de Datos de las AICAS*. CIPAMEX, CONABIO, FMCN y CCA, México. http://www.conabio.gob.mx.

4. Arellano, M., and P. Rojas. 1956. *Aves Acuaticas Migratorias en Mexico I*. IMRNR, Mexico, DF. 270 pp.

5. Sauer, J.R., J. E. Hines, and J. Fallon. 2005. *The North American Breeding Bird Survey, Results and Analysis 1966–2005*, Version 6.2.2006. USGS Patuxent Wildlife Research Center, Laurel, MD.

6. Sauer, J. R., S. Schwartz, and B. Hoover. 1996. *The Christmas Bird Count Home Page*. Version 95.1. Patuxent Wildlife Research Center, Laurel, MD.

7. Florida Fish and Wildlife Conservation Commission. 1999. *Mottled Duck Conservation Plan*. http://www.wildflorida.org/duck/Mottled_Ducks/modu_cons_plan.htm (accessed 8 April 2003).

8. U.S. Fish and Wildlife Service. 1998. *North American Waterfowl Management Plan—1998 Update*. U.S. Department of the Interior, Washington, DC.

9. Delany, S., and D. Scott. 2002. *Waterbird Population Estimates*, 3rd ed. Wetlands International Global Series No. 12, Wageningen, The Netherlands.

10. Wilson, B.C., and C.G. Esslinger. 2002. *North American Waterfowl Management Plan, Gulf Coast Joint Venture: Texas Mid-Coast Initiative*. North American Waterfowl Management Plan, Albuquerque, NM.

11. Moulton, D.W., T.E. Dahl, and D.M. Dall. 1997. *Texas Coastal Wetlands: Status and Trends, mid-1950s to early 1990s*. U.S. Department of the Interior, Fish and Wildlife Service. Albuquerque, NM.

12. SEMARNAP. 2000. *Áreas Naturales Protegidas de México*. SEMARNAP, Mexico, D.F. 64 pp.

13. U.S. Environmental Protection Agency. 2001. *Texas Prairie Wetlands Project Merits Gulf Guardian Award*. U.S. Environmental Protection Agency, Gulf of Mexico Program Office, Stennis Space Center, MS. http://www.epa.gov/gmpo/gulfguard/2001_tx prairiewetlandsrelease2.htm (accessed 7 November 2005).

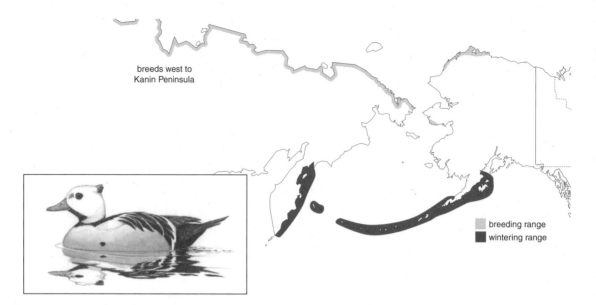

breeds west to
Kanin Peninsula

breeding range
wintering range

STELLER'S EIDER (*Polysticta stelleri*)

Steller's Eider is a small Arctic breeding eider whose U.S. population is now listed as Threatened because of declines in the Alaska portion of its breeding range.

STATUS AND DISTRIBUTION

Breeds along the Arctic coast of Siberia with a small population in western Siberia disjunct from larger eastern Siberian population, which is thought to be the bulk of the species' world population. In the U.S., it breeds along the Arctic Coastal Plain of Alaska with a concentration near Barrow. The species formerly bred in larger numbers in western Alaska at the Yukon-Kuskokwim Delta but now occurs in very small numbers. Most of the population breeding in eastern Siberia and Alaska winters in Alaska along Kodiak Island and the Alaskan peninsula and in the Aleutian Islands. Smaller numbers from the eastern Siberian population winter along Siberia's Kamchatkan coast. Birds from the western Siberian breeding range winter in northern Europe.

Important wintering and staging sites for the species in Alaska include Izembek National Wildlife Refuge (NWR), which has hosted as many 17,000 birds, Kodiak Island NWR, Alaska Peninsula NWR, and the Alaska Maritime NWR. The majority of the world's population of Steller's Eider uses the coastal habitats in or near these refuges for migratory staging and wintering.

Detecting trends in Steller's Eider populations has been hampered by the lack of survey data and the logistical hurdles in developing surveys within its Arctic breeding range. Historical records indicate that birds were once more common and widespread. Population was estimated at 400,000–500,000 individuals in the 1960s but was estimated at 200,000 in the 1990s. Aerial surveys in Russia from 1993 to 1995 resulted in an estimated breeding population there of 149,000 individuals. Aerial surveys during spring migration have been conducted annually since 1992 in the area in Alaska through which the majority of the Russian Pacific and Alaska breeding populations are known to migrate. Numbers detected in this survey have declined 6% annually, from 137,904 in 1992 to 77,369 in 2003. Annual surveys in or near the Izembek NWR from 1975 to 1990 show declines of 53–71%. During the 1950s and 1960s the nesting population of Steller's Eider in the Yukon-Kuskokwim Delta was estimated at 3,500 pairs but only five nests could be found during an intensive nesting biology study in the 1990s.[1–5]

ECOLOGY

Breeds in arctic tundra habitat near freshwater ponds typically within 20–30 km of coastline, but is sometimes found up to 150 km inland, especially in the Siberian breeding range. During migration this species uses shallow inshore coastal lagoons often with tidal flats and eelgrass beds. In the wintering range it seems to prefer similar habitats but also sometimes occurs in deep water bays. Wintering habitat use and preferences are poorly studied.[1]

THREATS

Reasons for declines are still a mystery but some factors have been proposed, including increased level of mortality from subsistence harvesting, oil pollution, incidental take in gillnet fisheries, and disturbance from fisheries and other maritime human activities. Estimates of survival rates from banding data indicate a decline from the 1970s to the 1990s and show a lower survival rate for males compared to females. Studies of Steller's Eider on the Lithuanian wintering grounds have shown that the species is susceptible to drowning in gill net fisheries, with estimates of the percentage of birds killed as high as 10%. No study of the effect of fisheries activities on Alaskan populations has been carried out. Subsistence harvesting mortality by native groups in Alaska is thought to be minimal. Illegal hunting in Russia is thought to be significant in some years and under certain conditions and is claimed to have involved thousands of birds killed in some years. In 2004, a plan was announced to open for oil and gas leases the 8.8-million-acre Northwest Planning Area of the National Petroleum Reserve–Alaska, which includes a large proportion of the Alaska breeding range of Steller's Eider. Loss of habitat from sea level rise and other habitat changes as a result of global warming may become the most difficult and pervasive threat.[1,4-9]

CONSERVATION ACTION

Steller's Eider received special protection status in Russia in 1993, and the Alaska-breeding population was federally listed as Threatened in the U.S. in 1997. The USFWS designated Critical Habitat areas for the species in 2001, including many important staging and wintering areas. The primary nesting areas in the Arctic Coastal Plain were not included due to the lack of information about which specific locations within this vast area were most important. The National Marine Fisheries Service has used these designations to consider whether certain fisheries are likely to adversely impact Steller's Eider populations on the staging and wintering grounds and they have hired a Seabird

Coordinator to focus on seabird-related fisheries issues.

To better manage the level of subsistence hunting mortality on Steller's Eiders and other birds the USFWS negotiated an amendment of the Migratory Bird Treaty with Canada and Mexico in 1999 to allow the USFWS to develop and implement spring and summer subsistence harvest regulations, which were disallowed by the original treaty. Following this, the USFWS convened an Alaska Migratory Bird Co-management Council with representation from the Native Migratory Bird Working Group and the Alaska Department of Fish and Game and developed proposed harvest regulations for 2003. The USFWS has provided ongoing funding for a Russian subsistence harvest survey in Chukotka to assess the harvest level.

The USFWS and the Seaduck Joint Venture have initiated a number of studies on the population status, biology, movements, and limiting factors of Steller's Eider populations but funding constraints still limit even the most basic surveys to determine trends and population size. Audubon Alaska has advocated for a "Wildlife Habitat Alternative" plan for protecting biological hotspots within the Northwest Planning Area of the National Petroleum Reserve when the area is opened for oil and gas leasing as a way to ensure healthy populations of Steller's Eider and other wildlife species.[1,4,5,7-10]

CONSERVATION NEEDS

- Slow production of global warming pollution.
- Ensure that oil and gas exploration and extraction activity within portions of the National Petroleum Reserve that support nesting Steller's Eider does not adversely impact habitat, productivity, and survival of Steller's Eiders.
- Encourage Russian conservation authorities to develop regulations to manage subsistence hunting and illegal take of Steller's Eider in Russia, perhaps as part of an international regional comanagement plan.
- Continue to decrease hunting pressure on Steller's Eider breeding populations in Alaska through efforts of Alaska Migratory Bird Co-management Council.
- Study wintering ecology of Steller's Eider to determine the limiting factors and importance of fisheries and oil pollutants to the survival of wintering birds.

- Increase funding for surveys designed to detect changes in abundance and distribution of the species.

References

1. Fredrickson, L.H. 2001. Steller's Eider (*Polysticta stelleri*). In *The Birds of North America*, No. 571 (A. Poole and F. Gill, eds.). Cornell Laboratory of Ornithology, Ithaca, NY, and the Academy of Natural Sciences, Philadelphia, PA.

2. USFWS. 2001. Endangered and Threatened Wildlife and Plants: Final Determination of Critical Habitat for the Alaska-breeding Population of the Steller's Eider. *Federal Register* 66 (23): 8850–8884. http://alaska.fws.gov/media/StellEider_FinalRule.htm (accessed 8 April 2003).

3. Larned, W.W. 2003. Steller's Eider Spring Migration Surveys Southwest Alaska 2003. Unpublished Report of the U.S. Fish and Wildlife Service, Migratory Bird Management Office, Waterfowl Branch, Anchorage, AK. 24 pp.

4. USFWS. 1999. *Population Status and Trends of Sea Ducks in Alaska*. USFWS, Migratory Bird Management, Waterfowl Management Branch, Anchorage, AK.

5. USFWS. 2002. *Steller's Eider Recovery Plan*. Fairbanks, AK.

6. Zydelis, R. 2002. *Ecology of Steller's Eider and a Recent Assessment of the Fishing Bycatch in Lithuania*. Abstracts of Presentations to the Wetlands International Seaduck Specialist Group Meeting, Estonia.

7. Audubon Alaska. 2002. *Alaska's Western Arctic: A Summary and Synthesis of Resources*. Audubon Alaska, Anchorage, AK. 240 pp. plus 49 maps.

8. BLM. 2003. Northwest National Petroleum Reserve–Alaska: draft integrated activity plan/environmental impact statement. Anchorage, AK.

9. BLM. 1998. Northeast National Petroleum Reserve–Alaska: final integrated activity plan/environmental impact statement. Anchorage, AK.

10. NMFS. 2005. *Program to Reduce Seabird Incidental Take in Longline Fisheries*. http://www.fakr.noaa.gov/protectedresources/seabirds.html (accessed 14 November 2005).

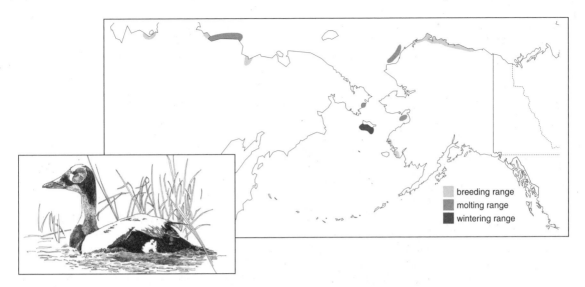

SPECTACLED EIDER (*Somateria fischeri*)

Males of this Arctic breeding eider are magnificently plumaged but to see a Spectacled Eider requires living in or visiting the remote Alaskan or Siberian breeding range. The location of the species' wintering range was an unsolved ornithological mystery until satellite telemetry studies were initiated after the species was federally listed in the U.S. as Threatened in 1993.

STATUS AND DISTRIBUTION

Breeds along the Arctic coasts of Siberia and Alaska. There are three known breeding concentration areas in Siberia. In Alaska, there are two spatially disjunct breeding populations: the Yukon-Kuskokwim Delta and the Arctic Coastal Plain from near Wainwright to Demarcation Point.

The wintering range and molting areas of the species were unknown until the 1990s, when satellite transmitters were implanted in birds on the breeding grounds and birds were tracked. Based on this work it is now known that the entire world population of Spectacled Eider winters in openings in the pack ice of the Bering Sea south of St. Lawrence Island. Molting areas in the U.S. include eastern Norton Sound and Ledyard Bay in Alaska. In Russia, birds molt in two regions of Arctic coastal Siberia.

From 1957 to 1992 the western Alaska breeding population declined by 96%, from a high of 96,000 in the 1970s to fewer than 5,000 in 1992. Aerial surveys of the western Alaska population

have shown an increase since 1992 with an estimated population of over 8,000 in 2002. An aerial survey of the northern Alaska population was started in 1992 and has indicated a slight decline through 2002, although the trend is not statistically significant. The northern Alaska population was estimated at 6,662 in 2002. Aerial surveys in Russia from 1993 to 1995 resulted in an estimated breeding population there of more than 140,000 individuals. Estimates of the number of birds found in wintering flocks in the Bering Sea from aerial surveys in the 1990s were of at least 333,000 birds.[1-5]

ECOLOGY

Breeds in arctic tundra habitat near brackish and freshwater ponds, lakes, and rivers. On Yukon-Kuskokwim Delta, birds breed within 20 km of the coastline, but elsewhere in their range they occur up to 120 km inland. Molting birds remain 2–45 km from shore in areas of the Arctic, Bering, and Chukchi Seas characterized by abundant bottom-dwelling mollusks, arthropods, and echinoderms. In winter, they are found in massive single-species flocks in small openings in the pack ice of the Bering Sea south of St. Lawrence Island. The species' ecology during this period has only recently begun to be studied but the birds are known to feed extensively on the thin-shelled clams that are abundant in this part of the Bering Sea. Other pack ice-wintering seaducks have been known to occasionally suffer massive mortality events when severe weather conditions cause openings in the pack ice to close rapidly and such an event could theoretically cause a major drop in numbers of Spectacled Eiders.[1,6]

THREATS

Reasons for declines are still a mystery but some factors have been proposed, including increased level of mortality as a result of ingestion of lead shot in areas of the Yukon-Kuskokwim Delta where there have been high levels of hunting. In this area, lead poisoning has reduced adult female annual survival by 34% or more. Subsistence harvesting and accidental mortality from sport hunters are thought to have a minimal effect, with estimates in the 1990s of about 190 birds taken annually in western Alaska. Speculative estimates of hunting mortality in Russia have been as high as 10% of breeding population but are open to debate. Expansion of human settlements and other factors may have caused an increase in numbers of predators like fox and gulls that could result in an increase in mortality to eggs and young of Spectacled Eiders.

Recent work shows that there has been a major shift in the species of clams available to Spectacled Eiders on the wintering grounds. The formerly abundant clams were of higher energy value than the clam species that now predominates, a factor that could have increased overwinter mortality in the birds. The decline in one species of clam (*Macoma calcarea*) and increase in another (*Nuculana radiata*) is thought to be the result of higher ocean temperatures caused by global warming.

Other potential threats are habitat degradation from expansion of human settlements and oil and gas exploration and extraction activities, oil pollution in molting and wintering habitats, and decreases in food supplies on wintering and molting areas from disturbance of marine environments. In 2004, a plan was announced to open for oil and gas leases the 8.8-million-acre Northwest Planning Area of the National Petroleum Reserve–Alaska, which includes a large proportion of the Alaska breeding range of Spectacled Eider. Loss of habitat from sea level rise and other habitat changes as a result of global warming may become the most difficult and pervasive threat.[1,3,6,7]

CONSERVATION ACTION

Spectacled Eider was federally listed as Threatened in the U.S. in 1993. The USFWS designated Critical Habitat areas for the species in 2001, including all important staging and wintering areas in the U.S. and the primary breeding area in western Alaska, but did not include any of the primary nesting area in the Arctic Coastal Plain because of the lack of information about which specific locations within this vast area were most important.

The USFWS and partners, through the Spectacled Eider Recovery Team, developed a Spectacled Eider Recovery Plan with recommended actions to benefit the species. A number of studies on the population status, biology, movements, and limiting factors of Spectacled Eider populations have been initiated but funding constraints still limit even the most basic surveys to determine trends and population size.

To better manage the level of subsistence hunting mortality on Spectacled Eiders and other birds the USFWS negotiated an amendment of the Migratory Bird Treaty with Canada and Mexico in 1999. The amendment allows the USFWS to develop and implement spring and summer subsistence harvest regulations, which were disallowed by the original treaty. Following this, the USFWS convened an Alaska Migratory Bird Co-management Council with representation from Native Migratory Bird Working Group, and the Alaska Department of Fish and Game and developed proposed harvest regulations for 2003.

Audubon Alaska has advocated for a "Wildlife Habitat Alternative" plan for protecting biological hotspots within the Northwest Planning Area of the National Petroleum Reserve when the area is opened for oil and gas leasing as a way to ensure healthy populations of Spectacled Eider and other wildlife species.[1,6–10]

CONSERVATION NEEDS

- Slow production of global warming pollution.
- Eliminate use of lead shot in Spectacled Eider breeding areas.
- Study impact of increased predator populations around human settlements in breeding range of Spectacled Eider.
- Ensure that oil and gas exploration and extraction activity within portions of the National Petroleum Reserve that support nesting

Spectacled Eider does not adversely impact habitat, productivity, and survival of Spectacled Eiders.

- Study migration, staging, and wintering ecology of Spectacled Eider to determine limiting factors and importance of fisheries and oil pollutants to survival of wintering birds.
- Continue funding for surveys designed to detect changes in abundance and distribution of the species.
- Encourage Russian conservation authorities to develop regulations to manage subsistence hunting of Spectacled Eider in Russia, perhaps as part of an international regional comanagement plan.
- Continue to decrease subsistence hunting pressure on Spectacled Eider breeding populations in Alaska through efforts of Alaska Migratory Bird Co-management Council.

References

1. Petersen, M.R., J.B. Grand, and C.P. Dau. 2000. Spectacled Eider (*Somateria fischeri*). In *The Birds of North America*, No. 547 (A. Poole and F. Gill, eds.). Cornell Laboratory of Ornithology, Ithaca, NY, and the Academy of Natural Sciences, Philadelphia, PA.

2. Petersen, M.R., W.W. Larned, and D.C. Douglas. 1999. At-sea distribution of Spectacled Eiders: A 120-year-old Mystery Resolved. *Auk* 116:1009–1020.

3. USFWS. 1999. *Population Status and Trends of Sea Ducks in Alaska*. USFWS, Migratory Bird Management, Waterfowl Management Branch, Anchorage, AK.

4. Platte, R.M., and R.A. Stehn. 2003. *Relative Abundance and Trends of Waterbirds from Aerial Breeding Pair Surveys, 1998–2002, on the Coastal Zone of the Yukon Kuskokwim Delta, Alaska*. USFWS, Migratory Bird Management, Anchorage, AK.

5. Larned, W., R. Stehn, and R. Platte. 2003. *Eider Breeding Population Survey: Arctic Coastal Plain, Alaska*. USFWS, Migratory Bird Management, Anchorage, AK.

6. U.S. Fish and Wildlife Service. 1996. *Spectacled Eider Recovery Plan*. Anchorage, Alaska. 157 pp.

7. Lovvorn, J.R., S. Richman, J. Grebmeier, and L. Cooper. 2003. Diet and Body Condition of Spectacled Eiders Wintering in Pack Ice of the Bering Sea. *Polar Biology* 26:259–267.

8. Audubon Alaska. 2002. *Alaska's Western Arctic: a summary and synthesis of resources*. Audubon Alaska, Anchorage, AK. 240 pp. plus 49 maps.

9. BLM. 2003. Northwest National Petroleum Reserve–Alaska: draft integrated activity plan/environmental impact statement. Anchorage, AK.

10. BLM. 1998. Northeast National Petroleum Reserve-Alaska: final integrated activity plan/environmental impact statement. Anchorage, AK.

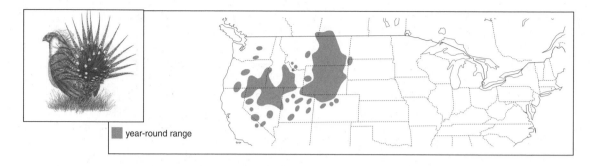

year-round range

GREATER SAGE-GROUSE (*Centrocercus urophasianus*)

One of the most well-known and dramatic of the suite of bird species of the sagebrush habitat of western North America, the Greater Sage-Grouse has shown major declines in abundance and shrinking of its range.

STATUS AND DISTRIBUTION

Range encompasses eleven states and two provinces from eastern California and Oregon, east to northcentral Colorado and north through eastern Montana to southeastern Saskatchewan and southern Alberta. Small isolated populations occur in central Washington and range barely extends into the northwestern corner of South Dakota and southwestern corner of North Dakota. Historically, this species occurred throughout most of eastern and central Washington to British Columbia and much more extensively in western portions of North and South Dakota to the northwestern corner of Nebraska. Populations now gone from Arizona, New Mexico, Oklahoma, and Kansas may have been this species or the recently recognized Gunnison Sage-Grouse.

Over 99% of the total population of Greater Sage-Grouse is found in the U.S., with 70% estimated to occur within the states of Idaho, Montana, Nevada, Oregon, and Wyoming. Important sites for the species include California's Surprise Valley Important Bird Areas (IBA) (largely private land), Colorado's Arapaho National Wildlife Refuge (NWR) where approximately 200 birds breed, Idaho's Curlew National Grassland, Montana's Charles M. Russell NWR and the BLM's 40 Complex, and Wyoming's Seedskadee NWR and Rock Springs District BLM land.

Along with a range reduction of at least 20–30%, having disappeared from six states where it formerly occurred, the species has shown an esti-

mated 86% decline in numbers. One expert has estimated a decline from at least 1.1 million birds in historic times to 142,000 today. Comparisons of surveys from before 1985 (some as early as the 1950s) to those after 1985 from ten states and one Canadian province show an average 33% decline in numbers across the range, and an assessment published in 2004 estimated a rangewide decline of more than 50% (2% per year) between 1965 and 2003. In some areas the decline has been even greater. For example, in Washington state the number of Greater Sage-Grouse harvested annually dropped from an average of 1,842 during the period 1951–1973 to <1,000 after 1974 and finally to 18 by 1987. The total estimated breeding population in the state in 1997 was less than the numbers harvested annually prior to 1974. In Saskatchewan and Alberta numbers have dropped by as much as 80% since the 1980s and the total population in Canada is estimated at fewer than 1,000 birds. In Oregon, numbers dropped by 60% between 1940 and 1983. In Idaho, numbers were down 40% from long-term averages. The total population size was estimated by one expert at 142,000 in 1998, though this estimate has been contested by others as too low.[1–9]

ECOLOGY

A species of sagebrush (*Artemisia* sp.) ecosystems, but uses a variety of types of sagebrush as well as wet meadows and riparian areas. Males display in groups (leks) in more open and elevated areas where females congregate to assess male status. These birds have a polygynous mating system in which only a few males mate with most of the females. Adults feed largely on sagebrush vegetation and are reliant on it during the winter when they may have to make small-scale migration movements to find sagebrush that is not snow-covered. Nests are placed in sagebrush vegetation or thick grasses on the ground. The female lay 6–9 eggs, which hatch in 25–29 days. Chicks are precocial and follow the female from the nest soon after hatching. Young feed themselves but are brooded by the female through the first week. Young are taken by the female to wetter, richer habitats, including meadows and riparian areas where they feed on insects and small flowering plants. Some populations are migratory in response to habitat availability with average movements of birds of 4–21 miles, though some birds may move 70 miles or more.[1]

THREATS

The greatest threat continues to be loss and degradation of native habitat largely through oil and gas extraction activities, spread of invasive plant species, changes in fire frequency and severity, road and building development, and overgrazing on rangeland. At least 50% of the original range of Greater Sage-Grouse can no longer support the species and in some states 70% or more of sagebrush habitat has been converted to cropland. Millions of acres of sagebrush have been destroyed for agricultural uses and on millions more sagebrush has been systematically removed. Less than 10% of the 84 million acres of the Great Basin Shrub Steppe ecoregion remains as intact habitat. Oil and gas well construction is expected to increase within the species' range. A 1996 report estimated that 6,000–11,000 new oil and gas wells would be developed in southwestern Wyoming by 2016, and in the Powder River Basin of Wyoming and Montana over 65,000 additional wells are being considered for development. A study in 2004 estimated that a minimum of 120 million acres of habitat in the western U.S. was impacted by oil and gas well pads, pipelines, and roads, including 28% of sagebrush habitats.

The variability in types of sagebrush-dominated ecosystems across the western U.S., including differences in which species of sagebrush is dominant, aridity, the impacts of fire, and the role of native herbivores, is astounding, especially for much of the American public whose experience with sagebrush is limited to its mention in movies or television shows of the Old West. This variability has even caused confusion and unintentional land management mistakes in some regions by land managers attempting to maintain sagebrush habitat or at least to balance management for healthy ecosystems with cattle grazing or other commercial activities. Greater Sage-Grouse require habitat that has 10–30% cover of sagebrush but with an understory of native grass. In sagebrush ecosystems used for grazing, burning is sometimes practiced to increase grass cover but certain species of sagebrush do not resprout after fire and will be eliminated. In such ecosystems, invasive grasses and other plants often appear after fires and outcompete native species. In other regions, fires are suppressed, allowing an increase in pinyon and other conifer species and/or allowing sagebrush to become so thick that it cannot be used by sage-grouse. Since cattle do not typically eat sagebrush, areas that are heavily grazed show a decrease in native grasses that are eaten, often resulting in the invasion of exotic grasses and the increase in density of sagebrush above levels used by sage-grouse. In many areas introduced cheatgrass (*Bromus tectorum*) has invaded, outcompeted, and eventually replaced sagebrush habitat. After cheatgrass becomes established fire frequency generally increases, to the detriment of most sagebrush habitat. Some of the isolated populations of Greater Sage-Grouse, like those in Washington, Utah, and western Nevada, are likely to begin having genetic inbreeding problems, especially as the species' polygynous mating system inherently decreases genetic variability. Hunting seasons continue in states throughout much of the species' range but the impact of hunting on populations is unclear and somewhat controversial. Beginning in 2003, Greater Sage-Grouse in some regions were found to have been infected with West Nile virus, which resulted in substantially higher mortality rates than in uninfected populations. The overall population level impact that West Nile virus will have on Greater Sage-Grouse is unknown but some small and isolated populations could potentially be at risk.[1,2,6,10,11]

CONSERVATION ACTION

Although concern for declining trends in the species has been expressed since the 1940s, the declines have continued. However, in the last 10 years an amazing surge in interest and conservation activity has taken place. Some of this flurry of activity has been spurred on by at least eight petitions submitted to the U.S. Fish and Wildlife Service (USFWS) to list the species as Endangered or Threatened under the Endangered Species Act and the resulting concern that such a listing would cause economic difficulty to private ranchers and other private commercial interests. The USFWS ruled in 2005 that listing was not warranted. A Memorandum of Understanding was signed in 2000 between the Western Association of Fish and Wildlife Agencies, U.S. Forest Service, U.S. Bureau of Land Management, and the USFWS in which the parties agreed to establish a team to co-ordinate conservation activities across the range of the species, including through the hiring of a full-time staff person to oversee the plan implementa-tion. A rangewide conservation strategy under de-velopment by the Western Association of Fish and Wildlife Agencies through a contract with the U.S. Fish and Wildlife Service was expected to be completed in 2006. Greater Sage-Grouse conser-vation plans have been completed and are being implemented in California, Idaho, Montana, Nevada, North Dakota, Oregon, Utah, Washing-ton, and Wyoming and are underway in other states within the species range. A Canadian Sage-Grouse Recovery Plan was completed by the provinces of Alberta and Saskatchewan in 2001. Additionally, at least 27 local plans had been com-pleted by 2005 across the species' range. At the federal level, the U.S. Bureau of Land Manage-ment has completed a Sage-Grouse Habitat Con-servation Strategy.

While much of the activity so far has centered on the development of plans with extensive com-munity involvement, in a few areas some specific conservation action has taken place. For example, in Utah a 5,000-acre area of dense sagebrush at Parker Mountain was treated to reduce sagebrush density and increase understory vegetation to lev-els preferred by Greater Sage-Grouse. Another sagebrush restoration project on an additional 1,000 acres at Parker Mountain was funded through a $36,000 grant from the Intermoun-tain–West Joint Venture. At the Department of Defense's Yakima Training Center—one of only two locations supporting significant populations of the species in Washington state—a 45,500-acre section has been designated a sage-grouse protec-tion area and sagebrush restoration activities are ongoing, including the planting of 300,000 sage-brush seedlings annually. The Nature Conservan-cy purchased the Crooked Creek Ranch in 2001— a 2,500-acre Idaho ranch with 70,000 acres of public land grazing allotments—to protect and manage a large Greater Sage-Grouse population. A new management plan recently adopted for Ida-ho's Curlew National Grassland outlines a goal of maintaining current acreage of sagebrush habitat within optimum density for sage-grouse by treating 9,600 acres of habitat mechanically or with herbi-cides over the next decade. Research on the spe-cies habitat requirements and limiting factors is ongoing throughout the range. In Idaho research is being carried out on BLM lands to assess whether burned areas can be restored through the planting of sagebrush seedlings and reduction in grazing pressure. A bill introduced but not passed in the U.S. Congress in 2003 would have reimbursed ranchers who wished to voluntarily give up their public land grazing permits and would have result-ed in the retiring of grazing permits on about 7.8 million acres.[1,2,8,11–24]

CONSERVATION NEEDS

- Incorporate Greater Sage-Grouse habitat ob-jectives into all BLM lease allotments within the range of the species and ensure that objec-tives are being reached in allotments with ex-isting habitat objectives.
- Continue purchase of conservation easements on private lands that support Greater Sage-Grouse populations.
- Develop sagebrush habitat corridors or step-ping stones to link disjunct populations.
- Consider relocations of birds from core popu-lation to disjunct populations to maintain ge-netic diversity, a practice that has already been done in some areas.
- Prevent oil and mineral development in areas with important or vulnerable existing Greater Sage-Grouse populations, and develop ways to minimize impacts on areas with oil and gas development.
- Increase monitoring and life-history research for the species.

References

1. Schroeder, M.A., J.R. Young, and C.E. Braun. 1999. Sage Grouse (*Centrocercus urophasianus*). In *The Birds of North America*, No. 425 (A. Poole and F. Gill, eds.). The Birds of North America, Inc., Philadelphia, PA.

2. Connelly, J. W., S. T. Knick, M. A. Schroeder,

and S. J. Stiver. 2004. Conservation Assessment of Greater Sage-grouse and Sagebrush Habitats. Western Association of Fish and Wildlife Agencies, Unpublished report, Cheyenne, WY.

3. Chipley, R.M., G.H. Fenwick, M.J. Parr, and D.N. Pashley. 2003. *The American Bird Conservancy Guide to the 500 Most Important Bird Areas in the United States.* Random House, New York, NY.

4. Cooper, D.S. 2004. *Important Bird Areas of California.* Audubon California, Pasadena, CA. 286 pp.

5. U.S. Fish and Wildlife Service. 2004. Endangered and Threatened Wildlife and Plants; 90-day Finding for a Petition to List the Eastern Subspecies of the Greater Sage-Grouse as Endangered. *Federal Register* 69(4): 933–936.

6. Braun, C.E. 1998. Sage Grouse Declines in Western North America: What Are the Problems? *Proceedings of the Western Association of State Fish and Wildlife Agencies* 78:139–156.

7. Connelly, J.W., and C.E. Braun. 1997. Long-term Changes in Sage Grouse *Centrocercus urophasianus* Populations in Western North America. *Wildlife Biology* 3/4:123–128.

8. Hays, D.W., M.J. Tirhi, and D.W. Stinson. 1998. *Washington State Status Report for the Sage Grouse.* Washington Deptartment of Fish and Wildlife, Olympia, WA. 62 pp.

9. Government of Alberta. No date. *Status of the Sage Grouse—Population Size and Trends.* http://www3 .gov.ab.ca/srd/fw/status/reports/sgrouse/pop.html (accessed 19 February 2004).

10. Ricketts, T.H., E. Dinerstein, D.M. Olson, C.J. Loucks, et al. 1999. *Terrestrial Ecoregions of North America: A Conservation Assessment.* Island Press, Washington, DC. 485 pp.

11. Connelly, J.W., M.A. Schroeder, A.R. Sands, and C.E. Braun. 2000. Guidelines to Manage Sage Grouse Populations and Their Habitats. *Wildlife Society Bulletin* 28:967–985.

12. Torrell, L.A., N. Rimbey, J. Tanaka, T. Darden, L. Van Tassell, and A. Harp. 2002. *Ranch-level Impacts of Changing Grazing Policies on BLM Land to Protect the Greater Sage-Grouse: Evidence from Idaho, Nevada, and Oregon.* PACWPL Policy Paper SG-01-02, Policy Analysis Center for Western Public Lands, Caldwell, ID. 20 pp.

13. Wambolt, C.L., A.J. Harp, B.L. Welch, N. Shaw, J.W. Connelly, K.P. Reese, C.E. Braun, D.A. Klebenow, E.D. McArthur, J.G. Thompson, L.A. Torell, and J.A. Tanaka. 2002. *Conservation of Greater Sage-Grouse on Public Lands in the Western U.S.: Implications of Recovery and Management Policies.* PACWPL Policy Paper SG-02-02, Policy Analysis Center for Western Public Lands, Caldwell, ID. 41 pp.

14. U.S. Fish and Wildlife Service. 2005. Endangered and Threatened Wildlife and Plants: 12-Month Finding for Petitions to List the Greater Sage-Grouse as Threatened or Endangered; Proposed Rule. *Federal Register* 70(8): 2244–2282.

15. U.S. Forest Service. 2002. *Record of Decision for the Curlew National Grassland Plan.* Caribou-Targhee National Forest, Idaho Falls, ID.

16. Governor's Sage Grouse Conservation Team. No date. *The Nevada Sage Grouse Conservation Strategy.* http://ndow.org/wild/sg/resources/index.shtm (accessed 20 February 2004).

17. Canadian Sage Grouse Recovery Team. 2001. *Canadian Sage Grouse Recovery Strategy.* http://www3 .gov.ab.ca/srd/fw/riskspecies/pdf/SageGrousePlan.pdf (accessed 20 February 2004).

18. Deibert, P. (USFWS). 2006. Personal communication.

19. Bureau of Land Management. 2004. Bureau of Land Management National Sage-Grouse Habitat Conservation Strategy. http://www.blm.gov/nhp/spotlight/ sage_grouse/ (accessed 21 March 2006).

20. Messmer, T.A., and J. Flory. 2002. Community-based Conservation Programs in Utah–State of Utah Contract #011530. Report submitted to Utah Division of Wildlife Resources, Utah State University Extension, and Utah State University College of Natural Resources.

21. Miller, M. 2003. *The Crooked Creek Project: A Cooperative Project for Sage Grouse Management.* http:// nature.org/wherewework/northamerica/states/idaho/ science/art8546.html (accessed 20 February 2004).

22. Yakima Training Center. No date. *Management of Sage Grouse on the Yakima Training Center.* Yakima, WA. 1 pp.

23. Idaho National Engineering and Environmental Laboratory, Environmental Surveillance Education and Research Program. No date. *Natural and Assisted Recovery of Sagebrush in Idaho's Big Desert: Effects of Seeding Treatments on Successional Trajectories of Sagebrush Communities.* http://www.stoller-eser.com/TinCup/Report.htm (accessed 20 February 2004).

24. National Public Lands Grazing Campaign. No date. *Voluntary Grazing Permit Buyout Legislation Introduced!* http://www.publiclandsranching.org/ (accessed 24 February 2004).

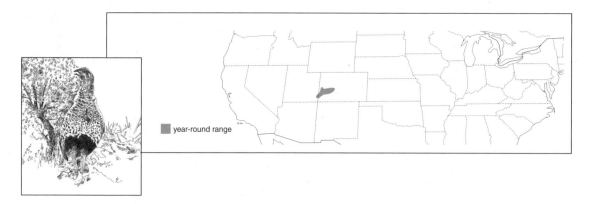

year-round range

GUNNISON SAGE-GROUSE (*Centrocercus minimus*)

Only recently recognized as a full species, the Gunnison Sage-Grouse has been the victim of major loss and alteration of its sagebrush habitat and the total population numbers in the low thousands.

STATUS AND DISTRIBUTION

These birds once occurred from southeastern Utah and southwestern Colorado south to northeastern Arizona and northwestern New Mexico (possibly also Oklahoma) but are now restricted to an estimated 8.5% of the historic range within Colorado and adjacent Utah. The Gunnison Basin Important Bird Area (IBA) supports more than 60% of the world population (3,000 birds in 2004), much of which is on land owned by the Bureau of Land Managment (BLM) and the U.S. Forest Service (USFS). The remainder of the birds are in six spatially disjunct populations, each with less than 300 individuals. The population has declined greatly since the 1970s and less than 10% of the species' original range is estimated to remain. At one site where only a single male had been detected in recent years, birds captured from the Gunnison Basin IBA population were released in an attempt to prevent the loss of that local population.[1-6]

ECOLOGY

The Gunnison Sage-Grouse is a species of the sagebrush (*Artemisia* sp.) ecosystem but uses a variety of types of sagebrush as well as wet meadows and riparian areas. Males display in groups (leks) in more open and elevated areas where females congregate to assess male status. These birds have a polygynous mating system in which only a few males mate with most of the females. Adults feed largely on sagebrush vegetation and are especially reliant on it during the winter, when they may have to make small-scale migration movements to find sagebrush that is not snow-covered. Nests are placed in thicker sagebrush vegetation or thick grasses on the ground. The females lay 6–9 eggs, which hatch in 25–29 days. Chicks are precocial and follow the female from nest soon after hatching. Young feed themselves but are brooded by the female through several weeks. Young are taken by the female to wetter, richer habitats, including meadows and riparian areas, where they feed on insects and, later, on small flowering plants.[1,5]

THREATS

The greatest threat continues to be loss and degradation of native habitat. A major concern is potential permanent habitat loss due to housing development subdivisions and the associated roads and business development. Additional concerns include overgrazing on rangeland, mineral and oil extraction activities, and fire suppression. The number of people living in the core breeding area in Gunnison County has been projected to increase by 41% from 2000 to 2030 and could cause further loss of sagebrush habitat. Several of the areas of BLM land leased for grazing within the Gunnison Basin were found to have substandard environmental assessments when reviewed in 2002 and an estimated 50% of sagebrush habitat in the Basin does not meet desirable habitat conditions for the species. Three of the populations outside of the Gunnison Basin are considered to have high potential for oil and gas development. Fire suppression has allowed pinyon-juniper habitat to overtake sagebrush habitat in some locations, making it unsuitable for Gunnison Sage-Grouse and increasing risks from avian predators that use pinyon-juniper. In some areas introduced cheatgrass (*Bromus tectorum*) has invaded, outcompeted, and eventually replaced sagebrush habitat. Isolated populations are likely to begin having genetic inbreeding problems, especially as the species' polygynous mating system inherently decreases genetic variability.[1,5–7]

CONSERVATION ACTION

A Gunnison Sage-Grouse Working Group formed in 1995 with representatives from a diversity of agencies and organizations, including the Bureau of Land Management, Colorado Division of Wildlife, Gunnison County Planning Commission, Gunnison County Stockgrowers, U.S. Fish and Wildlife Service, and Black Canyon Audubon Society. The group completed a conservation plan for the species' in 1997 that recommended 200 actions to increase the species' long-term probability of survival. Separate conservation plans have been developed for six additional areas within the species' range and the stakeholders completed a rangewide conservation plan for the species in 2005. In addition, the BLM completed a habitat conservation strategy for both species of sage grouse in 2004.

Gunnison County passed resolutions in 2001 that allow regulation of development on private land for conservation of habitat for Gunnison Sage-Grouse. About 41% of the species' current range is on lands managed by BLM, 5% by the state of Colorado, and 4% by U.S. Forest Service. Private land holdings account for 47% of the species' total range. However, the bulk of the population occurs on BLM and USFS lands within the Gunnison Basin. The Colorado Division of Wildlife spent about $250,000 per year from 1996 to 2001 on various conservation, research, and education activities for the species and secured $2.5 million for conservation easements in 2001. The BLM spent up to $1,000,000 rangewide for Gunnison Sage-Grouse conservation efforts in 2003. A significant amount of acreage on both public and private land has been restored or enhanced within the species' range through brush mowing, prescribed burns, planting of sagebrush mixtures, removal of pinyon-juniper, riparian fencing and stabilization. Objectives for sage-grouse habitat have been included in BLM grazing leases for 42% of the Gunnison Basin sagebrush habitat but objectives have not been met in some of the lease areas. The Colorado Division of Wildlife paid ranchers to stop grazing cattle on two BLM lease areas in 2001 totaling 38,000 acres so that the habitat could be managed for sage grouse. About 30,000 acres of private lands in the Gunnison Basin were protected by conservation easements for sage-grouse as of 2003. These easements cover 18% of the lek sites of the Gunnison Basin population. An additional $2.59 million had been allotted for sage grouse conservation work in Colorado in 2002 The hunting season for the species was closed in Colorado in 2000.[1,3,5–8]

CONSERVATION NEEDS

- Incorporate sage-grouse habitat objectives into all BLM lease allotments within the range of the species and ensure that objectives are being reached in allotments with existing sage-grouse habitat objectives.
- Continue purchase of conservation easements on private lands that support sage-grouse populations.
- Develop sagebrush habitat corridors or stepping stones to link disjunct populations.
- Continue relocations of birds from core population to disjunct populations to maintain genetic diversity.
- Prevent oil and mineral exploration in areas with existing Gunnison Sage-Grouse populations, and develop ways to minimize impacts on areas with existing oil and gas development.
- Increase monitoring and life-history research for the species.

References

1. Schroeder, M.A., J.R. Young, and C.E. Braun. 1999. Sage Grouse (*Centrocercus urophasianus*). In *The Birds of North America*, No. 425 (A. Poole and F. Gill, eds.). The Birds of North America, Inc., Philadelphia, PA.

2. Audubon Colorado. 2001. *Gunnison Basin IBA*. http://www.audubon.org/chapter/co/co/IBA/5.htm (accessed 26 August 2003).

3. BirdLife International. 2000. *Threatened Birds of the World*. Lynx Editions and BirdLife International, Barcelona, Spain, and Cambridge, UK.

4. Young, J. 2003. *The Gunnison Sage-Grouse.* http://www.western.edu/bio/young/gunnsg/gunnsg.htm (accessed 26 August 2003).

5. U.S. Fish and Wildlife Service. 2004. *Candidate and Listing Priority Assignment Form: Gunnison Sage Grouse.* http://ecos.fws.gov/docs/candforms_pdf/r6/B0B0_V01.pdf (accessed 20 March 2006).

6. Green, N. (USFWS biologist). 2006. Personal communication.

7. Bureau of Land Management. 2004. *Gunnison Sage Grouse Conservation Plan.* http://www.co.blm.gov/gra/sagegrouse.htm_(accessed 26 August 2003).

8. Gunnison Sage-grouse Rangewide Steering Committee. 2005. *Gunnison Sage-grouse Rangewide Conservation Plan.* Colorado Division of Wildlife, Denver, CO. http://wildlife.state.co.us/WildlifeSpecies/SpeciesOfConcern/Birds/GunnisonConsPlan.htm (accessed 20 March 2006).

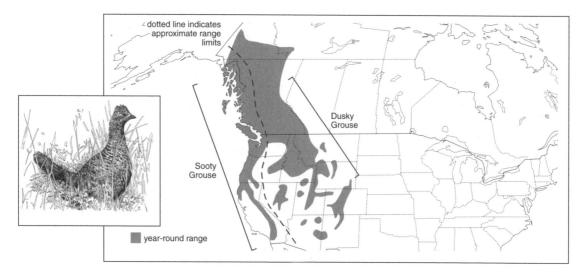

"BLUE" GROUSE including DUSKY GROUSE (*Dendragapus obscurus*) and SOOTY GROUSE (*Dendragapus fuliginosus*)

As this book was being finalized, the species formerly known as Blue Grouse was officially split into two species (Dusky Grouse and Sooty Grouse) based on agreement of new genetic evidence with recognized differences in voice, behavior, and plumage. This species account covers both of these new species.

STATUS AND DISTRIBUTION

The Sooty Grouse range extends from coastal southeastern Alaska south through coastal British Columbia, Washington, and Oregon to southern California. The Dusky Grouse range extends from southern Yukon and extreme southwestern Northwest Territories south through interior British Columbia and western Alberta through mountains of western U.S. south to Nevada, Arizona, and New Mexico. The range limits in the northern part of the distribution where the two species' ranges meet have yet to be delineated. In the southern part of the Dusky Grouse range, populations are often disjunct, small, and fragmented. Larger disjunct populations occur in eastern Wyoming and central Colorado extending north to Wyoming and south to New Mexico.

Breeding density maps for the former "Blue Grouse" produced from Breeding Bird Survey data indicate highest densities in southeast Alaska and coastal British Columbia. Important breeding sites for Sooty Grouse include Alaska's Misty Fiords National Monument and Tongass National Forest;

Washington's Olympic National Park, Olympic National Forest, and Wenatchee National Forest; Oregon's Siuslaw National Forest; and California's Sierra Meadows-Southern Important Bird Area (including Yosemite, Sequoia, and Kings Canyon National Parks). Sites known to support Dusky Grouse include Colorado's San Juan National Forest, Montana's Lewis and Clark National Forest, and Utah's Manti-La Sal and Dixie National Forests.

Breeding Bird Survey analysis for the former "Blue Grouse" shows a significant decrease of approximately 54% (2.0% per year) from 1966 to 2005 rangewide. An analysis of Christmas Bird Count data shows a nonsignificant decrease of 0.3% per year from 1959 to 1988. The total population of the two species combined was estimated at 2,600,000 individuals in 2004.[1-6]

ECOLOGY

During summer, Dusky Grouse occupy montane areas from lower elevation shrubsteppe to edges of coniferous forests mixed with high-elevation meadows to shrubby areas near treeline during summer. Sooty Grouse generally use similar habitats except that they seem to avoid shrubsteppe. In winter both species are found almost exclusively in dense coniferous forest where they subsist mainly on conifer needles. In coastal areas in the southern part of range, large local population increases of Sooty Grouse have been observed after clear-cutting, though numbers then decline over the ensu-ing 10–20 years. In most areas birds migrate rela-tively short distances from open, shrubby summer habitats to dense, coniferous forest wintering habi-tats. Like most grouse species, males perform an elaborate courtship display involving spreading the tail, flashing bright neck patches, hoots, and wing flutters. Males are thought to mate with many females. The female lays 5–9 eggs (some-times more or less) in a depression on the ground where she incubates them for 25–28 days. The male does not participate in incubation or brood rearing. Young leave nest within 24 hours after hatching, following the female but feeding on their own. They grow rapidly and by about 13 weeks of age they are nearly as large as one-year old birds. Mortality of chicks is high, with as many as 90% lost, primarily to mammalian and avian predators. Only one brood is produced each season and not all adults in an area may breed each year. Adults can live for as long as 14 years but on aver-age most birds probably reach only 2–5 years of age.[1]

THREATS

Reasons for the continued widespread declines in these species are not well understood. There is some indication that decreases could be related to major habitat losses in many regions. For example, about 96% of the forest habitat within the Central Pacific Coastal Forest ecoregion extending along the coast from Oregon north to Vancouver Island has been lost since prelogging days. Only about 25% of the coniferous forest ecoregion within cen-tral British Columbia remains as intact, natural habitat and 15–20% of the standing volume of timber is expected to be removed over the next 20 years. About 25% of the habitat in the Sierra Nevada of California remains intact. Similarly, in Alaska's Tongass National Forest approximately 90% of the high-volume old-growth forest has been logged and 30% of all old growth in the for-est is expected to be removed by about 2015. Per-haps of even more importance has been the tradi-tional forestry management in much of the region practiced through the 1980s in which, after log-ging, the remaining vegetation and slash was burned or treated with herbicide, then planted with fast-growing Douglas fir. These plantations

were sometimes sprayed with insecticides and competing vegetation was periodically removed to allow faster growth of planted tree species. This re-sulted in large expanses of forest that were homog-enous and did not have significant shrubby habitat that is a requirement for both species. Additional-ly, these managed forests would be harvested at much shorter intervals so that the necessary com-ponents of habitat for these species, including for-est gaps, may not have had the opportunity to be-come established before the forest would again be set back to an early successional stage following tree harvest. Healthy, stable bird populations will require forest harvest planning schemes that incor-porate ecological needs. Such plans need to be done at a broad landscape scale that provide a mo-saic of appropriate age-class forests and retain blocks of habitat that support source populations of birds.

Shrubsteppe habitats used by Dusky Grouse populations have shown similar losses through conversion to cropland, overgrazing on range-land, spread of invasive plant species, changes in fire frequency and severity, road and building de-velopment, and mineral and oil extraction activ-ities. Millions of acres of shrubsteppe habitat have been destroyed for agricultural uses and on millions more sagebrush and other shrubsteppe species have been systematically removed. Oil and gas well construction may be increasing in the region. A 1996 report estimated that 6,000–11,000 new oil and gas wells would be developed in southwestern Wyoming in the ensuing 20 years.

In some regions like the Sierra Nevada, cattle grazing continues to degrade mountain meadow habitats that are important for supporting Sooty Grouse and a host of other animal and plant species. Clearly much work needs to be done to understand which factors are most important in contributing to long-term declines in both spe-cies.[1,4,7–9]

CONSERVATION ACTION

The lack of understanding of the primary factors responsible for the long-term decrease in Sooty Grouse and Dusky Grouse populations has made it difficult to develop specific conservation activities to attempt to halt declines. Conservation activities aimed at protecting habitat for Marbled Murrelet, Spotted Owl, Northern Goshawk, Bald Eagle, brown bear, and Pacific salmon may have long-term benefits for both species in locations of overlap because of protection of large, intact functioning forest ecosystems that include naturally-occurring disturbance gaps. In addition, on federally managed lands there has generally been an increase in attempts to mimic natural disturbance regimes and to allow more habitat heterogeneity in logged areas.

Partners in Flight Bird Conservation Plans have been completed for Alaska, Arizona, California, Colorado, Idaho, Montana, Nevada, New Mexico, Oregon, Utah, Washington, and Wyoming and have identified habitats used by Sooty Grouse and Dusky Grouse as a priority. These plans have specific recommendations for improving habitat conditions for the suites of species from each of the habitat types within which the species regularly occurs.[1,7–18]

CONSERVATION NEEDS

- Increase acreage of forests managed as large, functioning ecosystems.
- Increase adoption of forestry management techniques that mimic natural disturbance.
- Develop baseline inventory of Sooty Grouse and Dusky Grouse populations, delineate distributions in areas where ranges seem to meet in northern part of range, and increase research to understand which factors are most important in determining abundance levels across landscape scales.

References

1. Zwickel, F.C. Blue Grouse. 1992. In *The Birds of North America*, No. 15 (A. Poole, P. Stettenheim, and F. Gill, Eds.). The Academy of Natural Sciences, Philadelphia, PA, and the American Ornithologists' Union, Washington, DC.

2. Sauer, J. R., J. E. Hines, and J. Fallon. 2005. *The North American Breeding Bird Survey, Results and Analysis 1966–2005*, Version 6.2.2006. USGS Patuxent Wildlife Research Center, Laurel, MD

3. Chipley, R.M., G.H. Fenwick, M.J. Parr, and D.N. Pashley. 2003. *The American Bird Conservancy Guide to the 500 Most Important Bird Areas in the United States*. Random House, New York, NY.

4. Cooper, D.S. 2004. *Important Bird Areas of California*. Audubon California, Pasadena, CA.

5. Sauer, J. R., S. Schwartz, and B. Hoover. 1996. *The Christmas Bird Count Home Page*, Version 95.1. Patuxent Wildlife Research Center, Laurel, MD.

6. Rich, T. D., C. Beardmore, H. Berlanga, P. Blancher, M. Bradstreet, G. Butcher, D. Demarest, E. Dunn, C. Hunter, E. Inigo-Elias, J. Kennedy, A. Martell, A. Panjabi, D. Pashley, K. Rosenberg, C. Rustay, S. Wendt, and T. Will. 2004. Partners in Flight North American Landbird Conservation Plan. Cornell Lab of Ornithology. Ithaca, NY.

7. Ricketts, T.H., E. Dinerstein, D.M. Olson, C.J. Loucks et al. 1999. *Terrestrial Ecoregions of North America: A Conservation Assessment*. Island Press, Washington, DC. 485 pp.

8. Oregon/Washington Partners in Flight. No date. Oregon/Washington Land Bird Conservation Plan: Westside Coniferous Forest. http://community.gorge.net/natres/pif/westside_plan.html (accessed 11 March 2004).

9. Braun, C.E. 1998. Sage Grouse Declines in Western North America: What Are the Problems? *Proceedings of the Western Association of State Fish and Wildlife Agencies* 78:139–156.

10. Casey, D. 2000. *Partners in Flight Draft Bird Conservation Plan Montana*, Version 1. American Bird Conservancy, c/o Montana Fish, Wildlife, and Parks, Kalispell, MT.

11. Ritter, S. 2000. *Idaho Bird Conservation Plan*, Version 1. Idaho Partners in Flight, Hamilton, MT.

12. Nevada Partners in Flight Working Group. 1999. *Nevada Partners in Flight Bird Conservation Plan*. Reno, NV.

13. Nicholoff, S.H., compiler. 2003. *Wyoming Bird Conservation Plan*, Version 2.0. Wyoming Partners in Flight. Wyoming Game and Fish Department, Lander, WY.

14. Parrish, J. R., F. P. and Howe, R. E. Norvell. 2002. *Utah Partners in Flight Avian Conservation Strategy*, Version 2.0. Utah Partners in Flight Program, Utah Division of Wildlife Resources, 1594 West North Temple, Salt Lake City, UT 84116, UDWR Publication Number 02–27. i–xiv + 302 pp.

15. Beidleman, C.A. 2000. *Partners in Flight Land Bird Conservation Plan Colorado*, Estes Park, CO.

16. New Mexico Partners in Flight. No date. *New Mexico Bird Conservation Plan*. http://www.hawksaloft.org/pif/ (accessed 12 June 2004).

17. Latta, M.J., C.J. Beardmore, and T.E. Corman. 1999. Arizona Partners in Flight Bird Conservation Plan,

Version 1.0. Nongame and Endangered Wildlife Program Technical Report 142. Arizona Game and Fish Department, Phoenix, Arizona.

18. Siegel, R.B., and D. F. DeSante. 1999. Version 1.0. *The Draft Avian Conservation Plan for the Sierra Nevada Bioregion: Conservation Priorities and Strategies for Safeguarding Sierra Bird Populations.* Institute for Bird Populations report to California Partners in Flight.

GREATER PRAIRIE-CHICKEN (*Tympanuchus cupido*)

A symbol of native grasslands of the U.S., the Greater Prairie-Chicken once occurred in at least 33 U.S. states and Canadian provinces but is now restricted to seven widely separated regions across 12 states.

STATUS AND DISTRIBUTION

Birds once occurred from Alberta east to Ontario south through the midwest U.S. to Texas and Louisiana. A disjunct population described as a subspecies, the Heath Hen, occurred along the coastal plain from Massachusetts south to Virginia. The Heath Hen declined quickly following European settlement, with the last population remaining on the island of Martha's Vineyard in Massachusetts until 1932 when it became extinct. Another distinct subspecies, the Attwater's Prairie-Chicken occurred in Texas and Louisiana with a population numbered at about a million individuals. It had disappeared from Louisiana by 1919 and numbers had declined to 8,700 in Texas by 1937 and to only 42 birds in 1996. As of 2001 there were just 25 males counted in the wild at two locations in Texas and nearly 200 birds in captivity. The Attwater Prairie Chicken National Wildlife Refuge (10,528 acres) and the Nature Conservancy's Texas City Preserve (2,303 acres) are the two sites currently supporting Attwater's Prairie-Chicken.

By the 1980s the subspecies making up the bulk of the population of Greater Prairie-Chicken had disappeared from 12 of the 22 states where it once occurred. The most recent losses were from Iowa and Michigan in the early 1980s, though the species was reintroduced to Iowa in the late 1980s, where 44 males were counted in 2000. In seven of the remaining ten states it was reported to have experienced declines over the 25-year period preceding 1993. In Illinois, the species declined from over 25,000 birds in 1933 to 46 in 1994. In Wisconsin, numbers dropped from an estimated population of 54,850 birds in 1930 to about 1,500 birds in recent years and 586 males were counted in 2001. In Missouri the population was estimated at 15,000 birds in the 1940s, had declined to less than 1,000 by the late 1990s, and the number of displaying males had declined 73% from 1993 to 2001 when 281 males were counted. Numbers in North Dakota were estimated at fewer than 1,000 by 2002. In Minnesota, spring 1999 counts found 1,419 males. The number in Oklahoma declined by 70–80% between 1981 and 1999. The highest numbers are found in Colorado (fall population estimated at 10,000–12,000 birds in 2002), Kansas, Nebraska, and South Dakota. Important sites for the species include Valentine National Wildlife Refuge in Nebraska, the National Park Service's Tallgrass National Preserve in Kansas, the Nature Conservancy's Anna Gronseth Prairie in Minnesota, and the Forest Service's Fort Pierre National Grassland in South Dakota. The species' total population was estimated at 690,000 individuals in 2004.[1–14]

ECOLOGY

Is a species of the tallgrass prairie, oak savanna, and formerly of scrub-oak barrens of the northeastern U.S. and coastal plain grasslands of Texas and

Louisiana. As native prairie habitat has been lost, the species has adapted in some areas to using a matrix of habitats that may mimic the preferred prairie and scrub mix of vegetation with some cropland. During the nonbreeding season, birds feed on leaves and seeds as well as waste grain in agricultural fields. Historically, acorns were an important food source in winter. Like other grassland grouse species, Greater Prairie-Chicken males display in groups (leks) in the late winter and spring on elevated and clear areas within their prairie habitat. Displays are quite elaborate and involve raising various feather tracts, inflating air sacs, shaking wings, and stamping the ground, all while making a low booming sound. At each lek only one or two males perform 70–90% of copulations. Females lay 8–13 eggs in a simple nest on the ground in thick grasses. Incubation lasts 23–25 days and young follow the female from the nest almost immediately after hatching. The chicks are fully feathered at hatching and can immediately begin feeding themselves by pecking for insects and vegetative material. Adults, young, and eggs are taken by a wide variety of avian and mammalian predators and average life span is less than two years.[1]

of native habitat largely through conversion to cropland, overgrazing on rangeland, housing development, mineral and oil extraction activities, and fire suppression. The Flint Hills of Kansas and the Nebraska Sand Hills are among the areas supporting the largest numbers of Greater Prairie-Chickens and neither area has been extensively plowed for row crops, but cattle overgrazing and loss of habitat to housing developments is an increasing problem. In regions where populations have become small and isolated there is an urgent need to increase the size, connectivity, and condition of grassland habitat patches. Hunting, though not thought to limit healthy populations of the species, has been suspended in many states because of low numbers. Limited lottery-based hunting seasons were reinstated in Colorado in 2000 and Minnesota in 2003 because numbers had reached levels thought to be sustainable.

Isolated populations in some areas have had genetic inbreeding problems especially as the species' polygynous mating system inherently decreases genetic variability, and researchers have warned that many isolated populations will become extinct unless managers move birds between populations.[1,2,7,8,15–19]

THREATS

Historically, overhunting was a major threat, including market hunting for sale of large numbers in city markets during 1800s. This was followed by the massive conversion of grassland habitats to agriculture. For example, 88–99% of the midwestern tallgrass prairie was estimated to have been lost since 1850. In some areas the loss has been even more severe. Less than 1% of original habitat in a forest/grassland ecozone extending from Illinois south to Texas is considered intact. Remnants of tallgrass prairie habitat in southern Iowa and northern Missouri are restricted to 20 sites, each less than 20 acres in size. Gulf coastal prairies were eliminated from Louisiana and only 1% of this habitat in Texas is now considered pristine. Native grasslands of the northeastern U.S. have been reduced to a few small, widely separated blocks. For example, the Hempstead Plains of Long Island, which once covered 60,000 acres, now consists of two patches, one 20 acres in size and the other 70 acres.

As in most grassland ecosystems, the greatest current threat continues to be loss and degradation

CONSERVATION ACTION

The species could clearly benefit from a rangewide conservation plan as conservation efforts in each state are at best only loosely coordinated. States in the eastern part of the range that each have fewer than about 1,000–2,000 birds, including Illinois, Iowa, Missouri, and Wisconsin, require major habitat restoration efforts and carefully planned releases of birds to ensure a reasonable chance that Greater Prairie-Chickens will remain a part of their avifauna over the long term.

Habitat management, especially through rotational grazing and prescribed burns, has been effective in maintaining and increasing the number of birds in areas where populations are relatively large and unfragmented. In most areas populations rely on privately owned farmland or ranchland and generally require at least 30–40% of grassland habitat within the landscape to maintain populations. The Colorado Division of Wildlife developed cooperative habitat projects with private landowners aimed at increasing desirable habitat for Greater Prairie-Chickens and numbers in that state increased from 600 birds in 1973 to at least

10,000 birds in 2002. In Missouri, the Nature Conservancy has acquired several parcels of grassland habitat and is managing them for the benefit of Greater Prairie-Chickens. Various habitat enhancement projects were supported with approximately $200,000 in grants in 2001. Similar efforts are underway in Wisconsin and North Dakota. The recently established Glacial Ridge National Wildlife Refuge (2,000 acres) in Minnesota provides important habitat and a link between Minnesota and North Dakota populations. In Iowa, the Kellerton Grasslands Bird Conservation Area was established in 2000 with the goal of establishing a 2,000 acre publicly owned prairie preserve within a 10,000 acre block that contains another 2,000 acres of privately-owned grasslands. The site supported at least 16 birds in 2003—the largest population in Iowa. Reintroduction of birds to sites where they had been lost and augmentation of declining populations with captured birds from healthy populations has continued in Illinois, Iowa, Minnesota, Missouri, North Dakota, and Wisconsin.

At the Fort Pierre National Grassland managers set guidelines that decreased cattle grazing pressure and protected 8% of the habitat annually from grazing. The guidelines were being appealed in court by a local cattle grazing association as of 2000. In addition, research is underway at sites in Oklahoma and Kansas to understand the movements and demographics of Greater Prairie-Chickens.

Attwater's Prairie-Chicken conservation has focused on captive breeding birds to augment rapidly declining wild populations. Five captive flocks have been founded, containing about 200 birds that produce about 150 young per year. All original wild males were thought to have disappeared from the Attwater Prairie Chicken National Wildlife Refuge by 1998 but releases of captive-bred birds have maintained a small population at the site, numbered at 11 males in 2001. Survival of released birds has been variable but in some years very low. For example, only 15% of released birds survived from 1999 to 2000. The U.S. Fish and Wildlife Service had entered into Safe Harbor Agreements with at least 13 private landowners by 2002 in the Texas coastal prairie region that encourages management of habitat to meet the requirements for Attwater's Prairie-Chicken. If the population increases sufficiently birds may eventually be released at some of these sites.[1-4,6-10,21-24]

CONSERVATION NEEDS

- Develop a rangewide conservation plan for Greater Prairie-Chicken that helps coordinate conservation work across the states that currently support the species.
- Incorporate Greater Prairie-Chicken habitat objectives into public land management where the species occurs on public lands.
- Provide incentives for private landowners to manage their lands to the benefit of prairie-chickens.
- Purchase land or conservation easements on private lands in areas like the Sand Hills and Flint Hills that still support healthy prairie-chicken populations.
- Develop habitat corridors or stepping stones to link disjunct populations within areas with dwindling prairie-chicken populations.
- Continue relocations of birds from core population to disjunct populations to maintain genetic diversity.
- Prevent oil and mineral exploration in areas with existing Greater Prairie-Chicken populations.
- Increase monitoring and life-history research for the species.
- For the severely endangered Attwater's Prairie-Chicken, increase control of small mammalian predators to decrease mortality within its restricted range.

References

1. Schroeder, M.A., and L.A. Robb. 1993. Greater Prairie-Chicken (*Tympanuchus cupido*). In *The Birds of North America*, No. 36 (A. Poole and F. Gill, eds.). The Academy of Natural Sciences, Philadelphia, PA, and the American Ornithologists' Union, Washington, DC.

2. Prairie Grouse Technical Council. 2001. *Prairie Grouse State Reports and Updates.* http://www.suttoncenter.org/PGTCNews.html (accessed 28 August 2003).

3. Silvy, N. No date. *On the Brink of Extinction: The Attwater's Prairie-Chicken.* The North American Grouse Partnership. http://gpn.8m.net/Articles/Attwaters Chickens.html (accessed 28 August 2003).

4. U.S. Fish and Wildlife Service. No date. *A Story of Loss and Hope.* Attwater Prairie Chicken National Wildlife Refuge. http://southwest.fws.gov/refuges/texas/attwater/story.html (accessed 27 August 2003).

5. Texas Parks and Wildlife. No date. *Attwater's*

Prairie Chicken. http://www.tpwd.state.tx.us/nature/endang/apc.htm (accessed 27 August 2003).

6. The Nature Conservancy. 2003. *Texas City Preserve.* http://nature.org/wherewework/northamerica/states/texas/preserves/texascity.html (accessed 27 August 2003).

7. Prairie Grouse Technical Council. 2000. *Prairie Grouse News: State Reports and Updates.* http://www.suttoncenter.org/PGTCNews.html (accessed 28 August 2003).

8. Colorado Division of Wildlife. 2003. *Greater Prairie Chicken.* http://wildlife.state.co.us/hunt/Greater_Prairie_Chicken/ (accessed 28 August 2003).

9. Iowa Department of Natural Resources. 2002. *The Reintroduction of Prairie Chickens to Iowa.* http://www.iowadnr.com/wildlife/files/FMAmay2000.html (accessed 27 August 2003).

10. Keir, J.R. 2001. *Central Wisconsin Prairie Chicken Census, 2001.* Wisconsin Department of Natural Resources, Madison, WI.

11. Wolfe, D.H. 1999. *Ecology of Greater Prairie Chickens.* Sutton Avian Research Center. http://www.suttoncenter.org/chicken.html (accessed 28 August 2003).

12. U.S. Fish and Wildlife Service. No date. *Valentine National Wildlife Refuge.* http://mountain-prairie.fws.gov/refuges/valentin/VALENTIN.HTM (accessed 26 August 2003).

13. The Nature Conservancy. 2003. *Anna Gronseth Prairie.* http://nature.org/wherewework/northamerica/states/minnesota/preserves/art6938.html (accessed 27 August 2003).

14. Rich, T.D., C. Beardmore, H. Berlanga, P. Blancher, M. Bradstreet, G. Butcher, D. Demarest, E. Dunn, C. Hunter, E. Inigo-Elias, J. Kennedy, A. Martell, A. Panjabi, D. Pashley, K. Rosenberg, C. Rustay, S. Wendt, and T. Will. 2004. *Partners in Flight North American Landbird Conservation Plan.* Cornell Lab of Ornithology, Ithaca, NY.

15. Vickery, P.D., P.B. Tubaro, J. M. Cardoso da Silva, B.G. Peterjohn, J.R. Herkert, and R.B. Cavalcanti. 1999. *Conservation of Grassland Birds in the Western Hemisphere.* Pages 2–26 in *Ecology and Conservation of Grassland Birds of the Western Hemisphere* (P.D. Vickery and J.R. Herkert, eds.). Studies in Avian Biology No. 19, Cooper Ornithological Society, Camarillo, CA.

16. Vickery, P.D., and P.W. Dunwiddie (eds.). 1997. *Grasslands of Northeastern North America.* Massachusetts Audubon Society, Lincoln, MA.

17. Ricketts, T.H. et al. 1999. *Terrestrial Ecoregions of North America: A Conservation Assessment.* Island Press, Washington, DC. 485 pp.

18. Bellinger, M.R., J.A. Johnson, J. Toepfer, and P. Dunn. 2003. Loss of Genetic Variation in Greater Prairie Chickens Following a Population Bottleneck in Wisconsin, U.S.A. *Conservation Biology* 17: 717–724.

19. Bouzat, J.L., H. Cheng, H.A. Lewin, R.L. Westemeier, J.D. Brawn, and K.N. Paige. 1998. Genetic Evaluation of a Demographic Bottleneck in the Greater Prairie Chicken. *Conservation Biology* 12: 836–843.

20. Sample, D.W., and M.J. Mossman. 1997. *Managing Habitat for Grassland Birds: A Guide for Wisconsin.* Wisconsin Department of Natural Resources, Madison, WI.

21. Missouri Department of Conservation. 2002. *Greater Prairie Chicken.* http://www.conservation.state.mo.us/nathis/birds/chickens/.

22. Moravek, G. No date. *Ft. Pierre National Grassland Mixed-Grass Prairie and Grouse.* The North American Grouse Partnership. http://gpn.8m.net/Articles/FT_Pierre.html (accessed 28 August 2003).

23. Loncarich, F.L. No date. *Survival and Movements of Greater Prairie Chickens Hens on the Tallgrass Prairie Preserve.* Arkansas Cooperative Fish and Wildlife Research Unit. http://biology.uark.edu/Coop/People/KrementzFormerStudents/loncarich.htm (accessed 26 August 2003).

24. Environmental Defense. 2002. *Texas Attwater's Prairie-Chicken/Coastal Prairie Safe Harbor Agreement.* http://www.environmentaldefense.org/article.cfm?contentid=141 (accessed 27 August 2003).

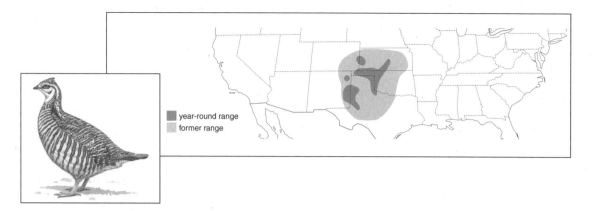

year-round range
former range

LESSER PRAIRIE-CHICKEN (*Tympanuchus pallidicinctus*)

Thought to have once numbered in the millions, the Lesser Prairie-Chicken population is now estimated at fewer than 25,000 individuals inhabiting pockets of shortgrass prairie and shrubland habitat in its limited southern Great Plains range.

STATUS AND DISTRIBUTION

Birds are permanent residents within their very limited range extending from eastern New Mexico and northwestern Texas north to southeastern Colorado and southwestern Kansas. An important area for the species is the U.S. Forest Service's Comanche National Grassland in Colorado, which is thought to hold as much as 5% of the world population of the species. Other important sites for the species managed by the U.S. Forest Service include the Black Kettle National Grassland in Texas and the Cimarron National Grassland in Kansas. Important sites in New Mexico include the Bureau of Land Management's Sand Ranch and the Nature Conservancy's Milnesand Prairie Preserve. The Nature Conservancy's Smokey Valley Ranch in Kansas and Four Canyon Preserve in Oklahoma also support populations of Lesser Prairie-Chicken.

The species' total range has declined by an estimated 78% since 1963, with only 8% of the original range remaining. The population is estimated to have dropped from approximately 60,000 individuals in the 1970s to 10,000–25,000 individuals in 1999. The species' range is now so limited that the Breeding Bird Survey cannot detect enough individuals to monitor the species' population trends.[1-5]

ECOLOGY

Is a species of southern portions of the shortgrass prairie where it occurs in areas with certain species of shrub oak or sagebrush. As native prairie habitat has been lost, the species has adapted in some areas to using a matrix of habitats that may mimic the preferred shortgrass and scrub mix of vegetation with some cropland. During the non-breeding season, flocks may feed on waste grain in agricultural fields. Like most grouse species, Lesser Prairie-Chicken males display in groups (leks) in the late winter and spring on elevated and clear areas within their prairie habitat. Females nest in areas of taller grasses near shrubs.[1,5,6]

THREATS

Loss and degradation of native shortgrass prairie habitat and other preferred native habitats was historically and continues to be the greatest threat to the species. Much grassland habitat within its limited range has been converted to agriculture and housing developments or has been disturbed by oil and mining operations. Approximately 40% of the shortgrass prairie native vegetation is estimated to have been lost across North America, and in some states the percentage lost is much higher (80% in Texas).

In some areas, reduction of shrub cover through the use of herbicides continues to be a problem. Landscapes with more than approximately 40% cultivated land do not seem to be able to support populations of the species, especially in years of drought when food supplies may be limited and nesting cover reduced.[1,2,6,9]

CONSERVATION ACTION

Because more than 70% of the species' habitat occurs on private land, the U.S. Fish and Wildlife Service has instituted Candidate Conservation Agreements with private landowners to protect and enhance habitat for the Lesser Prairie-Chicken as part of the High Plains Partnership. More than 80,000 acres in Oklahoma and Texas have been voluntarily enrolled in the program. The High Plains Partnership for Species at Risk was initiated by the Western Governor's Association to develop and implement cooperative interstate management plans for grassland species at risk in the western U.S. The first project was the Lesser Prairie-Chicken Interstate Working Group which includes state agency staff from Colorado, Kansas, New Mexico, Oklahoma, and Texas, federal agency staff from the USFWS, USFS, NRCS, BLM, EPA, and others, and conservation organizations, including Environmental Defense, the Nature Conservancy, and the National Fish and Wildlife Foundation. The High Plains Partnership has increased research for understanding the biology of the species, implemented an outreach strategy to ranchers, including newsletters and public meetings, and established a demonstration area on a 10,000-acre private ranch in New Mexico. The Nature Conservancy has recently completed several land-acquisition projects in New Mexico, Oklahoma, and Kansas specifically targeted at protecting the Lesser Prairie-Chicken and the shortgrass prairie shrubland ecosystem.[10–12]

CONSERVATION NEEDS

- Continue to protect large blocks of Lesser Prairie-Chicken habitat across the current range through land acquisition, conservation easements, or Farm Bill programs that reward private landowners for stewardship actions that benefit wildlife.
- In landscapes with existing Lesser Prairie-Chicken populations, maintain at least 60% of native habitat in large blocks (minimum size of 1000 hectares) or restore habitat to reach 60% minimum goal.
- Reduce grazing pressure on rangelands occupied by Lesser Prairie-Chickens by maintaining light grazing and rotational grazing schemes.
- Maintain native shrub oaks and sagebrush within native grassland habitats.
- Prevent habitat fragmentation by limiting oil and mineral exploration in areas with existing Lesser Prairie-Chicken populations,
- Increase monitoring and life-history research for the species.

References

1. Giesen, K.M. 1998. Lesser Prairie-Chicken (*Tympanuchus pallidicinctus*). In *The Birds of North America*, No. 364 (A. Poole and F. Gill, eds.). The Birds of North America, Inc., Philadelphia, PA.

2. BirdLife International. 2000. *Threatened Birds of the World*. Lynx Editions and BirdLife International, Barcelona, Spain and Cambridge, UK.

3. National Audubon Society. 2002. *Colorado's Important Bird Areas Program*. http://www.audubon .org/bird/iba/co.html (accessed 1 October 2003).

4. Chipley, R.M., G.H. Fenwick, M.J. Parr, and D.N. Pashley. 2003. *The American Bird Conservancy Guide to the 500 Most Important Bird Areas in the United States*. Random House, New York, NY.

5. Palis, J., M. Koenen, and D.W. Mehlman. 2000. *The Nature Conservancy Species Management Abstract: Lesser Prairie-Chicken* (Tympanuchus pallidicinctus). The Nature Conservancy, Arlington, VA.

6. Jamison, B. E., J. A. Dechant, D. H. Johnson, L. D. Igl, C. M. Goldade, and B. R. Euliss. 2002. *Effects of management practices on grassland birds: Lesser Prairie-Chicken*. Northern Prairie Wildlife Research Center, Jamestown, ND. Northern Prairie Wildlife Research Center Online. http://www.npwrc.usgs.gov/resource/ literatr/grasbird/lpch/lpch.htm (Version 28MAY2004).

7. Gauthier, D.A., A. Lafon, T. Tombs, J. Hoth, and E. Wilken. 2003. *Grasslands: Toward a North American Conservation Strategy*. Canadian Plains Research Center, University of Regina, Regina, Saskatchewan, and Commission for Environmental Cooperation, Montreal, QC, Canada. 99 pp.

8. Vickery, P.D., P.B. Tubaro, J. M. Cardoso da Silva, B.G. Peterjohn, J.R. Herkert, and R.B. Cavalcanti. 1999. Conservation of Grassland Birds in the Western Hemisphere. Pages 2–26 in *Ecology and Conservation of Grassland Birds of the Western Hemisphere* (P.D. Vickery and J.R. Herkert, eds.). Studies in Avian Biology No. 19, Cooper Ornithological Society, Camarillo, CA.

9. Ricketts et al. 1999. *Terrestrial Ecoregions of North America: A Conservation Assessment*. Island Press, Washington, DC. 485 pp.

10. U.S. EPA. 2000. *Region 8—Community Stew-*

ardship Projects. High Plains Partnership. http://www.epa .gov/region08/community_resources/steward/fact/hpp.ht ml (accessed 14, March 2003).

11. The Nature Conservancy. 2003. *The Prairie* *Wings Project.* http://nature.org/initiatives/programs/ birds/explore/ (accessed 21 October 2003).

12. Beidleman, C.A. 2000. *Partners in Flight Land Bird Conservation Plan Colorado.* Estes Park, CO.

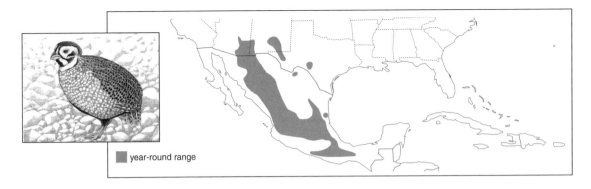

year-round range

MONTEZUMA QUAIL (*Cyrtonyx montezumae*)

A signature species of the oak-savanna grasslands of Mexico and adjacent regions of the southwest U.S., the Montezuma Quail is one of the most difficult bird species to observe because of its habit of remaining still and not flushing unless almost stepped on.

STATUS AND DISTRIBUTION

Range extends from southeastern Arizona and southwestern New Mexico south through Mexico's Sierra Madre mountains to Oaxaca. Small isolated populations occur in south-central Texas and adjacent Mexican state of Coahuila. At least 90% of the species' global population is thought to occur within Mexico.

Important U.S. sites for the species include Arizona's Buenos Aires National Wildlife Refuge (NWR), Coronado National Forest's Madera Canyon, the Chiricahua Mountains, and in New Mexico, the Animas Foundation's Gray Ranch and Lincoln National Forest. In Texas, where the species is state-listed as Endangered, the species occurs in Guadalupe Mountains National Park, the Davis Mountains, Kickapoo Cavern State Park, Devils River State Natural Area, and Dolan Falls Preserve.

Important sites for the species in Mexico include Sonora's Sistema de Islas Sierra Madre Occidental and Cuenca del Río Yaqui Important Bird Areas (IBA), Sinaloa's Alamos-Río Mayo IBA, Chihuahua's Sierra del Nido IBA, Zacatecas' Monte Escobedo IBA, and Oaxaca's Sierra Norte IBA. There are no available trend data for the species but its range has contracted greatly in Texas and it is said to be decreasing in its Mexican range as well. The species total population was estimated at 1,500,000 individuals in 2004 with 90% of population in Mexico and the remaining 10% in U.S.[1-4]

ECOLOGY

A very secretive species, the Montezuma Quail has been little studied and most of what is known comes only from the northern edge of the species' range in the southwest U.S. Occurs year-round in foothill oak forest, oak-savanna, and pine forest habitats with abundant native grasses. Occasionally also found in other habitats, including desert grasslands. Forages on the ground on acorns, grass seeds, and tubers that are dug up from underground, and in summer on insects. Birds are normally monogamous and raise one brood per season, with the young remaining with the adults through the winter until close to the beginning of the nesting season when they disperse. Females lay 10–11 eggs in a woven, covered ground nest, with incubation by both male and female for 24–26 days. The young are precocial and leave the nest within hours after hatching but are fed insects and small seeds and bulbs for the first two weeks, after which they have largely learned to feed on their own. Family groups remain together for 6–7 months after hatching, often remaining within an area as small as 2–5 acres. Nesting success of the Montezuma Quail is, like that of most quail species, almost certainly highly correlated with the amount of precipitation and subsequent food supply, and because the species can produce a large clutch, populations have the capacity to increase quickly in good years and within healthy ecosystems.[1]

THREATS

The greatest threat to this species has been the pervasive loss and degradation of habitat from intensive cattle grazing across vast stretches of the southwest U.S. and Mexico. A number of studies have shown that the species occurs in areas with at least 50% grass cover. Heavy cattle grazing removes the necessary native grass component of the pine-oak and oak savanna, rendering it unsuitable for the species and causing detrimental changes in fire frequency and increases in nonnative invasive plant species. In much of the Mexican range, logging has made large areas unsuitable for the species and continues to be a threat in many areas. In parts of the range where populations have become isolated and the habitat greatly fragmented, the sedentary nature of the species will undoubtedly increase rates of extirpation and problems from inbreeding. Habitat loss from urban and suburban developments has increased, as have problems related to increases in water removal from aquifers for agriculture coupled with increasing agricultural development. In some areas there is concern that hunting pressure could extirpate local populations and cause unknown effects to populations because the more visible males may be more readily observed and taken by hunters. Unfortunately, research on the species has been very limited and we are only beginning to understand the complex interactions between habitat, climate, and human-caused effects that determine the species' status.[1,5–10]

CONSERVATION ACTION

Partners in Flight Bird Conservation Plans in Arizona and New Mexico have identified Montezuma Quail and its associated suite of oak and pine-oak savanna species as a priority and have provided recommendations for management, research, monitoring, and outreach. Little conservation activity has been directed specifically toward Montezuma Quail habitat, but certain ecosystem-level conservation initiatives will likely prove beneficial for the species. For example, because the Chihuahuan ecoregion portion of the species' range has one of the greatest levels of species richness and endemism on Earth but has relatively few protected areas, the ecoregion has been the focus of a large-scale conservation planning effort by a consortium of groups including World Wildlife Fund,

CONABIO, The Nature Conservancy, Pronatura Noreste, and the Instituto Tecnológico y de Estudios Superiores de Monterrey. The Sierra Madre Alliance works on a variety of projects to decrease unsustainable logging pressure and to decrease grazing and agricultural practices detrimental to ecosystems of the Sierra Madre. Some research has been initiated more recently into the role of fire in the forests of the Sierra Madre Occidental and the influence of widespread cattle grazing within forests on fire frequency.[1,5–12]

CONSERVATION NEEDS

- Increase acreage of oak and pine-oak savanna habitat within the breeding range of Montezuma Quail that is managed to attain conditions beneficial to the species.
- Decrease acreage of oak and pine-oak savanna habitat degraded by cattle grazing and lack of prescribed burns.
- Develop baseline inventory of Montezuma Quail populations.

References

1. Stromberg, M.R. 2000. Montezuma Quail (*Cyrtonyx montezumae*). In *The Birds of North America*, No. 524 (A. Poole and F. Gill, eds.). The Birds of North America, Inc., Philadelphia, PA.

2. Chipley, R.M., G.H. Fenwick, M.J. Parr, and D.N. Pashley. 2003. *The American Bird Conservancy Guide to the 500 Most Important Bird Areas in the United States*. Random House, New York, NY.

3. CONABIO. 2002. *Áreas de Importancia para la Conservación de las Aves (AICAS)*. http://conabioweb .conabio.gob.mx/aicas/doctos/aicas.html (accessed 18 June 2003).

4. Rich, T.D., C. Beardmore, H. Berlanga, P. Blancher, M. Bradstreet, G. Butcher, D. Demarest, E. Dunn, C. Hunter, E. Iñigo-Elias, J. Kennedy, A. Martell, A. Panjabi, D. Pashley, K. Rosenberg, C. Rustay, S. Wendt, and T. Will. 2004. *Partners in Flight North American Landbird Conservation Plan*. Cornell Lab of Ornithology, Ithaca, NY.

5. Ricketts, T.H., E. Dinerstein, D.M. Olson, C.J. Loucks, et al. 1999. *Terrestrial Ecoregions of North America: A Conservation Assessment*. Island Press, Washington, DC. 485 pp.

6. World Wildlife Fund. 2001. *Sierra Madre Occidental Pine-Oak Forests (NA0302)*. http://www

.worldwildlife.org/wildworld/profiles/terrestrial/na/na03 02_full.html (Accessed 12 December 2003).

7. Johnson, D. 2003. Fighting Decades of Deforestation and Violence in the Mountains of Chihuahua. The Texas Observer, 7November 2003. http://www.texas observer.org/showArticle.asp?ArticleID=1482 (accessed 12 December 2003).

8. Pronatura Noreste. 2002. *Ecoregional Conservation Assessment of the Chihuahuan Desert*. www.conserve .online.

9. Rustay, C., C. Beardmore, M. Carter, C. Alford, and D. Pashley. 2003. *Partners in Flight Draft Land Bird Conservation Plan—New Mexico State Plan*, Version 1.2.

http://www.hawksaloft.org/pif.shtml (accessed 7 June 2004).

10. Latta, M.J., C.J. Beardmore, and T.E. Corman. 1999. *Arizona Partners in Flight Bird Conservation Plan*, Version 1.0. Nongame and Endangered Wildlife Program Technical Report 142. Arizona Game and Fish Department, Phoenix, AZ.

11. Sierra Madre Alliance. 2003. *Sierra Madre Alliance*. http://www.sierramadrealliance.org (accessed 12 December 2003).

12. Fule, P.Z., and W.W. Covington. 1999. Fire Regime Changes in La Michilia Biosphere Reserve, Durango, Mexico. *Conservation Biology* 13:1523–1739.

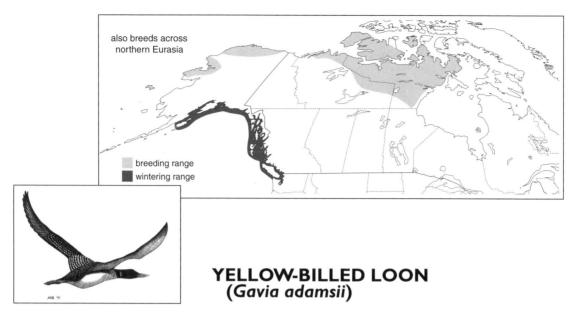

also breeds across
northern Eurasia

breeding range
wintering range

YELLOW-BILLED LOON
(*Gavia adamsii*)

An Arctic breeding loon with a restricted winter-ing range and relatively small total population, the Yellow-billed Loon is a prized sighting to birders from most of North America.

STATUS AND DISTRIBUTION

Breeds along the Arctic coasts of North America, Russia, and Europe. In North America, breeds in northern Alaska with the largest numbers along the North Slope and in western Arctic Canada. The highest densities are in the Alaska portion of breeding range from Coleville River west to Wain-wright, including much of National Petroleum Re-serve–Alaska. It has been estimated that nearly 100% of the U.S. breeding population and 24% of the North American breeding population of Yel-low-billed Loon occurs within the National Petro-leum Reserve–Alaska. Surveys of the North Slope of Alaska from 1986 to 1990 showed an average of 2,400 breeding birds. In Canada, important breed-ing areas include Banks Island, Northwest Territo-ries and Victoria Island, Nunavut as well as area between Great Slave Lake and northwestern Hud-son Bay.

The bulk of the North American population winters from Kodiak Island and the southern coast of Alaska Peninsula south along the coast to Van-couver Island and northwestern Washington. Birds occur rarely south to California and very rarely to Mexico. As birders have grown in num-bers and become more skilled in identification there have been an increasing number of records

of individual Yellow-billed Loons at lakes and reservoirs across much of the U.S.

No rangewide trend information is available for Yellow-billed Loon populations. Surveys along Alaska's North Slope from 1992 to 2002 found no significant trend. Since 1970 the numbers found on Christmas Bird Counts have ranged from 3 to 40 but Christmas Bird Count data show no obvi-ous trend. The population breeding in Russia and Europe has been estimated at fewer than 10,000 individuals. The North American population was estimated at 12,000–15,000 individuals in 2002.[1-6]

ECOLOGY

Breeds in arctic tundra habitat, nesting on islands or along shorelines of freshwater ponds, lakes, and rivers. In migration has been observed in large numbers on large freshwater lakes, rivers, and coastal areas. In winter is found in nearshore ma-rine habitats. In general the species' breeding and wintering ecology has been little-studied.[1]

THREATS

Potential threats identified include habitat degra-dation from expansion of human settlements and oil and gas exploration and extraction activities, oil pollution in molting and wintering habitats, and decreases in food supplies on wintering and molting areas from disturbance of marine envi-ronments. In 2004, a plan was announced to open for oil and gas leases the 8.8-million-acre

Northwest Planning Area of the National Petroleum Reserve–Alaska, which includes a large proportion of the Alaska breeding range of Yellow-billed Loon. Loss of habitat from sea level rise and other habitat changes as a result of global warming may become the most difficult and pervasive threat.[1,7]

CONSERVATION ACTION

The species has not been the focus of much research or conservation activity. An area within the Colville River Delta was identified as a location that should be protected for the benefit of Yellow-billed Loons, but the area was later leased for oil extraction.

Audubon Alaska has advocated for a "Wildlife Habitat Alternative" plan for protecting biological hotspots within the Northwest Planning Area of the National Petroleum Reserve when the area is opened for oil and gas leasing as a way to ensure healthy populations of Yellow-billed Loon and other wildlife species.[1,7]

CONSERVATION NEEDS

- Slow production of global warming pollution.
- Ensure that oil and gas exploration and extraction activity within portions of the National Petroleum Reserve that support nesting Yellow-billed Loon does not adversely impact habitat, productivity, and survival of the species.
- Study migration, staging, and wintering ecology of Yellow-billed Loon to determine limiting factors and importance of fisheries and oil pollutants to survival of wintering birds.
- Continue funding for surveys designed to detect changes in abundance and distribution of the species.

References

1. North, M.R. 1994. Yellow-billed Loon (*Gavia adamsii*). In *The Birds of North America*, No. 121 (A. Poole and F. Gill, eds.). The Academy of Natural Sciences; Philadelphia, PA, and The American Ornithologists' Union, Washington, DC.

2. Bureau of Land Management. 1997. *Waterfowl.* http://wwwndo.ak.blm.gov/npra/node33.html (accessed 21 April 2003).

3. Fair, J. 2002. *Status and Significance of Yellow-billed Loon* (Gavia adamsii) *Populations in Alaska.* The Wilderness Society and Trustees for Alaska, Anchorage, AK.

4. Mallek, E.J., R. Platte, and R. Stehn. *Aerial Breeding Pair Surveys of the Arctic Coastal Plain of Alaska—2002.* U.S. Fish and Wildlife Service, Waterfowl Management, Fairbanks, AK.

5. National Audubon Society (2002). *The Christmas Bird Count Historical Results* [Online]. http://www.audubon.org/bird/cbc (accessed 18 April 2003).

6. Wetlands International. 2002. *Waterbird Population Estimates*, 3rd ed. Wetlands International Global Series No. 12, Wageningen, The Netherlands.

7. Audubon Alaska. 2002. *Alaska's Western Arctic: A Summary and Synthesis of Resources.* Audubon Alaska, Anchorage, AK. 240 pp. plus 49 maps.

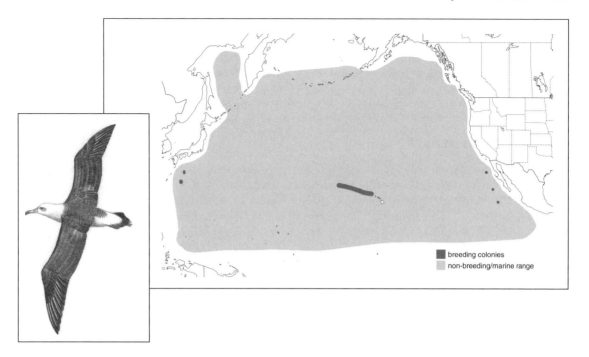

breeding colonies
non-breeding/marine range

LAYSAN ALBATROSS (*Phoebastria immutabilis*)

Like its close relatives the Black-footed Albatross and Short-tailed Albatross, the Laysan Albatross was heavily hunted on its breeding islands for the feather trade during the early 1900s and populations were seriously reduced. The species had bounced back but in more recent years large numbers have been killed accidentally by longline fisheries.

STATUS AND DISTRIBUTION

Almost the entire population breeds on islands in the northwestern Hawaiian Islands chain but small numbers nest on Bonin Islands off Japan and on Guadalupe Island and several other islands off Mexico's Pacific Coast. Colonies once were known to occur on several other Pacific islands but were wiped out by feather hunters and never returned. More than 75% of the breeding population (882,356 birds) was estimated in 2003 to be concentrated in the three islands that make up Midway Atoll.

During the nonbreeding season birds range north to the Bering Sea and the Gulf of Alaska and south along Pacific coasts of Asia to Japan and North America to California. Numbers off of continental U.S. coast are highest from October through February but there are records from virtu-

ally throughout the year. When birds are feeding young (January–July) satellite-tracked birds regularly traveled to the Aleutian Islands and the Gulf of Alaska from Hawaiian Islands.

Surveys completed in 2000–2001 indicate a decline of approximately 30% from 1991 to 1992 in numbers of breeding pairs for the three areas in the northwestern Hawaiian Islands with the bulk of the population. However, estimated breeding population in 2003 was about the level of that in 1991–92. The species' total population was estimated at 1.1 million breeders in 2002.[1-6]

ECOLOGY

Breeds on remote islands in the tropical northwestern Pacific where females lay their single egg on the ground in sandy areas or areas with short, turf grass. Both adults incubate the egg in shifts lasting 20–30 days. The eggs hatch in about 65 days and young leave nest at about 165 days after hatching. After fledging, young birds remain at sea for at least three years before returning to the breeding colony but do not breed until 8–9 years of age. Birds are long-lived in the absence of heightened human-induced mortality. In one banding study, 69% of females and 65% of males survived to 17 years. One bird recaptured in 2003 was known to be at least 51 years old. During the nonbreeding season the population ranges widely far from land over the Pacific Ocean and the Bering Sea. Forages largely at night for squid and flying fish eggs but also scavenges around fishing vessels for bait and discarded fisheries bycatch.[1,7]

THREATS

Historic losses of Laysan Albatross populations were primarily from direct killing of birds for the feather trade and for food. For example, 300,000 birds were killed on Laysan Island for the feather trade in 1909 and an estimated breeding population of a million birds had been wiped out from Marcus Island by the early 1900s. On Midway, tens of thousands of birds were killed by striking aircraft or were killed to prevent them from being an aircraft strike hazard, mostly during the 1950s and 1960s. The major threat today is from incidental take in fisheries, especially longline and gill-net fisheries in the northern Pacific. Driftnets, which are now illegal, resulted in the loss of an estimated 17,548 birds in 1990. The number of birds accidentally killed in the Hawaii-based longline fleet annually is estimated at 15,000 individuals. The birds are inadvertently hooked as they go after bait on longlines and subsequently drown on the submerged lines. More than 100 million hooks are set annually by the Japanese longline tuna fleet alone. Other potential threats include oil pollution and ingestion of floating plastics.[1,8,9]

CONSERVATION ACTION

Virtually the entire breeding population of Laysan Albatross is on islands that are part of the U.S. Fish and Wildlife Service Refuge system, so breeding sites are well protected.

U.S. Marine Fisheries Service has an active program to reduce seabird incidental take in longline fisheries, including regulations, monitoring, and education efforts. A National Plan of Action for Reducing the Incidental Catch of Seabirds in Longline Fisheries was published by the U.S. National Marine Fisheries Service in 2001. Certain simple measures have been developed that can reduce the number of birds killed by long-lining, including deployment of bird-scaring streamer lines, setting lines underwater through chutes, using heavier lines that drop below the surface quickly, and dying bait blue so that it is more difficult for

birds to see. Some of these measures have been implemented as regulations for certain U.S.-based fisheries but most of the world's fisheries are not required to use them.

BirdLife International has implemented a Save the Albatross Campaign that works to encourage governments with longline fisheries to implement international agreements to protect albatrosses and other seabirds. In particular, BirdLife is recommending that the U.S. and six other nations should sign on to the Agreement on the Conservation of Albatrosses and Petrels (ACAP) under the Convention on Migratory Species or Bonn Convention. National Audubon's Living Oceans Program participated in the Save the Albatross Campaign and has completed an educational video and other materials aimed at educating fishers about the impact of longlining on seabird populations and how simple measures can be deployed to minimize killing of seabirds. The Living Ocean's "Just Ask" campaign educates the public about which fish species are taken in unsustainable ways so that they can avoid purchasing those species at stores and restaurants.

The Cordell Banks and Monterey Bay, off the California coast, support small numbers of Laysan Albatross and have been designated as National Marine Sanctuaries that are managed by the National Oceanic and Atmospheric Administration. National Marine Sanctuaries generally prohibit oil and gas extraction activities within their boundaries and prohibit certain types of other human activities that may disturb marine life or marine habitats. These regulations should be beneficial to maintaining food supplies and a healthy ecosystem upon which Laysan Albatross depend.[1,8–15]

CONSERVATION NEEDS

- Decrease mortality from longline fisheries as quickly as possible.
- Continue efforts to limit amount of plastics, oil, and other pollutants within the marine ecosystem.

References

1. Whittow, G.C. 1993. Laysan Albatross (*Diomedea immutabilis*). In *The Birds of North America*, No. 66 (A. Poole and F. Gill, eds.). The Academy of Natural Sciences, Philadelphia, PA, and the American Ornithologists' Union, Washington, DC.

2. U.S. Fish and Wildlife Service. 2000. *Midway Atoll National Wildlife Refuge: Laysan Albatross*. http://midway.fws.gov/wildlife/laal.html (accessed 13 February 2004).

3. Thompson, W. 1998. *Albatross in WFU Study Circles the Globe in 90 Days*. Wake Forest University News Service. http://www.wfu.edu/wfunews/1998/051198a.htm (accessed 13 February 2004).

4. Environment Hawaii. 2001. *Goby Dreams, an Underwater Invasion, and Albatross Mysteries at Midway*. http://www.environment-hawaii.org/1201goby.htm (accessed 13 February 2004).

5. Honolulu Star Bulletin. 2004. *Albatross Population Increases at Midway*. http://starbulletin.com/2004/01/19/news/story5.html (accessed 13 February 2004).

6. Kushlan, J.A., M.J. Steinkamp, K.C. Parsons, J. Capp, M. Acosta Cruz, M. Coulter, I. Davidson, L. Dickson, N. Edelson, R. Elliot, R.M. Erwin, S. Hatch, S. Kress, R. Milko, S. Miller, K. Mills, R. Paul, R. Phillips, J.E. Saliva, B. Sydeman, J. Trapp, J. Wheeler, and K. Wohl. 2002. *Waterbird Conservation for the Americas: The North American Waterbird Conservation Plan*, Version 1. Waterbird Conservation for the Americas, Washington, DC. 78 pp.

7. Walker, C. 2003. 51-year-old Albatross Breaks North American Age Record. *National Geographic News*. http://news.nationalgeographic.com/news/2003/04/0417_030417_oldestbird.html (accessed 13 February 2004).

8. Cousins, K., P. Dalzell, and E.L. Gilman. 2001. Managing Pelagic Longline–Albatross Interactions in the North Pacific Ocean. *Marine Ornithology* 28(2): 159–174.

9. Montevicchi, W.A. 2002. Interactions Between Fisheries and Seabirds. Pages 527–557 In *Biology of Marine Birds* (E.A. Schreiber and J. Burger, eds.). CRC Press, Boca Raton, FL.

10. National Marine Fisheries Service. 2003. *Program to Reduce Seabird Incidental Take in Longline Fisheries*. http://www.fakr.noaa.gov/protectedresources/seabirds.html (accessed 28 April 2003).

11. National Marine Fisheries Service. 2001. *North Pacific Fishery Management Council Takes Final Action on Revisions to Seabird Avoidance Measures in Groundfish and Halibut Hook-and-Line Fisheries off Alaska*. National Marine Fisheries Service, Alaska Office, Anchorage, AK.

12. National Marine Fisheries Service. 2001. *Final United States National Plan of Action for Reducing the Incidental Catch of Seabirds in Longline Fisheries*. National Marine Fisheries Service, Silver Spring, MD.

13. National Audubon Society. 2003. *Fact Sheet: Save the Albatross Campaign*. http://www.audubon.org/campaign/lo/save_albatross.html (accessed 28 April 2003).

14. BirdLife International. 2003. *Save the Albatross*. http://www.birdlife.net/action/campaigns/save_the_albatross/index.html (accessed 28 April 2003).

15. National Ocean Service. 2003. *National Marine Sanctuaries*. http://www.sanctuaries.nos.noaa.gov/welcome.html (accessed 22 May 2003).

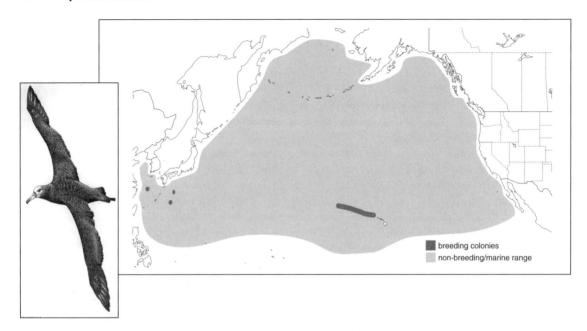

breeding colonies
non-breeding/marine range

BLACK-FOOTED ALBATROSS (*Phoebastria nigripes*)

Although the Black-footed Albatross is one of the most commonly observed albatrosses off the west coast of North America, the population is thought to have declined by nearly 20% since 1995 as a result of mortality caused by longline fisheries in the north Pacific.

STATUS AND DISTRIBUTION

Breeds on islands in the northwestern Hawaiian Islands chain and islands off Japan. Once bred more widely across islands in the northwest Pacific. More than 95% of the population now nests in the Hawaiian Islands. The largest colonies in the world occur at Laysan Island with about 23,000 pairs and Midway Atoll National Wildlife Refuge with over 20,000 pairs in 2000. The number of birds breeding on the three Japanese islands where they occur was estimated at less than 1,500 pairs in 1984.

During the nonbreeding season birds range north to the Bering Sea and Gulf of Alaska and south along the Pacific coast of North America to California. Numbers are highest off the Pacific coast of the U.S. from June through August, with pelagic birding trips regularly finding more than 100 individuals during the course of a day-long trip that may travel 30–40 miles offshore.

Surveys completed in 2000 indicated a 19% decline in numbers of breeding pairs for the three

areas in the northwestern Hawaiian islands with the bulk of the population. Worldwide population estimated at 278,000 pairs in 2000.[1-5]

ECOLOGY

Breeds on remote islands in the tropical northwestern Pacific where females lay their single egg on the ground in sandy areas or areas with short, turf grass. During the nonbreeding season ranges widely over Pacific Ocean and Bering Sea. An individual tracked with a satellite transmitter moved 5067 kilometers over 35 days from a location 400 kilometers off southern California to a location approximately 4000 kilometers north of Hawaii. Primary foods during nesting season are squid and flying fish eggs, but this bird also scavenges around fishing vessels for bait and discarded fisheries by-catch.[1,6]

THREATS

Historic losses of Black-footed Albatross populations were from direct killing of birds for the feather trade and for food. The major threat today is from incidental take in fisheries, especially longline fisheries in the northern Pacific. As many as 19,000 Black-footed Albatrosses are thought to be killed annually when they are inadvertently hooked as they go after bait on longlines and subsequently drown on the submerged lines. More than 100 million hooks are set annually by the Japanese longline tuna fleet alone. Other potential threats include oil pollution and ingestion of floating plastics.[1,3,7,8]

CONSERVATION ACTION

U.S. Marine Fisheries Service has an active program to reduce seabird incidental take in longline fisheries, including regulations, monitoring, and education efforts. Certain simple measures have been developed that can reduce the number of birds killed by long-lining, including deployment of bird-scaring streamer lines, setting lines underwater through chutes, using heavier lines that drop below the surface quickly, setting lines at night, and dying bait blue so that it is more difficult for birds to see. Some of these measures have been implemented as regulations for certain U.S.-based fisheries, but most of the world's fisheries are not required to use them.

BirdLife International has implemented a Save the Albatross Campaign that works to encourage governments with longline fisheries to implement international agreements to protect albatrosses and other seabirds. In particular, BirdLife is recommending that the U.S. and six other nations should sign on to the Agreement on the Conservation of Albatrosses and Petrels (ACAP) under the Convention on Migratory Species or Bonn Convention. National Audubon's Living Oceans Program participates in the Save the Albatross Campaign and has completed an educational video and other materials aimed at educating fishers about the impact of long-lining on seabird populations and how simple measures can be deployed to minimize killing of seabirds. The Living Ocean's "Just Ask" campaign is educating the public about which fish species are taken in unsustainable ways so that they can avoid purchasing those species at stores and restaurants.

Virtually the entire U.S. breeding population of Black-footed Albatross is on islands that are part of the U.S. Fish and Wildlife Service Refuge system so breeding sites are well protected.[3,6,8–10]

CONSERVATION NEEDS

- Decrease mortality from longline fisheries as quickly as possible.
- Continue efforts to limit amount of plastics, oil, and other pollutants within the marine ecosystem.

References

1. Whittow, G.C. 1993. Black-footed Albatross (*Diomedea nigripes*). In *The Birds of North America*, No. 65 (A. Poole and F. Gill, eds.). The Academy of Natural Sciences, Philadelphia, PA, and the American Ornithologists' Union, Washington, DC.

2. U.S. Fish and Wildlife Service. 2000. *Midway Atoll National Wildlife Refuge: Black-footed Albatross.* http://midway.fws.gov/wildlife/bfal.html (accessed 28 April 2003).

3. BirdLife International. 2000. *Threatened Birds of the World.* Lynx Editions and BirdLife International, Barcelona, Spain and Cambridge, UK.

4. Small, A. 1994. *California Birds: Their Status and Distribution.* Ibis Publishing Company, Vista, CA.

5. Wahl, T.R., and B. Tweit. 2000. Seabird Abundances off Washington, 1972–1998. *Western Birds* 31: 69–88

6. Montevicchi, W.A. 2002. Interactions Between Fisheries and Seabirds. Pages 527–557 In *Biology of Marine Birds* (E.A. Schreiber and J. Burger, eds.). CRC Press, Boca Raton, FL.

7. Cousins, K., P. Dalzell, and E.L. Gilman. 2001. Managing Pelagic Longline–Albatross Interactions in the North Pacific Ocean. *Marine Ornithology* 28(2): 159–174.

8. National Marine Fisheries Service. 2003. *Program to Reduce Seabird Incidental Take in Longline Fisheries.* http://www.fakr.noaa.gov/protectedresources/seabirds.html (accessed 28 April 2003).

9. National Audubon Society. 2003. *Fact Sheet: Save the Albatross Campaign.* http://www.audubon.org/campaign/lo/save_albatross.html (accessed 28 April 2003).

10. BirdLife International. 2003. *Save the Albatross.* http://www.birdlife.net/action/campaigns/save_the_albatross/index.html (accessed 28 April 2003).

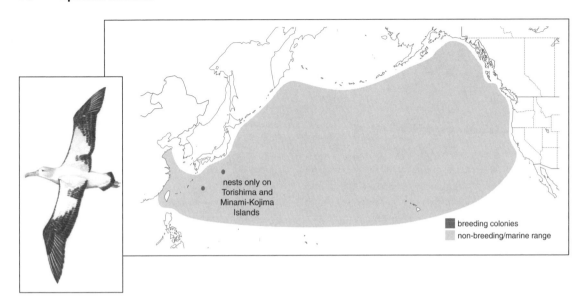

nests only on Torishima and Minami-Kojima Islands

■ breeding colonies
▨ non-breeding/marine range

SHORT-TAILED ALBATROSS (*Phoebastria albatrus*)

Once thought extinct, this species was rediscovered in the 1950s but still is one of the rarest seabirds in the world. Because of its extreme rarity, any loss of individuals is considered a major setback and efforts are underway to minimize such losses, especially in the offshore fishing industry.

STATUS AND DISTRIBUTION

Breeds on two islands off Japan and Taiwan but during the nonbreeding season ranges across the northern Pacific north to marine areas off of Russia and Alaska and east to the U.S. Pacific coast. The bulk of the population breeds on the island of Torishima, with 1,300 birds (700 adults, 800 subadults) and 193 chicks fledged in 2003–2004. Approximately 320 birds (145 adults, 175 subadults) were counted on Minami-Kojima Island, a Japanese-claimed island off the coast of Taiwan, in 2003–2004. The species was once abundant and widespread on islands in the northwest Pacific but was nearly wiped out by feather hunters who killed more than five million adults, so that birds were restricted to Torishima Island, which then began having volcanic eruptions, further decreasing numbers. There were an estimated 20 birds left in 1953 and birds began attempting to breed again in 1954. Work has been ongoing at Torishima Island to protect the birds and enhance the habitat. A pair was discovered nesting on Yomejima Island off Japan in 2000. Several un-

mated individuals have spent breeding seasons at Midway Atoll National Wildlife Refuge among colonies of Black-footed and Laysan albatross.

During the nonbreeding season (June–October) birds range from just south of Hawaii north to the Bering Strait, and from the coast of California west to the Pacific coasts of Japan and Russia. Because of the small size of population there are very few records of birds within this range, but fisheries vessels off Alaska and British Columbia report 20–30 individuals every year. Total population was estimated at 1,900–2,000 individuals in the 2003–2004 season.[1–8]

ECOLOGY

Breeding females lay their single egg on flat ground in sandy areas near clumps of grass. Most birds do not breed until they are six years old. Incubation lasts about 65 days and many birds apparently breed every other year. Primary foods are squid, flying fish eggs, and crustaceans, but these birds also scavenge around fishing vessels for bait and discarded fisheries bycatch.[1,3,4]

THREATS

Historic losses of Short-tailed Albatross populations were from direct killing of birds for the feather trade to stuff mattresses and pillows. More than five million adult Short-tailed Albatross were reportedly killed during the early part of the 1900s. The major threat today is from incidental take in fisheries, including longline fisheries and potentially from jig fishing and trawl fishing as well. Thousands of albatrosses of various species are killed annually when they are inadvertently hooked as they go after bait on longlines and subsequently drown on the submerged lines. Fortunately, there have been no documented deaths of Short-tailed Albatross from long-lining since two young birds were killed in 1998. More than 100 million hooks are set annually by the Japanese longline tuna fleet alone. Another major threat is loss of birds and habitat from erosion and from regular volcanic eruptions on Torishima Island. Other potential threats include oil pollution and ingestion of floating plastics and other marine contaminants.[1,2,4,8]

CONSERVATION ACTION

U.S. National Marine Fisheries Service has an active program to reduce seabird incidental take in longline fisheries, including regulations, monitoring, and education efforts. Certain simple measures have been developed that can reduce the number of birds killed by long-lining, including deployment of bird-scaring streamer lines. Seabird avoidance measures are required for U.S.-based longline fisheries, but not for other U.S. fisheries or any foreign North Pacific commercial fisheries. The U. S. Fish and Wildlife Service and the Pacific States Marine Fisheries Commission have provided 6,000 free bird-scaring streamer lines for use by commercial fishermen. Education efforts have included the development of posters and videos used in fisheries from Hawaii to Alaska. Alaska Sea Grant, Washington Sea Grant, and the University of Alaska produced a video describing the problems with incidental take of seabirds and demonstrating how to deploy streamer lines. The video is being distributed to all Alaska-based fisheries covered under current seabird avoidance regulations. World Wildlife Fund implemented a pilot project in 2004 to begin educating Russian longline fishermen about the problems with incidental take of seabirds in fisheries and seabird avoidance techniques currently used by U.S.-based longline fisheries.

BirdLife International has implemented a Save the Albatross Campaign that works to encourage governments with longline fisheries to im-plement international agreements to protect albatrosses and other seabirds. In particular, BirdLife is recommending that the U.S. and six other nations should sign on to the Agreement on the Conservation of Albatrosses and Petrels (ACAP) under the Convention on Migratory Species or Bonn Convention. Audubon's Living Ocean's "Just Ask" campaign has helped to educate the public about which fish species are taken in unsustainable ways so that they can avoid purchasing those species at stores and restaurants as a way to apply market pressure toward changing fishery practices.

The Japanese government has designated the Short-tailed Albatross a National Monument. The bulk of the breeding population of Short-tailed Albatross is on Torishima Island, which has been designated a National Wildlife Protection Area by Japan. Here work has been ongoing to restore habitat and to lure birds to a second site on the other side of the island that is less vulnerable to erosion and volcanic eruptions, through the use of decoys and recorded vocalizations. One albatross pair successfully reared six chicks at the new site from 1996 to 2004. Minami-Kojima and Yomejima Islands are claimed by both Japan and China, and while the islands are occasionally visited by tourists and biologists, no conservation work has been undertaken because of concerns over the territorial dispute. National Audubon's Seabird Restoration Program is partnering with the U.S. Fish and Wildlife Service to try to attract Short-tailed Albatrosses to Midway Island National Wildlife Refuge also using decoys and recorded vocalizations.[1,2,6,8–14]

CONSERVATION NEEDS

- Continue efforts to establish nesting colonies in areas on Torishima Island that are less vulnerable to loss of birds and habitat from volcanic eruptions.
- Continue habitat enhancement work and population monitoring on Torishima Island to increase fledging success.
- Establish regular monitoring of nesting colony on Minami-kojima Island.
- Monitor Yomejima Island to determine if Short-tailed Albatross continue to nest there.
- Continue research into distribution, movements, and life history of the species.
- Establish new colonies in the Bonin Islands or other suitable locations.

- Continue efforts to decrease mortality from incidental take in fisheries.
- Continue efforts to limit amount of plastics, oil, and other pollutants within the marine ecosystem.
- Continue efforts to encourage birds to establish new breeding colony in northwestern Hawaiian Islands.

References

1. BirdLife International. 2000. *Threatened Birds of the World*. Lynx Editions and BirdLife International, Barcelona, Spain, and Cambridge, UK.

2. Balogh, G. 2005. Personal communication.

3. National Marine Fisheries Service. 2001. NMFS *Reports on the Current Breeding Status of the Endangered Short-tailed Albatross*. http://www.fakr.noaa.gov/infobulletins/2001_infobulletins/albatrossbreeding.html (accessed 12 May 2003).

4. U.S. Fish and Wildlife Service. 2000. *Midway Atoll National Wildlife Refuge: Short-tailed Albatross*. http://midway.fws.gov/wildlife/stal.html (accessed 29 April 2003).

5. del Hoyo, J., A. Elliot, and J. Sargaral. 1992. *Handbook of Birds of the World*, Vol. 1. Lynx Editions, Barcelona, Spain.

6. Harrison, P. 1983. *Seabirds: An Identification Guide*. Houghton Mifflin, Boston, MA.

7. U.S. Fish and Wildlife Service. 2001. *Short-tailed Albatross* (Phoebastria albatrus). U.S. Fish and Wildlife Service Fact Sheet, U.S. Fish and Wildlife Service Ecological Services Field Office, Anchorage, AK.

8. International Pacific Halibut Commission. 2002. http://www.iphc.washington.edu/staff/tracee/shorttail.htm.

9. Montevicchi, W.A. 2002. Interactions Between Fisheries and Seabirds. Pages 527–557 in *Biology of Marine Birds* (E.A. Schreiber and J. Burger, eds.). CRC Press, Boca Raton, FL.

10. National Marine Fisheries Service. 2003. *Program to Reduce Seabird Incidental Take in Longline Fisheries*. http://www.fakr.noaa.gov/protectedresources/seabirds.html (accessed 28 April 2003).

11. World Wildlife Fund. 2005. *Bycatch Bygone: Saving the Bering Sea's Remarkable Birds*. http://www.worldwildlife.org/wildplaces/bs/projects.cfm (accessed 18 November 2005).

12. National Audubon Society. 2003. *Fact Sheet: Save the Albatross Campaign*. http://www.audubon.org/campaign/lo/save_albatross.html (accessed 28 April 2003).

13. BirdLife International. 2003. *Save the Albatross*. http://www.birdlife.net/action/campaigns/save_the_albatross/index.html (accessed 28 April 2003).

14. National Audubon Society. 2001. *Egg Rock Update*. National Audubon Society Seabird Restoration Program, Ithaca, NY.

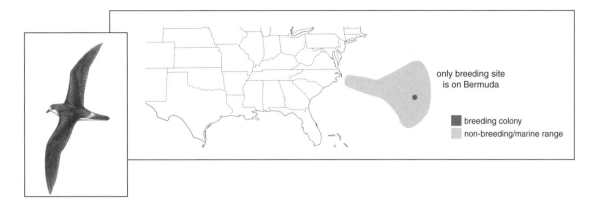

only breeding site
is on Bermuda

■ breeding colony
■ non-breeding/marine range

BERMUDA PETREL (*Pterodroma cahow*)

One of the world's rarest seabirds and thought to be extinct for 300 years, the Bermuda Petrel population was once reduced to a few dozen birds, but through extensive hands-on management, the population has increased to nearly 200 birds and a few individuals are seen annually by birders off the North Carolina coast.

STATUS AND DISTRIBUTION

Before human settlement of Bermuda the species was an abundant breeder on the main islands as well as surrounding small islands but rapidly declined as birds were taken for food by colonists and eggs and young were killed by introduced rats and other predators. Although the species was thought to number more than a million in the 1500s, by the 1600s it was considered extinct. It was not until the 1900s that the species was rediscovered, culminating with the discovery of breeding sites in 1951 that held 18 pairs. With intensive management, including the construction of artificial burrows on the four tiny rocky islands to which the species' breeding range is now restricted, the population has increased and was estimated at 180 individuals in 1997. In 2003 there were 70 nesting pairs that reared 40 young so that total population (with subadults) is likely greater than 200. The distribution at sea both in the breeding and nonbreeding season is poorly understood but a few birds (perhaps postbreeding adults) are seen annually in spring (usually late May) by pelagic birding trips in the Gulf Stream off of North Carolina.[1–5]

ECOLOGY

Begins nesting in January with young fledging normally in June. Nests in artificial burrows and crevices in four tiny rocky islands though formerly nested in burrows excavated in soil on the main island and larger outlying islands. Breeding sites are visited only at night when adults give moaning cries. Like related species, the Bermuda Petrel lays only a single egg and likely takes 5–7 years to reach breeding age (though birds were not regularly banded until recently to alleviate any possible stresses that could increase mortality of young or adults). The species' biology at sea is poorly known but birds are thought to eat squid as well as some shrimp and small fish. Young are slow to develop and reach peak weight at about two months, after which they lose weight (adults often stop feeding young in last weeks before fledging) before fledging at about three months of age.[1–4]

THREATS

Bermuda was uninhabited by humans prior to its discovery by European fishermen and explorers in the 1500s and the island had no native mammals, so Bermuda Petrel (and other species) were not adapted to survival against mammalian predators. The species disappeared from the main island by the 1600s primarily from predation by introduced pigs that ate eggs, young, and adults trapped in nesting burrows. They were still abundant on Cooper's Island and other small nearby islands but settlers began catching birds and taking eggs for food at these locations and rats, cats, and dogs were introduced as well. All of this led to the species' rapid decline so that by 1621 the Bermuda Petrel was considered extinct.

The current threats to the species are different but are the result of the historical problems. All nesting areas are confined to four tiny islands with only marginal habitat so that the birds have come to increasingly rely on artificial concrete nesting burrows. In early years it was discovered that White-tailed Tropicbirds were competing for nest sites (including artificial nest sites) with the petrels and often would even kill nestlings. Special baffles were eventually designed that allowed access to burrows by petrels but excluded tropicbirds. Rat predation continues to be a threat since, despite an active rat control program, rats regularly swim over to the islands and must be removed quickly before they destroy eggs or kill nestlings or adults. Light pollution from nearby U.S. government installations is thought to have disrupted the nocturnal breeding activities of the species in the past. Perhaps the greatest current threat is from increased hurricane and storm activity thought to be related to global warming. Since 1990 there have been at least five major overfloods of the nesting islands that have destroyed nesting burrows (as compared to no such events in the preceding 25 years). A major hurricane in 2003 swept away parts of two of the nesting islands and damaged more than 50 of the artificial concrete nesting burrows.

The waters off of North Carolina where birds have been seen annually and that support important concentrations of many seabirds (including the closely related Black-capped Petrel) are under consideration for gas and oil exploration. Oil spills, degradation of the food supply, and disturbance or mortality from attraction to lights on fishing boats or oil rigs are all potential threats. There is also an active longline fishery in this area but potential impacts with this species have not been studied.[1–7]

CONSERVATION ACTION

Bermuda Petrel has been the focus of more than 40 years of intensive, hands-on management efforts, led for most of that time by David Wingate of the Bermuda Department of Conservation Services. The nesting islands have been protected as a nature reserve since the 1960s. The development of artificial concrete burrows and baffles to prevent tropicbirds from entering them has increased nest success from 5% per year in the 1950s to about 50% in recent years. The Bermuda Department of Conservation Services has maintained this active management program over nearly 50 years so that the population of Bermuda Petrel has increased from 18 nesting pairs in 1952 to 70 in 2003. In recent years much work has gone into rebuilding artificial burrows destroyed or damaged by storms. The agency has also worked since the 1960s to restore the larger Nonsuch Island to its pre-human discovery condition and in 2004 transplanted 10 Bermuda Petrel chicks to the island in the hopes of establishing a new colony that can begin using traditional burrows in soil and be free from the effects of storm damage. Nonsuch Island is thought to have the capacity to sustain as many as 1000 nesting pairs using natural soil burrows and more with the use of artificial burrows. Sounds of the species will be played on Nonsuch during the nesting season to attract and encourage birds to nest on the island.

The at-sea concentration areas are not within any protected area and oil companies already hold leases for much of the area off of North Carolina. Audubon–North Carolina recently identified an Important Bird Area offshore of Cape Hatteras which encompasses some of the most important at-sea habitat for the many seabirds that rely on these waters. Bermuda Petrel is federally listed as Endangered in U.S. territorial waters so that any actions taken by U.S. government entities related to fisheries management and mineral rights should consider potential impacts on the species.[1–8]

CONSERVATION NEEDS

- Slow production of global warming pollution.
- Establish Marine Protected Areas encompassing at-sea seabird concentration areas off the coast of the southeast U.S.
- Continue measures to ensure protection of known breeding colonies and to establish new nesting colony on Nonsuch Island.
- Continue measures to effectively remove introduced mammalian predators from areas near breeding colonies.
- Continue efforts to limit amount of plastics, oil, and other pollutants within the marine ecosystem.

References

1. Collar, N.J., L.P. Gonzaga, N. Krabbe, A. Madroño Nieto, L.G. Naranjo, T.A. Parker III, and D.C. Wege. 1992. *Threatened Birds of the Americas*. International Council for Bird Preservation, Cambridge, UK.

2. BirdLife International. 2000. *Threatened Birds of the World*. Lynx Editions and BirdLife International, Barcelona and Cambridge, UK.

3. Madeiros, J. 2002. Bermuda's Remarkable Cahow. *World Birdwatch* 24:17–18.

4. BirdLife International. 2003. *Hurricane-torn Bermuda Rallies to Save Seabirds*. http://www.birdlife.net/news/news/2003/09/burmuda_petrel.html (accessed 28 July 2004).

5. Patteson, B. 2004. *Seabirding Pelagic Trips*. http://www.patteson.com (accessed 28 July 2004).

6. BirdLife International. 2004. *New Island Home for Cahow Chicks*. http://www.birdlife.net/news/news/2004/07/cahow_translocation.html (accessed 28 July 2004).

7. Audubon North Carolina. 2003. *Important Bird Areas of North Carolina*. http://www.ncaudubon.org/IBAs/Coast/OuterC_shelf.htm (accessed 20 May 2003).

8. Hunter, C. 2005. Personal communication.

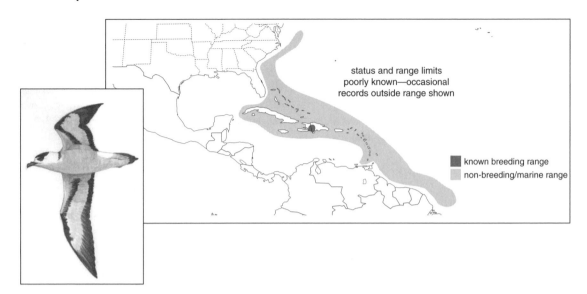

status and range limits
poorly known—occasional
records outside range shown

known breeding range
non-breeding/marine range

BLACK-CAPPED PETREL (*Pterodroma hasitata*)

Once thought to be extinct, the Black-capped Petrel is now seen regularly in Gulf Stream waters off of the southeastern U.S.—an area that supports the largest known concentrations of its still very small population.

STATUS AND DISTRIBUTION

Once bred in abundance in the mountains of both Greater and Lesser Antilles but the only known breeding sites now are in the mountains of Hispaniola. A total of 13 colonies is known from Massif de la Selle and Massif de la Hotte in Haiti and Sierra de Bahoruco in the Dominican Republic but the birds have been poorly surveyed because of nocturnal habits at breeding sites and inaccessibility of habitat. No other breeding locations have been confirmed but there is hope that the birds may still breed on Dominica. Surveys of colony sites in Haiti between 1961 and 1980 and 1984 indicated a decline in numbers at many colonies.

The birds' at-sea range extends from Gulf Stream waters off of North Carolina (occasionally further north) and south (at least historically) to waters off of northeastern Brazil. The most important at-sea location known for the species is Gulf Stream off of Cape Hatteras, North Carolina, where counts of 50–150 individuals are quite regular on pelagic boat trips from May though October.

Total population was estimated to range between 600 and 2000 individuals in 2000. Historically very abundant, but no estimates exist, though

there are accounts from the 1800s of hunters taking as many as 150–200 adults in a day of hunting the birds in their mountain breeding areas.[1-4]

ECOLOGY

Nests colonially between December and April in burrows and crevices in steep mountainous terrain at upper elevations of mountains that straddle the border between southeast Haiti and southwest Dominican Republic and historically in similar habitats on other Caribbean islands. These breeding sites are visited only at night when the birds give unusual, mournful calls. Although the species' biology has not been studied, it likely lays only a single egg and may take 5–7 years to reach breeding age. At-sea biology studied off of southeastern U.S. showed that birds concentrated along the western boundary of the Gulf Stream in association with upwellings. Birds were noted feeding most commonly in the early morning and late afternoon on fish and invertebrates and waste from fishing boats.[1,4,5]

THREATS

Historically, declines were apparently the result of a history of hunting birds at breeding sites and destruction of breeding habitat. Although this is not thought to be as major a problem today, some birds are apparently still taken in Haiti. Undoubtedly, they have also suffered mortality from introduced rats, mongoose, and other nonnative predatory mammals, a problem that is likely to continue. Many of the known breeding colonies are within national parks but tree harvesting for charcoal and small-scale agriculture continues within these areas, activities that could impact Black-capped Petrel habitat.

The waters off of North Carolina that represent the only known nonbreeding concentrations are under consideration for gas and oil exploration. Oil spills, degradation of the food supply, and disturbance or mortality from attraction to lights on fishing boats or oil rigs are all potential threats especially since apparently the bulk of the world's population of the species relies on these waters for survival. There is also an active longline fishery in this area but potential impacts with this species have not been studied.

Black-capped Petrels were found to be one of the seabirds with the highest concentrations of mercury in their tissues in a study that examined 27 seabird species but because the species is so little-studied it is unknown what affect this may have on the population.[1,2,6,7]

CONSERVATION ACTION

No direct conservation action has been taken on behalf of Black-capped Petrels within their breeding or at-sea ranges. Most of the known breeding colonies are within national parks of Haiti or the Dominican Republic but these parks are chronically underfunded and much illegal timber extraction, forest clearing, and other activities take place within park boundaries. The at-sea concentration areas are not within any protected area, and oil companies already hold leases for much of the area off of North Carolina. Audubon–North Carolina recently identified an Important Bird Area offshore of Cape Hatteras that encompasses some of the most important at-sea habitat for Black-capped Petrels and other seabirds.[6]

CONSERVATION NEEDS

- Establish Marine Protected Areas encompassing at-sea concentration areas for Black-capped Petrels off the coast of the southeast U.S.
- Develop and implement surveys, perhaps using radar and acoustic monitoring technologies, to detect and monitor breeding colonies of Black-capped Petrels on Hispaniola and other possible breeding locations in the Caribbean.
- Implement measures to ensure protection of known breeding colonies and to prevent possible take of birds at or near breeding sites.
- Implement measures to effectively remove introduced mammalian predators from areas near breeding colonies.
- Develop and implement at-sea surveys to monitor changes in abundance of Black-capped Petrels.
- Continue efforts to limit amount of plastics, oil, and other pollutants within the marine ecosystem.

References

1. Lee, D.S. 2000. Status of and Conservation Priorities for Black-capped Petrels in the West Indies. Pages 11–18 in (E.A. Schreiber and D.S. Lee, eds.) *Status and Conservation of West Indian Seabirds.* (E.A. Schreiber and D.S. Lee, eds.) Society of Caribbean Ornithology, Special Publication Number 1, Ruston, LA.

2. BirdLife International. 2000. *Threatened Birds of the World.* Lynx Editions and BirdLife International, Barcelona, Spain, and Cambridge, UK.

3. Mlodinow, S.G., and M. O'Brien. 1996. *America's 100 Most Wanted Birds.* Falcon Press Publishing Co., Helena and Billings, MT.

4. Bent, A.C. 1964. *Life Histories of North American Petrels and Pelicans and Their Allies.* Dover Publications, New York, NY.

5. Haney, J.C. 1987. Aspects of the Pelagic Ecology and Behavior of the Black-capped Petrel (*Ptredroma hasitata*). *Wilson Bulletin* 99:153–168.

6. Audubon North Carolina. 2003. *Important Bird Areas of North Carolina.* http://www.ncaudubon.org/IBAs/Coast/OuterC_shelf.htm (accessed 20 May 2003).

7. Hunter, C. 2005. Personal communication.

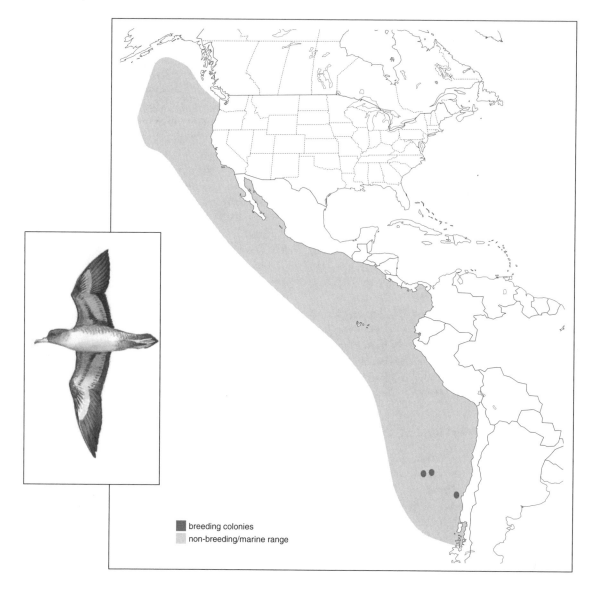

breeding colonies
non-breeding/marine range

PINK-FOOTED SHEARWATER (*Puffinus creatopus*)

Known to North American birders as a summer visitor to offshore waters of the Pacific coast, the Pink-footed Shearwater breeds on only three islands off Chile during the southern hemisphere summer where populations are threatened by introduced mammalian predators.

STATUS AND DISTRIBUTION

Breeds on Robinson Crusoe and Santa Clara Islands within the Juan Fernandez Islands and on Isla Mocha, all off the coast of Arauco, Chile. The largest colony at Isla Mocha is estimated at between 13,000 and 25,000 pairs. Colonies at other two islands were estimated in the range of 2,000–3,000 pairs in late 1980s and early 1990s.

During nonbreeding season (April–October), birds range north to the offshore waters of the Pacific coast of North America as far north as Gulf of Alaska. Day-long pelagic birding trips off of California, Oregon, and Washington regularly find hundreds and occasionally thousands of Pink-footed Shearwaters. Offshore locations like Monterey Bay and Cordell Banks, California and Perpetua and Heceta Banks off of Oregon are known concentration areas for the species. Birds have rarely been found west to the Hawaiian Islands, New Zealand, and Australia. Total population was estimated to range between 34,000 and 60,000 individuals in 2000. Historically poorly surveyed so no trend information is available.[1,2]

ECOLOGY

Nests colonially between November and May in burrows in sparsely vegetated habitat or within forest. Burrows are often more than six feet deep. Females lay a single egg, usually in November or December, with young fledging from March through April. At sea feeds on fish, squid, and some crustaceans.[1,3]

THREATS

The greatest current threats are direct nest depredation and adult mortality from introduced rats and cats, habitat degradation from introduced rabbits and goats, and possibly hunting of chicks by humans on Isla Mocha. Some birds are killed by entanglement in fisheries nets, but the extent of the problem is unclear.[1]

CONSERVATION ACTION

The Juan Fernandez Islands, where two of the three colonies are located, have been designated as a national park and biosphere reserve. These islands harbor many endemic plant and animal species but have been severely degraded by introduced animals and plants. The Chilean government has provided funds to attempt some habitat restoration and eradication of invasives but not enough resources have been made available to effectively counter the problems. The colony on Isla Mocha is within a national reserve that has a management plan and two guards as of 2000.

Cordell Banks and Monterey Bay have been designated as National Marine Sanctuaries and are managed by the National Oceanic and Atmospheric Administration. National Marine Sanctuaries generally prohibit oil and gas extraction activities within their boundaries and prohibit certain types of other human activities that may disturb marine life or marine habitats. These regulations should be beneficial to maintaining food supplies and a healthy ecosystem upon which Pink-footed Shearwaters depend.[1,4,5]

CONSERVATION NEEDS

- Implement measures to effectively remove introduced mammalian predators from areas near breeding colonies.
- Implement measures to remove introduced herbivores from areas near breeding colonies and stabilize eroding habitat.
- Develop and implement surveys, perhaps using radar and acoustic monitoring technologies, to detect and monitor breeding colonies of Pink-footed Shearwaters on Juan Fernandez Islands and Isla Mocha.
- Implement measures to ensure protection of known breeding colonies and to prevent harvest of chicks.
- Develop and implement at-sea surveys to monitor changes in abundance of Pink-footed Shearwater.
- Continue efforts to limit amount of plastics, oil, and other pollutants within the marine ecosystem.

References

1. BirdLife International. 2000. *Threatened Birds of the World.* Lynx Editions and BirdLife International, Barcelona and Cambridge, UK.

2. Harrison, P. 1983. *Seabirds: An Identification Guide.* Houghton Mifflin, Boston, MA.

3. Bent, A.C. 1964. *Life Histories of North American Petrels and Pelicans and Their Allies.* Dover Publications, New York, NY.

4. Bernardello, G., and T.F. Stuessy. 2001. *Juan Fernandez Islands Temperate Forests.* World Wildlife Fund. http://www.worldwildlife.org/wildworld/profiles/terrestrial/nt/nt0401_full.html (accessed 21 May 2003).

5. National Ocean Service. 2003. *National Marine Sanctuaries.* http://www.sanctuaries.nos.noaa.gov/welcome.html (accessed 22 May 2003).

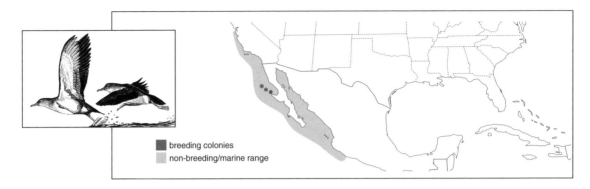

breeding colonies
non-breeding/marine range

BLACK-VENTED SHEARWATER (*Puffinus opisthomelas*)

Unusual among shearwaters, the Black-vented Shearwater occurs in waters within about 10 miles of shore and is commonly seen from points of land along the southern California coast where birds disperse from their Baja California breeding sites.

STATUS AND DISTRIBUTION

Breeds on Natividad Island and San Benito Islands and rocky islets off of Guadalupe Island, all off of Mexico's Baja California. Natividad Island is the most important breeding colony, supporting an estimated 95% of the world population—approximately 76,000 pairs—in 1997. San Benito Island has been estimated to support 250–500 pairs and the islets near Guadalupe Island 500–2,500 pairs, but surveys have been infrequent and unstandardized.

During the nonbreeding season (August–February), birds range north to the inshore waters of southern California, generally as far north as Monterey Bay, but exceptional records exist as far north as British Columbia. Pelagic birding trips off of southern California during this time period regularly find hundreds and sometime thousands of birds. It has been estimated that 20,000–30,000 birds may winter off of California in peak years.

Total population was estimated at 157,000 individuals in 2000. Although no trend information is available, massive flocks of the species were documented in the late 1800s off of Baja California, which suggests the species was formerly much more abundant. Studies on Natividad Island have estimated a 13–20% loss in nesting burrows between the 1970s and 1990s. Mortality from cats on Natividad was estimated at approximately 1,000 birds per month, resulting in a projected 4% annual decline in the population.[1,2]

ECOLOGY

Nests colonially between February and August in burrows in sandy soil or in rocky crevice. Females lay a single egg, usually in March or April, with young fledging from July through August. Thought to take 5–6 years to attain breeding age. At sea feeds on fish and squid, and will take some types of chum tossed overboard by boats trying to attract seabirds for birdwatching. The at-sea distribution is largely determined by the presence of warm coastal waters that the species prefers.[2]

THREATS

Greatest current threats are direct nest depredation and adult mortality from introduced cats and dogs. On Natividad Island the monthly mortality from cats was estimated at more than 1,000 birds per month in 1997. Other threats include habitat degradation from introduced rabbits, goats, sheep, and donkeys, and loss of burrow habitat from human development activity. Some birds may be killed by entanglement in increasing gill-net fisheries near some nesting colonies but extent of problem is unclear.[2]

CONSERVATION ACTION

Natividad Island is in the core area of the Vizcaino Biosphere Reserve. The Reserve, in partnership with Island Conservation, established programs to educate residents of Natividad Island about the impacts of introduced mammals on Black-vented Shearwaters. In addition, a program to remove introduced mammals from Natividad has been instituted with goats and sheep removed in 1997 and cats removed by 1999 and most dogs by 2004. San

Benito Islands are not legally protected but such protection, along with management actions to protect the breeding seabirds, is badly needed. Cats no longer occur on San Benito Island and introduced rabbits, goats, and donkeys were removed from the island between 1998 and 2004 by Island Conservation. At Guadalupe Island the species now occurs only on two small offshore islets due to predation by cats and dogs on the main island and soil erosion as a result of heavy grazing by introduced goats.

Monterey Bay, as one coastal area that supports nonbreeding Black-vented Shearwaters, has been designated as a National Marine Sanctuary and is managed by the National Oceanic and Atmospheric Administration. National Marine Sanctuaries generally prohibit oil and gas extraction activities within their boundaries and prohibit certain types of other human activities that may disturb marine life or marine habitats. These regulations should be beneficial to maintaining food supplies and a healthy ecosystem upon which Black-vented Shearwaters depend.[1-4]

CONSERVATION NEEDS

- Implement measures to remove introduced mammalian predators from Guadalupe Island and prevent further introductions on Natividad and San Benito Islands.
- Implement measures to remove introduced goats from Guadalupe Island and prevent further introductions.
- Obtain legal protection for the San Benito and Guadalupe Islands as well as other islands off the Pacific Coast of Baja California.
- Develop and implement surveys, perhaps using radar and acoustic monitoring technologies, to detect and monitor breeding colonies of Black-vented Shearwaters.
- Implement measures to ensure continued protection of known breeding colonies from loss of habitat and human disturbance.
- Develop and implement at-sea surveys to monitor changes in abundance of Black-vented Shearwater.
- Assess impact of gill-net fisheries on mortality of Black-vented Shearwaters.
- Continue efforts to limit amount of plastics, oil, and other pollutants within the marine ecosystem.

References

1. BirdLife International. 2000. *Threatened Birds of the World*. Lynx Editions and BirdLife International, Barcelona, Spain, and Cambridge, UK.

2. Keitt, B.S., B.R. Tershy, and D.A. Croll. 2000. Black-vented Shearwater (*Puffinus opisthomelas*). In *The Birds of North America*, No. 521 (A. Poole and F. Gill, eds.). The Academy of Natural Sciences, Philadelphia, PA, and the American Ornithologists' Union, Washington, DC.

3. National Ocean Service. 2003. National Marine Sanctuaries. http://www.sanctuaries.nos.noaa.gov/welcome.html (accessed 22 May 2003).

4. Tershy, B., B Keitt, and S. Wolf. 2005. Personal communication.

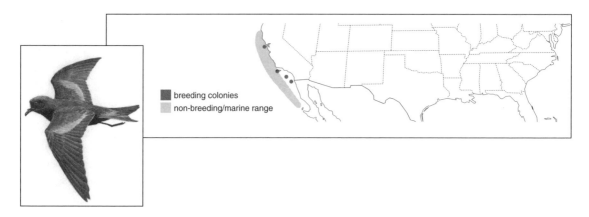

breeding colonies
non-breeding/marine range

ASHY STORM-PETREL (*Oceanodroma homochroa*)

Unlike most other species of storm-petrel throughout the world, this species is a resident within its very limited range in the cool waters off of coastal California, where it breeds on a handful of islands.

crevices in rocky, talus slopes. Diet is not well known but does include small fish, young squid, and crustaceans that are picked up off the ocean surface.[1]

STATUS AND DISTRIBUTION

Breeds at 16 locations (mostly islands) off of California and one island off of Mexico's Baja California. Occurs year-round in marine waters off of California coast, typically within 100 miles of shore. The largest breeding colony is thought to be at South Farallon Island, with at least 2,500 pairs estimated in 2000. Channel Islands National Park is thought to support more than 10% of the world population of the species.

Significant nonbreeding concentrations occur in Monterey Bay, with as many as 10,000 birds reported, and around Farallon Islands.

The species has been poorly surveyed so it has been difficult to assess trends. However, surveys on South Farallon Island analyzed by Point Reyes Bird Observatory indicated a 40% decline in breeding pairs between 1972 and 1992. Also, the species almost certainly had to be more abundant before many of its nesting islands where invaded by rats and other species that are known to cause high nestling mortality and egg depredation in other island nesting seabirds. The population was estimated at approximately 10,000 birds in 1995.[1-3]

ECOLOGY

Breeds on rocky islands and a few mainland peninsulas of coastal California where birds nest in deep

THREATS

Most breeding sites are publicly owned and protected from human intrusion and disturbance. Main current threat is continued depredation from introduced rat, mice, and cat populations and increased large gull populations at many of the breeding sites. Other potential threats include loss of habitat from encroachment of introduced grasses, oil pollution, and ingestion of floating plastics. Half of the oil spills that have occurred in California in the last two decades have occurred near the Farallon Islands.[1,2]

CONSERVATION ACTION

Farallon Islands are owned and managed by the U.S. Fish and Wildlife Service as part of the San Francisco Bay National Wildlife Refuge Complex, while the waters surrounding this important colony are part of the National Oceanic and Atmospheric Administration's (NOAA) Gulf of the Farallons National Marine Sanctuary. Efforts at discouraging gulls from nesting in certain areas using experimental gull exclosures have been ongoing at South Farallon Island.

Most of the Channel Islands are owned and managed by the Channel Islands National Park and the surrounding waters are part of NOAA's Channel Islands National Marine Sanctuary. The National Park Service developed its Anacapa Island Restoraton Project, which aimed to remove all Black Rats from the island to protect nesting seabirds on the island, including Ashy Storm-Petrels. The first application of rodenticide was on East Anacapa in 2001, with application on the remainder of the Anacapa Islands in 2002.

National Marine Sanctuaries generally prohibit oil and gas extraction activities within their boundaries and prohibit certain types of other human activities that may disturb marine life or marine habitats. These regulations should certainly be helpful to maintaining food supplies and a healthy ecosystem upon which Ashy Storm-Petrels depend.

A series of Marine Protected Areas was established near the Channel Islands in 2003 by the California Department of Fish and Game. These Marine Protected Areas provide further regulations on human recreational and fishing activities within the designated areas that may be beneficial to Ashy Storm-Petrel populations.[1-6]

CONSERVATION NEEDS

- Continue efforts to eradicate introduced rats and other invasive species from island nesting colonies.
- Continue efforts to limit amount of plastics, oil, and other pollutants within the marine ecosystem.

- Develop and implement survey methodologies to track the status of Ashy Storm-Petrel populations.
- Ensure that human visitation to island nesting colonies does not negatively impact Ashy Storm-Petrel nesting success and survival.

References

1. Ainley, D. 1995. Ashy Storm-Petrel (*Oceanodroma homochroa*). In *The Birds of North America*, No. 185 (A. Poole and F. Gill, eds.). The Academy of Natural Sciences, Philadelphia, PA, and the American Ornithologists' Union, Washington, DC.

2. Cooper, D.S. 2004. *Important Bird Areas of California*. Audubon California, Pasadena, CA.

3. Buffa, J. 1998. Managing the Farallones. *Point Reyes Bird Observatory Observer* 112.

4. National Ocean Service. 2003. *National Marine Sanctuaries*. http://www.sanctuaries.nos.noaa.gov/welcome .html (accessed 22 May 2003).

5. Faulkner, K.R. 2003. *Legacy of an Oil Spill: Eradicating Rats from Anacapa*. 2003 Department of the Interior Conference on the Environment. http://oepc .doi.gov/conference/abdetails2.cfm?ID=121 (accessed 16 May 2003).

6. State of California. 2003. *Channel Islands MPAs*. http://www.dfg.ca.gov/mrd/channel_islands/ (accessed 15 May 2003).

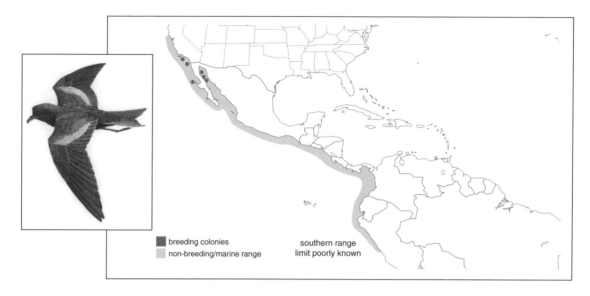

breeding colonies
non-breeding/marine range

southern range
limit poorly known

BLACK STORM-PETREL (*Oceanodroma melania*)

One of a set of Gulf of California/Pacific Baja California seabirds that has been hard-hit by introductions of cats and rats to its offshore nesting islands. Birders in the U.S. know the species primarily from pelagic boat trips off of southern California.

STATUS AND DISTRIBUTION

Known to breed at six locations: three in the Gulf of California (Cardinosa Island and Cardinosita, San Luis Island, and Roca Consag), two off the Pacific coast of Mexico's Baja California (Los Coronado Island and San Benito Island), and one off the coast of southern California (Santa Barbara Island and Sutil Island). Small numbers are suspected to breed at other islands in the region but have not been confirmed. Largest numbers are at the San Benito Islands (actually a collection of three islands) with numbers estimated on the largest island at 580,000 individuals in 1999. Very little information exists on numbers breeding at any locations, but estimates at all other sites are no more than low thousands and for many just a few hundred. Fewer than 400 birds were estimated to breed in the Channel Islands in 1991. In the non-breeding season the bulk of the population moves south to winter at sea off the Pacific coasts of Central American and northern South America but some birds also move north to winter off the coast of central and southern California.

The species has been poorly surveyed so it has been difficult to assess trends. Near Los Coronado Island numbers are thought to have declined since 1980. Historically, the species had to be more abundant before its nesting islands were invaded by cats and rats, which caused them to disappear from many islands. The population was estimated at 2,000,000 birds in 2002.[1–3]

ECOLOGY

The species' ecology is poorly known. Breeds on rocky islands where birds nest in deep crevices in rocky, talus slopes. On San Benito Island, begin arriving at breeding colony in late March with first documented egg laying in June. Females lay one egg, which is thought to hatch in 40–50 days. Young are fed by both parents and fledge 11–12 weeks after hatching. Birds are not thought to begin breeding until five years of age. Diet is not well known but does include small fish, young squid, and crustaceans that are picked up off the ocean surface. Prefers warm waters at all seasons but requirements and distribution are poorly known.[1]

THREATS

Main current threat is continued depredation from introduced rat and cat populations at many of the breeding sites. Oil pollution is considered a serious potential threat for birds wintering off California because of the high oil tanker traffic in the area. Other potential threats include disturbance from nighttime squid fisheries using high-powered lights and con-tamination from pesticides and other toxins.[1-3]

CONSERVATION ACTION

The breeding islands in the Gulf of California are included within the Gulf of California Biosphere Reserve and some have been designated as wildlife preserves. Work has been ongoing at some islands to eradicate introduced predators. A management plan for the Biosphere Reserve developed in 1994 began being implemented in 1999. Island Conser-vation with its partners, the Instituto de Ecología at the Universidad Nacional Autónoma de Mexi-co, Centro de Investigaciones Biológicas del Noroeste, and the Áreas Naturales Protegidas has worked with local communities to rid 23 islands in the breeding range of Black Storm-Petrel of one or more species of introduced mammals. Similar ef-forts are underway on at least seven more islands in the region. Plans are underway to restore Black Storm-Petrels to several islands where introduced mammals have been eradicated.

The International Division of the U.S. Fish and Wildlife Service provided funds to Island Con-servation to develop management plans for 19 of the islands of the Gulf of California Biosphere Re-serve in 1996. With the help of local conservation organizations Grupo Ecologista Antares (GEA) and Niparajá, the Nature Conservancy is working with local Biosphere Reserve staff and local fisher-men to patrol the protected areas and halt illegal fishing—activities that should benefit the ecosys-tem upon which Black Storm-Petrels depend.

The most important breeding colonies in the world, on the San Benito Islands, are not legally protected. Legal protection for the San Benito Is-lands and management actions to protect the breeding seabirds there are badly needed.

Monterey Bay, as one coastal area that sup-ports nonbreeding Black Storm-Petrel, has been designated as a National Marine Sanctuary and is managed by the National Oceanic and Atmos-pheric Administration. National Marine Sanctu-aries generally prohibit oil and gas extraction ac-tivities within their boundaries and prohibit certain types of other human activities that may disturb marine life or marine habitats. These regu-lations should be beneficial to maintaining food supplies and a healthy ecosystem upon which Black Storm-Petrels depend.

Most of the Channel Islands are owned and managed by the Channel Islands National Park and the surrounding waters are part of NOAA's Channel Islands National Marine Sanctuary. Na-tional Marine Sanctuaries generally prohibit oil and gas extraction activities within their bound-aries and prohibit certain types of other human ac-tivities that may disturb marine life or marine habitats. These regulations should certainly be helpful to maintaining food supplies and a healthy ecosystem upon which Black Storm-Petrels de-pend. The California Department of Fish and Game established a series of Marine Protected Ar-eas near the Channel Islands in 2003. These Ma-rine Protected Areas provide further regulations on human recreational and fishing activities with-in the designated areas, which may be beneficial to Black Storm-Petrel populations.[1-11]

CONSERVATION NEEDS

- Continue efforts to eradicate introduced rats and other invasive species from island nesting colonies.
- Obtain legal protection for the San Benito Is-lands and other islands off the Pacific Coast of Baja California.
- Develop and implement surveys, perhaps us-ing constant-effort mistnetting, radar, or acoustic monitoring technologies, to detect and monitor breeding colonies of Black Storm-Petrel.
- Investigate using seabird restoration tech-niques to lure birds to formerly occupied is-lands that are now predator free and protected or to protected areas within existing colony locations.
- Continue efforts to limit amount of plastics, oil, and other pollutants within the marine ecosystem.
- Ensure that human visitation to island nesting colonies does not negatively impact Black Storm-Petrel nesting success and survival.
- Continue efforts to limit amount of pesticides, oil, and other pollutants within the marine ecosystem.

References

1. Ainley, D.G., and W.T. Everett. 2001. Black Storm-Petrel (*Oceanodroma melania*). In *The Birds of North America*, No. 577 (A. Poole and F. Gill, eds.). The Birds of North America, Inc., Philadelphia, PA.

2. Wolf, S.G. 2002. The Relative Status and Con-

servation of Island Breeding Seabirds in California and Northwest Mexico. Unpublished master's thesis, University of California, Santa Cruz.

3. Kushlan J. A., M. J. Steinkamp, K. C. Parsons, J. Capp, M. Acosta Cruz, M. Coulter, I. Davidson, L. Dickson, N. Edelson, R. Elliot, R. M. Erwin, S. Hatch, S. Kress, R. Milko, S. Miller, K. Mills, R. Paul, R. Phillips, J. E. Saliva, B. Sydeman, J. Trapp, J. Wheeler, and K. Wohl. 2002. *Waterbird Conservation for the Americas: The North American Waterbird Conservation Plan*, Version 1. Waterbird Conservation for the Americas. Washington, DC.

4. Case, T., M. Cody, and E. Ezcurra. 2002. *Island Biogeography in the Sea of Cortez*. Oxford University Press, New York, NY.

5. BirdLife International. 2000. *Threatened Birds of the World*. Lynx Editions and BirdLife International, Barcelona, Spain, and Cambridge, UK.

6. Island Conservation. No Date. *Island Conserva-tion's Accomplishments*. http://www.islandconservation .org (accessed 28 January 2004).

7. Ocean Oasis. 2000. *Ocean Oasis—Conservation in the Sea of Cortes*. http://www.oceanoasis.org/conserva tion/study3.html (accessed 28 January 2004).

8. National Ocean Service. 2003. *National Marine Sanctuaries*. http://www.sanctuaries.nos.noaa.gov/welcome .html (accessed 22 May 2003).

9. U.S. Fish and Wildlife Service International Affairs. 1996. *Grants Awarded in 1996*. http://internation al.fws.gov/whp/annex4.html (accessed 3 November 2003).

10. The Nature Conservancy. 2003. *Baja & the Gulf of California*. http://nature.org/wherewework/ northamerica/mexico/work/art8618.html (accessed 3 November 2003).

11. State of California. 2003. *Channel Islands MPAs*. http://www.dfg.ca.gov/mrd/channel_islands/ (accessed 15 May 2003).

breeding colonies
non-breeding/marine range

LEAST STORM-PETREL (*Oceanodroma microsoma*)

A tiny storm-petrel that is most frequently seen by U.S. birders when it periodically appears in large numbers off of southern California, the Least Storm-Petrel is one of a suite of specialized marine species from Mexico's Gulf of California.

STATUS AND DISTRIBUTION

Breeds on islands in Mexico's Gulf of California and Pacific Coast of Baja California, including Archipiélago Salsipuedes and Espíritu Santo Island, and on the San Benito Islands (120,000–150,000 pairs estimated in 1999) off the west coast of Baja California.

In nonbreeding season (August–October) the bulk of the population moves south to winter at sea off the Pacific coasts of Central America and northern South America, but some birds also move north to winter off the coast of central and southern California. In warm-water years larger numbers move north, with thousands occasionally sighted off southern California and, rarely, hundreds even as far north as Monterey Bay.

The species has been poorly surveyed so it has been difficult to assess trends but the species is thought to have experienced a decline. Historically, the species had to be more abundant before its nesting islands were invaded by cats and rats, which are known to have caused them to disappear from many islands. The population was estimated at more than 1,000,000 birds in 2002.[1–7]

ECOLOGY

The species' ecology is poorly known. Breeds on rocky islands where birds nest in crevices in rocks and cliffs but come and go from nesting colonies only at night. Females lay one egg. Probably both parents incubate and feed the young as in other storm-petrels. Diet is not well known, but birds probably feed on small crustaceans and other small marine organisms that are picked up off the ocean surface. Prefers warm waters at all seasons but requirements and distribution are poorly known.[1,2,4,7,8]

THREATS

The greatest current threats are direct nest depredation and adult mortality from introduced rats, cats, and dogs on nesting islands, especially at the San Benito Islands colony. Other threats include habitat degradation from introduced rabbits, goats, sheep, and donkeys, and pollution and overfishing within the marine habitats upon which it depends. There have been major decreases in shrimp and a host of fish stocks in the Gulf of California as a result of overfishing and pollution.[7–12]

CONSERVATION ACTION

The breeding islands in the Gulf of California are included within the Gulf of California Biosphere Reserve and some have been designated as wildlife preserves. Work has been ongoing at some islands to eradicate introduced predators. The San Benito Islands and other Pacific islands off Baja California are not legally protetcted. Cats no longer occur on San Benito Island and introduced rabbits, goats, and donkeys were removed from the island in 1999 by Island Conservation. A management plan for the Gulf of California Biosphere Reserve developed in 1994 began being implemented in 1999. Island Conservation with its partners, the Instituto de Ecología at the Universidad Nacional Autónoma de Mexico, Centro de Investigaciones Biológicas del Noroeste, and the Áreas Naturales Protegidas has worked with local communities to rid islands within the breeding range of Least Storm-Petrel of one or more species of introduced mammals. Similar efforts are underway on at least seven more islands in the region.

The International Division of the U.S. Fish and Wildlife Service provided funds to Island Conservation to develop management plans for 19 of the islands of the Gulf of California Biosphere Reserve in 1996. With the help of local conservation organizations Grupo Ecologista Antares (GEA) and Niparajá, the Nature Conservancy is working with local Biosphere Reserve staff and local fishermen to patrol the protected areas and halt illegal fishing—activities that should benefit the ecosystem upon which Least Storm-Petrels depend.

World Wildlife Fund (WWF) has identified the Gulf of California as one of its focal ecoregions and is working with local partners to protect and restore the ecosystem. In 2003, the Mexican government set aside two more islands, including Espíritu Santo, within the Gulf of California as protected areas through the work of WWF and its partners. In addition WWF and the Scripps Institute of Oceanography have developed a proposal to establish a network of Marine Protected Areas within the Gulf of California that would protect the ecosystems upon which Least Storm-Petrels and other species (like the highly endangered Vaquita, a tiny porpoise) depend.

Monterey Bay, as one coastal area that sometimes supports nonbreeding Least Storm-Petrel, has been designated as a National Marine Sanctuary and is managed by the National Oceanic and Atmospheric Administration. National Marine Sanctuaries generally prohibit oil and gas extraction activities within their boundaries and prohibit certain types of other human activities that may disturb marine life or marine habitats. These regulations should be beneficial to maintaining food supplies and a healthy ecosystem upon which Least Storm-Petrels depend.[1,9–14]

CONSERVATION NEEDS

- Continue efforts to eradicate introduced rats and other invasive species from island nesting colonies.
- Obtain legal protection for the San Benito Islands and other islands off the Pacific Coast of Baja California.
- Develop and implement surveys, perhaps using constant-effort mistnetting, radar, or acoustic monitoring technologies, to detect and monitor breeding colonies of Least Storm-Petrel.
- Investigate using seabird restoration techniques to lure birds to formerly occupied islands that are now predator free and protected or to protected areas within existing colony locations.
- Ensure that human visitation to island nesting colonies does not negatively impact Least Storm-Petrel nesting success and survival.
- Continue efforts to limit amount of pesticides, oil, and other pollutants within the marine ecosystem.
- Develop and implement at-sea surveys to monitor changes in abundance of Least Storm-Petrel.

References

1. Wolf, S.G. 2002. The Relative Status and Conservation of Island Breeding Seabirds in California and Northwest Mexico. Unpublished master's thesis, University of California, Santa Cruz.

2. Howell, S.N.G., and S. Webb. 1995. *A Guide to the Birds of Mexico and Northern Central America*. Oxford University Press, New York, NY.

3. Harrison, P. 1983. *Seabirds: An Identification Guide*. Houghton Mifflin, Boston, MA.

4. CONABIO. 2002. Áreas de Importancia para la Conservación de las Aves (AICAS). http://conabioweb .conabio.gob.mx/aicas/doctos/aicas.html (accessed 28 January 2004).

5. del Hoyo, J., A. Elliott, and J. Sargatal, eds. (1992). *Handbook of the Birds of the World*, Vol. 1. Lynx Edicions, Barcelona, Spain.

6. Mlodinow, S.G., and M. O'Brien. 1996. *America's 100 Most Wanted Birds*. Falcon Press, Helena, MT.

7. Kushlan J. A., M. J. Steinkamp, K. C. Parsons, J. Capp, M. Acosta Cruz, M. Coulter, I. Davidson, L. Dickson, N. Edelson, R. Elliot, R. M. Erwin, S. Hatch, S. Kress, R. Milko, S. Miller, K. Mills, R. Paul, R. Phillips, J. E. Saliva, B. Sydeman, J. Trapp, J. Wheeler, and K. Wohl. 2002. *Waterbird Conservation for the Americas: The North American Waterbird Conservation Plan*, Version 1. Waterbird Conservation for the Americas. Washington, DC.

8. Kaufman, K. 1996. *Lives of North American Birds*. Houghton Mifflin, New York, NY.

9. World Wildlife Fund. 2004. *Gulf of California*. http://www.worldwildlife.org/wildplaces/goc/threats.cfm (accessed 9 June 2004).

10. The Nature Conservancy. 2004. *Baja & The Gulf of California*. http://nature.org/wherewework/ northamerica/mexico/work/art8618.html (accessed 10 June 2004).

11. Island Conservation. No Date. *Island Conservation's Accomplishments*. http://macarthur.ucsc.edu/Accomplishments.htm (accessed 28 January 2004).

12. Ocean Oasis. 2000. *Ocean Oasis—Conservation in the Sea of Cortes*. http://www.islandconservation.org (accessed 28 January 2004).

13. U.S. Fish and Wildlife Service International Affairs. 1996. *Grants Awarded in 1996*. URL:http:// international.fws.gov/whp/annex4.html (accessed 3 November 2003).

14. National Ocean Service. 2003. *National Marine Sanctuaries*. http://www.sanctuaries.nos.noaa.gov/welcome .html (accessed 22 May 2003).

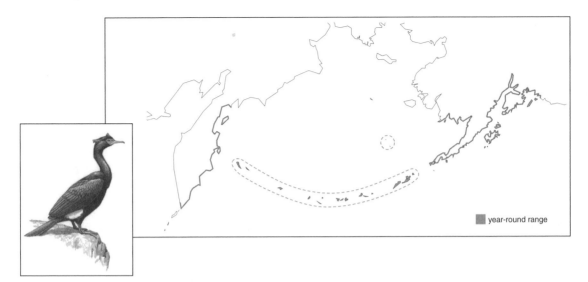

year-round range

RED-FACED CORMORANT (*Phalacrocorax urile*)

Living year-round along remote coasts of Alaska, Russia, and Japan, the Red-faced Cormorant is one of the least-studied birds of North America. The species' restricted range and relatively small estimated population size make it of conservation concern.

STATUS AND DISTRIBUTION

In North America occurs year-round along coast of Alaska peninsula and Aleutian Islands with a few colonies north of Alaska peninsula and in Gulf of Alaska. Range extends outside North America to Russia's Kuril Islands and eastern Kamchatka Peninsula and south to northern Japan. Approximately one-third of world population is estimated to occur in North America. Largest breeding colonies in North America are on the islands of Attu, Agattu, and Nizki-Alaid within the Aleutians. Winters largely within breeding range but may be more widely dispersed and move from areas that become iced-over.

No rangewide monitoring program is in place so it is difficult to estimate trends in overall abundance because colony sizes can vary greatly across years. There has been a shift in abundance from the Pribilofs to the outer Aleutians and some colonies have shown large decreases. For example, the number of breeding Red-faced Cormorants at Nizki-Alaid decreased from 1,200 in 1990 to 42 in 1992. On the other hand, the species has increased at colonies in the Gulf of Alaska since the

1960s. The total world breeding population of the species was estimated at 155,000 in 1993.[1,2]

ECOLOGY

Nests on cliffs on rocky islands and headlands along seacoast, laying 2–3 eggs. Feeds in relatively shallow nearshore coastal waters and generally always found within 20 km from land. Feeds exclusively on fish captured by diving.[1]

THREATS

Numbers were probably reduced on some Aleutian Islands by the introduction of foxes in the 1800s, but many of the islands have now been rid of these predators and breeding colonies have increased at these sites. However, some islands still have introduced fox populations. Throughout most of its range the Red-faced Cormorant comes into little contact with humans but in a few locations (Pribilofs and Komandorski Island) human disturbance could be a potential threat to colonies. Carcasses of 161 Red-faced Cormorants were collected following the Exxon Valdez oil spill and counts of all cormorant species in the oil spill area were lower after the spill. Contamination from oil spills and disturbance or mortality from fisheries activities or other industrial activity are potential threats in the southern portions of the species' North American range. At this time it appears that the areas where the species breeds in highest abundance are far from most human activity that would be a potential threat. Changes in marine ecosystems and the food base from higher ocean remperatures as a result of global warming may become the most difficult and pervasive threat.[1,3]

CONSERVATION ACTION

Most breeding colonies on islands in the Aleutians are part of the U.S. Fish and Wildlife Service's Alaska Maritime National Wildlife Refuge and the islands are managed for wildlife, including Red-faced Cormorants. This includes continuing efforts to eliminate introduced foxes from islands where they remain.

The U.S. Fish and Wildlife Service Division of International Affairs participates in a Russian–U.S. Working Group on Cooperation in the Field of Protection of the Environment and Natural Resources that involves specific joint activities related to the conservation and management of marine birds. These activities have included exchanges of biologists, educators, and managers and development of a joint database of seabird colonies, including Red-faced Cormorant colonies.

The U.S. Coast Guard and the U.S. Environmental Protection Agency with the cooperation of the National Marine Fisheries Service have developed an oil spill response plan to limit the mortality and ecological pollution from oil spills. For Red-faced Cormorants within areas that are susceptible to oil spills and oil pollution the rapid implementation of this plan in the event of an oil spill will be crucial to maintaining healthy populations.[1,2,4,5]

CONSERVATION NEEDS

- Slow production of global warming pollution.
- Study breeding, migration, staging, and wintering ecology of Red-faced Cormorant to determine limiting factors and importance of fisheries and oil pollutants to survival of wintering birds.
- Develop and implement surveys designed to detect changes in abundance and distribution of the species.
- Continue efforts to remove introduced foxes from islands hosting breeding seabirds.
- Maintain continued readiness of oil spill response team and plans.

References

1. Causey, D. 2002. Red-faced Cormorant (*Phalacrocorax urile*). In *The Birds of North America*, No. 617 (A. Poole and F. Gill, eds.). The Birds of North America, Inc., Philadelpia, PA.

2. Dragoo, D.E., G.V. Byrd, and D.B. Irons. 2000. *Breeding Status and Population Trends of Seabirds in Alaska in 1999*. U.S. Fish and Wildlife Service Report AMNWR 2000/02, Alaska Maritime National Wildlife Refuge, Homer, AK.

3. Exxon Valdez Oil Spill Trustee Council. No date. *Oil Spill Facts: Status of Injured Resources: Cormorants (Pelagic, Red-faced, & Double-crested)*. http://www.evostc.state.ak.us/facts/status_cormorants.html (accessed 2 June 2003).

4. U.S. Fish and Wildlife Service International Affairs. 2000. *Protection of Nature and the Organization of Reserves of the U.S.–Russia Agreement on Cooperation in the Field of Protection of the Environment and Natural Resources*, 2000 Working Group Protocol. http://international.fws.gov/laws/russia.html (accessed 2 June 2003).

5. Alaska Regional Response Team . No date. http://www.akrrt.org/index.shtml (accessed 19 November 2005).

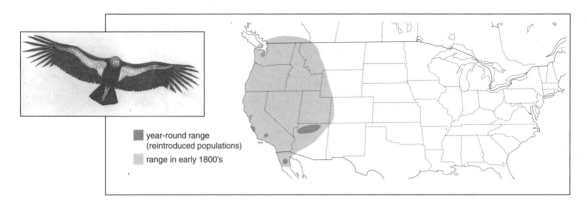

year-round range
(reintroduced populations)

range in early 1800's

CALIFORNIA CONDOR
(*Gymnogyps californianus*)

Seeing this, the largest North American landbird species, in flight over the mountains of central coastal or southern California or Arizona's Grand Canyon is a thrill that can be enjoyed only in recent years and only because of a major concerted effort to bring the species back from the brink of extinction.

STATUS AND DISTRIBUTION

Is one of the rarest birds in the world with the dubious distinction of being one of only about 200 species worldwide with population numbering fewer than 300 individuals. California Condors had already declined before ornithologists began trying to more accurately delimit the range and estimate numbers. In the early 1800s it ranged generally from southern British Columbia south to northern Baja California and west to Montana, Wyoming, Colorado, and Arizona. By the 1950s the species was restricted to southern California. Numbers declined steadily throughout the 1900s, with an estimated 150 birds in 1950, 60 birds in 1968, 30 in 1978, and 21 in 1982. As numbers were continuing to decline steadily, wild birds were taken into captivity along with eggs taken from wild nesting pairs. By 1987 the entire population consisted of 27 birds, all in captivity. Captive breeding efforts were quite successful so that in 1992 two birds were released in southern California. Releases have continued annually with release locations added in 1996 (Arizona), 1997 (Big Sur California), and 2002 (Mexico's Baja California Norte). As of August 2006 there were a total of 289 California Condors alive with 132 of those free-flying

in the wild in four locations: Arizona's Grand Canyon (58 birds), southern California's Sespe Condor Sanctuary and Hopper Mountain National Wildlife Refuge (19 birds), central California's Big Sur area (42 birds), and Mexico's Baja California Norte (13 birds). Wild birds first paired and successfully laid eggs in 2001 in both Arizona (1 pair) and California (2 pairs) but all were unsuccessful. From 2002 to 2006, the number of wild nesting pairs varied annually from 5 to 7 (in Arizona and California). Out of a total of 31 eggs laid by these pairs, six wild fledglings had been produced.[1–5]

ECOLOGY

Females lay their single egg on the ground within a cave or recess on a cliff face or occasionally within a cave-like hole in a giant sequoia tree. Birds generally do not breed until at least six years old. Incubation averages 57 days and young are dependent for about one year. Typically birds breed every other year. Birds forage over very large areas primarily of grassland and open country for carcasses of large mammals. In recent history, foods were primarily dead livestock, including range cattle, sheep, goats, and wild pigs, mule deer, coyotes, and ground squirrels, many of these having been poisoned or shot. Historically known to feed on whale and sea lion carcasses. Birds often ingest small bones and bone fragments, apparently as a calcium source—a behavior that may predispose them to take in lead fragments, which poison the birds. As they soar around, condors observe vultures, ravens, and eagles, which aid them in locating food sources. In the absence of recent human-caused increases in mortality, condors are long-lived—one bird survived in captivity for 45 years and a closely related Andean Condor in the Moscow Zoo was known to have lived to be at least 70 years old.[1]

THREATS

In at least the last 30–40 years the greatest overriding threat to the species appears to be from lead poisoning from lead bullet fragments ingested from unretrieved game carcasses. Many birds released over the last ten years have had to be recaptured and given emergency treatment for lead poisoning (16 cases through September 2000 and more continuing through 2006). At least eight released birds had died from lead poisoning as of 2003. Nine released birds were known to have died from electrocution or collisions with utility lines and other human-made structures as of 2003. A new program was instituted to teach newly released birds to avoid such structures by giving them a mild electric shock when they landed on a dummy pole in their rearing pen. A young bird died from electrocution after striking powerlines in the Big Sur area in 2003. Since that event, the local power company added plastic structures to the lines to make them easier for condors to see and avoid. In the recent past, condors often died from ingesting carcasses poisoned to kill predators like grizzly bears, mountain lions, and wolves, and from shooting either out of curiosity or, during the gold rush days, to obtain their flight feathers to make containers for storing gold dust. Five released birds were known to have been killed by shooting as of 2003. Sadly this includes one of the original wild birds that was taken into captivity in 1987 and that had subsequently been released back into the wild in 2000. Prior to European colonization of the western U.S., native tribes ritually sacrificed condors—a practice that may have become unsustainable as numbers of ceremonial sacrifices increased.[1,6–8]

CONSERVATION ACTION

Concern over the rapid pre-1980s decline of California Condors led to a number of actions and interventions by various conservation organizations and government agencies, primarily the National Audubon Society and the U.S. Fish and Wildlife Service. The Sespe Condor Sanctuary was established in 1947 and now encompasses about 53,000 acres within the Los Padres National Forest of southern California. The adjacent Hopper Mountain National Wildlife Refuge was established in 1974 to provide a buffer for the Sespe Condor Sanctuary. Research, education, and law enforcement activities were stepped up beginning in the 1960s. A California Condor Recovery Team that was formed in 1973 issued a recovery plan in 1975. Unfortunately, these efforts were not successful in reducing the continuing mortality of adults or increasing the low nesting success. Mortality rates have been shown to have been so high that few young birds produced during this time period would have even survived to reproductive age.[1,8]

A new cooperative conservation effort was started in 1980 with the U.S. Fish and Wildlife Service as the lead agency in the program. Partners included the California Department of Fish and Game, National Audubon Society, U.S. Forest Service, Bureau of Land Management, Zoological Society of San Diego, and the Los Angeles Zoo. The California Condor Recovery Team, composed of scientists and researchers from many disciplines, advises the U.S. Fish and Wildlife Service (USFWS) on the recovery efforts. The establishment of a captive population was a priority and a nestling condor was taken into captivity in 1982 to join a bird that had been at the Los Angeles Zoo since 1967. Captive breeding facilities were established at the Los Angeles Zoo and the San Diego Wild Animal Park, where the first successful captive breeding took place in 1988. In 1993 a third captive breeding program was established at the Peregrine Fund in Boise, Idaho and in 2003 a fourth was added at the Oregon Zoo. In recent years, about 25–30 young per year were being produced across the four locations. Pairings for breeding are planned to maintain the highest possible levels of genetic diversity and prevent problems from inbreeding. As of November 2005 there were 134 condors in breeding facilities and 11 in field pens at release sites.[1,3]

As of September 2004 a total of 181 condors had been released since 1992 (see Status and Distribution) at four sites by USFWS, Peregrine Fund, Ventana Wilderness Society, Zoological Society of San Diego, and Mexico's SEMARNAT, with a host of other partner organizations. Of the 181 released birds, 74 had died from a number of different causes. These included lead poisoning, collisions with powerlines, shooting, and predation by coyotes and Golden Eagles. Behavioral modification has begun to alleviate problems with birds associating with human-made structures and utility poles but the numbers of birds with life-threatening blood-lead levels that require emergency treatment continues to be surprisingly high. Lead-free carcasses are provided for the birds in all locations but as the condors foraging behavior becomes more natural they forage over wider areas and find food sources that have been contaminated with lead bullet fragments. During summer 2003 all or most free-flying condors were trapped to be inoculated against the West Nile virus and tested for lead poisoning and at least four required emergency treatment for lead poisoning. Probably the only sustainable solution will be to restrict use of lead shot within condor foraging areas. Several types of nontoxic ammunition are now available for hunting.[1,4,5,7,9,10]

CONSERVATION NEEDS

- Restrict use of lead shot for hunting in condor foraging areas.
- Continue captive breeding programs to maintain supply of birds for release in wild.
- Continue efforts to reduce human contact with captive-reared birds scheduled for release into the wild, including parent-rearing of birds in naturalistic zoo settings designed to mimic the natural environment.
- Continue education and outreach programs to prevent any further hunter mortality or human disturbance problems and to maintain public support of condor conservation programs.

References

1. Snyder, N.F.R., and N.J. Schmitt. 2002. California Condor (*Gymnogyps californianus*). In *The Birds of North America*, No. 610 (A. Poole and F. Gill, eds.). The Birds of North America, Inc., Philadelphia, PA.

2. BirdLife International. 2000. *Threatened Birds of the World*. Lynx Editions and BirdLife International, Barcelona, Spain, and Cambridge, UK.

3. The Peregrine Fund. 2003. *California Condor Fact Sheet*. http:www.peregrinefund.org/press/condor_chick_8_03.html (accessed 20 August 2003).

4. The Peregrine Fund. 2003. *Biologists Confirm California Condor Nestling in Arizona*. http:www.peregrinefund.org/press/condor_chick_8_03.html (accessed 20 August 2003).

5. California Department of Fish and Game. 2003. *California Condor Population Size and Distribution: July 1, 2003*. California Department of Fish and Game, Habitat Conservation Planning Branch. http://www.dfg.ca.gov/hcpb/species/t_e_spp/tebird/Condor%20Pop%20Stat.pdf (accessed 21 August 2003).

6. California Department of Fish and Game. 2006. *California Condor Population Size and Distribution: August 1, 2006*. California Department of Fish and Game, Habitat Conservation Planning Branch. http://www.ventanaws.org/pdf/CondorPopulationReport.pdf (accessed 13 November 2006).

7. U.S. Fish and Wildlife Service. 2003. *California Condor Population History*. Hopper Mountain National Wildlife Refuge Complex. http:hoppermountain.fws.gov/cacondor/Pophistory.html (accessed 21 August 2003).

8. Ventana Wilderness Society. 2003. *Condor Reintroduction Notes from the Field*. http://www.ventanaws.org/fldnotes.htm (accessed 20 August 2003).

9. U.S. Fish and Wildlife Service. 2003. *Milestones in the History of the California Condor*. Hopper Mountain National Wildlife Refuge Complex. http:hoppermountain.fws.gov/cacondor/milestone.html (accessed 21 August 2003).

10. Iñigo-Elias, E.E. 2002. *Bringing the California Condor Back to Mexico*. Cornell Lab of Ornithology, Birds in the Headlines. http://birds.cornell.edu/Birdnews/birdNews_condor_080102.html (accessed 21 August 2003).

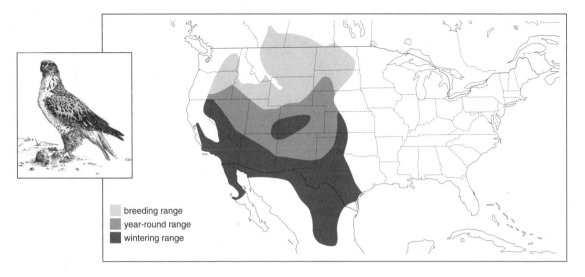

breeding range
year-round range
wintering range

FERRUGINOUS HAWK (*Buteo regalis*)

Like many species of shrubsteppe, grassland, and desert ecosystems of western North America, the Ferruginous Hawk has been greatly impacted by human changes in the landscape related to agriculture, grazing, invasive species, and fire frequency.

STATUS AND DISTRIBUTION

Species breeds from southeastern Alberta, southern Saskatchewan, and tiny portion of southwestern Manitoba south to Nevada, Arizona, and New Mexico. Approximately 80–90% of the breeding range occurs within the U.S. Important breeding sites for the species in the U.S. include Idaho's Snake River Birds of Prey National Conservation Area (55 nests) managed by the Bureau of Land Management, North Dakota's Little Missouri National Grassland and the Horsehead Lake region, Wyoming's Thunder Basin National Grassland, South Dakota's Fort Pierre National Grassland, Colorado's Pawnee National Grassland, Nevada's Great Basin National Park, and Washington's Fitzner-Eberhardt Arid Lands Ecology Reserve. Important breeding sites in Canada include Saskatchewan's Govenlock-Nashlyn-Battle Creek Grasslands Important Bird Area (IBA) (56 nests), Maple Creek Grasslands IBA (36 nests), Mantario Hills IBA (35 nests), Grasslands National Park (23 nests), and the Kindersley-Elna IBA (22 nests); and in Manitoba, the Southwestern Manitoba Mixed-Grass Prairie IBA (40–50 nests).

Birds winter from California east to southern Nebraska and south through Mexico to the state of Guanajuato. Birds occasionally winter within the southern part of breeding range. An estimated 80% of the winter range is thought to lie within the U.S. and the remaining 20% in Mexico. Christmas Bird Count data from the U.S. indicate highest wintering densities in eastern Colorado, western Nebraska, eastern New Mexico and western Texas. Important wintering areas in the U.S. include Colorado's Rocky Mountain Arsenal National Wildlife Refuge, New Mexico's Grulla National Wildlife Refuge, and Texas' Buffalo Lake National Wildlife Refuge and Muleshoe National Wildlife Refuge. Important wintering areas in Mexico include Sonora's El Pinacate y Gran-Desierto de Altar and Sistema de Islas Sierra Madre Occidental IBAs, Chihuahua's Janos-Nuevo Casas Grandes IBA, and Coahuala's Sierra de Arteaga and Pradera de Tokio IBAs.

Breeding Bird Survey data from 1966 to 2005 show a statistically significant increasing trend of approximately 61% (2.5% per year) as do Christmas Bird Count data from 1959 to 1988. Since 1990 the total number of Ferruginous Hawks counted annually on all Christmas Bird Counts together in the U.S. and Mexico has ranged from 634 to 919. An estimated 400–500 birds regularly winter in California but there are no estimates of numbers wintering in other portions of the wintering range. Despite this the species is thought to have declined on the peripheries of its range, and its populations must certainly be reduced from historical levels because of the massive loss and degradation of grassland and shrubland habitat and the extirpation of prairie dogs (its main food source) in many regions. The species is now thought to occupy approximately 50% of its former range in Canada and had apparently disappeared from Manitoba by the 1930s, though by 1982 it had nested in the province again and by 1990 there were more than 50 pairs. Alberta was estimated to have 800–1,000 breeding pairs in 2000 as compared to over 2000 in 1992. In study areas in Saskatchewan and Alberta the number of young produced per nest declined sharply between 1975 and 1995. The total population was estimated at 23,000 individuals in 2004.[1–13]

ECOLOGY

Breeds in grasslands, sagebrush, and other shrubby habitats where it builds its nest of sticks, twigs, and debris in lone trees or shrubs, on cliffs, utility poles, or outcroppings on the ground. In some areas artificial nest platforms have been used readily by the species. Females usually lay 2–4 eggs (more in years of high prey abundance) that are incubated by both sexes for 32–33 days. Males provide most food to females and nestlings, which fledge in 38–50 days. Apparently first breed at two years of age. Not all pairs nest in an area each year. Feeds on small mammals, especially prairie dogs, ground squirrels, and rabbits. In winter, small groups of Ferruginous Hawks often remain near prairie dog towns to feed. After breeding, they can show amazing long distance movements—likely a strategy for locating a source of abundant prey. For example, birds radio tracked from nesting areas in eastern Washington have moved many hundreds of miles into Montana, Alberta, and even as far east as South Dakota in the fall before moving to California, Mexico, or the southern Great Plains to winter.[1,14,15]

THREATS

Loss and degradation of native shortgrass prairie, sagebrush, desert grassland, and other preferred native habitats historically has been, and continues to be, the greatest threat to the species. Much habitat on both the breeding and wintering grounds has been converted to agriculture and housing developments or has been disturbed by oil and mining operations. Approximately 40% of the shortgrass prairie native vegetation is estimated to have been lost across North America and in some states the loss has been much higher (80% in

Texas). Millions of acres of sagebrush have been destroyed for agricultural uses and on millions more sagebrush has been systematically removed. Less than 10% of the 84 million acres of the Great Basin Shrub Steppe ecoregion remains as intact habitat. Oil and gas well construction may be increasing in the region; a 1996 report estimated that 6,000–11,000 new oil and gas wells would be developed in southwestern Wyoming in the ensuing 20 years. Similar problems exist in much of the Mexican wintering range as well. For example, Chihuahuan desert grasslands have been extensively altered through agricultural conversion, grazing, invasive plants, and shrub encroachment. There are few protected areas within the entire Chihuahuan Desert ecoregion.

Populations of prairie dogs have been systematically removed and reduced through both habitat loss and from poisoning; shooting and the use of rodenticides to kill prairie dogs have also increased. From 1980 to 1984 over $6 million dollars of federal funds were spent to poison prairie dogs in a 450,000 acre area stretching across Montana, Wyoming, and South Dakota. Shooting of prairie dogs continues in many states. An estimated 766,000 prairie dogs were shot in South Dakota in 2000 and 300,000 were shot in Nebraska in 1999. Only 2% of the original 250 million acres originally inhabited by prairie dogs continues to support them today. In addition, prairie dog populations in many areas have been decimated by an introduced disease (sylvatic plague—in humans sometimes called the black plague) toward which they have little or no immunity. The use of pesticides across much of the breeding and wintering range of Ferruginous Hawk has led to concerns about potential negative reproductive and physiological effects of accumulated pesticides and other pollutants. Throughout much of the breeding range pesticides are widely used to control grasshoppers on rangeland, although certain areas of public lands with prairie dog colonies have been excluded from pesticide application. In general, however, little is known about whether there are negative population level impacts from pesticides or other contaminants on Ferruginous Hawks.[1,3,12,16–23]

CONSERVATION ACTION

Ferruginous Hawk was assigned a national conservation status of Threatened in Canada and a recovery plan was approved in 1993. The species status has been regularly monitored in Canada and artificial nest platforms have been provided in a number of areas. A coalition of groups, including the Commission for Environmental Cooperation, the Nature Conservancy, Canadian Wildlife Service, Washington Department of Fish and Wildlife, Woodland Park Zoo, Pronatura, and many others, has developed a program to satellite track the movements of Ferruginous Hawks and to educate people about their life history and conservation needs, which they present through the website ferruginoushawk.org.

There has been a surge in conservation activity for Mountain Plover and black-tailed prairie dog in response to concerns about the possibility of federal endangered–threatened listing of both species. Ferruginous Hawk is another key member of this short-grass prairie habitat suite of animals and will benefit from activities targeted toward these species. For example, the Nature Conservancy has initiated a grassland conservation program called Prairie Wings, which hopes to target conservation activities toward key areas across the shortgrass prairie. Along with its other activities, the Rocky Mountain Bird Observatory has a Prairie Partners program that works with private landowners to monitor prairie bird species and provide outreach and habitat management advice for the benefit of prairie birds but within the farm management needs of the landowner. A number of Native American tribes have developed coalitions to develop management plans for the restoration of prairie dog populations and grassland ecosystems on tribal lands.

A multistate conservation plan for black-tailed prairie dog was completed in 2003. It hopes to slow or stop the loss of prairie dog populations through a variety of landowner incentives and regulations. Approximately 8% of shortgrass prairie habitat in the U.S. is under federal government ownership. In 1999 and 2000 the U.S. National Park Service and the U.S. Fish and Wildlife Service banned shooting and poisoning of prairie dogs on national parks and USFWS refuges. Many states have instituted hunting seasons and limits to control the number of prairie dogs being shot. Poisoning and shooting of prairie dogs has been halted on many lands managed by the Bureau of Land Management and National Grasslands managed by the U.S. Forest Service. Such activities should clearly benefit the Ferruginous Hawk. Various research and management activities have taken place on a number of federally owned lands, including National Grasslands where the species occurs. USDA-APHIS has agreed to avoid prairie dog colonies when applying grasshopper control pesticides to grasslands in Montana and Wyoming.

Within the species' wintering range a coalition of groups, including Pronatura Noreste, World Wildlife Fund, and the Nature Conservancy, has targeted the Chihuahuan Desert ecoregion for conservation and in 2002 the group completed a detailed conservation assessment for the region. The assessment includes a portfolio of sites that require protection to meet minimum requirements for conserving the highest priorities species and ecological communities. In 2000, Pronatura Noreste and the Nature Conservancy purchased a 7,000-acre ranch in Mexico's Cuatro Ciénegas Valley that includes desert grasslands.[1,3,11,12,14,15,17,19,21–26]

CONSERVATION NEEDS

- Ensure that management of publicly owned locations currently supporting Ferruginous Hawk continue to maintain habitat conditions beneficial to the species.
- Increase efforts at landowner education and outreach, incentives, and other activities that may increase productivity of Ferruginous Hawk on private lands.
- Increase protection and conservation of remaining native habitat within the wintering range of Ferruginous Hawk.
- Slow or halt declines in prairie dog populations across the species range.
- Restore native grassland ecosystems, including through reintroduction of native mammalian herbivores where possible.
- Work with National Resources Conservation Service in the implementation of Farm Bill conservation incentive programs so that the habitat conditions specified on lands potentially used by Ferruginous Hawk are beneficial to the species.
- Implement a rangewide survey designed to assess overall population status and trends.

References

1. Bechard, M.J., and J.A. Schmutz. 1995. Ferruginous Hawk (*Buteo regalis*). In *The Birds of North America*, No. 172 (A. Poole and F. Gill, eds.). The Academy of Natural Sciences, Philadelphia, PA, and The American Ornithologists' Union, Washington, DC.

2. Sauer, J. R., J. E. Hines, and J. Fallon. 2005. *The*

North American Breeding Bird Survey, Results and Analysis 1966–2005, Version 6.2.2006. USGS Patuxent Wildlife Research Center, Laurel, MD.

3. BirdLife International. 2000. *Threatened Birds of the World*. Lynx Editions and BirdLife International, Barcelona, Spain, and Cambridge, UK.

4. Igl, L. D. 2004. *Bird Checklists of the United States* (Version 12MAY03). Northern Prairie Wildlife Research Center Home Page, Jamestown, ND. http://www.npwrc.usgs.gov/resource/othrdata/chekbird/chekbird.htm (accessed 11 June 2004).

5. National Audubon Society. 2002. *Colorado's Important Bird Areas Program*. http://www.audubon.org/bird/iba/co.html (accessed 11 June 2004).

6. Lahontan Audubon Society. No date. *Nevada Important Bird Areas Program*. http://www.nevadaaudubon.org/Iba/iba.htm (accessed 11 June 2004).

7. Chipley, R.M., G.H. Fenwick, M.J. Parr, and D.N. Pashley. 2003. *The American Bird Conservancy Guide to the 500 Most Important Bird Areas in the United States*. Random House, New York, NY.

8. Bird Studies Canada. 2003. *Important Bird Areas of Canada*. http://www.bsc-eoc.org/iba/IBAsites.html (accessed 24 October 2003).

9. CONABIO. 2002. *Áreas de Importancia para la Conservación de las Aves (AICAS)*. http://conabioweb.conabio.gob.mx/aicas/doctos/aicas.html (accessed 11 June 2004).

10. Hunting, K. No date. *Ferruginous Hawk Species Account*. California Partners in Flight, Point Reyes Bird Observatory. http://www.prbo.org/calpif/htmldocs/species/grassland/fehaacct.html (accessed 14 June 2004).

11. Taylor, B.N. 2003. *Population Estimates and a Survey Protocol for Ferruginous Hawks in Alberta*. Alberta Sustainable Resource Development, Fish and Wildlife Division, Alberta Species at Risk Report No. 70, Edmonton, AB.

12. Houston, C.S., and J.K. Shmutz. 1999. Changes in Bird Populations on Canadian Grasslands. Pages 87–94 in *Ecology and Conservation of Grassland Birds of the Western Hemisphere* (P.D. Vickery and J.R. Herkert, eds.). Studies in Avian Biology No. 19, Cooper Ornithological Society, Camarillo, CA.

13. Rich, T. D., C. Beardmore, H. Berlanga, P. Blancher, M. Bradstreet, G. Butcher, D. Demarest, E. Dunn, C. Hunter, E. Inigo-Elias, J. Kennedy, A. Martell, A. Panjabi, D. Pashley, K. Rosenberg, C. Rustay, S. Wendt, and T. Will. 2004. *Partners in Flight North American Landbird Conservation Plan*. Cornell Lab of Ornithology, Ithaca, NY.

14. Woodland Park Zoo. 2004. *Ferruginous Hawk Field Study*. http://www.zoo.org/educate/hawks.html (accessed 14 June 2004).

15. FerruginousHawk.org. 2004. *Tri-National Migration Study*. http://www.ferruginoushawk.org/research/research.html (accessed 14 June 2004).

16. Ricketts, T.H., E. Dinerstein, D.M. Olson, C.J. Loucks, et al. 1999. *Terrestrial Ecoregions of North America: A Conservation Assessment*. Island Press, Washington, DC. 485 pp.

17. Gauthier, D.A., A. Lafon, T. Tombs, J. Hoth, and E. Wilken. 2003. *Grasslands: Toward a North American Conservation Strategy*. Canadian Plains Research Center, University of Regina, Regina, Saskatchewan, and Commission for Environmental Cooperation, Montreal, QC, Canada. 99 pp.

18. Vickery, P.D., P.B. Tubaro, J. M. Cardoso da Silva, B.G. Peterjohn, J.R. Herkert, and R.B. Cavalcanti. 1999. Conservation of Grassland Birds in the Western Hemisphere. Pages 2–26 in *Ecology and Conservation of Grassland Birds of the Western Hemisphere* (P.D. Vickery and J.R. Herkert, eds.). Studies in Avian Biology No. 19, Cooper Ornithological Society, Camarillo, CA.

19. Manzano-Fischer, P., R. List, and G. Ceballos. 1999. Grassland Birds in Prairie dog Towns in Northwestern Chihuahua, Mexico. Pages 263–271 in *Ecology and Conservation of Grassland Birds of the Western Hemisphere* (P.D. Vickery and J.R. Herkert, eds.). Studies in Avian Biology No. 19, Cooper Ornithological Society, Camarillo, CA.

20. Roemer, D.M., and S.C. Forrest. 1996. Prairie Dog Poisoning in Northern Great Plains: An Analysis of Programs and Policies. *Environmental Management* 20:349–359.

21. Predator Conservation Alliance. 2001. *Restoring the Prairie Dog Ecosystem of the Great Plains*. Predator Conservation Alliance, Bozeman, MT.

22. Pronatura Noreste, the Nature Conservancy, and the World Wildlife Fund. 2004. *Ecoregional Conservation Assessment of the Chihuahuan Desert*, 2nd ed. www.conserveonline.org.

23. The Nature Conservancy. 2004. *Chihuahuan Desert*. http://nature.org/wherewework/northamerica/mexico/work/art8620.html (accessed 29 January 2004).

24. Schmutz, J.K., et al., 1994. *National Recovery Plan for the Ferruginous Hawk*. Report No. 11. Recovery of Nationally Endangered Wildlife Committee: Ottawa. 35 pp.

25. Miller, B., C. Wemmer, D. Biggins, and R. Reading. 1990. A Proposal to Conserve Black-footed Ferrets and the Prairie Dog Ecosystem. *Environmental Management* 14:763–769.

26. Miller, B., G. Ceballos, and R.P. Reading. 1994. The Prairie Dog and Biotic Diversity. *Conservation Biology* 8:677–681.

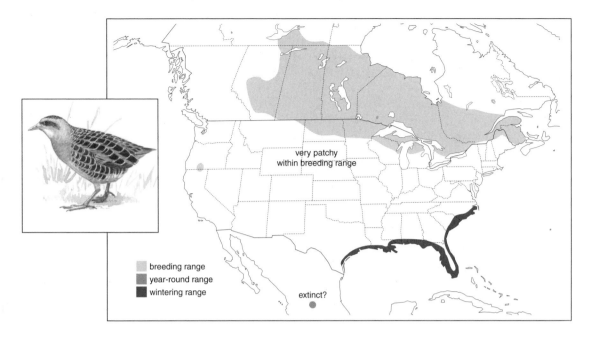

breeding range
year-round range
wintering range

very patchy
within breeding range

extinct?

YELLOW RAIL (*Coturnicops noveboracensis*)

A mysterious and little-studied species, even the breeding range of the Yellow Rail remains imperfectly known, though the species was first described more than 200 years ago.

STATUS AND DISTRIBUTION

Breeding range extends from southern Northwest Territories and Alberta east to southern Quebec and New Brunswick and south to northern Maine, Michigan, Wisconsin, Minnesota, North Dakota, and northeastern Montana. Within this range the species is patchily distributed but there has never been a systematic attempt to map its distribution. Approximately 90–95% of the species' breeding range occurs within Canada. An isolated population occurs in southcentral Oregon and an isolated subspecies that occurred in marshes near Mexico City may now be extinct. Birds winter in coastal marshes from North Carolina south to Florida and along Gulf Coast to Texas.

Important sites for the species in Canada include Manitoba's Douglas Marsh Important Bird Area (IBA) (estimated 500 pairs), New Brunswick's Lower St. John River IBA (at least 100 birds), and Ontario's Severn River Coastline IBA. Important breeding sites in the United States include Oregon's Klamath Marsh National Wildlife Refuge (NWR) (up to 65 birds heard during breeding season), North Dakota's Horsehead Lake, Minnesota's Neal Waterfowl Management Area (51 calling birds in 2003) and Rice Lake NWR, and Michigan's Seney NWR. Among many important wintering areas are Mississippi Sandhill Crane NWR, Grand Bay NWR in Mississippi and Alabama, Florida's Apalachicola NF, and Texas's Big Boggy NWR, Brazoria NWR, San Bernard NWR, and Anahuac NWR.

The species is not detected in sufficient numbers on Breeding Bird Survey routes or Christmas Bird Counts for analysis of trends. Clearly, massive amounts of the wetland habitats used by the species in migration and for breeding and wintering have been lost over the last 150 years, which would certainly have caused a decrease in populations. On the other hand, at the few sites where regular surveys have taken place the abundance of calling males can vary greatly from year-to-year and few banded birds are recaptured at the same locations in years following banding. The species' total population has been estimated at 10,000 to 25,000 individuals.[1–4]

ECOLOGY

In breeding season birds are typically found in wet meadows or brackish high marshes dominated by sedges and fine-stemmed grasses, but there has been limited research on the species' habitat preferences or needs. Such habitats are often kept open from encroaching shrubs through natural fire regimes. Nests are woven into sedges and grasses with an overhanging cover and are placed on or close to the ground. Presumably such nests would be very susceptible to increases in water levels from flooding or water management. Females lay 5–10 eggs that hatch in 17–18 days. Only females are thought to incubate. Young leave nest with the female within two days after hatching and are fed by the female for up to three weeks. Migration behavior is very poorly known but regularity of birds killed at communication towers at night demonstrates that the species migrates nocturnally. In winter range, occurs in drier portions of coastal saltmarshes, coastal prairies, and wet pine savannas, as well as in ricefields in coastal Louisiana and Texas.[1]

THREATS

Loss of breeding, wintering, and migratory stopover habitat from drainage and filling of wetlands for agriculture, hydroelectric projects, and development is major problem. More than 2.2 million acres of boreal wetlands in Canada have been lost due to hydroelectric projects. An estimated 40% of wetlands in the prairie region of Canada have been lost to agriculture. In Quebec, 40% of coastal marshlands along the St. Lawrence River were lost to agriculture between 1950 and 1978. More than 50% of wetlands in the continental U.S. have been lost since the 1700s. For example, the states of Minnesota, Michigan, and Wisconsin, which may harbor the bulk of the U.S. breeding population of Yellow Rail, have each lost between 2.5 million and 7.5 million acres of wetland habitat since European settlement. Changes in hydrology, fire frequency, siltation, and pollution from mining and logging may be affecting the species' rather specialized wetland habitats in some portions of its northern Canadian breeding range, but this has received little attention. Acidification of wetlands in the eastern portion of the breeding range from acid precipitation as a result of industrial air pollution in the eastern U.S. may have decreased availability of calcium-rich invertebrates crucial to egg production and chick rearing. In the upper Midwest, lack of protections or restoration activity for the rim of wet meadow habitats around protected lakes, ponds, and marshes, has resulted in a decrease of available Yellow Rail habitat. Modeling of current global warming trends predicts that much wetland habitat within the species breeding range will dry up and be lost over the next century.

Loss of habitat has also been severe within the species' wintering range. Florida and Texas have each lost at least 7.5 million acres of wetlands and Louisiana between 2.5 and 7.5 million acres over the last 200 years. In Louisiana and Texas coastal wetlands are continuing to be lost to erosion and subsequent saltwater intrusion. The Gulf coastal prairies and pine savannas where the species also winters have also been lost or degraded over vast regions. The Gulf coastal prairies were eliminated from Louisiana and only 1% of this habitat in Texas is now considered pristine. Similarly, longleaf pine ecosystems once occupied an estimated 60–90 million acres of the southeast U.S. but have been reduced to less than 3 million acres and are continuing to decline from loss of longleaf forests on private lands. Only about 3% (90,000 acres) is considered to still be in natural condition. Clearly, any activities that result in loss or degradation of habitat, including through alteration of water levels, destruction of buffer habitat, spraying of pesticides, ditching, fire suppression, plantation forestry, accumulation of contaminants, grazing, or spread of invasive species like phragmites, are continuing threats to the species. Sea level rise with global warming may become the most pervasive and difficult threat on the species' wintering grounds.[1,5–11]

CONSERVATION ACTION

While little direct conservation activity has focused on Yellow Rail, wetland preservation and restoration activities have been ongoing in a number of regions where the species occurs and which will likely provide benefits. A Community Conservation Plan for the Douglas Marsh IBA in Manitoba, which hosts the largest known concentration of Yellow Rail in the world, was completed in 2001 with specific recommendations to be carried out by members of a Douglas Marsh Working Group. Yellow Rail is listed as a high-priority species in Partners in Flight's Bird Conservation Plans for the Northern Mixed-grass Prairie and the Northern Tallgrass Prairie, both areas that encompass portions of the breeding range of the species. Both plans provide suggestions for maintaining wet sedge meadow habitat for Yellow Rail, including mowing or burning during dry years, to prevent the growth of cattails and woody vegetation.

In Canada, the Canadian Boreal Initiative and a broad coalition of conservation organizations, industry, and First Nations have announced the Boreal Forest Conservation Framework—a new national approach to conservation of habitats within the boreal ecoregion. The Framework calls for the establishment of large, interconnected, protected areas covering at least half of the boreal region and application of cutting-edge sustainable development practices on the lands that are developed. Some progress has been made with the establishment of protected areas, including the protection of 625,000 acres in Quebec since 2000.

The Boreal Songbird Initiative has spearheaded work by the Boreal Songbird Network—a coalition of international conservation groups—to reach the goals of the Boreal Forest Conservation Framework. This work has included outreach activities to increase awareness of the boreal region and the threats it faces. For example, the National Wildlife Federation and National Audubon Society have both conducted letter-writing campaigns asking large retail catalog companies to use recycled paper instead of paper made from virgin boreal forest. The Natural Resources Defense Council has designated the wetlands and forest of the eastern Lake Winnipeg area along the Ontario–Manitoba border as one of its twelve "Biogems" and is working to ensure that conservation plans developed by local indigenous peoples are not threatened by hydropower and other industrial development.

Montana Partners for Fish and Wildlife is working to secure perpetual grassland easements in the Upper Missouri Coteau, where Yellow Rail occurs, with the hope of restoring 300,000 acres of grasslands on private and tribal lands. The group has spent $3.4 million over 13 years on projects with over 230 private landowners to protect, restore, or enhance wetland and grassland habitat primarily for increasing waterfowl production but often also benefiting Yellow Rail and other wetland and grassland species.

Coastal wetland habitat restoration efforts within the wintering range of Yellow Rail should be beneficial to the species, though there are no known habitat initiatives focused on the species. The Coastal America Partnership, a coalition of federal agencies, state and local governments, and private organizations, identifies and implements local wetland restoration and protection projects throughout the U.S. The Partnership had initiated more than 500 projects impacting hundreds of thousands of acres of wetland habitat as of 2002. The North Carolina Coastal Federation is a private organization working to protect coastal ecosystems in that state. The group has initiated a number of projects, for example, the $1.2 million acquisition of nearly 2,000 acres along the North River, including 821 acres of coastal marsh.

NOAA's Fisheries Restoration Center Program and the Louisiana Department of Natural Resources through the Coastal Wetlands Planning, Protection, and Restoration Act have initiated projects benefiting 100,000 acres of coastal wetlands along Louisiana's coast within the wintering range of Yellow Rail at a cost of $120 million. Another example is the Texas Prairie Wetlands Project that was created by U.S. Fish and Wildlife Service, Texas Parks and Wildlife Department, USDA's Natural Resources Conservation Service, and Ducks Unlimited to provide technical assistance and financial incentives to private landowners for improving or restoring wetland habitats along the Gulf Coast. Through 2001, 299,000 acres of wetland projects in Texas had been completed or were under construction for more than 40 landowners.[1,7,8,12–20]

CONSERVATION NEEDS

- Slow production of global warming pollution.
- Within the breeding range of Yellow Rail implement broad, landscape scale forest management plans that maintain boreal wetlands and the forests bordering them.
- Increase the number of protected areas through national parks in Canada's boreal forest, including the implementation of proposed protections in the eastern Lake Winnipeg area along the Ontario–Manitoba border.
- Implement the Boreal Forest Conservation Framework, which calls for protection of 50% of Canada's boreal region and adoption of sustainable development practices in areas that are developed.
- Ensure that management of locations currently supporting Yellow Rail continues to maintain water levels and habitat conditions beneficial to the species.
- Increase acreage of coastal wetland habitat within the wintering range of Yellow Rail that

is managed to attain conditions beneficial to the species, including marsh restoration with special attention to "high" marsh habitat.

- Decrease acreage of wetland habitat degraded by erosion, pollution, invasive species, pesticides, and other factors.
- Decrease rates of acid deposition from air pollution, especially from sources impacting eastern portion of breeding range of Yellow Rail.
- Develop baseline inventory of Yellow Rail breeding and wintering populations and habitat needs on breeding and wintering grounds.

References

1. Bookhout, T.A. 1995. Yellow Rail (*Coturnicops noveboracensis*). In *The Birds of North America*, No. 139 (A. Poole and F. Gill, eds.). The Academy of Natural Sciences, Philadelphia, PA, and the American Ornithologists' Union, Washington, DC.

2. IBA Canada. 2004. *Important Bird Areas of Canada*. http://www.ibacanada.com/ (accessed 30 January 2004.)

3. Chipley, R.M., G.H. Fenwick, M.J. Parr, and D.N. Pashley. 2003. *The American Bird Conservancy Guide to the 500 Most Important Bird Areas in the United States*. Random House, New York, NY.

4. Wetlands International. 2002. *Waterbird Population Estimates*, 3rd ed. WetlandsInternational Global Series No. 12, Wageningen, The Netherlands.

5. Stein, B.A., L.S. Kutner, and J.S. Adams. 2000. *Precious Heritage: The Status of Biodiversity in the United States*. Oxford University Press, New York, NY. 399 pp.

6. Ricketts, T.H., E. Dinerstein, D.M. Olson, C.J. Loucks, et al. 1999. *Terrestrial Ecoregions of North America: A Conservation Assessment*. Island Press, Washington, DC. 485 pp.

7. Lindgren, C. 2001. *Community Conservation Plan for the Douglas Marsh Important Bird Area*. Manitoba IBA Program, Stonewall, MB.

8. Southwell, D.K. 2002. *Conservation Assessment for Yellow Rail* (Coturnicops noveboracensis). USDA Forest Service, Eastern Region, Escanaba, MI.

9. Sub-committee on Boreal Forest of the Standing Senate Committee on Agriculture and Forestry. 1999.

Competing Realities: The Boreal Forest at Risk. Government of Canada, Ottawa. http://www.parl.gc.ca/36/1/parlbus/commbus/senate/com-e/BORE-E/rep-e/rep09jun99-e.htm (accessed 24 June 2003).

10. Canadian Boreal Initiative. 2003. *The Boreal Forest at Risk: A Progress Report*. Canadian Boreal Initiative, Ottawa, ON.

11. Environmental Protection Agency. 2002. *Acid Rain*. http://www.epa.gov/airmarkets/acidrain/ (accessed 14 July 2003).

12. Fitzgerald, J. A., D. N. Pashley, S. J. Lewis, and B. Pardo. 1998. *Partners in Flight Bird Conservation Plan for the Northern Tallgrass Prairie (Physiographic Area 40)*. Missouri Department of Conservation, Jefferson City, MO.

13. Fitzgerald, J. A., D. N. Pashley, and B. Pardo. 1999. *Partners in Flight Bird Conservation Plan for the Northern Mixed-grass Prairie (Physiographic Area 37)*. Missouri Department of Conservation, Jefferson City, MO.

14. Montana Partners for Fish and Wildlife. No date. *Upper Missouri Coteau Focus Area, Conservation Strategies*. http://montanapartners.fws.gov/mt3f2.htm (accessed 22 January 2004).

15. Hunter, W.C., L. Peoples, and J. A. Collazo. 2001. *South Atlantic Plain Partners in Flight Bird Conservation Plan*. American Bird Conservancy, The Plains, VA. 158 pp.

16. Coastal America. 2002. *Coastal America: A Partnership for Action*. http://www.coastalamerica.gov (accessed 3 September 2003).

17. North Carolina Coastal Federation. No date. *Restoration and Protection of Key Coastal Habitats*. http://www.nccoast.org/skrestore.htm (accessed 3 September 2003).

18. NOAA. 2003. *About the CWPPRA*. http://www.nmfs.noaa.gov/habitat/restoration/projects_programs/CWPPRA/about.html (accessed 3 September 2003).

19. Texas Environmental Profiles. Undated. *Federal and State Nonregulatory Conservation Programs*. www.texasep.org/html/wld/wld_6hcp_nonreg.html (accessed 8 April 2003).

20. Boreal Songbird Initiative. 2005. http:www.borealbirds.org.

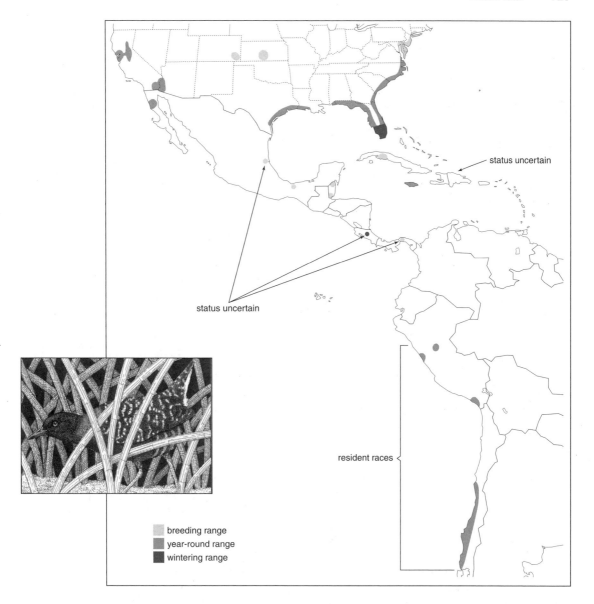

status uncertain

status uncertain

resident races

breeding range
year-round range
wintering range

BLACK RAIL (*Laterallus jamaicensis*)

One of the most secretive and little-known members of the rail family, the Black Rail has an unusually disjunct distribution, occurring in pockets of habitat from the U.S. south to Argentina, but throughout much of the U.S. range it is a characteristic species of large saltmarsh complexes.

STATUS AND DISTRIBUTION

Breeding range extends along the eastern coast of U.S. from Connecticut and New York (rarely) south to Florida and across Gulf Coast to Alabama, then with a gap until the southern Texas

coast. Birds winter from North Carolina south to Florida and across the Gulf Coast to Texas and perhaps at least occasionally in the Greater Antilles, Mexico, and Central America. There are a few summer records of birds in the interior of the eastern U.S., especially in the Midwest, but breeding has rarely been confirmed in the last 50 years. Isolated resident populations occur around California's San Francisco Bay (and at a few inland sites in that state) and along portions of the Lower Colorado River in California and Arizona. South of the U.S., isolated populations are known from Cuba, Jamaica, Mexico, Belize, Costa Rica, Panama, Peru, Chile, and Argentina. Concentrations of U.S. east coast population are thought to occur in Chesapeake Bay, in North Carolina, and along the St. John's River in Florida.

Important sites for the species include the St. Johns National Wildlife Refuge (NWR) in Florida, which is thought to support the largest population of Black Rails in that state; also in Florida, Steinhatchee State Wildlife Area (SWA) and Weekiwatchee SWA; Cedar Island NWR in North Carolina—thought to support the largest population in that state; Blackwater NWR and Fishing Bay Wildlife Management Area in Maryland; San Pablo Bay Wetlands Important Bird Areas in California, which may support 50% of the state's Black Rails; Arkansas River marshes in southeastern Colorado (as many as 74 calling birds in recent years), and Mittry Lake Wildlife Management Area in Arizona.

The species is not detected on enough Breeding Bird Survey routes or Christmas Bird Counts for analysis of trends. However, Black Rail populations are thought to have severely declined in the eastern U.S. and Midwest between the 1920s and 1970s because of the draining of wetlands prior to establishment of wetland regulations. Similarly, Black Rail numbers are thought to have drastically declined as a result of the loss of 95% of tidal marshes in San Francisco Bay by 1979. The population along the Lower Colorado River declined by 30% from 1973 to 1989. The population of Black Rail in California and Arizona is estimated at less than 10,000 individuals. The remainder of the global population is estimated to be between 25,000 and 100,000 individuals. The highest count ever documented within the eastern U.S. population was of approximately 100 birds at a site in Maryland in 1954.[1-11]

ECOLOGY

Black Rails have proved difficult to study because of their secretive habits and the inaccessibility of their habitat. Along the Atlantic and Gulf Coast breeding range, the species occurs along the upper, drier portions of saltmarshes that are only infrequently covered by high tides. Prefers areas with cordgrass or other rather fine-stemmed grasses or rushes usually in areas with a mix of small pools. In its California range it will occupy saltmarshes that flood more frequently than in the eastern coastal portion of range, but usually only if there is adja-

cent open, upland habitat to which birds can retreat safely during high tides; birds here also prefer the higher or more inland sections of the marsh. Birds may be area-sensitive as they seem to occur most consistently and in highest densities in the very largest of saltmarsh sites. Inland sites are usually wet meadows or marshes characterized by having fine-stemmed grasses, sedges, and/or rushes occurring in areas of shallow water with stable water levels. Nests are built in thicker clumps of vegetation just above ground or water. Females usually lay 6–9 eggs, though, on average, California Black Rails lay fewer eggs than Eastern Black Rails. Limited studies of the incubation period indicate a range of 17–20 days. Both sexes incubate the eggs. Birds are known to migrate from northern portions of east coast range to winter along entire Gulf Coast, Cuba, and possibly in parts of Mexico or Central America.[1]

THREATS

Loss of habitat from drainage and filling of wetlands for agriculture and development is a major problem. More than 50% of wetlands in the continental U.S. have been lost since the 1700s. For example, Florida is estimated to have lost 3.7 million hectares of wetland habitats since European settlement, representing 46% of the state's original wetlands, and California has lost 91% of its wetland habitats. All but one state within the U.S. range of Black Rail has lost a minimum of 25–50% of total wetland habitat. Apparently, most of the inland breeding population of the Midwest U.S. has been extirpated, presumably through the massive loss of wetlands to agriculture in that area. In Louisiana and Texas coastal wetlands are being lost to erosion and subsequent saltwater intrusion. Many estuarine systems within the range of the Black Rail are also showing degrading environmental conditions. For example, the percentage of the Delaware Estuary that tested above EPA ecological limits for metal contaminants increased from 5 to 22% from 1990–93 to 1997. Similarly, the percentage of the Chesapeake Bay that tested above EPA ecological limits for organic contaminants increased from 2 to 34% from 1990–93 to 1997. Along the Lower Colorado River, Black Rail habitat is threatened by water diversions, flood control projects, and invasive plant and animal species. The loss of the higher, more inland portions of coastal saltmarshes and any adjoining grassland buffer is thought to have been a factor in causing disappearance of Black Rails from many areas. Similarly, in the Midwest where the species used wet prairie meadows, often the wet meadow surrounding ponds and marshes is not protected or preserved, so there is little available Black Rail habitat. Clearly, any activities that result in loss or degradation of habitat, including through alteration of water levels, destruction of buffer habitat, spraying of pesticides, ditching, accumulation of contaminants, grazing, or spread of invasive species like phragmites, are continuing threats to the species. Sea level rise with global warming may become the most pervasive and difficult threat to the species and loss of saltmarsh habitat to sea level rise has already become a problem in some areas of the northeast U.S.[1,6,11–14]

CONSERVATION ACTION

Partners in Flight Bird Conservation Plans that have been completed for eastern U.S. physiographic regions have identified Black Rail and its associated suite of saltmarsh bird species as a high priority and have provided recommendations for management, research, and monitoring. Ideally, all sites where the species currently occurs would be managed to maintain proper habitat and water levels for the species. At National Wildlife Refuges and state-owned Wildlife Management Areas this could involve changes in timing of management of water levels to maintain sufficient high marsh habitat.

Coastal wetland habitat restoration efforts within the range of Black Rail should be beneficial to the species, though there are no known habitat initiatives focused on the species. For example, a major effort has been initiated in San Francisco Bay to restore tidal wetlands. Audubon's San Francisco Bay Campaign has proposed to restore over 100,000 acres of wetland habitat in the area over the next 20 years. A preliminary agreement with Cargill, Inc., would result in the public acquisition of 16,500 acres of salt ponds for $100 million. The ponds would eventually be restored to tidal wetlands. In 2003, the California State Coastal Conservancy, U.S. Army Corps of Engineers, and California Department of Fish and Game were proposing a habitat restoration project for the 9,460-acre Napa River Salt Marsh within the northern section of San Francisco Bay.

The Coastal America Partnership, a coalition of federal agencies, state and local governments, and private organizations, identifies and implements local wetland restoration and protection projects throughout the U.S. The Partnership had initiated more than 500 projects impacting hundreds of thousands of acres of wetland habitat as of 2002. In 2003, for example, the coalition awarded funds for the creation of 570 acres of tidal wetland at Poplar Island in Chesapeake Bay.

The North Carolina Coastal Federation is a private organization working to protect coastal ecosystems in that state. The group has initiated a number of projects, for example, the $1.2 million acquisition of nearly 2,000 acres along the North River, including 821 acres of coastal marsh.

NOAA's Fisheries Restoration Center Program and the Louisiana Department of Natural Resources, through the Coastal Wetlands Planning, Protection, and Restoration Act, have initiated projects benefiting 100,000 acres of coastal wetlands along Louisiana's coast within the wintering range of Black Rail at a cost of $120 million. Another example is the Texas Prairie Wetlands Project that was created by U.S. Fish and Wildlife Service, Texas Parks and Wildlife Department, USDA's Natural Resources Conservation Service, and Ducks Unlimited to provide technical assistance and financial incentives to private landowners for improving or restoring wetland habitats along the Gulf Coast. Through 2001, 299,000 acres of wetland projects in Texas had been completed or were under construction for more than 40 landowners.[11,15–22]

CONSERVATION NEEDS

- Slow production of global warming pollution.
- Ensure that management of locations currently supporting Black Rails continues to maintain water levels and habitat conditions beneficial to the species.
- Increase acreage of wetland habitat within the range of Black Rail that is managed to attain conditions beneficial to the species, including marsh restoration with special attention to "high" marsh habitat.
- In the Midwest, restore wet meadow habitats around ponds and marshes and develop clusters of wet prairie restoration sites.
- Decrease acreage of wetland habitat degraded by erosion, pollution, invasive species, pesticides, and other factors.

- Implement a rangewide survey designed to assess overall population status and trends.

References

1. Eddleman, W.R. , R.E. Flores, and M.L. Legare. 1994. Black Rail (*Laterallus jamaicensis*). In *The Birds of North America*, No. 123 (A. Poole and F. Gill, eds.). The Academy of Natural Sciences, Philadelphia, PA, and the American Ornithologists' Union, Washington, DC.

2. BirdLife International. 2000. *Threatened Birds of the World*. Lynx Editions and BirdLife International, Barcelona, Spain, and Cambridge, UK.

3. Taylor, B. 1998. *A Guide to the Rails, Crakes, Gallinules, and Coots of the World*. Yale University Press, New Haven, CT, and London, UK. 600 pp.

4. Pranty, B. 2002. The Important Bird Areas of Florida. Unpublished manuscript downloaded from website 9 April 2003.http://www.audubon.org/bird/iba/florida/

5. Audubon North Carolina. *North Carolina's Important Bird Areas*. http://www.ncaudubon.org/IBA1.htm (accessed 3 September 2003).

6. Davidson, L.M. 1992. Black Rail *Laterallus jamaicensis*. Pages 119–134 in *Migratory Nongame Birds of Management Concern in the Northeast* (K.J. Schneider and D.M. Pence, eds.). U.S. Dept. Interior, Fish and Wildlife Service, Newton Corner, MA. 400 pp.

7. Audubon Maryland. 2002. *Important Bird Areas*. http://www.audubon.org/chapter/md/md/conservation/iba/IBA_Program_Overview.htm (accessed 3 September 2003).

8. Cooper, D. 2001. Important bird areas of California. Unpublished manuscript available from Audubon California, 6042 Monte Vista St., Los Angeles, CA 90042.

9. Arizona Bureau of Land Management. 2002. *Mittry Lake*. http://azwww.az.blm.gov/yfo/mittry.html (accessed 29 August 2003).

10. Delany, S., and D. Scott. 2002. *Waterbird Population Estimates*, 3rd ed. Wetlands International Global Series No. 12, Wageningen, The Netherlands.

11. Russell, B. 2004. Personal communication.

12. Stein, B.A., L.S. Kutner, and J.S. Adams. 2000. *Precious Heritage: The Status of Biodiversity in the United States*. Oxford University Press, New York, NY. 399 pp.

13. Coachella Valley Association of Governments. No date. *Coachella Valley Multiple Species Habitat Conservation Plan: California Black Rail*. http://www.co.riverside.ca.us/CVAG/mshcp/sp_65.htm (accessed 27 August 2003).

14. U.S. EPA. 2002. *Mid-Atlantic Integrated Assessment 1997–98 Summary Report*, EPA/620/R-02/003. U.S. Environmental Protection Agency, Atlantic Ecology Division, Narragansett, RI. 115 pp.

15. Rosenberg, K.V., and J.V. Wells. 2003. *Conservation Priorities for Terrestrial Birds in the Northeastern United States*. Proceedings of the 4th International Partners in Flight Symposium, Asilomar, CA, March 2001.

16. Eddleman, W.R., F.L. Knopf, B. Meanley, F.A. Reid, and R. Zembal. 1988. Conservation of North American Rallids. *Wilson Bulletin* 100:458–475.

17. Hunter, W.C., L. Peoples, and J. A. Collazo. 2001. *South Atlantic Plain Partners in Flight Bird Conservation Plan*. American Bird Conservancy, The Plains, VA. 158 pp.

18. National Audubon Society. 2003. *San Francisco Bay Campaign*. http://www.audubonsfbay.org (accessed 3 September 2003).

19. Coastal America. 2002. *Coastal America: A Partnership for Action*. http://www.coastalamerica.gov (accessed 3 September 2003).

20. North Carolina Coastal Federation. No date. *Restoration and Protection of Key Coastal Habitats*. http://www.nccoast.org/skrestore.htm (accessed 3 September 2003).

21. NOAA. 2003. *About The CWPPRA*. http://www.nmfs.noaa.gov/habitat/restoration/projects_programs/CWPPRA/about.html (accessed 3 September 2003).

22. Texas Environmental Profiles. Undated. *Federal and State Nonregulatory Conservation Programs*. www.texasep.org/html/wld/wld_6hcp_nonreg.html (accessed 8 April 2003).

breeding range
introduced
wintering range

WHOOPING CRANE (*Grus americana*)

The Whooping Crane has served as the symbol of the plight of endangered species for several generations of conservationists. It declined to only 15 or 16 individuals before beginning a slow and continuing recovery.

STATUS AND DISTRIBUTION

The known breeding range of the species once extended from Illinois northwest to Alberta, where the species bred in marshes in tall and mixed-grass prairie. It disappeared from the U.S. portion of this range by 1890s and from Saskatchewan by 1930. A nonmigratory population occurred in Louisiana until 1950. Birds once wintered along the coast from southern New Jersey south to Florida and along Gulf Coast through Texas to northeastern Mexico. Some also wintered in interior Texas and central Mexico south to Jalisco and Guanajuato.

Populations were reduced from an estimated 500–1400 in the late 1800s to two small populations totaling fewer than 40 individuals by 1937. In Louisiana the nonmigratory population dropped from 13 to 6 after a hurricane in 1940 and continued to dwindle until a single individual was left. That individual was taken into captivity in 1950 and released into the other remaining population in Texas where it was subsequently found dead. The second population that winters along the central Texas coast near Aransas had dropped to 15 or 16 individuals by 1941. The breeding grounds of this, the only remaining self-sustaining migratory flock, were not discovered until 1954. This entire population is now known to breed in the boreal forest of Canada within Wood Buffalo National Park, which straddles the border between Alberta and Northwest Territories. Thanks to protection of their habitat on both breeding and wintering grounds, this population has shown a steady increase of nearly 5% per year since the 1940s and totaled 214 adults and 49 young in August 2006.

To decrease the risk of a catastrophe wiping out the single population in Texas, several captive flocks have been established and used to produce young birds for introduction in Florida and Wisconsin. Eggs were placed in Sandhill Crane nests at Grays Lake National Wildlife Refuge (NWR) in Idaho in the hope of developing a population in that area but the birds never developed pair bonds with other Whooping Cranes so the project was discontinued and there are no birds remaining in that population. As of October 2006 there were an estimated 54 birds in the Florida population—a nonmigratory population introduced in the Kissimmee Prairie region in which up to 14 pairs have now nested with fledged young produced starting in 2002. Young birds hatched in captivity have been released in Wisconsin since 2001 in an innovative attempt to develop a migratory population of Whooping Cranes. These released birds were initially taught their migration route by following an ultralight aircraft. After following the ultralight to their designated wintering grounds at Florida's Chassahowitzka NWR, the cranes returned on their own to Wisconsin the following spring. Although there has been some difficulty with individuals straying from the hoped-for migration route, a pair did hatch two eggs in the wild in Wisconsin in 2006. As of October 2006 there were 83 birds in the Wisconsin population and a total of 351 birds in the three extant wild populations. An additional 146 birds were in captivity at eleven locations as of October 2006.[1-6]

ECOLOGY

Historically, Whooping Crane breeding habitat was thought to be around small wetlands within tallgrass prairie and aspen parklands of the midwest U.S. and Canada. Wintering birds and former nonmigratory population occurred in coastal marshes and Gulf coastal plain prairies. They typically lay two eggs on a nest mound built in a shallow pond in a tall stand of emergent vegetation. Birds do not breed until at least three years old. Incubation lasts 30–35 days and young can fly 80–100 days after hatching. Young are fed by parents beginning 1–2 days after hatching and continuing until the young are 6–9 months old, though over that period the young become increasingly adept at feeding on their own. Most mortality of experimentally introduced populations has occurred at the chick or juvenal stage and has been the result of predation by bobcat, alligators, and coyotes, or bad weather. Young remain with parents throughout fall, winter, and spring—including through both the southward fall migration and usually the northward spring migration—but separate from the adults after arrival on the breeding grounds in spring. Whooping Cranes are omnivorous, eating blue crabs, clams, shrimp, insects, snakes, frogs, mice, plant roots, and grains among a great variety of foods. Pairs hold territories on both breeding and wintering grounds and return to the same territories each year. Subadults that have left family groups form small flocks on the wintering grounds outside territories occupied by adults. Birds in the wild are estimated to live to 22–30 years or more and one male in captivity lived to be 38 years old.[1]

THREATS

Historically, the species was apparently never numerous, though some have estimated that the population must have once numbered over 10,000 birds. A combination of hunting and habitat loss as prairie wetlands were drained and converted to agriculture caused the steep decline of the species so that there were only an estimated 500–1400 remaining in 1870. For example, 88–99% of the midwestern tallgrass prairie is estimated to have been lost since 1850. Gulf coastal prairies were eliminated from Louisiana and only 1% of this habitat in Texas is now considered pristine.

The current greatest threat is probably habitat and ecosystem degradation on wintering grounds of the original wild population at Aransas NWR in Texas. Perhaps the issue of greatest concern is the management of water removal from the Guadalupe River, which flows into the Aransas marshes. Whooping Cranes are particularly dependent on blue crabs for winter food and the crabs (and many other organisms of the marsh) require certain levels of freshwater from the river to maintain sufficient populations. When blue crab abundance declines the cranes feed on less nourishing food supplies that often cause them to lose weight instead of gain weight—weight that sustains them through their long spring migration and nesting season. In addition, if there is not enough freshwater coming into the marshes the water becomes too salty and the cranes must use extra energy to fly farther inland for freshwater to drink. Water is being taken out of the river for agriculture and for urban uses for the city of San Antonio. Water permit requests are expected to increase because the human population in South Texas is expected to double by about 2050.

The Gulf Intracoastal Waterway that was built through the refuge in 1941 resulted in the loss of 11% of wintering habitat for the species between 1941 and 1986. Additionally, shipping of petrochemical products through the Waterway poses a risk for spills that could cause major habitat and ecosystem degradation. Loss of habitat to housing development continues to be a threat. West Nile virus and other diseases are potentially important threats, especially as Whooping Cranes in captivity have been killed by eastern equine encephalitis, which is closely related to West Nile. Collisions with power lines have been a significant cause of death in Whooping Cranes that have made it past the fledging stage and is a growing threat as more power lines are constructed in the flyway. Perhaps the most insidious long-term threat is the drying out of nesting wetlands in the boreal forest and the loss of coastal wetlands from sea level rise, both as a result of global warming.[1,7–11]

CONSERVATION ACTION

The first major conservation action focused directly on the conservation of Whooping Cranes was the designation by President Franklin Roosevelt of the entire known wintering range of the species— 47,215 acres on the Texas coast—as the Aransas National Wildlife Refuge in 1937. The species continued to decline, however, and in 1945 the U.S. Fish and Wildlife Service and the National Audubon Society formed the Cooperative Whooping Crane Project to research the species' needs to increase the numbers and rescue it from eventual extinction. Audubon appointed Robert Porter Allen to study the birds in 1946. Allen was among those who tracked down the then unknown breeding site of the Texas-wintering birds in 1954–55 at Wood Buffalo National Park and published a monograph summarizing knowledge of the species life history in 1952. Efforts through the 1950s and early 1960s centered on education of hunters to prevent unintentional shooting of Whooping Cranes along the migratory route and education of the general public about the species' precarious situation. By the mid-1960s the species had increased to about 40 birds—only slightly more than had existed when Aransas NWR was established. To increase the population growth rate and lower the risk of extinction from a hurricane or disease, a captive population was initiated in 1967 when single eggs were taken from nests of birds in Wood Buffalo National Park that contained two-egg clutches and hatched at the Patuxent Wildlife Research Center in Maryland. Over a 27-year period 415 eggs were taken from the wild and 358 hatched in captivity or in Sandhill Crane nests in Idaho. The Patuxent Center captive population began producing eggs itself in 1975 and produced 310 fledged chicks from 771 eggs from 1975 to 2003. Captive populations have since been established at several locations, principally the International Crane Foundation in Wisconsin and the Calgary Zoo in Alberta. These populations produce 20–40 young per year for introductions to the Florida nonmigratory population and the experimental migratory population traveling between Wisconsin and Florida.

The U.S. Whooping Crane Recovery Plan sets out to maintain the Aransas/Wood Buffalo

population at current levels with the hope of eventually increasing it to 1,000 birds and to establish two other self-sustaining populations with at least 25 breeding pairs in each. Establishment of a nonmigratory population in the Kissimmee Prairie region of central Florida was initiated in 1993 with the release of captive-reared birds. As of October 2006 this population numbered 51 adults, with eight young produced from wild nests. A second experimental migratory population was initiated in 2001 by releasing captive-reared birds in Wisconsin and training them to migrate to Florida by following an ultralight aircraft. Flocks successfully followed the aircraft to Florida annually from 2001 to 2003 and made their way back to Wisconsin on their own in each successive spring. This work has been facilitated by a coalition called the Whooping Crane Eastern Partnership. Birds released through this project began to reach breeding age in 2004 and 2005 and it is hoped they will fledge young that they will teach the migratory route. Consideration has also been given to the idea of establishing a breeding population in another part of the Canadian boreal region (Ontario/Manitoba/Saskatchewan) that could be trained to migrate to coast of Louisiana or Mississippi. The efforts of the Canadian Boreal Initiative, the Boreal Songbird Initiative, and others to protect the boreal region are critical to ensuring that habit is available for expansion of Whooping Crane populations outside of Wood Buffalo National Park.

An attempt was made from 1975 through 1988 to establish a migratory population of Whooping Cranes traveling from Idaho to New Mexico by placing Whooping Crane eggs in Sandhill Crane nests in Idaho. Over that time period 289 eggs were placed in Sandhill nests and 85 young fledged. Unfortunately, the young Whooping Cranes imprinted on their Sandhill Crane parents and never successfully paired and mated with their own species. The egg transfers were discontinued after 1988 and all the Whooping Cranes in that population were gone by 2003.

Habitat management efforts have been ongoing at Aransas NWR and on surrounding lands and at various stopover locations along the migratory route of the Aransas/Wood Buffalo population. One of the most well-known efforts has been along the Platte River in Nebraska where Audubon's Rowe Sanctuary is located. A coalition of groups has worked to maintain open habitat in and around the river and to guarantee sufficient water levels in the river. The San Marcos River Foundation has attempted to obtain rights for the use of some water from the Guadalupe River that they would donate to the State of Texas to leave in the river for ecosystem protection. In March 2003, the group's application was denied because the Texas Commission on Environmental Quality (the governing authority) said that it could provide permits only to groups that would actually be removing water from the river for consumptive purposes. A research project had been established to study the relationships between water flows, blue crabs, cranes, and other ecosystem elements.[1,3-6,9-11]

CONSERVATION NEEDS

- Slow production of global warming pollution.
- Ensure that habitat and ecosystem elements are not lost and degraded on the Texas wintering grounds, or along the migratory route for Texas wintering birds or for birds in newly established populations.
- Increase the number of protected areas through national parks in Canada's boreal forest to allow for possible establishment of third migratory population.
- Continue captive breeding programs to maintain supply of birds for release in wild.
- Continue education and outreach programs to prevent hunting mortality from misidentification or human disturbance problems and to maintain public support of Whooping Crane conservation programs.

References

1. Lewis, J.C. 1995. Whooping Crane (*Grus americana*). In *The Birds of North America*, No.153 (A. Poole and F. Gill, eds.). The Academy of Natural Sciences, Philadelphia, PA, and the American Ornithologists' Union, Washington, DC.

2. BirdLife International. 2000. *Threatened Birds of the World*. Lynx Editions and BirdLife International, Barcelona, Spain, and Cambridge, UK.

3. Whooping Crane Conservation Association. 2006. *Current Whooping Crane Flock Status*. http://www.whoopingcrane.com/FLOCKSTATUS.HTM (Accessed 14 November 2006).

4. Whooping Crane Conservation Association. 2003. *Today's Whooper Report*. http://www.whoopingcrane.com/wccatodaybody.htm (accessed 4 September 2003).

5. U.S. Geological Survey Patuxent Wildlife Research Center. 2003. *The Whooping Crane Report*: 27. http://www.pwrc.usgs.gov/whoopers/ (accessed 4 September 2003).

6. International Crane Foundation. 2001. *The Whooping Crane*. http://www.savingcranes.org/species/whooping.asp (accessed 4 September 2003).

7. Vickery, P.D., P.B. Tubaro, J. M. Cardoso da Silva, B.G. Peterjohn, J.R. Herkert, and R.B. Cavalcanti. 1999. Conservation of Grassland Birds in the Western Hemisphere. Pages 2–26 in *Ecology and Conservation of Grassland Birds of the Western Hemisphere* (P.D. Vickery and J.R. Herkert, eds.). Studies in Avian Biology No. 19, Cooper Ornithological Society, Camarillo, CA.

8. Ricketts, T.H., et. al. 1999. *Terrestrial Ecoregions of North America: A Conservation Assessment*. Island Press, Washington, DC. 485 pp.

9. Stehn, T. 2003. *Water Issues Affect Whooping Cranes in Texas*. International Crane Foundation website. http://www.savingcranes.org/whatsnew/Announcements.asp (accessed 4 September 2003).

10. Whooping Crane Conservation Association. 2003. *San Marcos River Foundation Continues Struggle to Protect Whooping Crane Habitat*. http://www.whoopingcrane.com/WCURRENT.HTM (accessed 4 September 2003).

11. U.S. Geological Survey Northern Prairie Wildlife Research Center. No date. *Status Survey and Conservation Action Plan: Whooping Crane (Grus americana)*. http://www.npsc.nbs.gov/resource/distr/birds/cranes/grusamer.htm (accessed 4 September 2003).

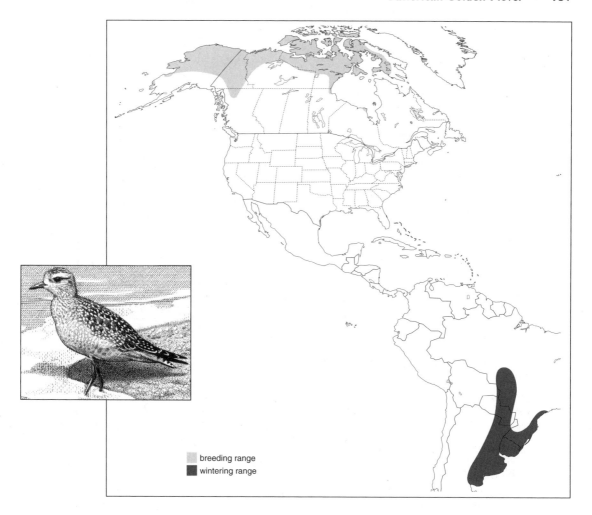

breeding range
wintering range

AMERICAN GOLDEN-PLOVER (*Pluvialis dominica*)

One of a trio of shorebirds that rely on central North American grasslands during migration and that winter in grasslands of southern South America, the American Golden-Plover also shares the dubious distinction of having suffered enormous losses in numbers from market hunting in the U.S. in the late 1800s.

STATUS AND DISTRIBUTION

The species has a rather extensive Arctic breeding range extending from northwestern Alaska to Baffin Island, Canada, though parts of the area are remote and little studied so the range may be less extensive than previously thought. An estimated 78% of the species total breeding range occurs in Canada. Several isolated breeding populations exist in southeastern Alaska and one in northern

Ontario. Birds winter primarily in campos and pampas grasslands of Argentina, southern Bolivia, southern Brazil, Uruguay, and Paraguay. The species' migration routes south of the U.S. are not well documented but pass through Barbados and Trinidad and northeastern South America. During spring migration, virtually the entire population passes through the Atlantic slope lowlands of Mexico and coastal Texas and the prairie grasslands of the central U.S. and Canada but small numbers occur along the Atlantic coast of the U.S. In the fall many birds, especially adults, move southeastward from breeding grounds and depart for South America from eastern Canada. Others, especially juveniles, travel south through the midwest U.S. and eastern U.S. and apparently fly over the Caribbean to South America. During migration small numbers are found along virtually the entire eastern Atlantic Coast of the U.S. and along Pacific Coast of British Columbia and Washington.

Important breeding sites for the species in Alaska include the Arctic National Wildlife Refuge (NWR), Bureau of Land Management's National Petroleum Reserve–Alaska, Kanuti NWR, and the National Park Service's Bering Land Bridge National Preserve. In Canada, important breeding sites include the Foxe Basin Islands Important Bird Area (IBA) in Nunavut, where more than 2% of the North American population is estimated to breed.

Important fall migratory stopover sites for American Golden-Plover in Canada include the Blow River Delta IBA in Yukon Territory (has hosted over 6,000 birds), Ekwan to Lakitusaki Shores IBA along James Bay, Ontario (up to 1,000 birds), and the Cape Pine and St. Shotts Barren, Newfoundland (hosts a minimum of 1,000 birds). Spring migratory stopover sites in Canada include the Shagamu River & Area IBA, Ontario (600 birds in 1993), Valeport Marsh IBA, Saskatchewan (500 birds in 1993), and the Greater Rondeau Area IBA on the shores of Lake Erie in Ontario (thousands in both spring and fall migration).

Important fall migratory stopover sites in the U.S. include Cheyenne Bottoms Wildlife Management Area in Kansas (has hosted over 500 birds) and the Saylorville Reservoir in Iowa (has hosted nearly 500 birds). High numbers have been reported in fall migration from parts of eastern North Dakota and Minnesota. Important coastal spring migratory stopover sites include the central coast of Veracruz, Mexico, rice fields of Cameron Parish in coastal Louisiana, Galveston Island State Park in Texas, the Corpus Christi Naval Air Station in Texas, and Anahuac National Wildlife Refuge in Texas. Inland locations that regularly host numbers of birds in spring migration include agricultural fields of northwestern Indiana and east central Illinois (4,000–25,000 birds counted 1980–86), the Coweta sod farms of Wagoner County, Oklahoma, the Fergus Falls Wetland Management District in Minnesota, and the Morris Wetland Management District in Minnesota. During both spring and fall migration, flocks of American Golden-Plovers often use different areas from year-to-year, probably depending on variation in food supplies and habitat condition at different sites.

Important wintering areas in South America include the Estancia Medaland, a 27,500-acre private ranch, in Argentina' Buenos Aires province, where an estimated 1,000+ birds wintered in the 1990s, and Brazil's Lagoa do Peixe National Park which has hosted up to 10,000 birds.

American Golden-Plovers suffered a major decline in abundance during the late 1800s from market and sport hunting during spring and fall migration in the U.S. and Canada. Various sources document cases of thousands of birds being killed in a single day at a site. Although there has been no systematic survey to estimate trends in modern times, surveys from several areas indicate a continuing decline in numbers. Unfortunately, the species' great variability in which sites are used during migration from year-to-year makes it difficult to test significance of changes. Breeding season counts from the Arctic Rasmussen Lowlands showed a statistically significant decline from the 1970s to 1990s. Surveys from the Maritime Provinces of Canada showed a statistically nonsignificant decline of 50% per year from 1974 to 1998. Both the Canadian and U.S. Shorebird Conservation Plans have given the species a population trend score of 4, indicating that experts believe the population has substantially declined but that there is not enough available data to verify the decline statistically. The total population size of American Golden-Plover is estimated at 150,000.[1–11]

ECOLOGY

Breeds in tundra habitat in the arctic and subarctic where the birds nest on drier, higher rocky slopes. Nests are depressions on ground where four eggs are laid, one clutch per season. The incubation period is 25–27 days. Typically, the male incubates eggs during the day and the female at night. Young are precocial and leave the nest within hours after hatching and forage on their own. Both adults defend the young and brood them. The young are estimated to fledge in 21–22 days.

During spring migration, the population primarily occurs in tallgrass and mixed-grass prairie regions and the prairie pothole region of the central U.S. and Canada but prefers very short grass or open agricultural fields. Likely once relied on recently burned areas and areas closely cropped by bison or perhaps by the now extinct Rocky Mountain Grasshopper. Sod farms, grazed pastures, and fallow corn fields have now become its preferred habitat. Also uses rice fields in coastal Texas and Louisiana, and golf courses, airports, recreational fields, and lake and ocean shorelines throughout U.S. migratory flyway. Diet has not been well studied but the species seems to feed mostly on small insects and other invertebrates and on eastern coast of Canada on crowberry. In winter, the species is seen in the pampas and campos regions of southern South America, especially in grazed pastures inland and along shores of marine and freshwater wetlands.[1]

THREATS

Historically, overhunting was a major threat, including market hunting for sale of large numbers in city markets. During the same time period, critical North American grassland migratory stopover habitat underwent massive conversion to agricultural land uses. For example, 88–99% of the midwestern tallgrass prairie is estimated to have been lost since 1850. In some areas the loss has been even more severe. Less than 1% of original habitat in a forest/grassland ecozone extending from Illinois south to Texas is considered intact. Remnants of tallgrass prairie habitat in southern Iowa and northern Missouri are restricted to 20 sites, each less than 20 acres in size. Gulf coastal prairies were eliminated from Louisiana and only 1% of this habitat in Texas is now considered pristine. Loss of northern mixed grass prairie has been estimated at 36–69% and southern mixed grass prairie at 27–65%. Conversion of habitat in concert with targeted use of pesticides and various habitat treatments also eventually led to the extinction of the Rocky Mountain Grasshopper, which may have created habitat and served as a major food source as it likely did for migrating Eskimo Curlew. Perhaps of even greater importance was the virtual extinction of many species and populations of grazing mammals, the most notable of which is the American Bison, and the loss of regular fire cycles. Grazers and fire helped create expanses of closely cropped grassland that is preferred by migrant American Golden-Plovers and other species.

As in most grassland ecosystems, the greatest current threat continues to be loss and degradation of native habitat largely through conversion to cropland, housing developments, mineral and oil extraction activities, and fire suppression. Most of the species' known wintering locations are on privately owned land that is generally managed for cattle production, producing the closely cropped grasslands that are preferred by American Golden-Plovers. Such areas near coastal lagoons are unlikely to be converted to cropland because of periodic flooding and high salinity. Inland grasslands areas, however, are more likely to be subject to conversion to cropland or pine plantations or subdivisions for housing. Particularly worrisome is that government programs in Argentina and Brazil are promoting, through financial incentives, commercial tree plantations, usually of exotic species. Commercial plantations occupied over 370,000 acres of former grassland habitat in 1994 within Argentina's Corrientes province and there was a 500% increase in forestry plantations between 1995 and 2000.

Other potential threats on the breeding grounds include habitat degradation from expansion of human settlements and oil and gas exploration and extraction activities. In 2004, a plan was announced to open for oil and gas leases the 8.8-million-acre Northwest Planning Area of the National Petroleum Reserve–Alaska, which includes a large proportion of the Alaska breeding range of American Golden-Plover. Proposals have also been brought before the U.S. Congress a number of times to override the conservation mandate for the Arctic National Wildlife Refuge to allow oil and gas extraction activities.

Pesticides and herbicides are a potentially major but poorly understood threat for the species during migration and on the wintering grounds. Birds regularly forage during migration in areas that receive high herbicide and pesticide applications, like sod farms, corn fields, rice fields, golf courses, and airports. The U.S. and Canada account for 36% of world pesticide use with 62% of all U.S. crop applications for corn and soybean and an average of 1,566 kg of pesticides used per 2.5 acres of cropland in the U.S. in 1996. Improper use of pesticides in grasslands in Argentina killed 5000 Swainson's Hawks in 1995–96.[1,12–19]

CONSERVATION ACTION

While little direct conservation activity has focused on American Golden-Plover, there has been increasing activity in grassland and wetland habitat conservation across the U.S. and Canada and involving a great many governmental and nongovernmental organizations. Throughout much of this region, state or provincial agencies own or manage the bulk of the conservation lands that are protected though often the percentage of the total area protected is quite small. In the Central Tallgrass Prairie ecoregion only 8% of recommended conservation acreage is protected. Partners in Flight and the Nature Conservancy have independently developed or are in the process of developing ecoregional plans for the tallgrass and mixed grass prairie regions across which American Golden-Plovers migrate. The Prairie Pothole Joint Venture has recently begun working toward protecting, restoring, and enhancing habitat specifically for migrant shorebirds, including American Golden-Plover.

The Western Hemisphere Shorebird Reserve Network has recognized Cheyenne Bottoms, Kansas as an important migratory shorebird staging area and Brazil's Lagoa do Peixe as an important shorebird wintering area. Much of the habitat at Cheyenne Bottoms is owned and managed by the Kansas Fish and Wildlife Agency and the Nature Conservancy but a major conservation problem at the site comes from management of water input from Arkansas River and Walnut Creek. Water withdrawals for irrigation from these two sources were so great in the early 1990s that no water was available for Cheyenne Bottoms and the area was dry much of the time. Later court rulings cut back on the amount removed from these sources and, with new water control structures and pumps, wetland habitat has been easier to maintain.

On the breeding grounds, Audubon Alaska has advocated for a "Wildlife Habitat Alternative" plan for protecting biological hotspots within the Northwest Planning Area of the National Petroleum Reserve. When the area is opened for oil and gas leasing the Audubon plan could help ensure healthy populations of American Golden-Plover and other wildlife species. In the wintering grounds, Aves Argentina has focused research activities on the pampas and campos grasslands of Argentina and initiated a new conservation program for the area in 2003 that will identify Important Bird Areas in the region and work toward their protection and proper management. The grasslands in this region also support 14 globally threatened bird species and wintering populations of Swainson's Hawk, Upland Sandpiper, and Bobolink. Lagoa de Peixe was established as a National Park by the Brazilian government in 1986 and various educational and research activities

have continued. About 10% of the land is owned by the Brazilian Institute for the Environment and Renewable Natural Resources (IBAMA) with the rest either private or Federal Community property. However, private lands are still being converted to rice and other forms of agriculture. [1,8,13,15–17,20–26]

CONSERVATION NEEDS

- Incorporate habitat objectives, including periodic prescribed burns, into public land management in areas where American Golden-Plover and other grassland-dependent bird species could occur or do occur on public lands.
- Slow or halt incentives for commercial forestry plantations on wintering ground grasslands in Argentina and Brazil.
- Provide incentives for private landowners to manage their lands to the benefit of grassland birds in areas where American Golden-Plover migrate or winter.
- Purchase land or conservation easements on private lands in areas in the U.S. that are important migratory staging areas for American Golden-Plover.
- Implement regular breeding, wintering, and migratory rangewide surveys designed to assess overall population status and trends.
- Prevent oil and mineral exploration in areas that are known to support breeding American Golden-Plover.

References

1. Johnson, O.W., and P.G. Connors. 1996. American Golden-Plover (*Pluvialis dominica*), Pacific Golden-Plover (*Pluvialis fulva*). In *The Birds of North America*, No. 201–202 (A. Poole and F. Gill, eds.). The Birds of North America, Inc., Philadelphia, PA, and the American Ornithologists' Union, Washington, DC.

2. Donaldson, G.M., C. Hyslop, R.I.G. Morrison, H.L. Dickson, and I. Davidson. 2000. *Canadian Shorebird Conservation Plan*. Canadian Wildlife Service, Environment Canada, Ottawa, ON.

3. Howell, S.N.G., and S.Webb. 1995. *A Guide to the Birds of Mexico and Northern Central America*. Oxford University Press, New York, NY.

4. Igl, L. D. 2003. *Bird Checklists of the United States* (Version 12MAY03). Northern Prairie Wildlife Research Center Home Page, Jamestown, ND. http://www.npwrc.usgs.gov/resource/othrdata/chekbird/chekbird.htm (accessed 24 October 2003).

5. U.S. Bureau of Land Management. 2003. *Northwest NPRA Final Integrated Activity Plan/Environmental Impact Statement*. http://wwwndo.ak.blm.gov/npra/ (accessed 24 October 2003).

6. Bird Studies Canada. 2003. *Important Bird Areas of Canada*. http://www.bsc-eoc.org/iba/IBAsites.html (accessed 24 October 2003).

7. Skagen, S.K., P.B. Sharpe, R.G. Waltermire, and M.B. Dillon. 1999. *Biogeographic Profiles of Shorebird Migration in Midcontinental North America*. Biological Science Report USGS/BRD/BSR—2000-0003. U.S. Government Printing Office, Denver, CO. 167 pp.

8. Manomet Bird Observatory. 2003. *Western Hemisphere Shorebird Reserve Network*. http://www.manomet.org/WHSRN/ (accessed 23 October 2003).

9. Isacch, J.P., and M.M. Martinez. 2002. Temporal Variation in Abundance and the Population Status of Non-breeding Nearctic and Patagonian Shorebirds in the Flooding Pampa Grasslands of Argentina. *Journal of Field Ornithology* 74:233–242.

10. Brown, S., C. Hickey, and B. Harrington, eds. 2000. *The U.S. Shorebird Conservation Plan*. Manomet Center for Conservation Sciences, Manomet, MA.

11. Delany, S., and D. Scott. 2002. *Waterbird Population Estimates*, 3rd ed. Wetlands International Global Series No. 12, Wageningen, The Netherlands.

12. Ricketts, T.H., et al. 1999. *Terrestrial Ecoregions of North America: A Conservation Assessment*. Island Press, Washington, DC. 485 pp.

13. Gauthier, D.A., A. Lafon, T. Tombs, J. Hoth, and E. Wilken. 2003. *Grasslands: Toward a North American Conservation Strategy*. Canadian Plains Research Center, University of Regina, Regina, Saskatchewan, and Commission for Environmental Cooperation, Montreal, QC, Canada. 99 pp.

14. Gill, R.E., Jr., P. Canevari, and E.H. Iverson. 1998. Eskimo Curlew (*Numenius borealis*). In *The Birds of North America*, No. 347 (A. Poole and F. Gill, eds.). The Birds of North America, Inc., Philadelphia, PA.

15. Di Giacomo, A., and S. Krapovickas. 2001. Afforestation Threatens Argentina's Grasslands. *World Birdwatch* 23:24–25.

16. Krapovickas, S., and A. Di Giacomo. 1998. Conservation of Pampas and Campos Grasslands in Argentina. *Parks* 8(3):47–53.

17. Audubon Alaska. 2002. *Alaska's Western Arctic: A Summary and Synthesis of Resources*. Audubon Alaska, Anchorage, AK. 240 pp. plus 49 maps.

18. United Nations Environment Programme. 2002. *North America's Environment: A Thirty-year State of the Environment and Policy Retrospective*. United Nations Environment Programme, Regional Office for North America, Washington, DC.

19. Goldstein, M.I., T.E. Lacher, Jr., B. Woodbridge, M.J. Bechard, S.B. Canavelli, M.E. Zaccagnini, G.P. Cobb, E.J. Scollon, R. Tribolet, and M.J. Hooper. 1999. Monocrotophos-induced Mass Mortality of Swainson's Hawks in Argentina, 1995–96. *Ecotoxicology* 8:201–214.

20. The Nature Conservancy Central Tallgrass Prairie Ecoregion Planning Team. 2000. *Conservation in a Highly Fragmented Landscape: The Central Tallgrass Prairie Ecoregional Conservation Plan*. The Nature Conservancy, Midwest Conservation Science Center, Minneapolis, MN.

21. Fitzgerald, J., B. Busby, M. Howery, R. Klataske, D. Reinking, and D. Pashley. 2000. *Partners in Flight Bird Conservation Plan for The Osage Plains*. American Bird Conservancy, The Plains, VA.

22. Fitzgerald, J.A., and D.N. Pashley. 2000. *Partners in Flight Bird Conservation Plan for the Dissected Till Plains*. American Bird Conservancy, The Plains, VA.

23. Fitzgerald, J.A., D.N. Pashley and B. Pardo. 1999. *Partners in Flight Bird Conservation Plan for the Northern Mixed-grass Prairie*. American Bird Conservancy, The Plains, VA.

24. Fitzgerald, J.A., D.N. Pashley, S.J. Lewis, and B. Pardo. 1998. *Partners in Flight Bird Conservation Plan for the Northern Tallgrass Prairie*. American Bird Conservancy, The Plains, VA.

25. Dinsmore, S., S.K. Skagen, and D.L. Helmers. No date. *Shorebirds: An Overview for the Prairie Pothole Joint Venture*. U.S. Fish and Wildlife Service, Colorado Fish and Wildlife Assistance Office, Lakewood, CO.

26. Wetlands International. 2002. *Ramsar Sites Database: Lagoa do Peixe*. http://www.wetlands.org/RDB/Ramsar_Dir/Brazil/BR002D02.htm (accessed 23 October 2003).

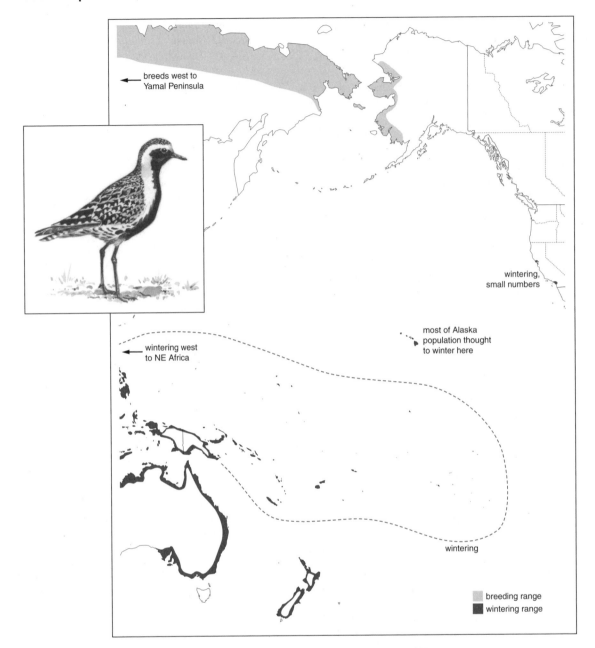

breeds west to
Yamal Peninsula

wintering,
small numbers

most of Alaska
population thought
to winter here

wintering west
to NE Africa

wintering

breeding range
wintering range

PACIFIC GOLDEN-PLOVER (*Pluvialis fulva*)

The Pacific Golden-Plover, unlike the closely related American Golden-Plover, has an extensive
wintering range across islands of the Pacific
Ocean, parts of southern Asia, northeast Africa,
and Australia. In the U.S. it breeds only in western Alaska and winters in the Hawaiian and Pacific islands with small numbers in southern California.

STATUS AND DISTRIBUTION

The species' breeding range extends from western
Alaska (where it overlaps with American Golden-
Plover) across Arctic Siberia to as far west as Yamal Peninsula. Most of the nesting area in Alaska
is south of the Arctic Circle. The species has a vast
wintering range extending from northeastern

Africa eastward through southeastern Asia to the Pacific Islands and south to Australia and New Zealand. Virtually the entire Alaskan breeding population is thought to winter in the Hawaiian Islands. Scattered birds winter along the Pacific Coast of North America from British Columbia south to Baja California, Mexico but with higher numbers in southern California.

Important breeding sites for the species in Alaska include Yukon Delta National Wildlife Refuge (NWR) and Togiak NWR. The species is widely distributed across locations and habitats within the Hawaiian Island wintering area, including military bases, airfields, cemeteries, golf courses, lawns, and natural areas. Hawaiian Islands NWR, Pu'uhonua o Honaunau National Historical Park, and Kaloko-Honokōhau National Historical Park on Hawaii are among many areas where the species is a common winterer. A few sites support small numbers of wintering Pacific Golden-Plover in California, including the offshore islands of southern California and Point Reyes National Seashore.

Likely suffered major declines in abundance during the late 1800s and early 1900s on wintering grounds from widespread hunting but little documentation is available. On Hawaii, species was legally hunted until 1941 with bag limits of 15 per day that were often exceeded. No recent information exists on trends overall, though Pacific Golden-Plovers monitored at locations in Australia showed a 72% decline from 1986 to 1995. The total population size of Pacific Golden-Plover is estimated at 150,000–200,000 but the Alaskan breeding population that winters in Hawaiian and Pacific Islands is estimated at 16,000.[1–4]

ECOLOGY

Breeds on arctic and subarctic tundra where the birds nest in a variety of habitats ranging from moist forest-tundra to drier lichen-tundra. Nests are depressions on the ground where four eggs are laid, one clutch per season, though replacement laying may occur if the first clutch is destroyed. Incubation period is 22–25 days. Typically the male incubates eggs during the day and the female at night. Young are precocial and leave the nest within hours after hatching and forage on their own. Both adults defend the young and brood them. The young are estimated to fledge in 26–28 days.

Diet has not been well studied but feeds mostly on small insects, crustaceans, and other invertebrates; also known to eat small reptiles and berries. In winter this bird is a species of a wide variety of open habitats either along marine shorelines (salt-marshes, mudflats, beaches) or areas with short grass (mowed airfields, military bases, pastures, lawns, cemeteries, etc.) throughout its expansive wintering range. In Hawaii the species has the same broad habitat preferences but the greatest numbers occur where there are large expanses of short-grass habitat, especially at military bases and airfields, but these birds even use small lawns in urban areas for feeding. Birds often hold winter territories for feeding but leave territories at night to roost communally on rooftops or islands.[1]

THREATS

Much of the species' breeding range is isolated and unlikely to experience major threats in near future, though there is always concern that activities like mineral and oil extraction activities could cause loss and degradation of habitat in some regions. The potential of such activity is unknown for the Siberian portion of range and low for the Alaskan breeding population. Perhaps the greatest threat to the species is from the major habitat and ecosystem changes already underway from global warming. Also of major concern is the continuing loss of wintering habitat, especially in southeast Asia. Another threat of unknown total impact comes from the commercial hunting of shorebirds in China, India, Indonesia, Thailand, Vietnam, and other Asian and Pacific regions but no information currently available on numbers taken. Pesticides and herbicides are a potentially major but poorly documented and understood threat for the species on the wintering grounds. In Hawaii, birds regularly forage during winter in areas that receive high herbicide and pesticide applications like golf courses, airports, and lawns.[1,5]

CONSERVATION ACTION

Pacific Golden-Plover is considered a species of High Conservation Concern by the U.S. Shorebird Conservation Plan, the U.S. Pacific Islands Regional Shorebird Conservation Plan, and the Alaska Regional Shorebird Conservation Plan. These plans were developed by partnership efforts of organizations committed to the conservation of shorebirds. Each plan provides a framework and background for conservation planning for shorebirds with specific objectives for research, monitoring, habitat conservation, and outreach.

Many wintering areas are protected within Hawaiian and Pacific Islands National Wildlife Refuge. While little direct conservation activity has focused on Pacific Golden-Plover within the U.S., there are a variety of efforts in Hawaii to protect and restore habitats for Hawaiian Goose and other species that may ultimately benefit Pacific Golden-Plover as well. For example, the U.S. Fish and Wildlife Service Endangered Species Program and the Hawaii Department of Land and Natural Resources entered into a Safe Harbor Agreement with the Umikoa Ranch on Hawaii. The owners of this privately owned site will continue wetland habitat restoration, watershed reforestation, and invasive species control for twenty years as part of the agreement with technical assistance provided by Ducks Unlimited. An unusual Safe Harbor Agreement was still being formulated in 2003 that would allow the Hawaii Department of Land and Natural Resources to enroll any interested landowner on Molokai with actual or potential habitat that an expanding reintroduced Hawaiian Goose population on that island could use—a program that may also benefit Pacific Golden-Plover.[1,5–11]

CONSERVATION NEEDS

- Slow production of global warming pollution.
- Identify, protect, restore, and enhance important habitats for Pacific Golden-Plover.
- Incorporate habitat objectives into public land management in areas where Pacific Golden-Plover breed and winter.
- Locate key wintering/migration stopover sites in Hawaii and the remote Pacific Islands.
- Implement regular breeding, wintering, and migratory rangewide surveys designed to assess overall population status and trends.
- Prevent oil and mineral exploration in areas that are known to support breeding Pacific Golden-Plover.

References

1. Johnson, O.W., and P.G. Connors. 1996. American Golden-Plover (*Pluvialis dominica*), Pacific Golden-Plover (*Pluvialis fulva*). In *The Birds of North America*, No. 201–202 (A. Poole and F. Gill, eds.). The Birds of North America, Inc., Philadelphia, PA, and the American Ornithologists' Union, Washington, DC.

2. Igl, L.D. 2003. *Bird Checklists of the United States* (Version 12MAY03). Northern Prairie Wildlife Research Center Home Page, Jamestown, ND. http://www.npwrc.usgs.gov/resource/othrdata/chekbird/chekbird.htm (accessed 24 October 2003).

3. Cooper, D. 2001. Important bird areas of California. Unpublished manuscript available from Audubon California, 6042 Monte Vista St., Los Angeles, CA 90042.

4. Delany, S., and D. Scott. 2002. *Waterbird Population Estimates*, 3rd ed. Wetlands International Global Series No. 12, Wageningen, The Netherlands.

5. Johnson, O.W. 2003. Pacific and American Golden-Plovers: reflections on conservation needs. *Wader Study Group Bulletin* 100:10–13.

6. Brown, S., C. Hickey, B. Harrington, and R. Gill, eds. 2001. *The U.S. Shorebird Conservation Plan*, 2nd ed. Manomet Center for Conservation Sciences, Manomet, MA.

7. Engilis, A., Jr., and M. Naughton. In press. *U.S. Pacific Islands Regional Shorebird Conservation Plan*, U.S. Shorebird Conservation Plan. U.S. Department of the Interior, Fish and Wildlife Service, Portland, OR.

8. Alaska Shorebird Working Group. 2000. A Conservation Plan for Alaska Shorebirds. Unpublished Report. Alaska Shorebird Working Group. Available though the U.S. Fish and Wildlife Service, Migratory Bird Management Program, Anchorage, AK.

9. Hawaii Department of Land and Natural Resources. 2002. *Annual Report to the Twenty-second Legislature State of Hawaii Regular Session 2003 on the Status of the Issuance of Incidental Take Licenses for Endangered, Threatened, Proposed, and Candidate Species; and the Condition of the Endangered Species Trust Fund for the Period July 1, 2001–June 30, 2002*. State of Hawaii, Department of Land and Natural Resources, Division of Forestry and Wildlife, Honolulu, HI.

10. Environmental Defense. 2001. *Safe Harbor Agreement for Endangered Hawaiian Waterfowl*. www.environmentaldefense.org (accessed 16 April 2003).

11. Hawaii Department of Land and Natural Resources. 2002. *Draft Programmatic Safe Harbor Agreement for Nene on the Island of Molokai, Hawaii*. State of Hawaii, Department of Land and Natural Resources, Division of Forestry and Wildlife, Honolulu, HI.

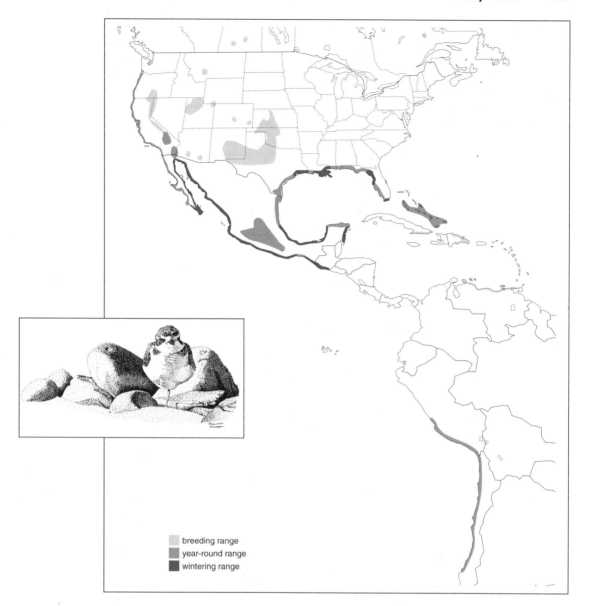

breeding range
year-round range
wintering range

SNOWY PLOVER (*Charadrius alexandrinus*)

A ghostly pale-plumaged shorebird of barren salt flats and coastal beaches, the Snowy Plover breeds in scattered populations across North America and the world but has declined in many areas from habitat loss and disturbance.

STATUS AND DISTRIBUTION

Species has an amazingly widespread range, occurring across North and South America, Europe, Africa, and Asia. In the U.S., the inland breeding population occurs in disjunct areas across at least 12 states west of the Mississippi River. A small inland breeding population also occurs in southern Saskatchewan. Birds from the inland population apparently move to the Gulf and Pacific coasts of the U.S. and to the Atlantic and Pacific coasts of Mexico and Central America to winter. Birds remain year-round along Pacific Coast from Oregon south to Baja California and along portions of the Gulf Coast from Florida to Mexico's Yucatan Peninsula. Year-round populations also occur on the central plains of Mexico and in the Bahamas and some Caribbean islands.

Most of the estimated U.S. breeding population of 16,000–21,000 birds occurs west of the Rocky Mountains (87%), with more than 50% (9,000) of those concentrated around Great Salt Lake, Utah. Other important breeding sites for the species include, in California, San Francisco Bay (200–300 birds), Mono Lake (300–400 birds), Vandenberg Air Force Base (100–200 birds), Salton Sea (200–300 birds), and Owens Lake (200–300 birds). In Oregon, Abert Lake supports 200–300 birds. Nevada's Lahonton Valley may support 300 or more birds and New Mexico's Bitter Lake National Wildlife Refuge (NWR) has recorded up to 300 birds. Important sites for the Gulf Coast breeding population include Laguna Madre, Texas and Tyndall Air Force Base, Eglin Air Force Base, Shell Island, and St. George State Park, Florida. Important breeding sites along Mexico's Baja California coast include Bahía San Quintín, Lagunas Ojo de Liebre and Guerrero Negro, Laguna San Ignacio, and Bahía Magdalena. In winter the Texas coast is estimated to support 1,500–2,000 birds, the U.S. Pacific Coast about 4,000 birds. and interior southern California about 500 birds.

The species is thought to have shown a significant population decline, especially the Pacific Coast and Gulf Coast populations, where loss of habitat and levels of human disturbance have been high. Numbers declined 20% from the late 1970s to the late 1980s on surveys of populations across California, Nevada, Oregon, and Washington. Surveys along California's coast indicate a 21% decline from around 1980 to 1995. Along the U.S. Pacific Coast the species disappeared as a breeder from 55 of 84 historical breeding locations. Its range on Gulf Coast has also shrunk and become more fragmented. Analysis of Christmas Bird Count data from 1959–1988 shows a significant 2.2% per year decline across the species' U.S. wintering range.[1–11]

ECOLOGY

Nests along sandy beaches and inland on barren flats and around shores of alkaline and saline lakes, ponds, reservoirs, and sandy rivers. In winter most of the U.S. population occurs in sandy beach habitats but some birds use similar inland habitats in southern California and south Texas. The birds feed on a variety of small invertebrates. Nests are simple depressions on the ground in which the three eggs are laid. Incubation lasts 25–32 days. Young are fully feathered when they hatch and leave the nest within a few hours. The chicks feed themselves but depend on the adults to brood them and lure predators away. Adults may stay with the young for as long as 47 days post-hatching. Young can fly by 28–33 days. In the early part of the nesting season, females from western U.S. populations typically leave the males to tend the chicks alone after the first week. Females may then depart and pair with a different male and lay another clutch in a different area. In some areas in the southern part of the range, Snowy Plovers may regularly have as many as three clutches per season and they will repeatedly renest (up to six times) if nests are lost. They can begin breeding at one year of age. Average life span of adults has been estimated at about 3 years but one bird was known to have survived to 15 years old.[1]

THREATS

Loss of habitat along the Pacific and Gulf coasts of U.S. from beachfront development and subsequent human disturbance and management for recreational purposes has been the most severe threat. Housing developments built along beaches have destroyed large amounts of Snowy Plover habitat, and subsequent increases in disturbance levels and rates of predation from cats and other predators contribute further to the loss of breeding populations. Many beaches are cleaned daily of vegetative debris that provides the substrate for the invertebrates upon which Snowy Plovers depend for food. The mechanical raking of beaches can also destroy nests if carried out during the nesting season. One of the most pervasive threats along the Pacific Coast has been from the introduction of European and American beachgrass, originally planted to stabilize sand dune systems. Neither species was native to the area and both form thick mats of vegetation that render it unsuitable for plovers. These introduced species also encourage the growth of shrubby vegetation behind the dune that provides habitat for a multitude of mammalian and avian predators of eggs and young plovers. Vast areas of habitat have been lost to the spread of these invasive plant species. Introduction of another nonnative species, the red fox, has also caused severe problems for Snowy Plovers as foxes are major predators of eggs and young in some areas. Threats along the Gulf Coast are generally similar to those of the Pacific Coast population, but also include, in Texas, excessive disturbance from driving of vehicles on the beaches.

Inland breeding habitat has been greatly reduced in some areas from changes in hydrology due to water management practices, which cause either draining or flooding of wetlands. For example, water levels in Mono Lake and Owens Lake, California have been greatly reduced as water has been removed for drinking supplies and agricultural irrigation. Loss of habitat from development along the eastern and southern shores of Great Salt Lake, Utah is a continuing threat. Plover habitat along rivers and streams has been lost as the open, sandy shores have been taken over by invasive plants (e.g., salt cedar) or plants that would have naturally been removed during natural flooding events that no longer occur due to water removal and flood control measures. Loss of habitat from sea level rise and other habitat changes as a result of global warming may become the most difficult and pervasive threat.[1,2,6,10,11]

CONSERVATION ACTION

The Pacific Coast population of Snowy Plover was federally designated as Threatened by the U.S. Fish and Wildlife Service in 1993; this designation is currently being reviewed. In addition, many states have designated the species as Endangered, Threatened, or Special Concern in their jurisdiction. A draft recovery plan for the Pacific Coast population was completed by the U.S. Fish and Wildlife Service in 2001. Significant work is ongoing in California, Oregon, and Washington for protection and enhancement of Snowy Plover populations and habitat. In many areas, segments of beaches have been roped off, fencing has been placed around plover nests, informational signs have been displayed, and people have been assigned to nesting sites to prevent disturbance by humans and dogs. Santa Barbara Audubon Society, for example, has a Snowy Plover Docent Program that involves as many as 70 volunteers. These trained volunteers are stationed at the Coal Oil Point Nature Reserve, where they educate people about the plovers and protect the birds from disturbance and avian predators, especially crows. Similar programs are carried out by a variety of organizations across the range of Snowy Plovers and have been quite effective in some areas in increasing productivity. The use of predator

fencing exclosures has proved quite successful in many areas in increasing numbers of plovers. For example, nest success for nests protected by exclosures in Oregon in 1992 was 84% compared to 5% for unprotected nests. Predator control has also been necessary to allow the increased survival of eggs and young in many regions, especially from nonnative red foxes and cats. Many beach areas that allow access to recreational vehicles have developed seasonal closures for sections of beaches used by plovers to prevent disturbance or destruction of nests by vehicles. This has been quite controversial in many locations as fishermen and other recreationists have their previously uncontrolled access curtailed for the benefit of plovers and other wildlife.

Various kinds of habitat management have been initiated specifically for the benefit of Pacific Coast breeding Snowy Plovers. In California, the Department of Parks and Recreation, which manages many of the beaches where plovers nest, has removed invasive European beachgrass from many areas. The Bureau of Land Management and the U.S. Forest Service have carried out similar work at plover nesting areas they manage in Oregon.

A great many organizations, agencies, and coalitions are working on general coastal habitat restoration and protection projects, many of which will likely eventually benefit Snowy Plovers. For example, the Coastal America Partnership, a coalition of federal agencies, state and local governments, and private organizations, identifies and implements local wetland restoration and protection projects throughout the U.S. The Partnership had initiated more than 500 projects impacting hundreds of thousands of acres of wetland habitat as of 2002.

Many of the sites that support inland nesting populations of Snowy Plovers are experiencing major problems from water diversion and water management for human consumption in expanding urban centers and for agricultural uses. The Mono Lake Committee has been working since the 1970s to maintain and restore the Mono Lake ecosystem, especially by working to decrease the amount of water removed from the lake for use in Los Angeles. Similarly, the Friends of Great Salt Lake was founded in 1994 to work to protect the Great Salt Lake ecosystem. Audubon–California and the Salton Sea Coalition are actively working to protect that ecosystem from a planned water diversion project.[1,2,12–17]

CONSERVATION NEEDS

- Slow production of global warming pollution.
- Ensure management of locations currently supporting Snowy Plover to maintain water levels and habitat conditions beneficial to the species.
- Increase efforts at education, volunteer patrols, predator and pet management, fencing, and other activities shown to increase productivity of plovers.
- Increase acreage of wetland and shoreline habitat that is managed to attain conditions beneficial to Snowy Plover.
- Continue removing invasive European and American beachgrass from Pacific Coast habitats and replace with native plants.
- Decrease acreage of wetland and shoreline habitat degraded by erosion, pollution, invasive species, pesticides, and other factors.
- Implement a rangewide survey designed to assess overall population status and trends.

References

1. Page, G.W., J.S. Warriner, J.C. Warriner, and P.W.C. Paton. 1995. Snowy Plover (*Charadrius alexandrinus*). In *The Birds of North America*, No. 154 (A. Poole and F. Gill, eds.). The Academy of Natural Sciences, Philadelphia, PA, and the American Ornithologists' Union, Washington, DC.

2. U.S. Fish and Wildlife Service. 2001. *Western Snowy Plover (Charadrius alexandrinus nivosus) Pacific Coast Population Draft Recovery Plan.* Portland, Oregon. 630 pp.

3. Ferland, C.L., and S.M. Haig. 2002. *2001 International Piping Plover Census.* U.S. Geological Survey, Forest and Rangeland Ecosystem Science Center, Corvallis, OR. 293 pp.

4. Florida Fish and Wildlife Conservation Commission. 2004. *Interim Report: Status and Distribution of the Snowy Plover in Florida.* USFWS Cooperative Agreement No. 1448-40181-01-J-002.

5. Page, G.W., L.E. Stenzel, W.D. Shuford, and C.R. Bruce. 1991. Distribution and Abundance of the Snowy Plover on Its Western North American Breeding Grounds. *Journal of Field Ornithology* 62:245–255.

6. Cooper, D. 2001. Important Bird Areas of California. Unpublished manuscript available from Audubon California, 6042 Monte Vista St., Los Angeles, CA 90042.

7. Pranty, B. 2002. The Important Bird Areas of Florida. Unpublished manuscript downloaded from website 9 April 2003. http://www.audubon.org/bird/iba/florida/

8. Brown, S., C. Hickey, and B. Harrington. 2000. *United States Shorebird Conservation Plan.* Manomet Center for Conservation Sciences, Manomet, MA.

9. Sauer, J. R., S. Schwartz, and B. Hoover. 1996. *The Christmas Bird Count Home Page*, Version 95.1. Patuxent Wildlife Research Center, Laurel, MD.

10. Western Hemisphere Shorebird Reserve Network. 2003. *Mono Lake.* http://www.manomet.org/WHSRN/viewsite.php?id=44 (accessed 10 September 2003).

11. Western Hemisphere Shorebird Reserve Network. 2003. *Great Salt Lake.* http://www.manaomet.org/WHSRN/viewsite.php?id=36 (accessed 10 September 2003).

12. Cooper, D.S. 2003. *Species Monitoring—Snowy Plover.* Audubon California. http://www.audubon-ca.org/snowy_plover.html (accessed 10 September 2003).

13. Santa Barbara Audubon Society. 2003. *Snowy Plover Docent Program.* http://www.rain.org/~audubon/sbasplvrdocents.html (accessed 10 September 2003).

14. Coastal America. 2002. *Coastal America: A Partnership for Action.* http://www.coastalamerica.gov (accessed 3 September 2003).

15. Mono Lake Committee. 2003. *Mono Lake Committee.* http://www.monolake.org/committee/ (accessed 11 September 2003).

16. Friends of Great Salt Lake. 2002. *Friends of Great Salt Lake.* http://www.xmission.com/~fogsl/ (accessed 11 September 2003).

17. Cooper, D.S. 2003. *Audubon California and the Salton Sea.* Audubon California. http://www.audubon-ca.org/salton_sea.html (accessed 11 September 2003).

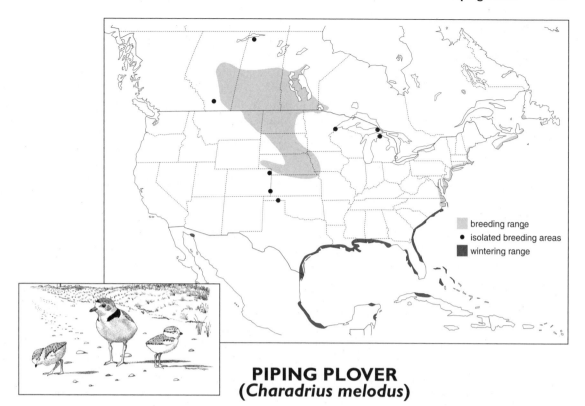

breeding range
isolated breeding areas
wintering range

PIPING PLOVER
(*Charadrius melodus*)

This small shorebird's requirement for beach nesting habitat has placed it in direct competition with human uses of beaches for development and recreation, causing declines that have led to the species federal listing as Endangered and Threatened.

STATUS AND DISTRIBUTION

An endemic breeding species of North America, the Piping Plover has three rather distinct breeding areas: prairie wetlands of the Great Plains of U.S. and Canada, the Great Lakes, and the Atlantic Coast of southern Canada and northeastern U.S. The Atlantic Coast breeding range extends from the southern tip of Newfoundland south to North Carolina. In the Great Lakes region of U.S. and Canada the species once bred along shores of all 5 lakes but is now restricted to small sections of the Lake Superior and Lake Michigan shorelines. The largest population occurs in the Great Plains, extending from southeastern Alberta east to southern Manitoba and the southwestern corner of Ontario and south to Nebraska, northern Kansas, and the northwestern corner of Missouri. Isolated breeding records exist from Colorado, Oklahoma, and northern Saskatchewan.

In 2001 when the last complete census was carried out, the population was estimated at 5,945 individuals, with 49% along the Atlantic Coast (2,920 birds), 50% in the Great Plains area (2,953 birds), and 1% in the Great Lakes area (70 birds). Within the Atlantic Coast population about 50% of the breeding birds occur in New England. Important breeding areas for that population include Cape Cod National Seashore, Monomoy National Wildlife Refuge (NWR) and the Duxbury/Plymouth Bays Complex Important Bird Area (IBA) in Massachusetts, West Hempstead Bay/Jones Beach West IBA in New York, and the North Brigantine Natural Area in New Jersey. Important sites in Canada include Prince Edward Island National Park and New Brunswick's Kouchibouguac National Park.

Virtually all of the Great Lakes population now breeds in Michigan, the most important site being the Sleeping Bear Dunes National Lakeshore. Largest concentrations of Piping Plovers of the Great Plains population are found in Saskatchewan and North Dakota. Important breeding sites for this population include Saskatchewan's Quill Lakes IBA, Chaplin Lake IBA, East Lake Diefenbaker IBA, and Willowbunch Lake IBA. These sites together support the majority of the

Canadian Great Plains population. In North Dakota, the Nature Conservancy's John E. Williams Preserve supports one of the largest populations of Piping Plovers in the world (sometimes more than 200 birds) and Lostwood NWR is also important for the species.

Winter range extends from the Atlantic Coast of North Carolina south to central Florida and across the Gulf Coast from southern Florida to Texas and the northern tip of the Mexican state of Tamaulipas. An unknown number of birds winter in the Bahamas, Cuba, and along the Gulf Coast of Mexico south to Quintana Roo. The International Piping Plover Winter Census located 63% in 1991, 42% in 1996, and 40% in 2001 of the known breeding population of Piping Plovers along beaches of the Atlantic and Gulf coasts of the U.S. It is suspected that many of the unaccounted-for birds are wintering along the Mexican coast, the Bahamas, and Cuba. The bulk of the birds found in the census were on the Gulf Coast (89%), with highest concentrations in Texas. Maximum counts of the species compiled from various sources from 1971 to 1996 show highest counts from Texas coast, including Matagorda NWR (303 birds), Bolivar Flats (300 birds), and South Padre Island (201 birds).

Numbers of Piping Plovers in the Atlantic Coast population more than doubled from 685–717 pairs in the 1980s to 1,676 pairs in 2003, but decreased slightly to 1,632 pairs in 2005. The Great Lakes population is the most imperiled, having decreased from historic estimates of 492–682 pairs during the 1800s to only 12 pairs by 1984. Numbers have increased since the species was federally listed as Endangered in 1986, with 32 pairs in 1999 and 55 pairs in 2004. The Great Plains population declined from 3,469 birds in 1991 to 2,953 in 2001.[1-14]

ECOLOGY

Breeds along sandy beaches and inland on barren flats and around shores of alkaline and saline lakes, ponds, reservoirs, and sandy rivers. In winter occurs in sandy beach habitats. Feeds on a variety of small invertebrates. Nests are simple depressions on the ground in which the 3–4 eggs are laid. Incubation lasts an average of 26–28 days. Young are fully feathered when born and leave the nest within a few hours after hatching, when they immediately begin feeding themselves. Young can fly by 21–35 days. These birds produce only a single brood per year but will renest several times if nests are lost early in the season. Nests are often lost to flooding from high tide events and storm surges as well as from predation and human destruction or disturbance. Can breed at one year. Adult survival rate is approximately 70% in populations studied. A number of population viability models have been developed for the three Piping Plover populations that have estimated annual productivity needed for population stability to range from 1.24 chicks per pair in the Atlantic Coast population to 1.25–2 chicks per pair for the Great Plains and Great Lakes populations. Average estimated productivity for the Atlantic Coast population was 1.63 chicks per pair from 1992 to 2001.[1,4,5,10,14]

THREATS

Loss of habitat along the Atlantic and Gulf coasts of the U.S. and shores of Great Lakes from beachfront development and subsequent human disturbance and management for recreational purposes has been the most severe threat. Housing developments built along beaches have destroyed large amounts of Piping Plover habitat, and subsequent increases in disturbance levels and rates of predation from cats and other predators contribute further to the loss of breeding populations. Many beaches are cleaned daily of vegetative debris that provides the substrate for the invertebrates upon which Piping Plovers depend for food. The mechanical raking of beaches can also destroy nests if carried out during the nesting season. Many beaches along the Atlantic and Gulf coasts are open to vehicle access, which can lead to crushed nests and chicks and disturbance of adults and fledglings. In many areas, hundreds of vehicles drive and park on beaches daily during the summer breeding season. A threat in some locations is from the planting of dense stands of beachgrass, originally planted to stabilize sand dune systems, but now forming thick mats of vegetation that render it unsuitable for plovers and encourage the growth of shrubby vegetation behind the dune that provides habitat for the multitude of mammalian and avian predators of eggs and young of the species.

The Great Plains breeding habitat has been greatly reduced in some areas from changes in hydrology from water management practices that cause either draining or flooding of wetlands. Pollution from agricultural runoff, disturbance from all-terrain vehicles, and in some areas, trampling of eggs and young by cattle have all been reported as threats in portions of the Great Plains population. Some plover habitat along rivers and streams has been lost as the open, sandy shores have been taken over by invasive plants or plants that would have naturally been removed during natural flooding events that no longer occur due to water removal and channelization projects. Loss of habitat from sea level rise and other habitat changes as a result of global warming may become the most difficult and pervasive threat.[1,2,5,6,8–10,12,14,15]

CONSERVATION ACTION

The Atlantic Coast and Great Plains populations of Piping Plover were federally designated as Threatened and the Great Lakes population as Endangered by the U.S. Fish and Wildlife Service (USFWS) in 1985. Recovery plans for all Piping Plover populations were published in 1988. A revised draft recovery plan for the Great Lakes population was completed in 2003. In 2001 and 2002 the USFWS officially designated critical habitat for the species on the Atlantic and Gulf Coast wintering grounds as well as for the Great Lakes and Great Plains breeding populations. In Canada the species was designated as Federally Threatened in 1978 and upgraded to Endangered in 1985. A recovery plan was completed in 1989 and updated in 2002. All of these recovery plans have detailed lists of actions to be initiated and specific numerical recovery goals for different population segments.

An amazing amount of on-the-ground conservation work is ongoing for the species across its breeding range, involving hundreds, perhaps thousands, of professionals and volunteers in public and private organizations from the federal to the local level. For example, the Massachusetts Audubon Society and the Maine Audubon Society both have had long-term programs involving 10–30 staff and interns annually and hundreds of volunteers that erect predator exclosures and fences, monitor plover nests and other beach-nesting species, and engage in a variety of education and outreach activities. In Massachusetts these efforts combined with those of the Massachusetts Department of Fish and Game and many other organizations have resulted in numbers of Piping Plovers increasing from 139 pairs in 1986 to 495 in 2001. Similar efforts by Maine Audubon have increased

numbers from 15 pairs in 1986 to 55 in 2001. The Nature Conservancy (TNC) has had similar programs in Rhode Island, on New York's Long Island, and in Maryland and Virginia. Generally, wherever these management and education activities are implemented annually with significant numbers of staff or volunteers, plover populations have shown major increases. Not all regions have significant programs and some of these regions have shown continuing declines in numbers or stable population levels. Many USFWS and TNC refuges protect breeding and wintering habitat for Piping Plovers.

Closing beaches to vehicle traffic has occurred in a number of areas but has proven very controversial because of organized recreational beach buggy associations and surf fishing associations, which oppose limits to their access. However, such closures have shown to be effective at increasing productivity rates and numbers of Piping Plovers. For example, at the Cape Cod National Seashore there were only a few records of nesting plovers prior to 1981 when regulations went into affect limiting vehicle access to the area, but there were 23 pairs nesting at the site by 1985 and 43 pairs by 1991.

Piping Plover conservation efforts are more limited across the range of the Great Plains population, but the Corps of Engineers has provided some education and outreach programs and signage, and USFWS and TNC work with private landowners at some sites in North Dakota and Montana to manage their lands for plovers. The Tern and Plover Conservation Partnership in Nebraska has an adopt-a-colony program focused on the lower Platte River and works with gravel mining operations to alleviate conflicts between mining activities and plover nests. The Nature Conservancy owns and manages the John E. Williams Memorial Nature Preserve in North Dakota, which supports one of the largest breeding populations of Piping Plovers in the world.

Some experimental work has been carried out to hatch eggs and raise chicks in captivity from abandoned nests (or occasionally by taking in abandoned chicks). Birds released back into the wild have survived and bred, but it has been difficult to assess the overall survival rates because of difficulties in resighting individuals the following year. A few zoos have been involved with this work and some now have a few birds that are maintained in captivity (a total of 14 in 2002), some of which have bred in captivity. The American Zoo and Aquarium Association formed a Piping Plover Specialist Group in 1995 to develop recommendations for maintaining and breeding Piping Plovers in captivity.

A great many organization, agencies, and coalitions are working on coastal habitat restoration and protection projects, many of which will likely eventually benefit Piping Plovers. For example, the Coastal America Partnership, a coalition of federal agencies, state and local governments, and private organizations, identifies and implements local wetland restoration and protection projects throughout the U.S. The Partnership had initiated more than 500 projects impacting hundreds of thousands of acres of wetland habitat as of 2002. A symposium on the wintering ecology and conservation of Piping Plovers was held in 2005.[1,5–10,12,14–17,18]

CONSERVATION NEEDS

- Slow production of global warming pollution.
- Ensure that management of locations currently supporting Piping Plover continues to maintain water levels and habitat conditions beneficial to the species.
- Increase efforts at education, volunteer patrols, predator and pet management, fencing, and other activities shown to increase productivity of plovers.
- Increase acreage of wetland and shoreline habitat within the range of Piping Plover that is managed to attain conditions beneficial to the species.
- Decrease acreage of wetland and shoreline habitat degraded by vehicle traffic, erosion, pollution, invasive species, pesticides, and other factors.
- Continue and expand rangewide surveys to Mexico and Caribbean designed to assess overall population status and trends.

References

1. Haig, S.M. 1992. Piping Plover (*Charadrius melodus*). In *The Birds of North America*, No. 2 (A. Poole, P. Stettenheim, and F. Gill, eds.). The Academy of Natural Sciences, Philadelphia, PA, and the American Ornithologists' Union, Washington, DC.

2. Ferland, C.L., and S.M. Haig. 2002. *2001 International Piping Plover Census*. U.S. Geological Survey, Forest and Rangeland Ecosystem Science Center, Corvallis, OR. 293 pp.

3. U.S. Fish and Wildlife Service. 2004. *2002–2003 Status Update: U.S. Atlantic Coast Piping Plover Population*. Sudbury, MA. 8pp.

4. Goossen, J.P., D.L. Amirault, J. Arndt, R. Bjorge, S. Boates, J. Brazil, S. Brechtel, R. Chiasson, G.N. Corbett, R. Curley, M. Elderkin, S.P. Flemming, W. Harris, L. Heyens, D. Hjertaas, M. Huot, B. Johnson, R. Jones, W. Koonz, P. Laporte, D. McAskill, R.I.G. Morrison, S. Richard, F. Shaffer, C. Stewart, L. Swanson, and E. Wiltse. 2002. *National Recovery Plan for the Piping Plover* (Charadrius melodus). National Recovery Plan No. 22. Recovery of Nationally Endangered Wildlife, Ottawa, ON. 47 pp.

5. Massachusetts Audubon Society. 2002. *Important Bird Areas*. http://www.audubon.org/bird/iba.ma.html (accessed 15 September 2003).

6. Wells, J.V. 1998. *Important Bird Areas in New York State*. National Audubon Society of New York State, Albany, NY. 243 pp.

7. Jenkins, C.D., and T. Pover. 2002. *2002 New Jersey Piping Plover Nesting Site Summaries: Current and Recommended Management*. New Jersey Division of Fish and Wildlife, Endangered and Nongame Species Program, Woodbine, NJ.

8. Bird Studies Canada. 2003. *Important Bird Areas of Canada*. http://www.bsc-eoc.org/iba/IBAsites.html (accessed 14 April 2003).

9. U.S. Fish and Wildlife Service. 2002. *Piping Plover (Charadrius melodus), Great Lakes Population, Agency Draft Recovery Plan*. Ft. Snelling, MN. 121 pp.

10. Svingen, D., and R. Martin. No date. *Birding North Dakota*. North Dakota Game and Fish Department, Bismarck, ND.

11. U.S. Fish and Wildlife Service. 2001. Endangered and Threatened Wildlife and Plants: Final Determination of Critical Habitat for Wintering Piping Plovers. *Federal Register* 66(132): 36038–36143.

12. Skagen, S.K., P.B. Sharpe, R.G. Waltermire, and M.B. Dillon. 1999. *Biogeographic Profiles of Shorebird Migration in Midcontinental North America*. Biological Science Report USGS/BRD/BSR—2000-0003. U.S. Government Printing Office, Denver, CO. 167 pp.

13. U.S. Fish and Wildlife Service. 2002. Endangered and Threatened Wildlife and Plants: Designation of Critical Habitat for the Northern Great Plains Breeding Population of the Piping Plover. *Federal Register* 67(176): 57638–57717.

14. Strucker, J. 2004. *Great Lakes Piping Plover Call*. Great Lakes Piping Plover Research and Recovery Team, University of Minnesota.

15. Primack, M. 1992. The Plovers' Paradise. *Sanctuary: The Journal of the Massachusetts Audubon Society* 31:9–10.

16. Tern and Plover Conservation Partnership. No date. *Tern and Plover Conservation Partnership.* http://ternandplover.unl.edu/trenandplover.shtml (accessed 12 September 2003).

17. Coastal America. 2002. *Coastal America: A Partnership for Action.* http://www.coastalamerica.gov (accessed 3 September 2003).

18. Rabon, D.R. (compiler). 2006. *Proceedings of the Symposium on the Wintering Ecology and Conservation of Piping Plovers.* U.S. Fish and Wildlife Service, Raleigh, NC.

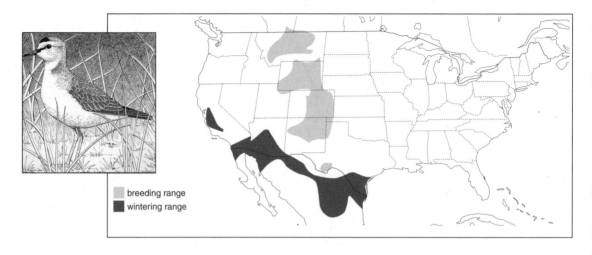

breeding range
wintering range

MOUNTAIN PLOVER (*Charadrius montanus*)

A species endemic to the shortgrass prairies of western North America, the Mountain Plover is well suited to the original native grassland communities that were grazed by bison, prairie dogs, and pronghorn. Loss and degradation of habitat has caused great declines in numbers of Mountain Plovers as well as other species of the shortgrass prairie habitat community.

STATUS AND DISTRIBUTION

Species breeds from central New Mexico and northwestern Texas north through the grasslands east of the Rocky Mountains to Montana. The majority of the population breeds in Colorado, Montana, and Wyoming. Recent estimates suggest that Colorado could support more than 60% of the global population and Wyoming 20% or more. Isolated populations occur in the Davis Mountains of Texas, in the Mexican state of Nuevo León, and possibly in the northern part of the Mexican states of Coahuila and Chihuahua. Formerly bred in southern Alberta and Saskatchewan but there have been no breeding records since 1990. Breeding range formerly extended further east but has retracted in South Dakota, Nebraska, Kansas, and Oklahoma. Birds winter from central California and northern Baja California east across southern Arizona to northern Mexico to southern Texas and northern Tamaulipas, Mexico.

Important breeding areas for the species include the South Park area in northwestern Colorado, which may support the largest population in the world (estimated at 2,310 adults in 2000–

2002). Other important sites include the Pawnee National Grasslands in Colorado, the Bureau of Land Management 40 Complex and Charles M. Russell National Wildlife Refuge (NWR) in Montana, the Bureau of Land Management's Rio Puerco Resource Area in New Mexico, and the Thunder Basin National Grassland and U.S. Forest Service's Great Divide Resource Area in Wyoming.

The largest wintering concentration is in central and southern California where 3,346 individuals were counted in a single day count in 1994 and 4,037 estimated in 2001, which is thought to be at least 50% of the global population. Virtually all of these birds are wintering in the Imperial Valley, an agriculturally dominated landscape extending from the southern end of the Salton Sea through Mexico almost to the Gulf of California. This represents a distributional shift in wintering areas within California as the species historically occurred in relative abundance in coastal southern California and the Central Valley. Records from remainder of wintering range are of relatively small numbers in scattered locations, though there has been no systematic attempt to survey across the species' entire winter range.

Assessing the species' overall population trend has been complicated by the lack of standardized survey protocol across the breeding or wintering range; however, all available data indicate a decline of 60% over the last 30–50 years. Most locations within the breeding range where long-term surveys have been completed have reported large declines over the last 10–20 years. For example, at the Pawnee National Grassland in Colorado the estimated population declined from 7,000 birds in the early 1970s to 1,280 in 1991 and 78 in 2002. At the Charles M. Russell NWR numbers declined by 50% from 1980 to 1996 and at the Thunder Basin National Grassland numbers dropped from 53 to 37 between 1993 and 2002. Analysis of California Christmas Bird Count data shows a decline of approximately 35% from 1955 to 1999. The species' total population was estimated at 11,000–14,000 individuals in 2005.[1-12]

ECOLOGY

Breeds in dry shortgrass prairie or semi-desert habitats that are heavily grazed with patches of bare ground, often amid prairie dog towns. Also breeds in recently plowed or fallow agricultural areas where native habitat is more fragmented. In winter uses plowed agricultural fields, heavily grazed grasslands, burned fields, and alkali flats. Feeds on a variety of small invertebrates, including grasshoppers and beetles. Nests are simple depressions on the ground in which three eggs are laid. Incubation lasts 28–31 days. Young are fully feathered when born and leave the nest within a few hours after hatching, when they immediately begin feeding themselves. Young can fly by 33–34 days. Number of clutches per season is not known but is thought to be as many as four. Can breed in their first year. Average life span of adults has been estimated at about 1.25 years, but one bird was known to have survived to 6 years old.[1,12,13]

THREATS

Loss and degradation of native shortgrass prairie habitat and other preferred native habitats was historically and continues to be the greatest threat to the species. Much grassland habitat on both the breeding and wintering grounds has been converted to agriculture and housing developments or has been disturbed by oil and mining operations. Approximately 40% of the shortgrass prairie native vegetation is estimated to have been lost across North America and in some states the percentage lost is much higher (80% in Texas). In California, the 4.4 million acres of native grassland habitat that existed historically in the San Joaquin Valley had been reduced to 1,500 acres by 1972. Perhaps of even greater importance was the virtual extinction of many species and populations of grazing

mammals, the most notable of which is the American bison. These grazers created large expanses of the heavily cropped and disturbed grassland habitat that is preferred by Mountain Plovers. Such habitats are also created naturally by prairie dogs, but populations of prairie dogs have been systematically removed and reduced through habitat loss, shooting, and poisoning with rodenticides. From 1980 to 1984 over $6 million of federal funds were spent to poison prairie dogs in a 450,000-acre area stretching across Montana, Wyoming, and South Dakota. Only 2% of the original 250 million acres originally inhabited by prairie dogs continues to support them today. In addition, prairie dog populations in many areas have been decimated by an introduced disease (sylvatic plague—in humans sometimes called the black plague) toward which they have little or no immunity.

Like many grassland-dependent species, Mountain Plovers have adapted to an ecosystem that is very dynamic and very likely the species has survived because of its ability to take advantage of newly created and modified habitats that occur as mosaics across the landscape. Cattle have replaced grazing from bison and other herbivores on grasslands throughout much of the shortgrass prairie region, but grazing management that allows grass to remain too high and/or that doesn't create barren openings results in habitat that is not suitable for Mountain Plovers. The species has been shown to be able to occasionally fledge young successfully in agricultural fields, but in some areas, nests can be destroyed in agricultural fields if planting operations begin after eggs are laid, and birds will abandon nests if crops grow too high before chicks hatch.

In some regions habitat has been lost to development. In the South Park area where the largest breeding population of Mountain Plovers now exists, housing development projects are expected to destroy some habitat now used by the species. The overall impact of this activity is difficult to quantify and is not well known.

On the wintering grounds in California where there is virtually no native habitat remaining, birds are now largely restricted to fallow agricultural fields, heavily grazed alfalfa fields, and burned Bermudagrass and asparagus fields, mostly within the Imperial Valley—a region that was once desert habitat and historically not used by plovers. In the Central Valley, where numbers of wintering birds have dropped significantly, the acreage of open cropland has also dropped with a doubling of acreage planted to vineyards—another habitat type that is not used by plovers. Little is known about wintering populations outside California, but many of the same issues are likely of concern throughout the species wintering range. For example, Chihuahuan Desert grasslands have been extensively altered through agricultural conversion, grazing, invasive plants, and shrub encroachment. There are few protected areas within the entire Chihuahuan Desert ecoregion.

The use of pesticides across much of the breeding and wintering range of Mountain Plover has led to concerns about potential negative reproductive and physiological effects of accumulated pesticides and other pollutants. Throughout much of the breeding range pesticides are widely used to control numbers of grasshoppers on rangeland, including areas where Mountain Plovers breed, though certain areas of public lands with prairie dog colonies have been excluded from pesticide application. Tests of Mountain Plover eggs collected in Colorado and Montana found DDE in all eggs and in four eggs levels were higher than those known to be detrimental in other bird species. In general, however, little is known about whether there are negative impacts from pesticides or other contaminants.[1,5,9–11,14–19]

CONSERVATION ACTION

In response to concern that Mountain Plover could become a federally threatened species, many local, state, and federal agencies and various farming and environmental organizations have initiated a number of conservation and monitoring projects. A conservation plan was drafted for the species in Colorado by a coalition involving the U.S. Fish and Wildlife Service (USFWS), Colorado Division of Wildlife, the Colorado Farm Bureau, Rocky Mountain Bird Observatory (RMBO), the Nature Conservancy, and the U.S. Department of Agriculture. As part of this plan RMBO implemented a toll-free number for farmers to call to have a biologist visit their fields before plowing in order to mark plover nests so that farmers could avoid destroying the eggs. More than 22,000 acres in Colorado and 2,000 acres in Nebraska were checked for birds in 2003. RMBO has also produced a video on Mountain Plover conservation that will be distributed and used for outreach and education activities across the species range. The Colorado Division of Wildlife is working toward the development and funding of a program to purchase conservation easements on privately owned shortgrass prairie habitat. A similar program by the Nebraska Game and Parks Commission is in the early stages of implementation. A number of Native American tribes have developed coalitions to develop management plans for the restoration of prairie dog populations and grassland ecosystems on tribal lands. The Nature Conservancy has initiated a grassland conservation program called Prairie Wings, which hopes to target conservation activities toward key areas across the shortgrass prairie and which will clearly be of benefit to Mountain Plovers.

A multistate conservation plan for black-tailed prairie dog was completed in 2003 that hopes to slow or stop the loss of prairie dog populations through a variety of landowner incentives and regulations. Such activities would clearly benefit Mountain Plovers. Approximately 8% of shortgrass prairie habitat in the U.S. is under federal government ownership. In 1999 and 2000, the U.S. National Park Service and the U.S. Fish and Wildlife Service banned shooting and poisoning of prairie dogs on national parks and USFWS refuges. Many states have instituted hunting seasons and limits to control the number of prairie dogs being shot. Poisoning and shooting of prairie dogs has been halted on many lands managed by the Bureau of Land Management and National Grasslands managed by the U.S. Forest Service. Various research and management activities have taken place on a number of federally owned lands, including National Grasslands where the species occurs. These activities include prescribed burns but success has been limited and mixed. USDA-APHIS has agreed to avoid prairie dog colonies and known Mountain Plover nesting areas when applying grasshopper control pesticides to grasslands in Montana and Wyoming. A proposal to list Mountain Plover as a federally threatened species was withdrawn by the USFWS in 2003.

In California, at least three counties are drafting Habitat Conservation Plans with the USFWS that will cover officially listed federally endangered and threatened species as well as Mountain Plover and other nonlisted species. These plans would target protection and management of wintering habitats for Mountain Plover and other species while allowing the loss of habitat for development in other areas.

Within the species' wintering range a coalition of groups, including Pronatura Noreste, World Wildlife Fund, and the Nature Conservancy, has targeted the Chihuahuan Desert ecoregion for conservation and in 2002 the group completed a detailed conservation assessment for the region. The assessment includes a portfolio of sites that require protection to meet minimum requirements for conserving the highest priorities species and ecological communities. In 2000, Pronatura Noreste and the Nature Conservancy purchased a 7,000-acre ranch in Mexico's Cuatro Ciénegas Valley that includes desert grasslands.[1,5,19–26]

CONSERVATION NEEDS

- Ensure that management of publicly owned locations currently supporting Mountain Plover continues to maintain habitat conditions beneficial to the species.
- Increase efforts at landowner education and outreach, incentives, and other activities that may increase productivity of plovers on private lands.
- Increase protection and conservation of remaining native habitat within the wintering range of Mountain Plover.
- Slow or halt declines in populations of all prairie dogs.
- Restore native grassland ecosystems, including the reintroduction of native mammalian herbivores where possible.
- Work with National Resources Conservation Service in the implementation of Farm Bill conservation incentive programs so that the habitat conditions specified on lands potentially used by Mountain Plovers are beneficial to the species.
- Implement a rangewide survey, including northern Mexico, designed to assess overall population status and trends.

References

1. Knopf, F.L. 1996. Mountain Plover (*Charadrius montanus*). In *The Birds of North America*, No. 211 (A. Poole and F. Gill, eds.). The Academy of Natural Sciences, Philadelphia, PA, and the American Ornithologists' Union, Washington, DC.

2. Plumb, R.E., F.L. Knopf, and S.H. Anderson. 2005. Minimum Population Size of Mountain Plovers Breeding in Wyoming. *Wilson Bulletin* 117:15–22.

3. Dreitz, V.J., M.B. Wunder, and F.L. Knopf. 2005. Movements and Home Ranges of Mountain Plovers Raising Broods in Three Colorado Landscapes. *Wilson Bulletin* 117:128–132.

4. Oyler-McCance, S.J., J. St. John, F.L. Knopf, and T.W. Quinn. 2005. Population Genetic Analysis of Mountain Plover Using Mitochondrial DNA Sequence Data. *Condor* 107:353–362.

5. U.S. Fish and Wildlife Service. 2001. Endangered and Threatened Wildlife and Plants; Withdrawal of the Proposed Rule to List the Mountain Plover as Threatened. *Federal Register* 68(174): 53083–53101.

6. National Audubon Society. 2002. *Colorado's Important Bird Areas Program*. http://www.audubon.org/bird/iba/co.html (accessed 1 October 2003).

7. Chipley, R.M., G.H. Fenwick, M.J. Parr, and D.N. Pashley. 2003. *The American Bird Conservancy Guide to the 500 Most Important Bird Areas in the United States*. Random House, New York, NY.

8. Igl, L. D. 2003. *Bird Checklists of the United States* (Version 12MAY03). Northern Prairie Wildlife Research Center Home Page, Jamestown, ND. http://www.npwrc.usgs.gov/resource/othrdata/chekbird/chekbird.htm (accessed 18 August 2003).

9. Wunder, M.B., F.L. Knopf, and C.A. Pague. 2003. The High-elevation Population of Mountain Plovers in Colorado. *Condor* 105: 654–662.

10. Wunder, M.B., and F.L. Knopf. 2003. The Imperial Valley of California Is Critical to Wintering Mountain Plovers. *Journal of Field Ornithology* 74:74–80.

11. Cooper, D. 2001. Important bird areas of California. Unpublished manuscript available from Audubon California, 6042 Monte Vista St., Los Angeles, CA 90042.

12. Dinsmore, S.J., G.C. White, and F.L. Knopf. 2003. Annual Survival and Population Estimates of Mountain Plovers in Southern Phillips County, Montana. *Ecological Applications* 13:1013–1026.

13. Dechant, J. A., M. L. Sondreal, D. H. Johnson, L. D. Igl, C. M. Goldade, M. P. Nenneman, and B. R. Euliss. 2003. *Effects of Management Practices on Grassland Birds: Mountain Plover*. Northern Prairie Wildlife Research Center, Jamestown, ND. Northern Prairie Wildlife Research Center Online. http://www.npwrc.usgs.gov/resource/literatr/grasbird/mopl/mopl.htm (Version 12DEC2003).

14. Gauthier, D.A., A. Lafon, T. Tombs, J. Hoth, and E. Wilken. 2003. *Grasslands: Toward a North American Conservation Strategy*. Canadian Plains Research Center, University of Regina, Regina, Saskatchewan, and Commission for Environmental Cooperation, Montreal, QC, Canada. 99 pp.

15. Ricketts, T.H., E. Dinerstein, D.M. Olson, C.J. Loucks, et al. 1999. *Terrestrial Ecoregions of North Ameri-*

ca: A Conservation Assessment. Island Press, Washington, DC. 485 pp.

16. Vickery, P.D., P.B. Tubaro, J. M. Cardoso da Silva, B.G. Peterjohn, J.R. Herkert, and R.B. Cavalcanti. 1999. Conservation of Grassland Birds in the Western Hemisphere. Pages 2–26 in Ecology and Conservation of Grassland Birds of the Western Hemisphere (P.D. Vickery and J.R. Herkert, eds.). Studies in Avian Biology No. 19, Cooper Ornithological Society, Camarillo, CA.

17. Manzano-Fischer, P., R. List, and G. Ceballos. 1999. Grassland Birds in Prairie Dog Towns in Northwestern Chihuahua, Mexico. Pages 263–271 in Ecology and Conservation of Grassland Birds of the Western Hemisphere (P.D. Vickery and J.R. Herkert, eds.). Studies in Avian Biology No. 19, Cooper Ornithological Society, Camarillo, CA.

18. Roemer, D.M., and S.C. Forrest. 1996. Prairie Dog Poisoning in Northern Great Plains: An Analysis of Programs and Policies. Environmental Management 20:349–359.

19. Colorado Division of Wildlife. 2003. Conservation Plan for Grassland Species in Colorado. 205 pp.

20. Montana Partners in Flight. 2000. Partners in Flight Draft Bird Conservation Plan Montana. American Bird Conservancy, Kalispell, MT.

21. Beidleman, C.A. 2000. Partners in Flight Land Bird Conservation Plan Colorado, Estes Park, CO.

22. Miller, B., C. Wemmer, D. Biggins, and R. Reading. 1990. A Proposal to Conserve Black-footed Ferrets and the Prairie Dog Ecosystem. Environmental Management 14:763–769.

23. Miller, B., G. Ceballos, and R.P. Reading. 1994. The Prairie Dog and Biotic Diversity. Conservation Biology 8:677–681.

24. Predator Conservation Alliance. 2001. Restoring the Prairie Dog Ecosystem of the Great Plains. Predator Conservation Alliance, Bozeman, MT.

25. Pronatura Noreste, The Nature Conservancy, and The World Wildlife Fund. 2004. Ecoregional Conservation Assessment of the Chihuahuan Desert, 2nd ed. www.conserveonline.org.

26. The Nature Conservancy. 2004. Chihuahuan Desert. http://nature.org/wherewework/northamerica/mexico/work/art8620.html (accessed 29 January 2004).

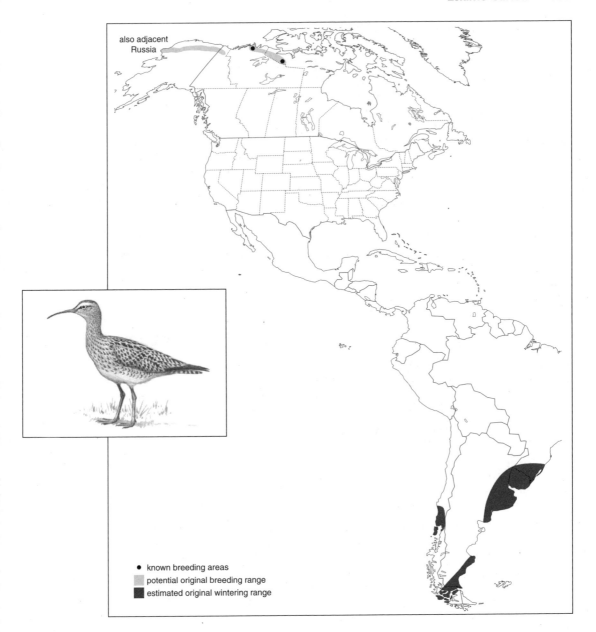

also adjacent
Russia

● known breeding areas
▨ potential original breeding range
■ estimated original wintering range

ESKIMO CURLEW (*Numenius borealis*)

Flocks of hundreds and occasionally thousands of Eskimo Curlews were once a common sight during spring migration in the central prairies of the U.S. and Canada but extensive loss of grassland habitat, market hunting, and the extinction of a major insect food source have brought the species to near or actual extinction.

STATUS AND DISTRIBUTION

The species was decimated before 1900 so knowledge of its range and numbers is fragmentary and has been pieced together only from diligent searching and compilation of many historical accounts. Breeding was documented at only two locations in northwestern Canada: at Bathurst Peninsula (Liverpool Bay at the mouth of Anderson River east to Horton River and Franklin Bay Lake north of Fort Enterprise) and near Point Lake (area between Melville Hills along the southern shore of Amundsen Gulf south to Coronation Gulf along the Copper River); but its range is surmised to have extended from the Arctic Coastal Plain of Alaska (and possibly portions of far eastern Siberia) east to northern Nunavut.

Eskimo Curlews migrated southeastward in the fall with most birds stopping over at sites along the coast of Labrador and Newfoundland to feed on crowberries and blueberries in heath shrubland and on a variety of insects and crustaceans in adjacent coastal habitats before departing for a nonstop flight to South America. Smaller numbers of birds occurred regularly across the Canadian Maritimes and northeast U.S., with larger numbers occasionally appearing after northeasterly storms. A few fall records exist in the midwest U.S., including Michigan, Illinois, and Nebraska, indicating a minor inland fall migratory pathway. Although unknown, birds may have stopped over at coastal locations in northeastern South America, especially in the Guianas, where large numbers of other shorebird species regularly concentrate during migration.

Birds were known to winter in the pampas of Argentina and likely in adjoining grassland regions containing permanent and ephemeral wetlands of southern Brazil, Uruguay, and Chile. There is some evidence that birds left the pampas in midwinter and moved to extreme southern Patagonia and northern Tierra del Fuego.

In the spring birds moved north through South and Central America (though only a few records exist from this area) reaching stopover locations in Texas by March. Birds continued north through the central U.S. and Canada, stopping off at locations in tallgrass and shortgrass prairies before eventually arriving at the breeding grounds in late May and June.

The total population size of Eskimo Curlew is estimated to have once numbered in the hundreds of thousands, perhaps similar in magnitude to the closely related Little Curlew of Siberia, which is estimated to number about 180,000 individuals. In the period 1850–1900, tens of thousands of Eskimo Curlews were killed annually during migration across the central U.S., packed in barrels, and shipped via train for sale in markets in metropolitan

centers like Chicago, Detroit, New York, St. Louis, and others. It was not uncommon for thousands of birds to be killed at one location in a single day. By 1900 sightings of the species were rare and from 1945–1985 there were reports in 23 different years, though it is difficult to ascertain their reliability and few have been substantiated with photographs. The last record confirmed with photographs in the U.S. was in Texas in 1962 and the last specimen was a bird killed by a hunter in Barbados in 1963. Unconfirmed sightings by reliable observers have continued since then, including a reported flock of 23 birds in Texas in 1981 and the report of an adult with a single young bird in May 1983 in the Arctic National Wildlife Refuge (NWR). Hope remains that a small number of birds may still survive. If the species is not extinct the population is thought to number fewer than 50 birds.[1-4]

ECOLOGY

The few historical breeding records for Eskimo Curlew are from tundra habitat in the arctic and subarctic where the birds probably nested on drier, higher areas within the tundra complex. Nests were reported as depressions on bare ground, where typically four eggs were laid, one clutch per season. Breeding season was said to have extended from May through mid-August with a hatching peak from the last week of June through the first two weeks of July. No information was ever recorded about the species' incubation period or fledging period. Both sexes are thought to have incubated and cared for young. Like all shorebirds, Eskimo Curlew chicks were precocial and could leave the nest within hours after hatching, feeding on their own.

During the fall migration southward, Eskimo Curlews preferred open heath–shrub habitat along the Labrador coast and Newfoundland as well as similar berry-producing habitats, including grasslands and blueberry barrens, in New England. Overwintered on southern South American pampas and Patagonia grasslands intermixed with small, shallow wetlands, where they probably foraged on insects, gastropods, and crustaceans, though mutilla berries (similar to crowberries) are abundant in Patagonia and may have served as an important food source.

During spring migration frequented tallgrass and mixed-grass prairie of the central U.S. and Canada. Fed on insects and may have specialized in finding locations with high concentrations of the now-extinct Rocky Mountain Grasshopper, extracting egg cases and emerging nymphs from sub-surface soils.[1]

THREATS

Historically, overhunting was a major threat, including market hunting for sale of large numbers in city markets, especially from 1860 to 1890. At the same time, critical grassland migratory stopover habitat underwent massive conversion to agricultural land uses. For example, 88–99% of the midwestern tallgrass prairie is estimated to have been lost since 1850. In some areas the loss has been even more severe. Less than 1% of original habitat in a forest/grassland ecozone extending from Illinois south to Texas is considered intact. Remnants of tallgrass prairie habitat in southern Iowa and northern Missouri are restricted to 20 sites each less than 20 acres in size. Gulf coastal prairies were eliminated from Louisiana and only 1% of this habitat in Texas is now considered pristine. Conversion of habitat in concert with targeted use of pesticides and various habitat treatments also eventually led to the extinction of the Rocky Mountain Grasshopper, which may have been a major food source for migrating Eskimo Curlew.

Currently, habitat encompassing historic Eskimo Curlew breeding locations appears to be generally undisturbed, though there is potential interest in mineral exploration and mining in the area, which could degrade or ultimately destroy the habitat. If the species still survives, remaining individuals will be reliant on grasslands in migration and on the wintering grounds. As in most grassland ecosystems greatest current threat continues to be loss and degradation of native habitat largely through conversion to cropland, overgrazing on rangeland, housing development, mineral and oil extraction activities, and fire suppression. In Argentina and Brazil, government programs are promoting, through financial incentives, commercial tree plantations composed primarily of exotic species that are often placed in native grassland habitat. Commercial plantations occupied over 370,000 acres of native grassland habitat in 1994 within Argentina's Corrientes province and there was a 500% increase in forestry plantations between 1995 and 2000. More catastrophic in the short-term could be the loss of remaining individuals from a pesticide poisoning event on the South American wintering grounds as occurred in 1995–96 when over 5000 Swainson's Hawks were killed by pesticides in Argentinean grasslands.[1,2,5–10]

CONSERVATION ACTION

Searches have continued for Eskimo Curlews within former breeding and wintering areas and in migratory corridors but without any definitive sightings of the species. There has been increasing activity in grassland habitat conservation within the former spring migration corridor for Eskimo Curlew, especially across the U.S. and Canada and involving a great many governmental and nongovernmental organizations. Throughout much of this region, state or provincial agencies own or manage the bulk of the conservation lands that are protected; however, the percentage of the total area protected is quite small. In the Central Tallgrass Prairie ecoregion, for example, only 8% of the desired conservation acreage is protected.

Partners in Flight and the Nature Conservancy have independently developed or are in the process of developing ecoregional plans for the tallgrass and mixed grass prairie regions across which Eskimo Curlews once migrated. These plans recommend both maintaining and enhancing existing conservation areas in the regions and developing projects to restore prairie habitat. A number of initiatives are underway within the region, many of them targeting tallgrass prairie habitat for populations of the rapidly declining Greater Prairie Chicken. For example, in Missouri the Nature Conservancy has acquired several parcels of grassland habitat and is managing for the benefit of Greater Prairie-Chickens and various habitat-enhancement projects were supported with approximately $200,000 in grants in 2001. Similar efforts are underway in Wisconsin and North Dakota. In Iowa, the Kellerton Grasslands Bird Conservation Area was established in 2000 with the goal of establishing a 2,000-acre publicly owned prairie preserve within a 10,000-acre block that contains another 2,000 acres of privately owned grasslands. Also in Iowa, the Neal Smith NWR is working to reestablish 8,000 acres of tallgrass prairie and oak savanna by connecting small prairie remnants through a program of plantings of native grasses and flowering plants.

On the wintering grounds, Aves Argentina is focusing research activities on the pampas and campos grasslands of Argentina. They also initiated a conservation program in 2003 that will identify Important Bird Areas in the region and work toward their protection and proper management. The grasslands in this region also support 14 globally threatened bird species and wintering populations of Swainson's Hawk, Upland Sandpiper, and Bobolink.[1,5–18]

CONSERVATION NEEDS

- Incorporate habitat objectives, including periodic prescribed burns, into public land management in areas where Eskimo Curlews could occur during migration.
- Slow or halt incentives for commercial forestry plantations on wintering ground grasslands in Argentina and Brazil.
- Provide incentives for private landowners to manage their lands to the benefit of grassland birds in areas where Eskimo Curlews migrated or wintered.
- Purchase land or conservation easements on private lands in areas in the U.S. like the Sand Hills and Flint Hills that still support healthy blocks of tallgrass prairie habitat.
- Continue intensive systematic searches of potential migratory corridors, breeding, and wintering areas in an effort to detect Eskimo Curlews.
- Prevent oil and mineral exploration in areas that were known to support breeding Eskimo Curlew.

References

1. Gill, R.E., Jr., P. Canevari, and E.H. Iverson. 1998. Eskimo Curlew (*Numenius borealis*). In *The Birds of North America*, No. 347 (A. Poole and F. Gill, eds.). The Birds of North America, Inc., Philadelphia, PA.

2. BirdLife International. 2000. *Threatened Birds of the World*. Lynx Editions and BirdLife International, Barcelona, Spain, and Cambridge, UK.

3. Gollop, J.B., T.W. Barry, and E.H. Iversen. 1986. *Eskimo Curlew: A Vanishing Species?* Saskatchewan Nat. Hist. Soc. Spec. Publ. 17.

4. Risdahl, G. Personal communication.

5. Ricketts et al. 1999. *Terrestrial Ecoregions of North America: A Conservation Assessment*. Island Press, Washington, DC. 485 pp.

6. Vickery, P.D., P.B. Tubaro, J. M. Cardoso da Silva, B.G. Peterjohn, J.R. Herkert, and R.B. Cavalcanti. 1999. *Conservation of Grassland Birds in the Western Hemisphere*. Pages 2–26 in Ecology and Conservation of Grassland Birds of the Western Hemisphere (P.D. Vickery and J.R.

Herkert, eds.). Studies in Avian Biology No. 19, Cooper Ornithological Society, Camarillo, CA.

7. Di Giacomo, A., and S. Krapovickas. 2001. Afforestation Threatens Argentina's Grasslands. *World Birdwatch* 23:24–25.

8. Krapovickas, S., and A. Di Giacomo. 1998. Conservation of Pampas and Campos Grasslands in Argentina. *Parks* 8(3):47–53.

9. Gauthier, D.A., A. Lafon, T. Tombs, J. Hoth, and E. Wilken. 2003. *Grasslands: Toward a North American Conservation Strategy*. Canadian Plains Research Center, University of Regina, Regina, SK, and Commission for Environmental Cooperation, Montreal, QC, Canada. 99 pp.

10. Goldstein, M.I., T.E. Lacher, Jr., B. Woodbridge, M.J. Bechard, S.B. Canavelli, M.E. Zaccagnini, G.P. Cobb, E.J. Scollon, R. Tribolet, and M.J. Hooper. 1999. Monocrotophos-induced Mass Mortality of Swainson's Hawks in Argentina, 1995–96. *Ecotoxicology* 8:201–214.

11. The Nature Conservancy Central Tallgrass Prairie Ecoregion Planning Team. 2000. *Conservation in a Highly Fragmented Landscape: The Central Tallgrass Prairie Ecoregional Conservation Plan*. The Nature Conservancy, Midwest Conservation Science Center, Minneapolis, MN.

12. Fitzgerald, J., B. Busby, M. Howery, R. Klataske, D. Reinking, and D. Pashley. 2000. *Partners in Flight Bird Conservation Plan for the Osage Plains*. American Bird Conservancy, The Plains, VA.

13. Fitzgerald, J.A., and D.N. Pashley. 2000. *Partners in Flight Bird Conservation Plan for the Dissected Till Plains*. American Bird Conservancy, The Plains, VA.

14. Fitzgerald, J.A., D.N. Pashley, and B. Pardo. 1999. *Partners in Flight Bird Conservation Plan for the Northern Mixed-grass Prairie*. American Bird Conservancy, The Plains, VA.

15. Fitzgerald, J.A., D.N. Pashley, S.J. Lewis, and B. Pardo. 1998. *Partners in Flight Bird Conservation Plan for the Northern Tallgrass Prairie*. American Bird Conservancy, The Plains, VA.

16. Iowa Department of Natural Resources. 2002. *The Reintroduction of Prairie Chickens to Iowa*. http:// www.iowadnr.com/wildlife/files/FMAmay2000.html (accessed 27 August 2003).

17. Sample, D.W., and M.J. Mossman. 1997. *Managing Habitat for Grassland Birds: A Guide for Wisconsin*. Wisconsin Department of Natural Resources, Madison, WI.

18. Missouri Department of Conservation. 2002. *Greater Prairie Chicken*. http://www.conservation.state .mo.us/nathis/birds/chickens/.

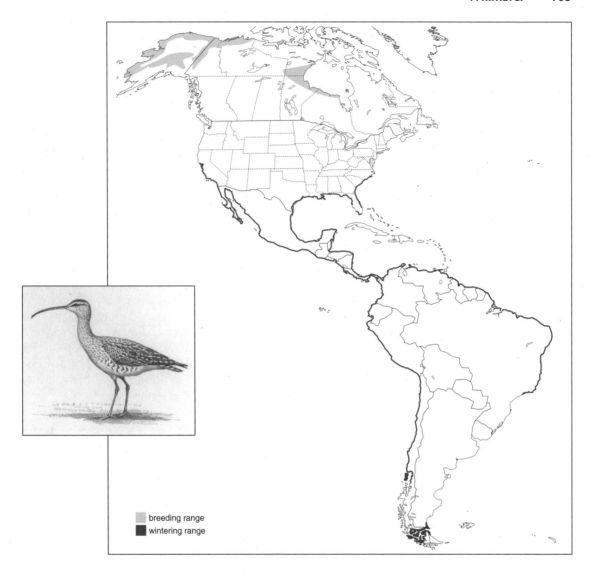

breeding range
wintering range

WHIMBREL (*Numenius phaeopus*)

Unlike its close relative, the Eskimo Curlew, this species survived the market hunting era of the 1800s but its numbers remain relatively low. Its reliance on intertidal marine habitats and mangrove ecosystems in South America during the winter puts it at risk as such habitats continue to be lost and degraded.

STATUS AND DISTRIBUTION

The species has two disjunct breeding areas in North America. One extends from western coastal Alaska west through Yukon to the northwestern coastal Northwest Territories. The other breeding area is found along the western side of the Hudson

Bay from southwestern Nunavut inland to the southeastern tip of Northwest Territories and south through northeastern Manitoba and northern Ontario. Approximately 65% of the species' North American population—about 40,000 of the 57,000—is estimated to breed in Alaska. Wintering range is extensive, extending from the southern Pacific and Atlantic coasts of U.S. south through Central America and the Caribbean to South America. Numbers in wintering range generally increase toward the southern portion. Larger numbers migrate long distances to southern South America, where there are concentrations along the coasts of Chile, Suriname, and northern central Brazil.

Important breeding sites for the species in Alaska include Yukon Delta National Wildlife Refuge (NWR), National Park Service's Bering Land Bridge National Preserve, Selawik NWR, Kanuti NWR, Arctic NWR, and the National Petroleum Reserve–Alaska. Although there is little specific information about breeding sites in Canada a number of protected areas encompass portions of the breeding range of the species, including Manitoba's Wapusk National Park (2.8 million acres) and Nunavut's Ijiraliq (Meliadine River) Territorial Park and McConnell River Bird Sanctuary.

Important migratory stopover locations in Canada include Ontario's Presqu'ile Provincial Park (2,350 acres—up to 1,000 birds have been recorded), Longridge Point Important Bird Area (IBA) (one-day counts of 225 birds during a study in 1993), Ekwan to Lakitusaki Shores IBA, and Greater Rondeau Area IBA (maximum of 250 recorded during spring migration). Up to 1,000 Whimbrels have been counted at Quebec's Lagune du Havre aux Basques et plage de l'Ouest Îles-de-la-Madeleine IBA. In British Columbia up to 700 have occurred at Tofino in spring and 750 in fall at Cleland Island.

Important spring migratory stopover locations in the U.S. include California's Central Valley, Imperial Valley, and Antelope Valley. Probably what are the largest regular concentrations in the U.S. (perhaps in all of North America) occur in the Imperial Valley where as many as 10,000 birds (representing nearly 20% of the population) have been recorded. Other spring concentration areas include the coastal saltmarshes of New Jersey (hundreds, perhaps thousands use the area), Washington's Skagit Flats (up to 450), and Oregon's Tillamook area (up to 350 birds). In Texas, up to 453 birds have been counted in spring migration at Anahuac NWR.

Important fall migratory stopover locations in the U.S. include the coastal Washington County region of Maine (400–700 birds use the area in fall migration), Georgia's Altamaha River Delta IBA (maximum 500), and Oregon's Yaquina Bay (up to 155 in fall). In Washington, Ocean Shores has hosted up to 600 in fall migration and Leadbetter Point up to 400.

The largest wintering concentrations occur south of the U.S. especially in South America where wintering population was estimated at 25,000 birds in late 1980s. This would suggest that 50–60% of the total population winters north of South America (since the total population was estimated at 57,000). If so, birds must either occur in small numbers at a vast number of locations from the U.S. south through the Caribbean and Central America or there are undiscovered major wintering locations in the region. In Mexico, the species winters at Ría Lagartos in Yucatán and occurs at the Laguna Madre and Delta del Río Bravo in Tamaulipas. Up to 504 have been found in January in Panama's Upper Bay of Panama, a site that in migration has hosted a maximum of 5,844 birds (10% of population). The Chiman Wetlands that adjoin the Upper Bay of Panama are also important, with fall migration counts as high as 994 and a January 1993 total of 176 birds. In northern South America, 1,000–2,000 have been recorded at Suriname's Bigi Pan, 850–1,500 at Suriname's Coppenamemonding Nature Reserve, and up to 1,000 at Suriname's Wia Wia Nature Reserve. An estimated 25% (6,000+) of the South American wintering population was found near Chiloé Island, Chile and 44% (11,000) at Reentráncias Maranhenses along the coast of northcentral Brazil.

There are no BBS data for this species. An analysis of Christmas Bird Count data shows a nonsignificant decrease of 0.2% per year from 1959 to 1988. Data from the International Shorebird Survey show a significant decline from 1972 to 1983 but an analysis of Maritimes Shorebird Survey data from 1974 to 1991 shows no clear trend. However, the U.S. Shorebird Conservation Plan classified the species as one showing a significant declining population trend. The species' total population was estimated at 57,000 individuals in 2000 with 40,000 in the western population and 17,000 in the eastern population.[1–16]

ECOLOGY

Breeds in subarctic and alpine tundra and various taiga wetlands and heath uplands. Nests are depressions on ground where four eggs are laid and are incubated by both male and female for 22–28 days. Young are precocial and leave nest within hours after hatching and forage on their own. Both adults defend the young and brood them. The young are estimated to fledge in 28–30 days. Only a single brood is produced each year. Feeds on a variety of foods, including berries, small insects, crabs and other marine crustaceans, and invertebrates. May not breed until 2–3 years old. On wintering grounds use a variety of coastal wetlands ranging from intertidal flats, saltmarshes, and beaches to rocky coastline to mangrove forests in South and Central America and the Caribbean.[1]

THREATS

On the breeding grounds, large areas of the species' habitat in Alaska are within National Wildlife Refuges or other protected areas. However, much of the species' range in Alaska and Canada is within areas that could be opened to oil and gas extraction activities. Such activities can cause habitat loss and degradation from establishment and expansion of infrastructure and pollution and increases in predatory mammals and birds (that capitalize on garbage). In 2004, a plan was announced to open for oil and gas development the 8.8-million-acre Northwest Planning Area of the National Petroleum Reserve–Alaska. Proposals were brought before the U.S. Congress a number of times, including in 2003, to override the conservation mandate for the Arctic National Wildlife Refuge to allow oil and gas extraction activities. Oil and gas exploration and mining activity is expected to show increases within portions of the Canadian breeding range as well. An interesting wildlife management paradox is that the massive increases in Snow Goose populations that nest along coastal Hudson Bay have resulted in major habitat destruction (from birds feeding on vegetation), which may impact Whimbrel populations that overlap with Snow Goose nesting areas.

In migration and on the wintering grounds the major threat is continued loss and degradation of coastal wetlands. In the U.S., such habitat loss has been dramatic. Florida and Texas have each lost at least 7.5 million acres of wetlands and Louisiana between 2.5 and 7.5 million acres over the last 200 years. In Louisiana and Texas coastal wetlands are continuing to be lost to erosion and subsequent saltwater intrusion. In California's San Francisco Bay, 80% of intertidal habitats have been destroyed. South of the U.S., loss of coastal wetland habitat in many countries continues to be a major threat. Loss of mangrove habitat is of particular concern as mangrove forests support the largest wintering concentrations of Whimbrel in South America (in Suriname and Brazil). Although the mangrove forests of Suriname and the Maranhão region of coastal north-central Brazil

are still relatively intact, throughout the species' wintering range much mangrove habitat has been lost or degraded by sedimentation and pollution from agricultural runoff and deforestation, changes in hydrology from road projects and developments, oil pollution, and cutting for fuel and charcoal production. For example, along Colombia's northwest coast mangrove forest declined by 64% between 1956 and 1995 from development, highway construction, agriculture, and aquaculture. In Venezuela's Lake Maracaibo, the loss of mangrove habitat was estimated at 90% between 1960 and 1993. In some areas large expanses of mangroves have been removed for shrimp farming or salt production. Between 1964 and 1989 in Costa Rica's Gulf of Nicoya 1,582 acres of mangroves were lost to shrimp farms and 287 acres to salt production.

In recent years there has been an increase in proposals for development of coastal tourism facilities that would destroy or degrade mangrove habitats. In general, mangrove habitat is underrepresented in parks and other protected areas throughout the wintering range. Several threatened bird species rely on these habitats, including the Mangrove Hummingbird, a species restricted to the Pacific coast of Costa Rica; the Yellow-billed Cotinga, occurring only on the Pacific coasts of Costa Rica and Panama; and the Sapphire-bellied Hummingbird, confined to the northern coast of Colombia. In addition, mangrove habitats support a host of other threatened animal species and marine species of economic importance.

Many estuarine systems within the migratory range of the Whimbrel are also showing degraded environmental conditions. For example, the percentage of the Delaware Estuary that tested above EPA ecological limits for metal contaminants increased from 5% to 22% from 1990–93 to 1997. Similarly, the percentage of the Chesapeake Bay that tested above EPA ecological limits for organic contaminants increased from 2 to 34% from 1990–93 to 1997. In northern Chile, high levels of cadmium were found in Whimbrels and their prey as a result of the discarding of large amounts of untreated mining wastes.

Clearly, any activities that result in loss or degradation of habitat, including through alteration of water levels, destruction of buffer habitat, spraying of pesticides, ditching, accumulation of contaminants, grazing, or spread of invasive species like phragmites, are continuing threats to the species. Sea level rise with global warming may become the most pervasive and difficult threat to the species and loss of saltmarsh habitat to sea level rise has already become a problem in some areas of the northeast U.S.[1,5,12,13,17–34]

CONSERVATION ACTION

U.S. and Canadian shorebird conservation plans have been developed that provide recommendations for management, research, outreach, and education for Whimbrel and other shorebird species. The Western Hemisphere Shorebird Reserve Network, RAMSAR, and the BirdLife International Important Bird Areas programs have identified many key breeding, wintering, and migratory stopover locations for the species and in some locations have initiated conservation and outreach projects. World Wildlife Fund–Canada, the Canadian Nature Federation, Canadian Parks and Wilderness Society, and many other organizations have been working with national and provincial governments to increase the number of protected areas in Canada, including within the breeding range of Whimbrel. For example, Wapusk National Park in Manitoba was established in 1996 and other potential parks continue to be planned for and discussed.

The primary wintering areas within Suriname are largely government-owned and considered protected areas, but, as in many South American countries, there are limited resources for enforcement of regulations. Similarly, much of the major Brazilian wintering area is within an official Area of Environmental Protection, which allows sustainable natural resource use, especially traditional uses. On the wintering grounds there is an urgent need for increased awareness of communities and governments to the ecological importance of coastal habitats, including mangrove forest and to increase acreage of mangroves within protected areas. Some limited work is being done to restore mangrove habitats in a few locations but few international conservation organizations seem to be working on the issue. There are laws in Costa Rica and Venezuela that make it illegal to remove mangroves but these laws are not enforced. A collaborative project to develop sustainable management alternatives for wetlands of the South American Pacific Coast, including Chile, Ecuador, and Colombia, was recently initiated that should benefit habitats used by Whimbrel. Ducks Unlimited

has funded waterfowl and waterbird surveys of the key wintering areas for Whimbrel in Suriname for many years that also monitor habitat conditions of these sites.

A great many organization, agencies, and coalitions are working on coastal habitat restoration and protection projects with the U.S., many of which will likely eventually benefit Whimbrels. For example, the Coastal America Partnership, a coalition of federal agencies, state and local governments, and private organizations, identifies and implements local wetland restoration and protection projects throughout the U.S. The Partnership had initiated more than 500 projects impacting hundreds of thousands of acres of wetland habitat as of 2002. NOAA's Fisheries Restoration Center Program and the Louisiana Department of Natural Resources through the Coastal Wetlands Planning, Protection, and Restoration Act have initiated projects benefiting 100,000 acres of coastal wetlands along Louisiana's coast within the migratory stopover and wintering range of Whimbrel at a cost of $120 million. Another example is the Texas Prairie Wetlands Project that was created by U.S. Fish and Wildlife Service (USFWS), Texas Parks and Wildlife Department, USDA's Natural Resources Conservation Service, and Ducks Unlimited to provide technical assistance and financial incentives to private landowners for improving or restoring wetland habitats along the Gulf Coast. Through January 1994, 4,901 acres of wetland projects had been completed or were under construction for 30 landowners, and 132 landowners controlling 1,231,023 acres had received on-site technical assistance. The Atlantic Coast Joint Venture (ACJV) has been very active in protecting wintering habitat through a multitude of land acquisition and habitat restoration projects involving more than $230 million in grants and matching funds and nearly 300,000 acres of habitat. Many of these ACJV-funded projects are within important migratory stopover areas for Whimbrel along the Atlantic coast. Ducks Unlimited has spearheaded a host of initiatives along the Atlantic coast to restore saltmarshes, which are used extensively by Whimbrels in spring migration. For example, Ducks Unlimited and USFWS partnered with Suffolk County Vector Control and the New York State Department of Environmental Conservation to restore hundreds of acres of saltmarsh on Long Island.[1,12,13,15,16,24–40]

CONSERVATION NEEDS

- Slow production of global warming pollution.
- Ensure that management of publicly owned locations currently supporting Whimbrel continues to maintain habitat conditions beneficial to the species.
- Increase protection and conservation of coastal habitat within the wintering range of Whimbrel.
- Restore coastal marine ecosystems within the migratory and wintering range of Whimbrel.
- Implement a rangewide wintering and migration survey designed to assess overall population status and trends and to determine if there are other unidentified key wintering and stopover locations for the species.

References

1. Skeel, M.A., and E. P. Mallory. 1996. Whimbrel (*Numenius phaeopus*). In *The Birds of North America*, No. 219 (A. Poole and F. Gill, eds.). The Academy of Natural Sciences, Philadelphia, PA, and the American Ornithologists' Union, Washington, DC.

2. Sauer, J. R., J. E. Hines, and J. Fallon. 2003. *The North American Breeding Bird Survey, Results and Analysis 1966–2002*. Version 2003.1, USGS Patuxent Wildlife Research Center, Laurel, MD.

3. Bird Studies Canada. 2003. *Important Bird Areas of Canada*. http://www.bsc-eoc.org/iba/IBAsites.html (accessed 16 June 2004).

4. Igl, L. D. 2003. *Bird Checklists of the United States* (Version 12MAY03). Northern Prairie Wildlife Research Center Home Page, Jamestown, ND. http://www.npwrc.usgs.gov/resource/othrdata/chekbird/chekbird.htm (accessed 18 August 2003).

5. Alaska Shorebird Working Group. 2000. *A Conservation Plan for Alaska Shorebirds*. Unpublished report, Alaska Shorebird Working Group. Available through U.S. Fish and Wildlife Service, Migratory Bird Management, Anchorage, AK. 47 pp.

6. Skagen, S.K., P.B. Sharpe, R.G. Waltermire, and M.B. Dillon. 1999. *Biogeographic Profiles of Shorebird Migration in Midcontinental North America*. Biological Science Report USGS/BRD/BSR—2000-0003. U.S. Government Printing Office, Denver, CO. 167 pp.

7. Paulson, D. 1993. *Shorebirds of the Pacific Northwest*, University of Washington Press, Seattle, WA.

8. Small, A. 1994. *California Birds: Their Status and Distribution*. Ibis Publishing Company, Vista, CA.

9. Cooper, D.S. 2004. *Important Bird Areas of California*. Audubon California, Pasadena, CA.

10. Chipley, R.M., G.H. Fenwick, M.J. Parr, and D.N. Pashley. 2003. *The American Bird Conservancy Guide to the 500 Most Important Bird Areas in the United States*. Random House, New York, NY.

11. CONABIO. 2002. *Áreas de Importancia para la Conservación de las Aves (AICAS)*. http://conabioweb.conabio.gob.mx/aicas/doctos/aicas.html (accessed 9 February 2004).

12. Angehr, G. 2003. *Directory of Important Bird Areas in Panama*. Panama Audubon Society, Balboa, Panama.

13. Manomet Bird Observatory. 2003. *Western Hemisphere Shorebird Reserve Network*. http://www.manomet.org/WHSRN/ (accessed 9 February 2004).

14. Sauer, J.R., S. Schwartz, and B. Hoover. 1996. *The Christmas Bird Count Home Page*, Version 95.1. Patuxent Wildlife Research Center, Laurel, MD.

15. Brown, S., C. Hickey, and B. Harrington, eds. 2000. *The U.S. Shorebird Conservation Plan*. Manomet Center for Conservation Sciences, Manomet, MA.

16. Donaldson, G.M., C. Hyslop, R.I.G. Morrison, H.L. Dickson, and I. Davidson. 2000. *Canadian Shorebird Conservation Plan*. Canadian Wildlife Service, Environment Canada, Ottawa, ON.

17. Ricketts T.H., et al. 1999. *Terrestrial Ecoregions of North America: A Conservation Assessment*. Island Press, Washington, DC. 485 pp.

18. Audubon Alaska. 2002. *Alaska's Western Arctic: A Summary and Synthesis of Resources*. Audubon Alaska, Anchorage, AK. 240 pages plus 49 maps.

19. U.S. Bureau of Land Management. 2003. *Northwest NPRA Final Integrated Activity Plan/Environmental Impact Statement*. http://wwwndo.ak.blm.gov/npra/ (accessed 24 Octpber 2003).

20. Batt, B.D.J., ed. 1997. *Arctic Ecosystems in Peril: Report of the Arctic Goose Habitat Working Group*. Arctic Goose Joint Venture Special Publication. U.S. Fish and Wildlife Service, Washington, DC, and Canadian Wildlife Service, Ottawa, ON. 120 pp.

21. Stein, B.A., L.S. Kutner, and J.S. Adams. 2000. *Precious Heritage: The Status of Biodiversity in the United States*. Oxford University Press, New York, NY. 399 pp.

22. National Audubon Society. 2003. *San Francisco Bay Campaign*. http://www.audubonsfbay.org (accessed 3 September 2003).

23. U.S. EPA. 2002. *Mid-Atlantic Integrated Assessment 1997–98 Summary Report*, EPA/620/R-02/003. U.S. Environmental Protection Agency, Atlantic Ecology Division, Narragansett, RI. 115 pp.

24. Manitobawildlands.org. 2004. *Manitoba Nation-

al Parks. http://manitobawildlands.org/pa_ntl_prks.htm (accessed 16 June 2004).

25. Nunavut Parks. 2004. *Welcome to Nunavut Parks.* http://www.nunavutparks.com/on_the_land/kivalliq.cfm (accessed 16 June 2004).

26. World Wildlife Fund–Canada. 2003. *WWF–Canada Congratulates Inuit and Federal Government: Ukkusiksalik National Park in Nunavut Is Designated.* http://www.wwf.ca/NewsAndFacts/NewsRoom (accessed 16 June 2004).

27. Ellison, A.M., and E.J. Farnsworth. 1996. Anthropogenic Disturbance of Caribbean Mangrove Ecosystems: Past Impacts, Present Trends, and Future Predictions. *Biotropica* 28:549–565.

28. World Wildlife Fund. 2001. *Maranhao mangroves (NT1419).* http://www.worldwildlife.org/wildworld/profiles/terrestrial/nt/nt1419_full.html (accessed 17 June 2004).

29. World Wildlife Fund. 2001. *Guianan mangroves (NT1411).* http://www.worldwildlife.org/wildworld/profiles/terrestrial/nt/nt1411_full.html (accessed 17 June 2004).

30. World Wildlife Fund. 2001. *Magdalena-Santa Marta mangroves (NT1417).* http://www.worldwildlife.org/wildworld/profiles/terrestrial/nt/nt1417_full.html (accessed 18 August 2003).

31. World Wildlife Fund. 2001. *Coastal Venezuelan mangroves (NT1408).* http://www.worldwildlife.org/wildworld/profiles/terrestrial/nt/nt1408_full.html (accessed 18 August 2003).

32. World Wildlife Fund. 2001. *Southern Dry Pacific Coast mangroves (NT1434).* http://www.worldwildlife.org/wildworld/profiles/terrestrial/nt/nt1434_full.html (accessed 18 August 2003).

33. World Wildlife Fund. 2001. *Moist Pacific Coast mangroves (NT1423).* http://www.worldwildlife.org/wildworld/profiles/terrestrial/nt/nt1423_full.html (accessed 18 August 2003).

34. Wege, D.C., and A.J. Long. 1995. *Key Areas for Threatened Birds in the Neotropics.* BirdLife International and Smithsonian Institution Press, Washington, DC. 311 pp.

35. Ducks Unlimited. 2002. *Waterfowl Surveys in Latin America.* http://www.ducks.org/conservation/latinamerica_surveys.asp (accessed 16 June 2004).

36. Eco-Index. 2002. *Conservation and Management of Coastal Wetlands in Coquimbo, Chile.* http:www.eco-index.org/search/results.cfm?projectID=412 (accessed 17 June 2004).

37. Coastal America. 2002. *Coastal America: A Partnership for Action.* http://www.coastalamerica.gov (accessed 3 September 2003).

38. NOAA. 2003. *About the CWPPRA.* http://www.nmfs.noaa.gov/habitat/restoration/projects_programs/CWPPRA/about.html (accessed 3 September 2003).

39. Texas Environmental Profiles. Undated. *Federal and State Nonregulatory Conservation Programs.* www.texasep.org/html/wld/wld_6hcp_nonreg.html (accessed 8 April 2003).

40. Ducks Unlimited. 2002. *Atlantic Coast Ecosystem Initiative.* http://www.ducks.org/conservation/Projects/GreatLakesAtlantic/AtlanticCoast/index.asp (accessed 18 June 2004).

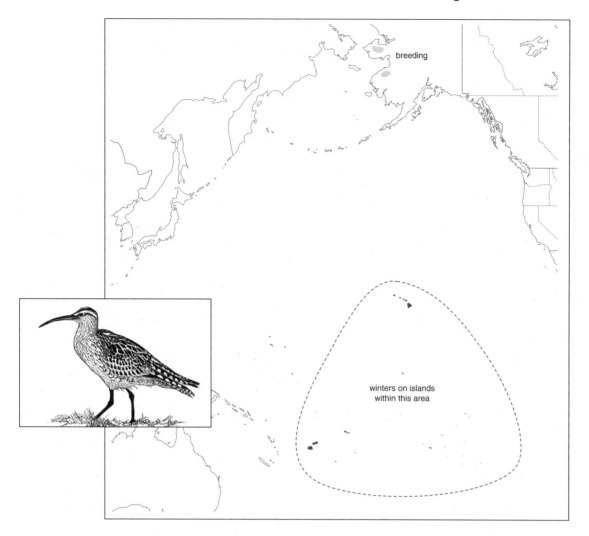

breeding

winters on islands
within this area

BRISTLE-THIGHED CURLEW (*Numenius tahitiensis*)

This species has one of the most restricted breeding ranges of any shorebird in North America, occurring only in southwestern coastal Alaska. Its wintering range is dramatically unusual, with birds spread across hundreds of islands both tiny and large throughout the southern Pacific where they are often killed by cats.

STATUS AND DISTRIBUTION

The species' breeding range is restricted entirely to southwestern Alaska, primarily along lower Yukon River and central Seward Peninsula. Wintering range extends across the south Pacific islands from the Hawaiian Islands south across the Polynesian islands to Pitcairn and Ducie Islands and Fiji. Va-

grants have appeared along the Pacific Coast of the U.S. and Canada and in Japan.

Important breeding sites for the species in Alaska include the Yukon Delta National Wildlife Refuge (NWR) and the National Park Service's Bering Land Bridge National Preserve. Important migration staging areas include the Yukon Delta NWR and Bristol Bay within the Togiak NWR. Important wintering areas include Laysan Island and Lisianski Island and other northwestern Hawaiian Islands within the Pacific/Remote Islands National Wildlife Refuge Complex. These islands are estimated to support about 800 birds, with largest concentrations on Laysan and Lisianski islands. Small numbers winter in the main Hawaiian Islands, including a flock of 10–20 birds that regularly winters at James Campbell National Wildlife Refuge on Oahu.

Likely suffered major declines in abundance over the last several hundred years from hunting on wintering grounds and from introduced predators that kill the birds when they are undergoing molt and cannot fly. Fossil evidence has shown that the species was abundant in Hawaiian Islands pre-Polynesian settlement and was apparently a major food source for early Poynesians. The only recent trend information is from one small wintering island in the northwestern Hawaiian Islands (Tern Island), where numbers declined significantly from 1988 to 2000, but it is unknown if this is indicative of rangewide decline. The total population size of the Bristle-thighed Curlew was estimated at 10,000 in 2000.[1-5]

ECOLOGY

Breeds in higher elevation tundra habitat of dwarf-shrub meadows within its restricted breeding range. Nests are depressions on the ground where a usual clutch of four eggs is laid, one clutch per season. The incubation period is 22–26 days and both sexes share in incubation duties. Young are precocial and leave the nest within hours after hatching and forage on their own. Both adults defend the young and brood them for about 3–4 weeks but the female departs a few days earlier than male. Broods from nearby nests begin to come together to form larger groups 2–3 weeks after hatching and as adults from some broods leave, other adults defend the entire group of young from predators. The young are estimated to fledge in 21–24 days but remain in the nesting area for another 2–3 weeks before joining adults at coastal staging areas. At fall staging areas birds use grassy meadows and dwarf-shrub habitat in coastal lowlands where they fatten on berries.

Diet includes small insects, marine invertebrates, berries, small reptiles, and occasionally small birds and mammals. On wintering grounds birds have adapted to eating seabird eggs, even having learned how to use a stone to break large albatross eggs. This is the only shorebird species known to use tools. In winter, the species occupies a wide variety of open habitats either along marine shorelines (saltpans, mudflats, mangroves, beaches) or areas with short vegetation. Birds seem to prefer more inland habitats, even on small islands where they often are found foraging in grasses and herbs within interior of islands rather than along shoreline. Species once may have occurred more commonly on the main Hawaiian Islands within habitats historically used by Hawaiian Goose and now by Pacific Golden-Plover, but their flightless molt period made them vulnerable to hunting and predators. Most birds apparently do not hold winter territories but will defend food sources from other individuals.[1]

THREATS

Much of the species' breeding range is isolated and unlikely to experience major threats in the near future though there is always concern that activities like mineral and oil extraction activities could cause loss and degradation of habitat in some regions and relatively large portion of breeding range is located on privately owned property. Similarly, a number of island wintering areas in the northwestern Hawaiian Islands are protected as U.S. National Wildlife Refuges. However, on the bulk of the Pacific islands supporting wintering Bristle-thighed Curlews the species is susceptible during its flightless period to capture and killing by introduced cats, dogs, and pigs and to habitat loss and degradation. Unfortunately, little is known about the locations of important wintering areas south of the Hawaiian Islands or the severity of these threats at these locations. Clearly, in any species with such a small population size, concern is warranted because losses at any major location could have a major effect on the total population.[1,6]

CONSERVATION ACTION

Many breeding areas are protected within the Yukon Delta National Wildlife Refuge and the Bering Land Bridge National Preserve but at least 25% of southern breeding population occurs on private land. Many wintering areas are protected within the Hawaiian Islands NWR. For example, Laysan Island, which was designated part of the Hawaiian Islands Bird Reservation in 1909 but without enforcement, is now part of the Hawaiian Islands NWR and access is restricted to authorized researchers and USFWS staff. USFWS and USGS staff and researchers continue efforts to eradicate introduced species and have implemented protocols to prevent further introductions. There has been a major increase in research activities, especially on the breeding grounds in the last two decades, that has vastly increased our understanding of the species' biology, ecology, and distribution. Unfortunately, little conservation, monitoring, or research activity has been undertaken in the wintering range south of the Hawaiian Islands.[1,6–8]

CONSERVATION NEEDS

- Incorporate habitat objectives into public land management in areas where Bristle-thighed Curlews breed and winter.
- Implement regular breeding, wintering, and migratory rangewide surveys designed to assess overall population status and trends and to determine key wintering and staging areas.
- Prevent oil and mineral exploration in areas that are known to support breeding Bristle-thighed Curlews.
- Eradicate or control introduced predators on islands that support wintering populations of Bristle-thighed Curlew and prevent further introductions of invasive species.
- Develop outreach and education materials to gain support of public for conservation efforts across Pacific islands wintering range.

References

1. Marks, J.S., T.L. Tibbitts, R.E. Gill, and B.J. McCaffery. 2002. Bristle-thighed Curlew (*Numenius tahitiensis*). In *The Birds of North America*, No. 705 (A. Poole and F. Gill, eds.). The Birds of North America, Inc., Philadelphia, PA.

2. Igl, L. D. 2003. *Bird Checklists of the United States* (Version 12MAY03). Northern Prairie Wildlife Research Center Home Page, Jamestown, ND. http://www.npwrc.usgs.gov/resource/othrdata/chekbird/chekbird.htm (accessed 24 October 2003).

3. Melgar, C. 2002. *The Bristle-thighed Curlew*. Birding Hawaii website. http://www.birdinghawaii.co,uk/XBTCurlew2.htm (accessed 27 October 2003).

4. Delany, S., and D. Scott. 2002. *Waterbird Population Estimates*, 3rd ed. Wetlands International Global Series No. 12, Wageningen, The Netherlands.

5. Brown, S., C. Hickey, and B. Harrington, eds. 2000. *The U.S. Shorebird Conservation Plan*. Manomet Center for Conservation Sciences, Manomet, MA.

6. BirdLife International. 2000. *Threatened Birds of the World*. Lynx Editions and BirdLife International, Barcelona, Spain, and Cambridge, UK.

7. Moulton, D.W., and A.P. Marshall. 1996. Laysan Duck (*Anas laysanensis*). In *Birds of North America*, No. 242 (A. Poole and F. Gill, eds.). The Academy of Natural Sciences, Philadelphia, PA, and the American Ornithologists' Union, Washington, DC.

8. Madge, S., and H. Burn. 1998. *Waterfowl: An Identification Guide to the Ducks, Geese, and Swans of the World*. Houghton Mifflin, Boston, MA.

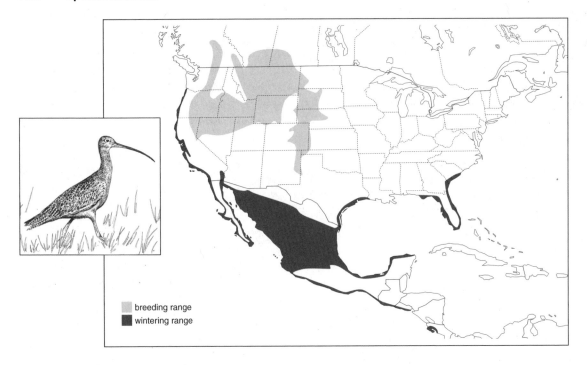

breeding range
wintering range

LONG-BILLED CURLEW (*Numenius americanus*)

One of the most dramatic of the grassland birds because of its large size and exceptionally long and decurved bill, the Long-billed Curlew once ranged over a much larger area of North America. Habitat loss and degradation, hunting, and perhaps pesticide effects all have contributed to a major decline in the species' range and abundance.

STATUS AND DISTRIBUTION

Species now breeds from northeastern New Mexico and northwestern Texas west to northern Utah, Nevada, and northeastern California north through the Great Basin to southern Alberta, Saskatchewan, and British Columbia. Across this range the species has a very patchy and discontinuous distribution. Breeding Bird Survey maps indicate a number of separate areas with high breeding densities, including southern Saskatchewan and western Montana, northwestern Utah and adjacent Nevada, western Nebraska, and northeastern New Mexico and adjacent portions of Colorado, Oklahoma, and Texas. The breeding range once extended into the tallgrass prairie regions east to Manitoba, Michigan, and Illinois and in coastal Texas. The species also bred historically in Arizona. Some early writers mentioned species breeding in the Carolinas, Georgia, and Florida, but the

reliability of these observations are unknown. Wintering range extends from California southeastward through Baja California, Mexico and across northern Mexico to Gulf Coast, extending from Texas south to Yucatán Peninsula. Small numbers occur in coastal Oregon and Washington, along the coast of the southeast U.S., and along the Pacific Coast of Central America to Costa Rica.

Important breeding areas for the species in Canada include Alberta's Canadian Forces Base Suffield National Wildlife Area, Saskatchewan's Skookumchuck Prairie Important Bird Area (IBA) which supported at least 22 pairs in the 1980s, and the South Saskatchewan River IBA (18 pairs in 1990). Important breeding areas in the U.S. include Red Rock Lakes NWR, Bowdoin NWR, and Medicine Lake NWR in Montana, Grays Lake National Wildlife Refuge (NWR) in Idaho, Bear River Migratory Bird Refuge in Utah, and Ruby Lake NWR in Nevada.

The largest wintering concentrations known are from central and southern California, coastal Texas, and Baja California, Mexico. Of individuals known to winter along Pacific Coast of California and Baja California, Mexico, nearly 50% occur in San Francisco Bay and 38% between San Francisco and Mexican border. Thousands also winter inland in shallow wetlands in California's Central and Imperial valleys. Other important wintering areas include California's Sonny Bono Salton Sea NWR, Imperial State Wildlife Area, Grasslands Ecological Area IBA, and Merced Grasslands IBA. In Texas, Laguna Atascosa NWR and the National Park Service's Padre Island National Seashore are among important wintering sites for Long-billed Curlew. In Mexico, the Bahía de San Quintín is an important coastal wintering area. An unknown, but significant proportion of the population winters in grasslands across the northern tier of Mexican states, including at sites like the Janos-Nuevos Casa Grandes IBA in Chihuahua and the Pradera de Tokio IBA, which straddles the Nuevo Leon/Coahuila border.

Breeding Bird Survey analysis showed a non-significant decrease of approximately 39% (1.3% per year) from 1966 to 2005 rangewide. Analysis of Christmas Bird Count data from 1959 to 1988 showed a stable population trend . The species' total population was estimated at 20,000 individuals in 2000.[1-10]

ECOLOGY

Breeds in shortgrass or mixed grass prairie avoiding areas with thick, tall grass or shrubs and trees. In some areas will use mowed or fallow agricultural areas with short, sparse vegetation structure. In winter and during migration uses shallow playa lakes and other inland wetlands, tidal wetlands and saltmarshes, pastures, agricultural fields, and grasslands. Feeds on a variety of small invertebrates, including grasshoppers and beetles, worms, crabs, shrimp, and other marine crustaceans, and invertebrates. Birds will take eggs and nestlings of small, ground-nesting birds if available. Nests are simple depressions on the ground in which the four eggs are laid. Incubation lasts 28–31 days. Young are fully feathered when born and leave the nest within 5–10 hours after hatching and begin feeding themselves. Fledging age is unknown. These birds lay only a single clutch per season. Do not breed until 2–4 years old. Average life span of adults has been estimated at about 8–10 years.[1,11]

THREATS

Loss and degradation of native shortgrass and mixed grass prairie habitat and other preferred native habitats was historically and continues to be the greatest threat to the species. Much grassland habitat on the breeding grounds has been converted to agriculture and housing developments or has been disturbed by oil and mining operations and invasive plant species. Approximately 40% of the shortgrass prairie is estimated to have been lost across North America and in some states the percentage lost is much higher (80% in Texas). Loss of northern mixed-grass prairie has been estimated at 36–69% and southern mixed-grass prairie at 27–65%. In some parts of the region only tiny fragments of native prairie are still in existence. Perhaps of even greater importance was the virtual extinction of many species and populations of grazing mammals, the most notable of which is the American bison. These grazers helped create mosaics of grassland habitat that included the short, sparse habitat that is preferred by Long-billed Curlews.

On the wintering grounds in California, habitat loss has also been dramatic. In San Francisco Bay, 80% of intertidal habitats have been destroyed and in the Central Valley region, 90% of wetlands have been drained. Similarly, the 4.4 million acres of native grassland habitat that existed historically in the San Joaquin Valley was reduced to 1,500 acres by 1972. Little is known about wintering populations outside the U.S., especially in interior Mexico, but many of the same issues are likely of concern throughout the species' wintering range.

The use of pesticides across much of the breeding and wintering range of Long-billed Curlew has led to concerns about potential negative reproductive and physiological effects of accumulated pesticides and other pollutants. There is one known instance of several birds dying from contaminants thought to have been picked up on wintering grounds. Throughout much of the breeding range pesticides are widely used to control numbers of grasshoppers on rangeland, including areas where Long-billed Curlews breed, but the effect is unknown.[1,12,13]

CONSERVATION ACTION

A rangewide breeding season survey for Long-billed Curlew was implemented by the USFWS and partners in 2004. Information obtained will help in understanding more about which areas are most important for the species and in detecting changes in abundance. In the U.S., a new version of the Farm Bill, which was first passed by Congress in 1985 and amended several times in the 1990s, was signed into law in 2002. The Farm Bill contains a number of conservation provisions that provide financial incentives to farmers to leave land with grassland cover and to create wildlife habitat. The Natural Resources Conservation Service's Wildlife Habitat Management Institute has produced and disseminated education and outreach materials about the habitat needs of Long-billed Curlew.

The Nature Conservancy (TNC) has initiated a grassland conservation program called Prairie Wings, which hopes to target conservation activities toward key areas across the shortgrass prairie and which will clearly be of benefit to Long-billed Curlew. One TNC program carried out with financial support from the Orvis Company has targeted the purchase of the 60,000-acre Matador Ranch in Montana, where the species breeds, along with protection of 100,000 acres of wintering habitat in the Saltillo Valley of northeastern Mexico. The Rocky Mountain Bird Observatory has a Prairie Partners program that works with private landowners to monitor prairie bird species and provide outreach and habitat management advice for the benefit of prairie birds but within the farm management needs of the landowner.

Approximately 8% of shortgrass prairie and 2% of mixed grass prairie in the U.S. is under federal government ownership. Various research and management activities have taken place on a number of federally owned lands but there has been no major focus on the needs of Long-billed Curlew.

A major effort has been initiated in San Francisco Bay, where a large proportion of the Pacific Coast population winters, to restore tidal wetlands. Audubon's San Francisco Bay Campaign has proposed to restore over 100,000 acres of wetland habitat in the area over the next 20 years. A preliminary agreement with Cargill, Inc., would result in the public acquisition of 16,500 acres of salt ponds for $100 million. The ponds would eventually be restored to tidal wetlands. In 2003, the California State Coastal Conservancy, U.S. Army Corps of Engineers, and California Department of Fish and Game proposed a habitat restoration project for the 9,460-acre Napa River Salt Marsh within the northern section of San Francisco Bay.[12,14–18]

CONSERVATION NEEDS

- Ensure that management of publicly owned locations currently supporting Long-billed Curlew continues to maintain habitat conditions beneficial to the species.
- Increase efforts at landowner education and outreach, incentives, and other activities that may increase productivity of Long-billed Curlew on private lands.
- Increase protection and conservation of remaining native habitat within the wintering range of Long-billed Curlew.
- Restore native grassland ecosystems, including through reintroduction of native mammalian herbivores where possible.
- Work with National Resources Conservation Service in the implementation of Farm Bill conservation incentive programs so that the habitat conditions specified on lands potentially used by Long-billed Curlew are beneficial to the species.
- Implement a rangewide winter survey designed to identify winter distribution and habitat.

References

1. Dugger, B.D., and K.M. Dugger. 2002. Long-billed Curlew (*Numenius americanus*). In *The Birds of North America*, No. 628 (A. Poole and F. Gill, eds.). The Birds of North America, Inc., Philadelphia, PA.

2. Sauer, J.R., J. E. Hines, and J. Fallon. 2005. *The North American Breeding Bird Survey, Results and Analysis 1966–2005*, Version 6.2.2006. USGS Patuxent Wildlife Research Center, Laurel, MD.

3. Hill, D.P. 1998. *Status of the Long-billed Curlew (Numenius americanus) in Alberta*. Alberta Environmental Protection, Fisheries & Wildlife Management Division, and Alberta Conservation Association, Wildlife Status Report No. 16, Edmonton, AB.

4. Bird Studies Canada. 2003. *Important Bird Areas of Canada*. http://www.bsc-eoc.org/iba/IBAsites.html (accessed 7 October 2003).

5. Igl, L. D. 2003. *Bird Checklists of the United States* (Version 12MAY03). Northern Prairie Wildlife Research Center Home Page, Jamestown, ND. http://www.npwrc.usgs.gov/resource/othrdata/chekbird/chekbird.htm (accessed 18 August 2003).

6. Cooper, D. 2001. Important bird areas of California. Unpublished manuscript available from Audubon

California, 6042 Monte Vista St., Los Angeles, CA 90042.

7. Skagen, S.K., P.B. Sharpe, R.G. Waltermire, and M.B. Dillon. 1999. *Biogeographic Profiles of Shorebird Migration in Midcontinental North America.* Biological Science Report USGS/BRD/BSR—2000-0003. U.S. Government Printing Office, Denver, CO. 167 pp.

8. CONABIO. 2002. *Áreas de Importancia para la Conservación de las Aves (AICAS).* http://conabioweb .conabio.gob.mx/aicas/doctos/aicas.html (accessed 8 December 2005).

9. Sauer, J.R., S. Schwartz, and B. Hoover. 1996. *The Christmas Bird Count Home Page,* Version 95.1. Patuxent Wildlife Research Center, Laurel, MD.

10. Delany, S., and D. Scott. 2002. *Waterbird Population Estimates,* 3rd ed. Wetlands International Global Series No. 12, Wageningen, The Netherlands.

11. Dechant, J. A., M. L. Sondreal, D. H. Johnson, L. D. Igl, C. M. Goldade, P. A. Rabie, and B. R. Euliss. 2003. *Effects of Management Practices on Grassland Birds: Long-billed Curlew.* Northern Prairie Wildlife Research Center, Jamestown, ND. Northern Prairie Wildlife Research Center Online. http://www.npwrc.usgs.gov/ resource/literatr/grasbird/lbcu/lbcu.htm (Version 12DEC2003).

12. Gauthier, D.A., A. Lafon, T. Tombs, J. Hoth, and E. Wilken. 2003. *Grasslands: Toward a North American Conservation Strategy.* Canadian Plains Research Center, University of Regina, Regina, SK, and Commission for Environmental Cooperation, Montreal, QC, Canada. 99 pp.

13. Ricketts, T.H., et al. 1999. *Terrestrial Ecoregions of North America: A Conservation Assessment. Island Press,* Washington, DC. 485 pp.

14. The Nature Conservancy. 2003. *The Prairie Wings Project.* http://nature.org/initiatives/programs/ birds/explore/ (accessed 21 October 2003).

15. The Orvis Company. 2003. *Help the Long-billed Curlew.* http://www.orvis.com (accessed 21 October 2003).

16. Rocky Mountain Bird Observatory. 2002. *Prairie Partners: Conserving Great Plains Birds and Their Habitats.* http://www.rmbo.org/conservation/partners .html (accessed 21 October 2003).

17. National Audubon Society. 2003. *San Francisco Bay Campaign.* http://www.audubonsfbay.org (accessed 3 September 2003).

18. Jones, S.L., T.R. Stanley, S.K. Skagen, and R.L. Redmond. 2003. *Long-Billed Curlew* (Numenius americanus) *Rangewide Survey and Monitoring Guidelines.* http://library.fws.gov/Bird_Publications/long-billed _curlew_survey03.pdf (accessed 8 December 2005).

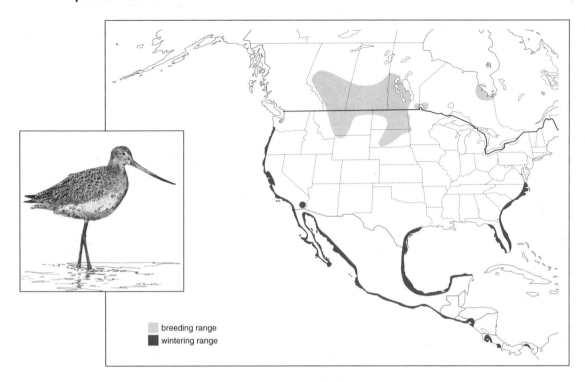

breeding range
wintering range

MARBLED GODWIT (*Limosa fedoa*)

A large, primarily grassland-breeding shorebird, the Marbled Godwit disappeared from the original eastern 25% of its former range primarily because of habitat loss and reached a low overall population level in the early 1900s because of its popularity with commercial market hunters.

STATUS AND DISTRIBUTION

The species now breeds from central Alberta east to southern Manitoba and south to Montana, North and South Dakota, and the northwestern edge of Minnesota. Disjunct populations occur in southwestern Ontario, along the western shore of James Bay, and on the Alaska Peninsula. Breeding Bird Survey maps indicate highest densities in southeastern Alberta. The breeding range once extended east to Wisconsin and Iowa and south to Nebraska. Approximately 60% of the breeding range occurs in Canada. Wintering range extends from California southeastward through Baja California and the Pacific Coast of Mexico to El Salvador and locally to Costa Rica and Panama. Also winters in smaller numbers along Atlantic Coast from North Carolina to Florida (including Florida's Gulf Coast) and from Texas south to the Yucatan Peninsula. Birds wintering along the At-

lantic Coast may represent individuals from the James Bay breeding population. Small numbers winter locally in coastal Oregon and Washington and inland California and Nevada. Important breeding areas for the species include Montana's Medicine Lake National Wildlife Refuge (NWR), South Dakota's Waubay NWR, and North Dakota's Chase Lake NWR, Arrowwood Lake NWR, Lostwood NWR, and Upper Souris NWR.

Important migratory stopover sites include Saskatchewan's Luck Lake (up to 12,225 birds have been reported during fall migration), Quill Lakes (over 1,000 in fall and spring migration), and Last Mountain Lake (over 1,000 in fall), Utah's Great Salt Lake (up to 35,000 on spring and fall migration), and Kansas's Cheyenne Bottoms Wildlife Area and Preserve, which has hosted over 3,000 birds in spring migration.

Wintering density maps produced from Christmas Bird Count data indicate highest densities in the U.S. along the coast of California. Key wintering and migratory stopover areas in California include Humboldt Bay (up to 8,000 birds), Morro Bay (regularly hosts over 2,000), San Francisco Bay (up to 20,000 birds, representing over 10% of the global population), Arcata Marsh, and Humboldt Bay NWR. A few locations in coastal

South Carolina, Florida (Everglades National Park), and Texas support wintering populations of hundreds of birds (occasionally as high as 700 in Texas). Mexico is thought to host the bulk of the world's population in winter (over 100,000), with most in Baja California and large numbers along coastal regions of Sonora and Sinaloa.

Important wintering areas in Mexico include Baja California's Bahía San Quintín Important Bird Area (IBA) (up to 7,800), Bahía Todos Santos IBA, and Complejo Lagunar Ojo de Liebre. In Sonora, the Sistema Tóbari IBA has hosted up to 3,000 birds and the Zonas Húmedas de Yávaros IBA up to 700. On the border between Sonora and Sinaloa the Agiabampo IBA has had as many as 2,000 birds. Marbled Godwits also winter at Nayarit's Marismas Nacionales IBA.

Breeding Bird Survey analysis shows a nonsignificant decrease of 27% (0.8% per year) from 1966 to 2005 rangewide. An analysis of Christmas Bird Count data shows a nonsignificant decrease of 1.3% per year from 1959 to 1988. The species' total population was estimated at 171,500 individuals in 2000.[1-12]

ECOLOGY

Breeds in shortgrass or mixed-grass prairie intermixed with small wetlands and avoids areas with thick, tall grass or shrubs and trees. In some areas will use grazed pastures or idle agricultural grasslands with short, sparse vegetation structure. In winter and during migration uses shallow playa lakes and other inland wetlands, tidal wetlands and saltmarshes, pastures, agricultural fields, and grasslands. Feeds on a variety of small invertebrates, including grasshoppers and beetles, worms, crabs, and leeches. Also small fish, and, unlike most other shorebirds, the roots of aquatic plants. Nests are simple depressions on the ground in which the four eggs are laid, where they are incubated by both sexes for 24–26 days. Young are fully feathered when born and leave the nest within 24 hours after hatching and begin feeding themselves. Young fledge approximately four weeks after hatching. These birds lay only a single clutch per season but they will renest if their clutch is destroyed early in the breeding season. Marbled Godwits are long-lived, with several studies showing annual survival rates of 80–90% and a number of records of banded birds still alive at 25 years (one more than 29 years old).[1]

THREATS

Loss and degradation of native shortgrass and mixed grass prairie habitat and other preferred native habitats was historically and continues to be the greatest threat to the species. Much grassland habitat on the breeding grounds has been converted to agriculture and housing developments or has been disturbed by oil and mining operations and invasive plant species. Approximately 40% of the shortgrass prairie native vegetation is estimated to have been lost across North America and in some states the percentage lost is much higher. Loss of northern mixed-grass prairie has been estimated at 36–69%. In some parts of the region only tiny fragments of native prairie are still in existence. Furthermore, nonnative plants are now estimated to account for 30–60% of grassland plant species. Perhaps of even greater importance was the near extinction of many species and populations of native grazing mammals, the most notable of which is the American bison. These grazers helped create mosaics of grassland habitat that included the short, sparse habitat that is preferred by Marbled Godwit and many other grassland birds.

On the wintering grounds in California, habitat loss has also been dramatic. In San Francisco Bay, 80% of intertidal habitats have been destroyed and in the Central Valley region 90% of wetlands have been drained. Little is known about wintering populations outside the U.S., especially in interior Mexico, but many of the same issues are likely of concern throughout the species' wintering range. The use of pesticides across much of the breeding and wintering range of Marbled Godwit has led to concerns about potential negative reproductive and physiological effects of accumulated pesticides and other pollutants. Throughout much of the breeding range pesticides are widely used to control numbers of grasshoppers on rangeland, including areas where Marbled Godwit breed, but effect is unknown.[1,15-18]

CONSERVATION ACTION

There has been no rangewide conservation plan or management program focused on maintaining or increasing Marbled Godwit populations, but some broad grassland restoration work has benefited the species. For example, at Lostwoods NWR, North Dakota, prescribed burns and light grazing of grasslands aimed at restoring the native habitat have benefited breeding Marbled Godwits. The Prairie Pothole Joint Venture initiated the Chase Lake Prairie Project to conserve and restore habitat in a 5.5-million-acre block surrounding Chase Lake NWR, North Dakota, where Marbled Godwit occur. The project area includes one of the largest intact pieces of native prairie in the state. Through the project the U.S. Fish and Wildlife Service has protected 12,890 acres of wetlands and grasslands through easements on private land and over 8,600 acres of habitat have been directly acquired. Rotational grazing systems have been implemented on over 35,000 acres of grasslands as well.

Ducks Unlimited's Grasslands for Tomorrow Initiative is striving to protect 2 million acres of grassland within the Prairie Pothole region, which encompasses much of the breeding range of Marbled Godwit. The Nature Conservancy has initiated a grassland conservation program called Prairie Wings, which targets conservation activities toward key areas across the shortgrass prairie and which will be of benefit to Marbled Godwit.

In the U.S., a new version of the Farm Bill, first passed by Congress in 1985 and amended several times in the 1990s, was signed into law in 2002. It contains a number of conservation provisions that provide financial incentives to farmers to leave land with grassland cover and to create wildlife habitat. For example, the Conservation Reserve Program pays farmers annually to set aside acreage from agricultural uses, and over 2 million acres could eventually be enrolled in the program.

A major effort has been initiated in San Francisco Bay, where a large proportion of the Pacific Coast population winters, to restore tidal wetlands. Audubon's San Francisco Bay Campaign has proposed to restore over 100,000 acres of wetland habitat in the area over the next 20 years. A preliminary agreement with Cargill, Inc., would result in the public acquisition of 16,500 acres of salt ponds for $100 million. The ponds would eventually be restored to tidal wetlands. In 2003, the California State Coastal Conservancy, U.S. Army Corps of Engineers, and California Department of Fish and Game were proposing a habitat restoration project for the 9,460-acre Napa River Salt Marsh within the northern section of San Francisco Bay.[1,15,18–22]

CONSERVATION NEEDS

- Ensure that management of publicly owned locations currently supporting Marbled God-

wit continues to maintain habitat conditions beneficial to the species.
- Increase efforts at landowner education and outreach, incentives, and other activities that may increase productivity of Marbled Godwit on private lands.
- Increase protection and conservation of remaining native habitat within the wintering range of Marbled Godwit.
- Manage native grassland ecosystems to include reintroduction of native mammalian herbivores where possible.
- Work with Natural Resources Conservation Service in the implementation of Farm Bill conservation incentive programs so that the habitat conditions specified on lands potentially used by Marbled Godwit are beneficial to the species.
- Implement rangewide surveys designed to assess overall population status and trends.

References

1. Gratto-Trevor, C.L. 2000. Marbled Godwit (*Limosa fedoa*). In *The Birds of North America*, No. 492 (A. Poole and F. Gill, eds.). The Birds of North America, Inc., Philadelphia, PA.

2. Sauer, J. R., J. E. Hines, and J. Fallon. 2005. *The North American Breeding Bird Survey, Results and Analysis 1966–2005*, Version 6.2.2006. USGS Patuxent Wildlife Research Center, Laurel, MD.

3. Donaldson, G.M., C. Hyslop, R.I.G. Morrison, H.L. Dickson, and I. Davidson. 2000. *Canadian Shorebird Conservation Plan*. Canadian Wildlife Service, Environment Canada, Ottawa, ON.

4. Igl, L.D. 2003. *Bird Checklists of the United States* (Version 12MAY03). Northern Prairie Wildlife Research Center Home Page, Jamestown, ND. http://www.npwrc.usgs.gov/resource/othrdata/chekbird/chekbird.htm (accessed 18 June 2004).

5. Chipley, R.M., G.H. Fenwick, M.J. Parr, and D.N. Pashley. 2003. *The American Bird Conservancy Guide to the 500 Most Important Bird Areas in the United States*. Random House, New York.

6. Bird Studies Canada. 2003. *Important Bird Areas of Canada*. http://www.bsc-eoc.org/iba/IBAsites.html (accessed 18 June 2004).

7. Manomet Bird Observatory. 2003. *Western Hemisphere Shorebird Reserve Network*. http://www.manomet.org/WHSRN/ (accessed 9 February 2004).

8. Sauer, J. R., S. Schwartz, and B. Hoover. 1996.

The Christmas Bird Count Home Page, Version 95.1. Patuxent Wildlife Research Center, Laurel, MD.

9. Cooper, D. S. 2004. *Important Bird Areas of California*. Audubon California, Pasadena, CA.

10. Skagen, S.K., P.B. Sharpe, R.G. Waltermire, and M.B. Dillon. 1999. *Biogeographic Profiles of Shorebird Migration in Midcontinental North America*. Biological Science Report USGS/BRD/BSR—2000-0003. U.S. Government Printing Office, Denver, CO. 167 pp.

11. National Audubon Society. 2002. *The Christmas Bird Count Historical Results*. http://www.audubon.org/bird/cbc (accessed 18 June 2004).

12. Audubon North Carolina. *North Carolina's Important Bird Areas*. http://www.ncaudubon.org/IBA1.htm (accessed 3 September 2003).

13. CONABIO. 2002. *Áreas de Importancia para la Conservación de las Aves (AICAS)*. http://conabioweb.conabio.gob.mx/aicas/doctos/aicas.html (accessed 18 June 2004).

14. Brown, S., C. Hickey, and B. Harrington, eds. 2000. *The U.S. Shorebird Conservation Plan*. Manomet Center for Conservation Sciences, Manomet, MA.

15. Gauthier, D.A., A. Lafon, T. Tombs, J. Hoth, and E. Wilken. 2003. *Grasslands: Toward a North American Conservation Strategy*. Canadian Plains Research Center, University of Regina, Regina, SK, and Commission for Environmental Cooperation, Montreal, QC, Canada. 99 pp.

16. Ricketts, T.H., et al. 1999. *Terrestrial Ecoregions of North America: A Conservation Assessment*. Island Press, Washington, DC. 485 pp.

17. Stein, B.A., L.S. Kutner, and J.S. Adams. 2000. *Precious Heritage: The Status of Biodiversity in the United States*. Oxford University Press, New York, NY. 399 pp.

18. National Audubon Society. 2003. *San Francisco Bay Campaign*. http://www.audubonsfbay.org (accessed 3 September 2003).

19. Greatplains.org. 2001. *Shorebird Management Manual*, Chapter 2: *Interior Region*. http://www.greatplains.org/resource/1998/multspec/casehist.htm (accessed 22 January 2004).

20. U. S. Fish and Wildlife Service. *Chase Lake Prairie Project*. http://chaselake.fws.gov/clpp.htm (accessed 22 January 2004).

21. Ducks Unlimited. 2003. *Protecting 2,000,000 Acres of Grasslands for Tomorrow*. http://prairie.ducks.org/index.cfm?&page=conservation/priorities/gft.cfm (accessed 18 June 2004).

22. The Nature Conservancy. 2003. *The Prairie Wings Project*. http://nature.org/initiatives/programs/birds/explore/ (accessed 21 October 2003).

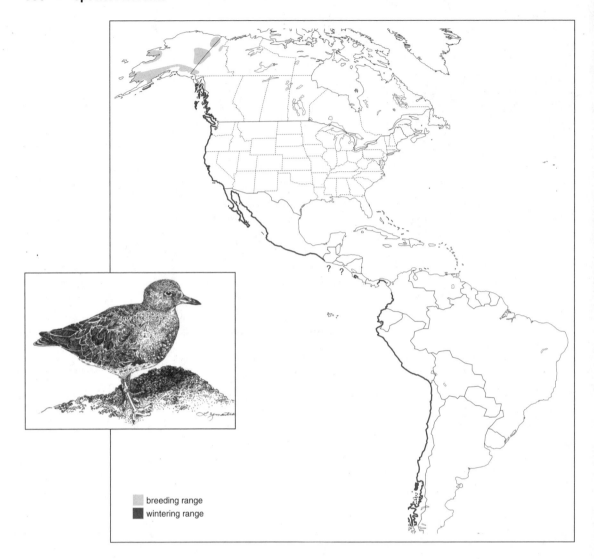

breeding range
wintering range

SURFBIRD (*Aphriza virgata*)

One of a suite of shorebirds specialized on feeding in the rocky intertidal zone of the Pacific coasts of the Americas, much of the Surfbird's life history and distribution has been difficult to decipher, including the location of its high-elevation tundra breeding area, which was not discovered until 1926.

STATUS AND DISTRIBUTION

Breeding range includes high-elevation tundra habitat throughout much of Alaska extending into western and northern Yukon but limits of distribution are poorly known. More than 75% of the global population is estimated to breed within Alaska. Important breeding areas in Alaska include Alaska's Yukon Delta National Wildlife Refuge (NWR), Yukon Flats NWR, Denali National Park and Preserve, Katmai National Park, Wrangell-St. Elias National Park and Preserve, and the Brooks Range area within the Arctic NWR.

Important migratory stopover locations include Alaska's Montague Island, Prince William Sound (max. 56,000 in spring migration), Kachemak Bay (max. 3,500 in spring), and Mitkof Island (max. 883 in fall); British Columbia's Turtle Island (4,500–5,000 max. in spring), Tzartus Island (max. 2,000+ in fall), and Fleming Island (max. 1,000 in fall); and Oregon's Seal Rock (max. 500 in fall).

Has an incredibly extensive wintering range, extending from south coastal Alaska along the Pacific Coast to Chile! Within much of its range, especially south of the U.S., the numbers and status are very poorly known. Wintering density maps produced from Christmas Bird Count data indicate highest densities along the coast of Oregon and southern British Columbia. Important wintering areas include Alaska's Prince William Sound, British Columbia's Tofino area, Oregon's Tillamook Bay and Yaquina Bay, and Washington's Gray's Harbor.

There are no Breeding Bird Survey data for this species. An analysis of Christmas Bird Count data shows a nonsignificant decrease of 1.2% per year from 1959 to 1988. The U.S. Shorebird Conservation Plan categorized the species as one with apparent population declines. The species' total population was estimated at 70,000 individuals in 2000.[1-8]

ECOLOGY

Much of the species' ecology and life history are poorly known, especially from the breeding season. Breeds in high-elevation alpine tundra of mountain ranges of Alaska and western Yukon. Lays its four eggs in a shallow depression on the ground. Incubation is thought to be 22–24 days, based on observation of a single nest. Male is known to incubate but it is unknown if the female incubates. There is no information on the fledging period. During the breeding season adults feed on insects, including beetles and flies. In winter and in migration birds are virtually never found outside of their rocky, coastal habitat, where they feed largely on mollusks and barnacles.[1]

THREATS

Major threats include oil pollution and oil spills along much of the U.S. and Canadian Pacific coast wintering area but perhaps especially in Prince William Sound and the Gulf of Alaska, where the bulk of the world population passes through on migration. Also of concern is increased development and recreational uses of coastal habitats, which may displace birds, degrade feeding habitats, and cause disturbance to birds. Little is known about potential threats on South American wintering grounds. Large parts of the species' breeding range are within protected areas and are unlikely to be targeted for major habitat altering resource-extraction activities.[1,2]

CONSERVATION ACTION

No specific conservation activities are focused on this species but much of its nesting habitat is protected within parks and refuges. U.S. and Canadian shorebird conservation plans have been developed that provide recommendations for management, research, outreach, and education for shorebirds. The Western Hemisphere Shorebird Reserve Network has identified some key breeding, wintering, and migratory stopover locations for the species and in some locations has initiated conservation and outreach projects.

The Alaska Department of Environmental Conservation, the U.S. Coast Guard, and the U.S. Environmental Protection Agency with the cooperation of the National Marine Fisheries Service have developed oil spill response plans to limit the mortality and ecological pollution from oil spills in coastal Alaska. The Olympic Peninsula National Marine Sanctuary, managed by the National Oceanic and Atmospheric Administration, harbors wintering Surfbirds (near Gray's Harbor, WA). National Marine Sanctuaries prohibit oil and gas extraction activities within their boundaries as well as certain types of other human activities that may disturb marine life or marine habitats. For example, a portion of the sanctuary within about 25 nautical miles of the coast is closed to ships carrying oil or other hazardous materials. These regulations should be beneficial to maintaining food supplies and a healthy ecosystem upon which Surfbirds depend. [1,2,8-12]

CONSERVATION NEEDS

- Greatly increase research on the breeding and wintering biology of Surfbird to better understand distribution and population limiting factors.
- Develop surveys to monitor changes in populations of Surfbird.
- Continue efforts to limit the amount of pesticides, oil, and other pollutants within the marine ecosystem.

References

1. Senner, S.E., and B. J. McCaffery. 1997. Surfbird (*Aphriza virgata*). In *The Birds of North America*, No. 266 (A. Poole and F. Gill, eds.). The Academy of Natural

Sciences, Philadelphia, PA, and the American Ornithologists' Union, Washington, DC.

2. Alaska Shorebird Working Group. 2000. *A Conservation Plan for Alaska Shorebirds*. Unpublished report, Alaska Shorebird Working Group. Available through U.S. Fish and Wildlife Service, Migratory Bird Management, Anchorage, AK. 47 pp.

3. Chipley, R.M., G.H. Fenwick, M.J. Parr, and D.N. Pashley. 2003. *The American Bird Conservancy Guide to the 500 Most Important Bird Areas in the United States*. Random House, New York, NY.

4. Igl, L. D. 2003. *Bird Checklists of the United States* (Version 12MAY03). Northern Prairie Wildlife Research Center Home Page, Jamestown, ND. http://www.npwrc.usgs.gov/resource/othrdata/chekbird/chekbird.htm (accessed 23 June 2004).

5. National Park Service. No date. *Wrangell-St. Elias National Park & Preserve*. http://www.nps.gov/wrst/home.htm (accessed 23 June 2004).

6. Paulson, D. 1993. *Shorebirds of the Pacific Northwest*. University of Washington Press, Seattle, WA.

7. Sauer, J. R., S. Schwartz, and B. Hoover. 1996. *The Christmas Bird Count Home Page*. Version 95.1. Patuxent Wildlife Research Center, Laurel, MD.

8. Brown, S., C. Hickey, and B. Harrington, eds. 2000. *The U.S. Shorebird Conservation Plan*. Manomet Center for Conservation Sciences, Manomet, MA.

9. Donaldson, G.M., C. Hyslop, R.I.G. Morrison, H.L. Dickson, I. Davidson. 2000. *Canadian Shorebird Conservation Plan*. Canadian Wildlife Service, Environment Canada, Ottawa, ON.

10. Manomet Bird Observatory. 2003. *Western Hemisphere Shorebird Reserve Network*. http://www.manomet.org/WHSRN/ (accessed 9 February 2004).

11. Alaska Department of Environmental Conservation. 2003. *Prevention and Emergency Response Program*. http://www.state.ak.us/dec/dspar/perp/about.htm (accessed 4 December 2003).

12. NOAA. No date. *Olympic Coast National Marine Sanctuary*. http://olympiccoast.noaa.gov/welcome.html (accessed 2 July 2004.)

also breeds in
Europe and Asia

breeding range
wintering range

RED KNOT (*Calidris canutus*)

Famous for its spring migratory concentrations along the shore of Delaware Bay, the Red Knot has shown massive declines in recent years that are linked to dramatic declines in horseshoe crabs as a result of overfishing along the mid-Atlantic coast.

STATUS AND DISTRIBUTION

Species has a circumpolar breeding range occurring in Arctic Russia as well as in North America and Greenland. Three of the five described subspecies breed in North America. The *roselaari* subspecies has a disjunct breeding population in northwestern Alaska, including the Seward Peninsula. The *rufa* subspecies breeds in northern Nunavut and Northwest Territories, mostly on Arctic islands. The *islandica* subspecies breeds further east in Arctic Canada and along the coasts of Greenland. The exact distributional limits between the *rufa* and *islandica* subspecies are poorly delimited. An estimated 64% of the species total North American population is thought to breed in Canada, the remaining 36% in Alaska. Important breeding sites for the species in Canada include

Southampton Island, King William Island (both for *rufa* subspecies), and northwestern Ellsmere Island (for *islandica* subspecies).

Perhaps the most important spring migratory stopover location in the U.S. is along the New Jersey and Delaware shores of Delaware Bay, where single-day counts as high as 96,000 have been recorded and an estimated 200,000 birds (50% of the North American population and virtually 100% of *rufa* subspecies) stop off to fatten up on horseshoe crab eggs. Other important spring staging areas include Alaska's Copper River and Yukon-Kuskokwim Deltas (up to 100,000 may use either site in some years, representing 25% of North American population), Washington's Gray's Harbor and Willapa Bay (hundreds and occasionally thousands), California's San Francisco Bay (up to 1,000), Texas' Mustang Island Beach, Matagorda National Wildlife Refuge (NWR), and Bolivar Flats (hundreds and occasionally thousands), Saskatchewan's Last Mountain Lake, Quill Lakes, and Chaplin Lakes (up to 2,500). Important stopover locations in South America include Argentina's Bahía San Antonio Oeste (up to 20,000) and Brazil's Lagoa do Peixe (up to 13,000). In fall migration, birds do not usually concentrate in high numbers at any one site and are more dispersed, though most of the spring staging areas are also used in fall.

Wintering range is extensive, extending from the Pacific and Atlantic coasts of U.S. south through Central America and the Caribbean to South America. Largest concentrations (*rufa* subspecies and possibly some of *roselaari* subspecies) are along the southern South American coast, with the largest numbers in coastal Chile and Argentina but significant numbers (estimated as high as 10,000) also in coastal Florida. A large proportion of the total wintering population of the *rufa* subspecies is thought to be concentrated within Chile's Bahía Lomas. Other important sites include Argentina's Bahía Lomas, Bahía San Sebastian, and Rio Grande.

Hundreds, sometimes thousands, winter along the coasts of California, Georgia, North Carolina, and South Carolina and in Baja California. Birds wintering in the U.S. and Mexico and at scattered locations throughout the Caribbean, Central America, and northern South America are thought to be from the *roselaari* subspecies. The bulk of the *islandica* subspecies winters along the coast of the North Sea in Europe and the United Kingdom, with nearly 90% of the wintering population in Britain and 50% in the Walsh Estuary alone.

Numbers of the *rufa* subspecies declined by more than 50% between the mid-1980s and 2003. The number of wintering *islandica* subspecies has stabilized in recent years but remains about 40% lower than in the 1970s. There is no information on trends in the *roselaari* subspecies. The species' total North American population was estimated in 2000 at 400,000, with 170,000 in *rufa* subspecies, 150,000 in *roselaari* subspecies, and 80,000 in *islandica* subspecies. However, more recent estimates of the *rufa* subspecies put the total population as low as 35,000–40,000, which would put the total North American population at 265,000–270,000.[1-13]

ECOLOGY

Breeds in Arctic lowlands near coasts on hummocks within wet habitats and in some locations and some years on higher ridges or gravel eskers. Nests are depressions on the ground where four eggs are laid and incubated by both the male and female for 21–22 days. Young are precocial and leave the nest within hours after hatching and forage on their own. Usually only the male defends and broods the young. The young are estimated to fledge in 18 days. Only a single brood is produced each year. Feeds mostly on marine invertebrates, especially mussels in many areas. In Delaware Bay birds feed almost exclusively on the eggs of horseshoe crabs. When birds arrive in spring at Delaware Bay after their 9,000 mile journey from the southern South American wintering grounds they are very lean and must double their weight to be able to reach the Arctic breeding grounds and survive. Most birds are not thought to breed until at least two years old. On wintering grounds and during migration they prefer sandy beaches and intertidal flats.[1,11]

THREATS

The major overriding threat has been human-caused decimation of horseshoe crab egg food supply at the key Delaware Bay staging area for the entire population of the *rufa* subspecies. The annual harvest of horseshoe crabs (to be used for bait) along the Atlantic Coast increased from about 800,000 pounds in 1993 to 6.38 million pounds in 1998 while towing surveys of horseshoe crab numbers in Delaware Bay went from an average of 6.8 crabs per tow in 1991 to 0.2 crabs per tow in 2002. In recent years an increasingly large proportion of the population passing through Delaware Bay has not been able to find enough horseshoe crab eggs to increase weight sufficiently for breeding and survival. This has resulted in a 37% decrease in adult survival rates and is thought to account for the dramatic declines in the population of the *rufa* subspecies.

Much of the species' range in Alaska and Canada is within protected areas or areas with relatively undisturbed habitat. However, many breeding areas could be opened to oil and gas extraction activities. Such activities can cause habitat loss and degradation from establishment and expansion of infrastructure and pollution and increases in predatory mammals and birds (that capitalize on garbage). In 2004 a plan was released for consideration to open the 8.8-million-acre Northwest Planning Area of the National Petroleum Reserve–Alaska to leasing for oil and gas development. Oil and gas exploration and mining activity is expected to show increases within portions of the Canadian breeding range as well.

In migration and on the wintering grounds the major threat is continued loss and degradation of coastal wetlands. In the U.S., such habitat loss has been dramatic. Florida and Texas have each lost at least 7.5 million acres of wetlands and Louisiana between 2.5 and 7.5 million acres over the last 200 years. In Louisiana and Texas coastal wetlands are continuing to be lost to erosion and subsequent saltwater intrusion. In California's San Francisco Bay, 80% of intertidal habitats have been destroyed. South of the U.S., loss of coastal wetland habitat in many countries continues to be a major threat. At the major wintering area in Argentina, there is offshore oil exploration and extraction activity nearby, a spill from which would threaten the estuary.

Many estuarine systems used by Red Knot in migration and winter are showing degraded environmental conditions. For example, the percentage of the Delaware Estuary that tested above EPA ecological limits for metal contaminants increased from 5 to 22% from 1990–93 to 1997. The amount of land lost to development with the Delaware Bay Estuary increased 20% from 1970 to 1990. Clearly, any activities that result in loss or degradation of habitat, including alteration of water levels, de-

struction of buffer habitat, spraying of pesticides, ditching, accumulation of contaminants, grazing, or spread of invasive plants like phragmites, are continuing threats to the species. In many areas the species uses beach habitats that are increasingly threatened by development, beach armoring, and so-called beach renourishment projects. All of these activities reduce the invertebrate food supply that Red Knots and other beach-inhabiting birds rely upon. Sea level rise with global warming may become the most pervasive and difficult threat to the species. An estimated 16–33% of the species Arctic breeding habitat could be lost from global warming-induced sea level rise.[1,9–12,14–23]

CONSERVATION ACTION

A coalition of conservation organizations has been actively working to decrease or stop the massive harvest of horseshoe crabs along the mid-Atlantic coast of the U.S. The National Marine Fisheries Service closed a 1,500-square-mile area at the mouth of Delaware Bay to harvesting of horseshoe crabs in 2001 and reduced harvest levels by 30%. Because horseshoe crabs do not begin breeding until 7–8 years of age it may require years before we know whether populations can reach former levels. The New Jersey Division of Fish and Wildlife established closures on important beach feeding areas for the species in May 2003 that restricted human presence on the beaches to prevent disturbance of feeding knots and other shorebirds.

Research efforts on the species on breeding, wintering, and migratory ranges have increased dramatically in the last decade. Thousands of birds have been banded in southern South America and during migration in Delaware Bay. Radio transmitters affixed to birds migrating through Delaware Bay allowed the discovery of the primary breeding areas and a research team has carried out annual studies of the species' breeding biology since that time.

U.S. and Canadian shorebird conservation plans have been developed that provide recommendations for management, research, outreach, and education for Red Knot and other shorebird species. The Western Hemisphere Shorebird Reserve Network, RAMSAR Treaty on Wetlands, and the Birdlife International Important Bird Areas programs have identified many key breeding, wintering, and migratory stopover locations for the species and in some locations have initiated conservation and outreach projects.

A great many organizations, agencies, and coalitions are working on coastal habitat restoration and protection projects within the U.S., many of which will likely eventually benefit Red Knot. For example, the Coastal America Partnership, a coalition of federal agencies, state and local governments, and private organizations, identifies and implements local wetland restoration and protection projects throughout the U.S. The Partnership had initiated more than 500 projects impacting hundreds of thousands of acres of wetland habitat as of 2002. The Delaware Estuary Program is a broad partnership that is working to improve the health of the Delaware Bay ecosystem through a great variety of habitat restoration, conservation, outreach, and education projects. The Texas Prairie Wetlands Project was created by U.S. Fish and Wildlife Service, Texas Parks and Wildlife Department, USDA's Natural Resources Conservation Service, and Ducks Unlimited to provide technical assistance and financial incentives to private landowners for improving or restoring wetland habitats along the Gulf Coast. Through January 1994, 4,901 acres of wetland projects had been completed or were under construction for 30 landowners, and 132 landowners controlling 1,231,023 acres had received on-site technical assistance. The Atlantic Coast Joint Venture (ACJV) has been very active in protecting wintering habitat through a multitude of land acquisition and habitat restoration projects involving more than $230 million in grants and matching funds and nearly 300,000 acres of habitat. Audubon's San Francisco Bay Campaign has proposed to restore over 100,000 acres of wetland habitat in the area over the next 20 years. A preliminary agreement with Cargill, Inc., would result in the public acquisition of 16,500 acres of salt ponds for $100 million. The ponds would eventually be restored to tidal wetlands.[1,2–4,13,14,16,17,20,24–28]

CONSERVATION NEEDS

- Slow production of global warming pollution.
- Continue efforts to decrease commercial harvesting of horseshoe crabs along the mid-Atlantic coast of U.S.
- Continue efforts to reduce disturbance of birds at important migratory feeding areas.
- Ensure that management of publicly owned locations currently supporting the Red Knot

continues to maintain habitat conditions beneficial to the species.
- Increase protection, conservation, and restoration of coastal habitat within the migration and wintering range of the Red Knot.
- Implement further wintering surveys of the species in U.S., Mexico, the Caribbean, and Central and South America.

References

1. Harrington, B.A. 2001. Red Knot (*Calidris canutus*). In *The Birds of North America*, No. 563 (A. Poole and F. Gill, eds.). The Academy of Natural Sciences, Philadelphia, PA, and the American Ornithologists' Union, Washington, DC.

2. Donaldson, G.M., C. Hyslop, R.I.G. Morrison, H.L. Dickson, and I. Davidson. 2000. *Canadian Shorebird Conservation Plan*. Canadian Wildlife Service, Environment Canada, Ottawa, ON.

3. New Jersey Department of Fish and Wildlife. 2000. *The 2000 Arctic Search for the Red Knot*. http://www.njfishandwildlife.com/ensp/2000end.htm (accessed 21 June 2004).

4. Canadian Wildlife Service. 2003. *Research—Shorebirds*. http://www.ces-scf.ec.gc.ca/nwrc-cnrf/migb/shor_e.cfm (accessed 21 June 2004).

5. Paulson, D. 1993. *Shorebirds of the Pacific Northwest*. University of Washington Press, Seattle, WA.

6. Skagen, S.K., P.B. Sharpe, R.G. Waltermire, and M.B. Dillon. 1999. *Biogeographic Profiles of Shorebird Migration in Midcontinental North America*. Biological Science Report USGS/BRD/BSR—2000-0003. U.S. Government Printing Office, Denver, CO. 167 pp.

7. Cooper, D. S. 2004. *Important Bird Areas of California*. Audubon California, Pasadena, CA.

8. Chipley, R.M., G.H. Fenwick, M.J. Parr, and D.N. Pashley. 2003. *The American Bird Conservancy Guide to the 500 Most Important Bird Areas in the United States*. Random House, New York, NY.

9. Manomet Bird Observatory. 2003. *Western Hemisphere Shorebird Reserve Network*. http://www.manomet.org/WHSRN/ (accessed 9 February 2004).

10. Morrison, R.I.G., R.K. Ross, and L.J. Niles. 2004. Declines in Wintering Populations of Red Knots in Southern South America. *Condor* 106:60–70.

11. Baker, A.J., P.M.Gonzalez, T. Piersma, L.J. Niles, I. de Lima Serrano do Nascimento, P.W. Atkinson, N.A. Clark, C.D.T. Minton, M.K. Peck, and G. Aarts. 2004. Rapid Population Decline in Red Knots: Fitness Consequences of Decreased Refuelling Rates

and Late Arrival in Delaware Bay. *Proceedings of the Royal Society of London* 271:875–882.

12. Tucker, G.M., and M.F. Heath. 1994. *Birds in Europe: Their Conservation Status*. BirdLife International, Cambridge, UK.

13. Brown, S., C. Hickey, and B. Harrington, eds. 2000. *The U.S. Shorebird Conservation Plan*. Manomet Center for Conservation Sciences, Manomet, MA.

14. Alaska Shorebird Working Group. 2000. A Conservation Plan for Alaska Shorebirds. Unpublished report, Alaska Shorebird Working Group. Available through U.S. Fish and Wildlife Service, Migratory Bird Management, Anchorage, AK. 47 pp.

15. Ricketts et al. 1999. *Terrestrial Ecoregions of North America: A Conservation Assessment*. Island Press, Washington, DC. 485 pp.

16. Canadian Wildlife Service. 2001. *Shorebird Conservation Strategy and Action Plan*. Canadian Wildlife Service, Northern Conservation Division, Yellowknife, NT, Canada.

17. Audubon Alaska. 2002. *Alaska's Western Arctic: A Summary and Synthesis of Resources*. Audubon Alaska, Anchorage, AK. 240 pages plus 49 maps.

18. U.S. Bureau of Land Management. 2003. *Northwest NPRA Final Integrated Activity Plan/Environmental Impact Statement*. http://wwwndo.ak.blm.gov/npra/ (accessed 24 October 2003).

19. Stein, B.A., L.S. Kutner, and J.S. Adams. 2000. *Precious Heritage: The Status of Biodiversity in the United States*. Oxford University Press, New York, NY. 399 pp.

20. National Audubon Society. 2003. *San Francisco Bay Campaign*. http://www.audubonsfbay.org (accessed 3 September 2003).

21. U.S. EPA. 2002. *Mid-Atlantic Integrated Assessment 1997–98 Summary Report*, EPA/620/R-02/003. U.S. Environmental Protection Agency, Atlantic Ecology Division, Narragansett, RI. 115 pp.

22. Delaware Estuary Program. No date. *Delaware Estuary Indicators*. http://www.delep.org/indicators/population.pdf (accessed 23 June 2004).

23. World Wildlife Fund–UK. 2001. No *Place to Go for Some of Britain's Best-loved Winter Birds*. http://www.wwf-uk.org/News/n_0000000465.asp (accessed 21 June 2004).

24. Coastal America. 2002. *Coastal America: A Partnership for Action*. http://www.coastalamerica.gov (accessed 3 September 2003).

25. Delaware Estuary Program. No date. *The Delaware Estuary Program*. http://http://www.delep.org/ (accessed 23 June 2004).

26. Texas Environmental Profiles. Undated. *Federal and State Nonregulatory Conservation Programs*. www.texasep.org/html/wld/wld_6hcp_nonreg.html (accessed 8 April 2003).

27. American Bird Conservancy. No date. *Horseshoe Crabs*. http://www.abcbirds.org/policy/crabs.htm (accessed 22 June 2004).

28. New Jersey Audubon Society. 2003. *State of New Jersey Announces Delaware Bay Beach Closures to Protect Shorebirds and Allows Wildlife Watching: May 17 & 18 and May 24 thru June 1, 2003*. New Jersey Audubon Society, Department of Conservation, Bernadsville, NJ.

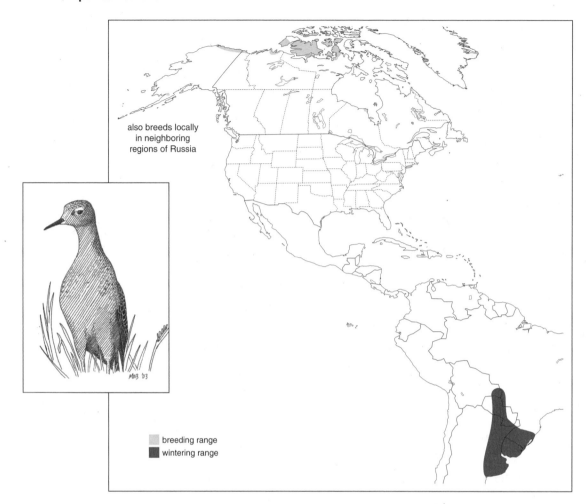

also breeds locally
in neighboring
regions of Russia

breeding range
wintering range

BUFF-BREASTED SANDPIPER (*Tryngites subruficollis*)

Like the Eskimo Curlew, this species was heavily hunted during the late 1800s and this, combined with massive loss of its grassland stopover habitat, resulted in a decline from hundreds of thousands or millions of individuals to an estimated 15,000 birds in 2002.

STATUS AND DISTRIBUTION

The species breeds in the high Arctic with its range extending from the Arctic Coastal Plain of northern Alaska eastward to Canada's Queen Elizabeth Islands, but densities vary widely across the range and from year to year. Also breeds locally in western Chukotka, Russia. Birds winter primarily in the pampas grasslands of Argentina, Brazil, and Uruguay, but some occur in the altiplanos of southwestern Bolivia and northwestern Argentina. The species' migration routes south of the U.S.

are not well documented but largely seem to bypass Central America and instead pass over the Gulf of Mexico and through Venezuela, Guyana, and Suriname. Large concentrations have rarely been found between the U.S. and the southern South American wintering grounds. During spring migration the entire population passes through the prairie grasslands and agricultural fields of the central U.S. and Canada. The bulk of the population uses the same route in fall but small numbers (mostly juveniles) occur at locations west and east to both coasts.

Although there is little detailed information available about rangewide densities, known breeding sites for the species include, in Canada's Northwest Territories, Banks Island (including the Banks Island Migratory Bird Sanctuary) and Prince Patrick Island and in Alaska, the Arctic National Wildlife Refuge and the National Petroleum Reserve. Important migratory stopover sites for Buff-breasted Sandpiper include Beaverhill Lake in Alberta, where 1,500 birds were counted in 1978, Riverton Wildlife Area in Iowa, where up to 257 birds have been counted; and Cheyenne Bottoms Wildlife Management Area in Kansas, which has hosted up to 182 birds. High counts have come from sod farms during migration, including 800–1,000 birds at a sod farm in Burleson County, Texas in August 2004 and over 200 in Dakota County, Minnesota in August 2002. Important wintering areas in South America include the Estancia Medaland, a 27,500-acre private ranch, in Argentina's Buenos Aires Province, Brazil's Lagoa do Peixe National Park and fields near Ilha da Torotama, and Uruguay's Laguna de Rocha and Laguna de Castillos.

Although there has been no systematic survey to estimate trends, repeated counts at several sites indicate a continuing decline in numbers. At Estancia Medaland in Argentina surveys in 1973 indicated approximately 2,000 birds using the area while surveys from 1996 to 2000 estimated only 200 birds. Densities of breeding birds on Somerset Island, Canada showed a significant decrease from 1995 and 1997 to 2001. Declines in numbers of migrant birds have also been noted at several regular stopover sites in the midwest U.S. and Canada. The total population size of Buff-breasted Sandpiper is estimated to have once numbered in the hundreds of thousands or millions but had declined to an estimated 15,000 in 2000.[1-7]

ECOLOGY

Breeds in tundra habitat in the high arctic, where the birds nest on drier, higher areas within tundra complex. Has one of the most unusual breeding systems of any shorebird. Males defend small territories (leks) in clusters where groups of females come to watch the males' mating display, which involves rather elaborate positionings of open wings. Locations of leks seems to vary widely from year to year and even within a season and males may move many kilometers between leks. A male may mate with several females who will each leave the lek to build a nest and raise the young on her own. Females also mate with several males, frequently resulting in mixed paternity clutches. Nests are depressions on grounds where four eggs are laid, one clutch per season. The incubation period is 23–25 days. Young are precocial and leave the nest within hours after hatching but may take several days before beginning to forage successfully. The adult female incubates the eggs by herself and broods and defends the young for 2–3 weeks. Adults and young seem to show relatively little site fidelity. No young banded birds were ever resighted (though sample sizes were small) and only 17% of males and 9% of females were resighted in subsequent years in one study. Locations of leks seem to vary widely from year to year and even within a season, males seem to move many kilometers between lekking areas.

During migration the species occurs in mixed grass prairie regions and Prairie Pothole Region of the central U.S. and Canada but prefers moist areas with very short grass and muddy margins of prairie lakes. Sod farms and grazed pastures have become a preferred habitat in many areas with large numbers noted at sod farms in Minnesota, Oklahoma, and Texas. Also uses rice fields in coastal Texas and Louisiana and golf courses and airports throughout U.S. migratory flyway. Diet has not been well studied but this bird seems to feed mostly on small insects and other invertebrates. In winter the species occurs in the pampas region of southern South America, especially in grazed pasture grasslands and grasslands along shores of marine and freshwater wetlands.[1,4,5]

THREATS

Historically, overhunting was a major threat, including market hunting for sale of large numbers in city markets. During the same time period critical North American grassland migratory stopover habitat underwent massive conversion to agricultural land uses. Loss of northern mixed grass prairie has been estimated at 36–69% and southern mixed grass prairie 27–65%. In some parts of the region there are only tiny fragments of native prairie still in existence. Furthermore, nonnative plants are now estimated to account for 30–60% of grassland plant species. Perhaps of even greater importance was the practical extinction of many species and populations of grazing mammals, the most notable of which is the American bison. These grazers helped create expanses of closely cropped grassland that is preferred by migrant Buff-breasted Sandpipers.

As in most grassland ecosystems greatest current threat continues to be loss and degradation of native habitat largely through conversion to cropland, housing developments, mineral and oil extraction activities, and fire suppression. Most of the species' known wintering locations are on privately owned land that is generally managed for cattle production, producing the closely cropped grasslands that are preferred by Buff-breasted Sandpipers. Such areas near coastal lagoons are unlikely to be converted to cropland because of periodic flooding and high salinity. Inland grasslands areas, however, are more likely to be subject to conversion to cropland or pine plantations or subdivision for housing. Particularly worrisome is that government programs in Argentina and Brazil are promoting, through financial incentives, commercial tree plantations usually of exotic species. Commercial plantations occupied over 370,000 acres of former grassland habitat in 1994 within Argentina's Corrientes Province and there was a 500% increase in forestry plantations between 1995 and 2000. A mine was proposed for an important wintering area in Brazil but negotiations apparently succeeded in moving the mine to habitat not used by Buff-breasted Sandpipers. There are also increasing problems from beach property development for recreational uses in Brazil and Uruguay.

Currently, habitat in the species' known breeding locations is generally undisturbed, though there is interest in mineral exploration and mining in the area, which could eventually destroy or degrade the habitat. For example, proposals have been brought before the U.S. Congress a number of times to override the conservation mandate for the Arctic National Wildlife Refuge to allow oil and gas extraction activities, especially within the Coastal Plain where Buff-breasted Sandpipers breed. Buff-breasted Sandpipers are also known to breed within the Alaska National Petroleum Reserve.

Pesticides and herbicides are a potentially major but poorly documented and understood threat for the species during migration and on the wintering grounds. Birds regularly forage during migration in areas that receive high herbicide and pesticide applications, like sod farms, rice fields, golf courses, and airports. Three birds were known to have died from ingesting pesticides applied to a rice field in Texas and birds were observed foraging in rice fields on the South American wintering grounds while pesticides were being sprayed on the fields. Improper use of pesticides in grasslands in Argentina killed nearly 6000 Swainson's Hawks in 1995–96. A similar event in one of the primary wintering areas for Buff-breasted Sandpiper could result in loss of a large proportion of the global population of the species.[1,4,8-13]

CONSERVATION ACTION

While little direct conservation activity has focused on Buff-breasted Sandpiper, there has been increasing activity in grassland habitat conservation across the U.S. and Canada and involving a great many governmental and nongovernmental organizations. Throughout much of this region, state or provincial agencies own or manage the bulk of the conservation lands that are protected, though often the percentage of the total area protected is quite small. Partners in Flight and the Nature Conservancy have independently developed or are in the process of developing ecoregional plans for the mixed grass prairie regions across which Buff-breasted Sandpipers migrate. These plans recommend both maintaining and enhancing existing conservation areas in the regions and developing projects to restore prairie habitat. The Prairie Pothole Joint Venture has recently begun working toward protecting, restoring, and enhancing habitat specifically for migrant shorebirds, including Buff-breasted Sandpiper.

The Western Hemisphere Shorebird Reserve Network has recognized Beaverhill Lake, Alberta and Cheyenne Bottoms, Kansas as important migratory shorebird staging areas and Brazil's Lagoa do Peixe as an important shorebird wintering area. Much of the habitat at Cheyenne Bottoms is owned and managed by the Kansas Fish and Wildlife Agency and the Nature Conservancy but major conservation problem at the site comes from management of water input from Arkansas River and Walnut Creek. Water withdrawals for irrigation from these two sources were so great in the early 1990s that no water was available for Cheyenne Bottoms and the area was dry much of the time. Later court rulings cut back on amount removed from these sources and along with new water control structures and pumps, wetland habitat has been easier to maintain.

In the wintering grounds, Aves Argentina has focused research activities on the pampas and campos grasslands of Argentina and initiated a new conservation program for the area in 2003 that will identify Important Bird Areas in the region and work toward their protection and proper management. The grasslands in this region also support 14 globally threatened bird species and wintering populations of Swainson's Hawk, Upland Sandpiper, and Bobolink. Lagoa de Peixe was established as a National Park by the Brazilian government in 1986 and various educational and research activities have continued. About 10% of the land is owned by the Brazilian Institute for the Environment and Renewable Natural Resources (IBAMA), with the rest either private or Federal Community property. Private lands are still being converted to rice and other forms of agriculture.[1,10,11,14–18]

CONSERVATION NEEDS

- Ensure that management of publicly owned lands currently used by Buff-breasted Sandpipers continues to maintain habitat conditions beneficial to the species.
- Slow or halt incentives for commercial forestry plantations on wintering ground grasslands in Argentina and Brazil as well as for mining, agriculture, and shoreline development in wintering areas.
- Provide incentives for private landowners to manage their lands to the benefit of grassland birds in areas where Buff-breasted Sandpipers migrate or winter.
- Purchase land or conservation easements on private lands in areas in the U.S., Canada, and Central and South America that are important migratory staging and wintering areas for Buff-breasted Sandpiper.
- Implement regular breeding, wintering, and migratory rangewide surveys designed to assess overall population status and trends.
- Prevent oil and mineral exploration in areas that are known to support breeding Buff-breasted Sandpipers in Alaska and Canada and in wintering areas in South America.
- Restore native grassland ecosystems including through reintroduction of native mammalian herbivores where possible.
- In the U.S., work with National Resources Conservation Service in the implementation of Farm Bill conservation incentive programs so that the habitat conditions specified on lands potentially used by Buff-breasted Sandpipers are beneficial to the species.
- Assess effects of pesticides and other contaminants encountered by Buff-breasted Sandpipers on their survival and reproductive health.

References

1. Lanctot, R.B., and C.D. Laredo. 1994. Buff-breasted Sandpiper (*Tryngites subruficollis*). In *The Birds of North America*, No. 91 (A. Poole and F. Gill, eds.). The Birds of North America, Inc., Philadelphia, PA, and the American Ornithologists' Union, Washington, DC.

2. Bird Studies Canada. 2003. *Important Bird Areas of Canada*. http://www.bsc-eoc.org/iba/IBAsites.html (accessed October 2003).

3. Skagen, S.K., P.B. Sharpe, R.G. Waltermire, and M.B. Dillon. 1999. *Biogeographic Profiles of Shorebird Migration in Midcontinental North America*. Biological Science Report USGS/BRD/BSR—2000-0003. U.S. Government Printing Office, Denver, CO. 167 pp.

4. Lanctot, R.B., D.E. Blanco, R.A. Dias, J.P. Isacch, V.A. Gill, J.B. Almeida, K. Delhey, P.F. Petracci, G.A. Bencke, and R.A. Balbueno. 2002. Conservation Status of the Buff-breasted Sandpiper: Historic and Contemporary Distribution and Abundance in South America. *Wilson Bulletin* 114:44–72.

5. Isacch, J.P., and M.M. Martinez. 2002. Temporal Variation in Abundance and the Population Status of Non-breeding Nearctic and Patagonian Shorebirds in the Flooding Pampa Grasslands of Argentina. *Journal of Field Ornithology* 74:233–242.

6. BirdLife International. 2000. *Threatened Birds of the World*. Lynx Editions and BirdLife International, Barcelona, Spain, and Cambridge, UK.

7. Delany, S., and D. Scott. 2002. *Waterbird Population Estimates*, 3rd ed. Wetlands International Global Series No. 12, Wageningen, The Netherlands.

8. Gauthier, D.A., A. Lafon, T. Tombs, J. Hoth, and E. Wilken. 2003. *Grasslands: Toward a North American Conservation Strategy*. Canadian Plains Research Center, University of Regina, Regina, Saskatchewan, and Commission for Environmental Cooperation, Montreal, QC, Canada. 99 pp.

9. Ricketts T.H., et al. 1999. *Terrestrial Ecoregions of North America: A Conservation Assessment*. Island Press, Washington, DC. 485 pp.

10. Di Giacomo, A., and S. Krapovickas. 2001. Afforestation Threatens Argentina's Grasslands. World Birdwatch 23:24–25.

11. Krapovickas, S., and A. Di Giacomo. 1998. Conservation of Pampas and Campos Grasslands in Argentina. *Parks* 8(3):47–53.

12. Wilbor, S. No date. *Review of Rare and Sensitive*

Vertebrate Species in the National Petroleum Reserve–Alaska. Proceedings of NPR-A Symposium, Bureau of Land Management, Northern District Office, Fairbanks, AK. http://wwwndo.ak.blm.gov/npra/sympos/html/paper18 .html (accessed 23 October 2003).

13. Goldstein, M.I., T.E. Lacher, Jr., B. Woodbridge, M.J. Bechard, S.B. Canavelli, M.E. Zaccagnini, G.P. Cobb, E.J. Scollon, R. Tribolet, and M.J. Hooper. 1999. Monocrotophos-induced Mass Mortality of Swainson's Hawks in Argentina, 1995–96. *Ecotoxicology* 8:201–214.

14. Fitzgerald, J.A., and D.N. Pashley. 2000. *Partners in Flight Bird Conservation Plan for the Dissected till Plains.* American Bird Conservancy, The Plains, VA.

15. Fitzgerald, J.A., D.N. Pashley, and B. Pardo. 1999. *Partners in Flight Bird Conservation Plan for the Northern Mixed-grass Prairie.* American Bird Conservancy, The Plains, VA.

16. Dinsmore, S., S.K. Skagen, and D.L. Helmers. No date. *Shorebirds: An Overview for the Prairie Pothole Joint Venture.* U.S. Fish and Wildlife Service, Colorado Fish and Wildlife Assistance Office, Lakewood, CO.

17. Manomet Bird Observatory. 2003. *Western Hemisphere Shorebird Reserve Network.* http://www .manomet.org/WHSRN/ (accessed 23 October 2003).

18. Wetlands International. 2002. *Ramsar Sites Database: Lagoa do Peixe.* http://www.wetlands.org/ RDB/Ramsar_Dir/Brazil/BR002D02.htm (accessed 23 October 2003).

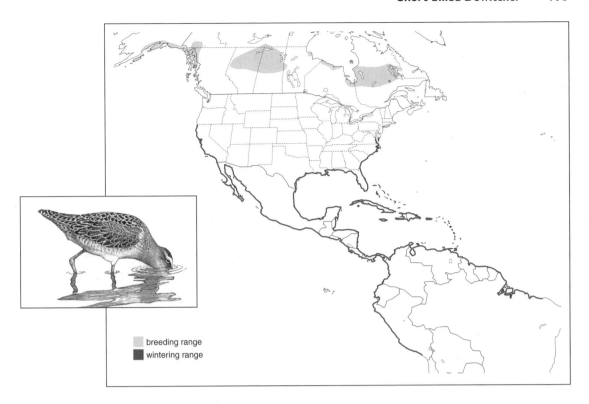

breeding range
wintering range

SHORT-BILLED DOWITCHER (*Limnodromus griseus*)

For most birders the memory of watching Short-billed Dowitchers brings back the smell of salty mudflats and saltmarshes where the birds often congregate in large numbers during migration. It is, however, the marshy wetlands within the boreal forest of Canada where an estimated 90% of the population breeds. An apparent decline of approximately 50% in the eastern population has placed the species in the conservation concern category.

STATUS AND DISTRIBUTION

This species has four disjunct breeding areas. One (the *caurinus* subspecies) extends along southern coastal Alaska from Kodiak Island east to southern Yukon and northwestern British Columbia and south to Charlotte Island, British Columbia. Another (subspecies *hendersoni*) extends from northern Alberta east to the central western edge of Manitoba. A small population (subspecies unknown) breeds along the shore of Hudson Bay in northern Manitoba. A fourth major population (subspecies *griseus*—though some on western edge may have characteristics of *hendersoni*) occurs from northeastern Ontario along the shore of James Bay

east across central Quebec to the western edge of Labrador. Approximately 90% of the species' total breeding range is within Canada's boreal. Wintering range is extensive, extending from the southern Pacific and Atlantic coasts of the U.S. south through Central America and the Caribbean to northern South America.

Although little specific information is available about important breeding sites for the species, a number of parks and protected areas lie within the breeding range of the species and likely harbor breeding populations. In Canada these include Wood Buffalo National Park in Alberta and Northwest Territories, Alberta's Prince Albert National Park, Saskatchewan's Lac La Ronge Provincial Park, Manitoba's Wapusk National Park, Ontario's Polar Bear Provincial Park, Québec's Assinica and des Lacs-Albanel-Mistassini-et-Waconichi Faunal Reserves, and British Columbia's Tatshenshini-Alsek Park. In the U.S., the Chugach National Forest and Wrangell-St. Elias National Park and Preserve harbor breeding populations of Short-billed Dowitcher.

Important migratory stopover sites for this species in Canada include British Columbia's Tofino area (max. 10,000–15,000 in spring), Nova Scotia's Eastern Cape Sable Island (up to 15,000 birds), Québec's Lagune du Havre aux Basques et plage de l'Ouest Important Bird Area (IBA) (up to 7,600 birds), and Manitoba's Oak Hammock Marsh WMA IBA (up to 5,000 birds). Important migratory stopover sites for this species in the U.S. include Washington's Gray's Harbor (max. 34,000 in spring/12,000 in fall) and Willapa Bay (max. 26,000 in spring); North Carolina's Pea Island Nationl Wildlife Refuge (NWR) (max. 15,000); and Delaware Bay (max. 10,000), New Jersey's Forsythe NWR (max. 11,000), Massachusetts' Monomoy NWR (max. 6,000), rice fields of western Louisiana and eastern Texas (single site maximums of up to 3,500 in spring), Ohio's Winous Point (max. 6,400), Texas' Bolivar Flats (max. 1,500) and Anahuac NWR (max. 1,600), and Kansas' Cheyenne Bottoms Wildlife Management Area (max. 3,200). In Central America, the Upper Bay of Panama has hosted up to 6,273 Short-billed Dowitchers during migration.

Important wintering sites in the U.S. include California's Salton Sea (max 10,000 dowitchers of both this species and Long-billed Dowitcher) and Florida's Ding Darling National Wildlife Refuge (1,370 in March 2000). Important wintering sites in Mexico include Ensenada Pabellones and Bahía Santa Maria in Sinaloa and Ojo de Liebra/Guerrero Negro (42,000 dowitcher sp. in January 1994) and Bahía San Quintín (3,300 dowitcher sp. in January 1992) in Baja California. Important South American wintering sites include Suriname's Bigi Pan (max. 30,000) and Wia Wia Nature Reserve (max. 50,000), Venezuela's Chacopata Lagoon (thousands), and Brazil's Baia de Tiracu (max. 1,100) and Baia dos Lencois (max. 3,000).

Prior to the period of intense market hunting in the late 1800s and early 1900s when dowitchers were a popular game species, the species was incredibly common with some descriptions that suggest numbers could have been as high 500,000–1,000,000. For example, an observer in Scarborough, Maine, described a May 1868 flight of Short-billed Dowitcher as extending 12 miles wide and 100 miles long. The numbers dropped precipitously by the early 1900s but after market hunting ceased the species increased in numbers again. However, the International Shorebird Survey shows a decline of 46% from 1972 to 1983. The Maritime Shorebird Survey has also shown significant declines over the last 30 years. The spe-

cies' total population was estimated in 2000 at 320,000, with 150,000 in *caurinus* subspecies, 110,000 in *griseus* subspecies, and 60,000 in *hendersonii* subspecies. However, an independent estimate based on numbers on wintering sites and maximums at migration sites has suggested that the total population could be as low as 150,000–175,000.[1,2–19]

ECOLOGY

Breeds in muskeg, bogs, and sedge meadows in the boreal forest and taiga of Canada and Alaska. Nests are depressions on ground where four eggs are laid; incubation is performed by both the male and female for about 21 days. Young are fully feathered when hatched (precocial) and leave nest within hours after hatching and forage on their own. Virtually all defense and brooding of young is by male as female departs within days after hatching of eggs. The male leaves the young after 12–14 days, when they can fly. Immatures begin migrating at 4–6 weeks. Only a single brood is produced each year. Feeds on a variety of foods, especially aquatic invertebrates, including insect larvae, marine worms, small clams, crabs, and other marine crustaceans and invertebrates, but also some plant seeds and tubers. Probably first breeds at 1–2 years of age. On wintering grounds and during migration uses a variety of coastal wetlands, but especially intertidal flats and saltmarshes, and in South and Central America and the Caribbean, also uses mangrove forests.[1]

THREATS

The reasons for the decline in numbers of Short-billed Dowitcher are unknown, though there are a number of possible or probable causes. Portions of the breeding range of the species in Alaska and Canada lie within various protected areas where, barring any major changes in management policy, the species' habitat should remain in good condition. Acidification of wetlands in the eastern portion of the breeding range from acid precipitation as a result of industrial air pollution in the eastern U.S. could impact species by degrading wetlands. In the western part of the breeding range there is increasing evidence that wetland habitats are drying and shrinking as a result of global warming.

In addition there has been much habitat loss within the species' breeding range. Habitat loss and degradation from development for oil and gas industry and mining is increasing. Plans are underway for increased development of the Alberta Oil Sands, the world's second largest oil and gas deposit in the world. More than 2.2 million acres of boreal wetlands in Canada have been lost due to hydroelectric projects already and energy and forest products industries are increasing their activities in the boreal region of Canada.

Throughout the breeding range much of the habitat is within areas managed for forestry and it is unclear how current forestry practices are impacting the species. Though more than 90% of the Canadian boreal forest is publicly owned, almost 1/3 of the boreal is currently allocated to forestry companies for timber production amounting to tens of millions of acres that will be logged. Clearcutting has been used in over 80% of forest harvest operations in Canada.

In migration and on the wintering grounds the major threat is continued loss and degradation of coastal wetlands. In the U.S., such habitat loss has been dramatic. Florida and Texas have each lost at least 7.5 million acres of wetlands and Louisiana between 2.5 and 7.5 million acres over the last 200 years. In Louisiana and Texas coastal wetlands are continuing to be lost to erosion and subsequent saltwater intrusion. In California's San Francisco Bay, 80% of intertidal habitats have been destroyed. South of the U.S., loss of coastal wetland habitat in many countries continues to be a major threat. Loss of mangrove habitat is of particular concern as mangrove forests support the largest wintering concentrations of Short-billed Dowitcher in South America (in Suriname and Brazil). Although the mangrove forests of Suriname and the Maranhão region of coastal north-central Brazil are still relatively intact, throughout the species' wintering range much mangrove habitat has been lost or degraded by sedimentation and pollution from agricultural runoff and deforestation, changes in hydrology from road projects and developments, oil pollution, and cutting for fuel and charcoal production. For example, along Colombia's northwest coast mangrove forest declined by 64% between 1956 and 1995 from development, highway construction, agriculture, and aquaculture. In Venezuela's Lake Maracaibo, the loss of mangrove habitat was estimated at 90% between 1960 and 1993. In some areas large expanses of mangroves have been removed for shrimp farming or salt production. Between 1964 and 1989 in Costa Rica's Gulf of Nicoya 1,582 acres of mangroves were lost to shrimp farms and 287 acres to salt production. In recent years there has been an increase in proposals for development of coastal tourism facilities that would destroy or degrade mangrove habitats. In general, mangrove habitat is underrepresented in parks and other protected areas throughout the wintering range. Several threatened bird species rely on these habitats, including the Mangrove Hummingbird, a species restricted to the Pacific coast of Costa Rica; the Yellow-billed Cotinga, occurring only on the Pacific coasts of Costa Rica and Panama; and the Sapphire-bellied Hummingbird, confined to the northern coast of Colombia. In addition, mangrove habitats support a host of other threatened animal species and marine species of economic importance.

Many estuarine systems within the migratory range of the Short-billed Dowitcher are also showing degraded environmental conditions. For example, the percentage of the Delaware Estuary that tested above EPA ecological limits for metal contaminants increased from 5 to 22% from 1990–93 to 1997. Similarly, the percentage of the Chesapeake Bay that tested above EPA ecological limits for organic contaminants increased from 2 to 34% from 1990–93 to 1997.[20-32]

CONSERVATION ACTION

U.S. and Canadian shorebird conservation plans have been developed that provide recommendations for management, research, outreach, and education for Short-billed Dowitcher and other shorebird species. The Western Hemisphere Shorebird Reserve Network, RAMSAR, and the Birdlife International Important Bird Areas programs have identified many key breeding, wintering, and migratory stopover locations for the species and in some locations have initiated conservation and outreach projects. World Wildlife Fund–Canada, the Canadian Nature Federation, and many other organizations have been working with national and provincial governments to increase the number of protected areas in Canada, including within the breeding range of Short-billed Dowitcher. For example, Wapusk National Park in Manitoba was established in 1996 and other potential parks continue to be planned for and discussed.

In Canada, a broad community of conservation organizations, industry and First Nations have announced the Boreal Forest Conservation Framework—a new national boreal conservation approach. The plan protects the ecological integrity of the region while integrating sustainable forestry and other development activities. The Framework calls for the establishment of large, interconnected protected areas covering at least half of the boreal region and application of cutting-edge sustainable development practices in the remaining lands. The Canadian Boreal Initiative and its partners advocate for the adoption of Framework principles on the vast, and largely publicly owned, boreal landscape.

A Canadian Senate subcommittee developed a comprehensive report in 1999 that recommended a set of actions needed to ensure the protection and sustainable use of Canada's boreal forests. Since then the Canadian Boreal Initiative has been advocating for adoption and implementation of these recommendations in addition to promoting the Framework and working with Provincial governments to adopt the principles of the Framework on their lands. Some progress was reported in the establishment of protected areas including the protection of 625,000 acres of boreal forest habitat in Québec since 2000.

The Boreal Songbird Initiative has spearheaded work by a network of U.S. conservation groups to support the Boreal Forest Conservation Framework. This work includes outreach activities to increase awareness of the boreal wilderness and the threats it faces. For example, the National Wildlife Federation and National Audubon Society both have conducted letter-writing campaigns asking large retail catalog companies to use recycled paper and purchase from environmentally and socially responsible sources instead of using paper from trees harvested from the boreal forest.

The primary wintering areas within Suriname are largely government-owned and considered protected areas, but, as in many South American countries, there are limited resources for enforcement of regulations. Similarly, much of the major Brazilian wintering area is within an official Area of Environmental Protection, which allows sustainable natural resource use, especially traditional uses. On the wintering grounds there is an urgent need for increased awareness of communities and governments to the ecological importance of coastal habitats, including mangrove forest, and to increase acreage of mangroves within protected areas. Some limited work is being done to restore mangrove habitats in some locations but few international conservation organizations seem to be working on the issue. There are laws in Costa Rica and Venezuela that make it illegal to remove mangroves but these laws are not enforced. Ducks Unlimited has funded waterfowl and waterbird surveys of the key wintering areas for Short-billed Dowitcher in Suriname for many years that also monitor habitat conditions of these sites.

A great many organization, agencies, and coalitions are working on coastal habitat restoration and protection projects within the U.S., many of which will likely eventually benefit Short-billed Dowitchers. For example, the Coastal America Partnership, a coalition of federal agencies, state and local governments, and private organizations, identifies and implements local wetland restoration and protection projects throughout the U.S. The Partnership had initiated more than 500 projects impacting hundreds of thousands of acres of wetland habitat as of 2002. The Atlantic Coast Joint Venture (ACJV) has been very active in protecting migratory habitat for the species through a multitude of land acquisition and habitat restoration projects involving more than $230 million in grants and matching funds and nearly 300,000 acres of habitat. Many of these ACJV-funded projects are within important migratory stopover areas for Short-billed Dowitcher along the Atlantic Coast. Ducks Unlimited has spearheaded a host of initiatives along the Atlantic Coast to restore saltmarshes that are used extensively by Short-billed Dowitchers in spring migration. For example, Ducks Unlimited and USFWS partnered with Suffolk County Vector Control and the New York State Department of Environmental Conservation to restore hundreds of acres of saltmarsh on Long Island.[17–19,22,23,25,26,33–37]

CONSERVATION NEEDS

- Slow production of global warming pollution.
- Within the breeding range of Short-billed Dowitcher implement broad, landscape-scale forest management plans that maintain boreal wetlands and the forests bordering them.
- Increase the number of protected areas through national parks in Canada's boreal forest.
- Implement the Boreal Forest Conservation Framework that calls for protection of 50% of

Canada's boreal region and adoption of leading-edge sustainable development practices in parts of the boreal that are developed.

- Decrease rates of acid deposition from air pollution, especially from sources impacting eastern portion of breeding range of Short-billed Dowitcher.
- Ensure that management of publicly owned locations currently supporting Short-billed Dowitcher continues to maintain habitat conditions beneficial to the species.
- Increase protection and conservation of coastal habitat within the wintering range of Short-billed Dowitcher.
- Restore coastal marine ecosystems within the migratory and wintering range of Short-billed Dowitcher.
- Implement a rangewide wintering and migration survey designed to assess overall population status and trends and to determine if there are other unidentified key wintering and stopover locations for the species.

References

1. Jehl, J.R., Jr., J. Klima, and R. E. Harris. 2001. Short-billed Dowitcher (*Limnodromus griseus*). In *The Birds of North America*, No. 564 (A. Poole and F. Gill, eds.). The Birds of North America, Inc., Philadelphia, PA.

2. Parks Canada. 2003. *Prince Albert National Park of Canada.* http://www.pc.gc.ca/pn-np/sk/princealbert/natcul/natcul2_e.asp (accessed 23 June 2004).

3. Parks Canada. 2003. *Wood Buffalo National Park.* http://www.pc.gc.ca/pn-np/nt/woodbuffalo/natcul/natcul1_e.asp (accessed 23 June 2004).

4. Ontario Parks, 2004. *Polar Bear Provincial Park.* http://www.ontarioparks.com/english/pola.html (accessed 23 June 2004).

5. British Columbia Ministry of Water, Land, and Air Protection. No date. *Tatshenshini-Alsek Park.* http://wlapwww.gov.bc/bcparks/explore/parpgs/tatshen.htm (accessed 23 June 2004).

6. Tourism Saskatchewan. No date. *Lac La Ronge Provincial Park.* http://interactive.usask.ski/tourism/sask_parks/laronge.html (accessed 23 June 2004).

7. Wildlife Reserves Quebec. No date. *Reserves Fauniques Assinica et des lacs-Albanel-Mistassini-et-Waconichi.* http://www.sepaq.com (accessed 23 June 2004).

8. National Park Service. No date. *Wrangell-St. Elias National Park & Preserve.* http://www.nps.gov/wrst/home.htm (accessed 23 June 2004).

9. Igl, L.D. 2003. *Bird Checklists of the United States* (Version 12MAY03). Northern Prairie Wildlife Research Center Home Page, Jamestown, ND. http://www.npwrc.usgs.gov/resource/othrdata/chekbird/chekbird.htm (accessed 23 June 2004).

10. Paulson, D. 1993. *Shorebirds of the Pacific Northwest.* University of Washington Press, Seattle, WA.

11. Bird Studies Canada. 2003. *Important Bird Areas of Canada.* http://www.bsc-eoc.org/iba/IBAsites.html (accessed 23 June 2004).

12. Skagen, S.K., P.B. Sharpe, R.G. Waltermire, and M.B. Dillon. 1999. *Biogeographic Profiles of Shorebird Migration in Midcontinental North America.* Biological Science Report USGS/BRD/BSR—2000-0003. U.S. Government Printing Office, Denver, CO. 167 pp.

13. Chipley, R.M., G.H. Fenwick, M.J. Parr, and D.N. Pashley. 2003. *The American Bird Conservancy Guide to the 500 Most Important Bird Areas in the United States.* Random House, New York, NY.

14. Page, G.W., E. Palacios, A. Lucia, S. Gonzalez, L.E. Stenzel, and M. Jungers. 1997. Numbers of Wintering Shorebirds in Coastal Wetlands of Baja California, Mexico. *Journal of Field Ornithology* 68:562–574.

15. Angehr, G. 2003. *Directory of Important Bird Areas in Panama.* Panama Audubon Society, Balboa, Panama.

16. Morrison, R.I.G., and R.K. Ross. 1989. *Atlas of Nearctic Shorebirds on the Coast of South America*, Vols. I & II. Canadian Wildlife Service, Ottawa, ON.

17. Manomet Bird Observatory. 2003. *Western Hemisphere Shorebird Reserve Network.* http://www.manomet.org/WHSRN/ (accessed 9 February 2004).

18. Brown, S., C. Hickey, and B. Harrington, eds. 2000. *The U.S. Shorebird Conservation Plan.* Manomet Center for Conservation Sciences, Manomet, MA.

19. Donaldson, G.M., C. Hyslop, R.I.G. Morrison, H.L. Dickson, and I. Davidson. 2000. *Canadian Shorebird Conservation Plan.* Canadian Wildlife Service, Environment Canada, Ottawa, ON.

20. Environment Canada. 2003. *Acid Rain—What Is Being Done?* http://www.ec.gc.ca/acidrain/done-canada.html (accessed 14 July 2003).

21. Greenberg, R., and S. Droege. 1999. On the Decline of the Rusty Blackbird and the Use of Ornithological Literature to Document Long-term Population Trends. *Conservation Biology* 13:553–559.

22. Sub-committee on Boreal Forest of the Standing Senate Committee on Agriculture and Forestry. 1999. *Competing Realities: The Boreal Forest at Risk.* Government of Canada, Ottawa, ON. http://www.parl.gc.ca/36/1/parlbus/commbus/senate/com-e/BORE-E/rep-e/rep09jun99-e.htm (accessed 24 June 2003).

23. Canadian Boreal Initiative. 2003. *The Boreal Forest at Risk: A Progress Report*. Canadian Boreal Initiative, Ottawa, ON.

24. Stein, B.A., L.S. Kutner, and J.S. Adams. 2000. *Precious Heritage: The Status of Biodiversity in the United States*. Oxford University Press, New York, NY. 399 pp.

25. National Audubon Society. 2003. *San Francisco Bay Campaign*. http://www.audubonsfbay.org (accessed 3 September 2003).

26. Ellison, A.M., and E.J. Farnsworth. 1996. Anthropogenic Disturbance of Caribbean Mangrove Ecosystems: Past Impacts, Present Trends, and Future Predictions. *Biotropica* 28:549–565.

27. World Wildlife Fund. 2001. *Maranhao mangroves (NT1419)*. http://www.worldwildlife.org/wildworld/profiles/terrestrial/nt/nt1419_full.html (accessed 17 June 2004).

28. World Wildlife Fund. 2001. *Guianan mangroves (NT1411)*. http://www.worldwildlife.org/wildworld/profiles/terrestrial/nt/nt1411_full.html (accessed 17 June 2004).

29. World Wildlife Fund. 2001. *Magdalena-Santa Marta mangroves (NT1417)*. http://www.worldwildlife.org/wildworld/profiles/terrestrial/nt/nt1417_full.html (accessed 18 August 2003).

30. World Wildlife Fund. 2001. *Coastal Venezuelan mangroves (NT1408)*. http://www.worldwildlife.org/wildworld/profiles/terrestrial/nt/nt1408_full.html (accessed 18 August 2003).

31. Wege, D.C., and A.J. Long. 1995. *Key Areas for Threatened Birds in the Neotropics*. BirdLife International and Smithsonian Institution Press, Washington, DC. 311 pp.

32. U.S. EPA. 2002. *Mid-Atlantic Integrated Assessment 1997–98 Summary Report*, EPA/620/R-02/003. U.S. Environmental Protection Agency, Atlantic Ecology Division, Narragansett, RI. 115 pp.

33. Manitobawildlands.org. 2004. *Manitoba National Parks*. http://manitobawildlands.org/pa_ntl_prks.htm (accessed 16 June 2004).

34. National Wildlife Federation. 2004. *Help the Boreal Forest*. http://www.nwf.org/ (accessed 30 June 2004).

35. Ducks Unlimited. 2002. *Waterfowl Surveys in Latin America*. http://www.ducks.org/conservation/latin america_surveys.asp (accessed 16 June 2004).

36. Coastal America. 2002. *Coastal America: A Partnership for Action*. http://www.coastalamerica.gov (accessed 3 September 2003).

37. Ducks Unlimited. 2002. *Atlantic Coast Ecosystem Initiative*. http://www.ducks.org/conservation/Projects/GreatLakesAtlantic/AtlanticCoast/index.asp (accessed 18 June 2004).

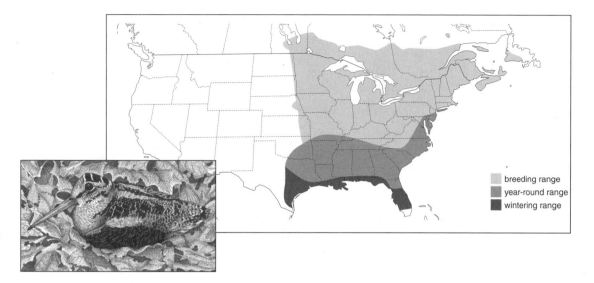

AMERICAN WOODCOCK (*Scolopax minor*)

The mating display of this odd-looking shorebird is one of the signs of spring to many inhabitants of the rural eastern U.S., but the distinctive nasal "peent" sound that the males give as part of the display has disappeared from many areas as the population has declined.

STATUS AND DISTRIBUTION

Species breeds from southeastern Manitoba east to southern Québec and southwestern Newfoundland south to northern Florida and west to eastern Texas. The southern third of the breeding range is inhabited year round, though it is unknown whether the same birds stay throughout the year. An estimated 80% of the breeding population occurs within the U.S. but highest densities seem to occur in the northern portion of the range from the northern U.S. extending into Canada. The species is widely distributed and there is little specific information available about important breeding sites for the species. Parks and protected areas that lie within the breeding range of the species and harbor breeding populations include New Brunswick's Kouchibouguac National Park, Ontario's Pukaskwa National Park, Maine's Moosehorn National Wildlife Refuge (NWR), Michigan's Seney NWR, New Jersey's Great Swamp NWR, and New York's Iroquois NWR. Wintering range extends from eastern Oklahoma and Texas eastwards across the Gulf states and along the Atlantic coast to New Jersey and Long Island, New York. Species is also widely distributed in

winter and among a great many wintering sites are North Carolina's Pee Dee NWR and Louisiana's Atchafalaya River Basin, which is claimed to support one of the largest wintering populations.

The species has shown significant long-term declines, at least in the northern portion of the breeding range. The U.S. Fish and Wildlife Service's Singing-ground Survey, which covers the northern part of the breeding range, has documented a significant decline of approximately 52% (1.9% per year) from 1968 to 2006 in the eastern portion of the surveyed range and 50% (1.8% per year) in the western portion. In addition, the number of young produced per female based on estimates from collections of wings from hunted birds has shown a steady decline since the mid-1980s. The species' total population has been estimated at 5,000,000 individuals.[1-6]

ECOLOGY

Breeds in areas with young forests, shrubs, and forest openings interspersed. Males use open areas as singing grounds from which they initiate aerial displays to attract multiple females for mating. Birds feed in moist soils of young forests and shrubby areas, especially on earthworms but also some seeds, small insects, and other invertebrates. After mating, males do not participate in any part of nesting or care of the young. Nests are depressions on ground where four eggs are laid and incubated for about 21 days. Young are precocial and leave the nest within hours after hatching. The female feeds the young during the first week but within a few days the young are actively probing for food. The young are independent of the female by 31–38 days. No evidence for production of more than one brood per year. Breeds in the first year.[1]

THREATS

The greatest threat to the species on the breeding and wintering grounds is continued loss of shrub-scrub, early-successional habitat as the proportion of the landscape that is in an early successional state continues to decline across much of the east. For example, as of 1988 only 8% of forest land in New England was made up of young trees. This decline in amount of shrub-scrub habitat is attributable to a variety of factors, including the maturation of second-growth habitat after widespread farmland abandonment across the region as well as loss of habitat to development, and is a widespread issue impacting a suite of bird species of early-successional habitats. In addition, much of the forested wetland habitats used by American Woodcock in breeding and wintering areas has been lost in the last 150 years. The loss of southern bottomland habitats in the Mississippi alluvial valley has been estimated at 75%, and 25% of forested wetland habitat in the southeastern U.S. was lost between the 1950s and 1980s. In many areas the destruction of bottomland forests continues to the present time. For example, in South Carolina 28% of bottomland hardwood forest acreage was lost between 1952 and 2000.

The bulk of habitat for the species lies on private lands. In the northeast U.S. most habitat is owned by timber companies. Balancing the needs of early-successional species like American Woodcock against the needs of species that require mature forest is one of the greatest challenges facing conservation in the eastern U.S. A forest can be harvested and it will provide habitat for early-successional species within a year or two but it may take dozens or even hundreds of years before species requiring mature forests can survive and reproduce there. Decisions about the size, configuration, and location of areas to convert or maintain in early successional habitat and whether natural disturbance regimes are adequate to meet the needs of these species in some areas is difficult and requires a landscape level perspective.

Other issues that could potentially impact American Woodcock include the effects of acid rain on the invertebrate fauna of forested wetlands, especially in the northeast U.S. and adjacent Canada, where there is significant acidification from power plan emissions in the Midwest U.S. The effects of various pesticides and pollutants on the species are also unknown but could be an issue since the species has been known to accumulate high levels of certain contaminants (e.g., DDT). Woodcock from eastern Canada have been found to have elevated levels of lead in their bodies that may be from ingesting spent lead shot. The effect of hunting mortality on populations is not well studied but is thought to be minimal. An estimated 2 million birds were taken annually in the U.S. in late 1980s but recent estimates place U.S. annual take at about 300,000 birds.[1,2,7–11]

CONSERVATION ACTION

The U.S. Fish and Wildlife Service published a national American Woodcock Management Plan in 1990 that included some recommendations for protection of key migratory stopover locations. Several of these sites, including Canaan Valley, WV, and Cape May, NJ, have since had National Wildlife Refuges established there. A number of other National Wildife Refuges in the eastern U.S. have active habitat management programs to benefit American Woodcock and other species of early-successional habitats. Moosehorn NWR in eastern Maine, in particular, has hosted an active research and management program targeted at improving conditions for the species and understanding its biology. Within the Mississippi Alluvial Valley many projects to purchase or reforest lands are ongoing through many partner agencies and organizations, including the Mississippi Valley Joint Venture, U.S. Fish and Wildlife Service Partners for Wildlife program, the National Resources Conservation Service Wetland Reserve Program, Ducks Unlimited, and the Nature Conservancy.

The International Association of Fish and Wildlife Agencies has created a task force to develop a multistate conservation plan for the species. Partners in Flight Bird Conservation Plans that have been completed for eastern U.S. physiographic regions have identified American Woodcock and its associated suite of shrub-scrub bird species as a high priority and have provided recommendations for management, research, and monitoring. Healthy, stable bird populations will require forest harvest planning schemes that incorporate ecological needs at a broad landscape scale that provides a mosaic of appropriate age-class habitat, including early-successional habitat.

The U.S. Environmental Protection Agency's Acid Rain Program has worked toward reducing sulfur dioxide and nitrogen oxide emissions from industrial sources, especially coal-fired power generating facilities, the primary contributor to acid rain. By 1996 emissions from U.S. sources had decline by about 27% compared to 1980 levels. Similarly, Environment Canada's Eastern Canada Acid Rain Program had resulted in a 58% reduction in emissions by 1999 compared to 1980 levels. Unfortunately, further research has also shown that eastern Canadian wetland ecosystems are more sensitive to acid rain than first thought and further reductions in emissions are necessary to preserve these wetland systems. In 1998 various Canadian government agencies signed The Canada-wide Acid Rain Strategy for Post-2000 to reduce emissions to levels that would not harm Canadian ecosystems.[1,2,5,7,10–15]

CONSERVATION NEEDS

- Increase acreage of shrub-scrub forest habitat within the breeding range of American Woodcock that is managed to attain conditions beneficial to the species within the context of large, landscape level habitat management plans, especially on public lands.
- Compare early successional habitats resulting from natural disturbances vs. forestry and other management practices, with regard to suitability for high-priority species.
- Develop management guidelines/policy for utility right-of-ways and other shrub habitats maintained in early-successional states.
- Carry out more research to understand whether acid rain is having an impact on reproduction in the species.
- Increase research efforts to understand the source and implications of elevated lead levels in American Woodcock bone tissues.

References

1. Keppie, D.M. and R. M. Whiting, Jr. 1994. American Woodcock (*Scolopax minor*). In *The Birds of North America*, No. 100 (A. Poole and F. Gill, Eds.). Philadelphia: The Academy of Natural Sciences; Philadelphia, PA, and the American Ornithologists' Union, Washington, DC.

2. Robertson, B. 2002. *American Woodcock Species Management Abstract*. The Nature Conservancy, Arlington, VA. http://www.conserveonline.org/2002/09/b/en/amwo.doc

3. Igl, L. D. 2003. *Bird Checklists of the United States* (Version 12MAY03). Northern Prairie Wildlife Research Center Home Page, Jamestown, ND. http://www.npwrc.usgs.gov/resource/othrdata/chekbird/chekbird.htm (accessed 23 June 2004).

4. Chipley, R.M., G.H. Fenwick, M.J. Parr, and D.N. Pashley. 2003. *The American Bird Conservancy Guide to the 500 Most Important Bird Areas in the United States*. Random House, New York, NY.

5. Kelley, J.R., Jr., and R. D. Rau. 2004. *American woodcock population status*, 2006. U.S. Fish and Wildlife Service, Laurel, MD. 15pp.

6. Donaldson, G.M., C. Hyslop, R.I.G. Morrison, H.L. Dickson, and I. Davidson. 2000. *Canadian Shorebird Conservation Plan*. Canadian Wildlife Service, Environment Canada, Ottawa, ON.

7. Rosenberg, K.V., and J.V. Wells. 2004. *Conservation Priorities for Terrestrial Birds in the Northeastern United States*. Proceedings of the 4th International Partners in Flight Symposium; Asilomar, CA; March, 2001.

8. Ricketts, T.H., E. Dinerstein, D.M. Olson, C.J. Loucks, et al. 1999. *Terrestrial Ecoregions of North America: A Conservation Assessment*. Island Press, Washington, DC. 485 pp.

9. Twedt, D.J., and C.R. Loesch. 1999. Forest Area and Distribution in the Mississippi Alluvial Valley: Implications for Breeding Bird Conservation. *Journal of Biogeography* 26:1215–1224.

10. Greenberg, R., and S. Droege. 1999. On the Decline of the Rusty Blackbird and the Use of Ornithological Literature to Document Long-term Population Trends. *Conservation Biology* 13:553–559.

11. McAuley, D., and D.A. Clugston. No date. *American Woodcock*. U.S. Geological Survey, Northeast Research Group, Orono, ME. http://biology.usgs.gov/s+t/SNT/noframe/ne122.htm (accessed 19 July 2004).

12. Kelley, J. 2004. Personal communication.

13. Mueller, A.J., D.J. Twedt, and C.R. Loesch. 2000. Development of Management Objectives for Breeding Birds in the Mississippi Alluvial Valley. Pages 12–17 in *Strategies for Bird Conservation: The Partners In Flight Planning Process: Proceedings of the 3rd Partners in Flight Workshop; 1995 October 1–5, Cape May, NJ* (R.

Bonney, D.N. Pashley, and R.J. Niles, eds.). Proceedings RMRS-P-16, U.S. Department of Agriculture, Forest Service, Rocky Mountain Reserach Station, Ogden, UT.

14. Environmental Protection Agency. 2002. *Acid Rain.* http://www.epa.gov/airmarkets/acidrain/ (accessed 14 July 2003).

15. Environment Canada. 2003. *Acid Rain—What Is Being Done?* http://www.ec.gc.ca/acidrain/done-cana da.html (accessed 14 July 2003).

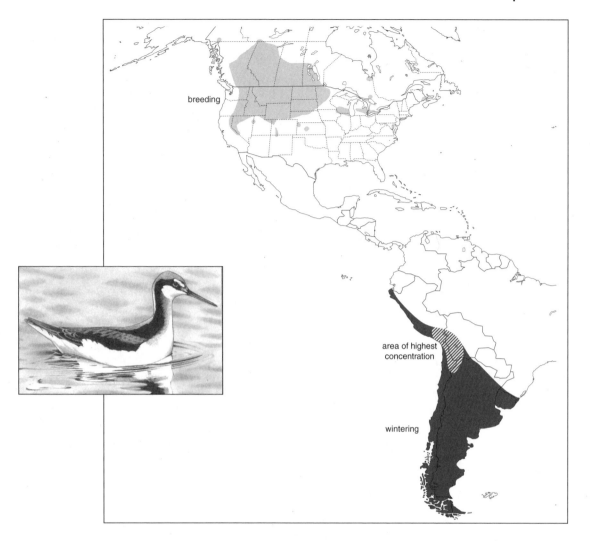

WILSON'S PHALAROPE (*Phalaropus tricolor*)

Phalaropes are well known for their mating system in which females are larger, more colorful, and compete among themselves for males, who do all egg incubation and caring of young. The Wilson's Phalarope, the only one of the three phalarope species restricted to the Western Hemisphere, is vulnerable because virtually the entire population congregates at a few saline lakes in the western U.S. to molt and feed before traveling to the South American wintering grounds.

STATUS AND DISTRIBUTION

The northern edge of the breeding range extends from British Columbia and Northwest Territories east to southern Manitoba and Minnesota and the southern edge from California east to Nebraska, with a smaller disjunct population extending from Wisconsin eastward through Michigan and southern Ontario to extreme southwestern Quebec. Isolated populations occur in Yukon, Ontario, New Brunswick, Kansas, and southern Colorado. Occasional isolated breeding records exist beyond normal range. An estimated 55% of the species' breeding range lies within the U.S., with the remaining 45% in Canada. Breeding density maps produced from Breeding Bird Survey data indicate the highest densities in southern Saskatchewan, northwestern Montana, central North Dakota, northern Utah, and northern California/southern Oregon. Important breeding sites for this species include Montana's Medicine Lake National Wildlife Refuge (NWR), North Dakota's Lostwood Lake NWR, J. Clark Salyer NWR, Chase Lake

NWR and the Horsehead Lake region (privately owned), Colorado's Monte Vista NWR, and the Klamath Basin NWR Complex in Oregon and California.

After breeding, birds move south with the bulk of the adult population congregating on a few large saline lakes of the western U.S. where they molt and fatten up for an apparently nonstop flight across open Pacific Ocean to the southwestern coast of South America. Young birds move south along a broad front, with individuals appearing virtually throughout the U.S. The species winters in South America in scattered wetlands from Peru south to Chile and southern Argentina but the highest numbers are found in the high elevation saline lakes of the Andes Mountains in southern Peru, northern Chile, Bolivia, and northwest Argentina. In spring, birds migrate overland north through the Andes and into Central America and Mexico and across the Great Plains of the U.S.

Important migratory stopover locations include Utah's Great Salt Lake (one-day maximum of 600,000 birds in July 1991), California's Mono Lake (up to 80,000), Oregon's Lake Abert (up to 70,000), Nevada's Lahontan Valley area, including Stillwater NWR (up to 67,000), Kansas' Cheyenne Bottoms Wildlife Management Area (one-day maximum of 146,000 in spring), Nebraska's Crescent Lake NWR (up to 8,000), Texas' Muleshoe NWR (up to 4,500), Alberta's Pakowki Lake Important Bird Area (IBA) (up to 3,000), and Saskatchewan's Last Mountain Lake IBA (up to 2,000) and Chaplin Lake IBA (up to 7,100). Important South American wintering sites include Argentina's Laguna Mar Chiquita (maximum reported 500,000 birds), Bolivia's Laguna Loromayu (100,000+), and Peru's Laguna del Indio.

The species is thought to have experienced major declines based on surveys at two large staging areas (Mono Lake and Lake Abert), which indicate a 50% decline from 1980 to 1997. The species' total population was estimated at 1,500,000 individuals in 2000.[1-10]

ECOLOGY

During breeding season, birds occupy wet meadows and marshy grasslands adjacent to ponds and lakes. Species occurs in higher densities in areas that are not grazed (or are lightly grazed) or mowed. Groups of females chase males and compete for dominance. Females lay eggs in shallow depression on the ground, which the male lines with grass. Females leave males after the clutch is completed and may go on to mate with other males. Males do all incubation, which lasts 18–27 days. Young are precocial and leave nest within hours of hatching and can feed on their own. Birds breed in first year. Adults and young show fairly low site fidelity, with fewer than 20% (lower in females and young) returning to the same location where they were banded the previous year. During migration, these birds occur in largest concentrations at alkaline lakes where they feed on aquatic invertebrates, primarily brine flies and brine shrimp. In winter they congregate at saline lakes and freshwater marshes in South America.[1,11]

THREATS

The greatest current threat continues to be loss and degradation of native habitat largely through conversion to cropland, overgrazing on rangeland, housing development, mineral and oil extraction activities, and fire suppression. Loss of northern mixed grass prairie has been estimated at 36–69% and virtually no unaltered habitat persists in much of the breeding range. In some parts of the region only tiny fragments of native prairie are still in existence. Although much conversion of prairie habitat was historical, large amounts continue to be lost today. From 1982 to 1997, 1.1 million acres of native prairie were lost in South Dakota alone. The recently enacted Farm Bill has provided incentives for further conversion of native prairie to cropland (especially for wheat production) and has worked against the smaller conservation provisions of the bill that encourage farmers to set aside acreage for conservation. Furthermore, nonnative plants are now estimated to account for 30–60% of grassland plant species.

Loss of breeding habitat from drainage and filling of wetlands for agriculture and development is also a major problem. An estimated 40% of wetlands in the prairie region of Canada have been lost to agriculture. More than 50% of wetlands in the continental U.S. have been lost since the 1700s. In the Midwest where the species uses wet prairie meadows, often the wet meadow surrounding ponds and marshes is not protected or preserved so there is little available nesting habitat for Wilson's Phalaropes.

Migratory staging habitat has been greatly reduced in some areas from changes in hydrology from water management practices. For example, water levels in Mono Lake in California and in the Lahontan Valley of Nevada have been greatly reduced as water was removed for drinking supplies and agricultural irrigation. Loss of habitat from development along the eastern and southern shores of Great Salt Lake, Utah is a continuing threat. Similarly, some wintering areas in South America (e.g., Argentina's Laguna Mar Chiquita) are threatened by changes in hydrology from water diversions for agriculture.

Pollution from agricultural runoff and pesticides occurs at many of the wetland areas used by Wilson's Phalarope throughout its breeding, migratory, and wintering range, but its impact on the species is unstudied. At Argentina's Laguna Mar Chiquita, which has hosted as many as 500,000 birds, untreated sewage and industrial wastes flow into the lake with an unknown effect on Wilson's Phalarope and the many other species that rely on the wetlands. At least one nonnative fish species has been introduced into the lake as well and, though a commercial fishery for the fish now exists, its effect on the aquatic ecosystem (and in turn the food supply for Wilson's Phalarope) is apparently unstudied.[1,7,11–17]

CONSERVATION ACTION

While little direct conservation activity has focused on Wilson's Phalarope, there has been increasing activity in grassland habitat conservation across the U.S. and Canada involving many governmental and nongovernmental organizations. The Prairie Pothole Joint Venture initiated the Chase Lake Prairie Project to conserve and restore habitat in a 5.5-million-acre block surrounding the Chase Lake NWR where Wilson's Phalaropes occur in North Dakota. The project area includes one of the largest intact pieces of native prairie in the state. Through the project the U.S. Fish and Wildlife Service has protected 12,890 acres of wetlands and grasslands through easements on private land and over 8,600 acres of habitat have been directly acquired. Rotational grazing systems have been implemented on over 35,000 acres of grasslands as well. Montana Partners for Fish and Wildlife is working to secure perpetual grassland easements in the Upper Missouri Coteau, where Wilson's Phalarope are found, with the hope of restoring 300,000 acres of grasslands on private and tribal lands. The group has spent $3.4 million

over 13 years on projects with over 230 private landowners to protect, restore, or enhance wetland and grassland habitat. Ducks Unlimited's Grasslands for Tomorrow Initiative is striving to protect 2 million acres of grassland within the Prairie Pothole region, which encompasses much of the species' breeding range. Within all these areas, it is important to restore wet prairie habitat and shallow water wetlands surrounding any wetlands that are established or restored.

The Western Hemisphere Shorebird Reserve Network has recognized Mono Lake, California; Lahontan Valley, Nevada; Great Salt Lake, Utah; Cheyenne Bottoms, Kansas; and Chaplin Lake, Saskatchewan as important migratory shorebird staging areas and Argentina's Laguna Mar Chiquita as an important shorebird wintering area. Much of the habitat at Cheyenne Bottoms is owned and managed by the Kansas Fish and Wildlife Agency and the Nature Conservancy but major conservation problem at the site comes from management of water input from Arkansas River and Walnut Creek. Water withdrawals for irrigation from these two sources were so great in the early 1990s that no water was available for Cheyenne Bottoms and the area was dry much of the time. Later court rulings cut back on the amount removed from these sources and along with new water control structures and pumps, wetland habitat has been easier to maintain.

The Mono Lake Committee has been working since the 1970s to maintain and restore the Mono Lake ecosystem, especially by working to decrease the amount of water removed from the lake for use in Los Angeles through a series of legal challenges. This work resulted in a decision in 1994 by the governmental board in charge of setting water resource policy to allow less water to be removed from the lake so that a higher water level would be maintained in the lake.

Similarly, the Friends of Great Salt Lake was founded in 1994 to work to protect the Great Salt Lake ecosystem. The Utah Division of Wildlife Resources, with help from the U.S. Fish and Wildlife Service, is currently working to identify lands important, or potentially important, to the management of shorebirds around Great Salt Lake. These lands will be recommended for acquisition as funds become available. In the Lahontan Valley of Nevada, millions of dollars have been made available for the acquisition of water rights by the U.S. Fish and Wildlife Service from willing sellers in an attempt to restore the wetland ecosystem.

The Universidad Nacional de Córdoba was awarded a grant in 2004 from the U.S. Neotropical Migratory Bird Conservation Act Program to develop a management plan for Argentina's Laguna Mar Chiquita. [1,2,5,7,9,11,12,16,18,–24]

CONSERVATION NEEDS

- Ensure that management of publicly owned locations currently supporting Wilson's Phalarope continues to maintain habitat conditions, including sufficient water resources, to continue meeting the needs of the species.
- In the Midwest, restore wet meadow habitats around ponds and marshes and develop clusters of wet prairie restoration sites.
- Increase efforts at landowner education and outreach, incentives, and other activities that may increase breeding productivity of Wilson's Phalarope on private lands.
- Increase protection and conservation of wetlands at migratory stopover sites and within the wintering range of Wilson's Phalarope.
- Work with National Resources Conservation Service in the implementation of Farm Bill conservation incentive programs so that the habitat conditions specified on lands potentially used by Wilson's Phalarope are beneficial to the species.
- Implement rangewide surveys designed to assess overall population status and trends.

References

1. Colwell, M.A., and J. R. Jehl, Jr. 1994. Wilson's Phalarope (*Phalaropus tricolor*). In *The Birds of North America*, No. 83 (A. Poole and F. Gill, Eds.). Philadelphia: The Academy of Natural Sciences, Philadelphia, PA, and the American Ornithologists' Union, Washington, DC.

2. Donaldson, G.M., C. Hyslop, R.I.G. Morrison, H.L. Dickson, I. Davidson. 2000. *Canadian Shorebird Conservation Plan*. Canadian Wildlife Service, Environment Canada, Ottawa, ON.

3. Sauer, J. R., J. E. Hines, and J. Fallon. 2003. The North American Breeding Bird Survey, Results and Analysis 1966–2002, *Version 2003.1, USGS Patuxent Wildlife Research Center, Laurel, MD*.

4. Chipley, R.M., G.H. Fenwick, M.J. Parr, and D.N. Pashley. 2003. *The American Bird Conservancy Guide to the 500 Most Important Bird Areas in the United States*. Random House, New York, NY.

5. Bird Studies Canada. 2003. *Important Bird Areas of Canada*. URL: http://www.bsc-eoc.org/iba/IBAsites.html (accessed 7 October 2003).

6. Skagen, S.K., P.B. Sharpe, R.G. Waltermire, and M.B. Dillon. 1999. *Biogeographic Profiles of Shorebird Migration in Midcontinental North America*. Biological Science Report USGS/BRD/BSR—2000-0003. U.S. Government Printing Office, Denver, CO. 167 pp.

7. Manomet Bird Observatory. 2003. *Western Hemisphere Shorebird Reserve Network*. http://www.manomet.org/WHSRN/ (accessed 9 February 2004).

8. Jehl, J.R. 1999. Population Studies of Wilson's Phalaropes at Fall Staging Areas, 1980–1997: A Challenge for Monitoring. *Waterbirds* 22:37–46.

9. Brown, S., C. Hickey, and B. Harrington, eds. 2000. *The U.S. Shorebird Conservation Plan*. Manomet Center for Conservation Sciences, Manomet, MA.

10. U.S. Fish and Wildlife Service. *Bird List— Chase Lake National Wildlife Refuge*. http://www.fws.giv/arrowwood/chaselake_nwr/bird_list.html

11. Dechant, J.A., D.H. Johnson, L.D. Igl, C.M. Goldade, A.L. Zimmerman, and B.R. Euliss. 1999. *Wilson's Phalarope Species Management Abstract*. The Nature Conservancy, Arlington, VA. http://www.conserveonline.org/2002/09/b/en/wiph.doc

12. Gauthier, D.A., A. Lafon, T. Tombs, J. Hoth, and E. Wilken. 2003. *Grasslands: Toward a North American Conservation Strategy*. Canadian Plains Research Center, University of Regina, Regina, Saskatchewan, and Commission for Environmental Cooperation, Montreal, QC, Canada. 99 pp.

13. Ricketts T.H., et al. 1999. *Terrestrial Ecoregions of North America: A Conservation Assessment*. Island Press, Washington, DC. 485 pp.

14. Stein, B.A., L.S. Kutner, and J.S. Adams. 2000. *Precious Heritage: The Status of Biodiversity in the United States*. Oxford University Press, New York, NY. 399 pp.

15. Delta Waterfowl Foundation. 2003. *The Great American Plowout Threatens Duck Production*. http://www.deltawaterfowl.org/home/archive/2003/030818_plowout.html (accessed 28 January 2004).

16. Mono Lake Committee. 2004. *Political History*. http://www.monolake.org/politicalhistory/index.html (accessed 23 July 2004).

17. RAMSAR. 2000. *The Annotated Ramsar List*: Peru. http://www.ramsar.org/profiles_peru.htm (accessed 21 July 2004).

18. U. S. Fish and Wildlife Service. No date. *Prairie Potholes Shorebird Watch*. http://216.149.9.196/Tracking/prairie_potholes.cfm (accessed 10 February 2004).

19. U. S. Fish and Wildlife Service. *Chase Lake Prairie Project.* http://chaselake.fws.gov/clpp.htm (accessed 22 January 2004).

20. Montana Partners for Fish and Wildlife. No date. *Upper Missouri Coteau Focus Area, Conservation Strategies.* http://montanapartners.fws.gov/mt3f2.htm (accessed 22 January 2004).

21. Ducks Unlimited. 2003. *Protecting 2,000,000 Acres of Grasslands for Tomorrow.* http://prairie.ducks .org/index.cfm?&page=conservation/priorities/gft.cfm (accessed 18 June 2004).

22. Friends of Great Salt Lake. 2002. *Friends of Great Salt Lake.* http://www.xmission.com/~fogsl/ (accessed 11 September 2003).

23. Utah Division of Wildlife Resources. 1999. *Wildlife Notebook Series No. 6: Wilson's Phalarope.* www .wildlife.utah.gov/publications/pdf/phalrnew99.pdf (accessed 10 February 2004).

24. U.S. Fish and Wildlife Service. 2004. *The Neotropical Migratory Bird Conservation Act Grants Program.* http://birdhabitat.fws.gov/NMBCA/projectsNar .htm (accessed 23 July 2004).

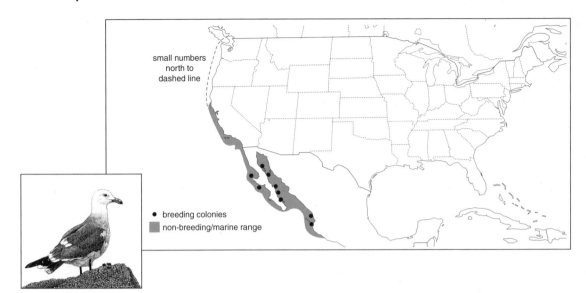

small numbers
north to
dashed line

● breeding colonies
▪ non-breeding/marine range

HEERMANN'S GULL *(Larus heermanni)*

One of the most strikingly beautiful gulls in North America, the Heermann's Gull also has one of the strangest migration patterns, traveling north after breeding in the spring to spend summer and fall along the Pacific Coast north to southern British Columbia. The species is of conservation concern because virtually the entire breeding population occurs at a single site, making it vulnerable to a natural or manmade disaster.

STATUS AND DISTRIBUTION

Breeds in Mexico's Gulf of California at about seven sites and two sites along the Pacific coast of Baja California but occasionally also at other small islands. Isla Rasa is the most important breeding colony, with early 1990s estimates of 300,000 individuals, representing 90–95% of the total breeding population. Also in the early 1990s Isla Partida was estimated to support 8,000 birds and Isla Cholluda 1,000 birds.

Beginning in May, birds begin moving northward along the Pacific coast, with peak numbers off of California in mid-June and off of Washington and Vancouver, BC in July and August. Birds begin moving south again in August, with a few birds remaining off of southern California after December. Birds arrive at breeding sites in March. An estimated 13,000 birds were found in southern and central California in 1982.

Although no trend information is available, numbers on Isla Rasa were estimated at 110,000 in

1975 and total population was estimated at 300,000 individuals in the 1990s.[1–4]

ECOLOGY

Nests colonially between March and July on dry, rocky islands in Gulf of California and Baja California. Females lay 1–3 eggs, usually in April or May, on the ground in a small depression, sometimes with a few shells, twigs, or debris in and around it. Young hatch at 28 days and fledge by 45 days of age. They first breed in their fourth year.

A very marine species, during nonbreeding season it occurs along the coastline and far out to sea but only rarely inland. Feeds on a variety of fish and marine invertebrates, but especially small fish, including sardine, anchovy, and smelt. Often steals fish from other bird species, especially Brown Pelicans. Will also eat insects, lizards, bird eggs, and, like most gulls, refuse.[1]

THREATS

Species was once threatened by widespread egg harvesting at nesting colonies, with as many as 50,000 eggs known to have been taken in a single year. This practice is now discontinued, at least at Isla Rasa, as the island is now a preserve and is protected by wardens and the presence of researchers. It is unknown if illegal egg harvesting or other human disturbance is a concern at other breeding sites, but the area is popular among recreational sailors and many sites are not monitored regularly by wardens. Prey depletion by fisheries, mortality as fisheries bycatch, pollutants, disturbance, habitat conversion, introduced predators, exploitation, and oceanographic change pose significant threats to current populations. The impact of introduced predators is unknown, but on islands with populations of introduced rats, cats, dogs, and other species some number of eggs and young are killed annually. The greatest conservation concern stems from the fact that virtually the entire population is concentrated on a single island during the breeding season so that any natural or human-induced disaster could eliminate a large proportion of the global population.

Other threats include the accumulation of pesticides and environmental contaminants. Tissue samples of Heermann's Gull found high levels of DDE, PCBs, and other contaminants, but it is unknown if there were any negative physiological effects. Some areas off the California coast that host nonbreeding concentrations of the species have high oil tanker traffic, so that a large oil spill during these times could cause a major mortality event.[1-4]

CONSERVATION ACTION

Isla Rasa was designated as a wildlife santuary in 1964 by the Mexican government and is protected by wardens. At Isla Rasa, efforts to eradicate introduced rats and mice had apparently succeeded by 1995. Many other breeding islands in the Gulf of California are included within the Gulf of California Biosphere Reserve and some have been designated as wildlife preserves. Work has been ongoing at some islands to eradicate introduced predators. A management plan for the Biosphere Reserve developed in 1994 began being implemented in 1999.

The International Division of the U.S. Fish and Wildlife Service provided funds to Island Conservation to develop management plans for 19 of the islands of the Gulf of California Biosphere Reserve in 1996. With the help of local conservation organizations Grupo Ecologista Antares (GEA) and Niparajá, the Nature Conservancy is working with local Biosphere Reserve staff and local fishermen to patrol the protected areas and halt illegal fishing—activities that should benefit the ecosystem upon which Heermann's Gull depends.

Monterey Bay, as one coastal area that sup-

ports nonbreeding Heermann's Gull, has been designated as a National Marine Sanctuary and is managed by the National Oceanic and Atmospheric Administration. National Marine Sanctuaries generally prohibit oil and gas extraction activities within their boundaries and prohibit certain types of other human activities that may disturb marine life or marine habitats. These regulations should be beneficial to maintaining the food supplies and a healthy ecosystem upon which Heermann's Gull depends.[1,5-8]

CONSERVATION NEEDS

- Increase numbers of breeders on other islands besides Isla Rasa through protection efforts, removal of introduced predators, and seabird social attraction techniques.
- Implement measures to remove introduced mammalian predators from islands with breeding colonies and prevent further introductions.
- Obtain legal protection for the San Benito Islands and other islands off the Pacific coasts of Baja California.
- Develop and implement surveys to detect and monitor breeding colonies of Heermann's Gull.
- Implement measures to ensure continued protection of known breeding colonies from loss of habitat and human disturbance.
- Develop and implement coastal and at-sea surveys to monitor changes in abundance of Heermann's Gull.
- Continue efforts to limit amount of plastics, oil, and other pollutants within the marine ecosystem.

References

1. Islam, K. 2002. Heermann's Gull (*Larus heermanni*). In *The Birds of North America*, No. 643 (A. Poole and F. Gill, eds.). The Academy of Natural Sciences, Philadelphia, PA.

2. BirdLife International. 2000. *Threatened Birds of the World.* Lynx Editions and BirdLife International, Barcelona, Spain, and Cambridge, UK.

3. Mellinck, E. 2001. History and Status of Colonies of Heermann's Gull in Mexico. *Waterbirds* 24:188–194.

4. Cooper, D. 2001. Important Bird Areas of Cali-

fornia. Unpublished manuscript available from Audubon California, 6042 Monte Vista St., Los Angeles, CA 90042.

5. Case, T., M. Cody, and E. Ezcurra. 2002. *Island Biogeography in the Sea of Cortez.* Oxford University Press, New York, NY.

6. U.S. Fish and Wildlife Service International Affairs. 1996. *Grants Awarded in 1996.* http://international.fws.gov/whp/annex4.html (accessed 3 November 2003).

7. The Nature Conservancy. 2003. *Baja & the Gulf of California.* http://nature.org/wherewework/northamerica/mexico/work/art8618.html (accessed 3 November 2003).

8. National Ocean Service. 2003. *National Marine Sanctuaries.* http://www.sanctuaries.nos.noaa.gov/welcome.html (accessed 22 May 2003).

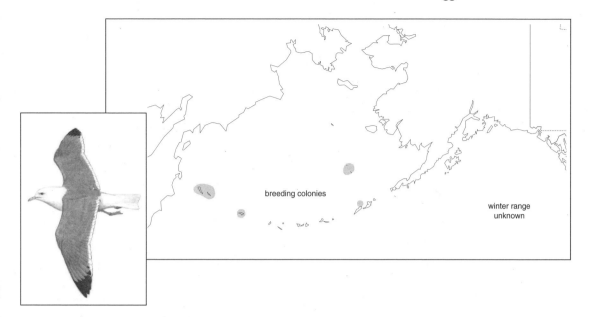

breeding colonies

winter range
unknown

RED-LEGGED KITTIWAKE (*Rissa brevirostris*)

A little-known close relative of the more abundant Black-legged Kittiwake, this species has a
tiny breeding range on islands in the Bering Sea
but its wintering range is virtually unknown.

STATUS AND DISTRIBUTION

Breeds on four island groups in the Bering Sea. St.
George and St. Paul islands in the Pribilofs host
more than 70% (100,000+ individuals) and Bering
Island and Commander Islands, Russia about 18%
(30,000+ individuals) of the global population.
Smaller breeding populations occur on Buldir Island (4,400 birds in the 1970s) and Bogoslof Island (200 birds in 1973). During the breeding season birds feed over deep water within 70–90 miles
of breeding islands. Winter distribution is poorly
understood but most sightings have been from the
northern Gulf of Alaska and near the ice edge in
the Bering Sea.

Numbers at primary breeding site at St.
George Island declined by 44% between the 1970s
and 1990s. Declines have also been noted on St.
Paul Island and increases at Buldir and Bogoslof
but populations on these islands remain relatively
small (none hold more than 2% of population).
Total population had declined 35% from an estimated 259,000 individuals in the 1970s to 168,000
individuals by the 1990s.[1-3]

ECOLOGY

Nests colonially beginning in June on high, steep
cliffs on rocky islands in the Bering Sea. Lays one
(occasionally two) eggs in June or July in simple
mud and vegetation nest on narrow ledge on cliff
face. Both parents incubate. Young hatch at 25–32
days and fledge at about 37 days of age.

A very marine species, it feeds well offshore
even during the breeding season. Feeds on a variety of fish and marine invertebrates but during the
breeding season seems to prefer lampfish, pollock,
and squid. Both of the latter prey species migrate
to the surface at night when Red-legged Kittiwake's large eyes apparently help them to see and
catch prey effectively.[1]

THREATS

Archeological evidence suggests that the species
was once more abundant and widespread in the
Bering Sea region, but it is unclear why the species'
range became more restricted though historical
harvesting of eggs or young, disturbance, or introduction of alien predators may have played some
role. Subsistence harvesting of eggs and young may
still occur in the Pribilof Islands and other areas
but at levels thought to be too low to impact population. The reasons for its decline in last two
decades are unknown but a major concern is that

commercial fishing levels may be so high that food supplies for marine birds and other animals will be insufficient to sustain populations. Over 1,300 vessels were operating in the U.S. portion of the Alaska groundfish fishery in 2001, and in 2002 1.53 million tons of pollock were netted in Alaska waters, amounting to perhaps a billion individual fish. Half of the seafood consumed in the U.S. originates in the Bering Sea region and a number of commercial fisheries have seen major declines in all or part of the region over the last 20 years. Within the so-called "Donut Hole"—the 10% of the Bering Sea that is beyond the 200 mile limits of the U.S. and Russia—the pollock population crashed in the early 1990s and has not recovered. Other wildlife populations have declined, the most notable being the Steller's sea lion which has seen an 80% drop in numbers. Harbor development activities in the Pribilofs increase the possibility of accidental introduction of rats to islands, which would pose a serious threat to eggs and young of kittiwakes and other nesting seabirds.[1,2,4-7]

CONSERVATION ACTION

Most breeding sites are included in Alaska Maritime National Wildlife Refuge, including Pribilof Island nesting cliffs, which were purchased in 1982. The U.S. Fish and Wildlife Service has an active program to prevent rats from establishing themselves on islands through education campaigns and continuing placement of poison-baited traps in the event that rats do inadvertently make it to an island.

National Marine Fisheries Service has many different rules and regulations governing the fisheries in the Bering Sea and Gulf of Alaska and had released a Draft Programmatic Supplemental Impact Statement for Alaska Groundfish Fisheries in fall 2003 for public comment. To monitor the various regulations all vessels larger than 124 feet have been required since 1990 to carry a NMFS observer who records information on amounts and types of fish taken. A large area north of Bogoslof Island has been closed to fishing for pollock, cod, and mackerel as a measure to protect Steller's sea lions. A closure of areas around the Pribilof Islands from commercial groundfish trawling has been suggested. An international treaty was signed by the U.S., Russia, China, Japan, South Korea, and Poland in 1994 to collectively regulate pollock fisheries in the "Donut Hole" area of the central Bering Sea,

and the fishery has been closed since that time because pollock stocks have not reached the level indicated in the treaty for resumption of commercial fisheries. However, at the 2002 and 2003 meetings of the treaty signatories, China, Japan, South Korea, and Poland requested that a minimal allowable harvest level be set for symbolic reasons and that limited numbers of trial fishing vessels (as allowed by the treaty) from some countries be allowed to continue to harvest pollock. Enforcement of fishing regulations, closures, and international treaties is extremely difficult in an area as large and remote as the Bering Sea region and some level of illegal activity takes place throughout the region, perhaps especially in the Russian-controlled western side. On the U.S. side, the U.S. Coast Guard is responsible for enforcing most of the rules, regulations, and territorial boundaries and does so through its Ocean Guardian fisheries enforcement strategic plan.

The Alaska Department of Fish and Game developed a set of recommendations for a public process to consider the establishment of Marine Protected Areas in the state which would likely be of benefit to Red-legged Kittiwake. A nonprofit organization, the International Bering Sea Forum, advocates with governmental agencies responsible for the Bering Sea for policies and positions beneficial to the ecosystem and to providing sustainable resources for local communities. The Nature Conservancy and World Wildlife Fund recently concluded an ecoregional planning process for the Bering Sea, which brought together scientists from Russia, the U.S., and Japan to determine conservation priorities, assess threats, and identify important areas for conservation throughout the region.[1,2,4-10]

CONSERVATION NEEDS

- Continue regular surveys to detect and monitor breeding colonies of Red-legged Kittiwake and to assess winter range limits and densities.
- Implement measures to ensure continued protection of known breeding colonies from loss of habitat and human disturbance.
- Continue efforts to prevent rats or other predators from becoming introduced and established on islands supporting Red-legged Kittiwake.
- Continue efforts to maintain sustainable commercial fisheries levels to protect the marine ecosystems of the Bering Sea.

References

1. Byrd, G.V., and J.C. Williams. 1993. Red-legged Kittiwake (*Rissa brevirostris*). In *The Birds of North America*, No. 60 (A. Poole and F. Gill, eds.). The Academy of Natural Sciences, Philadelphia, PA, and the American Ornithologists' Union, Washington, DC.

2. BirdLife International. 2000. *Threatened Birds of the World*. Lynx Editions and BirdLife International, Barcelona, Spain, and Cambridge, UK.

3. Byrd, G.V., J.C. Williams, Y.B. Artukhin, and P.S. Vyatkin. 1997. Trends in Populations of Red-legged Kittiwake *Rissa brevirostris*, a Bering Sea Endemic. *Bird Conservation International* 7:167–180.

4. National Marine Fisheries Service. 2003. *Draft Programmatic Supplemental Environmental Impact Statement for Alaska Groundfish Fisheries*. National Marine Fisheries Service, Alaska Regional Office, Juneau, AK.

5. Alaska Fisheries Science Center–National Marine Fisheries Service. 2003. *Walleye Pollock Research*. http://www.afsc.noaa.gov/species/pollock.htm. (accessed 5 November 2003).

6. Alaska Fisheries Science Center National Marine Fisheries Service. 2003. *Convention on the Conservation and Management of Pollock Resources in the Central Bering Sea.* http://www.afsc.noaa.gov/refm/cbs/convention_description.htm (accessed 5 November 2003).

7. The International Bering Sea Forum. 2002. *About Us.* http://beringseaforum.org/issues.html (accessed 5 November 2003).

8. U.S. Coast Guard. No date. *OCEAN GUARDIAN: Coast Guard Fisheries Enforcement Strategic Plan.* http://www.uscg.mil/hq/g-o/g-opl/mle/OceanG/OceanGuard.html (accessed 5 November 2003).

9. Woodby, D., S. Meyer, K. Mabry, V. O'Connell, C. Trowbridge, J.H. Schempf, E. Krygier, and D. Lloyd. 2002. Marine Protected Areas in Alaska: Recommendations for a Public Process. Alaska Department of Fish and Game, Division of Commercial Fisheries, Juneau, AK.

10. Banks, D., M. Williams, J. Pearce, A. Springer, R. Hagenstein, and D. Olson, eds. No date. *Ecoregion-based Conservation in the Bering Sea: Identifying Important Areas for Biodiversity Conservation.* www.conservationonline.org.

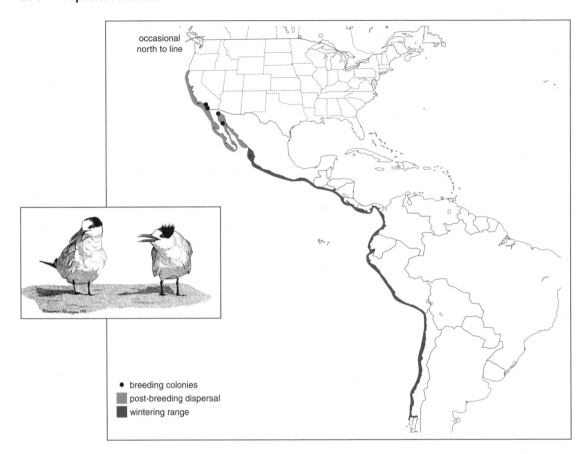

occasional
north to line

• breeding colonies
post-breeding dispersal
wintering range

ELEGANT TERN (*Thalasseus elegans*)

The tern species with the most restricted range of any in North America, the Elegant Tern is also one of the least studied. The species is vulnerable because the bulk of its global population breeds on only a single island in the Gulf of California.

STATUS AND DISTRIBUTION

Breeds in Mexico's Gulf of California at two sites and at two sites along the Pacific Coast of southern California but occasionally also at other small islands. Isla Rasa, in the Gulf of California, is the most important breeding colony, with early 1990s estimates of 44,000 individuals, representing 90–95% of the total breeding population.

A small colony of 550 individuals was found breeding at Isla Montague in the Gulf of California in the early 1990s. A colony at the Bolsa Chica Ecological Reserve, California held an estimated 8,000 birds in 1995 but the bulk of the colony had shifted to islands in Los Angeles Harbor in 1998. A colony at San Diego Bay, California was

estimated at 3,740 birds in 1996 but held fewer than 30 birds in 1998.

Beginning in late May postbreeding adults with juveniles and failed breeders from Isla Rasa begin appearing in south coastal California. Numbers continue to increase along coast to northern California and peak in July–September. Smaller numbers occur north to southern British Columbia, though number of birds and northern extent of occurrence is variable from year to year, depending on ocean temperatures and food supplies. Most birds depart the U.S. coast by October, migrating south to a wintering range that extends along the Pacific coast from Nayarit, Mexico south to Chile. Greatest wintering abundances are from Ecuador south. Important wintering areas include Peru's Paracas National Reserve. Vagrants have been recorded from U.S. Gulf and Atlantic coasts and in Europe.

The species was once a more widespread breeder on islands in the Gulf of California but commercial egg harvesting and introduced predators caused populations to decrease so that a survey of Isla Rasa in 1975 estimated 9,400–15,500 individuals. With protection the colony had increased to an estimated 44,000 birds in the 1990s. The total population was estimated at 60,000 breeding individuals in the early 1990s.[1,2]

ECOLOGY

Nests colonially between March and July on dry, rocky or sandy islands in the Gulf of California and coastal southern California. Lays one egg, usually in April or May, on the ground in a small depression sometimes with a few shells, twigs, or debris in and around it. Both sexes incubate. Young hatch at 23–33 days and fledge by 30–35 days of age. Thought to first breed in the third year. Feeds on a variety of small fish, including sardine, anchovy, and smelt.[1]

THREATS

Species was once threatened by widespread egg harvesting at nesting colonies. This practice is now discontinued at Isla Rasa, as the island is a preserve and is protected by wardens and the presence of researchers. Illegal egg harvesting and other human disturbance is a concern at other potential breeding sites but the area is popular among recreational sailors and many sites are not monitored regularly by wardens. Stray dogs killed more than 100 Elegant Tern chicks at the San Diego colony in 1982. Introduced rats, cats, dogs, and other species on islands in the Gulf of California would likely prevent birds from becoming established on other islands. The greatest conservation concern stems from the fact that virtually the entire population is concentrated on a single island during the breeding season so that any natural or human-induced disaster could eliminate a large proportion of the global population.

Declines in prey abundance as a result of commercial overfishing is a concern on both breeding and wintering grounds. Other threats include the accumulation of pesticides and environmental contaminants and continued degradation of estuarine ecosystems upon which the species is reliant for food. Egg and tissue samples of Elegant Tern from California found various contaminants, including DDE, but no known negative physiological effects.[1–3]

CONSERVATION ACTION

Isla Rasa was designated as a wildlife sanctuary in 1964 by the Mexican government and is protected by wardens. At Isla Rasa, efforts to eradicate introduced rats and mice succeeded by 1995. Many other potential breeding islands in the Gulf of California are included within the Gulf of California Biosphere Reserve and some have been designated as wildlife preserves. Work has been ongoing at some islands to eradicate introduced predators. A management plan for the Biosphere Reserve developed in 1994 began being implemented in 1999.

Rats were removed from San Jorge Island and rats and cats from San Roque Island, both of which were historical breeding sites for Elegant Terns. Active social attraction using decoys and playback of colony sound could facilitate recolonization of these islands.

The International Division of the U.S. Fish and Wildlife Service provided funds to Island Conservation to develop management plans for 19 of the islands of the Gulf of California Biosphere Reserve in 1996. With the help of local conservation organizations Grupo Ecologista Antares (GEA) and Niparajá, the Nature Conservancy is working with local Biosphere Reserve staff and local fishermen to patrol the protected areas and halt illegal fishing—activities that should benefit the ecosystem upon which Elegant Tern depends.

In Peru's Paracas National Reserve, Pro Naturaleza and the Nature Conservancy are collaborating with and assisting the Peruvian park service in creating and implementing a management plan for the park to better manage tourism, overfishing, and pollution from fish-processing plants in and around the park. They have recently helped refurbish a ranger station and provide vehicles at the park.[1,2,4–7]

CONSERVATION NEEDS

- Increase numbers of breeders on other islands beside Isla Rasa through protection efforts, removal of introduced predators, and seabird social attraction techniques.
- Implement measures to remove introduced mammalian predators from islands with current or historic breeding colonies and prevent further introductions.

- Develop and implement surveys to detect and monitor breeding colonies of Elegant Tern.
- Implement measures to ensure continued protection of known breeding colonies from loss of habitat and human disturbance.
- Develop and implement coastal non-breeding surveys to map distribution and monitor changes in abundance of Elegant Tern.
- Continue efforts to limit amount of pollutants within the marine ecosystems on breeding and wintering grounds and throughout migratory flyway.

References

1. Burness, G.P., K, Lefevre, and C.T. Collins. 1999. Elegant Tern (*Sterna elegans*). In *The Birds of North America*, No. 404 (A. Poole and F. Gill, eds.). The Academy of Natural Sciences, Philadelphia, PA.

2. BirdLife International. 2000. *Threatened Birds of the World*. Lynx Editions and BirdLife International, Barcelona, Spain, and Cambridge, UK.

3. Duffy, D.C., C. Hays, and M.A. Plenge. 1984. The Conservation Status of Peruvian Seabirds. Pages 245–259 in *International Council for Bird Preservation Technical Publication No. 2* (J.P. Croxall, P.G.H. Evans, and R.W. Schreiber, eds.). Cambridge, UK.

4. Case, T., M. Cody, and E. Ezcurra. 2002. *Island Biogeography in the Sea of Cortez*. Oxford University Press, New York, NY.

5. U.S. Fish and Wildlife Service International Affairs. 1996. *Grants Awarded in 1996*. http://international.fws.gov/whp/annex4.html (accessed 3 November 2003).

6. The Nature Conservancy. 2003. *Baja & the Gulf of California*. http://nature.org/wherewework/northamerica/mexico/work/art8618.html (accessed 3 November 2003).

7. The Nature Conservancy. 2003. *Paracas National Reserve*. http://nature.org/wherewework/south america/peru/work/art5307.html (accessed 7 November 2003).

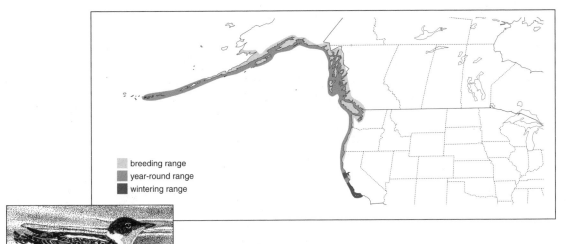

breeding range
year-round range
wintering range

MARBLED MURRELET
(*Brachyramphus marmoratus*)

Unlike most alcids (or even most seabirds), the Marbled Murrelet nests solitarily rather than in colonies but perhaps most astonishingly, its nests are usually placed on the branches of towering old-growth coniferous trees along the Pacific Coast of Canada, and the U.S.

STATUS AND DISTRIBUTION

Breeding range extends from Alaska's Aleutian Islands through coastal regions of southern Alaska and British Columbia to northern California (Humboldt County) with an isolated population 270 miles further south at Half Moon Bay. Breeding range generally extends inland no further than about 50 miles from coastline. Birds also tend to stay relatively close to shore when feeding, usually within about 3 miles except up to 30 miles in Alaska and occasionally as far as 45 miles from shore. Breeding range is, therefore, essentially a narrow corridor encompassing nearshore waters and coastal lands. Bulk of population breeds in Alaska (67–90% of total population), with most of those in the Alexander Archipelago, Prince William Sound, and Kodiak Archipelago areas. Highest densities in British Columbia are in the Queen Charlotte Island area and the western coast of Vancouver Island. More than 50% of birds in Washington occur in Puget Sound and the Straits of Juan de Fuca and Georgia.

Some sites that are known to support important nesting concentrations of Marbled Murrelet include Tongass National Forest, Chugach National Forest, and Kodiak National Wildlife Refuge in Alaska, Olympia National Park and Olympia National Forest in Washington State, Siuslaw National Forest in Oregon, and Gwaii Haanas National Park Reserve and Carmanah-Walbran Provincial Park in British Columbia. Important marine foraging concentration areas for the species include the Olympic Coast National Marine Sanctuary in Washington, the Monterey Bay National Marine Sanctuary in California, Glacier Bay in Alaska, and Desolation Sound, Clayoquot Sound, and Barkley Sound in British Columbia.

Surveys in the northern Gulf of Alaska have shown a 50–73% decline in numbers of Marbled Murrelets from the late 1970s to the late 1990s. Surveys off of Vancouver Island suggest a 40% decline between the 1980s and 1990s. A demographic modeling analysis suggested that populations were declining rangewide at a rate of 4–7% per year. The population was estimated at approximately 559,000 individuals in 2000.[1-9]

ECOLOGY

Breeds in old growth and mature coniferous forests along the Pacific Coast, both on the mainland and on islands. Rather incredibly, usually lays its single egg on a large branch of very large, tall tree (for example, Douglas-fir, Alaska yellow cedar, Sitka spruce, western hemlock, or coast redwood) in the top third of the tree. In parts of the Alaska breeding range some small number of birds nest on the ground among rocky slopes or tree roots. Incubation lasts 28–30 days, with males and females alternating incubation duties every 24 hours. Young are brooded for only 1–2 days. Adults carry a single small fish from ocean feeding grounds to feed the nestling up to eight times a day, with most feedings at dawn and dusk. Young grow rapidly and fly from the nest site to the ocean at 27–40 days. After young leave nest they are not fed or cared for by parents and they learn to catch fish on their own. Overall nest success has been quite low in nests studied—only 28% of eggs laid produce young that fledge. Birds remain in nearshore and protected waters year-round, feeding on small fish and marine invertebrates.[1]

THREATS

The main threat causing long-term population declines is continued loss of old growth and mature forest breeding habitat to commercial logging. This type of habitat requires a minimum of 100–200 years to attain sufficient height, structure, and other features so any acreage of old growth forests that is cut is essentially lost to the breeding population. About 96% of the forest habitat within the Central Pacific Coastal Forest ecoregion extending along the coast from Oregon north to Vancouver Island has been lost since prelogging days. Similarly, over 95% of the northern California Redwood forest has been removed. About 50% of the habitat in the Queen Charlotte Islands has been altered, mostly by logging. In the Tongass National Forest approximately 90% of the high-volume old growth forest has been logged and 30% of all old growth in the forest is expected to be removed by about 2015.

Other major threats include birds drowning in commercial fishing nets, especially inshore gill-nets, and mortality from oil spills. Approximately 0.5–2% (3,300 birds) of the Alaska population were estimated to be killed annually from gill-netting operations as of 1995. Hundreds of birds are also lost to gill-netting in British Columbia and Washington. The species is also very susceptible to oil spills because individuals remain relatively close to shore within major shipping channels. For example, 8,400 murrelets, mostly this species, representing 3.4% of the Alaska population, were estimated to have been killed by the Exxon Val-

dez oil spill. Dead Marbled Murrelets have also been recovered from a number of smaller oil spills.[1,2,5,7–11]

CONSERVATION ACTION

The species was federally listed as Threatened in the U.S. (excluding Alaska) in 1992, an action that resulted in increased funding for research and monitoring of the species and consideration of the species' needs in various land management decisions. Critical habitat for the species was designated for California, Oregon, and Washington by the U.S. Fish and Wildlife Service in 1996. This designation requires land managers to consider effects of land management on Marbled Murrelet populations. Most of the critical habitat designated was on federal lands where the species occurs but also on some private lands (48,000 acres across the three states). About 3.9 million acres were included in the critical habitat designation, most of it within areas already designated as reserve land within the Northwest Forest Plan. The Pacific Seabird Group designed a survey protocol to detect whether Marbled Murrelets were breeding in a forest tract so that trees could be harvested in areas where the species was not detected. A variety of habitat models have also been developed to predict areas that will be preferred by the species for nesting with the idea that these areas could be set aside as protected areas and not be logged. In California a Habitat Conservation Plan was developed under the Endangered Species Act for 219,298 acres of lands owned by Pacific Lumber and the Elk River Timber Company that would set aside 17,000 acres of the best habitat for Marbled Murrelets for 50 years and allow the harvesting of timber from the remaining acreage. Various organizations have contested aspects of the plan in court and through protests, including "tree-sitting," to try to prevent trees from being cut down. Habitat Conservation Plans have also been developed for state lands in Washington and Oregon.

A number of regulations have been put in place in California and Washington (gill-netting has not been allowed in Oregon since 1942) to reduce the number of Marbled Murrelets and other seabirds killed by commercial salmon gill-netting operations. These include closures of certain areas and not allowing fishing at dawn and dusk when the birds are most actively feeding or at certain seasons when they are most concentrated in fishing areas. In addition, research has been conducted to find ways of making the birds avoid gill-nets by making the nets more visible or by connecting devices to the nets that make a "pinging" sound underwater. These various efforts are thought to have reduced mortality of murrelets in the Puget Sound region of Washington where they have been implemented. There have been no regulatory changes in gill-net fisheries in British Columbia or Alaska aimed specifically at reducing the numbers of Marbled Murrelets killed.

Across the range of Marbled Murrelet there have been increasing efforts at developing marine protected areas and various commercial fisheries regulations to ensure healthy, long-term marine ecosystems and sustainable harvests of fish. For example, Monterey Bay National Marine Sanctuary and Olympic Coast National Marine Sanctuary both support Marbled Murrelet and are managed by the National Oceanic and Atmospheric Administration. National Marine Sanctuaries generally prohibit oil and gas extraction activities within their boundaries and prohibit certain types of other human activities that may disturb marine life or marine habitats. These regulations should be beneficial to maintaining food supplies and a healthy ecosystem upon which Marbled Murrelet depends. The Alaska Department of Fish and Game developed a set of recommendations for a public process to consider the establishment of Marine Protected Areas in the state that would likely be of benefit to Marbled Murrelet.[1,5,7,11–19]

CONSERVATION NEEDS

- Protect remaining old-growth nesting habitat from any further loss from logging.
- Continue refining radar and other survey techniques to better monitor changes in populations of Marbled Murrelet.
- Continue research on effects of predators on nest survival of Marbled Murrelets in relation to fragmentation and isolation of nesting habitat patches and work toward developing landscape level conservation plans to buffer patches and decrease predator effects.
- Assess impact of salmon gill-net fisheries on mortality of Marbled Murrelet in British Columbia and Alaska and implement changes to reduce mortality as has been done in Washington State.
- Continue efforts to maintain sustainable commercial fisheries levels to protect the marine ecosystems within the breeding range of Marbled Murrelet.
- Continue efforts to limit amount of pesticides, oil, and other pollutants within the marine ecosystem.

References

1. Nelson, S.K. 1997. Marbled Murrelet (*Brachyramphus marmoratus*). In *The Birds of North America*, No. 276 (A. Poole and F. Gill, eds.). The Academy of Natural Sciences, Philadelphia, PA, and the American Ornithologists' Union, Washington, D.C.

2. DeGange, A.R. 1996. *The Marbled Murrelet: A Conservation Assessment*. Gen. Tech. Rep. PNW-GTR-388. U.S. Dept. of Agriculture, Forest Service, Pacific Northwest Research Station, Portland, OR.

3. Igl, L. D. 2003. *Bird Checklists of the United States* (Version 12MAY03). Northern Prairie Wildlife Research Center Home Page, Jamestown, ND. http://www.npwrc.usgs.gov/resource/othrdata/chekbird/chekbird.htm (accessed 12 November 2003).

4. Chipley, R.M., G.H. Fenwick, M.J. Parr, and D.N. Pashley. 2003. *The American Bird Conservancy Guide to the 500 Most Important Bird Areas in the United States*. Random House, New York, NY.

5. U.S. Fish and Wildlife Service. 1997. *Recovery Plan for the Threatened Marbled Murrelet* (Brachyramphus marmoratus) *in Washington, Oregon, and California*. Portland, OR.

6. Bird Studies Canada. 2003. *Important Bird Areas of Canada*. http://www.bsc-eoc.org/iba/IBAsites.html (accessed 13 November 2003).

7. Burger, A.E. 2002. *Conservation Assessment of Marbled Murrelets in British Columbia: A Review of the Biology, Populations, Habitat Associations, and Conservation*. Technical Report Series No. 387. Canadian Wildlife Service, Pacific and Yukon Region, Delta, BC.

8. Ralph, C.J., G.L. Hunt, M.G. Raphael, and J.F. Piatt (eds.). 1995. *Ecology and Conservation of the Marbled Murrelet*. Gen. Tech. Rep. PSW-GTR-152. U.S. Dept. of Agriculture, Forest Service, Pacific Southwest Research Station, Albany, CA.

9. BirdLife International. 2000. *Threatened Birds of the World*. Lynx Editions and BirdLife International, Barcelona, Spain, and Cambridge, UK.

10. Ricketts et al. 1999. *Terrestrial Ecoregions of North America: A Conservation Assessment*. Island Press, Washington, DC. 485 pp.

11. Canadian Marbled Murrelet Recovery Team. 2003. *Marbled Murrelet Conservation Assessment 2003,*

Part B: Marbled Murrelet Recovery Team Advisory Document on Conservation and Management. Canadian Marbled Murrelet Recovery Team Working Document No. 1. Canadian Wildlife Service, Pacific and Yukon Region, Delta, BC.

12. U.S. Fish and Wildlife Service. 1996. *Primarily Federal Lands Identified as Critical Habitat for Rare Seabird; Minimal Effects Predicted from Habitat Designation.* http://pacific.fws.gov/news/1996/9625nr.htm (accessed 14 November 2003).

13. Pacific Lumber Company. 1999. *Habitat Conservation Plan for the Properties of The Pacific Lumber Company, Scotia Pacific Holding Company, and Salmon Creek Corporation.* http://www.palco.com/hcp.pdf (accessed 17 November 2003).

14. Environmental Protection Information Center. 2003. *Court Rules Against Pacific Lumber's Headwaters Permits Over 600 Acres of Ancient Forest Logged Using Illegal Permits.* http://www.wildcalifornia.org/press_releases/2003/pr052003.html (accessed 14 November 2003).

15. Pacific Lumber Company. 2003. *PALCO Resumes Removing Tree-sitters and Trees.* http://www.palco.com/news_releases_2003_0805.cfm (accessed 17 November 2003).

16. Pacific Lumber Company. 2003. *Statement by Robert E. Manne, President and CEO PALCO, Regarding Judge Golden's Decision Not to Enjoin Previously Exempted Timber Harvest Plans.* http://www.palco.com/news_releases_2003_0926.cfm (accessed 17 November 2003).

17. Norris, S. 2002. Ecological Lessons from Marine Bycatch. *Conservation in Practice Online.* http://www.conbio.org/InPractice/article34THI.html (accessed 13 November 2003).

18. Melvin, E.F., J.K. Parrish, and L.L. Conquest. 1999. Novel Tools to Reduce Seabird Bycatch in Coastal Gillnet Fisheries. *Conservation Biology* 13(6): 1386–1397.

19. Woodby, D., S. Meyer, K. Mabry, V. O'Connell, C. Trowbridge, J.H. Schempf, E. Krygier, D. Lloyd. 2002. *Marine Protected Areas in Alaska: Recommendations for a Public Process.* Alaska Department of Fish and Game, Division of Commercial Fisheries, Juneau, AK.

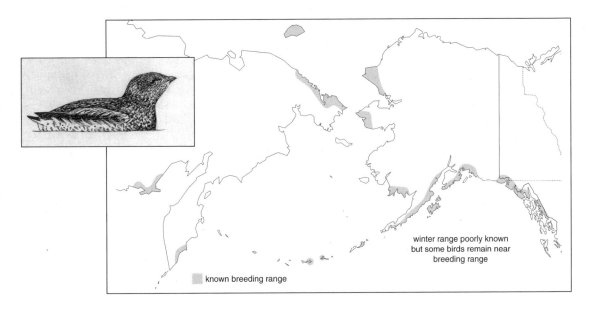

known breeding range

winter range poorly known
but some birds remain near
breeding range

KITTLITZ'S MURRELET (*Brachyramphus brevirostris*)

One of the poorest known of the North American alcids, this species has a spotty and restricted breeding range in isolated and hard-to-access mountainous habitat in Alaska and adjacent coastal Siberia. Its wintering range is still essentially unknown.

STATUS AND DISTRIBUTION

Breeding range extends from Juneau area northwest along the southern coast of Alaska through the larger Aleutian Islands to Attu and along the Siberian coast from the Okhotsk Sea to the Chukchi Sea. North of the Alaska Peninsula the species is known to breed along Bristol Bay, Seward Peninsula, and Lisburne Peninsula. Limits of breeding distribution are poorly known because few nests have ever been found (25 as of 1999), but generally nest near areas with glaciers. Important breeding areas in Alaska include Glacier Bay National Park and Preserve, the outer coast of Wrangel St. Elias National Park (including Icy Bay), northern and western Prince William Sound areas, Katmai National Park, Alaska Peninsula National Wildlife Refuge, Lower Cook Inlet/Lake Clark National Park and Preserve, Kenai Fjords National Park, Kachemak Bay State Park and State Wilderness Park, and the Aniakchak National Monument and Preserve.

Winter range is largely unknown. Some birds previously wintered in Prince William Sound, but none have been recorded there since March surveys in 1998. Very few birds have been documented wintering near inshore areas that they frequent in spring and summer, so the population is generally thought to winter somewhere offshore. There are records of occasional winter sightings in southeast and western Alaska and more frequent sightings in a few local areas in south coastal Alaska. Some birds have been seen during winter over open continental shelf waters in the northern Gulf of Alaska.

Surveys in Prince William Sound show an 84% decline from 1989 (6,436 birds) to 2000 (1,033). In Glacier Bay density estimates indicate an 89% decline between 1991 and 2000; along the Malaspina Forelands coast, surveys show a decline of from 38–75% during this same time period. The population was estimated at approximately 20,000 individuals in 1999 and models developed from recent surveys have placed the total population at between 9,505 and 26,767 birds.[1–7]

ECOLOGY

Breeds in high elevation boulder fields near glaciers where it lays its single egg on the ground, often in the lee of a large boulder that provides protection from falling rocks and blowing snow. Of the 25 nests found as of 1999, distance from the ocean varied from 0.3 to 45 miles but most were within about 20 miles of coastline. Incubation is not known but is expected to be similar to the closely related Marbled Murrelet (28–30 days), with both sexes known to incubate. Information from the one nest closely studied as of 1999 showed adults bringing a single fish to the nestling 4–6 times per day, with most feedings at night. Young studied in two nests fledged at around 24 days. Birds are thought to reach breeding age in 2–4 years based on studies of the similar Marbled Murrelet. During breeding season, adults and immatures feed in icy nearshore areas, especially near icebergs from glaciers. They primarily eat small fish but also eat some invertebrates. Although some birds remain in bays and fjords in winter, most birds are thought to leave, but wintering area is unknown.[1]

THREATS

Major threats include birds drowning in commercial fishing nets, especially inshore gill-nets, and mortality from oil spills. Approximately 3–10% of the global population of this species was estimated to have been killed by oil in the Exxon *Valdez* oil spill. Numbers killed in salmon gill-nets are not monitored but more than 100 individuals are estimated to have been killed in gill-nets in Prince William Sound in 1991. Of concern is the possibility that frequent disturbance from cruise ships, recreational boaters, and kayakers in preferred feeding areas near glaciers may disrupt birds' foraging or cause other problems but this has not been studied. Loss of glaciers from global warming and changes in fish abundance and distribution from global warming may become the most severe threats.[1]

CONSERVATION ACTION

The U.S. Fish and Wildlife Service (USFWS) added Kittlitz's Murrelet to its candidate list in May 2004, indicating that there is sufficient information available to propose endangered or threatened status for the species. USFWS also held a workshop in March 2004 to determine and prioritize the species' information and management needs. In partnership with the U.S. National Park Service, the USFWS is funding offshore surveys for murrelets in the Gulf of Alaska.

Much of the species' nesting habitat is protected within parks and refuges. The Alaska Department of Fish and Game developed a set of rec-

ommendations for a public process to consider the establishment of Marine Protected Areas in the state that would likely be of benefit to Kittlitz's Murrelet. The USFWS Division of International Affairs participates in a Russian–U.S. Working Group on Cooperation in the Field of Protection of the Environment and Natural Resources that involves specific joint activities related to the conservation and management of marine birds. The Alaska Department of Environmental Conservation, the U.S. Coast Guard, and the U.S. Environmental Protection Agency with the cooperation of the National Marine Fisheries Service have developed oil spill response plans to limit the mortality and ecological pollution from oil spills in coastal Alaska. The rapid implementation of these plans in the event of an oil spill will be crucial to maintaining healthy populations of Kittlitz's Murrelet and other susceptible wildlife occupying areas affected by a spill.[1,5–10]

CONSERVATION NEEDS

- Slow production of global warming pollution.
- Greatly increase research on the foraging habits and breeding biology of Kittlitz's Murrelet to better understand distribution and population limiting factors.
- Develop survey techniques (perhaps including radar) to monitor changes in populations of Kittlitz's Murrelet.
- Obtain better population estimates for core areas that are not surveyed and continue to monitor key population sites to better assess trends.
- Develop techniques to delimit wintering range of the species.
- Monitor direct and indirect impacts to murrelets from vessel traffic, especially large, fast vessels (including fast ferries), tour boats (especially jet boats), and cruise ships, that operate in fjords with glaciers.
- Assess impact of salmon gill-net fisheries on mortality of Kittlitz's Murrelet in Alaska and implement changes to reduce mortality.
- Continue efforts to maintain sustainable commercial fisheries levels to protect the marine ecosystems within the breeding range of Kittlitz's Murrelet.
- Continue efforts to limit amount of pesticides, oil, and other pollutants within the marine ecosystem.

References

1. Day, R.H., K.J. Kuletz, and D.A. Nigro. 1999. Kittlitz's Murrelet (*Brachyramphus brevirostris*). In *The Birds of North America*, No. 435 (A. Poole and F. Gill, eds.). The Birds of North America, Inc., Philadelphia, PA.

2. Alaska Natural Heritage Program. 1998. *Status report on the Kittlitz's Murrelet* (Brachyramphus brevirostris) *in Alaska*. The Alaska Natural Heritage Program, University of Alaska Anchorage, Anchorage AK. http://www.uaa.alaska.edu/enri/aknhp_web/index.html (accessed 18 November 2003).

3. Igl, L. D. 2003. *Bird Checklists of the United States* (Version 12MAY03). Northern Prairie Wildlife Research Center Home Page, Jamestown, ND. http://www.npwrc.usgs.gov/resource/othrdata/chekbird/chekbird.htm (accessed 18 November 2003).

4. Chipley, R.M., G.H. Fenwick, M.J. Parr, and D.N. Pashley. 2003. *The American Bird Conservancy Guide to the 500 Most Important Bird Areas in the United States*. Random House, New York, NY.

5. USFWS. 2004. *Kittlitz's Murrelet Fact Sheet*. USFWS, Alaska Region, Branch of Fisheries and Ecological Services, 1011 E. Tudor Rd., Anchorage, AK.

6. BirdLife International. 2003. *Kittlitz's Murrelet: Upgrade to Critical?* BirdLife International's Globally Threatened Bird Forums. http://www.birdlife.net/ (accessed 19 November 2003).

7. USFWS. 2004. *Species Assessment and Listing Priority Form for Kittlitz's Murrelet*. USFWS, Alaska Region, Branch of Fisheries and Ecological Services, 1011 E. Tudor Rd., Anchorage, AK.

8. Woodby, D., S. Meyer, K. Mabry, V. O'Connell, C. Trowbridge, J.H. Schempf, E. Krygier, and D. Lloyd. 2002. *Marine Protected Areas in Alaska: Recommendations for a Public Process*. Alaska Department of Fish and Game, Division of Commercial Fisheries, Juneau, AK.

9. U.S. Fish and Wildlife Service International Affairs. 2000. *2000 Working Group Protocol, Area V, Protection of Nature and the Organization of Reserves of the U.S.—Russia Agreement on Cooperation in the Field of Protection of the Environment and Natural Resources*. http://international.fws.gov/laws/russia.html (accessed 4 December 2003).

10. Alaska Department of Environmental Conservation. 2003. *Prevention and Emergency Response Program*. http://www.state.ak.us/dec/dspar/perp/about.htm (accessed 4 December 2003).

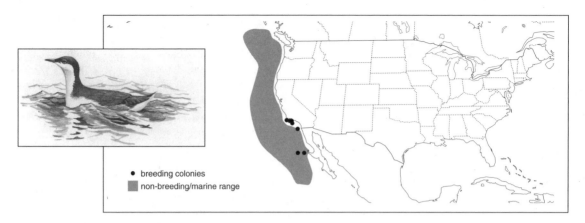

- breeding colonies
- non-breeding/marine range

XANTUS'S MURRELET (*Synthliboramphus hypoleucus*)

Unusual among alcids, Xantus's Murrelet occurs further south and in warmer waters than all but the related Craveri's Murrelet and the southern subspecies of the Cassin's Auklet. It breeds on a few islands off of California and Mexico's Baja California peninsula but it has been extirpated or its numbers have been severely reduced by introduced cats and rats.

STATUS AND DISTRIBUTION

Breeds regularly on 5–6 islands off of California and 4–6 islands off of Mexico's Baja California. Largest breeding colonies are on Santa Barbara Island within California's Channel Islands National Park (500–1,250 pairs estimated from 2000–2003), Mexico's Guadalupe Islands (1,200 pairs estimated from surveys in 1967–68 on small islets offshore from main islands), Mexico's San Benitos Islands (250–500 pairs estimated in 2003), and Mexico's Los Coronados Islas (750–1,500 pairs estimated in 1999). There are two subspecies. The southern subspecies currently breeds only on the San Benitos Islands and a few offshore islets of Guadalupe Island.

Birds disperse from breeding colonies to offshore waters of Pacific Coast from southern British Columbia to Baja California but with highest numbers 20–100 km offshore of central and southern California.

The species has been poorly surveyed so it has been difficult to assess trends. However, the species was severely reduced or extirpated by introduced cats on Todos Santos, San Martin, and San Geronimo but has since begun to recover, and is thought extirpated on mainland Guada-

lupe and has been greatly reduced on Mexico's Islas Los Coronados. Surveys at Santa Barbara Island in the Channel Islands National Park indicated a 2.5–5.3% decline in numbers from 1991 to 1997 and declining burrow occupancy rates since the early 1990s. The population was estimated at approximately 5,600 birds in 2000 but estimated to range between 5,000 and 11,500 in 2002.[1–5]

ECOLOGY

Breeds on offshore islands where birds nest in caves and crevices, under boulders, or on the ground under thick vegetation. Xantus's Murrelets lay two eggs and, quite unique in seabirds, the young are fully-feathered at hatching and leave the nest within 1–2 days after hatching. Diet is not well known but consists mainly of small, larval fish that are captured in the bill as the bird uses its wings to "fly" underwater. Prefers warm waters at all seasons, tending to avoid the cooler inshore waters, and occurs in higher numbers in deeper, warmer waters more than 20 km offshore.[1–3]

THREATS

The main current threat is continued depredation from introduced rat and cat populations at many of the breeding sites. Remains of 174 cat-killed Xantus's Murrelets were found at Islas Los Coronados in 1989. Cats had severely reduced or extirpated the species from Islas Todos Santos, Isla San Martin, Isla San Geronimo, and the main island of Isla Guadalupe. Rats had virtually extirpated

Xantus's Murrelet from Anacapa Island where the species was once common. Oil pollution is considered a serious potential threat for the California breeding segment of the population because of the high oil tanker traffic passing within 25 km of the breeding colonies. An increase in the number of boats engaged in night fishing for squid using bright lights near Xantus's Murrelet colonies has raised concerns about disruption of breeding activities and increases in mortality. An increase in mortality results from birds striking boats due to light attraction or being depredated by diurnal avian predators, especially gulls, that are able to feed in the artificial light that attracts the murrelets. New threats include light pollution from the proposed development of liquefied natural gas (LNG) regasification terminals along the Pacific Coast of the Baja California peninsula by foreign oil companies. In 2003, ChevronTexaco Corporation proposed construction of an LNG receiving and regasification terminal terminal only 500 m offshore of South Coronado Island. Light pollution from the long proposed platform and from docking supertankers will likely disrupt breeding activities of the species in addition to disturbance by construction and general operation of the terminal, increased opportunity for spills and discharge of petroleum products, and increased potential for rat introduction to the islands. Other potential threats include mortality from gillnetting, and contamination from pesticides and other toxins.[1–5]

CONSERVATION ACTION

The Pacific Seabird Group filed petitions in May 2002 to consider Xantus's Murrelet for listing under both the Federal Endangered Species Act and the California Endangered Species Act. The California Fish and Game Commission designated the species a candidate threatened species in November 2002 and adopted emergency regulations governing incidental take of the species and the petition was officially accepted in 2004. The U.S. Fish and Wildlife Service added Xantus's Murrelet to its candidate list in 2004, indicating that there is sufficient information available to propose endangered or threatened status for the species. The species is listed as Threatened by the Mexican government as well.

Most of the Channel Islands are owned and managed by the Channel Islands National Park and the surrounding waters are part of NOAA's Channel Islands National Marine Sanctuary. The National Park Service removed all introduced cats from Santa Barbara Island in 1978 where the species had ceased breeding by 1939 and numbers had increased to 1,544 by 1992. The National Park Service developed its Anacapa Island Restoraton Project and worked with Island Conservation to successfully remove all black rats from the island in 2001 and 2002. Island Conservation and their partners have removed introduced predators and herbivores from all Mexican islands in the species breeding range except for Guadalupe and Cedros islands.

National Marine Sanctuaries generally prohibit oil and gas extraction activities within their boundaries and prohibit certain types of other human activities that may disturb marine life or marine habitats. These regulations should certainly be helpful to maintaining food supplies and a healthy ecosystem upon which Xantus's Murrelet depend.

A series of Marine Protected Areas were established near the Channel Islands in 2003 by the California Department of Fish and Game. These Marine Protected Areas provide further regulations on human recreational and fishing activities within the designated areas, which may be beneficial to Xantus's Murrelet populations.[4–7]

CONSERVATION NEEDS

- Continue efforts to eradicate introduced rats and other invasive species from island nesting colonies.
- Prevent inappropriate development and fishing activities near breeding islands since such activities can increase mortality of Xantus's Murrelets because of the birds' attraction to artificial light sources.
- Develop and implement surveys, perhaps using radar and acoustic monitoring technologies, to detect and monitor breeding colonies of Xantus's Murrelet.
- Ensure that human visitation to island nesting colonies does not negatively impact Xantus's Murrelet nesting success and survival.
- Assess impact of gill-net fisheries on mortality of Xantus's Murrelet.
- Continue efforts to limit amount of pesticides, oil, and other pollutants within the marine ecosystem.

References

1. Drost, C.A., and D. B. Lewis. 1995. Xantus' Murrelet (*Synthliboramphus hypoleucus*). In *The Birds of North America*, No. 164 (A. Poole and F. Gill, eds.). The Academy of Natural Sciences, Philadelphia, PA, and the American Ornithologists' Union, Washington, DC.

2. BirdLife International. 2000. *Threatened Birds of the World*. Lynx Editions and BirdLife International, Barcelona, Spain, and Cambridge, UK.

3. Wolf, S.G. 2002. *The Relative Status and Conservation of Island Breeding Seabirds in California and Northwest Mexico*. Thesis, University of California, Santa Cruz.

4. Keitt, B., Tershey, B., and S. Wolf. 2005. Personal communication.

5. Pacific Seabird Group. 2002. *Petition to List the California Fish and Game Commission to List the Xantus's Murrelet as Threatened Under the California Fish and Game Code*. http://www.pacificseabirdgrou.org/XAMU_PETITION_STATE.pdf (accessed 28 May 2003).

6. Pacific Seabird Group. 2003. Pacific Seabird Group website. http://www.pacificseabirdgroup.org/committees.html (accessed 28 May 2003).

7. California Department of Fish and Game. 2002. *Xantus's Murrelet Becomes a Candidate for Listing in California*. California Department of Fish and Game Press Release. http://www.dfg.ca.gov/mrd/pressrelease_110402.html (accessed 28 May 2003).

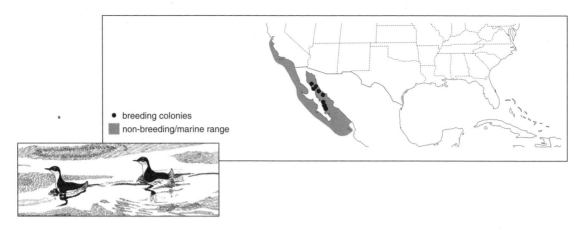

CRAVERI'S MURRELET (*Synthliboramphus craveri*)

Although not a species that nests within the U.S., Craveri's Murrelet regularly occurs off the coast of southern California where it is sometimes seen in good numbers by birders on pelagic boat trips. The species breeds on relatively few islands within Mexico's Gulf of California and the Pacific Coast of Baja California and has been severely reduced by depredation from introduced rats, cats, and other mammals.

STATUS AND DISTRIBUTION

Breeds regularly at 10–11 islands or island groups, most within Mexico's Gulf of California, but also thought to breed on the Pacific coast of Baja at Islas San Benito, though no nests have ever been documented there. The islands of Partida, Rasa, and Tiburón are thought to support 90% of the breeding population.

Birds disperse from breeding colonies to offshore waters of the Pacific Coast from southern California to Baja California, but nonbreeding distribution has been little studied.[1] Peak counts from birding trips off San Diego and Monterey Bay, California have occurred in September–October and range from 15 to 45.

The species has been poorly surveyed so it has been difficult to assess trends. The species has disappeared or been greatly reduced at several breeding locations. The population was estimated in the 1990s at approximately 10,000 breeding birds, with an additional 5,000–10,000 prebreeding individuals.[1–4]

ECOLOGY

Breeds on offshore islands where birds nest in caves and crevices, under boulders, or on the ground under thick vegetation. Lays two eggs and, quite unique in seabirds, the young are fully-feathered at hatching and leave the nest within 1–2 days after hatching. Diet is not well known but consists mainly of small, larval fish that are captured in the bill as the bird uses its wings to "fly" underwater. Prefers warm waters at all seasons but requirements and distribution are poorly known.[1]

THREATS

The main current threat is continued depredation from introduced rat and cat populations at many of the breeding sites. Oil pollution is considered a serious potential threat for birds wintering off California because of the high oil tanker traffic in the area. Other potential threats include mortality from gillnetting, human disturbance at breeding sites, and contamination from pesticides and other toxins.[1,2]

CONSERVATION ACTION

The breeding islands in the Gulf of California are included within the Gulf of California Biosphere Reserve and some have been designated as wildlife preserves. Work has been ongoing at some islands to eradicate introduced predators. At Isla Rasa, efforts to eradicate introduced rats and mice had succeeded by 1995. A management plan for the

Biosphere Reserve developed in 1994 began being implemented in 1999.

The International Division of the U.S. Fish and Wildlife Service provided funds to Island Conservation to develop management plans for 19 of the islands of the Gulf of California Biosphere Reserve in 1996. With the help of local conservation organizations Grupo Ecologista Antares and Niparajá, the Nature Conservancy is working with local Biosphere Reserve staff and local fishermen to patrol the protected areas and halt illegal fishing—activities that should benefit the ecosystem upon which Craveri's Murrelet depends.

The San Benito Islands currently have no protected status despite their importance to seabirds. Legal protection for the San Benito Islands and additional research on the status of Craveri's Murrelets there are needed.

Monterey Bay, as one coastal area that sometimes supports nonbreeding Craveri's Murrelets, has been designated as a National Marine Sanctuary and is managed by the National Oceanic and Atmospheric Administration. National Marine Sanctuaries generally prohibit oil and gas extraction activities within their boundaries and prohibit certain types of other human activities that may disturb marine life or marine habitats. These regulations should be beneficial to maintaining food supplies and a healthy ecosystem upon which Craveri's Murrelet depends.[1,4–7]

CONSERVATION NEEDS

- Continue efforts to eradicate introduced rats, cats, and other invasive species from island nesting colonies.
- Develop and implement surveys, perhaps using radar and acoustic monitoring technologies, to detect and monitor breeding colonies of Craveri's Murrelet.
- Investigate using seabird restoration tech-

niques to lure birds to formerly occupied islands that are now predator free and protected or to protected areas within existing colony locations.

- Ensure that human visitation to island nesting colonies does not negatively impact Craveri's Murrelet nesting success and survival.
- Assess impact of gill-net fisheries on mortality of Craveri's Murrelet.
- Continue efforts to limit amount of pesticides, oil, and other pollutants within the marine ecosystem.
- Increase protection for San Benito Islands and research on the status of Craveri's Murrelets there.

References

1. BirdLife International. 2000. *Threatened Birds of the World*. Lynx Editions and BirdLife International, Barcelona, Spain, and Cambridge, UK.

2. Nettleship, D.N. 1996. Family Alcidae (Auks). Pages 678–724 in *Handbook of the Birds of the World*, Vol. 3, *Hoatzins to Auks* (J. del Hoyo, A. Elliot, and J. Sargatal, eds.). Lynx Edicions, Barcelona, Spain.

3. Mlodinow, S.G., and M. O'Brien. 1996. *America's 100 Most Wanted Birds*. Falcon Press, Helena, MT.

4. Keitt, B., B. Tershey, and S. Wolf. 2005. Personal communication.

5. U.S. Fish and Wildlife Service International Affairs. 1996. *Grants Awarded in 1996*. http://international.fws.gov/whp/annex4.html (accessed 3 November 2003).

6. The Nature Conservancy. 2003. *Baja & the Gulf of California*. http://nature.org/wherewework/northamerica/mexico/work/art8618.html (accessed 3 November 2003).

7. National Ocean Service. 2003. *National Marine Sanctuaries*. http://www.sanctuaries.nos.noaa.gov/welcome.html (accessed 22 May 2003).

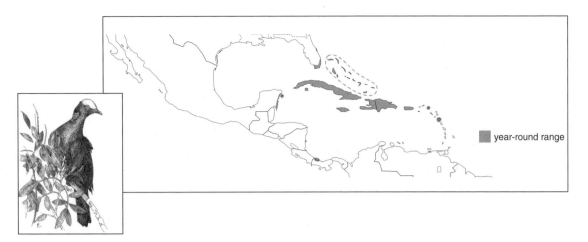

year-round range

WHITE-CROWNED PIGEON (*Patagioenas leucocephala*)

The White-crowned Pigeon, a Caribbean species with a small breeding population in the southern tip of Florida, has been negatively impacted by habitat loss throughout its range and overhunting in parts of the Caribbean.

STATUS AND DISTRIBUTION

The White-crowned Pigeon is essentially restricted to the Caribbean, ranging from the Florida Keys and Everglades through the Bahamas and Greater Antilles, the northern Lesser Antilles (to Guadeloupe), and with small populations along the coast of Yucatán, Mexico, and the Caribbean coast of Panama. The bulk of the world population is thought to occur in Cuba, the Bahamas, Jamaica, and the Dominican Republic, with less than 5% in the continental U.S. In nonbreeding season, some birds make short-distance migratory movements, including among islands. For example, only a small proportion of Florida's breeding population occurs there in winter, with most birds apparently migrating to Cuba and the Bahamas. On larger islands some birds move into upland forests during winter. Banding records have shown nestlings banded in Bahamas being found in Florida, Cuba, Puerto Rico, and Dominican Republic.

Although no specific information exists on densities of the species across its range, a number of sites are known to support the species. These include Florida's Everglades National Park (5,055 nests in 1991), Key West National Wildlife Refuge (NWR) (>2,000 nesting pairs May–Aug 2001), and Great White Heron NWR (1,608 pairs in June/July 2001), Cuba's Desembarco del Granma

National Park, Santa María–Los Caimanes National Park, and Ciénaga de Zapata Biosphere Reserve, Dominican Republic's Del Este National Park and Jaragua National Park and Mexico's Sian Ka'an Biosphere Reserve. In the Bahamas large breeding colonies are known to occur on Big Green Cay, Finley Cay, Joulters Cay, Schooner Cays, Deadman's Cay, Goat Cay, Duck Cay, Samana Cay, and Red Shank Cay.

While there is no rangewide survey program in existence to assess changes in abundance, the species is thought to have experienced a significant decline in most of its range. The species' total population was estimated at 550,000 individuals in 2004.[1-7]

ECOLOGY

Builds nests in mangroves, often on islands, but feeds on fruits of tropical deciduous trees and shrubs that occur in upland areas, often on the mainland. Nests typically built in trees or bushes (often in mangroves) and from ground level to 20 feet above ground and are little more than loose platforms of twigs. Females lay 2 eggs that are incubated by both male and female for 13–14 days. Young are cared for by both parents and fledge at about 20 days when undisturbed. In the few populations studied to date there is a high rate of predation of eggs and young. In Florida, birds avoid areas with raccoons, probably because they are such efficient nest predators. Feeds on variety of fruits of tropical deciduous trees and shrubs. In Florida, birds seem to rely especially on poisonwood fruits, so that more birds nest when there are good crops of the fruit. Like all pigeons, young are first fed "crop milk," a milk-like substance formed from the sloughed-off cells of the crop. After a few days, adults add fruits to the diet of nestlings and gradually move toward an all-fruit diet. In the non-breeding season these birds form flocks and make short-distance migratory movements to track the cycle of fruiting of different trees and shrubs. Tropical storms and hurricanes can destroy and damage nesting and foraging habitat.[1,8]

THREATS

The greatest threat to the species on the breeding grounds is continued loss and degradation of mangroves and tropical deciduous forest within its restricted range. Hunting of adults and nestlings has been a problem historically, but is probably a threat in only some limited parts of the range. Habitat loss has been severe across many habitats of south Florida and the Greater Antilles of the Caribbean. For example, 98.5% of forest has been lost in Haiti, 75% in Jamaica. Hispaniolan Dry Forest habitat is estimated to have declined by more than 50% and Cuban Dry Forest habitat by more than 90%. These habitats harbor many endemic plant and animal species as well as providing foraging habitat for White-crowned Pigeon. Forest habitats have been lost across the Caribbean from clearing for charcoal production and agriculture. In many areas the cutting of forests has continued and occurs even within the borders of National Parks and other protected areas. Lack of resources to monitor and patrol parks and political difficulty of enforcing park regulations has hampered conservation efforts in many parks within the species' range. Mangrove habitats have been destroyed in many areas for tourism development and for development of commercial shrimp farms. In many areas they are being negatively impacted by sedimentation and pollution. An evaluation of conservation priorities for the Neotropics places the Greater Antilles in the second highest category (of five) of concern—"immediate action needed in all ecosystems to stem widespread declines."[1,4,9–14]

CONSERVATION ACTION

The species has been the focus of conservation work in its Florida range but there has been only limited activity in other parts of range. A program is in place to purchase key land parcels in the Florida Keys and 6,400 acres were targeted for acquisition by Florida's state government in 2003. A joint project involving the Nature Conservancy, U.S. Geological Survey, and various partners called the Atlas of Bahamian Environments is in development and will result in a set of conservation goals to benefit White-crowned Pigeon and other species. Hunting seasons and regulations were established in 1987 in the Bahamas and these are likely to have decreased hunting pressure in some areas, though bag limits are liberal (50 birds per day). Harvesting of nestlings for food for people and to feed livestock is still considered a serious threat in some parts of the Dominican Republic. The effect of hunting pressure in other parts of the range is poorly known.

Pronatura, a nongovernmental organization in the Dominican Republic, is working with the Nature Conservancy to develop and implement effective management and protection infrastructure for Jaragua National Park. Three guard stations and two docks were built, boundaries of the park were marked, and meetings to discuss ecotourism were initiated with local communities and government officials. In Cuba, World Wildlife Fund Canada has provided grants to promote sustainable development activities by villagers living in and near the Ciénaga de Zapata Biosphere Reserve and to support national park staff working to halt poaching and habitat loss in the area.

With funding ($8 million Canadian) from the Canadian International Development Agency, the Jamaican Forestry Department has been engaged since 1992 in the Trees for Tomorrow Project. The Project has trained forestry department employees, allowed the demarcation and marking of park boundaries, instituted forest management plans, developed an environmental education program, and upgraded reforestation infrastructure. All of these activities are expected to decrease loss of habitat and encroachment into national parks.

In Belize, a variety of habitat protection activities are underway. For example, in 1998 the 100-acre Caye Caulker Forest Reserve was established to protect mangrove habitat that supports a variety of wildlife, including White-crowned Pigeon.[1,4,5,15–20]

CONSERVATION NEEDS

- Preserve remaining acreage of mangroves and tropical deciduous forest habitats used by the species for nesting and foraging.

- Prevent spread of nonnative mammals (rats, mongoose, etc.) to mangrove nesting islands and remove nonnative predators if already established.
- Increase enforcement of existing hunting regulations in areas of the Caribbean where they are in place and develop regulations in areas where they are lacking.
- Increase education and outreach to convince people to leave native fruiting tree species on their property and to make them aware of the habitat needs of the species.
- Develop baseline inventory of White-crowned Pigeon breeding and wintering populations from across the species' range.

References

1. Bancroft, G. T., and R. Bowman. 2001. White-crowned Pigeon (*Columba leucocephala*). In *The Birds of North America*, No. 596 (A. Poole and F. Gill, eds.). The Birds of North America, Inc., Philadelphia, PA.

2. Pranty, B. 2002. *The Important Bird Areas of Florida: 2000–2002*. http://www.audubon.org/bird/iba/florida/ (accessed 2 February 2004).

3. Centro Nacional de Áreas Protegidas Cuba. No date. *Áreas Protegidas de Significación Nacional*. http://www.cuba.cu/ciencia/citma/ama/cnap/areasfr.htm (accessed 23 July 2004).

4. Parks in Peril. No date. *Where the Parks in Peril Program Works: Dominican Republic*. http://parksin peril .org/03g_dominicanrepublic.shtml (accessed 21 July 2003).

5. United Nations Educational, Scientific, and Cultural Organization. 2002. *Man and the Biosphere Reserves Directory*. http://www2.unesco.org/mab/bios1-2 .htm (accessed 22 July 2003).

6. University of Miami. 2003. *Atlas of Bahamian Environments: Conservation Targets: White-crowned Pigeon Description and Distribution*. http://islands.bio.miami .edu/Targets/White-Crowned%20Pigeon/Description %20and%20Distribution/index.html (accessed 26 July 2004).

7. Rich, T. D., C. Beardmore, H. Berlanga, P. Blancher, M. Bradstreet, G. Butcher, D. Demarest, E. Dunn, C. Hunter, E. Inigo-Elias, J. Kennedy, A. Martell, A. Panjabi, D. Pashley, K. Rosenberg, C. Rustay, S. Wendt, and T. Will. 2004. *Partners in Flight North American Landbird Conservation Plan*. Cornell Lab of Ornithology, Ithaca, NY.

8. Bancroft, G.T., R. Bowman, and R.J. Sawicki.

2000. Rainfall, Fruiting Phenology, and the Nesting Season of White-crowned Pigeons in the Upper Florida Keys. *Auk* 117:416–426.

9. World Wildlife Fund. 2001. *Cuban dry forests (NT0213)*. http://www.worldwildlife.org/wildworld/ profiles/terrestrial/nt/nt0213_full.html (accessed 21 July 2003).

10. World Wildlife Fund. 2001. *Hispaniolan Dry Forests (NT0215)*. http://www.worldwildlife.org/wildworld/ profiles/terrestrial/nt/nt0215_full.html (accessed 21 July 2003).

11. World Wildlife Fund. 2001. *Jamaican dry forests (NT0218)*. http://www.worldwildlife.org/wildworld/ profiles/terrestrial/nt/nt0218_full.html (accessed 21 July 2003).

12. World Wildlife Fund. 2001. *Bahamian Dry Forests (NT0203)*. http://www.worldwildlife.org/wildworld/ profiles/terrestrial/nt/nt0203_full.html (accessed 21 July 2003).

13. World Wildlife Fund. 2001. *Greater Antilles mangroves (NT1410)*. http://www.worldwildlife.org/ wildworld/profiles/terrestrial/nt/nt1410_full.html (accessed 21 July 2003).

14. Stotz, D.F., J.W. Fitzpatrick, T.A. Parker III, and D. K. Moskovits. 1996. *Neotropical Birds: Ecology and Conservation*. University of Chicago Press, Chicago, IL. 481 pp.

15. Florida Department of Environmental Protection. 2003. *Acquisitions in The Florida Keys Placed On Fast-Track*. http://www.dep.state.fl.us/secretary/comm/ 2003/dec/1216_acquisitions.htm (accessed 2 February 2004).

16. University of Miami. 2003. *Atlas of Bahamian Environments*. http://islands.bio.miami.edu/ (accessed 26 July 2004).

17. University of Miami Department of Biology. No date. *White-crowned Pigeon: Current Conservation, Information Gaps, and Research Needs*. http://islands.bio .miami.edu/Targets/White-Crowned%20Pigeon/ Conservation%20and%20Research/index.html (accessed 2 February 2004).

18. World Wildlife Fund-Canada. No date. *Conservation Programs-International*. http://www.wwfcanada .org/AboutWWF/WhatWeDo/ConservationPrograms/ Conservation.asp (accessed 22 July 2003).

19. Jamaican Forestry Department. No date. *The Trees for Tomorrow Project*. http://www.forestry.gov .jm/tft_info.htm (accessed 22 July 2003).

20. Naturealight Productions. 2004. *Caye Caulker Forest and Marine Reserve*. http://www.gocayecaulker .com/conserv.html (accessed 26 July 2004).

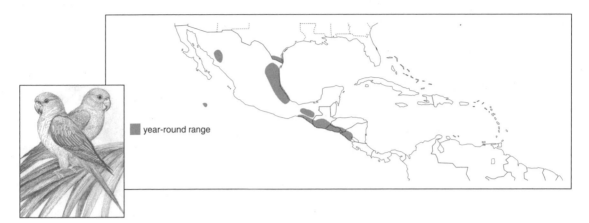

year-round range

GREEN PARAKEET (*Aratinga holochlora*)

The northernmost naturally occurring parakeet in North America (since the extinction of the Carolina Parakeet), the Green Parakeet is most familiar to U.S. birders from the Rio Grande Valley of south Texas, where it occurs in suburban and agricultural habitats. The species limits are confusing, with some authors splitting the taxon into as many as four species, but the American Ornithologists' Union considers all populations to be a single species ranging from southeastern Texas through Mexico to Nicaragua.

STATUS AND DISTRIBUTION

There are four described subspecies within the currently recognized species, each with a disjunct range. The northeastern subspecies (*A. h. holochlora*), which recent studies suggest should be considered a separate species and about which this account is focused, occurs in urban areas of the Rio Grande Valley of southeastern Texas and the Mexican states of Tamaulipas and Nuevo León south to central Veracruz. A disjunct population occurs from southern Veracruz and Oaxaca south to Chiapas and possibly adjacent regions of Guatemala. Another subspecies (*A.h. brewsteri*) occupies a rather restricted region of western Mexico where the borders of Sonora, Chihuahua, and Sinaloa come together. A third subspecies (*A.h. strenua*) occurs from eastern Oaxaca, Mexico south to Nicaragua. The fourth subspecies (*A.h. brevipes*) occurs only on Socorro Island, Mexico. Some of these subspecies are considered full species by certain authors, although not currently by the American Ornithologists' Union.

Populations in the urban Rio Grande Valley of southeastern Texas are thought to number from hundreds to low thousands. The origin of the population in Texas is unclear. It was once thought to be exclusively from escaped or released captive birds, but it is now thought that at least some of these birds may have wandered north from naturally occurring populations in the bordering Mexican state of Tamaulipas. Small introduced and increasing populations also occur in south Florida and southern California, where breeding has been documented. The species is resident but some populations may make irregular seasonal movements based on food availability.

Important sites for the northeastern subspecies include the Sierra de Tamaulipas Important Bird Area and the El Cielo Biosphere Reserve (356,442 acres) both in the Mexican state of Tamaulipas. In the U.S. the species occurs most commonly in urban and suburban areas around Brownsville, Weslaco, and McAllen, Texas but does occur rarely at some natural areas, including the Santa Ana National Wildlife Refuge, which abuts the Mexican border. Christmas Bird Count totals for the species in south Texas have ranged from 119 to 469 birds since 1998, but up to 300 birds have been counted at a single roost in Brownsville. Between 1990 and 2003 the CBC at Gómez Farías within the El Cielo Biosphere Reserve has shown wide variability in the numbers of Green Parakeets tallied, ranging from 0 to 319. There is no trend information available for the species but it is thought to have declined because of the loss of habitat to agriculture as well as from capture for the wild bird trade. The species' total population size was estimated at 200,000 in 2004.[1–10]

ECOLOGY

In the south Texas portion of its range, occurs in urban areas with large shade trees and palms, which are favored for roosting and nesting. The northeastern subspecies in Mexico uses a variety of forest habitats from sea level up to 1500 m and has been found nesting in cavities in large trees and in crevices in a large cave, but the ecology is generally not well studied. Birds breeding in captivity laid four eggs that were incubated for 23 days. Young left the nest 50 days after hatching and were independent in another two weeks. Birds eat a variety of fruit, seeds, nuts, and berries and in Mexico have occasionally been found eating cultivated corn. In the nonbreeding season birds gather in flocks that may contain more than 100 individuals, and roosts in south Texas have been reported to reach as high as 300 individuals. In Mexico, flocks of the species are said to fly higher than other parrot species and to have a slower wingbeat than co-occurring parakeet species.[1,3,4,8,11]

THREATS

In northeastern Mexico the greatest threats are from loss of forest habitat from clearing for agriculture or forestry and from capture of birds for the caged bird trade. A habitat model for the species developed from specimen records suggests that 30% of its habitat in Mexico has been lost. In much of the range the loss and degradation of habitat has been severe. Only an estimated 2% of the Tamaulipan Mezquital Ecoregion that encompasses the northern portion of the range of the northeastern subspecies is considered intact habitat and no blocks of habitat larger than 62,500 acres remain. This loss of native habitat has been largely through conversion to agriculture and as much as a quarter of the little remaining habitat may be altered by this activity in the next two decades. Protected areas within the region are small and mostly confined to the U.S. side of the Rio Grande River. About 20% of the Veracruz Moist Forests Ecoregion that encompasses the southern portion of the range of the northeastern subspecies is considered intact habitat. Over 4.6 million acres of forest were logged in the Mexican state of Veracruz between 1900 and 1987. The only protected area within the ecoregion, El Cielo Biosphere Reserve, is chronically underfunded and continues to suffer from unregulated cattle grazing and illegal harvest of plants and animals. The Lower Rio Grande Valley of Texas, where the species now occurs, has little remaining natural habitat. For example, the sabal palm, a species native to this area, once occurred extensively along the river up to 80 miles inland, but the only remaining groves of these palms are at the 172 acre Audubon Sabal Palm Grove Sanctuary and the Nature Conservancy's Southmost Preserve, both near Brownsville. Montezuma bald cypress trees were also once common along the Rio Grande but are now rare; further south in Mexico this tree provides nesting cavities for Green Parakeets.

Green Parakeets are taken from the wild legally within Mexico for sale within that country. It is technically illegal to export the species but they are regularly illegally exported to various countries around the world. An estimated 25,000 parrots of various species are smuggled across the U.S.–Mexico border annually and another 25,000 die in transport. An unknown number of these are undoubtedly Green Parakeets.[3,11–16]

CONSERVATION ACTION

Within the Lower Rio Grande Valley of Texas there are several initiatives underway to increase the amount of natural habitat for wildlife through purchase of remaining fragments of native habitat and through restoration of degraded habitat. The U.S. Fish and Wildlife Service has continued to purchase lands to connect the natural existing tracts of habitat left along the Lower Rio Grande within the Lower Rio Grande National Wildlife Refuge, which has grown to 90,000 acres in 112 separate parcels since its establishment in 1979. In 2003 it was announced that an additional $1 million had been allocated by Congress for additional land acquisition from willing sellers.

Nongovernmental conservation groups are also active in the Lower Rio Grande Valley of Texas, including the Nature Conservancy, which has purchased the 1,035-acre Southmost Preserve near Brownsville and the 243-acre Chihuahua Woods Preserve near Mission. Another organization, the Valley Land Fund, has worked with partners since 1987 to protect over 5,000 acres within the Valley. The World Birding Center began development in the 1990s in Texas to promote birding and conservation within the Lower Rio Grande Valley as a way to show local communities that land conservation has great economic and social benefits for those communities.

In northeastern Mexico, conservation initiatives within habitats used by Green Parakeets are more limited. The State of Tamaulipas declared El Cielo a biosphere reserve in 1985 and in 1987 it was recognized within the UNESCO–Man and the Biosphere reserve network. However, there is little funding (one employee) for reserve management, education, enforcement, and research activities within the reserve. Fortunately, the remoteness of the area has allowed the habitat to remain relatively undisturbed and commerical logging ceased in 1985. The Rancho del Cielo Research Station, located within the higher elevation cloud forest at El Cielo, was established in 1964 and is now operated by the Gorgas Research Foundation and Texas Southmost College from near Brownsville, Texas. Texas Southmost College has continued to maintain programs that bring students from the university for short-term in-depth course offerings and, in addition, various birding groups have been allowed to use the facilities for a fee. In the 1980s the Gorgas Research Foundation also acquired the 250-acre Rancho el Cielito to protect some of the last remaining lowland tropical forest in the area. The U.S. Fish and Wildlife Service Division of International Affairs has provided funding to a local nongovernmental organization called Terra Nostra over several years for a project to develop and promote ecotourism as a conservation tool for El Cielo. Through this work a small hotel and restaurant/store were built in one community within the reserve. The area has become increasingly popular for birding because of its relatively close proximity to the U.S. border (within a day's drive) but most visitors to the reserve are Mexican citizens.[17–25]

CONSERVATION NEEDS

- Develop baseline inventory of Green Parakeet populations in northeastern Mexico and in southern Texas.
- Implement research on limiting factors for Green Parakeet populations.
- Study the ecology and genetics of Green Parakeets in south Texas and Mexico.
- Increase land conservation efforts within northern Tamaulipas region of Mexico and continue land conservation initiatives in U.S. side of Lower Rio Grande Valley.

References

1. Forshaw, J.M. 1989. *Parrots of the World*: 3rd ed. Lansdowne Editions, Willoughby, Australia.

2. American Ornithologists Union. 1998. *Check-List of North American Birds*. Allen Press, Inc., Lawrence, KS.

3. Juniper, T., and M. Parr. 1998. *Parrots: A Guide to Parrots of the World*. Yale University Press, New Haven, CT.

4. Howell, S.N.G., and S. Webb. 1995. *A Guide to the Birds of Mexico and Northern Central America*. Oxford University Press, New York, NY.

5. Pranty, B., and K.L. Garrett. 2003. The Parrot Fauna of the ABA Area: A Current Look. *Birding* 35:248–261.

6. CONABIO. 2002. *Áreas de Importancia para la Conservación de las Aves (AICAS)*. http://conabioweb .conabio.gob.mx/aicas/doctos/aicas.html (accessed 9 December 2003).

7. Igl, L.D. 2003. *Bird Checklists of the United States* (Version 12MAY03). Northern Prairie Wildlife Research Center Home Page, Jamestown, ND. http://www .npwrc.usgs.gov/resource/othrdata/chekbird/chekbird .htm (accessed December 2003).

8. World Birding Center. No date. *Green Parakeet*. http://www.tpwd.tx.us/worldbirdingcenter/bird_info/ green_parakeet.phtml (accessed 9 December 2003).

9. National Audubon Society. 2002. *The Christmas Bird Count Historical Results*. http://www.audubon.org/ bird/cbc (accessed 9 December 2003).

10. Rich, T. D., C. Beardmore, H. Berlanga, P. Blancher, M. Bradstreet, G. Butcher, D. Demarest, E. Dunn, C. Hunter, E. Inigo-Elias, J. Kennedy, A. Martell, A. Panjabi, D. Pashley, K. Rosenberg, C. Rustay, S. Wendt, and T. Will. 2004. *Partners in Flight North American Landbird Conservation Plan*. Cornell Lab of Ornithology, Ithaca, NY.

11. Muñoz, C.A.R. 2002. *Caracterizacion Geografica de la Familia Psittacidae (Aves) Utilizando un Modelo Predictivo*. Thesis, Universidad Nacional Autónoma de México.

12. World Wildlife Fund. 2001. *Veracruz Moist Forests (NT0176)*. http://www.worldwildlife.org/wild world/profiles/terrestrial/nt/nt0176_full.html (accessed 9 December 2003).

13. World Wildlife Fund. 2001. *Tamaulipan Mesquital (NA1312)*. http://www.worldwildlife.org/wild world/profiles/terrestrial/na/na1312_full.html (accessed 9 December 2003).

14. SEMARNAP. 2000. *Proyecto Para la Conservacion, Manejoy Approvechamiento Sustentable de Los*

Psitacidos en Mexico. Instituto Nacional de Ecologia, Mexico City, Mexico.

15. Mumford, D.L. 1992. Parrot Trade. *TED Case Studies*, Volume 2, Number 1. http://www.american.edu/TED/PARROT.HTM (accessed 10 December 2003).

16. The Nature Conservancy. 2003. *Lennox Foundation Southmost Preserve.* The Nature Conservancy. http://nature.org/wherewework/northamerica/states/texas/preserves/art6685.html (accessed 10 December 2003).

17. U.S. Fish and Wildlife Service. 2001. *Lower Rio Grande Valley National Wildlife Refuge.* http://southwest.fws.gov/refuges/texas/lrgv.html (accessed 10 December 2003).

18. Williamson, R. 2003. $1M Tapped for Refuge—Funds Set to Aid Purchase of New Land. *The Monitor*, Monday, 3 November 2003. http://www.themonitor.com/NewsPub/News/Stories/2003/11/03/10679210872.shtml (accessed 10 December 2003).

19. The Nature Conservancy. 2001. *3M Foundation Gives $5.1 Million to Protect Vanishing Habitat.* The Nature Conservancy. http://nature.org/pressroom/press/press237.html (accessed 10 December 2003).

20. The Valley Land Fund. No date. *Land Conservation.* http://www.valleylandfund.com/conservation.html (accessed 10 December 2003).

21. The World Birding Center. No date. *A Grand Vision Takes Flight.* http://www.tpwd.state.tx.us/worldbirdingcenter/about_us/index.phtml (accessed 9 December 2003).

22. Sosa, V.J., A. Hernandez, and A. Contreras. No date. *Gomez Farias Region and El Cielo Biosphere Reserve.* http://www.nmnh.si.edu/botany/projects/cpd/ma/ma9.htm (accessed 9 December 2003).

23. Chilton, C.S. No date. *The First 70 Years—A History of Higher Education in Brownsville.* http://pubs.utb.edu/anniversary/first70years/chapter-6.htm (accessed 10 December 2003).

24. Walker, S.L. 1997. *Ecotourism Demand and Supply in El Cielo Biosphere Reserve, Tamaulipas, Mexico.* Thesis, Southwest Texas State University.

25. U.S. Fish and Wildlife Service International Affairs. 1999. *Grants Awarded in 1999.* http://international.fws.gov/whp/annex1.html (accessed 9 December 2003).

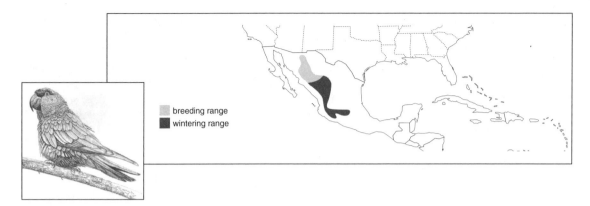

legend:
breeding range
wintering range

THICK-BILLED PARROT (*Rhynchopsitta pachyrhyncha*)

Breaking the traditional stereotype of the tropical nature of parrots, the Thick-billed Parrot inhabits high-elevation coniferous forests of northwestern Mexico and formerly occurred at least occasionally in the border regions of the southwest U.S. Intensive logging of its habitat (which it once shared with the now extinct Imperial Woodpecker) and continued taking of birds for the wild bird trade have resulted in major declines.

STATUS AND DISTRIBUTION

Current breeding range within the Sierra Madre Occidental of Mexico extends from northwest Chihuahua and northeast Sonora south to northwest Durango. Historically, birds may have also bred in mountains of southern Arizona and southwest New Mexico though the species had essentially disappeared from the U.S. before any thorough ornithological investigations of its status there were carried out. Flocks containing up to 1,500 individuals did sometimes occur in the U.S. and the species was reliably reported from Arizona until at least 1938. A small flock was also seen in the Animas Mountains of New Mexico in 1964. A program to reintroduce the species to the U.S. using individuals confiscated from the illegal bird trade was started in Arizona in 1986 but was unsuccessful because of behavioral problems and disease associated with captive birds and was discontinued in 1993. Some reintroduced birds did breed in the wild and some were known to have persisted into the late 1990s. A single Thick-billed Parrot that was discovered at the southwestern New Mexico ranch of Ted Turner in 2003 may have been a survivor or offspring from these introduced birds or an escape from an illegal bird trader

(though it is possible that it was a wild bird from Mexico as well). Although not well studied, it is thought that in winter populations usually (but not always) retreat south and occur in high-elevation forests of the Mexican states of Durango, Sinaloa, Nayarit, Jalisco, Colima, and Michoacán. The species is also thought to make irregular movements in response to low food supplies, sometimes moving relatively large distances (perhaps as much as 100 miles or more).

Important sites for the species in Mexico include the following Important Bird Areas (IBAs) in the state of Chihuahua: Cebadillas (100+ nests), Maderas Chihuahua (50+ individuals in 2003), Mesa de Guacamayas (100 individuals), and Sierra del Nido. Important sites in other Mexican states include the Sistema de Islas Sierra Madre Occidental IBA in Sonora, the Alamos-Río Mayo IBA in Sinaloa, the Baserac-Sierra Tabaco-Río Bavispe IBA in Sonora and Chihuahua, the Las Bufas, Parte Alta del Río Humaya, San Juan de Camarones, Río Presidio-Pueblo Nuevo, and Guacamayita IBAs all in Durango, El Carricito IBA in Jalisco, and the Tancitaro IBA in Michoacán. Although not identified as an IBA, several areas of old-growth forest in the Sierra Tarahumara region of southwest Chihuahua are known to host migrating groups of Thick-billed Parrots, including Pino Gordo and Coloradas de la Virgen. The lands within these areas are virtually all private or communally owned lands and there are few protected areas within the range and habitat of the species.

Although there has been no standardized survey in place to detect changes in abundance of Thick-billed Parrots, it is clear that the species has greatly declined. An estimated 99.5% of the pine-oak forest within the species' breeding range had been at least partially logged by 1995. In the U.S., the species once appeared in flocks as high as 1,500 birds but birds had virtually disappeared by the 1930s. A waterfall that was frequented by thousands of the birds in Chihuahua hosted only a small number of birds in recent years. The species' total population size was estimated at 1,000–4,000 in 1996.[1-10]

ECOLOGY

The thick-billed Parrot could well be called the "Pine Parrot" as it, like the closely related Maroon-fronted Parrot, relies almost solely on pine seeds for food. The birds occur in pine-oak, pine, fir, and Douglas fir forests in Sierra Madre Occidental mountains at elevations ranging from 4,000 to 11,500 feet. Most nests of the species have been found at elevations above 7,500 feet. Females lay 2–3 eggs in a cavity in a dead tree snag or dead portion of a live tree. Most nests are in Douglas fir or one of several species of pine but also sometimes in aspen, firs, and oaks and possibly in holes in cliffs. Incubation lasts 25–28 days and only the female incubates. Young leave the nest 59–65 days after hatching but are dependent on adults for many months as the young must learn the apparently difficult task of extracting pine seeds from cones before they are fully independent. Birds feed almost exclusively on pine seeds but occasionally also eat seeds from Douglas fir as well as acorns, conifer buds, and cherries. Nesting of the birds is closely tied to the periods of availability of pine seeds with egg laying in late June and July and young fledging in October. After the breeding season they aggregate into flocks that once numbered in the hundreds or thousands. Birds seem to leave the breeding range in October and November and return in April and May. It is speculated that some birds may travel as much as 600 miles between breeding and wintering areas but movements are poorly understood. Birds can survive in forests that have been partially logged or logged over long cycles if large standing nesting trees remain and there are adequate mature pines in the area for foraging. However, because of the difficulty young birds have in learning to feed on their own, the young may suffer from high mortality if pine forest foraging areas are fragmented, scattered, or unhealthy, or do not contain enough large, mature trees.[1,3,6,11]

THREATS

The greatest current threats are from continued logging of remaining mature and old-growth pine-oak forest within Sierra Madre Occidental and from illegal capture of birds for wild bird trade. An estimated 99.5% of the original old-growth forest within the region had been logged at least once between 1880 and 1995. Approximately 140,000 acres of old-growth pine-oak forest were estimated to remain in 1995 but only about 5,500 acres of old-growth habitat remained on high-elevation plateaus (above 7,500 feet) that once provided the largest expanses of the prime habitat for Thick-billed Parrots as well as for the now extinct Imperial Woodpecker. Virtually all habitat within the species' breeding and wintering ranges is within communally owned land cooperatives (ejidos) or under private ownership and is subject to continued logging. The only two of the handful of small protected areas in the region in which Thick-billed Parrots are known to occur are the Ajos Bavispe National Forest and Wildlife Refuge (450,000 acres) within the Sistema de Islas Sierra Madre Occidental IBA in Sonora and the Tancitaro National Park (58,000 acres) in Michoacán. Some patches of old-growth forest are known to remain in the Cebadillas, El Carricito, Las Bufas, and Baserac-Sierra Tabaco-Rio Bravispe IBAs. In addition, in many forests the dead trees used by parrots for nesting have virtually all been removed for use in paper mill operations. In the southern part of the state of Chihuahua there was much loss of habitat from drug-growing operations, logging, and cattle-grazing in the early 1990s. The Pino Gordo Ejido and the Communidad Coloradas de la Virgen have been the victims of a series of corrupt activities of various government agencies and commissions, some recently involving a local drug cartel, all carried out to establish control over the remaining old-growth forest to continue commercial logging of the site. The Pino Gordo Ejido is a cooperative of an indigenous group (the Tarahumaras) who, beginning in 1994, decided to maintain the 71,0000-acre site as a protected area. Similarly, the Communidad Coloradas de la Virgen is made up of indigenous Tarahumaras who want to protect the remaining old-growth forests in the area from logging. In recent years Tarahumaras leaders from Coloradas de la Virgen have been killed or jailed following protests to stop logging operations. Much of the deforestation is fueled by the need to provide timber for a paper mill in Chihuahua that expanded its capacity using a $175 million dollar loan from Chase Manhattan Bank. Most of the paper produced by the mill is shipped north into the U.S.

Although apparently somewhat less of a threat than in the past, trapping of adult birds and capture of young from nests for the caged bird trade does continue. Both within-country sale and export of the species is illegal. During recent studies of nesting biology of the species some nest trees were robbed of young, including some in which the nest trees were felled to obtain the birds.

Human-induced changes in fire regimes within the pine-oak ecosystems of the Sierra Madre Occidental have only recently been studied and may have had an influence on ecosystem dynamics that, in association with widespread logging, may reduce food supplies and availability of snags for nesting for Thick-billed Parrots.

In the U.S. portion of the former range the species was indiscriminately shot whenever it appeared during the late 1800s and early 1900s. For example, in 1917–1888 about 100 of the 300 Thick-billed Parrots that were found at Pinery Canyon, Arizona were shot. Hunting is not considered a major threat anywhere in the range today.[1,6,8–10,12–18]

CONSERVATION ACTION

Perhaps the most significant conservation action for the species that has been achieved to date is the negotiation of a 15-year conservation easement on 6,000 acres owned by a local ejido within the Cebadillas IBA that harbors one of the largest known breeding populations of Thick-billed Parrots. The agreement, which took several years to negotiate, provided $240,000 to the ejido cooperative for not allowing any logging in the tract for 15 years (until 2015). Funds were provided by the Wildlands Project, Pronatura, and Naturalia.

A 1996 report recommended pursuing active protection of the three largest remaining areas of old-growth habitat in the Sierra Madre Occidental. These were Sierra Tabaco-Río Bavispe in Sonora (the largest roadless area in the region), Las Bufas in Durango, and El Carricito in Jalisco. The Sierra Madre Alliance was reportedly working to protect an old-growth stand within the Baserac-Sierra Tabaco-Río Bavispe IBA in Sonora. A logging contract had been obtained to log 375 acres of old-growth forest in Sierra Tabaco but cutting

had not started as of 1995 because of logistical difficulties. A nonprofit organization, Bosque Antiguo, is working with indigenous communities in El Carricito to prevent logging of the old-growth forests there as well as to develop a protected area designation for some or all of the area. The local indigenous community declared part of the area a conservation area and Bosque Antiguo purchased 921 acres in the area and has hired a guard and started construction of a research facility.

The Sierra Madre Alliance and CASMAC (Consejo Asesor de la Sierra Madre) are among organizations that have spearheaded efforts to return ownership and control of land illegally taken from Tarahumara ejido cooperatives at Pino Gordo and Coloradas de la Virgen so that remaining old-growth forest stands can be preserved.

In the U.S. the species' long-term prospects rely completely on ensuring a healthy population within its Mexican breeding range. Much of the remaining appropriate habitat within the U.S. is already within protected areas. A reintroduction program using birds confiscated from illegally held cage birds resulted in several successful nests but introduced birds experienced high mortality from predators and many were found to be diseased and in weakened state. Several zoos maintain captive flocks of Thick-billed Parrots and have successfully bred birds in captivity. It has been recommended that future reintroduction efforts in the U.S. use wild birds relocated from healthy populations of Thick-billed Parrots in Mexico.

There is an intensive ongoing research program to study the nesting ecology and status of Thick-billed Parrots in several regions of Mexico led by researchers at the Instituto Tecnológico de Estudios Superiores de Monterrey (ITESM) with funding from a variety of sources including the Division of International Affairs of the U.S. Fish and Wildlife Service. Some research has been initiated more recently into the role of fire in the forests of the Sierra Madre Occidental and the influence of widespread cattle grazing within forests on fire frequency.[1,6,11,14–24]

CONSERVATION NEEDS

- Protect remaining areas of old-growth forest and IBAs supporting Thick-billed Parrots within the Sierra Madre Occidental.
- Prohibit further cutting of dead snags within Thick-billed Parrot nesting areas.

- Develop nonforestry-related economic incentives for local communities within the Sierra Madre Occidental to relieve logging pressure.
- Develop long-term landscape level forest management plan for areas that will continue to be used as industrial forest land to maintain a mosaic of different age stands of pine-oak forest including mature forest.
- Develop baseline inventory of Thick-billed Parrot populations in the Sierra Madre Occidental of Mexico.
- Implement research on limiting factors for Thick-billed Parrot populations.
- Continue research on the ecological need for fire within the Sierra Madre Occidental pine-oak ecosystem.

References

1. Snyder, N.F.R., E.C. Enkerlin-Hoeflich, and M.A. Cruz-Nieto. 1999. Thick-billed Parrot (*Rhynchopsitta pachyrhyncha*). In *The Birds of North America*, No. 406 (A. Poole and F. Gill, eds.). The Birds of North America, Inc., Philadelphia, PA.

2. American Bird Conservancy. 2003. Ted Turner Hosts Rare Parrot. *Bird Calls* 7:6.

3. Forshaw, J.M. 1989. *Parrots of the World*, 3rd. ed. Lansdowne Editions, Willoughby, Australia.

4. Juniper, T., and M. Parr. 1998. *Parrots: A Guide to Parrots of the World*. Yale University Press, New Haven, CT.

5. Howell, S.N.G., and S. Webb. 1995. *A Guide to the Birds of Mexico and Northern Central America*. Oxford University Press, New York, NY.

6. Lammertink, J.M., J.A. Rojas-Tome, F.M. Cassillas-Orona, and R.L. Otto. 1996. *Status of Conservation of Old-growth Forests and Endemic Birds in the Pine-Oak Zone of the Sierra Madre Occidental, Mexico*. Technical Report No. 69, Institute for Systematics and Population Biology, University of Amsterdam, The Netherlands.

7. CONABIO. 2002. *Áreas de Importancia para la Conservación de las Aves (AICAS)*. http://conabioweb .conabio.gob.mx/aicas/doctos/aicas.html (accessed 9 December 2003).

8. Miller, A.M., and R. Gingrich. No date. *Ejido Pino Gordo: Endangered Habitat and Biological Diversity of Southwestern Chihuahua, Mexico*. Sierra Madre Alliance, El Paso, TX.

9. Sierra Madre Alliance. 2003. *Sierra Madre Alliance*. http://www.sierramadrealliance.org_(accessed 12 December 2003).

10. BirdLife International. 2000. *Threatened Birds of the World*. Lynx Editions and BirdLife International, Barcelona, Spain, and Cambridge, UK.

11. Monterrubio, T., E. Enkerlin-Hoeflich, and R.B. Hamilton. 2002. Productivity and Nesting Success of Thick-billed Parrots. *Condor* 104:788–794.

12. World Wildlife Fund. 2001. *Sierra Madre Occidental Pine-Oak Forests (NA0302)*. http://www.world wildlife.org/wildworld/profiles/terrestrial/na/na0302_full .html (accessed 12 December 2003).

13. The Nature Conservancy. No date. *Ajos Bavispe National Forest and Wildlife Refuge, Mexico*. Parks In Peril Program, the Nature Conservancy, Arlington, VA.

14. Sierra Club. 2003. *International Campaigns: Mexico*. http://www.sierraclub.org/human-rights/mexico/ activists_framed.asp (accessed 12 December 2003).

15. Johnson, D. 2003. Fighting Decades of Deforestation and Violence in the Mountains of Chihuahua. *The Texas Observer*, 7 November 2003. http://www.texas observer.org/showArticle.asp?ArticleID=1482 (accessed 12 December 2003).

16. Hitt, S. 1995. Mexico's Tarahumara Fight Drugs and Loggers. *Earth Island Journal*, Spring 1995.

17. Monterrubio, T. 2001. *Efforts to Preserve the Thick-billed Parrot in Northwestern Mexico*. http://www .theparrotsocietyuk.org/thickbilled.htm (accessed 11 December 2003).

18. Fule, P.Z., and W.W. Covington. 1999. Fire Regime Changes in La Michilia Biosphere Reserve, Durango, Mexico. *Conservation Biology* 13:1523–1739.

19. Enkerlin-Hoeflich, E.C. 2000. *Conservation Triumph for the Thick-billed Parrot*. WorldTwitch. http:// worldtwitch.virtualave.net/thick-billed_parrot.htm (accessed 11 December 2003).

20. McDonnell, A., and K. Vicariu. 2000. Ejidos Cebadillas, Imperiled Parrots, and an Historic Conservation Partnership. *WildEarth*, Spring 2000.

21. Biodiversity Support Program. No date. *BSP's Latin America & Caribbean Program*. http://www.bspon line.org/programs/latin/elcarricito.html (accesed 16 December 2003).

22. Eco-Index. 2002. *Biological Conservation and Culture of El Carricito*. http://www.eco-index.org/ search/results.cfm?projectID=1 (accessed 16 December 2003).

23. Sacremento Zoo. 2002. *Sacramento Zoo's Naturalistic Habitat Opens: New Aviary for Thick-billed Parrots*. http://www.saczoo.com/2_new/press_releases/ (accessed 11 December 2003).

24. U.S. Fish and Wildlife Service International Affairs. 1999. *Grants Awarded in 1999*. http://interna tional.fws.gov/whp/annex1.html (accessed 12 December 2003).

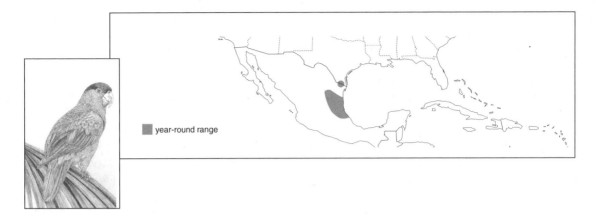

year-round range

RED-CROWNED PARROT (*Amazona viridigenalis*)

A species with a very restricted natural range in northeastern Mexico, Red-crowned Parrot has been a popular cage bird, with the result that escaped birds have established breeding populations in several urban centers within the U.S. Sadly, there may now be more birds in feral populations than in populations within the native range.

STATUS AND DISTRIBUTION

A very restricted range species that now occurs in urban areas of the Rio Grande Valley of southeastern Texas and in the Mexican states of Tamaulipas and Nuevo León south to northeast Veracruz. Populations now breeding in the urban Rio Grande Valley of southeastern Texas are probably mainly attributable to escaped or released captive birds but some proportion are now thought to have come from the native Mexican population located 180 miles south. Introduced populations now also breed in several cities in northeastern Mexico, in southern California, and in southern Florida as well as in Hawaii and Puerto Rico. The species is resident but some populations may make irregular seasonal movements based on food availability.

Important sites include the Sierra de Tamaulipas, Parras de la Fuente, Cerro del Metate, and Desembocadura del Rio Soto La Marina Important Bird Areas (IBA) and the El Cielo Biosphere Reserve, all in the Mexican state of Tamaulipas. Other sites where the species occurs include the Sierra del Abra IBA in San Luis Potosí and the Sierra Gorda Biosphere Reserve in Querétaro. In the U.S. the species occurs most commonly in urban and suburban areas around Brownsville, Weslaco, and McAllen, Texas but does occur rarely at some natural areas, including the Santa Ana National Wildlife Refuge, which abuts the Mexican border. Christmas Bird Count (CBC) totals for the species in south Texas have ranged from 9 to 272 birds since 1990. More than 2,600 birds occur in southern California and several hundred are estimated from southern Florida.

Between 1990 and 2003 the CBC at Gómez Farías within the El Cielo Biosphere Reserve has shown wide variability in the numbers of Red-crowned Parrots tallied, ranging from 0 to 124. There is no trend information available for the species but it is thought to have declined because of the loss of habitat to agriculture, but, especially over the last several decades, from capture for the wild bird trade. The species' total population size in its native range was estimated at 3,000–6,500 individuals from 1992 to 1994.[1–10]

ECOLOGY

In the south Texas portion of the range, this bird occurs in urban areas with large shade trees, which are favored for roosting and nesting. In Mexico, it occurs most commonly in lowland (below 1600 feet) subtropical deciduous forest, but also uses Tamaulipan thorn scrub, especially in areas with larger trees along streams and rivers and in ravines. Nests in cavities of a wide variety of tree species. Often uses cavities excavated by other bird species, especially woodpeckers. Birds lay 2–5 eggs that are incubated for 25–31 days. Young are typically fed twice a day. Young leave the nest 53 days after hatching but remain dependent on adults for another 3–4 months. Birds eat a variety of fruit, seeds, nuts, and berries and in Mexico have occasionally been found eating cultivated corn. In the nonbreeding season birds gather in large flocks.[1–3,11]

THREATS

In northeastern Mexico the greatest threats are from capture of birds for the cage bird trade and from loss of forest habitat from clearing for agriculture or forestry. Capture of birds for cage bird trade is now thought to be the greatest threat to the species. Red-crowned Parrots are popular cage birds and more than 30,000 birds were estimated to have been legally or illegally exported from Mexico between 1970 and 1982. Another 25,000 were estimated to have died in the process of capture and captivity during that same time period. It is now illegal to export the species but they are regularly illegally exported to various countries around the world. An estimated 25,000 parrots of various species are smuggled across the U.S.–Mexico border annually, with at least another 25,000 that die in transport. An unknown number of these are Red-crowned Parrots.

A habitat model for the species developed from specimen records suggests that 31% of its habitat in Mexico has been lost and another study of habitat within the species range estimated that less than 17% of the original vegetation remains. Clearly the loss and degradation of habitat has been severe throughout most of the species range. Only an estimated 2% of the Tamaulipan Mezquital Ecoregion that encompasses the northern portion of the range is considered intact habitat and no blocks of habitat larger than 62,500 acres remain. This loss of native habitat has been largely through conversion to agriculture and as much as a quarter of the little remaining habitat may be altered by this activity in the next two decades. Protected areas within the region are small and mostly confined to the U.S. side of the Rio Grande in southernmost Texas. About 20% of the habitat within the Veracruz Moist Forests Ecoregion that encompasses the southern portion of the range is considered intact. Over 4.6 million acres of forest were logged in the Mexican state of Veracruz between 1900 and 1987. The only protected area within the ecoregion, El Cielo Biosphere Reserve, is chronically underfunded and continues to suffer from unregulated cattle grazing and illegal harvest of plants and animals. The core areas of the reserve are mostly high-elevation habitat that is not used extensively by Red-crowned Parrot. The Lower Rio Grande Valley of Texas, where the species now occurs, has little remaining natural habitat.[1,11–16]

CONSERVATION ACTION

The species is listed in Appendix I and II of the Convention on International Trade in Endangered Species of Wild Fauna and Flora (CITES). CITES is an international agreement between federal governments to regulate and monitor international trade in species listed in the Appendices. It is now illegal to capture and export the species from Mexico. Unfortunately, the species is still widely taken illegally, especially on private lands where perhaps the bulk of the population occurs.

At the Sierra Gorda Biosphere Reserve a conservation group called the Grupo Ecológico Sierra Gorda has implemented a major series of education, outreach, and conservation initiatives throughout the 600 communities within the reserve. From 1989 to 1998 courses on ecology and conservation had reached more than 17,000 students in 193 schools and more than 20,000 environmental awareness meetings were held with adults. Over 3,700 acres of land have been reforested by planting more than three million native trees on lands originally cleared for agriculture. This multifaceted approach is undoubtedly improving habitat and hopefully decreasing parrot poaching activity within the Reserve.

In northeastern Mexico, conservation initiatives within the low-elevation habitats used by Red-crowned Parrots are limited. The State of Tamaulipas declared El Cielo a Biosphere Reserve in 1985, and in 1987 it was recognized within the UNESCO-Man and the Biosphere Reserve Network. However, there is little funding (one employee) for reserve management, education, enforcement, and research activities within the reserve and most of the protected habitat is at higher elevations. In the 1980s the Gorgas Research Foundation acquired the 250-acre Rancho el Cielito to protect some of the last remaining lowland tropical forest in the area. The U.S. Fish and Wildlife Service Division of International Affairs has provided funding to a local nongovernmental organization called Terra Nostra over several years for a project to develop and promote ecotourism as a conservation tool for El Cielo. Through this work a small hotel and restaurant/

store were built in one community within the Reserve. The area has become increasingly popular for birding because of its relatively close proximity to the U.S. border (within a day's drive) but most visitors to the reserve are Mexican citizens.

Within the Lower Rio Grande Valley of Texas there are several initiatives underway to increase the amount of natural habitat for wildlife through purchase of remaining fragments of native habitat and through restoration of degraded habitat. The U.S. Fish and Wildlife Service has continued to purchase lands to connect the natural existing tracts of habitat left along the Lower Rio Grande within the Lower Rio Grande National Wildlife Refuge, which has grown to 90,000 acres in 112 separate parcels since its establishment in 1979. In 2003 it was announced that an additional $1 million had been allocated by Congress for additional land acquisition from willing sellers.

Nongovernmental conservation groups are also active in the Lower Rio Grande Valley of Texas, including the Nature Conservancy, which has purchased the 1,035-acre Southmost Preserve near Brownsville and the 243-acre Chihuahua Woods Preserve near Mission. Another organization, the Valley Land Fund, has worked with partners since 1987 to protect over 5,000 acres within the valley. The World Birding Center was established in Harlingen, Texas in the 1990s to promote birding and conservation within the Lower Rio Grande Valley as a way to show local communities that land conservation has great economic and social benefits for those communities.[1,6,16–26]

CONSERVATION NEEDS

- Develop incentives for private landowners to maintain forest habitat on their lands and to prevent illegal harvesting of nestling parrots for cage bird trade.
- Provide education and outreach about the need for landowners with private forest lands used by parrots to allow growth of tree seedlings for long-term maintenance of healthy forests.
- Develop baseline inventory of Red-crowned Parrot populations in northeastern Mexico and in southern Texas.
- Continue research on limiting factors for Red-crowned Parrot populations.

- Study the ecology and genetics of Red-crowned Parrots in south Texas and Mexico.
- Increase land conservation efforts within Tamaulipas and Veracruz in Mexico and continue land conservation initiatives in the U.S. side of Lower Rio Grande Valley.

References

1. Enkerlin-Hoeflich, E.C., and K.M. Hogan. 1997. Red-crowned Parrot (*Amazona viridigenalis*). In *The Birds of North America*, No. 292 (A. Poole and F. Gill, eds.). The Academy of Natural Sciences, Philadelphia, PA, and the American Ornithologists' Union, Washington, DC.

2. Forshaw, J.M. 1989. *Parrots of the World*, 3rd ed. Lansdowne Editions, Willoughby, Australia.

3. Juniper, T., and M. Parr. 1998. *Parrots: A Guide to Parrots of the World*. Yale University Press, New Haven, CT.

4. Howell, S.N.G., and S. Webb. 1995. *A Guide to the Birds of Mexico and Northern Central America*. Oxford University Press, New York, NY.

5. Pranty, B., and K.L. Garrett. 2003. The Parrot Fauna of the ABA Area: A Current Look. *Birding* 35:248–261.

6. BirdLife International. 2000. *Threatened Birds of the World*. Lynx Editions and BirdLife International, Barcelona, Spain, and Cambridge, UK.

7. CONABIO. 2002. *Áreas de Importancia para la Conservación de las Aves (AICAS)*. http://conabioweb .conabio.gob.mx/aicas/doctos/aicas.html (accessed 9 December 2003).

8. Igl, L. D. 2003. *Bird Checklists of the United States* (Version 12MAY03). Northern Prairie Wildlife Research Center Home Page, Jamestown, ND. http:// www.npwrc.usgs.gov/resource/othrdata/chekbird/chek bird.htm (accessed 9 December 2003).

9. World Birding Center. No date. *Green Parakeet*. http://www.tpwd.tx.us/worldbirdingcenter/bird_info/ green_parakeet.phtml (accessed 9 December 2003).

10. National Audubon Society. 2002. *The Christmas Bird Count Historical Results*. http://www.audubon .org/bird/cbc (accessed 9 December 2003).

11. Muñoz, C.A.R. 2002. *Caracterizacion Geografica de la Familia Psittacidae (Aves) Utilizando un Modelo Predictivo*. Thesis, Universidad Nacional Autonoma de Mexico.

12. Iñigo-Elias, E.E., and M.A. Ramos. 1991. The Psittacine Trade in Mexico. Pages 380–392 in *Neotropical Wildlife Use and Conservation* (J.G. Robinson and K.H. Redford, eds.). University of Chicago Press, Chicago, IL.

13. Mumford, D.L. 1992. *Parrot Trade*. TED Case Studies, Volume 2, Number 1. http://www.american.edu/TED/PARROT.HTM (accessed 10 December 2003).

14. World Wildlife Fund. 2001. *Veracruz Moist Forests (NT0176)*. http://www.worldwildlife.org/wildworld/profiles/terrestrial/nt/nt0176_full.html (accessed 9 December 2003).

15. World Wildlife Fund. 2001. *Tamaulipan Mesquital (NA1312)*. http://www.worldwildlife.org/wildworld/profiles/terrestrial/na/na1312_full.html (accessed 9 December 2003).

16. Walker, S.L. 1997. *Ecotourism Demand and Supply in El Cielo Biosphere Reserve, Tamaulipas, Mexico*. Thesis, Southwest Texas State University.

17. Rich, T. 2001. Holistic Conservation in the Sierra Gorda Biosphere Reserve. *Birdscapes*, Fall 2001.

18. Sosa, V.J., A. Hernandez, and A. Contreras. No date. *Gomez Farias Region and El Cielo Biosphere Reserve*. http://www.nmnh.si.edu/botany/projects/cpd/ma/ma9.htm (accessed 9 December 2003).

19. Chilton, C.S. No date. *The First 70 Years—A History of Higher Education in Brownsville*. http://pubs.utb.edu/anniversary/first70years/chapter-6.htm (accessed 10 December 2003).

20. U.S. Fish and Wildlife Service International Affairs. 1999. *Grants Awarded in 1999*. http://international.fws.gov/whp/annex1.html (accessed 9 December 2003).

21. U.S. Fish and Wildlife Service. 2001. *Lower Rio Grande Valley National Wildlife Refuge*. http://southwest.fws.gov/refuges/texas/lrgv.html (accessed 10 December 2003).

22. Williamson, R. 2003. $1M Tapped for Refuge—Funds Set to Aid Purchase of New Land. *The Monitor*, Monday, 3 November 2003. http://www.themonitor.com/NewsPub/News/Stories/2003/11/03/10679210872.shtml (accessed 10 December 2003).

23. The Nature Conservancy. 2003. *Lennox Foundation Southmost Preserve*. The Nature Conservancy. http://nature.org/wherewework/northamerica/states/texas/preserves/art6685.html (accessed 10 December 2003).

24. The Nature Conservancy. 2001. *3M Foundation Gives $5.1 Million to Protect Vanishing Habitat*. The Nature Conservancy. http://nature.org/pressroom/press/press237.html (accessed 10 December 2003).

25. The Valley Land Fund. No date. *Land Conservation*. http://www.valleylandfund.com/conservation.html (accessed 10 December 2003).

26. The World Birding Center. No date. *A Grand Vision Takes Flight*. http://www.tpwd.state.tx.us/worldbirdingcenter/about_us/index.phtml (accessed 9 December 2003).

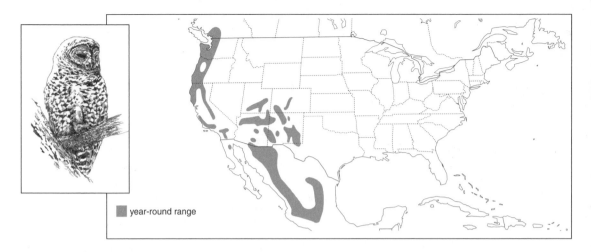

year-round range

SPOTTED OWL (*Strix occidentalis*)

A species of mature and old-growth forests of regions of the western U.S. and Mexico, the Spotted Owl became an icon for the protection of such forests and, therefore, hated by those wishing to harvest those forests because of their high economic value. Despite its federal listing as a Threatened species in the U.S., populations continue to decline.

STATUS AND DISTRIBUTION

Three subspecies (Northern, California, Mexican) have been described that are quite distinct, though there is some very limited intergradation between the Northern and California subspecies in northern California. Northern Spotted Owl is resident from southern British Columbia south through Pacific slope forests to northern California. California Spotted Owl occurs from northern California south through Pacific slope forests and the Sierra Nevadas in increasingly isolated populations to southern California and northern Baja California, Mexico. Mexican Spotted Owl occurs from Utah and Colorado south through the Sierra Madre Occidental and Oriental mountains of Mexico to Michoacán. The range of Mexican Spotted Owl in the U.S. is distributed as a series of isolated populations. In Mexico, populations may be similarly fragmented but they are poorly documented.

Some sites that are known to support concentrations of Northern Spotted Owl include Washington State's Wenatchee National Forest (150 pairs), and the Olympia National Park and Olympia National Forest that together support an estimated 230 pairs of birds, Oregon's Siuslaw National Forest (100 pairs), and California's Klamath National Forest (280 pairs) and Shasta-Trinity National Forest (230 pairs).

Sites supporting California Spotted Owls include a series of 12 National Parks or National Forests stretching across 8.7 million acres of the Sierra Nevadas of California that supports the bulk of the California Spotted Owl population (2,000–3,000 pairs). These sites include the Plumas National Forest (255 pairs), Eldorado National Forest (200 pairs), and the Sierra National Forest (224 pairs). Other sites important for this subspecies include the San Bernardino National Forest (70+ pairs).

The bulk of the population of Mexican Spotted Owl occurs within a band of forest extending from central Arizona east to east central New Mexico. Within this region New Mexico's Gila National Forest and Cibola National Forest and Arizona's Kaibab and Apache Sitgreaves National Forests support the species. Other important sites for the species include Arizona's Coronado National Forest and Fort Huachuca Army Base, New Mexico's Lincoln National Forest (130 pairs), Utah's Zion and Canyonlands National Parks and Manti-La Sal National Forest and Colorado's Mesa Verde National Park. In Mexico the species is known from a number of Important Bird Areas, including the Sistema de Islas Sierra Madre Occidental in Sonora, El Carricito in Jalisco, and Las Bufas in Durango.

In recent years there has been increasing attention to monitoring rangewide population and demographic trends for the species, although monitoring programs have been underway in some local areas for decades. Spotted Owls certainly had to have undergone major declines in abundance since historical times given the extreme loss of its preferred habitat within its range (see threats below). A meta-analysis in 2004 concluded that populations of Northern Spotted Owls were declining overall but that trends varied regionally. Other studies have indicated that adult female survival in the Northern Spotted Owl may be showing a continuing rate of decline, which is indicative of a decline in abundance. No obvious change has occurred in numbers of the Sierra Nevada population of the California Spotted Owl but two populations in southern California have declined. Few data are available for assessing changes in abundance of Mexican Spotted Owl, though in the Mexican portion of the range most of the old-growth habitat it once used has been logged. The species' total population size was estimated at 15,000 individuals in 2000.[1-7]

ECOLOGY

Northern Spotted Owl subspecies breeds in mature and old-growth coniferous forests within coastal mountain ranges of the Pacific coast and northern Sierra Nevada Mountains of California. California Spotted Owl uses a wider habitat spectrum from oak forests at lower elevations to coniferous forests at higher elevations but also requires mature forests. Mexican Spotted Owl occurs in coniferous forests but also in riparian and canyon forests that often contain at least a few coniferous tree species. In all subspecies, birds show preference for older forest ecosystems with diverse structural components. All subspecies nest in cavities in trees or on platforms formed from old raptor or squirrel nests, mistletoe brooms, or accumulated vegetation caught in branches. The 1–4 eggs are incubated by the female for about 30 days. Young normally leave the nest 34–36 days after hatching but are cared for by both parents for an additional 60–90 days. Thereafter, the young disperse at random to locate new territories. A few birds breed in first year but typically show lower nest success than older birds. Most pairs do not breed every year. Major food items are small mammals, especially woodrats and flying squirrels, but Spotted Owls capture a great variety of prey, including insects, small birds, and small reptiles and amphibians.[1]

THREATS

The main threat causing long-term population declines is continued loss of mature and old-growth forest breeding habitat to commercial logging. In some areas owls will use selectively harvested forests that are 40–100 years old (postharvest) if some large trees, snags, and other features remain after harvest, but the majority of forest harvested over last 100 years was rendered unsuitable for the species. Harvest plans for many national forests continue to allow removal of most mature trees, forming forest stands of young trees without the diversity required to support owl populations. About 96% of the forest habitat within the Central Pacific Coastal Forest ecoregion extending along the coast from Oregon north to British Columbia has been lost since prelogging days. Similarly, over 95% of the northern California Redwood forests have been removed. In the Sierra Nevada Mountains of California an estimated 25% of intact natural habitat remains, much of it in the alpine zone above treeline. In Mexico's Sierra Madre Occidental an estimated 99.5% of the original old-growth forest had been logged at least once between 1880 and 1995. In addition, in many forests in the Sierra Madre Occidental dead trees which can be an important component of owl habitat, have virtually all been removed for use in paper mill operations. Catastrophic wildfires that result from decades of fire suppression in forests that are fire-adapted have become a threat in recent years in a few areas. Other potential threats include West Nile virus and competition with expanding Barred Owl populations.[1,3,5-9]

CONSERVATION ACTION

The Northern and Mexican subspecies were federally listed as Threatened in the U.S. in 1990 and 1993. The listing led to increased funding for research and monitoring of the species and consideration of the species' needs in various land management decisions. Similarly, the Northern Spotted Owl is listed as Endangered in Canada and the Mexican Spotted Owl as Threatened in Mexico. Various recovery plans for the Northern Spotted Owl have been developed over several decades and have led to rancorous debate and litigation. The U.S. Fish and Wildlife Service (USFWS) designated critical habitat on public lands for the Northern Spotted Owl in Washington, Oregon, and California in 1992. This designation requires land managers to consider the effects of land management on Spotted Owl populations within these critical habitats. The Northwest Forest Plan adopted in 1994 under the Clinton administration was an attempt to manage the forests in the region using an ecosystem approach and included 16 million acres where logging was to be restricted. However, several organizations filed suit against the USFWS in 2003 charging that some areas designated as critical habitat were being logged in violation of the designations. Several organizations sued and reached an agreement with the USFWS to have a new status review completed for the Northern Spotted Owl because they contend that owls are more abundant than once thought and that more forests could be opened for logging. Fifteen Habitat Conservation Plans had been approved by the USFWS for Northern Spotted Owl as of 2003.

Critical habitat was designated by the US-FWS for the Mexican Spotted Owl in 1995 and 2001 but these designations were challenged in court because the designation did not include 8.7 million acres of public lands that are used by the subspecies. USFWS proposed a new critical habitat designation in November 2003 to comply with a court order from the most recent legal challenge.

The Sierra Nevada Framework was a management plan developed in the 1990's for the federally-owned forests of the Sierra Nevadas that included specific recommendations for the protection of California Spotted Owl habitats. Several groups petitioned the USFWS in 2000 to consider listing the California Spotted Owl as Threatened because of evidence of declines in some populations of the subspecies. The USFWS decided in 2003 that the subspecies would not be listed because the Sierra Nevada Framework provided adequate protection. The petitioning organizations had filed papers in Fall 2003 indicating their intent to sue the USFWS over this decision.

All in all, the conservation and management of the species has been one of the most hotly debated and legally contested of species conservation issues in the history of U.S. conservation. The listing of the species certainly increased the understanding of the species' biology and focused attention on the management of the forest habitats in which it occurs. The subsequent slowdown in the loss of its preferred habitats and changes in forest harvesting strategies logically must have also slowed the species' overall decline. Debate continues as to whether or not existing protections are adequate to maintain populations throughout the species' range over the long term, especially as populations in British Columbia and Washington have shown major declines.[1,10-15]

CONSERVATION NEEDS

- Protect remaining old-growth nesting habitat from any further loss from logging.
- Continue survey techniques to better monitor changes in populations of Spotted Owl.
- Continue research on nest success and survival of Spotted Owl in relation to fragmentation and isolation of nesting habitat patches.
- Implement landscape-level conservation plans.

References

1. Gutiérrez, R.J., A.B. Franklin, and W.S. Lahaye. 1995. Spotted Owl (*Strix occidentalis*). In *The Birds of North America*, No. 179 (A. Poole and F. Gill, eds.). The Academy of Natural Sciences, Philadelphia, PA, and the American Ornithologists' Union, Washington, DC.

2. Howell, S.N.G., and S. Webb. 1995. *A Guide to the Birds of Mexico and Northern Central America*. Oxford University Press, New York, NY.

3. Courtney, S.P., J. A. Blakesley, R. E. Bigley, M. L. Cody, J. P. Dumbacher, R. C. Fleischer, A.B. Franklin, J. F. Franklin, R. J. Gutiérrez, J. M. Marzluff, and L. Sztukowski. 2004. *Scientific Evaluation of the Status of the Northern Spotted Owl*. Sustainable Ecosystems Institute, Portland, OR. http://www.sei.org/owl/finalreport/Owl FinalReport.pdf (accessed 5 January 2006).

4. Chipley, R.M., G.H. Fenwick, M.J. Parr, and D.N. Pashley. 2003. *The American Bird Conservancy Guide to the 500 Most Important Bird Areas in the United States*. Random House, New York, NY.

5. U.S. Fish and Wildlife Service. 1995. *Recovery Plan for the Mexican Spotted Owl*, Vol. 1. Albuquerque, NM.

6. CONABIO. 2002. *Áreas de Importancia para la Conservación de las Aves (AICAS)*. http://conabioweb .conabio.gob.mx/aicas/doctos/aicas.html (accessed 9 December 2003).

7. BirdLife International. 2000. *Threatened Birds of the World*. Lynx Editions and BirdLife International, Barcelona, Spain, and Cambridge, UK.

8. Ricketts T.H., et al. 1999. *Terrestrial Ecoregions of North America: A Conservation Assessment*. Island Press, Washington, DC. 485 pp.

9. World Wildlife Fund. 2001. *Sierra Madre Occidental Pine-Oak Forests (NA0302)*. http://www.world wildlife.org/wildworld/profiles/terrestrial/na/na0302_full .html (accessed 12 December 2003).

10. U.S. Fish and Wildlife Service. 1992. Endangered and Threatened Wildlife and Plants: Determination of Critical Habitat for the Northern Spotted Owl. *Federal Register* 57(10): 1796–1838.

11. U.S. Fish and Wildlife Service. 2003. *California Spotted Owl Doesn't Require ESA Protection, Wildlife Service Concludes*. http://news.fws.gov/newsreleases/r1/ D35554E6-8BC4-44DC-A445B1D42FB29E2C.html (accessed 6 January 2004).

12. U.S. Fish and Wildlife Service. 2003. *Critical Habitat Proposed for Mexican Spotted Owl*. http://news .fws.gov/newsreleases/r2/4CA41277-167E-4FC2-8BB A07AB07ED8A0A.HTML (accessed 19 December 2003).

13. Earthjustice. 2003. *Groups Challenge Logging of Spotted Owl Critical Habitat*. http://www.earthjustice .org/news/display.html?ID=621 (accessed 6 January 2004).

14. Silicon Valley/San Jose Business Journal. 2003. *Spotted Owl Goes to Court*. http://ww.bizjournals.com/ sanjose/stories/2003/09/01/daily20.html (accessed 6 January 2004).

15. U.S. Fish and Wildlife Service. 2003. *More Time Provided to Submit Information for 5-year Reviews of Northern Spotted Owl and Marbled Murrelet*. http://pacific .fws.gov (accessed 6 January 2004).

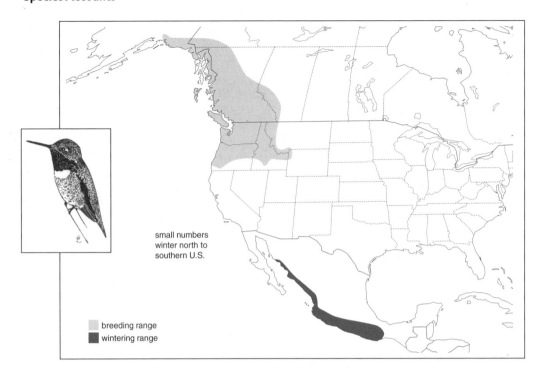

small numbers
winter north to
southern U.S.

breeding range
wintering range

RUFOUS HUMMINGBIRD (*Selasphorus rufus*)

While this species has shown continuing long-term declines in its overall population, there has been an unexplained corresponding increase in winter sightings across the southeastern U.S. Banding studies have begun to unravel some of the mysteries of Rufous Hummingbird migration but reasons for its decline and many aspects of its life history and wintering status are poorly known.

STATUS AND DISTRIBUTION

The Rufous Hummingbird breeding range extends from southern Alaska south through British Columbia and western Saskatchewan to western Montana, Idaho, and northwestern corner of California. Breeding density maps produced from Breeding Bird Survey data indicate highest densities along the coasts of Oregon, Washington, British Columbia, and southeast Alaska. Important breeding sites for this species include Alaska's Tongass and Chugach National Forests, Washington's Olympic National Park and Olympic National Forest, and Oregon's Siuslaw National Forest, Mount Hood National Forest, Willamette National Forest, and Umpqua National Forest.

The species' wintering range (Dec–Jan) extends along Mexico's Pacific coast south to Oaxa-

ca. Small numbers occur from southern California through Arizona and from coastal Texas to northern Florida. There is no available information on wintering densities of Rufous Hummingbird. This species is a winter resident in Sierra de Manantlán Biosphere Reserve in the Mexican states of Jalisco and Colima and occurs during migration in the Sierra Gorda Biosphere Reserve in the Mexican state of Querétaro.

Breeding Bird Survey analysis shows a significant decrease of approximately 55% (2.1 per year) from 1966 to 2005 rangewide. The species' total population was estimated at 6,500,000 individuals in 2004.[1-6]

ECOLOGY

On the breeding range occurs in successional shrub-scrub habitat in openings within forests of the Pacific Northwest and northern Rockies, often on the edges of streams, rivers, and mountain meadows. Males mate with many females and do not participate in nesting or parental care for their young. Females usually lay 2 eggs in an open cup nest built 5–30 feet above ground often in lower branches of conifers but sometimes in hardwoods or shrubs. Eggs are incubated by the female alone for 15–17 days. Only the female feeds the young, which fledge in about 21 days. One brood is produced each season. Species is thought to migrate north from Mexico along Pacific coast from February through April then return south largely through the Rocky Mountains in July and August. On the wintering grounds it has been little studied but is usually found in higher elevation pine-oak forests.[1]

THREATS

Reasons for the continued widespread declines in this species are not well understood. There is some indication that decreases could be related to major habitat losses in parts of the species' range. For example, about 96% of the forest habitat within the Central Pacific Coastal Forest ecoregion extending along the coast from Oregon north to Vancouver Island has been lost since prelogging days. Similarly, in Alaska's Tongass National Forest approximately 90% of the high-volume old growth forest has been logged and 30% of all old growth in the forest is expected to be removed by about 2015. Although flowering plants that provide food often greatly increase in abundance immediately after an area has been logged, studies in some portions of the species' range have shown that the birds are most abundant in either second-growth forests that are 16–120 years of age or in mature forests that are more than 120 years old. Perhaps of even more importance has been the traditional forestry management in much of the region practiced through the 1980s in which after logging, the remaining vegetation and slash was burned or treated with herbicide, then planted with fast-growing Douglas fir. These plantations then were sometimes sprayed with insecticides, and competing vegetation was periodically removed to allow faster growth of planted tree species. This resulted in large expanses of forest that was homogenous and did not have the significant understory or secondary-successional habitat that is a requirement for Rufous Hummingbird. Additionally, these managed forests would be harvested at much shorter intervals so that the necessary components of habitat for the species, including forest gaps, may not have had the opportunity to become established before the forest would again be set back to an early successional stage following tree harvest. Other possible threats include susceptibility to pesticide poisoning, loss of native flowering plant food source from competition with invasive plant species, and habitat loss on wintering grounds. Clearly much work needs to be done to understand which factors are most important in contributing to the species' long-term decline.[1,7,8]

CONSERVATION ACTION

The lack of understanding of the primary factors responsible for the long-term decrease in Rufous Hummingbird populations has made it difficult to develop specific conservation activities to attempt to halt declines. Conservation activities aimed at protecting habitat for Marbled Murrelet and Spotted Owl have likely benefited Rufous Hummingbird in locations of overlap because of protection of large, intact functioning forest ecosystems that include naturally occurring disturbance gaps. In addition, on federally managed lands there has generally been an increase in attempting to mimic natural disturbance regions and to allow more habitat heterogeneity in logged areas.

Partners in Flight Bird Conservation Plans have been completed for Alaska, Idaho, Montana, Oregon, and Washington and have identified Rufous Hummingbird as a priority species in appropriate habitats. These plans have specific recommendations for improving habitat conditions for the suites of species from each of the habitat types within which Rufous Hummingbird regularly occurs.

Conservation activities that are likely to be beneficial to the species are taking place at many locations in the Mexican migratory and wintering range. For example, at the Sierra Gorda Biosphere Reserve a conservation group called the Grupo Ecológico Sierra Gorda has implemented a major series of education, outreach, and conservation initiatives throughout the 600 communities within the reserve. From 1989 to 1998 courses on ecology and conservation had reached more than 17,000 students in 193 schools and more than 20,000 environmental awareness meetings were held with adults. Over 3,700 acres of land have been reforested by the planting of more than three million native trees on lands originally cleared for agriculture.

A coalition of nonprofit organizations, universities, and businesses called Partners in Pollination/Alianza para Polinización was formed in 1995 to increase public awareness of the crucial role of pollinators to ecosystems, to facilitate further research on plant/pollinator interactions, and to increase conservation activities that benefit plant/pollinator conservation. The Arizona-Sonora Desert Museum has a program called Migratory Pollinators and Their Corridors that is carrying out education, community stewardship development, and conservation activities for plant/pollinator systems ranging from Mexico to the U.S.[1,7-13]

CONSERVATION NEEDS

- Increase acreage of forests managed as large, functioning ecosystems.
- Increase adoption of forestry management techniques that mimic natural disturbance regimes and allow maintenance of significant secondary successional understory plant species including flowering plant species important for food supplies.
- Develop baseline inventory of Rufous Hummingbird wintering populations and increase research into limiting factors and causes for declines.

References

1. Calder, W.A. 1993. Rufous Hummingbird (*Selasphorus rufus*). In *The Birds of North America*, No. 53 (A. Poole and F. Gill, eds.). The Academy of Natural Sciences, Philadelphia, PA, and the American Ornithologists' Union, Washington, D.C.

2. Sauer, J. R., J. E. Hines, and J. Fallon. 2005. *The North American Breeding Bird Survey, Results and Analysis 1966–2005*. Version 6.2.2006. USGS Patuxent Wildlife Research Center, Laurel, MD.

3. Rich, T. D., C. Beardmore, H. Berlanga, P. Blancher, M. Bradstreet, G. Butcher, D. Demarest, E. Dunn, C. Hunter, E. Inigo-Elias, J. Kennedy, A. Martell, A. Panjabi, D. Pashley, K. Rosenberg, C. Rustay, S. Wendt, and T. Will. 2004. *Partners in Flight North American Landbird Conservation Plan*. Cornell Lab of Ornithology, Ithaca, NY.

4. Chipley, R.M., G.H. Fenwick, M.J. Parr, and D.N. Pashley. 2003. *The American Bird Conservancy Guide to the 500 Most Important Bird Areas in the United States*. Random House, New York.

6. CONABIO. 2002. *Áreas de Importancia para la Conservación de las Aves (AICAS)*. http://conabioweb.conabio.gob.mx/aicas/doctos/aicas.html (accessed 18 June 2003).

7. Ricketts, T.H., E. Dinerstein, D.M. Olson, C.J. Loucks, et al. 1999. *Terrestrial Ecoregions of North America: A Conservation Assessment*. Island Press, Washington, DC. 485 pp.

8. Oregon/Washington Partners in Flight. No date. *Oregon/Washington LandBird Conservation Plan: Westside Coniferous Forest*. http://community.gorge.net/natres/pif/westside_plan.html (accessed 11 March 2004).

9. Casey, D. 2000. *Partners in Flight Draft Bird Conservation Plan Montana*, Version 1. American Bird Conservancy, c/o Montana Fish, Wildlife, and Parks, Kalispell, MT.

10. Ritter, S. 2000. *Idaho Bird Conservation Plan*, Version 1. Idaho Partners in Flight, Hamilton, MT.

11. Boreal Partners in Flight Working Group. 1999. *Landbird Conservation Plan for Alaska Biogeographic Regions*, Version 1.0. Unpubl. Rep. U.S. Fish and Wildlife Service, Anchorage, AK.

12. Rich, T. 2001. Holistic Conservation in the Sierra Gorda Biosphere Reserve. *Birdscapes* Fall 2001.

13. Arizona-Sonora Desert Museum. 2003. *Migratory Pollinators Program*. http://www.desertmuseum.org/pollination/executive_summary.html (accessed 31 January 2004).

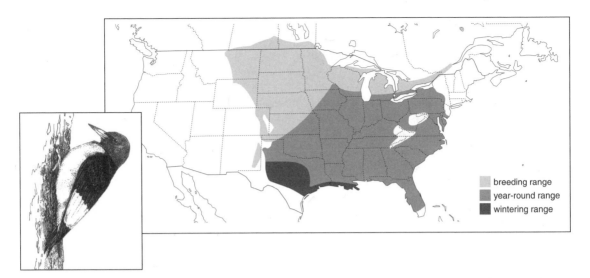

breeding range
year-round range
wintering range

RED-HEADED WOODPECKER (*Melanerpes erythrocephalus*)

One of the most charismatic of birds familiar to backyard birders, the Red-headed Woodpecker is endemic to the eastern U.S. and southern Canada. Once one of the most common birds of towns and cities, it has experienced a long-term rangewide decline.

STATUS AND DISTRIBUTION

The northern edge of the species' range extends from southern Saskatchewan east to southern Québec. From there the range extends south to Texas and east to Florida. Small isolated populations occur in eastern New Mexico. Birds vacate the northern 20% of range and winter slightly to the southwest of the breeding range in Texas. Breeding density maps produced from Breeding Bird Survey data indicate the highest densities in northeastern Missouri and northeastern Nebraska. Wintering density maps produced from Christmas Bird Count data indicate highest densities in northern Missouri, southern Illinois, and southeastern Missouri, eastern Kansas, and northeastern Oklahoma.

Important breeding sites for this species include Wisconsin's Necadah National Wildlife Refuge (NWR); Iowa and Nebraska's DeSoto NWR; Missouri's Swan Lake NWR and Mingo NWR; the Mark Twain NWR Complex (111,000 acres in Illinois, Iowa, and Missouri); Indiana's Jasper Pulaski Fish and Wildlife Area; Tennessee and Kentucky's Reelfoot Lake NWR; and Arkansas's Big Lake NWR.

Breeding Bird Survey analysis shows a significant decrease of approximately 63% (2.6% per year) from 1966 to 2005 rangewide. An analysis of Christmas Bird Count data shows a nonsignificant decrease of 1.0% per year from 1959 to 1988. The species' total population was estimated at 2,500,000 individuals in 2004.[1–6]

ECOLOGY

Occurs in a range of deciduous forest habitats, oak savanna, open pine forest, and grasslands with hedgerows or scattered trees. The main components of these habitats seem to be presence of dead trees or mature trees with dead branches and tops and often a rather open park-like forest with limited understory or along edges near openings. The birds nest in cavities excavated in dead trees or dead branches, usually 20–35 feet above ground. The male does most of the excavation of the cavity. Often will reuse the same nest cavity or the same nest tree for several years. Females lay 4–7 eggs that are incubated by both sexes for 12–14 days. The male does all the incubation at night, the female most during the day. Young are fed by both parents and fledge from the nest in 24–31 days. Young are fed by parents for some time after fledging but are independent by about three weeks. In some part of the range birds will raise a second brood. Said to be the most omnivorous of North American woodpeckers, Red-headed Woodpeckers eat insects, nuts, seeds, fruit, and occasionally eggs, nestlings, and mice. The species is adept at the unwoodpecker-like habitat of flying out from the tops of trees to catch flying insects. Often will key in on outbreaks of insects and was seen to feed on outbreaks of the now extinct Rocky Mountain Grasshopper in the late 1800s. In winter, birds may move unpredictably to find areas with good supplies of acorns, nuts, or other food supplies. Similarly, after fire or some other event that creates a large expanse of appropriate habitat, many birds will arrive and begin nesting. Many aspects of the species' ecology are surprisingly poorly studied given its conspicuous nature.[1]

THREATS

The greatest threat is loss, fragmentation, and degradation of savanna and deciduous forest habitat. Oak-savanna habitat in the midwest U.S., where the species reaches its highest abundance, is one of the most endangered habitats in the U.S., with more than 98% lost since European settlement. In the upper midwest, less than 7,000 acres of the original 7.3 million acres are still in existence today. Much of the remaining oak-savanna habitat is severely degraded by invasive shrubs and lack of fires. The historic loss of habitat from clearing of large tracts of mature southeastern bottomland forest beginning in the 1800s was responsible for the extinction of Ivory-billed Woodpecker and Bachman's Warbler and contributed to a decline of other species associated with this habitat, including the Red-headed Woodpecker. The loss of such habitat in the Mississippi alluvial valley is estimated at 75% or more and in the lower Mississippi valley at more than 80%. Similarly, longleaf pine ecosystems once occupied an estimated 60–90 million acres of the southeast U.S. but have been reduced to less than 3 million acres and are continuing to decline from loss on private lands.

Perhaps of equal concern for the species' survival is the loss of large landscape level functioning ecosystems where small and large-scale natural disturbance patterns can exist in a mosaic that provides enough dead trees for nesting and various nuts, seeds, and fruit for food. Some elements of these disturbance patterns have been mimicked by human changes to the landscape, including development of small-scale family farms in the 1800s with woodlots, fence posts, and shelterbelts as well as some modern forestry practices and urban parks. However, many of these land management practices have changed in the last 50–100 years so that there is less habitat available over the entire range. Habitat loss and fragmentation has increased in certain areas for development of homes, businesses, and the associated infrastructure (roads, utility corridors, etc.). In areas with existing forest land the problem has been further exacerbated by a decrease in frequency and size of fires, which can provide abundant nest sites. Fires are often still seen as negative events by the general public, making it difficult to carry out the crucial controlled fires needed to mimic natural disturbance patterns necessary to provide habitat for the species. Forestry practices that do not allow forests to reach ages where there are abundant dead trees and limbs or that do not leave enough dead and dying trees after harvest limit the number of potential nesting cavities. The required nuts and seeds may also be lacking in forests that have not matured.[1,7–13]

CONSERVATION ACTION

Partners in Flight Bird Conservation Plans have identified Red-headed Woodpecker and the associated suite of oak savanna, bottomland, and upland forest and pine forest bird species as high priorities and have provided recommendations for management, research, and monitoring. No conservation activity has focused solely on the species but a variety of habitat restoration projects for oak savanna, native pine ecosystems, and deciduous forests are likely beneficial to the species. A major movement to restore remaining acreage of oak savanna to healthy condition has been ongoing in the upper midwest and in southern Ontario since the 1980s. Restoration projects are underway at many sites impacting thousands of acres across that region. In Minnesota, the Sherburne NWR has been using prescribed burns to restore its oak-savanna habitat. The Minnesota Department of Natural Resources has an Oak Savanna Landscape Project that has enlisted many private landowners and public land managers in restoring oak-savanna habitat. In Ohio, the Toledo Metroparks maintains the 3,600-acre Oak Openings Preserve, and the Nature Conservancy is working to continue adding acreage to its 575-acre Kitty Todd Preserve. Both organizations are part of the Oak Openings Region Preservation Alliance that focuses on teaching people from local communities how they can help to preserve oak-savanna species. In Illinois, the Chicago

Wilderness coalition has spearheaded numerous oak-savanna restoration projects within the greater Chicago area. In Iowa, the Illinois Natural Heritage Foundation has an ongoing project to restore 80 acres of savanna habitat at its Snyder-Heritage Farm. In Wisconsin, the Pleasant Valley Conservancy has used prescribed burns and manual removal of invasive shrubs to restore oak savanna within its 140 acres. These are just a few examples of many projects that are underway and that demonstrate the high interest in oak-savanna restoration across the region.

Within the Mississippi alluvial valley many projects to purchase or reforest lands are ongoing through many partner agencies and organizations, including the Lower Mississippi Valley Joint Venture, U.S. Fish and Wildlife Service Partners for Wildlife program, the National Resources Conservation Service Wetland Reserve Program, Ducks Unlimited, and the Nature Conservancy. The more widespread adoption of prescribed burns to maintain healthy pine forests on public lands in the southeast U.S. has probably benefited the species. The U.S. Forest Service in its pine forest holdings in the southeast U.S. has implemented longer periods between harvesting of trees and the retention of some old growth trees within harvested areas, which will likely benefit Red-headed Woodpecker.[1,8–10,12,14–25]

CONSERVATION NEEDS

- Increase acreage of restored oak-savanna habitat and maintain it in healthy condition through prescribed burns and other means.
- Increase acreage of forested habitat within the range of Red-headed Woodpecker that is managed to attain conditions beneficial to the species within the context of large, landscape level habitat management plans, especially on public lands.
- Compare habitats resulting from natural disturbances, forestry, and other management practices, and in suburban areas with regard to suitability for Red-headed Woodpecker.
- Increase purchases of land or easements on acreage supporting Red-headed Woodpecker by private conservation groups and government agencies when possible and appropriate.
- Continue research efforts for further refining understanding of the species biology, ecology, and management.
- Develop rangewide inventory and monitoring survey to assess species' status.

References

1. Smith, K.G., J. H. Withgott, and P. G. Rodewald. 2000. Red-headed Woodpecker (*Melanerpes erythrocephalus*). In *The Birds of North America*, No. 518 (A. Poole and F. Gill, eds.). The Birds of North America, Inc., Philadelphia, PA.

2. Sauer, J. R., J. E. Hines, and J. Fallon. 2005. *The North American Breeding Bird Survey, Results and Analysis 1966–2005*, Version 6.2.2006. USGS Patuxent Wildlife Research Center, Laurel, MD.

3. Sauer, J. R., S. Schwartz, and B. Hoover. 1996. The Christmas Bird Count Home Page, Version 95.1. *Patuxent Wildlife Research Center, Laurel, MD.*

4. Chipley, R.M., G.H. Fenwick, M.J. Parr, and D.N. Pashley. 2003. *The American Bird Conservancy Guide to the 500 Most Important Bird Areas in the United States.* Random House, New York, NY.

5. Igl, L. D. 2003. *Bird Checklists of the United States* (Version 12MAY03). Northern Prairie Wildlife Research Center Home Page, Jamestown, ND. http://www.npwrc.usgs.gov/resource/othrdata/chekbird/chekbird.htm (accessed 27 July 2004).

6. Rich, T.D., C. Beardmore, H. Berlanga, P. Blancher, M. Bradstreet, G. Butcher, D. Demarest, E. Dunn, C. Hunter, E. Inigo-Elias, J. Kennedy, A. Martell, A. Panjabi, D. Pashley, K. Rosenberg, C. Rustay, S. Wendt, and T. Will. 2004. *Partners in Flight North American Landbird Conservation Plan.* Cornell Lab of Ornithology, Ithaca, NY.

7. Stein, B.A., L.S. Kutner, and J.S. Adams. 2000. *Precious Heritage: The Status of Biodiversity in the United States.* Oxford University Press, New York, NY. 399 pp.

8. Henderson, R.A., and E.J. Epstein. No date. *Oak Savannas in Wisconsin.* http://biology.usgs.gov/s+t/noframe/m1106.htm (accessed 27 July 2004)

9. Fitzgerald, J.A., J.R. Herkert, and J.D. Brawn. 2000. *Partners in Flight Bird Conservation Plan for the Prairie Peninsula.* American Bird Conservancy, The Plains, VA.

10. Fitzgerald, J.A., B. Busby, M. Howery, R. Klataske, D. Reinking, and D. Pashley. 2000. *Partners in Flight Bird Conservation Plan for the Osage Plains.* American Bird Conservancy, The Plains, VA.

11. Ricketts, T.H., E. Dinerstein, D.M. Olson, C.J. Loucks, et al. 1999. *Terrestrial Ecoregions of North America: A Conservation Assessment.* Island Press, Washington, DC. 485 pp.

12. Hunter, W.C., L. Peoples, and J. Callazo. 2001.

South Atlantic Coastal Plain Partners in Flight Bird Conservation Plan. U.S. Fish and Wildlife Service, Atlanta, GA.

13. Twedt, D.J., and C.R. Loesch. 1999. Forest Area and Distribution in the Mississippi Alluvial Valley: Implications for Breeding Bird Conservation. *Journal of Biogeography* 26:1215–1224.

14. Fitzgerald, J.A., D.N. Pashley, S.J. Lewis, and B. Pardo. 1998. *Partners in Flight Bird Conservation Plan for the Northern Tallgrass Prairie.* American Bird Conservancy, The Plains, VA.

15. Fitzgerald, J.A., and D.N. Pashley. 2000. *Partners in Flight Bird Conservation Plan for the Dissected Till Plains.* American Bird Conservancy, The Plains, VA.

16. Green Legacy. No date. *Transforming Damaged Landscapes.* http://www.rbg.ca/greenlegacy/pages/transforming_central.html (accessed 27 July 2004).

17. U.S. Fish and Wildlife Service. No date. *Sherburne National Wildlife Refuge—Oak Savanna.* http://midwest.fws.gov/sherburne/Oak.htm (accessed 27 July 2004).

18. Minnesota Department of Natural Resources. 2004. *Oak Savanna Landscape Project.* http://www.dnr.state.mn.us/rprp/oaksavanna/challenges.html (accessed 27 July 2004).

19. The Nature Conservancy. 2000. *Oak Openings Region Designated One of America's "Last Great Places."* http://oakopen.org/oLastGreat.htm (accessed 27 July 2004).

20. The Nature Conservancy. 2004. *Kitty Todd Nature Preserve.* http://nature.org/wherewework/north america/states/ohio/preserves/art162.html (accessed 27 July 2004).

21. Stein, S. 1999. *Chicago Wilderness. Illinois Parks and Recreation* 30(5). http://www.lib.niu.edu/ipo/ip990926.html (accessed 27 July 2004).

22. McGovern, M. 2004. *Iowa's Oak Savannas: Rekindling a Relationship.* Iowa Natural Heritage Foundation. http://www.inhf.org/oaksavannas.htm (accessed 27 July 2004).

23. Savanna Oak Foundation, Inc. No date. *Pleasant Valley Conservancy.* http://www.savannaoak.org/history.html (accessed 27 July 2004).

24. Mueller, A.J., D.J. Twedt, and C.R. Loesch. 2000. Development of Management Objectives for Breeding Birds in the Mississippi Alluvial Valley. Pages 12–17 in *Strategies for Bird Conservation: The Partners In Flight Planning Process.* Proceedings of the 3rd Partners in Flight Workshop; 1995 October 1–5; Cape May, NJ (R. Bonney, D.N. Pashley, and R.J. Niles, eds.). Proceedings RMRS-P-16, U.S. Department of Agriculture, Forest Service, Rocky Mountain Reserach Station, Ogden, UT.

25. U.S. Fish and Wildlife Service. 2003. *Recovery Plan for the Red-cockaded Woodpecker* (Picoides borealis), 2nd revision. U.S. Fish and Wildlife Service, Atlanta, GA. 296 pp.

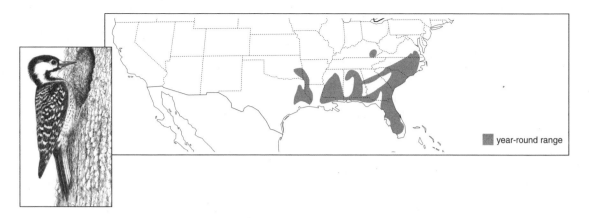

year-round range

RED-COCKADED WOODPECKER (*Picoides borealis*)

This and the Brown-headed Nuthatch, as species endemic to native pine forests of the southeast U.S., are excellent indicator species whose declines mirror the almost catastrophic loss of the native pine ecosystems of the region.

STATUS AND DISTRIBUTION

The southern extent of the Red-cockaded Woodpecker range extends from Florida west to eastern Texas, while the northern edge now extends from Oklahoma east to Virginia. Across the range populations have become extensively fragmented and isolated and now occur as about 75 distinct populations. The species once ranged further north but disappeared from Missouri by 1946, Maryland by 1958, Tennessee by 1994, and Kentucky by 2001 (the last individuals were moved to Arkansas, Georgia, and South Carolina by the U.S. Forest Service).

Among many important breeding areas for the species are Florida's Apalachicola (world's largest population with 619 active clusters) and Osceola National Forests (77 active clusters), and Eglin Air Force Base (313 active clusters). In North Carolina, Croatan National Forest (602 active clusters) and Fort Bragg (384 active clusters) support large populations. South Carolina's Francis Marion National Forest supported 361 active clusters in 2003. In Georgia important sites include Fort Benning (251 active clusters), Fort Stewart (268 active clusters), and Okefenokee National Wildlife Refuge (38 active clusters). Sam Houston National Forest (largest population in Texas, 152 active clusters) and Angelina Na-

tional Forest (58 active clusters) in Texas, Bienville National Forest in Mississippi (95 active clusters), and Kisatchie National Forest in Louisiana (315 active clusters) support core populations, as does the Oakmulgee Division of the Talladega National Forest in Alabama (101 active clusters).

The species is inferred to have suffered massive declines from historic levels as only an estimated 3% of its native pine forest habitat remains intact today and the species is gone from much of the historic range, including loss from some states in recent decades. During the 1970s and 1980s most monitored populations had continued to decline but many populations had stabilized in the 1990s and some showed increases. The species' total population was estimated at 14,500 individuals in 2003.[1-5]

ECOLOGY

Occurs only in mature pine forests in southeast U.S. that have fires at 1- to 5-year intervals. Throughout much of range occurs in long-leaf pine but can also occur in loblolly, slash, shortleaf, Virginia, pond, and pitch pine especially at northern edges of range. Excavates cavities in live 80- to 100-year old pines that are used for roosting and nesting. Are cooperative breeders, a social system unique among North American woodpeckers, in which birds live in family groups (clusters) of 2–5 individuals and in which helpers (usually males from previous broods) provide assistance to the single breeding pair. The nesting cavity is usually the roost cavity of the dominant male. All active roost cavities have small holes—"resin wells"—excavated by the birds in the trunk above and below the hole that exude sap. This forms a sticky barrier that prevents snakes from accessing the cavities to prey on the eggs, young, or adults. Approximately 10–40% of family groups do not breed in any given year. Females lay 2–5 eggs that are incubated by the breeding pair and occasionally by helpers. The incubation period is 10–11 days. Young are fed by both parents and by helpers. Young fledge at 26–29 days but remain at least partially dependent on parents for 2–5 months.[1]

THREATS

The greatest threat is loss, fragmentation, and degradation of mature pine forest habitat. Longleaf pine ecosystems once occupied an estimated 60–90 million acres of the southeast U.S. but have been reduced to less than 3 million acres and are continuing to decline from loss of longleaf forests on private lands. Only about 3% (90,000 acres) of the remaining forest is considered to still be in natural condition and of that, only 3,000–5,000 acres is virgin old-growth habitat. Much of the remaining pine forests are of young age trees and with a greater hardwood component than in the original forests, primarily today because of the lack of fires. Red-cockaded Woodpecker is thought to have survived this major loss of habitat because early logging operations typically left trees with red heart fungus disease or those that would be used for resin production—types of trees favored by woodpeckers for roosting and nesting cavities.

Today the greatest threats to the species in the surviving habitat are from fire suppression and detrimental forestry practices. With fire suppression, not only do hardwood species increase in frequency (to the detriment of the species), but, in the case of longleaf pine, no young trees grow to replace the older trees as they eventually die. Fires continue to be seen as negative events by the general public, making it difficult to carry out the crucial controlled fires needed to ensure the survival of the pine ecosystems upon which Red-cockaded Woodpecker depends. Small populations of the species have continued to disappear from some areas into the 1990s because of habitat degradation caused by fire suppression. Most of the second-growth pines relied upon today by Red-cockaded Woodpecker began growing between 1900 and 1930. As these trees age and die there may be a bottleneck in some forests with a long history of fire suppression during which the species will be increasingly reliant on artificial cavities until enough trees reach appropriate ages.

Forestry practices that have been and remain a threat to the species include the conversion of longleaf pine forests to pine plantations of various species, a practice that began in earnest in the 1940s so that by 1993 there were an estimated 15 million acres in plantations in the Southeast U.S. These plantations do not support Red-cockaded Woodpecker for a variety of reasons, including the fact that the trees are harvested before they reach sufficient age to provide nesting and roosting cavities, but also because virtually all trees are removed at the time of harvest. Logging practices on public lands have been modified over the last several decades so that the needs of Red-cockaded Woodpecker and other species are considered.[1–3,5]

CONSERVATION ACTION

Red-cockaded Woodpecker was federally listed as Endangered in 1973 and recovery plans were written in 1979 and 1985, though the 1979 plan was never adopted. A revised and very detailed recovery plan was adopted in 2003. The listing of the species resulted in a flurry of research activity, making it the most-studied woodpecker species in the world. Despite this, many aspects of its biology and management of pine ecosystems have become well-understood only in the last decade. As a result, many populations of the species declined or disappeared in the first 20 years after the species was listed as Endangered. However, a combination of increases in prescribed burns and hardwood removal from pine ecosystems and the widespread use of artificial nesting and roosting cavities has resulted in stabilization or increases in most of these populations. The increased attention paid to this species on public lands, including many military installations and national forests, is a testament not only to the success of the Endangered Species Act but also to the great ability of a diversity of public agencies to fullfill their missions while maintaining the health of our nation's resources. For example, the U.S. Forest Service has implemented longer periods between harvesting of trees and the retention of some mature trees within harvested areas for the benefit of Red-cockaded Woodpeckers. It is clear, however, that the survival of Red-cockaded Woodpecker is now reliant on the intensive management measures that have been developed, especially provision of artificial cavities, burn management, and mechanical removal of hardwoods in forests that have not been burned. Although many state-owned sites that are important for the species have instituted prescribed burns and removal of hardwoods, many do not have adequate surveys underway to assess the status of populations on their lands so that modifications of management plans or increased efforts can be implemented if numbers are declining. Detailed descriptions of the intricacies of management required to sustain populations of the species are included in the 2003 Red-cockaded Woodpecker Recovery Plan.

While intensive management efforts have continued for the species on public lands, an estimated 23% of the world's Red-cockaded Woodpeckers occurred on private lands as of 2003. Various activities have been targeted toward populations on private lands. The Nature Conservancy, for example, purchased 1,160 acres of mature pine forest in 2000 in Virginia to create the 2,695-acre Piney Grove Preserve that supports 5 active clusters—the northernmost population of the species. The U.S. Fish and Wildlife Service (USFWS) began implementing a private lands conservation strategy in 1992 that focused on entering into cooperative agreements with landowners to stabilize and eventually increase populations on private lands, but also allows landowners some flexibility in managing their lands, especially for timber production. As of 2003, the USFWS had entered into various agreements with 139 private landowners, resulting in protection of 347,439 acres and 509 clusters of Red-cockaded Woodpeckers. The most recent type of private landowner agreement used by the USFWS is called a Safe Harbor Agreement and it allows landowners who work to increase populations of the species on their lands to have the option of engaging in management at a later date that could decrease the population back to the level at the time of the signing of the agreement without worry of prosecution under the Endangered Species Act. Over 200,000 acres of habitat supporting Red-cockaded Woodpecker on private lands from 125 different landowners were enrolled in the Safe Harbor Agreement in 2003. Other agreements include Habitat Conservation Plans, which allow some incidental take of the species in return for efforts to mitigate by establishing new breeding groups at other locations.[1-6]

CONSERVATION NEEDS

- Implement the 2003 Recovery Plan for the species and monitor the success of implementation to ensure that recommendations continue to be followed and that recovery is continuing at a rate that will allow delisting by 2075 as estimated in the Recovery Plan.
- Increase acreage of pine forest habitats especially on private lands and state-owned lands within the range of Red-cockaded Woodpecker that is managed to attain conditions beneficial to the species.
- Continue efforts to provide artificial cavities for Red-cockaded Woodpeckers especially on public lands.
- Increase the number of private landowners enrolled in Safe Harbor Agreements for Red-cockaded Woodpecker.
- Increase annual surveys on state-owned lands and continue surveys on federally-owned lands and private lands covered by USFWS agreements to monitor the health of Red-cockaded Woodpecker populations.
- Increase purchases of land or easements on acreage supporting Red-cockaded Woodpeckers by private conservation groups and government agencies when possible and appropriate.
- Monitor success of mitigation as a tool for maintaining populations of the species.
- Continue research efforts for further refining understanding of the species' biology, ecology, and management.

References

1. Jackson, J.A. 1994. Red-cockaded Woodpecker (*Picoides borealis*). In *The Birds of North America*, No. 85 (A. Poole and F. Gill, eds.). The Academy of Natural Sciences, Philadelphia, PA, and the American Ornithologists' Union, Washington, DC.

2. Costa, R. 2004. Personal communication.

3. BirdLife International. 2000. *Threatened Birds of the World*. Lynx Editions and BirdLife International, Barcelona, Spain, and Cambridge, UK.

4. Chipley, R.M., G.H. Fenwick, M.J. Parr, and D.N. Pashley. 2003. *The American Bird Conservancy Guide to the 500 Most Important Bird Areas in the United States*. Random House, New York, NY.

5. U.S. Fish and Wildlife Service. 2003. *Recovery Plan for the Red-cockaded Woodpecker* (Picoides borealis), 2nd Revision. U.S. Fish and Wildlife Service, Atlanta, GA. 296 pp.

6. The Nature Conservancy. 2000. *Nature Conservancy Adds 1,160 Acres to Red-cockaded Woodpecker Preserve*. http://nature.orb/wherewework/northamerica/states/virginia/press/press130.html (accessed 15 January 2004).

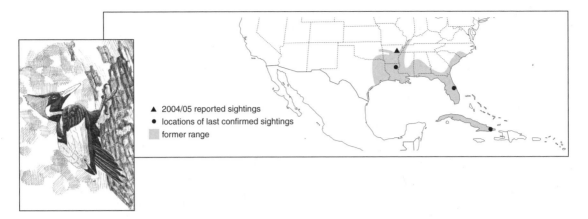

▲ 2004/05 reported sightings
● locations of last confirmed sightings
  former range

IVORY-BILLED WOODPECKER (*Campephilus principalis*)

The reported rediscovery of this thought-to-be extinct species in 2004 in a cypress swamp in Arkansas captured the world's attention. While efforts to obtain further proof of its existence continue, the lessons learned from the history of the Ivory-billed Woodpecker's decline will hopefully never be forgotten.

STATUS AND DISTRIBUTION

The Ivory-billed Woodpecker range once spanned from eastern Texas across the Gulf states to Florida and north along the coastal plain to southeastern North Carolina, then up the Mississippi River and its tributaries to eastern Oklahoma, Arkansas, southeastern Missouri, and southern Indiana and Illinois. Last unquestionably confirmed individuals persisted to 1944 in the Singer Tract along Louisiana's Tensas River in what is now the Tensas Nation Wildlife Refuge (NWR). By 1942 it was thought that only two other locations besides the Tensas River Basin had any chance of harboring the species. These were the Apalachicola River in northern Florida and the Big Cypress region of southern Florida. Occasional unconfirmed reports, some with seemingly credible details, continued from Florida, Texas, and, in 1999, from the Pearl River area in southeast Louisiana. An in-depth search of the Pearl River area for Ivory-billed Woodpecker with teams of observers and automated-recording units designed and deployed by the Cornell Lab of Ornithology carried out from January to March 2002 did not find any evidence of the species.

In February 2004, a lone kayaker reported seeing an Ivory-billed Woodpecker along the Bayou DeView, a small tributary within the Cache River NWR of eastern Arkansas. Following up on the report a few weeks later, two birders reported a simultaneous sighting of an Ivory-bill in the same area. A secret search effort, coordinated by the Cornell Lab of Ornithology and the Nature Conservancy, was immediately mounted. Three further single-person sightings were reported from team members in April 2004 within several miles of the original sighting location. A short video sequence purporting to show an Ivory-billed Woodpecker was also obtained in April 2004. A larger search effort was initiated in November 2005 that expanded to include the White River NWR. At least two other single-person sightings had been reported. Sounds that may have been produced by Ivory-billed Woodpeckers were heard by several observers and captured on automated recording units deployed in the area in 2005. A paper published in 2006 reported to have found possible audio evidence of several Ivory-billed Woodpeckers and claimed a number of sighting records all from the Choctawhatchee River basin of nothwestern Florida. Unequivocal proof of the species' existence had not been reported as of 2006 but a major search effort continues.

In Cuba, the species was found nesting and last photographed in 1948. Several birds were observed in 1986 in the Ojito de Agua area of northeastern Cuba. Searches since that time yielded several glimpses of what were thought to be Ivory-billed Woodpeckers, but there has been no confirmation and no more reports from Cuba since 1991.

It goes without saying that this species showed a massive decline in abundance since the time of

European settlement of the southeast U.S. that has resulted in its near or complete extinction. By 1891 ornithologists recognized that the species' distribution had already been greatly reduced and by 1939 it was estimated that only 22–24 individuals existed in the U.S. The last documented bird was a lone female that persisted, apparently alone, for several years in the Singer Tract of Louisiana until at least 1944. Similarly, in Cuba ornithologists recognized that the species was declining rapidly as early as 1876. In 1956 it was estimated that 12 birds remained and the last confirmed sighting in Cuba was in 1986.[1–9]

ECOLOGY

Only a single life-history study was ever completed on the species and this was of the last few known nesting pairs in the Singer Tract of Louisiana, so information about the species' ecology is sketchy. In the U.S. it was known from old-growth bottomland forest, cypress swamps, and longleaf pine forests of the southeast U.S. The species required very large tracts of forest with very large trees and patches where trees were killed by storms, fire, flooding, disease, and insect outbreaks to provide food sources and nesting cavities. In Cuba, birds probably historically also occurred in extensive lowland forests but by the time ornithologists began to learn about the species they were largely restricted to old-growth mountain pine forests. Nested in a cavity excavated in large tree and laid 1–6 eggs. Both parents incubated the eggs and brooded and fed the young. Young left the nest about five weeks after hatching.[1]

THREATS

The loss of habitat from clearing of large tracts of bottomland forest beginning in the 1800s was responsible for the extinction of Ivory-billed Woodpecker and Bachman's Warbler and for the decline of other species associated with this habitat. The loss and degradation of such habitat in the southeast U.S. has been estimated at 90% and in the Lower Mississippi Valley at more than 80%. A major increase in logging of remaining southeastern old-growth forests occurred during the period 1880–1910 when the federal government sold large tracts of land confiscated after the Civil War. During World Wars I and II, politicians passed bills to ensure forest owners would receive financial contracts for timber used in various industrial and war uses. These actions succeeded in decimating many of the remaining large tracts of old-growth bottomland forest and made conservation efforts difficult because such efforts could be portrayed as unpatriotic by business interests. In many areas the destruction of bottomland forests continues to the present time. For example, in South Carolina 28% of bottomland hardwood forest acreage was lost between 1952 and 2000.[1–4,6,9–13]

CONSERVATION ACTION

While efforts have been ongoing since the 1940s to try to protect tracts of land where the species had occurred, most of these were unsuccessful or too late. The National Audubon Society and the American Ornithologists' Union worked to try to protect the Singer Tract from logging while the species still persisted there but were unsuccessful. It was not until 1980 that the area became a National Wildlife Refuge. The Ivory-billed Woodpecker was federally listed as Endangered in 1967 and 1970.

Conservation of land in the lower White River of eastern Arkansas began with the establishment of the White River National Wildlife Refuge (NWR) in 1935. Much of the conservation work in the area was driven by a desire to protect habitat for Mallards and other waterfowl since the region hosts one of the largest wintering concentrations of Mallards in North America. There are now about 550,000 acres of bottomland forest in the region and, of those, about 300,000 acres are contiguous forest—one of the largest remaining blocks of southern bottomland forest in the world. The White River NWR encompasses about 160,000 acres and Cache River NWR another 63,000 acres. The Nature Conservancy has acquired 18,500 acres just since the reported rediscovery in 2004. A coalition of groups called the Big Woods Conservation Partnership, which includes the U.S. Fish and Wildlife Service, Arkansas Game and Fish Commission, the Nature Conservancy, and the Cornell Lab of Ornithology, is working to protect an additional 120,000 acres of existing bottomland forest and restore 50,000 acres of cleared land by planting trees.

As both a legacy to the Ivory-billed Woodpecker and as insurance in case the species does survive in any other areas, the preservation of any remaining unprotected large tracts of mature bottomland forest in the southeastern U.S. is essential. Partners in Flight Bird Conservation Plans that have been completed for southeastern U.S. physiographic regions have identified a suite of bottomland and upland forest bird species as a high priority and have provided recommendations for management, research, and monitoring. These suggestions have included specific goals for increasing the acreage of bottomland forest in large blocks across the landscape. Within the Mississippi Alluvial Valley many projects to purchase or reforest lands are ongoing through many partner agencies and organizations, including the Mississippi Valley Joint Venture, U.S. Fish and Wildlife Service Partners for Fish and Wildlife Program, the Natural Resources Conservation Service Wetland Reserve Program, Ducks Unlimited, the Nature Conservancy, and many others. Similar programs are underway throughout the former range of Ivory-billed Woodpecker.

The State of Florida started an ambitious conservation land acquisition program in the 1990s and has spent $3.2 billion on land acquisition—much more than the federal government spent on land acquisition during the same time period throughout the entire country. Many areas protected through the initiative include regions that historically supported Ivory-billed Woodpecker.[1–4,6,11–14]

CONSERVATION NEEDS

- Protect remaining large tracts of bottomland forest habitat in southeast U.S.
- Restore areas of former bottomland forest through reforestation to connect isolated forest blocks.
- Increase acreage of bottomland and upland forest habitats within southeastern U.S. that is managed for wildlife, including for the special needs of Ivory-billed Woodpckers.
- Continue efforts to follow up on credible reports of the species and use new tools like automated recording units to confirm presence or absence of the species.

References

1. Jackson, J.A. 2002. Ivory-billed Woodpecker (*Campephilus principalis*). In *The Birds of North America*, No. 711 (A. Poole and F. Gill, eds.). The Birds of North America, Inc., Philadelphia, PA.

2. Chipley, R.M., G.H. Fenwick, M.J. Parr, and D.N. Pashley. 2003. *The American Bird Conservancy Guide to the 500 Most Important Bird Areas in the United States*. Random House, New York, NY.

3. Hoose, P. 2004. *The Race to Save the Lord God Bird*. Farrar, Straus, and Giroux, New York, NY.

4. Jackson, J.A. 2004. In *Search of the Ivory-billed Woodpecker*. Smithsonian Institution, Washington, DC.

5. Fitzpatrick, J.W. 2002. Ivory-bill Absent from Sounds of the Bayous. *Birdscope*, newsletter of the Cornell Lab of Ornithology, Summer 2002.

6. USFWS. 2005. *The Ivory-billed Woodpecker*. http://www.fws.gov/ivorybill/IBW-general-brochure.pdf (accessed 20 January 2006).

7. Cornell Lab of Ornithology. 2006. Rediscovering the Ivory-billed Woodpecker. http://www.birds.cornell/edu/ivory/ (accessed 20 January 2006).

8. Gallagher, T. 2005. *The Grail Bird*. Houghton Mifflin Company, New York, NY.

9. Hill, G.E., D. J. Mennill, B. W. Rolek, T. L. Hicks, and K. A. Swiston. 2006. Evidence Suggesting That Ivory-billed Woodpeckers (*Campephilus principalis*) Exist in Florida. *Avian Conservation and Ecology–Écologie et conservation des oiseaux* 1(3): 2. [online] http://www.ace-eco.org/vol1/iss3/art2/

10. Ricketts, T.H., E. Dinerstein, D.M. Olson, C.J. Loucks, et al. 1999. *Terrestrial Ecoregions of North America: A Conservation Assessment*. Island Press, Washington, DC. 485 pp.

11. Twedt, D.J., and C.R. Loesch. 1999. Forest Area and Distribution in the Mississippi Alluvial Valley: Implications for Breeding Bird Conservation. *Journal of Biogeography* 26:1215–1224.

12. Mueller, A.J., D.J. Twedt, and C.R. Loesch. 2000. Development of Management Objectives for Breeding Birds in the Mississippi Alluvial Valley. Pages 12–17 in *Strategies for Bird Conservation: The Partners in Flight Planning Process*; Proceedings of the 3rd Partners in Flight Workshop; 1995 October 1–5; Cape May, NJ (R. Bonney, D.N. Pashley, and R.J. Niles, eds.). Proceedings RMRS-P-16, U.S. Department of Agriculture, Forest Service, Rocky Mountain Reserach Station, Ogden, UT.

13. Stein, B.A., L.S. Kutner, and J.S. Adams. 2000. *Precious Heritage: The Status of Biodiversity in the United States*. Oxford University Press, New York, NY. 399 pp.

14. The Nature Conservancy. 2006. *The Ivory-billed Woodpecker Has Returned*. http://www.nature.org/ivorybill/ (Accessed 20 January 2006).

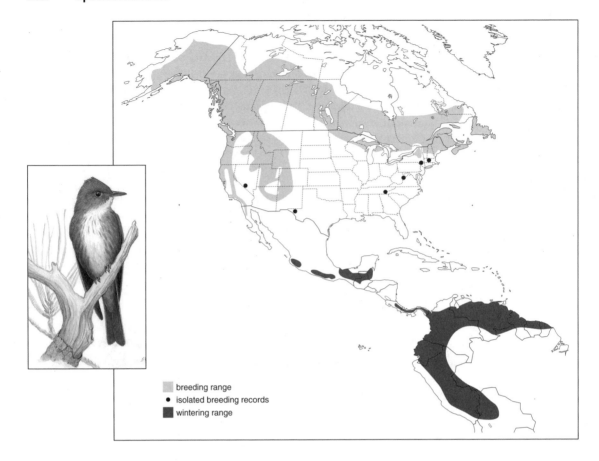

breeding range
• isolated breeding records
wintering range

OLIVE-SIDED FLYCATCHER (*Contopus cooperi*)

The loud, snappy "Quick-three-beers!" song of the Olive-sided Flycatcher is usually the first indication of the presence of this species within its coniferous forest breeding habitat. Its breeding range extends across the boreal zone of Alaska and Canada (almost 60% of its entire population breeds in the boreal region) and the northeastern U.S. and south at high elevations through the western U.S. Within this range the species has experienced significant declines that may be linked to loss of habitat on its South American wintering grounds.

STATUS AND DISTRIBUTION

The breeding range extends from Alaska across the boreal forest of Canada to Labrador and Newfoundland and south through northern Minnesota, Michigan, New York, and northern New England and in the western states south through mountainous regions to California, Arizona, New Mexico, and the northern part of the Mexican state of Baja

California. Small, isolated populations occur at high elevations within the Appalachians south to North Carolina and Tennessee.

Breeding density maps produced from Breeding Bird Survey data indicate highest densities in the western portion of the range, especially in British Columbia, Washington, and Oregon but there are no Breeding Bird Survey routes through much of the northern boreal forest. Canada was estimated to support 68% of the global population. Another analysis estimated that 57% of the global population occurred in the boreal forest of Canada and Alaska.

Although no systematic survey has been completed to identify sites that are of particular importance for breeding populations of Olive-sided Flycatcher there are many areas that have large expanses of appropriate habitat within the species' breeding range. These include British Columbia's Kootenay National Park and Yoho National Park, Yellowstone National Park in Wyoming, Montana, and Idaho, Washington State's Gifford Pinchot National Forest, and Oregon's Deschutes National Forest.

In winter, birds migrate to Central and South America, occurring in the foothills and mountains. They are rare to uncommon winterers in southern Mexico, Guatemala, and Belize and on both slopes of Costa Rica and Panama. Most of the population is thought to winter in the lower slopes and foothills of the Andes from western Venezuela south to Bolivia but there are occasional records from Guyana and even Amazonian Brazil.

A number of parks and protected areas exist across parts of the winter range and likely provide important wintering habitat for the species, though few data are available on occurrence (much less density) of the species at these locations. In Panama, Darien National Park is one of the largest protected areas in that country that encompass habitat within the wintering range of Olive-sided Flycatcher. Sites known or expected to support Olive-sided Flycatchers include Bolivia's Madidi National Park, Colombia's Los Katios and Tayrona National Parks, Ecuador's Cotacachi-Cayapas Ecological Reserve and Sangay National Park, Peru's Santiago-Comaina and Tumbes Reserves and Cordillera Azul and Manú National Park, and Venezuela's Sierra Nevada and Guatopo National Parks.

Breeding Bird Survey analysis shows a significant decrease of approximately 74% (3.5% per year) from 1966 to 2005 rangewide. The species' total population was estimated at 1,200,000 individuals in 2004.[1-10]

ECOLOGY

On the breeding range occurs in openings in coniferous forest ranging from spruce-fir forest in the boreal zone of Alaska and Canada to montane spruce-fir, lodgepole pine, and ponderosa pine forests in the western U.S. In the boreal forest is often found near bogs, ponds, and streams that provide natural openings and edge habitat. Throughout the range it prefers areas a number of years after fires, wind damage, or after certain types of tree harvesting. In all cases, needs open areas that have scattered standing tall trees or snags that can be used for perches or nesting. Many studies in the western U.S. have shown an increase in density of Olive-sided Flycatchers in proper habitat following burns or forestry operations that leave standing trees or snags. There is some evidence

that although birds seem to equally prefer burned and harvested forests, reproductive success may be lower in harvested forests compared to burned forests but more research is needed to clarify this relationship. Birds also use old-growth habitat in parts of the western U.S. when such habitat includes natural openings and edges. Nesting territories for the species can be as large as 100 acres. Typically builds nest high off ground, but occasionally as low as 3–4 feet, on branch of spruce or fir tree, laying 3–4 eggs.

On the wintering grounds the species has been little studied but occurs in openings and edges of primary forest and lightly forested areas usually in primary montane forests between 1,000 and 2,000 m but occasionally at lower or higher elevations. Birds are usually solitary and apparently territorial, as individuals are often resighted at same location over many weeks.[1]

THREATS

The major issues impacting this species on the breeding grounds are all related to trends in management of public lands in Canada and the western U.S. Throughout the range much of the habitat is within areas managed for forestry. Though more than 90% of the Canadian boreal forest is publicly owned, almost a third of the boreal forest is currently allocated to forestry companies for timber production, amounting to tens of millions of acres that will be logged during this century. For example, one logging license area of 375,000 acres in Québec is scheduled to be harvested over the next twenty years and logging rights to 24.7 million acres of Alberta's boreal forest were leased to two Japanese firms in 1987–88. Clearcutting has been used in over 80% of forest harvest operations in Canada.

In the western U.S., there has been a decrease in the volume of trees harvested since the 1970s and 1980s and the acreage logged has probably decreased, though on average just under 2 million acres of western U.S. forest lands have been harvested annually since 1950. Largely as a result of concerns for the survival and health of populations of Spotted Owls, Marbled Murrelets, and Northern Goshawks, some blocks of mature, coniferous forest habitat on public lands have not been logged over the past decade. On U.S. National Forest lands the proportion of total acreage harvested by clearcutting versus other logging methods had decreased to about 50% by 1992. Certain types of logging can make what are sometimes called "ecological traps"—habitat that attracts birds to set up breeding territories but within which they will experience lower reproductive success because of higher numbers of predators in fragmented adjoining habitat. Healthy, stable bird populations will require forest harvest planning schemes that incorporate ecological needs at a broad landscape scale that provide a mosaic of appropriate age-class forests and retain blocks of habitat that support source populations of birds.

Other forestry-related trends that may impact Olive-sided Flycatcher include the suppression of forest fires, which may decrease preferred habitat for the species. The U.S. Forest Service has had a fire-suppression policy in place for most of the last 100 years—a policy that has resulted in many detrimental habitat changes and that has increased severity of forest fires when they do occur. The broadscale application of pesticides to control various forest insects could have direct negative physiological effects on the birds and indirect effects by decreasing insect food supplies. Other issues affecting habitats supporting breeding Olive-sided Flycatchers include development and prospecting for minerals and oil across the area and, in some areas, the building of hydroelectric facilities.

On the wintering grounds, the middle and lower elevation foothill forests of southern Central America and the northern Andes where the species prefers to winter provide excellent conditions for growing various agricultural crops, including coffee as well as illicit coca plantations, and forests in this zone are full of commercially valuable trees. These foothill habitats are being lost and fragmented, perhaps faster than any other forest habitat in the Neotropics, and already harbor large assemblages of endangered and threatened species.[1,11-17]

CONSERVATION ACTION

Partners in Flight Bird Conservation Plans that have been completed for many western U.S. states have identified Olive-sided Flycatcher and its associated suite of coniferous forest bird species as a high priority and have provided recommendations for management, research, and monitoring.

In Canada a broad community of conservation organizations, industry, and First Nations have announced the Boreal Forest Conservation Framework—a new national conservation approach for Canada's boreal forest region. The Framework plan would protect the ecological integrity of the region while integrating sustainable forestry and other development activities. The Framework calls for the establishment of large, interconnected, protected areas covering at least half of the boreal region and application of cutting-edge sustainable development practices on the lands that are developed. The Canadian Boreal Initiative and its partners are working to encourage the adoption of Framework principles by Canadian national and provincial government agencies and policy makers as a vision for the future of the vast, and largely publicly owned, boreal landscape.

A Canadian Senate subcommittee developed a comprehensive report in 1999 that recommended a set of actions needed to ensure the protection and sustainable use of Canada's boreal forests. Since then the Canadian Boreal Initiative has been advocating for adoption and implementation of these recommendations in addition to promoting the Framework and working with provincial governments to adopt the principles of the Framework on their lands. Some progress was reported in the establishment of protected areas, including the protection of 625,000 acres of boreal forest habitat in Québec since 2000.

The Boreal Songbird Initiative has spearheaded work by a network of U.S. conservation groups to support the Boreal Forest Conservation Framework. This work has included outreach activities to increase awareness of the boreal wilderness and the threats it faces. For example, the National Wildlife Federation and National Audubon both have conducted letter-writing campaigns asking large retail catalog companies to use recycled paper and paper purchased from environmentally and socially responsible sources instead of using paper made from virgin boreal forest. The Natural Resources Defense Council has also designated the intact boreal forest in the Ontario–Manitoba border region as one of its twelve "BioGems" and is working to ensure that the conservation plans of local indigenous peoples are not threatened by hydropower and industrial development.

On the wintering grounds a number of government agencies and conservation groups are involved in efforts to protect and manage parks and other protected areas within the wintering range of Olive-sided Flycatcher. The U.S. National Park

Service Office of International Affairs conducted a training workshop for Venezuela's National Institute for Parks in 2002 to help in management Venezuela's National Parks. In 2001, the Peruvian government established the country's second largest national park known as Cordillera Azul National Park, protecting a 5.1-million-acre expanse of habitat used by wintering Olive-sided Flycatcher and a host of rare resident species. The area's importance was identified through the efforts of the Chicago Field Museum's Environmental and Conservation program and the Peruvian Association for the Conservation of Nature. These organizations are assisting the newly formed Center for the Conservation, Investigation, and Management of Natural Areas to develop a management plan for the park and raise the funds necessary to implement the plan. Already rangers have been deployed along the park's western boundary to prevent or slow illegal logging within the park.[11,12,18–23]

CONSERVATION NEEDS

- Within the breeding range of Olive-sided Flycatcher implement broad, landscape-scale forest management plans that maintain large tracts of old-growth forest with natural openings and large tracts of managed forest in which mature trees and snags are retained.
- Increase the acreage of public lands in which fire is allowed to occur as part of the natural ecological cycle.
- Increase the number of protected areas through national and provincial parks in Canada to encompass at least 50% of the boreal forest region.
- Increase the number of wilderness and roadless areas in appropriate habitat in the western U.S.
- Implement the Protected Areas Strategy in the Northwest Territories prior to the development of the Mackenzie Gas Project, and implement the proposed protections near Lake Winnipeg to maintain the intact boreal forest in the Ontario–Manitoba border region.
- Implement the Boreal Forest Conservation Framework.
- Slow or halt deforestation of wintering habitat for Olive-sided Flycatcher and restore habitat where possible.
- Increase the number of protected areas within

the species' wintering range and increase support for management and on-the-ground enforcement of regulations within existing protected areas.
- Develop baseline inventory of Olive-sided Flycatcher breeding and wintering populations, habitat needs on breeding and wintering grounds, and factors responsible for continuing population declines.

References

1. Altman, B., and R. Sallabanks. 2000. Olive-sided Flycatcher (*Contopus cooperi*). In *The Birds of North America*, No. 502 (A. Poole and F. Gill, eds.). The Birds of North America, Inc., Philadelphia, PA.

2. Sauer, J.R., J. E. Hines, and J. Fallon. 2005. *The North American Breeding Bird Survey, Results and Analysis 1966–2005*, Version 6.2.2006. USGS Patuxent Wildlife Research Center, Laurel, MD.

3. Rosenberg, K.V., and J.V. Wells. 2000. Global Perspectives in Neotropical Migratory Bird Conservation in the Northeast: Long-term Responsibility Versus Immediate Concern. Pages 32–43 in *Strategies for Bird Conservation: The Partners in Flight Planning Process*. Proceedings of the 3rd Partners in Flight Workshop; 1995 October 1–5; Cape May, NJ (R. Bonney, D.N. Pashley, and R.J. Niles, eds.). Proceedings RMRS-P-16, U.S. Department of Agriculture, Forest Service, Rocky Mountain Reserach Station, Ogden, UT.

4. Blancher, P., and J.V. Wells. 2005. *The Boreal Forest Region: North America's Bird Nursery*. Canadian Boreal Initiative, Boreal Songbird Initiative, Bird Studies Canada, Ottawa, ON, Seattle, WA, and Port Rowan, ON. 10 pp.

5. Parks Canada. 2003. *National Parks of Canada*. http://parkscanada.gc.ca/progs/np-pn/index_E.asp (accessed 25 June 2003).

6. Hilty, S.L., and W.L. Brown. 1986. *Birds of Colombia*. Princeton University Press, Princeton, NJ. 836 pp.

7. Hilty, S.L. 2003. *Birds of Venezuela*, 2nd ed. Princeton University Press, Princeton, NJ. 878 pp.

8. Panama Travel. No date. *Panama's National Parks*. http://www.panamatravel.com/natparks.htm (accessed 25 June 2003).

9. BirdLife International. 2006. *Neotropical Migrants in the Tropical Andes—Olive-sided Flycatcher*, Contopus cooperi. http://www.birdlife.org/action/science/species/neotrops/andes/species/olive-sided_flycatcher.html?language=en (accessed 19 January 2006).

10. Rich, T. D., C. Beardmore, H. Berlanga, P.

Blancher, M. Bradstreet, G. Butcher, D. Demarest, E. Dunn, C. Hunter, E. Inigo-Elias, J. Kennedy, A. Martell, A. Panjabi, D. Pashley, K. Rosenberg, C. Rustay, S. Wendt, and T. Will. 2004. *Partners in Flight North American Landbird Conservation Plan.* Cornell Lab of Ornithology, Ithaca, NY.

11. Sub-committee on Boreal Forest of the Standing Senate Committee on Agriculture and Forestry. 1999. *Competing Realities: The Boreal Forest at Risk.* Government of Canada, Ottawa, ON. http://www.parl.gc.ca/36/1/parlbus/commbus/senate/com-e/BORE-E/rep-e/rep09jun99-e.htm (accessed 24 June 2003).

12. Canadian Boreal Initiative. 2003. *The Boreal Forest at Risk: A Progress Report.* Canadian Boreal Initiative, Ottawa, ON.

13. Ricketts T.H., et al. 1999. *Terrestrial Ecoregions of North America: A Conservation Assessment.* Island Press, Washington, DC. 485 pp.

14. U.S. Forest Service. 2001. *U.S. Forest Service Facts and Historical Trends.* U.S. Department of Agriculture, U.S. Forest Service. http: www.fs.fed.us (accessed 30 June 2003).

15. Thompson, F.R., J.R. Probst, and M.G. Raphael. 1995. Impacts of Silviculture: Overview and Management Recommendations. Pages 201–219 In *Ecology and Management of Neotropical Migratory Birds* (T.E. Martin and D.M. Finch, eds.). Oxford University Press, New York, NY.

16. Askins, R.A. 2000. *Restoring North America's Birds.* Yale University Press, New Haven, CT. 320 pp.

17. Stotz, D.F., J.W. Fitzpatrick, T.A. Parker III, and D. K. Moskovits. 1996. *Neotropical Birds: Ecology and Conservation.* University of Chicago Press, Chicago, IL. 481 pp.

18. Latta, M.J., C.J. Beardmore, and T.E. Corman. 1999. *Arizona Partners in Flight Bird Conservation Plan.* Version 1.0. Nongame and Endangered Wildlife Program Technical Report 142. Arizona Game and Fish Department, Phoenix, AZ.

19. Neel, L.A. (ed.). 1999. *Nevada Partners in Flight Bird Conservation Plan.* Nevada Partners in Flight Working Group.

20. Colorado Partners in Flight. 2000. *Colorado Partners In Flight Land Bird Conservation Plan.* http://www.rmbo.org/pif (accessed 30 June 2003).

21. Casey, D. 2000. *Partners in Flight Draft Bird Conservation Plan: Montana.* American Bird Conservancy, The Plains, VA.

22. National Park Service Office of International Affairs. No date. *Latin America and Caribbean.* http://www.nps.gov/oia/around/lac.htm (accessed 25 June 2003).

23. The Field Museum. 2002. *Parque Nacional Cordillera Azul.* http://www.fmnh.org/cordilleraazul/park story.html (accessed 30 June 2003).

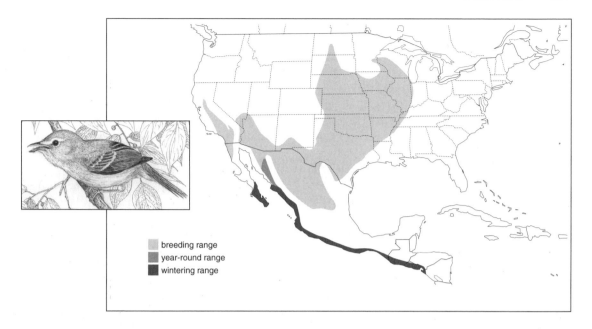

breeding range
year-round range
wintering range

BELL'S VIREO (*Vireo bellii*)

A species characteristic of shrubby habitats of the midwest and southwest U.S. and northern Mexico, especially along rivers and streams, the Bell's Vireo has declined by more than 50% since the 1960s.

STATUS AND DISTRIBUTION

The Bell's Vireo breeding range encompasses much of the Mississippi River drainage in the midwest U.S. extending from south central North Dakota, southern Wisconsin, southern Michigan, and western Ohio south through Texas into northern Mexico and west across southern New Mexico, Arizona, and southern Nevada to California. The endangered Least Bell's Vireo subspecies occurs only in the southern half of California. Breeding density maps produced from Breeding Bird Survey data indicate highest densities in central and western Texas and southeastern Arizona. An estimated 75% of the breeding population is found in the U.S., with the remaining 25% in Mexico.

Among many important breeding areas for the species are Arizona's Buenos Aires National Wildlife Refuge (NWR) and the San Pedro Riparian National Conservation Area, which is estimated to hold 350–400 pairs of Bell's Vireo. In Texas, Big Bend NP and the Nature Conservancy's Davis Mountain Preserve are known to support breeding populations. Important breeding areas in California for the Least Bell's Vireo include the Camp Pendleton military base, which is estimated to support 50% of the population of the subspecies (600+ birds) and the San Luis Rey River area (400 birds).

In winter, birds migrate to western Mexico and Central America where they occur along the Pacific Coast from southern Sonora to Nicaragua. There is no available information on wintering densities of Bell's Vireo. The species is known from a number of Important Bird Areas in Mexico, including the Sierra de la Laguna IBA in Baja California Sur, the Marismas Nacionales IBA in Nayarit, and the Coalcomán-Pómaro IBA in Michoacán.

Breeding Bird Survey analysis showed a significant decrease of approximately 64% (2.7% per year) from 1966 to 2005 rangewide. The species' total population was estimated at 1,500,000 individuals in 2004.[1-6]

ECOLOGY

On the breeding range occurs in early successional shrub-scrub habitat, often on the edges of streams and rivers. Females lay 3–5 eggs in an open cup nest built in low shrubs. Eggs are incubated by both sexes for about 14 days. Both adults feed young, which fledge in 10–12 days. Adults continue to feed young for as many as 20 days after fledging. In some parts of the range Bell's Vireo regularly produce two broods per season, in other regions only one. The species is heavily parasitized by Brown-headed Cowbirds throughout much of the range and in nests that are parasitized the cowbirds often outcompete the vireos so that all vireo nestlings die. Cowbird parasitism rates are as high as 30–70% in many parts of the species' range. Most Bell's Vireo are thought to survive only 3–4 years. On the wintering grounds it has been little studied but is usually found in dry scrub vegetation or tropical forests near streams and rivers. Whether it defends winter territories is unknown.[1]

THREATS

The greatest threat is loss, fragmentation, and degradation of shrubby riparian habitats across the midwest and southwest U.S. It has been estimated that 95% of western riparian habitats have been lost or degraded in the last 100 years. For example, an estimated 90% of original riparian habitat in Arizona has been lost and 95% of riparian habitat has been lost from the Central Valley of California. Shrubby habitats within the tallgrass prairie ecoregion of the midwest U.S. were historically thought to be maintained by periodic fires and, as in the southwest, were often along stream corridors or within wet areas. These habitats have been lost and fragmented due to conversion to cropland and rangeland, suppression of fires, loss of and change in water flow from dams and irrigation, urban development, and increases in invasive plant species. Many of these habitat effects have also resulted in higher levels of Brown-headed Cowbird parasitism. Preliminary research has indicated that Bell's Vireo may exhibit area sensitivity, occurring mostly in shrubland patches greater than 80 acres. In the southwest U.S., many riparian areas have been heavily degraded by cattle that are attracted to the cooler conditions and lusher vegetation in such areas and use them in high densities when such areas are unfenced. Along the Lower Colorado River an estimated 99% of native cottonwood-willow forest has disappeared since the 1930s, much of it as a result of introduced salt cedar outcompeting the native plants. In a 1990 report, the U.S. Environmental Protection Agency concluded that riparian areas in the western U.S. where in their poorest condition in history.

On the wintering grounds, the dry scrub forest preferred by the species has seen great losses, with only an estimated 2% of dry forest remaining in Central America and Mexico. Some of the largest remaining blocks of this habitat persist in the Mexican states of Sonora and Sinaloa. The greatest loss of wintering habitat and the greatest continuing threat is from conversion and degradation of habitat for cattle ranching. Many large areas of habitat have been converted to nonnative grasses for cattle over the last 30 years.[1,4,7–11]

CONSERVATION ACTION

Partners in Flight Bird Conservation Plans in Arizona, California, Nevada, and New Mexico have identified Bell's Vireo and its associated suite of lowland riparian habitat bird species as a high priority and have provided recommendations for management, research, monitoring, and outreach. Many efforts are underway to restore and protect riparian habitats along major river systems in Arizona, California, and New Mexico. For example, the Upper San Pedro Partnership is a a consortium of 20 agencies and organizations working together to meet the water needs of area residents while protecting the San Pedro River. The Nature Conservancy (TNC) owns several preserves along the San Pedro. TNC acquired a 2,000 acre ranch along the river in 2002 and an easement on a 900-acre ranch in 2003 and announced that both ranches would stop all groundwater pumping. Congress designated 40 miles of the river managed by the Bureau of Land Management as a National Conservation Area in 1988. All grazing and farming in this stretch of the river were halted, allowing the vegetation to be restored, and numbers of many bird species have increased. The Commission for Environmental Cooperation initiated a joint Mexican–U.S. conservation initiative for the San Pedro in 1999. Along the Colorado River that delineates the border between California and Arizona efforts are underway at Havasu and Bill Williams National Wildlife Refuges (both support Bell's Vireo populations) to control the spread of invasive salt cedar in riparian areas and to restore native cottonwood-willow communities.

Although less conservation attention has been focused on the species in the Midwest, U.S. Partners in Flight Bird Conservation Plans that have been completed for physiographic regions have identified Bell's Vireo and its associated suite of shrub habitat bird species as a priority and have provided some recommendations for management, research, and monitoring, though there are large gaps in our current understanding of management needs for the species. In some areas, Bell's Vireo has benefited from habitat management focused on improving conditions for Black-capped Vireo.

The Least Bell's Vireo was federally listed as Endangered in 1986 and, under the Endangered Species Act, critical habitat for this subspecies was designated in 1994 encompassing about 38,000 acres along 10 streams in southern California. A Draft Recovery Plan was published by the U.S. Fish and Wildlife Service in 1998. Extensive Brown-headed Cowbird trapping has been carried out in some areas with significant populations, including at Camp Pendeleton in California where nest parasitism rates dropped from 47% in the 1980s to less than 1% by 1990. In 1994 California Partners in Flight started the Riparian Habitat Joint Venture project that has enlisted 18 state and private organizations in a cooperative agreement to protect and restore riparian habitat in California and resulted in a Riparian Bird Conservation Plan published in 2000. The number of Least Bell's Vireo in southern California was estimated at 330 pairs in 1986 and in 1996 estimates had increased to 1,346 pairs. Although some of the increase could be due to better survey efforts, much of it is thought to be attributable to cowbird trapping and habitat conservation efforts.

Audubon California bird surveys in 2001 discovered a previously unknown breeding population of Least Bell's Vireo along San Gabriel River and Tujunga Wash within the Los Angeles Flood Control Basins. Negotiations between Audubon, the U.S. Army Corps of Engineers, and Los Angeles County Department of Public Works to ensure beneficial management of the area for the vireo are continuing.[1,4,8,11–21]

CONSERVATION NEEDS

- Increase acreage of healthy riparian and shrub-scrub habitat within the breeding range of Bell's Vireo that is managed to attain conditions beneficial to the species.
- Decrease acreage of lowland riparian habitat degraded by cattle grazing and invasive plant species and lack of regular flooding regimes.
- Develop baseline inventory of Bell's Vireo breeding and wintering populations.

References

1. Brown, B.T. 1993. Bell's Vireo (*Vireo bellii*). In *The Birds of North America*, No. 35 (A. Poole and F. Gill, eds.). The Academy of Natural Sciences, Philadelphia, PA, and the American Ornithologists' Union, Washington, D.C.

2. Sauer, J. R., J. E. Hines, and J. Fallon. 2005. *The North American Breeding Bird Survey, Results and Analysis 1966–2005*, Version 6.2.2006. USGS Patuxent Wildlife Research Center, Laurel, MD.

3. Rich, T. D., C. Beardmore, H. Berlanga, P. Blancher, M. Bradstreet, G. Butcher, D. Demarest, E. Dunn, C. Hunter, E. Inigo-Elias, J. Kennedy, A. Martell, A. Panjabi, D. Pashley, K. Rosenberg, C. Rustay, S. Wendt, and T. Will. 2004. *Partners in Flight North American Landbird Conservation Plan*. Cornell Lab of Ornithology, Ithaca, NY.

4. Chipley, R.M., G.H. Fenwick, M.J. Parr, and D.N. Pashley. 2003. *The American Bird Conservancy Guide to the 500 Most Important Bird Areas in the United States*. Random House, New York, NY.

5. Cooper, D. 2001. Important bird areas of California. Unpublished manuscript available from Audubon California, 6042 Monte Vista St., Los Angeles, CA 90042.

6. CONABIO. 2002. *Áreas de Importancia para la Conservación de las Aves (AICAS)*. http://conabioweb .conabio.gob.mx/aicas/doctos/aicas.html (accessed 18 June 2003).

7. Ricketts, T.H., E. Dinerstein, D.M. Olson, C.J. Loucks, et al. 1999. *Terrestrial Ecoregions of North America: A Conservation Assessment*. Island Press, Washington, DC. 485 pp.

8. Latta, M.J., C.J. Beardmore, and T.E. Corman. 1999. *Arizona Partners in Flight Bird Conservation Plan*, Version 1.0. Nongame and Endangered Wildlife Program Technical Report 142. Arizona Game and Fish Department, Phoenix, AZ.

9. World Wildlife Fund. 2001. *Sonoran–Sinaloan Transition Subtropical Dry Forest (NA0201)*. http://www .worldwidelife.org/wildworld/profiles/terrestrial/na/na02 01_full.html (accessed 20 January 2004).

10. Ceballos, G., and A. García. 1995. Conserving Neotropical Diversity: The Role of Dry Forests in Western Mexico. *Conservation Biology* 9:1349–1356.

11. Fitzgerald, J.A., J.R. Herkert, and J.D. Brawn. 2000. *Partners in Flight Bird Conservation Plan for the Prairie Peninsula*. American Bird Conservancy, The Plains, VA.

12. Neel, L.A. (ed.). 1999. *Nevada Partners in Flight*

Bird Conservation Plan. Nevada Partners in Flight Working Group.

13. Riparian Habitat Joint Venture. 2000. Version 1.0. *The Riparian Bird Conservation Plan: A Strategy for Reversing the Decline of Riparian Associated Birds in California.* California Partners in Flight. http://www.prbo.org/CPIF/Riparian/Riparian.html (accessed 20 January 2004).

14. Bureau of Land Management. 21 September 2003. *San Pedro Riparian National Conservation Area.* http://azwww.az.blm.gov/tfo/spnca/spnca-info.html (accessed 19 January 2004).

15. Commission for Environmental Cooperation. 1999. *Ribbon of Life: An Agenda for Preserving Transboundary Migratory Bird Habitat on the Upper San Pedro River.* Commission for Environmental Cooperation, Montreal, QC, Canada.

16. Fitzgerald, J.A., and D.N. Pashley. 2000. *Partners in Flight Bird Conservation Plan for The Dissected till Plains.* American Bird Conservancy, The Plains, VA.

17. Fitzgerald, J.A., B. Busby, M. Howery, R. Klataske, D. Reinking, and D. Pashley. 2000. *Partners in Flight Bird Conservation Plan for the Osage Plains.* American Bird Conservancy, The Plains, VA.

18. U.S. Fish and Wildlife Service. 1998. *Draft Recovery Plan for the Least Bell's Vireo.* U.S. Fish and Wildlife Service, Portland, OR. 139 pp.

19. U.S. Fish and Wildlife Service. No date. *Least Bell's Vireo species account.* http://ventura.fws.gov/SpeciesAccount/birds/lbv_acct.htm (accessed 19 January 2004).

20. Scoggin, S., and D. Barton. No date. *Riparian Habitat Joint Venture.* http://www.prbo.org/calpif/htmldocs/rhjv/ (accessed 19 January 2004).

21. Audubon California. 2004. *Important Bird Areas: AIM Surveys.* http://ca.audubon.org/IBA.htm (accessed 20 January 2004).

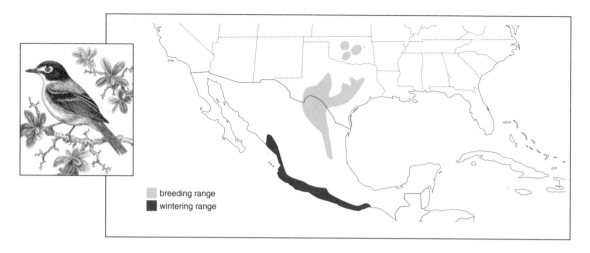

breeding range
wintering range

BLACK-CAPPED VIREO (*Vireo atricapillus*)

A strikingly handsome songbird of the hot, dry scrub vegetation of the southern Midwest, the Black-capped Vireo has experienced a 50% reduction in its range and is now federally listed as Endangered.

STATUS AND DISTRIBUTION

The Black-capped Vireo breeding range once extended from south central Kansas south through Oklahoma and central Texas through the Mexican state of Coahuila to southern Nuevo León. The species had disappeared from Kansas by the 1950s, had been reduced to three small populations in Oklahoma and was gone from much of northern portion of former Texas range by the 1990s. An estimated 60% of the breeding population is found in the U.S., with the remaining 40% in Mexico. Important breeding sites for the species include Oklahoma's Wichita Mountains National Wildlife Refuge (NRW) (200 pairs) and in Texas, Fort Hood (2,500+ adults in 2003), Kerr Wildlife Management Area (422 singing males in 2002), Balcones Canyonlands NWR (100 pairs), and Kickapoo Cavern State Park (100+ pairs in 1993). In the Mexican state of Coahuila, the species breeds in the Sierra Maderas del Carmen Important Bird Area (IBA) and the Sierra del Burro IBA, where at least 28 pairs were counted in 1989.

In winter, birds migrate to western Mexico and though the limits of the wintering range are poorly known they are thought to winter mainly along the Pacific slope from Sinaloa to Oaxaca. There is no available information on wintering densities of Black-capped Vireo. The species is known from a number of Important Bird Areas in Mexico such as the Marismas Nacionales IBA in Nayarit and the Sierra de Manantlán IBA in Colima. No trend information is available for the species as a whole but the breeding range has declined by more than 50% since historical times and many remaining populations are fragmented and small. In several areas where the habitat has been actively managed for Black-capped Vireo and where there has been active trapping and removal of Brown-headed Cowbirds, populations have shown great increases. The species' total population was estimated at 8,000 individuals in 2004.[1-6]

ECOLOGY

On the breeding range occurs in shrub-scrub habitat often in an early-successional state after a fire or mechanical removal of vegetation but in some areas such habitat persists without disturbance because of poor soil conditions. Females lay 3–4 eggs in an open cup nest built in low shrubs. Eggs are incubated by both sexes for about 15 days. Both adults feed young which fledge in 10–12 days. Adults continue to feed young for as many as 35–45 days after fledging. Most breeders attempt to produce a second brood. The species is heavily parasitized by Brown-headed Cowbirds throughout the range and occasionally by Bronzed Cowbirds in some areas. In nests that are parasitized the cowbirds often outcompete the vireos so that all vireo nestlings die. Cowbird parasitism rates are as high as 90% in many parts of the species' range.

Annual survival rates estimated at 55–75%. On the wintering grounds it has been little studied and habitat information is somewhat conflicting but apparently in winters in both arid and more humid scrub vegetation. Whether it defends winter territories is unknown.[1]

THREATS

The greatest threat is loss, fragmentation, and degradation of shrub-scrub habitats across range. Across the northern half of the species' breeding range it is estimated that 90% or more of the natural habitat has been converted to cropland or rangeland. Much of the habitat type was historically maintained by regular fires and fire suppression is one of the most significant threats to the species. Highest concentrations are typically in areas that have experienced recent fires. These shrub-scrub habitats have also been lost and fragmented due to conversion to cropland and rangeland and urban development. Many of these habitat affects have also resulted in extraordinarily high levels of Brown-headed Cowbird parasitism in many populations. In the short-term cowbird parasitism is often the most overriding threat to the survival of some populations.

Because the species' wintering range limits and habitat preferences are essentially unknown it is difficult to assess threats on the wintering grounds. However, it is known that there has been a great loss of scrub habitat and many forest types within portions of the wintering area.[1,7–9]

CONSERVATION ACTION

The species was federally listed as Endangered in 1987 and a Recovery Plan was completed in 1991. Extensive efforts at trapping and removing Brown-headed Cowbirds from at least three of the major populations (Fort Hood, Wichita Mountains NWR, Kerr WMA) have been very successful in lowering parasitism rates and increasing vireo numbers. For example, at Fort Hood, cowbird parasitism rates went from nearly 90% in 1988 to 6% in 1998 after intensive removal of cowbirds and consequently numbers of Black-capped Vireo there have greatly increased. Texas Parks and Wildlife received a grant from the National Fish and Wildlife Foundation in 2002 to implement cowbird trapping programs on private lands in the state to benefit Black-

capped Vireo, Golden-cheeked Warbler, and other birds.

Management efforts at several sites have also been focused on improving habitat conditions through prescribed burns, including at Kerr WMA, where such work combined with cowbird trapping increased vireo numbers from 27 singing males in 1986 to 422 in 2002. Safe Harbor Agreements in the Texas Hill Country approved by the U.S. Fish and Wildlife Service and administered by a private organization called Environmental Defense provide an incentive for landowners to create habitat for Black-capped Vireo and Golden-cheeked Warbler. Over 500 acres had been enrolled by 2003. Environmental Defense also offers another program called the Landowner Conservation Assistance Program that provides technical and financial assistance to landowners who wish to manage habitats for endangered animals and plants, including the Black-capped Vireo. As of 2003, over 70,000 acres from 43 private landowners had used the program.

Some work has also focused on protecting remaining habitat patches from conversion to housing developments or agricultural uses. For example, Balcones Canyonlands NWR near Austin, TX was created in 1992 with the goal of acquiring and protecting 46,000 acres of nesting habitat for Black-capped Vireo and Golden-cheeked Warbler. About 16,000 acres had been acquired from willing sellers as of 2003. Similarly, the Bexar Land Trust received a grant in 2004 to purchase 150-acres of land adjacent to a private 500-acre ranch in Kendall County, Texas, that is managing habitat for Black-capped Vireo and Golden-cheeked Warbler under a Safe Harbor Agreement.[1,4,5,9–16]

CONSERVATION NEEDS

- Increase acreage of healthy shrub-scrub habitat within the breeding range of Black-capped Vireo that is managed to attain conditions beneficial to the species, especially through prescribed burns.
- Continue acquisition of remaining intact habitat from willing sellers within species' range by conservation agencies and organizations, including at Balcones Canyonlands NWR, which is authorized to expand by 30,000 acres from its present size.
- Develop baseline inventory of Black-capped Vireo breeding and wintering populations.

- Invest in further research into the species' winter range limits, habitat requirements, and ecology.

References

1. Grzybowski, J.A. 1995. Black-capped Vireo (*Vireo atricapillus*). In *The Birds of North America*, No. 181 (A. Poole and F. Gill, eds.). The Academy of Natural Sciences, Philadelphia, and the American Ornithologists' Union, Washington, DC.

2. Howell, S.N.G., and S. Webb. 1995. *A Guide to the Birds of Mexico and Northern Central America*. Oxford University Press, New York, NY.

3. Rich, T. D., C. Beardmore, H. Berlanga, P. Blancher, M. Bradstreet, G. Butcher, D. Demarest, E. Dunn, C. Hunter, E. Iñigo-Elias, J. Kennedy, A. Martell, A. Panjabi, D. Pashley, K. Rosenberg, C. Rustay, S. Wendt, and T. Will. 2004. *Partners in Flight North American Landbird Conservation Plan*. Cornell Lab of Ornithology, Ithaca, NY.

4. Chipley, R.M., G.H. Fenwick, M.J. Parr, and D.N. Pashley. 2003. *The American Bird Conservancy Guide to the 500 Most Important Bird Areas in the United States*. Random House, New York, NY.

5. The Nature Conservancy. 2003. *Endangered Species Monitoring and Management at Fort Hood, Texas: 2003 Annual Report*. The Nature Conservancy, Fort Hood Project, Fort Hood, Texas, USA.

6. CONABIO. 2002. *Áreas de Importancia para la Conservación de las Aves (AICAS)*. http://conabioweb .conabio.gob.mx/aicas/doctos/aicas.html (accessed 18 June 2003).

7. Ricketts, T.H., E. Dinerstein, D.M. Olson, C.J. Loucks, et al. 1999. *Terrestrial Ecoregions of North America: A Conservation Assessment*. Island Press, Washington, DC. 485 pp.

8. Stotz, D.F., J.W. Fitzpatrick, T.A. Parker III, and D. K. Moskovits. 1996. *Neotropical Birds: Ecology and Conservation*. University of Chicago Press, Chicago, IL. 481 pp.

9. U.S. Fish and Wildlife Service. 1991. *Black-capped Vireo (Vireo atricapillus) Recovery Plan*, Austin, TX. 74 pp.

10. U.S. Fish and Wildlife Service. 20 January 2004. *Species Profile for Black-capped Vireo*. https://ecos .fws.gov/species_profile/SpeciesProfile?spcode=B07T (accessed 20 January 2004).

11. National Fish and Wildlife Foundation. 2002. *National Fish and Wildlife Foundation Grants in Fiscal Year 2002—Texas*. http://www.nfwf.org/programs/grant_TX.htm (accessed 22 January 2004).

12. Environmental Defense. 2003. *The Texas Hill Country Endangered Songbird Safe Harbor Agreement*. http://www.environmentaldefense.org/article.cfm? contentid=142 (accessed 22 January 2004).

13. Environmental Defense. 2003. *The Landowner Conservation Assistance Program*. http://www.environ mentaldefense.org/article.cfm?contentid=154 (accessed 22 January 2004).

14. Texas Parks and Wildlife Department. May 20, 2003. *Black-capped Vireo Trends—Kerr WMA*. http:// www.tpwd.state.tx.us/wma/find_a_wma/list/wildlife _management/kerr_wma/bcv_trends.phtml (accessed 20 January 2004).

15. U.S. Fish and Wildlife Service. No date. "*Wildlife—Balcones Canyonlands NWR*." http://southwest.fws .gov/refuges/texas/balcones/wildlife.html (accessed 20 January 2004).

16. Land Trust Alliance. 2004. *Grant Benefits the Black-capped Vireo in Texas*. http://www.lta.org/regionlta/ s_sw.htm (accessed 22 January 2004).

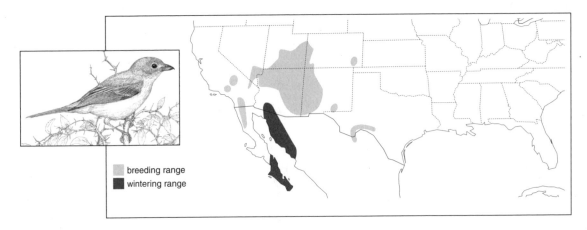

breeding range
wintering range

GRAY VIREO (*Vireo vicinior*)

With its very limited breeding and wintering range in the southwestern U.S. and northwestern Mexico, its preference for dry scrubby habitats that are being destroyed and degraded, and the lack of knowledge about its status, Gray Vireo is a species that warrants national conservation concern.

Breeding Bird Survey analysis shows a non-significant increase of approximately 45% (1.6% per year) from 1966 to 2005 rangewide but the species was detected on very few Breeding Bird Survey routes. The species' total population was estimated at 410,000 individuals in 2004.[1-6]

STATUS AND DISTRIBUTION

Endemic to southwestern North America, the Gray Vireo breeding range extends from Nevada, Utah, and Colorado south through the U.S.–Mexico border states to Mexico's northern Baja California and northern Coahuila. Within this range the species has a very patchy and discontinuous distribution.

Breeding density maps produced from the rather limited amount of Breeding Bird Survey data available for the species indicate highest densities in southern Utah and northwestern Arizona. Important breeding areas for the species include Colorado's Canyons of the Ancients National Monument—a site managed by the Bureau of Land Management that supports at least 500 pairs of Gray Vireo—and the National Park Service's Colorado National Monument, which supports more than 150 pairs. Other important breeding sites include Utah's Zion and Arches National Parks and Texas's Big Bend National Park and Kickapoo Cavern State Park.

In winter, birds move south, inhabiting a range extending from southwestern Arizona south through the Mexican state of Sonora with a disjunct wintering population in southern Baja California. There is no available information on wintering densities of Gray Vireo.

ECOLOGY

On the breeding range this bird occurs in dry scrubby habitats, especially pinyon-juniper (juniper savannah and open juniper slopes) and oak-juniper woodlands, generally at elevations between 4,400 and 6,500 feet, and in some areas, chaparral habitats. Females lay 2–4 eggs in an open cup nest usually built 3–10 feet above ground. Eggs are incubated by both sexes for 12–14 days. Both adults feed young which fledge in 13–14 days. Most probably produce two broods per year. Insects are the primary food source in the breeding season and part of the diet in the non-breeding season. On the wintering grounds, the species occurs in dry thorn scrub habitat often with a particular species of elephant tree (*Bursera microphylla*) with which it seems to have a mutualistic ecological relationship. Gray Vireo is one of only two bird species known to regularly eat the fruits of *B. microphylla* while on its winter range.[1]

THREATS

On breeding and wintering grounds, loss of habitat from clearing of pinyon-juniper, chaparral, and other scrub habitat for cattle grazing, firewood, and housing developments is a major threat. An estimated 3 million acres of pinyon-juniper habitat was converted to cattle pasture in the southwest U.S. between 1950 and 1964. In many areas, pinyon-juniper habitat is used for intensive livestock grazing, which reduces the shrub and ground cover densities below those required by Gray Vireos. The species also seems to be susceptible to increased levels of Brown-headed Cowbird parasitism when habitat is fragmented and cattle are introduced.[1,7–10]

CONSERVATION ACTION

Partners in Flight Bird Conservation Plans in Arizona, California, Colorado, Nevada, New Mexico, and Utah have identified Gray Vireo and its associated suite of pinyon-juniper or chaparral bird species as a high priority and have provided recommendations for management, research, monitoring, and outreach. Unfortunately, the species has been poorly monitored and little studied so many recommendations have centered on increased research and monitoring efforts. Rocky Mountain Bird Observatory has initiated a study of Gray Vireo in Colorado based on these recommendations and has collected several years of baseline data, including some that indicate a higher level of cowbird nest parasitism in areas where cattle grazing occurs. The U.S. Forest Service had a now-discontinued outreach effort to teach people, especially those who directly impacted pinyon-juniper habitat, the importance of this habitat type to wildlife and ways to manage it for the benefit of birds and other wildlife.

The National Park Service has an agreement with Mexico's National Commission for Protected Natural Areas (CONANP) to provide training in natural resource management and park management and development of "sister park" relationships. Areas in Mexico like the El Pinacate Biosphere Reserve and the El Vizcaino Biosphere Reserve provide habitat for wintering Gray Vireo and could benefit from this exchange program between NPS and CONANP staff.[1,9–16]

CONSERVATION NEEDS

- Increase acreage of pinyon-juniper (specifically juniper savannah) and oak-juniper habitat within the breeding range of Gray Vireo that is managed to attain conditions beneficial to the species.
- Decrease acreage of pinyon-juniper and oak-

juniper habitat degraded by cattle grazing and lack of prescribed burns.
- Develop baseline inventory of Gray Vireo breeding populations.

References

1. Barlow, J.C., S. N. Leckie, and C. T. Baril. 1999. Gray Vireo (*Vireo vicinior*). In *The Birds of North America*, No. 447 (A. Poole and F. Gill, eds.). The Birds of North America, Inc., Philadelphia, PA.

2. Sauer, J.R., J. E. Hines, and J. Fallon. 2005. *The North American Breeding Bird Survey, Results and Analysis 1966–2005*, Version 6.2.2006. USGS Patuxent Wildlife Research Center, Laurel, MD.

3. National Audubon Society. 2002. *Colorado's Important Bird Areas Program*. URL: http://www.audubon.org/bird/iba/co.html (accessed 1 October 2003).

4. Chipley, R.M., G.H. Fenwick, M.J. Parr, and D.N. Pashley. 2003. *The American Bird Conservancy Guide to the 500 Most Important Bird Areas in the United States*. Random House, New York, NY.

5. Northern Prairie Wildlife Research Center. No Date. *Bird Checklists of the United States*. URL: http://www.npwrc.usgs.gov/resource/orthrdata/chekbird/chekbird.htm (accessed January 30, 2004).

6. Rich, T. D., C. Beardmore, H. Berlanga, P. Blancher, M. Bradstreet, G. Butcher, D. Demarest, E. Dunn, C. Hunter, E. Inigo-Elias, J. Kennedy, A. Martell, A. Panjabi, D. Pashley, K. Rosenberg, C. Rustay, S. Wendt, and T. Will. 2004. *Partners in Flight North American Landbird Conservation Plan*. Cornell Lab of Ornithology, Ithaca, NY.

7. Arnold, J.F., D.A. Jamison, and E.H. Reid. 1964. *The Pinyon-Juniper Type of Arizona: Effects of Grazing, Fire, and Tree Control*. U.S. Dept. of Agric. Prod. Res. Rep. 84.

8. Balda, R.P. 2002. Pinyon Jay (*Gymnorhinus cyanocephalus*). In *The Birds of North America*, No. 605 (A. Poole and F. Gill, eds.). The Birds of North America, Inc., Philadelphia, PA.

9. Latta, M.J., C.J. Beardmore, and T.E. Corman. 1999. *Arizona Partners in Flight Bird Conservation Plan*, Version 1.0. Nongame and Endangered Wildlife Program Technical Report 142. Arizona Game and Fish Department, Phoenix, AZ.

10. Winter, K., and L. Hargrove. 2004. Gray Vireo (*Vireo vicinior*). In *The Coastal Scrub and Chaparral Bird Conservation Plan: A Strategy for Protecting and Managing Coastal Scrub and Chaparral Habitats and Associated Birds in California*. California Partners in Flight. http://www.prbo.org/calpif/htmldocs/scrub.html

11. Rustay, C., C. Beardmore, M. Carter, C. Alford, and D. Pashley. 2003. *Partners in Flight Draft Land Bird Conservation Plan—New Mexico State Plan*, Version 1.2. http://www.hawksaloft.org/pif.shtml (accessed 7 June 2004).

12. Brockway, D.G., R.G. Gatewood, and R.B. Paris. 2002. Restoring Grassland Savannas from Degraded Pinyon-Juniper Woodlands: Effects of Mechanical Overstory Reduction and Slash Treatment Alternatives. *Journal of Environmental Management* 64:179–197.

13. Beidleman, C.A. 2000. *Partners in Flight Land Bird Conservation Plan Colorado*. Estes Park, CO.

14. Nevada Partners in Flight Working Group. 1999. *Nevada Partners in Flight Bird Conservation Plan*. Reno, NV.

15. Parrish, J.R., F. P. Howe, and R. E. Norvell. 2002. *Utah Partners in Flight Avian Conservation Strategy*, Version 2.0. Utah Partners in Flight Program, Utah Division of Wildlife Resources, 1594 West North Temple, Salt Lake City, UT 84116, UDWR Publication Number 02-27. i-xiv + 302 pp.

16. National Park Service Office of International Affairs. 2005. *The NPS Sister Parks Initiative*. http://www.nps.gov/oia/topics/sister.htm (accessed 2 February 2006).

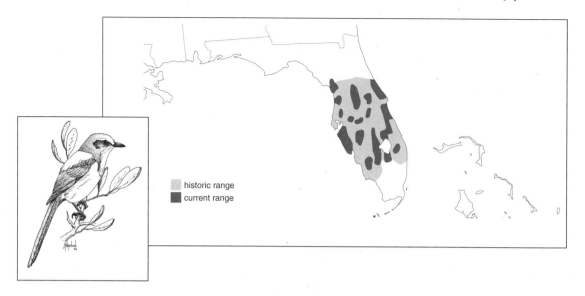

historic range
current range

FLORIDA SCRUB-JAY (*Aphelocoma coerulescens*)

The signature species of Florida's highly endangered native shrub-scrub habitat, the Florida Scrub-Jay is also one of the most intensely studied bird species in the world. Sadly, populations of the species continue to decline in the face of continued habitat destruction and habitat degradation caused by fire suppression.

STATUS AND DISTRIBUTION

Found only in Peninsular Florida once occupying 39 of the 40 counties but now restricted to 31 counties. Populations are highly fragmented, with fewer than 10 breeding pairs estimated from 6 of the remaining counties. Important sites for the species include Ocala National Forest, which supports an estimated 19% of the population (763 groups in 2001), the Brevard Scrub Ecosystem Important Bird Area (IBA) (286 groups in 2002 but most land privately owned), Cape Canaveral Air Force Station (111 groups in 2002), Merritt Island National Wildlife Refuge (<697 groups in 2004), and the Lake Wales Ridge IBA, including the Archbold Biological Station (265 groups in 1990s). The species is estimated to have declined by more than 90% since pre-European settlement times and by 25% since 1983. The species total population size was estimated at 4,000 breeding pairs and 10,000 individuals (including nonbreeders) in 1993.[1–5]

ECOLOGY

Restricted to oak-dominated Florida shrub-scrub habitat that was historically maintained by frequent fires and occurs only on very well-drained sand deposits. Habitat becomes unsuitable for the species if not burned within about 20 years after last fire. Mechanical removal of trees and other vegetation appears to mimic fires sufficiently in some areas so that jay populations can persist, though the long-term ecological effect of replacing fires with this type of habitat treatment is unknown. Like most jays feeds on a variety of items, including acorns, various berries and seeds, insects and other arthropods, small snakes, frogs, lizards, mice, and eggs and young of other birds. Acorns are an especially important component of diet as they are stored by birds in sand and recovered months later when other food supplies are scarce. Amazingly, birds can remember where they have individually stored thousands of acorns. Females usually lay 3–4 eggs in their open-cup nest placed in dense bush or tree. Eggs are incubated by the female only for about 18 days. Florida Scrub-Jay is famous for its cooperative breeding behavior in which just over half of breeding pairs have one or more helpers in some years. Helpers are usually offspring from previous years, and those breeding pairs with helpers produce more young than those with no helpers. Both members of breeding pair and helpers assist in feeding young, territory defense, and mobbing of predators. Young leave nest at about 18 days but are at least partially dependent on adults for another 85 days.[1]

THREATS

The greatest threat has been and continues to be direct loss of habitat and degradation of existing habitat mainly because of fire suppression. Beginning in the mid-1800s Florida shrub-scrub habitat began being extensively cleared for building homes, pastures, citrus groves, and later for airfields and various types of urban development. An estimated 10–15% of the original shrub-scrub habitat remains today and much of the remaining acreage that is under private ownership continues to be destroyed. In addition, many of the tracts of habitat that remain have become degraded because of lack of fire and have lost scrub-jays or have declining populations. In many areas, housing developments abut shrub-scrub habitat and prevent the use of fire as a management tool so that the only management alternative is mechanical removal of trees and shrubs. In addition, because the species is nonmigratory it has limited dispersal abilities, and populations that become separated by more than about six miles of non-scrub habitat are fully isolated and will not receive immigrants from other populations. Over the next 100 years, the most pervasive threat to the species may come from loss of habitat from sea level rise as a result of global warming.[1,6,7]

CONSERVATION ACTION

Florida Scrub-Jay was listed as a Threatened species by the Florida Game and Fresh Water Fish Commission (now the Florida Fish and Game Conservation Commission) in 1975, and was federally listed as Threatened in 1987. A Recovery Plan was published for the species in 1990 outlining a set of recommendations to stabilize or increase populations, including land acquisition and habitat improvement through prescribed burns and mechanical removal of trees and shrubs. The State of Florida started an ambitious conservation land acquisition program in the 1990s and had spent $3.2 billion on land acquisition—much more than the federal government spent on land acquisition during the same time period throughout the entire country. Many parcels of shrub-scrub habitat were purchased using these funds and funds from other sources as well, amounting to thousands of acres protected through direct acquisition. For example, the state purchased a 737-acre parcel of shrub-scrub habitat in Lake Placid in 2003 and a 181-acre tract in Altamonte Springs in 2003. The Nature Conservancy negotiated both deals on behalf of the state. The U.S. Fish and Wildlife Service established the Lake Wales Ridge National Wildlife Refuge in 1990 to assist in the protection of the shrub-scrub ecosystem and has acquired over 1,000 acres.

Management of habitat on existing preserves through fire and mechanical removal of vegetation is also increasing. The Lake Wales Ridge Ecosystem Working group was established in 1997 to share information and coordinate activities to promote the protection and management of Lake Wales Ridge Ecosystem. The group has many participating organizations and has helped further proper management of shrub-scrub habitat. The Archbold Biological Station has managed its 5,200-acre property for years using prescribed burns and has maintained habitat for about 100 pairs of Florida Scrub-Jays. The organization now also manages habitat at the adjoining 3,000-acre state-owned Lake Placid Scrub Preserve and the 10,300-acre Buck Island Ranch. Audubon of Florida is assisting Pinellas County Utilities as it works to restore habitat for Florida Scrub-Jays on its 12,023-acre Cross Bar Ranch Wellfield and Al-Bar Ranch. The County restored 200 acres in 1999–2000 and hopes to increase the number of jays from the current baseline of 21 groups. The Nature Conservancy has a Florida Scrub-Jay Fire Strike Team of six prescribed burn professionals that provides assistance in carrying out fire management in Florida shrub-scrub habitats. The team assisted with 140 burns of 9,168 acres of land between 1999 and 2003. At Ocala National Forest, which supports the state's largest population of Florida Scrub-Jay, a forest management plan was approved in 1999 with a goal of clearcutting 40,000 acres of sand pine scrub to provide 45,000 to 55,000 acres of habitat for between 742 and 907 breeding groups of scrub-jays.[1,2,4,5,7–16]

CONSERVATION NEEDS

- Slow production of global warming pollution.
- Continue efforts to acquire remaining parcels

of native shrub-scrub habitat within range of Florida Scrub-Jay.

- Continue efforts to restore and maintain proper habitat conditions (often with prescribed burns) for Florida Scrub-Jay where they occur.
- Continue research and monitoring of Florida Scrub-Jay to quickly detect any problems that could cause declines and to proactively manage the species and its habitats.

References

1. Woolfenden, G.E., and J. W. Fitzpatrick. 1996. Florida Scrub-Jay (*Aphelocoma coerulescens*). In *The Birds of North America*, No. 228 (A. Poole and F. Gill, eds.). The Academy of Natural Sciences, Philadelphia, PA, and the American Ornithologists' Union, Washington, DC.

2. Pranty, B. 2002. The Important Bird Areas of Florida. Unpublished manuscript downloaded from website 9 April 2003. http//www.audubon.org/bird/iba/florida/

3. Zattau, D. 2004. Personal communication.

4. Stevens, T., and J. Young. 2002. *Status and Distribution of the Florida Scrub-Jay* (Aphelocoma coerulescens) *at Cape Canaveral Air Force Station, Florida.* Annual Report 2001–2002. Prepared for 45th CES/CEV, Patrick Air Force Base, FL. 66 pp.

5. Breininger, D., B. Toland, D. Oddy, M. Legare, J. Elseroad, and G. Carter. 2003. *Biological Criteria for the Recovery of Florida Scrub-Jay Populations on Public Lands in Brevard and Indian River County.* Final report to Endangered Species Office, USFWS, Jacksonville, FL. 104 pp.

6. Ricketts, T.H., E. Dinerstein, D.M. Olson, C.J. Loucks, et al. 1999. *Terrestrial Ecoregions of North America: A Conservation Assessment.* Island Press, Washington, DC. 485 pp.

7. U.S. Fish and Wildlife Service. 1990. *Recovery Plan for the Florida Scrub Jay.* U.S. Fish and Wildlife Service, Atlanta, GA. 23pp.

8. Stein, B.A., L.S. Kutner, and J.S. Adams. 2000. *Precious Heritage: The Status of Biodiversity in the United States.* Oxford University Press, New York, NY. 399 pp.

9. U.S. Fish and Wildlife Service. No date. *Lake Wales Ridge National Wildlife Refuge.* U.S. Fish and Wildlife Service, Merritt Island NWR, Titusville, FL.

10. The Nature Conservancy. 2003. *Governor and Cabinet Make Students Happy With Protection of Undeveloped Land Adjacent to Lake Wales Ridge School.* http://nature.org/wherewework/northamerica/states/florida/press/press953.html (accessed 22 January 2004).

11. *EcoFlorida Magazine.* 2002. *Florida Scrub Purchase to Preserve Important Habitat in Lake Wales Ridge.* http://www.ecofloridamag.com/archived/spring02_news.htm (accessed 22 January 2004).

12. Audubon of Florida. No Date. *Florida Scrub-Jay Population Monitoring and Habitat Restoration.* http://www.audubonofflorida.org/conservation/jay.htm (accessed 21 January 2004).

13. Archbold Biological Station. 2000. *Lake Wales Ridge Ecosystem Working Group.* http://www.archbold-station.org/lwrewg/ecosystem.html (accessed 22 January 2004).

14. Archbold Biological Station. 2003. *Land Management: Stewardship of the Station's Greatest Asset.* http://www.archbold-station.org/abs.landmanage/landmgmt.htm (accessed 22 January 2004).

15. The Nature Conservancy. 2003. *Florida Scrub-Jays Get Help from the Nature Conservancy and Disney.* http://nature.org/wherewework/northamerica/states/florida/press/press1131.html (accessed 22 January 2004).

16. U.S. Forest Service. 1999. *Record of Decision for the Revised Land and Resource Management Plan for National Forests in Florida.* USDA-Forest Service, Atlanta, GA.

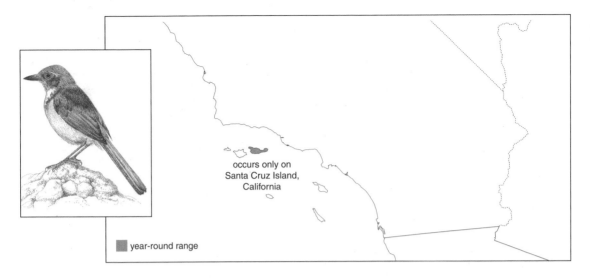

occurs only on
Santa Cruz Island,
California

year-round range

ISLAND SCRUB-JAY (*Aphelocoma insularis*)

One of only two species that do not occur anywhere outside of California, the Island Scrub-Jay occurs only on Santa Cruz Island off of southern California where its population currently appears stable.

STATUS AND DISTRIBUTION

Found only on Santa Cruz Island (60,645 acres) within the Channel Islands off of southern California. The largest part of the island (76%) is owned by the Nature Conservancy (TNC), with the remainder under National Park Service ownership as part of Channel Islands National Park. The species total population size was estimated at 12,500 individuals in 1997.[1,2]

ECOLOGY

Occurs in several habitat types on the island, including chaparral and woodlands dominated by various species of oak but also in Bishop pine forest and occasionally other habitats. Feeds opportunistically on a great variety of items, including acorns, various seeds, insects, lizards, and eggs and young of other birds. Females usually lay 3–4 eggs in their open cup nest placed in dense bush or tree. Eggs are incubated by the female only for about 18 days. Both adults feed young. Unlike in the Florida Scrub-Jay, territories are occupied by only single pair of birds, and helpers at the nest have never been observed. Over 40% of the population was estimated to be made up of nonbreeding birds that did not maintain territories and occurred in flocks frequenting habitats not occupied by breeding birds.[1]

THREATS

Santa Cruz Island has a long history of human use and impact. Starting in the early 1800s the island was used for a large cattle and sheep ranching operation. Over the years this resulted in major loss and degradation of the original native habitats on the island and is likely to have caused a decrease in the number of Island Scrub-Jays. However, despite these changes, the species has persisted with a reasonably healthy population on the island.

Today the species is thought to be generally quite secure on the island as no development or major habitat modification is expected to occur, especially since the largest part of the island is now owned by the Nature Conservancy and the remainder by the National Park Service. However, small, range-restricted species like the Island Scrub-Jay are always susceptible to unexpected calamities, including from inadvertently introduced plants, animals, or diseases. The number of introduced plants on the island had increased from 36 in 1900 to 170 in 1995, demonstrating how easily species can be unknowingly introduced. An estimated 5% of the island is covered by introduced fennel that is now being controlled.[1-4]

CONSERVATION ACTION

The Nature Conservancy and the National Park Service have active programs underway to rid the island of some of the most widespread and potentially harmful introduced plant species. All of these efforts to restore native habitats on Santa Cruz are expected to benefit Island Scrub-Jay. Both organizations worked together to rid the island of introduced or domestic species, including sheep and cattle, which were gone by 2000. Plans are now underway to rid the island of feral pigs.

The Nature Conservancy-owned portion of the island requires a permit for access and visits by the general public to the interior of the island are generally not allowed. A research station operated by the University of California is located within the TNC-owned portion of the park and supports a great many research efforts on the flora and fauna of the island, including research on Island Scrub-Jay. The National Park Service portion is open to visitation and there are several campsites and hiking trails. Regulations and recommendations are in effect to lessen the risk of unintentional fires or introduction of exotic plants and animals, though visitation is not tightly controlled and does not require a permit.[1-6]

CONSERVATION NEEDS

- Continue efforts to eradicate feral pigs from Santa Cruz Island and restore natural habitats.
- Continue efforts to control and eradicate introduced plant species on Santa Cruz Island.
- Develop or maintain regulations to prevent inadvertent introduction of harmful plants, animals, or diseases to Santa Cruz Island from staff or visitors and to prevent accidental uncontrolled fires.
- Continue research and monitoring of Island Scrub-Jays to quickly detect any problems that could cause declines and to proactively manage the species and the natural habitats on the island.

References

1. Curry, R.L., and K. S. Delaney. 2002. Island Scrub-Jay (*Aphelocoma insularis*). In *The Birds of North America*, No. 713 (A. Poole and F. Gill, eds.). The Birds of North America, Inc., Philadelphia, PA.

2. The Nature Conservancy of California. 2002. *The Nature Conservancy of California—Our Projects—Santa Cruz Island*. http://www.tnccalifornia.org/our_proj/santa_cruz_island/ (accessed 20 January 2004).

3. Channel Islands National Park. 2003. *Final Environmental Impact Statement For Santa Cruz Island Restoration Plan*. Channel Islands National Park, Santa Barbara, CA.

4. BirdLife International. 2000. *Threatened Birds of the World*. Lynx Editions and BirdLife International, Barcelona, Spain, and Cambridge, UK.

5. Santa Cruz Island Foundation. No date. *History of Santa Cruz Island*. http://www.west.net/~scifmail/sanhhisto.html (accessed 22 January 2004).

6. U.S. National Park Service. 2001. *Santa Cruz Island—Channel Islands National Park*. http://www.nps.gov/chis/scipage.htm (accessed 22 January 2004).

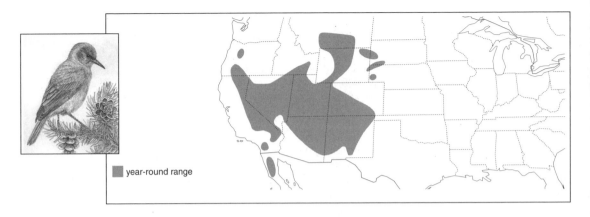

year-round range

PINYON JAY (*Gymnorhinus cyanocephalus*)

A highly social jay endemic to pinyon pine habitats of the western U.S. and (barely) Mexico, flocks can number in the hundreds. The conversion of millions of acres of pinyon pine to grasslands for cattle grazing has resulted in a decline in abundance estimated at more than 80% over the last 40 years.

STATUS AND DISTRIBUTION

Endemic to southwestern North America, the Pinyon Jay breeding range extends from central Oregon, southern Idaho and Montana south to southeastern California, Arizona, and New Mexico. Small isolated populations occur in South Dakota, Nebraska, and in Mexico's Baja California Norte. In years with little or no seeds available from pines, birds may disperse widely beyond normal range.

Breeding density maps produced from Breeding Bird Survey data indicate highest densities in northeastern and northwestern Arizona, northwestern New Mexico, southern Utah, and eastern Nevada. Important breeding sites for the species include New Mexico's El Malpais National Monument and National Conservation Area and Nevada's Desert National Wildlife Range and Great Basin National Park.

Breeding Bird Survey analysis showed a significant decrease of approximately 83% (4.6% per year) from 1966 to 2005 rangewide. The species total population was estimated at 4,100,000 individuals in 2004.[1–5]

ECOLOGY

Occurs year-round in foothill and middle-elevation pinyon-juniper, ponderosa, and Jeffrey pine forests as well as in sagebrush, chaparral, and scrub oak habitats. Forages on a variety of foods, including pine seeds, acorns, berries, grains, insects and other arthropods, small snakes, frogs, lizards, mice, and eggs and young of other birds. Pine seeds are an especially important food source, especially pinyon pine seeds. When pine seeds are abundant birds spend significant amounts of time extracting the seeds from the cones and carrying them to locations where they are cached in the ground. Birds have a remarkable ability to remember the locations of these caches so that they can feed on the seeds in them later in the season. It has been estimated that a single jay may cache as many as 2,600 seeds in a season, and a flock of 250 about 4.5 million seeds. Birds remain in large more-or-less permanent flocks within a home range except in years with few or no pine cone production when they may move large distances in search of food and join together with other flocks to form large groups containing as many as 1,000 birds. Birds pair in second year, building an open cup nest in a pine or juniper tree and laying 3–5 eggs, Only the female incubates the eggs, which hatch in about 17 days. The female broods young for the first ten days while male does all feeding of young and female. Later both parents feed young. In a few cases, yearling males will help at nests by providing food to young, removing fecal sacs, and guarding the nest. Young leave the nest at 21–22 days.[1]

THREATS

Loss of habitat from clearing of pinyon-juniper, chaparral, and other scrub habitat for cattle grazing, firewood collection, and housing developments has been a major threat. An estimated 3 million acres of pinyon-juniper habitat was converted to cattle pasture in the southwestern U.S. between 1950 and 1964. Human-caused effects on pinyon-juniper habitat across the western U.S. over the last 150 years have been significant and have resulted in complex ecosystem interactions. For example, heavy grazing reduced understory vegetation over vast acreages of pinyon-juniper and resulted in reduced fire frequency. Without regular fires, densities of juniper and pines increased. In some areas this allowed junipers to expand into lower-elevation grasslands. At the same time, any fires that moved through these higher density pinyon-juniper habitat would be larger, hotter, and more lethal to the normally fire-resistant pines. Such fires destroyed thousands of acres of Pinyon Jay habitat in the late 1990s. Most pinyon-juniper forests today are less than 100 years old. These complicated interactions and the lack of a full understanding of the ecological needs of Pinyon Jays and other animals tied to such habitats has made it difficult to understand the threats and issues impacting them.[1,6–10]

CONSERVATION ACTION

Partners in Flight Bird Conservation Plans in Arizona, California, Colorado, Idaho, Nevada, and New Mexico have identified Pinyon Jay and its associated suite of pinyon-juniper or chaparral bird species as a high priority and have provided recommendations for management, research, monitoring, and outreach. Unfortunately, the species has been poorly monitored and little-studied so many recommendations have centered on increased research and monitoring efforts. The U.S. Forest Service had a now-discontinued outreach effort to teach people, especially those who directly impacted pinyon-juniper habitat, the importance of this habitat type to wildlife and ways to manage it for the benefit of birds and other wildlife.[1,6–10]

CONSERVATION NEEDS

- Increase acreage of pinyon-juniper habitat within the breeding range of Pinyon Jay that is managed to attain conditions beneficial to the species.
- Decrease acreage of pinyon-juniper habitat de-

graded by cattle grazing and lack of prescribed burns.
- Develop baseline inventory of Pinyon Jay breeding populations

References

1. Balda, R.P. 2002. Pinyon Jay (*Gymnorhinus cyanocephalus*). In *The Birds of North America*, No. 605 (A. Poole and F. Gill, eds.). The Birds of North America, Inc., Philadelphia, PA.

2. Sauer, J. R., J. E. Hines, and J. Fallon. 2005. *The North American Breeding Bird Survey, Results and Analysis 1966–2005*, Version 6.2.2006. USGS Patuxent Wildlife Research Center, Laurel, MD.

3. Northern Prairie Wildlife Research Center. No Date. *Bird Checklists of the United States*. http://www.npwrc.usgs.gov/resource/othrdata/chekbird/chekbird.htm (accessed 30 January 2004).

4. Lahontan Audubon Society. No date. *Nevada Important Bird Areas Program*. http://www.nevadaaudubon.org/Iba/iba.htm (accessed 4 June 2004).

5. Rich, T.D., C. Beardmore, H. Berlanga, P. Blancher, M. Bradstreet, G. Butcher, D. Demarest, E. Dunn, C. Hunter, E. Iñigo-Elias, J. Kennedy, A. Martell, A. Panjabi, D. Pashley, K. Rosenberg, C. Rustay, S. Wendt, and T. Will. 2004. *Partners in Flight North American Landbird Conservation Plan*. Cornell Lab of Ornithology, Ithaca, NY.

6. Rustay, C., C. Beardmore, M. Carter, C. Alford, and D. Pashley. 2003. *Partners in Flight Draft Land Bird Conservation Plan—New Mexico State Plan*, Version 1.2. http://www.hawksaloft.org/pif.shtml (accessed 7 June 2004).

7. Brockway, D.G., R.G. Gatewood, and R.B. Paris. 2002. Restoring Grassland Savannas from Degraded Pinyon-Juniper Woodlands: Effects of Mechanical Overstory Reduction and Slash Treatment Alternatives. *Journal of Environmental Management* 64:179–197.

8. Nicholoff, S. H., compiler. 2003. *Wyoming Bird Conservation Plan*, Version 2.0. Wyoming Partners in Flight. Wyoming Game and Fish Department, Lander, WY.

9. Beidleman, C.A. 2000. *Partners in Flight Land Bird Conservation Plan Colorado*. Estes Park, CO.

10. Nevada Partners in Flight Working Group. 1999. *Nevada Partners in Flight Bird Conservation Plan*. Reno, NV.

11. Ritter, S. 2000. *Idaho Bird Conservation Plan*, version 1. Idaho Partners in Flight, Hamilton, MT.

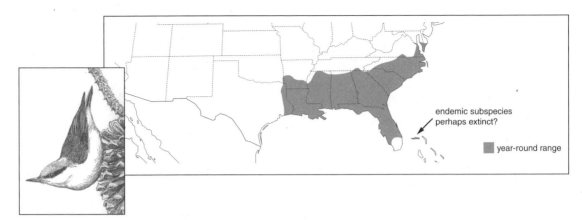

endemic subspecies
perhaps extinct?

year-round range

BROWN-HEADED NUTHATCH (*Sitta pusilla*)

This species has shown a consistent long-term rangewide decline over the last three decades but is inferred to have suffered massive declines in the late 1800s and early 1900s as virtually all of its southern pine habitat was removed by logging.

STATUS AND DISTRIBUTION

The species breeds in pine forests from eastern Texas and southeastern Oklahoma east across southern Arkansas and southeastern Tennessee to southern Virginia and Delaware south through the Gulf states, but is more patchily distributed in Peninsular Florida. An isolated population occurs on Grand Bahama Island in the Bahamas but was thought to be nearly extirpated by 1998. Breeding density maps produced from Breeding Bird Survey data indicate highest densities in the Piedmont region from North Carolina south to Georgia.

Many important breeding areas for the species are also strongholds for Red-cockaded Woodpecker, including Florida's Apalachicola National Forest and Eglin Air Force Base, North Carolina's Croatan National Forest and Fort Bragg, South Carolina's Frances Marion National Forest, and Georgia's Fort Stewart.

The species is inferred to have suffered massive declines from historic levels as only an estimated 3% of its native pine forest habitat remains intact today. Breeding Bird Survey analysis shows a significant decrease of approximately 46% (1.6% per year) from 1966 to 2005 rangewide. The species total population was estimated at 1,500,000 individuals in 2004.[1–5]

ECOLOGY

Occurs only in pine forests in southeast U.S. in areas with mature trees, little hardwood understory, and/or small natural or artificially created openings with snags. Such habitat is associated in much of range with pine ecosystems that have fires at 1- to 5-year intervals. Throughout much of range it occurs in longleaf/slash pine and loblolly/shortleaf pine habitats. Excavates nesting cavity (occasionally uses existing cavity) in decayed snags typically often within 3–10 feet above ground. May excavate several cavities before selecting one for nesting. Will also use nest boxes when snags are limited. Females usually lay 4–5 eggs that are incubated only by the female for about 14 days. Young are fed small insects or other arthropods and fledge at 18–19 days but are dependent on adults for another 2–4 weeks. Birds live in family groups and breeding pair often has one or more helpers from previous year's brood. Helpers assist in cavity excavation and feeding of incubating female and young. Normally raise only a single brood each year.[1]

THREATS

Greatest threat is loss, fragmentation, and degradation of mature pine forest habitat. Longleaf pine ecosystems once occupied an estimated 60–90 million acres of the southeast U.S. but have been reduced to less than 3 million acres and are continuing to decline from loss of longleaf forests on private lands. Only about 3% (90,000 acres) is considered to still be in natural condition. Much of the remaining pine forests are of young age trees with fewer snags and with a greater hardwood component than in the original forests, primarily today because of the lack of fires.

Today the greatest threats to the species in the surviving habitat are from fire suppression and detrimental forestry practices, especially on private lands. With fire suppression fewer snags are created and not only do hardwood species increase in frequency (to the detriment of the species) but, in the case of longleaf pine, no young trees grow to replace the older trees as they eventually die or are logged. Fires continue to be seen as negative events by the general public, often making it difficult to carry out the crucial controlled fires needed to ensure the survival of the pine ecosystems upon which Brown-headed Nuthatch, Red-cockaded Woodpecker, Bachman's Sparrow, and other species depend.

Forestry practices that have been and remain a threat to the species include the conversion of longleaf pine forests to pine plantations of various species, a practice that began in earnest in the 1940s so that by 1993 there were an estimated 15 million acres in plantations in the southeast U.S. These plantations generally either do not support Brown-headed Nuthatches or do so at very low densities for a variety of reasons including the fact that the trees are harvested before they reach sufficient age to provide nesting and roosting cavities, but also because virtually all trees are removed at the time of harvest. Logging practices on public lands have been modified over the last several decades to accommodate the needs of Red-cockaded Woodpecker, which is also beneficial to Brown-headed Nuthatch. However, logging of mature pine forests on private lands continues to occur at a high rate.[1,3,6-8]

CONSERVATION ACTION

Brown-headed Nuthatch has certainly been the recipient of a great many positive management actions aimed initially at improving habitat conditions for the federally Endangered Red-cockaded Woodpecker. The more widespread adoption of prescribed burns and the mechanical removal of encroaching hardwoods to maintain healthy pine forests on public lands in particular has greatly benefited the species. Certain modifications of logging practices on public and private lands can allow the Brown-headed Nuthatch to maintain populations. For example, the U.S. Forest Service has implemented longer periods between harvesting of trees and the retention of some old-growth trees within harvested areas for the benefit of Red-cockaded Woodpecker but also of benefit to Brown-headed Nuthatch.

A variety of activities have been targeted at private lands. The Nature Conservancy has purchased a number of parcels of pine forest with Brown-headed Nuthatch populations, including a 150-acre tract of longleaf pine in 2003 for addition to the Frances Marion National Forest in South Carolina and 1,160 acres of mature pine forest in 2000 in Virginia to create the 2,695-acre Piney Grove Preserve. As another example of how Brown-headed Nuthatch has benefited work targeting the Red-cockaded Woodpecker, the U.S. Fish and Wildlife Service (USFWS) began implementing a private lands conservation strategy for the woodpecker in 1992. As of 2003, the USFWS had entered into various agreements with 139 private landowners, resulting in protection of 347,439 acres of southern pine forest habitat.

The National Forest Service and the Nature Conservancy are working together to restore shortleaf pine habitat in the Mark Twain National Forest in Missouri so that Brown-headed Nuthatch and Red-cockaded Woodpecker can be reintroduced to the state. At Big Pine Key in Florida's Everglades National Park where the species had disappeared by the 1940s, a reintroduction program has been ongoing since 1997 using individuals from a population at Big Cypress National Preserve.

Partners in Flight Bird Conservation Plans that have been completed for southeastern U.S. physiographic regions have identified Brown-headed Nuthatch and its associated suite of southern pine forest bird species as a high priority and have provided recommendations for management, research, and monitoring. For example, the South Atlantic Coastal Plain plan recommended increasing the acreage of longleaf pine from 1.5 million acres to 2.2. million acres by 2025.[1,6-11]

CONSERVATION NEEDS

- Increase acreage of pine forest habitats, especially on private lands and state-owned lands, within the range of Brown-headed Nuthatch that is managed to attain conditions beneficial to the species.
- Provide nest boxes for Brown-headed Nuthatch where appropriate.

- Increase the number of private landowners enrolled in Safe Harbor Agreements for Red-cockaded Woodpecker.
- Increase purchases of land or easements on acreage supporting Brown-headed Nuthatch and other pine forest species by private conservation groups and government agencies when possible and appropriate.
- Continue research efforts for further refining understanding of the species biology, ecology, and management.

References

1. Withgott, J.H., and K.G. Smith 1998. Brown-headed Nuthatch (*Sitta pusilla*). In *The Birds of North America*, No. 349 (A. Poole and F. Gill, eds.). The Birds of North America, Inc., Philadelphia, PA.

2. Sauer, J. R., J. E. Hines, and J. Fallon. 2005. *The North American Breeding Bird Survey, Results and Analysis 1966–2005*, Version 6.2.2006. USGS Patuxent Wildlife Research Center, Laurel, MD.

3. Jackson, J.A. 1994. Red-cockaded Woodpecker (*Picoides borealis*). In *The Birds of North America*, No. 85 (A. Poole and F. Gill, eds.). The Academy of Natural Sciences, Philadelphia, PA, and the American Ornithologists' Union, Washington, D.C.

4. Chipley, R.M., G.H. Fenwick, M.J. Parr, and D.N. Pashley. 2003. *The American Bird Conservancy Guide to the 500 Most Important Bird Areas in the United States*. Random House, New York, NY.

5. Rich, T. D., C. Beardmore, H. Berlanga, P. Blancher, M. Bradstreet, G. Butcher, D. Demarest, E. Dunn, C. Hunter, E. Iñigo-Elias, J. Kennedy, A. Martell, A. Panjabi, D. Pashley, K. Rosenberg, C. Rustay, S. Wendt, and T. Will. 2004. *Partners in Flight North American Landbird Conservation Plan*. Cornell Lab of Ornithology, Ithaca, NY.

6. Catlin, D. 1999. *Brown-headed Nuthatch Species Management Abstract*. The Nature Conservancy, Arlington, VA.

7. U.S. Fish and Wildlife Service. 2003. *Recovery Plan for the Red-cockaded Woodpecker* (Picoides borealis), 2nd revision. U.S. Fish and Wildlife Service, Atlanta, GA. 296 pp.

8. Hunter, W.C., L. Peoples, and J. Callazo. 2001. *South Atlantic Coastal Plain Partners in Flight Bird Conservation Plan*. U.S. Fish and Wildlife Service, Atlanta, GA.

9. The Nature Conservancy. 2003. *Conservancy Acquires Strategic Tract as Addition to Frances Marion National Forest*. http://nature.org/wherewework/north america/states/southcarolina/press/press1276.html (accessed 18 January 2004).

10. The Nature Conservancy. 2000. *Nature Conservancy Adds 1,160 Acres to Red-cockaded Woodpecker Preserve*. http://nature.org/wherewework/northamerica/states/virginia/press/press130.html (accessed 15 January 2004).

11. The Nature Conservancy. 2003. *Missouri-Lower Ozarks*. http://nature.org/wherewework/fieldguide/project profiles/low.html (accessed 18 January 2004).

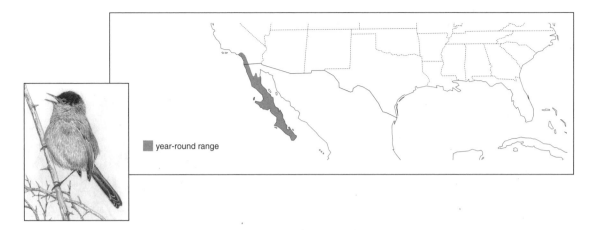

year-round range

CALIFORNIA GNATCATCHER (*Polioptila californica*)

A tiny bird with an inconspicuous wheezy call, the California Gnatcatcher occurs only in Mexico's Baja Peninsula and adjacent border regions of southwestern coastal California, where it has become one of the most well-known representative species of the globally unique community of endemic plants and animals of Baja California.

STATUS AND DISTRIBUTION

Endemic to Baja California, the California Gnatcatcher year-round range extends from extreme southwestern California south to the southern tip of Mexico's Baja Peninsula. Important breeding areas for the species in California include Camp Pendleton Marine Corp base (600 pairs in 1998), Lake Hodges/San Dieguito River Park (80 pairs), and the San Diego National Wildlife Refuge complex (over 500 pairs in 1998), and the Southern Orange County Important Bird Area (IBA) (over 350 pairs in 1998). In Mexico where the species is much more widely distributed it is known to occur within the Important Bird Areas of Sierra San Pedro Martir and Sierra La Giganta, and on the islands of Espiritu Santo, San Jose, Santa Margarita, and Magdalena. No trend estimates are available for the species but habitat is known to have decreased in U.S. by 70–90% since pre-European settlement and by 33% since 1993. The species' total population was estimated at 77,000 individuals in 2004.[1–7]

ECOLOGY

On the breeding range it occurs in dry scrubby habitats from sea level to 4,500 feet (but only to 2,400 feet in California). In California and northwestern portion of Mexico's Baja California it primarily inhabits coastal sage scrub dominated by California sagebrush (*Artemisia californica*). Most research on the species has been within California so the species distribution, ecology, and biology in Mexico are poorly understood. Female lays 3–4 eggs in an open cup nest usually built within three feet above ground. Eggs are incubated by both sexes for about 14 days. Both adults feed young, which fledge in about 13 days. These birds are very persistent breeders and may attempt as many as three broods per year, though high nest failure rates cause few pairs to produce more than one or two broods per season. Insects are the primary food source.[1,2,5]

THREATS

Loss of habitat from clearing of coastal sage and other scrub habitat for housing development is a major threat in the U.S. portion of the range and in Mexico near the U.S.–Mexico border. In some of the Mexican portion of the range, land clearing for cattle ranching and human settlements has eliminated or degraded much dry scrub habitat. In many areas introduced buffel grass (*Cechrus ciliaris*) has invaded, outcompeted, and eventually replaced dry scrub habitat. After buffel grass becomes established, fire frequency generally increases to the detriment of most dry scrub habitat. The species also seems to be susceptible to increased levels of Brown-headed Cowbird parasitism when habitat is fragmented.[1,3–5,8–10]

CONSERVATION ACTION

The species was federally listed as Threatened within its U.S. range in 1993. Within the U.S., much of the habitat it requires for survival occurs on lands in heavily populated southern coastal California—lands that could yield millions of dollars to private land owners if developed for housing. The question that the California Gnatcatcher forced society (at least in California) to consider was whether it is okay to prevent destruction of habitat that supports an endangered species on private lands and therefore potentially reduce the economic benefit that the landowner could receive if allowed to destroy the species' habitat. The flurry of lawsuits and media attention related to this question eventually resulted in the adoption of California's Natural Communities Conservation Planning (NCCP) process. Through this process, private land developers are allowed to destroy habitat and "take" some small number of California Gnatcatchers or other of the 77 Endangered or Threatened plant and animal species that occur in the region. In return the developer must set aside a larger amount of sage scrub habitat as conservation lands. As of 2001, at least 110,000 acres of natural habitat including 72,000 acres of coastal sage shrub had been placed in conservation status under six plans approved through the NCCP process.

The Mexican government has established a number of protected areas within Baja California to conserve the amazing and globally unique natural communities that occur there. Clearly, this should preserve habitat important for the survival of California Gnatcatcher populations.[1,10–12]

CONSERVATION NEEDS

- Evaluate success of California's Natural Communities Conservation Planning process in ensuring long-term viability of California Gnatcatcher populations in the U.S.
- Within Mexican portion of breeding range decrease acreage of dry scrub habitat degraded by cattle grazing and invasive plants, especially buffel grass.
- Increase acreage of coastal sage scrub habitat reclaimed and restored within the U.S. breeding range of California Gnatcatcher.

- Continue basic research into the species ecology and population biology especially within Mexican portion of range.
- Develop baseline inventory of California Gnatcatcher abundance and distribution in Mexico.

References

1. Atwood, J.L., and D. R. Bontrager. 2001. California Gnatcatcher (*Polioptila californica*). In *The Birds of North America*, No. 574 (A. Poole and F. Gill, eds.). The Birds of North America, Inc., Philadelphia, PA.

2. Howell, S.N.G., and S. Webb. 1995. *A Guide to the Birds of Mexico and Northern Central America*. Oxford University Press, New York, NY.

3. Chipley, R.M., G.H. Fenwick, M.J. Parr, and D.N. Pashley. 2003. *The American Bird Conservancy Guide to the 500 Most Important Bird Areas in the United States*. Random House, New York, NY.

4. Cooper, D.S. 2004. *Important Bird Areas of California*. Audubon California, Pasadena, CA.

5. Mock, P. 2004. California Gnatcatcher (*Polioptila californica*). In *The Coastal Scrub and Chaparral Bird Conservation Plan: A Strategy for Protecting and Managing Coastal Scrub and Chaparral Habitats and Associated Birds in California*. California Partners in Flight. http://www.prbo.org/calpif/htmldocs/scrub.html.

6. CONABIO. 2002. *Áreas de Importancia para la Conservación de las Aves (AICAS)*. http://conabioweb.conabio.gob.mx/aicas/doctos/aicas.html (accessed 3 February 2006).

7. Rich, T. D., C. Beardmore, H. Berlanga, P. Blancher, M. Bradstreet, G. Butcher, D. Demarest, E. Dunn, C. Hunter, E. Inigo-Elias, J. Kennedy, A. Martell, A. Panjabi, D. Pashley, K. Rosenberg, C. Rustay, S. Wendt, and T. Will. 2004. *Partners in Flight North American Landbird Conservation Plan*. Cornell Lab of Ornithology, Ithaca, NY.

8. Ricketts, T.H., E. Dinerstein, D.M. Olson, C.J. Loucks, et al. 1999. *Terrestrial Ecoregions of North America: A Conservation Assessment*. Island Press, Washington, DC. 485 pp.

9. Stattersfield, A.J., M.J. Crosby, A.J. Long, and D.C. Wege. 1998. *Endemic Bird Areas of the World, Priorities for Biodiversity Conservation*. BirdLife International, Cambridge, UK.

10. World Wildlife Fund. 2001. *California Coastal Sage and Chapparral (NA1201)*. http://www.worldwildlife.org/wildworld/profiles/terrestrial/na/na1201_full.html (accessed 6 February 2006).

11. World Wildlife Fund. 2001. *Baja California Desert (NA1301)*. http://www.worldwildlife.org/wildworld/profiles/terrestrial/na/na1301_full.html (accessed 6 February 2006).

12. World Wildlife Fund. 2001. *Gulf of California Xeric Shrub (NA1306)*. http://www.worldwildlife.org/wildworld/profiles/terrestrial/na/na1306_full.html (accessed 6 February 2006).

breeding range
wintering range

BICKNELL'S THRUSH (*Catharus bicknelli*)

One of the bird species with the most restricted breeding range in the eastern U.S., the Bicknell's Thrush's specialization on high-elevation habitat in most of its breeding range has made it difficult for researchers to study and for birders to observe.

STATUS AND DISTRIBUTION

The Bicknell's Thrush breeding range extends from a restricted portion of southeastern Québec, northern New Brunswick, and Nova Scotia's Cape Breton Island south through restricted high elevation habitats of central and western Maine, New Hampshire, Vermont, and the Adirondack and Catskill Mountains of New York. Throughout the U.S. portion of range, populations occur as a series of island-like patches of high-elevation habitat often separated by large-expanses of unsuitable lower elevation habitat. More than 90% of birds are thought to breed in the U.S., with largest expanses of available habitat in the Adirondack Mountains of New York and the White Mountains of New Hampshire.

Sites known to support important breeding populations of the species include the High Peaks Wilderness Area within New York's Adirondack Park, the White Mountain National Forest in New Hampshire and western Maine, Nova Scotia's Cape Breton Highlands National Park, and Québec's Forillon National Park.

In winter, birds migrate to the Caribbean occurring in eastern Cuba, Hispaniola, eastern Jamaica, and, rarely, eastern Puerto Rico. The bulk of the population is thought to winter in the Dominican Republic on the island of Hispaniola.

A number of parks and protected areas exist across parts of the winter range and likely provide important wintering habitat for the species, though limited data are available on occurrence and density of the species at these locations. In the Dominican Republic, sites that still have intact habitat that is known to harbor wintering Bicknell's Thrush include Sierra de Bahoruco National Park and the Madre de las Aguas Conservation Area. Other sites at which the species is known to occur include Cuba's Parque Nacional Turquino, Jamaica's Blue and John Crow Mountains National Park, and Haiti's Parc Nacional Macaya.

The species is detected on too few Breeding Bird Survey routes to estimate trends. Few other data are available to assess changes in abundance but the species has disappeared as a breeder from a number of coastal breeding locations in the Canadian Maritimes and possibly eastern coastal

Maine. The species' total population was estimated at 40,000 individuals in 2004.[1–9]

ECOLOGY

In the U.S. portion of the breeding range it occurs in stunted, high-elevation coniferous forest with high densities of balsam fir. In Canada, species breeds in montane balsam fir forests but also at lower-elevation stunted coastal spruce-fir forests and, in the Central Highlands of New Brunswick, regenerating clearcuts with high densities of deciduous tree species but with significant amounts of balsam fir. Species has been difficult to study because of remoteness and inhospitableness of habitat but researchers at Vermont Institute of Natural Sciences have vastly increased knowledge of the species in the last decade. Males do not defend territories on breeding grounds but have preferred song perches, though several males may sing from same area within same day. Females are thought to be territorial on breeding grounds. A single female may have young in the same nest from several males. Nests are typically built in thick, low stands of balsam fir within 10 feet of ground and at the base of a branch against the trunk of a tree. Females lay 3–4 eggs. The nests suffer a high loss of eggs and young from red squirrels when spruce and fir cone crops are low, which happens every other year in many areas.

On the wintering grounds the preferred habitat is montane broadleaf deciduous forest but birds have been found at elevations from sea level to 7,000 feet and in pine forests and, more rarely, in dry forest habitat. Although most records on wintering grounds come from mature forest, some birds occur in regenerating second-growth woodland. Studies of a small sample of radio-tagged individuals show that they often moved from broadleaf forest to pines to roost at night.[1]

THREATS

The majority of breeding habitat lies within protected areas and is generally secure from major loss or fragmentation of habitat. There are some cases of high-elevation forests being cut or fragmented for ski area development or placement of communication towers or windmills for power generation. Areas in New Brunswick that are managed for commercial forestry have created successional habitat for the species.

The greatest threat to the species and its habitat on the breeding grounds may come from the indirect effects of acid rain and deposition of heavy metals from air pollution originating largely from industrial coal-fired energy plants in the eastern U.S. High-elevation forests throughout the eastern U.S. have suffered increased mortality since the 1960s and air pollution has been implicated as one of the causes.

The most pressing threat to the species survival is the extensive habitat loss on the wintering grounds. For example, 98.5% of forest has been lost in Haiti, 90% in Dominican Republic, 80–85% in Cuba, and 75% in Jamaica. These habitats have been identified as among those of highest global conservation concern because of the great loss of habitat and the many endemic animal and plants species that also occur in these habitats. In many areas the cutting of forests has continued and occurs even within the borders of National Parks and other protected areas. Lack of resources to monitor and patrol parks and political difficulty of enforcing park regulations has hampered conservation efforts in many parks within the Caribbean wintering range of the species.[1,5,10]

CONSERVATION ACTION

Partners in Flight Bird Conservation Plans that have been completed for eastern U.S. physiographic regions have identified Bicknell's Thrush as one of the highest priority landbirds of the region and have provided recommendations for management, research, and monitoring. Vermont Institute of Natural Sciences has instituted a monitoring program for Bicknell's Thrush and other bird species that occur at high-elevation sites called Mountain Birdwatch.

On the wintering grounds a number of government agencies and conservation groups are involved in efforts to protect and manage parks and other protected areas within the wintering range of Bicknell's Thrush. Within the Dominican Republic's Madre de las Aguas Conservation Area, Fundación Moscoso Puello and the Nature Conservancy are developing plans for hiring and training park rangers, planting trees, and training local people in sustainable agriculture and foresty practices. In Jamaica, the Jamaican Conservation Development Trust and the Nature Conservancy are working to protect the forests in the Blue and John Crow Mountains National Park by posting and securing park boundaries, hiring and training park rangers and providing them with guard stations, two-way radios and vehicles, and monitoring short- and long-term changes in the park's plant and animal species.

. The U.S. Environmental Protection Agency's Acid Rain Program has worked toward reducing sulfur dioxide and nitrogen oxide emissions from industrial sources, especially coal-fired power generating facilities, the primary contributor to acid rain. By 1996 emissions from U.S. sources had declined by about 27% compared to 1980 levels. Similarly, Environment Canada's Eastern Canada Acid Rain Program had resulted in a 58% reduction in emissions by 1999 compared to 1980 levels. Unfortunately, further research has also shown that eastern Canadian wetland ecosystems are more sensitive to acid rain than first thought and further reductions in emissions are necessary in order to preserve these wetland systems. In 1998 various Canadian government agencies signed the Canada-wide Acid Rain Strategy for Post-2000 to reduce emissions to levels that would not harm Canadian ecosystems.[6,8,11–14]

CONSERVATION NEEDS

- Slow or halt deforestation of wintering habitat for Bicknell's Thrush and restore habitat where possible.
- Develop broad, landscape-scale forest management plans for the Central Highlands region of New Brunswick that ensure that tracts of successional habitat suitable for Bicknell's Thrush are always available somewhere within the region.
- Decrease rates of acid deposition from air pollution impacting Bicknell's Thrush breeding habitat.
- Develop baseline inventory of Bicknell's Thrush breeding and wintering populations, habitat needs on breeding and wintering grounds, and limiting factors.

References

1. Rimmer, C.C., K. P. McFarland, W. G. Ellison, and J. E. Goetz. 2001. Bicknell's Thrush (*Catharus bicknelli*). In *The Birds of North America*, No. 592 (A. Poole and F. Gill, eds.). The Academy of Natural Sciences, Philadelphia, PA, and the American Ornithologists' Union, Washington, D.C.

2. Wells, J.V. 1998. *Important Bird Areas in New York State*. National Audubon Society, Albany, NY. 243 pp.

3. USDA Forest Service. No date. *White Mountain National Forest—About Us*. http://www.fs.fed.us/r9/white/about_us/index.html (accessed 16 July 2003).

4. Parks Canada. 2003. *National Parks of Canada*. http://parkscanada.gc.ca/progs/np-pn/index_E.asp (accessed 15 July 2003).

5. World Wildlife Fund. 2001. *Hispaniolan moist forests (NT0127)*. http://www.worldwildlife.org/wildworld/profiles/terrestrial/nt/nt0127_full.html (accessed 16 July 2003).

6. The Nature Conservancy. 2003. *Dominican Republic—Places We Work*. http://nature.org/wherewework/caribbean/dominicanrepublic/work/ (accessed 16 July 2003).

7. Centro Nacional de Áreas Protegidas Cuba. No date. *Áreas Protegidas de Significación Nacional*. http://www.cuba.cu/ciencia/citma/ama/cnap/areasfr.htm (accessed 16 July 2003).

8. The Nature Conservancy. 2003. *Blue and John Crow Mountains*. http://nature.org/wherewework/caribbean/jamaica/work/art8665.html (accessed 16 July 2003).

9. Rich, T.D., C. Beardmore, H. Berlanga, P. Blancher, M. Bradstreet, G. Butcher, De. Demarest, E. Dunn, C. Hunter, E. Iñigo-Elias, J. Kennedy, A. Mortell, A. Panjabi, D. Pashley, K. Rosenberg, C. Rustay, S. Wendt, and T. Will. 2004. *Partners in Flight North American Conservation Plan*. Cornell Lab of Ornithology, Ithaca, NY.

10. Stotz, D.F., J.W. Fitzpatrick, T.A. Parker III, and D. K. Moskovits. 1996. *Neotropical Birds: Ecology and Conservation*. University of Chicago Press, Chicago, IL. 481 pp.

11. Rosenberg, K.V., and J.V. Wells. 2003. *Conservation Priorities for Terrestrial Birds in the Northeastern United States*. Proceedings of the 4th International Partners in Flight Symposium, Asilomar, CA, March 2001.

12. Vermont Institute of Natural Sciences. 2003. *Mountain Birdwatch*. http://www.vinsweb.org/cbd/mtn_birdwatch.html (accessed 16 July 2003).

13. Environmental Protection Agency. 2002. *Acid Rain*. http://www.epa.gov/airmarkets/acidrain/ (accessed 14 July 2003).

14. Environment Canada. 2003. Acid Rain—What Is Being Done? http://www.ec.gc.ca/acidrain/done-canada.html (accessed 14 July 2003).

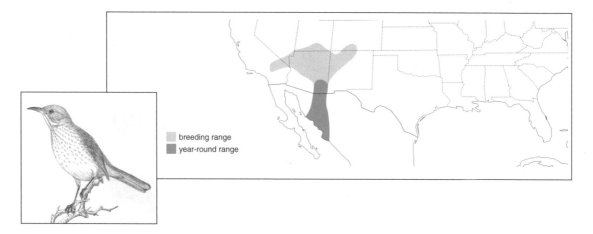

breeding range
year-round range

BENDIRE'S THRASHER (*Toxostoma bendirei*)

A poorly known species that is cryptic enough that leading ornithologists of the late 1800s didn't recognize the first specimen as a new species and thought it was instead a female Curve-billed Thrasher. The species' limited southwestern U.S. and Mexican desert breeding range and declining trend make it of conservation concern.

STATUS AND DISTRIBUTION

The limits of the Bendire's Thrasher range remains poorly documented because of difficulties in identification and lack of observers throughout much of its range. Breeding range extends from southwestern California east across southern Nevada and Utah to the southwestern corner of Colorado then south through Arizona and western New Mexico and then in Mexico to the northwestern corner of the state of Chihuahua and through Sonora to northern Sinaloa. Birds move south from the northern half of the breeding range in winter. Throughout this range birds are patchily distributed. In California, the species is distributed in a few isolated populations and does not occupy seemingly appropriate habitat in many areas. Breeding density maps produced from Breeding Bird Survey data indicate highest densities in northwestern New Mexico and southwestern Arizona.

Important breeding areas for the species include California's Mojave National Preserve, Joshua Tree National Park, and Death Valley National Park. Bendire's Thrasher is found year-round in Arizona's Cabeza Prieta National Wildlife Refuge (NWR), Organ Pipe Cactus National Monument, Buenos Aires NWR, and Madera Canyon. In Mexico the species is known from several Important Bird Areas, including the Sistema de Sierras de la Sierra Madre Occidental IBA and the Cuenca del Rio Yaqui IBA, both in Sonora, and the Babicora IBA in Chihuahua.

Breeding Bird Survey analysis shows a significant decrease of approximately 87% (5.3% per year) from 1966 to 2005 in the U.S. portion of its range. The species' total population was estimated at 170,000 individuals in 2004.[1–7]

ECOLOGY

Throughout its range occurs in desert scrub vegetation but types of plant associations occupied seem to vary across range. In the northern part of the range and at higher elevations it will use sagebrush habitat, while at lower elevations and further south it is typically found in desert grassland with scattered shrubs and cacti and desert shrubland. In the northern portion of the range it returns from wintering areas by February and begins nesting in March. Females lay 3–4 eggs in an open cup nest built in low shrubs. Very little information is known about the species' breeding biology but young are thought to fledge about 12 days after hatching. Normally at least two broods are raised per season. There is almost no information from its Mexican range or about its wintering ecology.[1]

THREATS

Analysis of threats is difficult because of lack of basic information on species' habitat preferences and life history. In many parts of its range its habitat has been lost or degraded from urban development, agricultural development, off-road vehicle use, mining, excessive pumping of groundwater, and invasive plant species. Some authors have suggested that excessive cattle grazing has been detrimental to the species but others have postulated that the species has benefited from the practice. In much of the Mojave Desert portion of the range, habitats are generally intact and well protected but lower-elevation valleys (which may have more Bendire's Thrasher habitat) are mostly in private hands and are not protected and many are threatened by potential development. In the Sonoran Desert region of the species range about 60% of the ecoregion has been degraded especially by urban and suburban development in many parts of Arizona. The human population of Arizona increased by 64% between 1980 and 1996 and this growth (and resulting loss of habitat to development) is expected to continue. Introduced buffel grass has taken over large areas of habitat to the detriment of native plant species and therefore also to birds and other wildlife. In Mexico the greatest loss of wintering habitat and the greatest continuing threat is from conversion and degradation of habitat for cattle ranching. Many large areas of habitat have been converted to nonnative grasses for cattle over the last 30 years.[1,5,8,9]

CONSERVATION ACTION

Partners in Flight Bird Conservation Plans in California and New Mexico have identified Bendire's Thrasher and its associated suite of species as a priority and have provided recommendations for management, research, monitoring, and outreach. However, in general, there has been little conservation activity focused on the species because of a lack of understanding of its requirements and reasons for its decline. Fortunately, much of its Mojave Desert and Sonoran Ecoregion range is protected within public lands and large expanses of intact habitat still exist.

A great deal of effort has been and continues to be focused on protecting and managing habitats within the Mojave Desert and Sonoran Desert regions. A 25-million acre expanse of southwestern California desert habitat was designated by Congress in 1976 as the California Desert Conservation Area to be managed by the Bureau of Land Management (BLM). In 1994 Congress passed the California Desert Protection Act that designated 3.5

million acres of the area as wilderness and establishing Death Valley National Park and Joshua Tree National Park. Both areas are important breeding sites for Bendire's Thrasher in California. In recent years, sections of the Conservation Area have been closed to mining, road-building, and off-road vehicle use and the BLM has increased efforts to control introduced burros and plants that are degrading habitat. Issues related to changes in land management policies for sections of the California Desert Conservation Area continue to be discussed and debated. For example, at the Algodone Dunes within the Mojave National Preserve—an ecologically unique site that supports breeding Bendire's Thrasher—thousands of off-road vehicle enthusiasts have protested restrictions on their use of the area and a rollback of protections was proposed and under public discussion in 2004. The Center for Biological Diversity has made environmental protection of the California Desert Conservation Area a major focus of its activities.

Within the Arizona portion of the Sonoran Desert, Pima County has been working with various groups over six years to develop the Sonoran Desert Conservation Plan—an ambitious plan that will attempt to direct development pressures away from the most ecologically sensitive areas and will establish a regional conservation reserve. The Coalition for Sonoran Desert Protection (made up of about 40 conservation and community groups) has been participating in the development of the plan and has been actively advocating for a county-level bond act to provide $250 million for land protection as a component of the plan. Various organizations promoting off-road vehicle use and other activities have objected to many of the plan's components because some areas would have restrictions on off-road activities.

The Nature Conservancy has spearheaded the development of a conservation plan for the entire Sonoran Desert Ecoregion that will identify priorities for conservation action in the area. A research project was recently initiated in Death Valley National Park to learn more about the population dynamics and breeding biology of California populations of Bendire's Thrasher.[1,2,5,8–17]

CONSERVATION NEEDS

- Continue existing conservation initiatives within the species breeding and wintering ranges.

- Increase research activities aimed at understanding the species habitat preferences and breeding and wintering ecology.
- Develop baseline inventory of Bendire's Thrasher breeding and wintering populations.

References

1. England, A.S., and W.F. Laudenslayer, Jr. 1993. Bendire's Thrasher (*Toxostoma bendirei*). In *The Birds of North America*, No. 71 (A. Poole and F. Gill, eds.). The Academy of Natural Sciences, Philadelphia, PA, and the American Ornithologists' Union, Washington, D.C.

2. Nelson, K. N., and J. M. Ellis. 2003. *Status and Breeding Biology of an Isolated Population of Bendire's Thrashers in California: A Study Proposal.* http://www.oikonos.org/projects/beth.htm accessed 26 January 2004).

3. Sauer, J. R., J. E. Hines, and J. Fallon. 2005. *The North American Breeding Bird Survey, Results and Analysis 1966–2005*, Version 6.2.2006. USGS Patuxent Wildlife Research Center, Laurel, MD.

4. Chipley, R.M., G.H. Fenwick, M.J. Parr, and D.N. Pashley. 2003. *The American Bird Conservancy Guide to the 500 Most Important Bird Areas in the United States.* Random House, New York, NY.

5. Cooper, D. 2001. Important Bird Areas of California. Unpublished manuscript available from Audubon California, 6042 Monte Vista St., Los Angeles, CA 90042.

6. CONABIO. 2002. *Áreas de Importancia para la Conservación de las Aves (AICAS).* http://conabioweb.conabio.gob.mx/aicas/doctos/aicas.html (accessed 18 June 2003).

7. Rich, T. D., C. Beardmore, H. Berlanga, P. Blancher, M. Bradstreet, G. Butcher, D. Demarest, E. Dunn, C. Hunter, E. Iñigo-Elias, J. Kennedy, A. Martell, A. Panjabi, D. Pashley, K. Rosenberg, C. Rustay, S. Wendt, and T. Will. 2004. *Partners in Flight North American Landbird Conservation Plan.* Cornell Lab of Ornithology, Ithaca, NY.

8. Ricketts, T.H., E. Dinerstein, D.M. Olson, C.J. Loucks. et al. 1999. *Terrestrial Ecoregions of North America: A Conservation Assessment.* Island Press, Washington, DC. 485 pp.

9. World Wildlife Fund. 2001. *Sonoran Desert (NA1310).* http://www.worldwildlife.org/wildworld/profiles/terrestrial/na/na1310_full.html (accessed 5 February 2004).

10. CalPIF (California Partners in Flight). 2006. Version 1.0. *The Desert Bird Conservation Plan: A Strategy for Protecting and Managing Desert Habitats and Associated Birds in the Mojave and Colorado Deserts.* California Partners in Flight. http://www.prbo.org/calpif/plans.html.

11. New Mexico Partners in Flight. No date. *New Mexico Bird Conservation Plan: Chihuahuan Desert Scrub.* http://www.hawksaloft.org/pif.cds.htm (accessed 5 February 2004).

12. Center for Biological Diversity. No date. *California's Grand Deserts.* http://www.biologicaldiversity.org/swcbd/goldenstate/cdca/ (accessed 5 February 2004).

13. Bureau of Land Management. 2003. *The California Desert Conservation Area (CDCA).* http://www.ca.blm.gov/cdd/cdca_q-a.html (accessed 5 February 2004).

14. Huckelberry, C. 2002. The Sonoran Desert Conservation Plan. *Endangered Species Bulletin* 27:12–15.

15. Campbell, C. 2003. *The Sonoran Desert Conservation Plan and 2004 Open Space Bond: Our Land, Our Water, Our Way of Life.* http:www.tucsonaudubon.org/conservation/sdcp2.htm (accessed 5 February 2004).

16. Burkhardt, G.A. 2003. *Pima County, Arizona Sonoran Desert Conservation Plan Threatens OHV Use.* http://www.off-road.com/land/sdcp.html (accessed 5 February 2004).

17. The Nature Conservancy. 2004. *Sonoran Desert Ecoregion.* http://nature.org/wherewework/northamerica/states/arizona/preserves/art7717.html (accessed 5 February 2004).

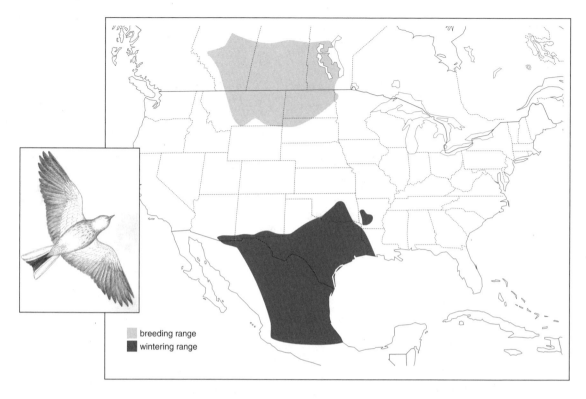

breeding range
wintering range

SPRAGUE'S PIPIT (*Anthus spragueii*)

A poorly known species perhaps because of its rather plain plumage and preference for open, windswept grasslands, the Sprague's Pipit is also one of the fastest declining songbirds of North America.

STATUS AND DISTRIBUTION

The species' restricted breeding range extends from southeastern Alberta across southern Saskatchewan to southwestern Manitoba then south to northwestern South Dakota and the eastern two-thirds of Montana. A small extension of the eastern range extends barely over the border into northwestern Minnesota. Range is known to have contracted in Minnesota and Manitoba. Breeding density maps produced from Breeding Bird Survey data indicate highest densities in southeastern Alberta.

Important breeding sites for this species include Saskatchewan's Grasslands National Park and the Govenlock-Nashlyn-Battle Creek Grasslands Important Bird Area (IBA), Alberta's Canadian Forces Base Suffield National Wildlife Area, Montana's Bowdoin National Wildlife Refuge (NWR) and Medicine Lake

NWR, and, in North Dakota, Lostwood NWR, Upper Souris NWR, and Little Missouri National Grassland.

The species' wintering range extends from southeastern Arizona across southern New Mexico (where rare) through Texas and southern Oklahoma to southern Arkansas and Louisiana. Wintering range extends south through Mexico to Mexican states of Michoacán, Puebla, and Veracruz. Wintering density maps produced from Christmas Bird Count data indicate highest densities in northern Texas though maps do not cover the Mexican portion of range where the bulk of the population winters.

Among many important wintering sites for this species are Texas's Attwater Prairie-Chicken NWR, Anahuac NWR, and Mid-Coast NWR Complex IBAs. In Mexico, the Saltillo Grasslands Protected Area in Nuevo León and the Janos-Nuevos Casas Grandes IBA in Chihuahua are known to host Sprague's Pipits in winter.

Breeding Bird Survey analysis shows a significant decrease of approximately 79% (4.1% per year) from 1966 to 2005 rangewide. The species' total population was estimated at 870,000 individuals in 2004.[1–6]

ECOLOGY

During the breeding season, this bird is a species of the mixed-grass and shortgrass prairie and avoids areas with more than a few shrubs. Prefers areas with grass of medium height and thickness. Generally not found in areas that are heavily grazed or in cropland. Occurs in highest densities in native grasslands and only rarely in agricultural grasslands. Originally native habitat was likely maintained through regular fires and bison grazing in a large landscape matrix with areas rotating in suitability as they burned or were grazed then grew thicker and eventually became unsuitable over time. Female lays 4–5 eggs in nest built on the ground among thick grass and often partly concealed by grass tuft. Eggs are incubated by the female for 11–17 days. Both adults feed young that fledge in 10–14 days. Normally only a single brood is raised per season. The species' migration and wintering ecology and habitat requirements are poorly known but it is found in grasslands, pastures, and sometimes in fallow cropland.[1,7,8]

THREATS

As in most species of grassland ecosystems, the greatest current threat continues to be loss and degradation of native habitat largely through conversion to cropland, overgrazing on rangeland, mineral and oil extraction activities, and fire suppression. Loss of northern mixed-grass prairie has been estimated at 36–69% and virtually no unaltered habitat persists in much of the breeding range. In some parts of the region only tiny fragments of native prairie still exist. Although much conversion of prairie habitat was historical, large amounts continue to be lost today. The virtual extinction of bison in the area has also changed the dynamics of plant succession so that mixed-grass prairie ecosystems must be maintained through fire and carefully managed cattle grazing. Invasion of exotic plants species, like leafy spurge, is a continuing threat as well. Within the species' wintering range grassland habitat loss has been even more severe. For example, Gulf coastal prairies were eliminated from Louisiana and only 1% of this habitat in Texas is now considered pristine. Chihuahuan desert grasslands have been extensively altered through agricultural conversion, grazing, urban development, invasive plants, and shrub encroachment. There are few protected areas within the entire Chihuahuan desert ecoregion.[1,9,10]

CONSERVATION ACTION

No rangewide conservation plan or management program has been focused on maintaining or increasing Sprague's Pipit populations but some broad grassland restoration work has benefited the species. Habitat management, especially through rotational grazing and prescribed burns has been effective in maintaining and increasing number of birds in areas where populations are relatively large and unfragmented. For example at Lostwoods NWR prescribed burns and light grazing of grasslands aimed at restoring the native habitat have increased Sprague's Pipit populations at the site.

The Canadian Government designated 112,500 acres of its Canadian Forces Base Suffield, a military installation, as a National Wildlife Area in 2003 to increase the number of acres of officially protected critical habitats in Canada. Grasslands National Park in Saskatchewan, established in 1981, is the only national park in Canada that protects a significant amount of mixed-grass prairie habitat. The park continues to add new acreage purchased from willing sellers and is planned to eventually include 226,500 acres—nearly double its current size.

The Prairie Pothole Joint Venture initiated the Chase Lake Prairie Project to conserve and restore habitat in a 5.5-million-acre block surrounding the Chase Lake NWR, where Sprague's Pipit occurs in North Dakota. The project area includes one of the largest intact pieces of native prairie in the state. Through the project the U.S. Fish and Wildlife Service has protected 12,890 acres of wetlands and grasslands through easements on private land and over 8,600 acres of habitat have been directly acquired.

In parts of the Texas wintering range, the species has likely benefited from conservation work focused on restoring habitat for Attwater's Prairie-Chicken. The U.S. Fish and Wildlife Service had entered into Safe Harbor Agreements with at least 13 private landowners by 2002 in the Texas coastal prairie region, which encourage management of grassland habitat to meet the requirements for Attwater's Prairie-Chicken.

Within part of the species' Mexican wintering range a coalition of groups, including Pronatura Noreste, World Wildlife Fund, and the Nature

Conservancy, has targeted the Chihuahuan Desert ecoregion for conservation and in 2002 the group completed a detailed conservation assessment for the region. The assessment includes a portfolio of sites that require protection to meet minimum requirements for conserving the highest priorities species and ecological communities. In 2000, Pronatura Noreste and the Nature Conservancy purchased a 7,000-acre ranch in Mexico's Cuatro Ciénegas Valley that includes desert grasslands.[1,8,10–17]

CONSERVATION NEEDS

- Develop a rangewide conservation plan for Sprague's Pipit that helps coordinate conservation work across the states and provinces that currently support the species.
- Incorporate Sprague's Pipit habitat objectives into public land management where the species occurs on public lands.
- Provide incentives for private landowners to manage their lands to the benefit of Sprague's Pipit and other native grassland species.
- Purchase land or conservation easements on private lands in areas that still support healthy populations of Sprague's Pipit and other native grassland species.
- Increase monitoring and life-history research for the species, including on the wintering grounds and during migration.

References

1. Robbins, M.B., and B. C. Dale. 1999. Sprague's Pipit (*Anthus spragueii*). In *The Birds of North America*, No. 439 (A. Poole and F. Gill, eds.). The Birds of North America, Inc., Philadelphia, PA.

2. Sauer, J. R., J. E. Hines, and J. Fallon. 2005. *The North American Breeding Bird Survey, Results and Analysis 1966–2005*, Version 6.2.2006, USGS Patuxent Wildlife Research Center, Laurel, MD.

3. Bird Studies Canada. 2003. *Important Bird Areas of Canada*. http://www.bsc-eoc.org/iba/IBAsites.html (accessed 24 October 2003).

4. Chipley, R.M., G.H. Fenwick, M.J. Parr, and D.N. Pashley. 2003. *The American Bird Conservancy Guide to the 500 Most Important Bird Areas in the United States*. Random House, New York, NY.

5. National Audubon Society. 2001. *North Dakota's Important Bird Areas Program*. http://www.audubon.org/bird/iba/nd.html (accessed 22 January 2004).

6. Rich, T. D., C. Beardmore, H. Berlanga, P. Blancher, M. Bradstreet, G. Butcher, D. Demarest, E. Dunn, C. Hunter, E. Iñigo-Elias, J. Kennedy, A. Martell, A. Panjabi, D. Pashley, K. Rosenberg, C. Rustay, S. Wendt, and T. Will. 2004. *Partners in Flight North American Landbird Conservation Plan*. Cornell Lab of Ornithology, Ithaca, NY.

7. Drilling, N., J. Griffin, and J.D. Reichel. 1998. *Sprague's Pipit (Anthus spragueii) Species Management Abstract*. The Nature Conservancy, Arlington, VA.

8. Dechant, J. A., M. L. Sondreal, D. H. Johnson, L. D. Igl, C. M. Goldade, M. P. Nenneman, and B. R. Euliss. 2003. *Effects of Management Practices on Grassland Birds: Sprague's Pipit*. Northern Prairie Wildlife Research Center, Jamestown, ND. Northern Prairie Wildlife Research Center Online. http://www.npwrc.usgs.gov/resource/literatr/grasbird/sppi/sppi.htm (Version 28MAY2004).

9. Ricketts, T.H., E. Dinerstein, D.M. Olson, C.J. Loucks, et al. 1999. *Terrestrial Ecoregions of North America: A Conservation Assessment*. Island Press, Washington, DC. 485 pp.

10. World Wildlife Fund. 2001. *Chihuahuan Desert (NA1303)*. http://www.worldwildlife.org/wildworld/profiles/terrestrial/na/na1303_full.html (accessed 28 January 2004).

11. Greatplains.org. 2001. *Shorebird Management Manual*, Chapter 2: *Interior Region*. http://www.greatplains.org/resource/1998/multspec/casehist.htm (accessed 22 January 2004).

12. Canada National Defense Department. 2003. *Government of Canada Designates Canadian Forces Base Suffield National Wildlife Area*. http://www.dnd.ca/site/newsroom/view_news_e.asp?id=1118 (accessed 21 February 2004).

13. Parks Canada. 2003. *Grassland National Park of Canada—Park Management*. http://www.parkscanada.ca/ (accessed 12 February 2004).

14. U. S. Fish and Wildlife Service. 2004. *Chase Lake Prairie Project*. http://chaselake.fws.gov/clpp.htm (accessed 22 January 2004).

15. Environmental Defense. 2002. *Texas Attwater's Prairie-Chicken/Coastal Prairie Safe Harbor Agreement*. http://www.environmentaldefense.org/article.cfm?contentid=141 (accessed 27 August 2003).

16. Pronatura, The Nature Conservancy, and World Wildlife Fund. 2004. *Ecoregional Conservation Assessment of the Chihuahuan Desert*, 2nd ed. www.conserveonline.org.

17. The Nature Conservancy. 2004. *Chihuahuan Desert*. http://nature.org/wherewework/northamerica/mexico/work/art8620.html (accessed 29 January 2004).

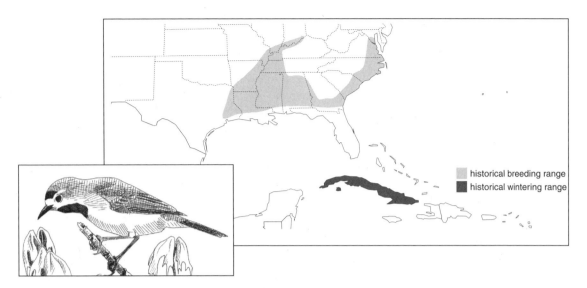

legend:
historical breeding range
historical wintering range

BACHMAN'S WARBLER (*Vermivora bachmanii*)

This species, like its counterpart the Ivory-billed Woodpecker, was doomed by the massive clearing of southern bottomland forest for agriculture and logs and from similar loss of habitat on its Cuban wintering grounds.

STATUS AND DISTRIBUTION

The Bachman's Warbler breeding range was restricted to the southeastern U.S. from eastern Texas across the Gulf states to Georgia (but excluding Florida) and north along the coastal plain to Virginia and southern Maryland then up the Mississippi and its tributaries to the southeastern corner of Oklahoma, Arkansas, southeastern Missouri, Tennessee, Kentucky, and southern Indiana and Illinois. From the limited information available it is thought that the species might have been most abundant in the Mississippi alluvial valley of Arkansas and Missouri. Protected areas that once supported breeding populations of the species include Tensas National Wildlife Refuge (NWR) in Louisiana, Francis Marion National Forest in South Carolina, and Big Lake NWR and Wapanoca NWR in Arkansas. In winter, birds moved south to Cuba and the Isle of Pines and, though data are limited, apparently were widely distributed there.

Bachman's Warbler was relatively abundant before 1900 and still locally common in a few areas until about 1920. In March 1886–88, 38 birds (presumably migrants) were collected near Lake Ponchartrain in southern Louisiana. In March of 1890, 46 individuals were collected along a 50-mile (113-km) stretch, and 50 were counted in one 10- to 12-acre area along the Suwanee River in northern Florida. In the same region another 50 were collected in March of 1892 and 1893. At Key West, Florida, where the species was a migrant, an estimated 150–200 birds were seen in July and August of 1887–89. Also in the Florida Keys, 21 birds were found dead after striking the light at Sombrero Key while migrating north on 3 March 1889. At the I'On Swamp, much of which is now within the Francis Marion National Forest, 32 nests of Bachman's Warbler were located between 1906 and 1918. In Kentucky, two breeding sites held 22 pairs of the species in 1906.

Records of the species became rare after about 1920. The last well-documented records from the wintering grounds in Cuba were in 1938 and 1940. The last documented Missouri record was in 1948, the last in Mississippi in 1949, in Florida in 1951, in Maryland in 1954, and in Virginia in 1958. There were records at I'On Swamp and Charleston, South Carolina, through the 1950s, with the last documented record in 1962 of a singing male at Moore's Landing near I'On Swamp. Reports of sightings of the species have continued intermittently since 1962 to the present day (a possible bird was reported from Congaree Swamp National Park in South Carolina in 2001) but none have been unequivocally documented. The species is generally considered extinct.[1–5]

ECOLOGY

On the breeding range, the species occurred in bottomland floodplain forest with thick understory typically along rivers and in swampy areas, though it is thought to have preferred the slightly higher, drier ground. It built its nests in thickets of cane, blackberry, and other shrubby species that grow in small openings in or along edges of the forest. Such habitat is often disturbance-related, kept open from regular flooding, or occurring in gaps caused by fallen trees or from severe windstorms or hurricanes. In the so-called Sunken Lands of Missouri and Arkansas, a location where a population is thought to have persisted into the 1940s, the severe New Madrid earthquakes of 1811–1812 apparently created habitat for the species when in some areas the land dropped as much as 15 feet in elevation, causing sudden flooding and tree falls. It has been postulated that the species was a cane specialist, though while it was often associated with cane thickets, available evidence suggests that it also occurred in other types of dense shrubby habitats. Although there is little information on feeding habits, the birds were known to probe dead-leaf clusters for insects like the closely related Golden-winged and Blue-winged warblers.

Nests were built low to the ground (<10 feet) in dense thickets often in cane or blackberries. Females laid 3–5 eggs. No information is available about length of incubation period or time to fledging, but is likely similar to other Vermivora warblers. Even less information is available on its habitat preferences on the wintering grounds, but it was found in a variety of forested lowland habitat. The species was one of the earlier migrants, passing through Florida and coastal Louisiana in February and March and arriving on breeding territory in March. Birds began migrating south as early as July.[1,4,6]

THREATS

On breeding grounds, the loss of habitat from clearing of large tracts of bottomland forest beginning in the 1800s was responsible for the extinction of both the Bachman's Warbler and its unfortunate habitat partner, the Ivory-billed Woodpecker as well as for the decline of other species associated with this habitat. The loss of such habitat in the southeastern U.S. has been estimated at 90% and in the Lower Mississippi Valley more than 80%. Most of the habitat in the Mississippi Valley was converted to agriculture and often the higher, drier portions of land that the Bachman's Warbler required were the first to be cleared because they were more accessible and least prone to flooding. An increase in logging of remaining southeastern old-growth forests occurred during the period 1880–1910 when the federal government sold large tracts of land confiscated after the Civil War. During World War I and II, politicians passed bills to ensure that forest owners would receive financial contracts for timber used for various industrial and war purposes. These actions succeeded in decimating many of the remaining large tracts of old-growth bottomland forest and made conservation efforts difficult because such efforts could be portrayed as unpatriotic by business interests. In many areas the destruction of bottomland forests continues to the present time. For example, in South Carolina 28% of bottomland hardwood forest acreage was lost between 1952 and 2000. One area that once supported the species near Tuscaloosa, Alabama, became the site of a four-lane bridge and highway development in the late 1990s. An undocumented but potential added detrimental effect could have been from nest parasitism by Brown-headed Cowbirds as the species' breeding habitats became increasingly fragmented and isolated.

On the wintering grounds, there has been extensive loss of primary forest wintering habitat. In Cuba, 80–85% of forest habitat has been lost to agriculture, especially sugarcane. The loss of Cuban Dry Forest habitat has been estimated at more than 90%. These habitats have been identified as among those of highest global conservation concern because of the great loss of habitat and the many endemic animal and plants species that also occur there.[1,7–11]

CONSERVATION ACTION

As both a legacy to the Bachman's Warbler and as insurance in case the species has survived, the preservation of any remaining unprotected large tracts of mature bottomland forest in the southeastern U.S. is essential. Partners in Flight Bird Conservation Plans that have been completed for southeastern U.S. physiographic regions have identified surviving bottomland forest bird species as a high priority and have provided recommendations for management, research, and monitoring.

These suggestions have included specific goals for increasing the acreage of bottomland forest in large blocks across the landscape. Within the Mississippi Alluvial Valley many projects to purchase or reforest lands are ongoing through many partner agencies and organizations, including the Mississippi Valley Joint Venture, U.S. Fish and Wildlife Service Partners for Wildlife program, the Natural Resources Conservation Service Wetland Reserve Program, Ducks Unlimited, and the Nature Conservancy. Through these efforts habitat loss within the Mississippi Alluvial Valley has halted and may have even begun to reverse. Additionally, similar efforts are occurring with support from the Atlantic Coast Joint Venture in the states of North Carolina, South Carolina, Georgia, and Florida.

The State of Florida started an ambitious conservation land acquisition program in the 1990s and has spent $3.2 billion on land acquisition—much more than the federal government spent on land acquisition during the same time period throughout the entire country. Many areas protected through the initiative include regions that historically supported Bachman's Warbler.

Unsuccessful searches for the species have been carried out at a number of historic locations over the years, including an extensive search from 1975 to 1979 that covered 20,000 acres of habitat in South Carolina, Missouri, and Arkansas using song playback. Less in-depth searches have been carried out during the last decade at Big Lake National Wildlife Refuge, Francis Marion National Forest, and Congaree Swamp National Park. Undoubtedly these searches will continue and the use of new technologies like automated recording units and recording devices operated from weather balloons may allow systematic surveys of otherwise inaccessible habitat.

Various conservation activities are ongoing in Cuba to protect forest habitat. For example, World Wildlife Fund Canada has provided grants to promote sustainable development activities by villagers living in and near the Ciénaga de Zapata Biosphere Reserve and to support national park staff working to halt poaching and habitat loss in the area. Cuban ornithologists have initiated monitoring of the resident and migrant birds at Cuba's Guanahacabibes Peninsula Biosphere Reserve to evaluate different land management strategies that will be implemented in the area.[1,12–15]

CONSERVATION NEEDS

- Protect remaining large tracts of bottomland forest habitat in southeastern U.S.
- Increase acreage of bottomland and upland forest habitats within southeastern U.S. that is managed for wildlife.
- Continue efforts to restore cane thickets within appropriate habitats in former breeding range.
- Preserve and restore native tropical hardwood stopover habitat in Florida Keys.
- Continue efforts to follow up on credible reports of the species and use new tools like automated recording units to confirm presence or absence of the species in the former breeding range.

References

1. Hamel, P.B. 1995. Bachman's Warbler (*Vermivora bachmannii*). In *The Birds of North America*, No. 150 (A. Poole ånd F. Gill, eds.). The Academy of Natural Sciences, Philadelphia, PA, and the American Ornithologists' Union, Washington, DC.

2. King, W.B. 1981. *Endangered Birds of the World: The ICBP Red Data Book*. Smithsonian Institution Press and International Council for Bird Preservation, Washington, DC.

3. U.S. Fish and Wildlife Service. No date. *Bachman's Warbler Species Account*. http://endangered.fws .gov/i/b/sab0z.html (accessed 18 February 2004).

4. Dunn, J., and K. Garrett. 1997. *A Field Guide to Warblers of North America*. Houghton Mifflin Co., New York, NY.

5. Chipley, R.M., G.H. Fenwick, M.J. Parr, and D.N. Pashley. 2003. *The American Bird Conservancy Guide to the 500 Most Important Bird Areas in the United States*. Random House, New York, NY.

6. U.S. Geological Survey. 2003. *Large Earthquakes in the United States: New Madrid 1811–1812*. http://neic .usgs.gov/neis/eq_depot/usa/1811-1812.html (accessed 19 February 2004).

7. Ricketts, T.H., E. Dinerstein, D.M. Olson, C.J. Loucks, et al. 1999. *Terrestrial Ecoregions of North America: A Conservation Assessment*. Island Press, Washington, DC. 485 pp.

8. Twedt, D.J., and C.R. Loesch. 1999. Forest Area and Distribution in the Mississippi Alluvial Valley: Implications for Breeding Bird Conservation. *Journal of Biogeography* 26:1215–1224.

9. Jackson, J.A. 2002. Ivory-billed Woodpecker

(*Campephilus principalis*). In *The Birds of North America*, No. 711 (A. Poole and F. Gill, eds.). The Birds of North America, Inc., Philadelphia, PA.

10. Stotz, D.F., J.W. Fitzpatrick, T.A. Parker III, and D. K. Moskovits. 1996. *Neotropical Birds: Ecology and Conservation*. University of Chicago Press, Chicago, IL. 481 pp.

11. World Wildlife Fund. 2001. *Cuban dry forests (NT0213)*. http://www.worldwildlife.org/wildworld/profiles/terrestrial/nt/nt0213_full.html (accessed 21 July 2003).

12. Mueller, A.J., D.J. Twedt, and C.R. Loesch. 2000. Development of Management Objectives for Breeding Birds in the Mississippi Alluvial Valley. Pages 12–17 in *Strategies for Bird Conservation: The Partners in Flight Planning Process*. Proceedings of the 3rd Partners in Flight Workshop, 1995 October 1–5, Cape May, NJ (R. Bonney, D.N. Pashley, and R.J. Niles, eds.). Proceedings RMRS-P-16, U.S. Department of Agriculture, Forest Service, Rocky Mountain Research Station, Ogden, UT.

13. Stein, B.A., L.S. Kutner, and J.S. Adams. 2000. *Precious Heritage: The Status of Biodiversity in the United States*. Oxford University Press, New York, NY. 399 pp.

14. World Wildlife Fund-Canada. No date. *Conservation Programs-International*. http://www.wwfcanada.org/AboutWWF/WhatWeDo/ConservationPrograms/Conservation.asp (accessed 22 July 2003).

15. Optics for the Tropics. 2002. *Migratory Birds and Forest Conservation in Western Cuba*. http://www.opticsforthetropics.org/projects4.shtml (accessed 22 July 2003).

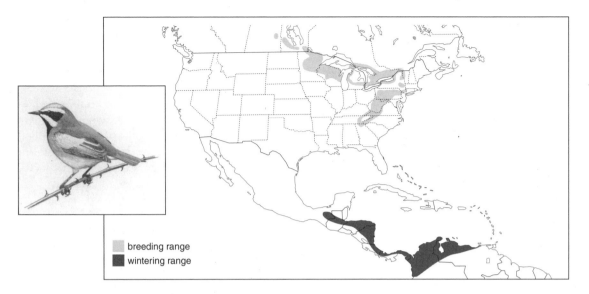

breeding range
wintering range

GOLDEN-WINGED WARBLER (*Vermivora chrysoptera*)

The Golden-winged Warbler is perhaps the most imperiled of a suite of declining bird species restricted to shrub-scrub habitats of the eastern U.S. and adjacent Canada.

STATUS AND DISTRIBUTION

The Golden-winged Warbler breeding range is restricted to the eastern U.S. and adjacent Canada from southern Manitoba east to the southeastern corner of Quebec and south to Vermont, New York, Michigan, and Minnesota and south through the Appalachians to Georgia. The range expanded northward in the last decades of the 20th century while disappearing from many areas in the central part of range. Small numbers may still occasionally breed in northern Illinois, Indiana, and Ohio. Throughout much of this range populations are fragmented and isolated. Breeding density maps produced from Breeding Bird Survey data indicate the highest densities in central Minnesota and northern Wisconsin. Data from the Cornell Lab of Ornithology's Golden-winged Warbler Atlas project also show high densities in high-elevation habitats in southern West Virginia. The states of Minnesota, Wisconsin, and Michigan were estimated to support 65% of the global population, the northeast U.S. and Appalachians 30%, and Canada about 3%.

Among many important breeding areas for the species are West Virginia's Guyandotte Mountain area; Minnesota's Tamarac National Wildlife Refuge (NWR), Sherburne NWR, and Carlos Avery Wildlife Management Area; Wisconsin's Crex Meadows Wildlife Area and Brule River State Forest; and Tennessee's Southern Cumberland Mountains Important Bird Area.

In winter, birds migrate to Central America and northern South America, occurring most regularly in mid-elevation montane forests from southernmost Mexico (Chiapas) and Guatemala south to Colombia and Venezuela and are thought to be more abundant on Caribbean slopes but no studies of this species status and biology on the wintering range have been published.

A number of parks and protected areas exist across parts of the winter range and likely provide important wintering habitat for the species, though few data are available on occurrence (much less density) of the species at these locations. Guatemala's Maya Biosphere Reserve, Costa Rica's and Panama's La Amistad Biosphere Reserves, Colombia's Sumapaz National Park, and Venezuela's Sierra Nevada National Park are among the protected areas that encompass habitat within the wintering range of Golden-winged Warbler.

Breeding Bird Survey analysis shows a significant decrease of approximately 61% (2.5% per year) from 1966 to 2005 rangewide. The species' total population was estimated at 210,000 individuals in 2004.[1–14]

ECOLOGY

On the breeding range it occurs in early successional shrub-scrub habitat, often on the edges of streams, swamps, and beaver ponds, and throughout the Appalachian portion of the range it occurs more typically at high elevations. In the northern portion of the range it often occurs in regenerating clearcuts and abandoned agricultural land, and in the southern Appalachians it is found in regenerating reclaimed contour mines. In some areas it occurs along power-line right-of-ways, where habitat is maintained in an early successional state. Throughout much of the breeding range it hybridizes with Blue-winged Warblers and in many areas it eventually disappears after Blue-winged Warblers become established. Nests are typically built on the ground. Female lays 4–6 eggs.

On the wintering grounds it has been little studied but is usually found in the canopy of mature forest or along woodland edges and perhaps is not as tolerant of second-growth habitat as the Blue-winged Warbler. Birds are thought to be territorial on wintering grounds, apparently maintaining spacing through chipping but not through song, and associating with resident flocks.[1]

THREATS

The greatest threat to the species on the breeding grounds is continued loss of shrub-scrub, early successional habitat as proportion of landscape in an early successional state continues to decline across much of the east. This decline in amount of shrub-scrub habitat is attributable to a variety of factors, including the maturation of second-growth habitat after widespread farmland abandonment across the region as well as loss of habitat to development in some areas.

On the wintering grounds, the middle and lower elevation foothill forests of southern Central America and the northern Andes where the species prefers to winter provide excellent conditions for growing various agricultural crops, including coffee, as well as illicit coca plantations, and forests in this zone are full of commercially valuable trees. These foothill habitats are being lost and fragmented, perhaps faster than any other forest habitat in the Neotropics and already harbor large assemblages of endangered and threatened species.[1,15]

CONSERVATION ACTION

Partners in Flight Bird Conservation Plans that have been completed for eastern U.S. physiographic regions have identified Golden-winged Warbler and its associated suite of shrub-scrub bird species as a high priority and have provided recommendations for management, research, and monitoring. Healthy, stable bird populations will require forest harvest planning schemes that incorporate ecological needs at a broad landscape scale that provides a mosaic of appropriate age-class habitat, including early-successional habitat. Developing such planning schemes is not simple because, while harvested forests can provide shrub-scrub habitat within a few years after clearing, it may take decades or even hundreds of years for forests to reach stages that provide habitat for birds that require mature forests.

The Tennessee Wildlife Resources Agency is working with a coalition of partners in an attempt to purchase an additional 80,000 acres within the boundaries of the Southern Cumberland Mountains Important Bird Area, which will create a contiguous protected area of over 141,000 acres in public ownership. At the Maya Biosphere Reserve in Guatemala, the Nature Conservancy, working with the Guatemalan government and Defensores de la Naturaleza, entered into an agreement to cooperatively manage the Sierra del Lacandon National Park within the Reserve and helped purchase 22,500 acres of additional habitat in the park. The Amistad/Talamanca highlands of Costa Rica and Panama is a priority of the Nature Conservancy's Parks in Peril program, which is working to improve the long-term protection, infrastructure, community integration, and management capacity of the multiple agencies responsible for managing the area.[2,7,16–18]

CONSERVATION NEEDS

- Increase acreage of shrub-scrub forest habitat within the breeding range of Golden-winged Warbler that is managed to attain conditions beneficial to the species within the context of large, landscape level habitat management plans, especially on public lands.
- Compare early successional habitats resulting from natural disturbances vs. forestry and other management practices, with regard to suitability for high-priority species.

- Develop management guidelines/policy for utility right-of-ways and other shrub habitats maintained in early-successional states.
- Identify sites where significant populations of Golden-winged Warblers coexist with Blue-winged Warblers; manage these sites as potential "safe havens" for sustaining Golden-wings within their historic range.
- Slow or halt deforestation of wintering habitat for Golden-winged Warbler and restore habitat where possible.
- Develop baseline inventory of Golden-winged Warbler breeding and wintering populations.

References

1. Confer, J.L. 1992. Golden-winged Warbler (*Vermivora chrysoptera*). In *The Birds of North America*, No. 511 (A. Poole and F. Gill, eds.). The Academy of Natural Sciences, Philadelphia, PA, and the American Ornithologists' Union, Washington, DC.

2. Rosenberg, K.V., and S.E. Barker. 2002. *Range-wide Population Status and Present-day Hybrid Zone of Golden-winged Warbler*. American Ornithologists' Union Annual Meeting, Poster Presentation, New Orleans, LA.

3. Sauer, J. R., J. E. Hines, and J. Fallon. 2005. *The North American Breeding Bird Survey, Results and Analysis 1966–2005*, Version 6.2.2006, USGS Patuxent Wildlife Research Center, Laurel, MD.

4. Rosenberg, K.V., and J.V. Wells. 2000. Global Perspectives in Neotropical Migratory Bird Conservation in the Northeast: Long-term Responsibility Versus Immediate Concern. Pages 32–43 in *Strategies for Bird Conservation: The Partners In Flight Planning Process*. Proceedings of the 3rd Partners In Flight Workshop, 1995 October 1–5, Cape May, NJ (R. Bonney, D.N. Pashley, and R.J. Niles, eds.). Proceedings RMRS-P-16, U.S. Department of Agriculture, Forest Service, Rocky Mountain Research Station, Ogden, UT.

5. National Audubon Society. 2002. *West Virginia's Important Bird Areas Program*. http://www.audubon.org/bird/iba/wv.html (accessed 17 July 2003).

6. Minnesota Ornithologists' Union. No date. *Birding Hotspots*. http://www.cbs.umn.edu/~mou/birdloc.html (accessed 16 July 2003).

7. National Audubon Society. 2002. *Tennessee's Important Bird Areas Program*. http://www.audubon.org/bird/iba/tn.html (accessed 17 July 2003).

8. Stiles, F. G., and A. F. Skutch. 1989. *A Guide to the Birds of Costa Rica*. Cornell University Press, Ithaca, NY.

9. Ridgely, R.S., and J.A. Gwynne, Jr. 1989. *A Guide to the Birds of Panama*, revised. Princeton University Press, Princeton, NJ.

10. Howell, S.N.G., and S. Webb. 1995. *A Guide to the Birds of Mexico and Northern Central America*. Oxford University Press, Oxford, UK.

11. United Nations Educational, Scientific, and Cultural Organization. 2002. *Man and Biosphere Reserves Directory*. http://www.unesco.org/mab/BR-WH.htm (accessed 17 July 2003).

12. Hilty, S.L. 2003. *Birds of Venezuela*, 2nd ed. Princeton University Press, Princeton, NJ. 878 pp.

13. Unidad Administrativa Especial del Sistema de Parques Nacionales Naturales. No date. *Parques Nacionales de Colombia*. http://www.parquesnacionales.gov.co/areas.htm (accessed 23 June 2003).

14. Rich, T. D., C. Beardmore, H. Berlanga, P. Blancher, M. Bradstreet, G. Butcher, D. Demarest, E. Dunn, C. Hunter, E. Iñigo-Elias, J. Kennedy, A. Martell, A. Panjabi, D. Pashley, K. Rosenberg, C. Rustay, S. Wendt, and T. Will. 2004. *Partners in Flight North American Landbird Conservation Plan*. Cornell Lab of Ornithology, Ithaca, NY.

15. Stotz, D.F., J.W. Fitzpatrick, T.A. Parker III, and D. K. Moskovits. 1996. *Neotropical Birds: Ecology and Conservation*. University of Chicago Press, Chicago, IL. 481 pp.

16. Rosenberg, K.V., and J.V. Wells. 2003. *Conservation Priorities for Terrestrial Birds in the Northeastern United States*. Proceedings of the 4th International Partners in Flight Symposium, Asilomar, CA, March 2001.

17. The Nature Conservancy. 2002. *Maya Biosphere Reserve*. http://nature.org/wherewework/centralamerica/guatemala/work/art8858.html (accessed 19 June 2003).

18. The Nature Conservancy. 2003. *Amistad/Talamanca Region*. http://nature.org/wherewework/centralamerica/costarica/work/art8690.html (accessed 18 July 2003).

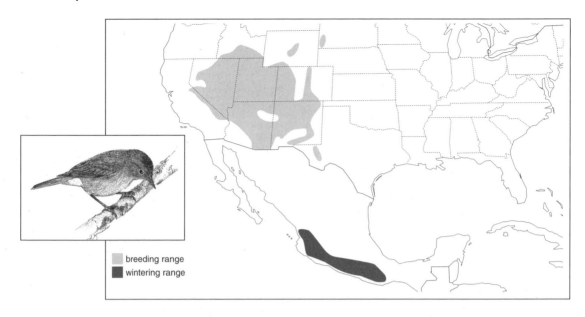

breeding range
wintering range

VIRGINIA'S WARBLER (*Vermivora virginiae*)

Within its western U.S. breeding range, Virginia's Warbler occupies habitats, especially pinyon-juniper woodlands, that are becoming increasingly destroyed and degraded by human activity.

STATUS AND DISTRIBUTION

The Virginia's Warbler breeding range extends from southern Idaho and Wyoming south through Arizona and New Mexico and west to Calfornia. Isolated populations are also known from South Dakota and Texas. Within this range the species has a very patchy and discontinuous distribution. Breeding density maps produced from the rather limited amount of Breeding Bird Survey data available for the species indicate highest densities in central Arizona, western Colorado, and north-central New Mexico.

Important breeding areas for the species include the Rocky Mountain National Park in Colorado, which is thought to support at least 1,000 individuals, Utah's Grand Staircase-Escalante National Monument (a site managed by the Bureau of Land Management), Arizona's Kaibab, Coconino, Tonto, and Apache-Sitgreaves National Forests, and the Gila National Forest in New Mexico.

In winter, birds move south to Mexico, inhabiting a range extending through the western mountains from southern Jalisco south to Oaxaca. There is no available information on wintering densities of Virginia's Warbler. Sierra de Manantlán Biosphere Reserve in the Mexican states of Jalisco and Colima supports wintering populations of Virginia's Warbler, as do the Tancitaro and Tacámbaro Important Bird Areas in the Mexican state of Michóacan.

Breeding Bird Survey analysis shows a non-significant decrease of approximately 29% (0.9% per year) from 1966 to 2005 rangewide, though the species was detected on relatively few Breeding Bird Survey routes. The species' total population was estimated at 410,000 individuals in 2004.[1-4]

ECOLOGY

On the breeding range it occurs most commonly in pinyon-juniper and oak-dominated woodlands but may inhabit a variety of scrubby habitats. Nests on the ground, usually laying four eggs. On the wintering grounds it has been little studied, but occurs in mountainous regions, utilizing thorn scrub and tropical deciduous forest.[1]

THREATS

On breeding and wintering grounds, loss of habitat from clearing of pinyon-juniper, other scrub habitat, and tropical deciduous forest for cattle grazing, firewood, and housing developments is a major threat. In many areas, scrub habitats are used for intensive livestock grazing, which reduces the shrub and ground cover densities below those required by Virginia's Warbler. The species also seems to be susceptible to increased levels of Brown-headed Cowbird parasitism when habitat is fragmented and degraded.[1,4–6]

CONSERVATION ACTION

Partners in Flight Bird Conservation Plans in Colorado, Nevada, New Mexico, and Utah have identified Virginia's Warbler and its associated suite of pinyon-juniper, oak, and scrub bird species as a high priority and have provided recommendations for management, research, monitoring, and outreach. Unfortunately, the species has been poorly monitored and little studied so many recommendations have centered on increased research and monitoring efforts. The U.S. Forest Service had a now-discontinued outreach effort to teach people, especially those who directly impacted pinyon-juniper habitat, the importance of this habitat type to wildlife and ways to manage it for the benefit of birds and other wildlife.

The National Park Service (NPS) has an agreement with Mexico's National Commission for Protected Natural Areas (CONANP) to provide training in natural resource management and park management and development of "sister park" relationships. Areas in Mexico like the Sierra de Manantlán Biosphere Reserve provide habitat for wintering Virginia's Warbler and could benefit from this exchange program between NPS and CONANP staff.[4–8]

CONSERVATION NEEDS

- Increase acreage of pinyon-juniper, oak, and scrub habitats within the breeding range of Virginia's Warbler that is managed to attain conditions beneficial to the species.
- Decrease acreage of pinyon-juniper, oak, and scrub habitat degraded by cattle grazing or lost to development activities.
- Develop baseline inventory of Virginia's Warbler breeding and wintering populations.

References

1. Olson, C.R., and T.E. Martin. 1999. Virginia's Warbler (*Vermivora virginiae*). In *The Birds of North America*, No. 477 (A. Poole and F. Gill, eds.). The Academy of Natural Sciences, Philadelphia, PA, and the American Ornithologists' Union, Washington, D.C.

2. Sauer, J. R., J. E. Hines, and J. Fallon. 2005. *The North American Breeding Bird Survey, Results and Analysis 1966–2005*, Version 6.2.2006. USGS Patuxent Wildlife Research Center, Laurel, MD.

3. CONABIO. 2002. *Áreas de Importancia para la Conservación de las Aves (AICAS)*. http://conabioweb .conabio.gob.mx/aicas/doctos/aicas.html (accessed 6 June 2003).

4. Rich, T. D., C. Beardmore, H. Berlanga, P. Blancher, M. Bradstreet, G. Butcher, D. Demarest, E. Dunn, C. Hunter, E. Iñigo-Elias, J. Kennedy, A. Martell, A. Panjabi, D. Pashley, K. Rosenberg, C. Rustay, S. Wendt, and T. Will. 2004. *Partners in Flight North American Landbird Conservation Plan*. Cornell Lab of Ornithology, Ithaca, NY.

5. Latta, M.J., C.J. Beardmore, and T.E. Corman. 1999. *Arizona Partners in Flight Bird Conservation Plan*, Version 1.0. Nongame and Endangered Wildlife Program Technical Report 142. Arizona Game and Fish Department, Phoenix, AZ.

6. Neel, L.A. (ed.). 1999. *Nevada Partners in Flight Bird Conservation Plan*. Nevada Partners in Flight Working Group.

7. Colorado Partners in Flight. 2000. *Colorado Partners in Flight Land Bird Conservation Plan*. http:// www.rmbo.org/pif (accessed 6 June 2003).

8. National Park Service Office of International Affairs. 2005 *The NPS Sister Parks Initiative*. http:// www.nps.gov/oia/topics/sister.htm (accessed 2 February 2006).

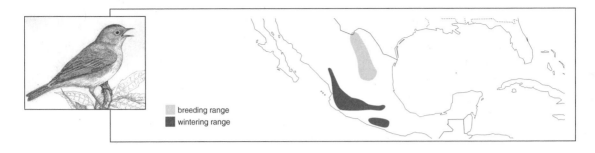

breeding range
wintering range

COLIMA WARBLER (*Vermivora crissalis*)

The breeding range of this essentially Mexican warbler barely reaches into the U.S. within the Chisos Mountains of Big Bend National Park along the Texas–Mexico border. Its very limited breeding range and relatively small estimated population make it a species of conservation concern.

STATUS AND DISTRIBUTION

The Colima Warbler breeding range extends from barely over the Texas border in the Chisos Mountains south through the Mexican states of Coahuila and Nuevo León south to southwestern Tamaulipas, northeast Zacatecas, and northern San Luis Potosi, but populations are patchily distributed across the range. An estimated 1% of the breeding population is found in the U.S., with the remaining 99% in Mexico. The entire U.S. breeding population of Colima Warbler (<250 birds) is found within Big Bend National Park (801,163 acres) in Texas. Important breeding sites in Mexico include the El Potos' Important Bird Area (IBA) and the the San Antonio Peña Nevada IBA both in Nuevo León, and the Sierra Maderas del Carmen IBA in Coahuila.

In winter, birds migrate to the mountains of the central and Pacific slope of western Mexico, where they occur from southeast Sinaloa and southwest Durango south to southern Jalisco and east to near Mexico City, and in western and central Guerrero south to northern Oaxaca. Sites that support wintering populations of Colima Warbler include the Nevado de Colima IBA in Colima and Jalisco and the Sierra de Atoyac IBA in Guerrero. There is no trend information for the species. The species' total population was estimated at 25,000 individuals in 2004.[1–6]

ECOLOGY

The species has been little studied, so most information has been gleaned from small numbers of observations or limited research. Breeds in pine-oak, oak, and pinyon-juniper habitats at elevations between 5,000 and 10,500 feet in the Chisos Mountains of Texas and Sierra Madre Oriental mountains of Mexico. Female builds nest on the ground under the edge of a grass clump, tree root, rock, or other concealing overhang and often on relatively steep slopes. Usually lays 4 eggs, which are incubated only by the female for about 12 days. Young are fed by both parents and fledge at about 11 days.

On the wintering grounds it has been even less studied but is usually found in brushy habitat within humid to semi-humid montane forest between 5,000 and 10,500 feet elevation. It is unknown whether birds are territorial on wintering grounds but it does occur in resident, mixed species flocks.[1,2]

THREATS

Habitats in the breeding range of the species in Texas are all protected within Big Bend National Park. Habitats throughout much of the range in Mexico have been subjected to much logging and clearing for agriculture, but the extent of loss of habitat for Colima Warbler is poorly quantified. One study estimated that 40% of pine-oak forests had been logged or converted to agriculture. Similarly, forested habitats for the species in its wintering range continue to be lost to logging, clearing for agriculture, grazing, and development.[1,2,7,8]

CONSERVATION ACTION

Little conservation work has focused on the Colima Warbler or its habitats. However, along with Big Bend National Park in Texas there are a number of protected areas within Mexico where the species occurs. The U.S. Department of the Interior and SEMARNAP, its agency counterpart in Mexico, have had an ongoing initiative for working together in the Big Bend region of Texas and Mexico that has resulted in a number of meetings and cross-border exchanges.[1,2,7,9]

CONSERVATION NEEDS

- Develop baseline inventory of Colima Warbler breeding and wintering populations.
- Initiate research on the species' ecology and breeding biology.

References

1. Beason, R.C., and R. H. Wauer. 1998. Colima Warbler (*Vermivora crissalis*). In *The Birds of North America*, No. 383 (A. Poole and F. Gill, eds.). The Birds of North America, Inc., Philadelphia, PA.

2. BirdLife International. 2000. *Threatened Birds of the World.* Lynx Editions and BirdLife International, Barcelona, Spain, and Cambridge, UK.

3. Chipley, R.M., G.H. Fenwick, M.J. Parr, and D.N. Pashley. 2003. *The American Bird Conservancy Guide to the 500 Most Important Bird Areas in the United States.* Random House, New York, NY.

4. CONABIO. 2002. *Áreas de Importancia para la Conservación de las Aves (AICAS)*. http://conabioweb .conabio.gob.mx/aicas/doctos/aicas.html (accessed 21 January 2004).

5. Howell, S.N.G. 1999. *A Bird-finding Guide to Mexico.* Cornell University Press, Ithaca, NY. 365 pp.

6. Rich, T. D., C. Beardmore, H. Berlanga, P. Blancher, M. Bradstreet, G. Butcher, D. Demarest, E. Dunn, C. Hunter, E. Iñigo-Elias, J. Kennedy, A. Martell, A. Panjabi, D. Pashley, K. Rosenberg, C. Rustay, S. Wendt, and T. Will. 2004. *Partners in Flight North American Landbird Conservation Plan.* Cornell Lab of Ornithology, Ithaca, NY.

7. BirdLife International. 2003. *BirdLife's Online World Bird Database: the Site for Bird Conservation*, Version 2.0. BirdLife International, Cambridge, UK. http://www.birdlife.org (accessed 23 January 2004).

8. World Wildlife Fund. 2001. *Sierra Madre Oriental Pine-Oak Forests (NA0303)*. http://www.worldwildlife .org/wildworld/profiles/terrestrial/na/na0303_full.html (accessed 23 January 2004).

9. U.S. Department of the Interior. 2001. *U.S. Mexico Sister Areas Issue Team*. http://www.cerc.usgs .gov/FCC/issue%220teams/US_Mexico_Sister_Areas .html (accessed 23 January 2004).

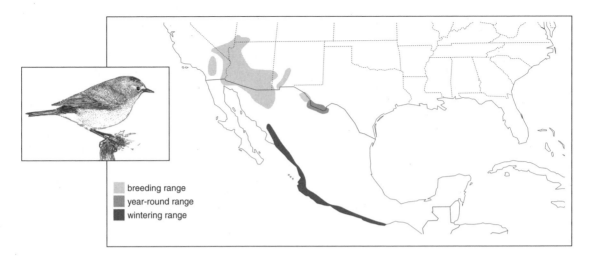

breeding range
year-round range
wintering range

LUCY'S WARBLER (*Vermivora luciae*)

This inconspicuous warbler has a limited breeding range in the southwestern U.S. and adjacent Mexico and breeds in mesquite woodlands and riparian habitats that have been severely degraded in much of its range. It is one of the poorest-known warblers of North America.

STATUS AND DISTRIBUTION

Endemic to southwestern North America, the Lucy's Warbler breeding range extends from California, Nevada, Utah, and Colorado south through Arizona and New Mexico (rare in southwestern Texas) to Mexico's northern Baja California and northern Sonora and barely extending into the northwestern corner of Chihuahua. Within this range the species has a very patchy and discontinuous distribution.

Breeding density maps produced from the rather limited amount of Breeding Bird Survey data available for the species indicate highest densities in southeastern Arizona. Important breeding areas for the species include the Lower Colorado River Valley in Arizona and California where Havasu, Cibola, and Imperial National Wildlife Refuges are located; Arizona's San Pedro National Conservation Area, a stretch of some 40 miles (56,000 acres) along the San Pedro River managed by the Bureau of Land Management (BLM); Arizona's Grand Canyon National Park; and New Mexico's Gila Box Riparian National Conservation Area, also managed by the BLM.

In winter, birds move south to western Mexico, inhabiting a range extending along the Pacific coast from southern Sonora south to Oaxaca. There is no available information on wintering densities of Lucy's Warbler.

Breeding Bird Survey analysis shows a non-significant decrease of approximately 8% (0.2% per year) from 1966 to 2005 rangewide, though the species was detected on very few Breeding Bird Survey routes. However, riparian habitat within its breeding range has been severely degraded or lost from large areas since the late 1800s so the species must have declined greatly since that time. Within areas where it occurs, the species has one of the highest densities reported for North American warblers and these high densities and clumped distribution make surveying for the species quite difficult. The species' total population was estimated at 1,200,000 individuals in 2004.[1-6]

ECOLOGY

On the breeding range it occurs most commonly in dense mesquite woodlands but also in willows and cottonwoods along rivers and streams. More recently it has been found nesting in habitats along rivers dominated by introduced tamarisk (salt cedar). Occurs in lower densities in shrubby vegetation in dry desert washes. Unusual among warblers, the Lucy's Warbler nests in tree cavities and behind slabs of loose bark and thus generally requires woodland with some mature trees. On the wintering grounds it has been little studied. Studies that have been done show that the species is relatively specialized in its habitat usage and occurs in habitats similar to those on the breeding grounds.[1]

THREATS

On breeding and wintering grounds, loss of habitat from clearing of riparian forests for cattle grazing, firewood collection, agricultural interests, and housing developments is a major threat. It has been estimated that 95% of western riparian habitats have been lost or degraded in the last 100 years. The loss of water flow in major rivers as water is taken for agriculture and to supply urban areas is a major problem that degrades riparian habitats, as is the loss of flooding regimes caused by damming the rivers and regulating the flow of water.[1,7]

CONSERVATION ACTION

Partners in Flight Bird Conservation Plans in Arizona, Nevada, and New Mexico have identified Lucy's Warbler and its associated suite of lowland riparian or mesquite habitat bird species as a high priority and have provided recommendations for management, research, monitoring, and outreach. Many efforts are underway to restore and protect riparian habitats along major river systems in Arizona and New Mexico. For example, the Upper San Pedro Partnership is a consortium of 20 agencies and organizations working together to meet the water needs of area residents while protecting the San Pedro River. The Nature Conservancy owns several preserves along the Lower San Pedro. The Conservancy acquired a 2,000-acre ranch along the river in 2002 and an easement on a 900-acre ranch in 2003 and announced that both ranches would stop all groundwater pumping.[7–11]

CONSERVATION NEEDS

- Increase acreage of healthy riparian and associated habitats within the breeding range of Lucy's Warbler that is managed to attain conditions beneficial to the species.
- Eliminate livestock grazing within lowland riparian habitats.
- Eliminate or decrease acreage impacted by invasive plant species.
- Restore regular flooding and fire regimes to habitats used by Lucy's Warbler.

- Develop baseline inventory of Lucy's Warbler breeding and wintering populations.

References

1. Johnson, R.R., H.K. Yard, and B. T. Brown. 1997. Lucy's Warbler (*Vermivora luciae*). In *The Birds of North America*, No. 318 (A. Poole and F. Gill, eds.). The Academy of Natural Sciences, Philadelphia, PA, and the American Ornithologists' Union, Washington, D.C.

2. Sauer, J. R., J. E. Hines, and J. Fallon. 2005. *The North American Breeding Bird Survey, Results and Analysis 1966–2005*, Version 6.2.2006. USGS Patuxent Wildlife Research Center, Laurel, MD.

3. Cooper, D.S. 2002. *California Important Bird Areas*. Audubon California, Sacramento, CA.

4. Rich, T. D., C. Beardmore, H. Berlanga, P. Blancher, M. Bradstreet, G. Butcher, D. Demarest, E. Dunn, C. Hunter, E. Iñigo-Elias, J. Kennedy, A. Martell, A. Panjabi, D. Pashley, K. Rosenberg, C. Rustay, S. Wendt, and T. Will. 2004. *Partners in Flight North American Landbird Conservation Plan*. Cornell Lab of Ornithology, Ithaca, NY.

5. Rosenberg, K.V., R.D. Ohmart, W.C. Hunter, and B.W. Anderson. 1991. *Birds of the Lower Colorado River Valley*. University of Arizona Press, Tucson, AZ.

6. Ricketts, T.H., E. Dinerstein, D.M. Olson, C.J. Loucks, et al. 1999. *Terrestrial Ecoregions of North America: A Conservation Assessment*. Island Press, Washington, DC.

7. Latta, M.J., C.J. Beardmore, and T.E. Corman. 1999. *Arizona Partners in Flight Bird Conservation Plan*, Version 1.0. Nongame and Endangered Wildlife Program Technical Report 142. Arizona Game and Fish Department, Phoenix, AZ.

8. Neel, L.A. (ed.). 1999. *Nevada Partners in Flight Bird Conservation Plan*. Nevada Partners in Flight Working Group.

9. Rustay, C., C. Beardmore, M. Carter, C. Alford, and D. Pashley. 2003. *Partners in Flight Draft Land Bird Conservation Plan–New Mexico State Plan*, Version 1.2. http://www.hawksaloft.org/pif.shtml (accessed 7 June 2004).

10. Bureau of Land Management. 21 September 2003. *San Pedro Riparian National Conservation Area*. http://azwww.az.blm.gov/tfo/spnca/spnca-info.html (accessed 19 January 2004).

11. Commission for Environmental Cooperation. 1999. *Ribbon of Life: An Agenda for Preserving Transboundary Migratory Bird Habitat on the Upper San Pedro River*. Commission for Environmental Cooperation, Montreal, QC, Canada.

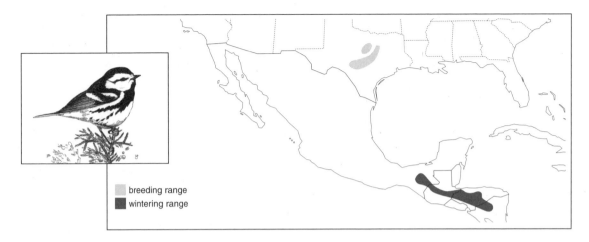

breeding range
wintering range

GOLDEN-CHEEKED WARBLER (*Dendroica chrysoparia*)

One of the bird species with the most restricted breeding ranges in the U.S., the Golden-cheeked Warbler nests only within central Texas, where its mature juniper-oak habitat has been greatly reduced from clearing for agriculture and development.

STATUS AND DISTRIBUTION

The entire Golden-cheeked Warbler breeding range lies within central Texas. It is known to breed in 25 of the state's 254 counties but even over this small area the species is patchily distributed with populations becoming increasingly fragmented in some areas. Important breeding sites for the species include Fort Hood Military Installation (4,500 pairs), Balcones Canyonlands National Wildlife Refuge (800 singing males), Pedernales Falls State Park (70 pairs), Barton Creek Habitat Preserve (60–65 pairs), Kerr Wildlife Management Area (55 birds in 1999), and Lost Maples State Natural Area (95 singing males).

In winter, birds migrate to southern Mexico and northern Central America, occuring from the Mexican state of Chiapas south through Guatamala and Honduras, possibly to northwestern Nicaruagua. Golden-cheeked Warbler is known to occur in migration in the Nacimiento Río Sabinas/SE Sierra de Santa Rosa Important Bird Area (IBA) in the Mexican state of Coahuila. Important wintering areas for the species in Chiapas include the Cerros de Tapalapa IBA, the Cerro Blanco/La Yerbabuena, y Jotolchén IBA, the Cerros de San Cristóbal de las Casas IBA, the Lagos de Montebello IBA, and the Montañas del Norte de Chiapas IBA. This species also winters in the Sierra de las Minas Biosphere Reserve in Guatemala and may winter in the Celaque, Cusuco, and Santa Barbara National Parks in Honduras.

No trend information is available for the species as a whole but analysis of available habitat inferred a reduction of 25% in available territories from 1962 to 1981. The species' total population was estimated at 9,600–32,000 individuals in 1990 and at 21,000 in 2004.[1–7]

ECOLOGY

On the breeding range it occurs in old-growth and mature juniper-oak woodlands that are at least 25–50 years old. Females lay 3–4 eggs in an open cup nest built in an ashe juniper or hardwood tree about 15-20 feet above ground. Eggs are incubated only by the female for 10–12 days. Both adults feed young, which fledge in 9–12 days. Adults continue to feed young for as many as 28 days after fledging. Some pairs under good conditions are thought to attempt to produce a second brood but most breeders produce only a single brood. The species is parasitized by Brown-headed Cowbirds throughout its range but there seems to be much variability in level of parasitism in different areas. On the wintering grounds it has been poorly studied but occurs in pine, pine-oak, and deciduous forests at elevations between 4,500 and 10,000 feet. In one study, birds were shown to prefer to feed in oaks over the more common pines within the study area. Whether it defends winter territories is unknown.[1]

THREATS

The greatest threat is loss, fragmentation, and degradation of mature juniper-oak woodlands across the range. Within the Edwards Plateau portion of the breeding range (the bulk of the range) an estimated 90% or more of the natural habitat has been lost to development, cropland, or rangeland, and only a few relatively small areas of intact habitat remain. The major cities of Austin and San Antonio are located in this area and around both cities much habitat has been lost and fragmented from development of houses, businesses, roads, and associated infrastructure. Habitat has also been degraded from invasive species and overgrazing in many areas. In some areas with highly fragmented habitat Brown-headed Cowbird nest parasitism rates have been very high.

Within the species' southern Mexican and northern Central American wintering range pine-oak forests have been extensively cleared for agriculture and logging. This ecoregion is also home to the largest number of endemic bird species of any ecoregion in Mexico or Central America. In the Guatemalan portion of the wintering range, much of the human population is concentrated in this ecoregion and the human population there is expected to double in the next thirty years so there will be increasing pressure to harvest forests. There are few protected areas within the species wintering range and most protect primarily higher-elevation cloud forest not the primary habitat for wintering Golden-cheeked Warbler. There are still large areas of pine-oak forest remaining in Honduras but they are not protected.[1,8–10]

CONSERVATION ACTION

The species was federally listed as Endangered in 1990 and a Recovery Plan was completed in 1992. Conservation activity has focused on protecting remaining habitat patches from conversion to housing developments or agricultural uses. Balcones Canyonlands NWR near Austin, Texas was created in 1992 with the goal of acquiring and protecting 46,000 acres of nesting habitat for Golden-cheeked Warbler and Black-capped Vireo. About 16,000 acres had been acquired from willing sellers as of 2003. The U.S. Fish and Wildlife Service approved the Balcones Canyonlands Conservation Plan in 1996 that allowed Travis County, the City of Austin, and the Lower Colorado River Authori-

ty to remove some habitat for Golden-cheeked Warbler and other endangered species in return for assembling a 30,000-acre preserve and monitoring the species to ensure that populations remain healthy in the new reserve. About 27,000 acres had been acquired as of 2003 with the help of various partners, including private landowners, Travis County Audubon, and the Nature Conservancy.

Safe Harbor Agreements in the Texas Hill Country approved by the U.S. Fish and Wildlife Service and administered by a private organization called Environmental Defense provide an incentive for landowners to protect and create habitat for Golden-cheeked Warbler and other species. Over 500 acres had been enrolled by 2003. Environmental Defense also offers another program called the Landowner Conservation Assistance Program, which provides technical assistance and financial assistance to landowners who wish to manage habitats for endangered animals and plants including the Golden-cheeked Warbler. As of 2003, over 70,000 acres from 43 private landowners had used the program. The Bexar Land Trust received a grant in 2004 to purchase 150-acres of land adjacent to a private 500-acre ranch in Kendall County, Texas, that is managing habitat for Black-capped Vireo and Golden-cheeked Warbler under a Safe Harbor Agreement.

Texas Parks and Wildlife and a number of other organizations have developed and disseminated education and information materials, including management guidelines and a video, all aimed at reaching more private landowners and the public about the status and needs of Golden-cheeked Warbler. Intensive research and monitoring has been carried out at Fort Hood in cooperation with the Nature Conservancy. In 2003, the Cornell Lab of Ornithology's Bioacoustic Research Department implemented an innovate new technique to survey areas on Fort Hood closed to human entry using microphone arrays operated from remotely controlled weather balloons.

On the wintering grounds there is an urgent need for further conservation activities not only for Golden-cheeked Warbler but for the suite of endemic species that co-occur within the ecoregion. A symposium on the conservation of pine-oak forest and the Golden-cheeked Warbler in Mesoamerica was convened in November 2003 by Pronatura Chiapas, SalvaNATURA (El Salvador), and Defensores de la Naturaleza (Guatemala).

Some conservation projects have been initiated by Defensores de la Naturaleza working in Guatemala's Sierra de las Minas Biosphere Reserve.[1,8–17]

Conservation Needs

- Continue acquisition of remaining intact habitat from willing sellers within species breeding range by conservation agencies and organizations, including at Balcones Canyonlands NWR, which is authorized to expand by 30,000 acres from its present size.
- Implement conservation actions to benefit Golden-cheeked Warbler at current protected areas within the wintering range and determine new areas for protected area status.
- Develop baseline inventory of Golden-cheeked Warbler breeding and wintering populations.
- Invest in further research into the species' winter range limits, habitat requirements, and ecology.

References

1. Ladd, C., and L. Gass. 1999. Golden-cheeked Warbler (*Dendroica chrysoparia*). In *The Birds of North America*, No. 420. (A. Poole and F. Gill, eds.). The Birds of North America, Inc., Philadelphia, PA.

2. Chipley, R.M., G.H. Fenwick, M.J. Parr, and D.N. Pashley. 2003. *The American Bird Conservancy Guide to the 500 Most Important Bird Areas in the United States*. Random House, New York, NY.

3. Anders, A.D., and D. C. Dearborn. 2003. *Population Trends of the Endangered Golden-cheeked Warbler on Fort Hood, Texas, from 1992–2001*. Unpublished manuscript, the Nature Conservancy, Fort Hood, TX.

4. The Nature Conservancy. 2003. *Endangered Species Monitoring and Management at Fort Hood, Texas: 2003 Annual Report*. The Nature Conservancy, Fort Hood Project, Fort Hood, TX.

5. CONABIO. 2002. *Áreas de Importancia para la Conservación de las Aves (AICAS)*. http://conabioweb.conabio.gob.mx/aicas/doctos/aicas.html (accessed 18 June 2003).

6. BirdLife International. 2000. *Threatened Birds of the World*. Lynx Editions and BirdLife International, Barcelona, Spain, and Cambridge, UK.

7. Rich, T.D., C. Beardmore, H. Berlanga, P. Blancher, M. Bradstreet, G. Butcher, D. Demarest, E. Dunn, C. Hunter, E. Iñigo-Elias, J. Kennedy, A. Martell, A. Panjabi, D. Pashley, K. Rosenberg, C. Rustay, S. Wendt, and T. Will. 2004. *Partners in Flight North American Landbird Conservation Plan*. Cornell Lab of Ornithology, Ithaca, NY.

8. Ricketts, T.H., E. Dinerstein, D.M. Olson, C.J. Loucks, et al. 1999. *Terrestrial Ecoregions of North America: A Conservation Assessment*. Island Press, Washington, DC. 485 pp.

9. BirdLife International. 2003. *BirdLife's Online World Bird Database: The Site for Bird Conservation*, Version 2.0. BirdLife International, Cambridge, UK. http://www.birdlife.org (accessed 26 January 2004).

10. World Wildlife Fund. 2001. *Central American Pine-Oak Forests (NT0303)*. http://www.worldwildlife.org/wildworld/profiles/terrestrial/nt/nt0303_full.html (accessed 26 January 2004).

11. U.S. Fish and Wildlife Service. No date. *Wildlife—Balcones Canyonlands NWR*. http://southwest.fws.gov/refuges/texas/balcones/wildlife.html (accessed 20 January 2004).

12. Travis County, TX. 4 September 2003. *The Balcones Canyonlands Conservation Plan*. http://www.co.travis.tx.us/tnr/bccp/default.asp (accessed 22 January 2004.)

13. Environmental Defense. 2003. *The Texas Hill Country Endangered Songbird Safe Harbor Agreement*. http://www.environmentaldefense.org/article.cfm?contentid=142 (accessed 22 January 2004).

14. Environmental Defense. 2003. *The Landowner Conservation Assistance Program*. http://www.environmentaldefense.org/article.cfm?contentid=154 (accessed 22 January 2004).

15. Land Trust Alliance. 2004. *Grant Benefits the Black-capped Vireo in Texas*. http://www.lta.org/regionlta/s_sw.htm (accessed 22 January 2004).

16. The Nature Conservancy. 2003. *Fort Hood Center for Cooperative Ecological Research*. http://nature.org/wherewework/northamerica/states/texas/science/art6223.html (accessed 22 January 2004).

17. American Bird Conservancy. No date. *Project Profile—Golden-cheeked Warbler*. http://www.abcbirds.org/counterparts/project_golden-cheeked_warbler.htm (accessed 22 January 2004).

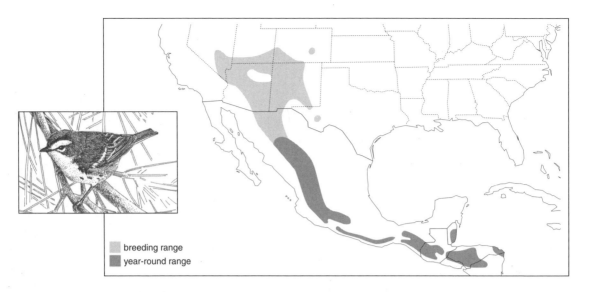

breeding range
year-round range

GRACE'S WARBLER (*Dendroica graciae*)

The sweet song of the Grace's Warbler drifts down from the tops of tall ponderosa pines in the open mountain forests of the southwestern U.S., where it reaches its northern range limit. One of the least-studied warblers, the Grace's Warbler is identified by Partners in Flight as a species of concern because of its limited U.S. breeding range, threats to wintering habitat in Mexico and Central America, and its possible decline on the breeding range.

STATUS AND DISTRIBUTION

In the U.S., it occurs only in the southwestern states, the breeding range extending from southern Colorado, Nevada, and Utah south through Mexico to Nicaragua. Important breeding areas for the species include New Mexico's Gila National Forest and Cibola National Forest and Arizona's Coconino and Kaibab National Forests. The Kaibab National Forest is part of the largest contiguous ponderosa pine forest in the U.S. In Mexico the species seems to have a rather patchy distribution but there is limited information. It is known to occur within the Santiaguillo Important Bird Area in Durango and the Sierra Gorda Biosphere Reserve in Querétaro.

Birds breeding in the U.S. withdraw to mountains of western and central Mexico south to at least Belize and Guatemala, though exact wintering distribution is unknown because wintering birds overlap with the resident Mexican population. Occasionally, single birds have wintered in southern California. Breeding Bird Survey analysis shows a nonsignificant decline of approximately 52% (1.9% per year) from 1966 to 2005 in the U.S portion of the species' range. No trend information is available from portions of the range south of the U.S. The species' total population was estimated at 2,000,000 individuals in 2004, with half in the U.S. and half in Mexico.[1-6]

ECOLOGY

This bird is a species of mature pine and pine-oak forests throughout its range but especially ponderosa pine in the mountains of the southwestern U.S. Normally feeds and nests in pines in breeding and wintering season as well as migration. Arrives on southwestern U.S. breeding grounds in April and normally departs by September. Very little basic research into the species' biology and ecology has been carried out.[1,7]

THREATS

The greatest threats are degradation of pine and pine-oak forest habitat from fire suppression and loss and alteration of habitat from logging practices and, in some areas, urban development. Habitats throughout much of range in Mexico have been subjected to much logging and clearing for agriculture but the extent of loss of habitat for Grace's Warbler is poorly quantified. In Mexico's

Sierra Madre Occidental an estimated 99.5% of the original old-growth forest was logged at least once between 1880 and 1995. Human-induced changes in fire regimes within the pine-oak ecosystems of the Sierra Madre Occidental have only recently been studied and may have had an influence on ecosystem dynamics that, in association with widespread logging, may have reduced populations of Grace's Warbler.[1,7–9]

CONSERVATION ACTION

Partners in Flight conservation plans for Arizona, Colorado, Nevada, and New Mexico have identified this species as a priority for ponderosa pine habitats and have encouraged increased monitoring of the species because it is detected on relatively few Breeding Bird Survey routes. The U.S. Forest Service, within its multiple-use mandate, manages very large acreages of pine and pine-oak habitat within its National Forests to maintain sufficient mature forest habitat for Mexican Spotted Owls, which likely also provides essential habitat for Grace's Warbler. Areas that have been designated as wilderness within National Forests that include ponderosa pine habitats are likely to support Grace's Warbler.

Some research has been initiated more recently into the role of fire in the forests of Mexico's Sierra Madre Occidental and the influence of widespread cattle grazing within forests on fire frequency. The U.S. Forest Service International Division and the Nature Conservancy have worked with the Mexican Ministry of the Environment to provide training in forestry management, including fire management, impacting millions of acres of communally-owned lands as well as government-owned protected areas that include important breeding and wintering habitat for Grace's Warbler.[1,7,9–15]

CONSERVATION NEEDS

- Manage pine and pine-oak habitat for large pines and open, mature canopy conditions.
- Increase monitoring and life-history research for the species.
- Protect wintering habitat in Mexico and Central America by eliminating unsustainable logging practices.
- Continue research on the ecological need for fire within Mexico's Sierra Madre Occidental pine-oak ecosystem.

References

1. Stacier, C.A., and M. J. Guzy. 2002. Grace's Warbler (Dendroica graciae). In The Birds of North America, No. 677 (A. Poole and F. Gill, eds.). The Birds of North America, Inc., Philadelphia, PA.

2. Howell, S.N.G., and S. Webb. 1995. A Guide to the Birds of Mexico and Northern Central America. Oxford University Press, New York, NY.

3. Audubon New Mexico. 2005. Important Bird Areas of New Mexico. http://nm.audubon.org/iba/iba.html (accessed 1 February 2006).

4. CONABIO. 2002. Áreas de Importancia para la Conservación de las Aves (AICAS). http://conabioweb.conabio.gob.mx/aicas/doctos/aicas.html (accessed 9 December 2003).

5. Sauer, J.R., J. E. Hines, and J. Fallon. 2005. The North American Breeding Bird Survey, Results and Analysis 1966–2005, Version 6.2.2006. USGS Patuxent Wildlife Research Center, Laurel, MD.

6. Rich, T.D., C. Beardmore, H. Berlanga, P. Blancher, M. Bradstreet,G. Butcher, D. Demarest, E. Dunn, C. Hunter, E. Iñigo-Elias, J. Kennedy, A. Martell, A. Panjabi, D. Pashley, K. Rosenberg, C. Rustay, S. Wendt, and T. Will. 2004. Partners in Flight North American Landbird Conservation Plan. Cornell Lab of Ornithology, Ithaca, NY.

7. Paige, C., M. Koenen, and D.W. Mehlman. 1999. Grace's Warbler (Dendroica graciae) Species Management Abstract. The Nature Conservancy, Arlington, VA.

8. World Wildlife Fund. 2001. Sierra Madre Oriental Pine-Oak Forests (NA0303). http://www.worldwildlife.org/wildworld/profiles/terrestrial/na/na0303_full.html (accessed 23 January 2004).

9. Fule, P.Z., and W.W. Covington. 1999. Fire Regime Changes in La Michilia Biosphere Reserve, Durango, Mexico. Conservation Biology 13:1523–1739.

10. Latta, M.J., C.J. Beardmore, and T.E. Corman. 1999. Arizona Partners in Flight Bird Conservation Plan, Version 1.0. Nongame and Endangered Wildlife Program Technical Report 142. Arizona Game and Fish Department, Phoenix, AZ.

11. Rustay, C., C. Beardmore, M. Carter, C. Alford, D. Pashley. 2003. Partners in Flight Draft Land Bird Conservation Plan—New Mexico State Plan, Version 1.2. http://www.hawksaloft.org/pif.shtml (accessed 7 June 2004).

12. Beidleman, C.A. 2000. *Partners in Flight Land Bird Conservation Plan Colorado*. Estes Park, CO.

13. Nevada Partners in Flight Working Group. 1999. *Nevada Partners In Flight Bird Conservation Plan*. Reno, NV.

14. U.S. Fish and Wildlife Service International Affairs. 1999. *Grants Awarded in 1999*. http://inter national.fws.gov/whp/annex1.html (accessed 12 December 2003).

15. USDA Forest Service International Programs. 2000. *Latin America and the Caribbean: Mexico*. http://www.fs.fed.us/global/globe/l_amer/mexico.htm#2c (accessed 2 February 2006).

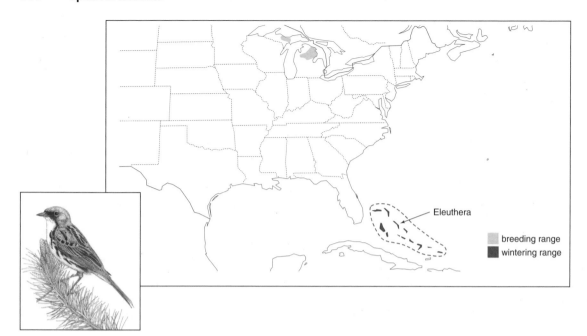

Eleuthera

breeding range

wintering range

KIRTLAND'S WARBLER (*Dendroica kirtlandii*)

The rarest breeding songbird of the U.S. (excluding the presumed extinct Bachman's Warbler), Kirtland's Warbler is one of a suite of rare species in North America that depend on regular fires to maintain proper habitat and that have suffered from the misguided policies of fire suppression in ecological systems.

STATUS AND DISTRIBUTION

The entire Kirtland's Warbler breeding range lies within northern Michigan. It is known to breed in 13 of the state's Lower Peninsula counties and three counties in the state's Upper Peninsula. Unpaired singing males have occasionally occurred in neighboring Wisconsin and Ontario and in Québec. Virtually the entire population breeds within the 140,000-acre Kirtland's Warbler Management Area, which includes the Huron National Forest, the Kirtland's Warbler National Wildlife Refuge, and various Michigan state forests.

In winter, birds migrate to the Bahamas but their exact range within the 35 major and 700 small islands that make up the Bahamas is poorly known. In winter 2002–2003 ornithologists were surprised to discover the largest concentration of the species located since the late 1800s on the island of Eleuthera—a total of at least 30 birds at 12 sites.

No historical trend information is available for the species, but based on the number of specimens acquired by collectors in the Bahamas in the late 1800s it was certainly more common. Regular surveys began in 1951 when 432 singing males were counted. The population continued to decline until reaching a low point of 167 males in 1974 followed by a slow increase and a second drop to 167 males in 1987. Since then the population has steadily increased and reached an all-time high of 1,478 singing males in 2006. The species' total population was estimated at 2,830 individuals in 2005.[1–7]

ECOLOGY

On the breeding range it occurs only in large tracts of young (<15-year-old) jack pine. This habitat was maintained historically by frequent natural fires but in most areas today is mimicked by clearcutting followed by planting of young jack pines. Females lay 3–6 eggs in a nest built on the ground partly concealed by grass tufts or other vegetation. Eggs are incubated only by the female for 13–15 days. Both adults feed young, which fledge in 9–10 days. Adults continue to feed young for as many as 44 days after fledging. Some pairs under good conditions are thought to attempt to produce a second brood but most breeders produce only a single brood. The species was heavily parasitized by Brown-headed Cowbirds before trapping of cowbirds began in the 1970s. Because parasitized nests usually produce no young, Kirtland's Warbler was thought to be in danger of extinction by the 1980s unless cowbird parasitism rates were decreased. On the wintering grounds it has been difficult to study because very few individuals could be located and it is unclear whether the birds prefer pine forests in the northern Bahamas or broad-leaved scrub habitat that is more common in the central and southern Bahamas. The discovery in 2002 and 2003 of relatively high numbers of birds wintering on Eleuthera has provided more opportunities for study. The 30 birds found on Eleuthera were all in broad-leaved habitat. Five of six birds color-banded on Eleuthera in 2002 were found at the same site on the island in 2003 and three birds banded on Eleuthera were resighted the following season in Michigan. A seven-year-old bird originally banded in Michigan was also subsequently resighted on Eleuthera. About 65% of adult population survives from one breeding season to the next.[1,7]

THREATS

The greatest historical threat is loss and degradation of breeding habitat from fire suppression and forestry practices inadequate to maintain proper habitat. Homes are scattered throughout much of the breeding habitat for the species so prescribed burning is generally not carried out in most areas and must be replaced with intensive forestry practices. The greatest current threat remains from Brown-headed Cowbird nest parasitism. Over 120,000 cowbirds have been trapped over the course of the program since the 1970s, decreasing parasitism rates from as high as 70% to about 3%. However, numbers of cowbirds in the area remain stable so that any decrease in trapping effort would result in an increase in parasitism rates and a drop in productivity for Kirtland's Warbler populations. Because of the uncertainty in preferred wintering habitat in the Bahamas, it is unclear whether the large decline in pine forest habitat in the northern Bahamas was a major factor in the species' original decline and its current small population size. Pine forest habitat in the Bahamas has begun to recover[1,4,7–9]

CONSERVATION ACTION

The species was federally listed as Endangered in 1973 and a Recovery Plan was completed in 1976 and revised in 1986. Conservation activity carried out by the Michigan Department of Natural Resources, the U.S. Forest Service, the U.S. Fish and Wildlife Service, and others has centered on managing habitat on federal and state lands within the Kirtland's Warbler Managment Area in northern Michigan. A combination of clearcutting, seeding, and replanting of jack pines is carried out on approximately 2,000–2,500 acres of the 140,000-acre area each year. This, combined with intensive trapping of Brown-headed Cowbirds, has resulted in great increases in the Kirtland's Warbler population since the late 1980s.

Most of the remaining pine forest acreage in the Bahamas is now government-owned and much is within national parks and national forests. The Bahamas National Trust is responsible for the management of the 25 national parks encompassing more than 700,000 acres that have been established in the Bahamas. On Andros Island in the northern Bahamas, the Andros Conservancy and Trust and the Nature Conservancy are working with the Bahamas National Trust to develop management plans for the newly established Central Andros National Park. The Bahamas National Trust, U.S. Forest Service, and the Nature Conservancy have also initiated the Kirtland's Warbler Research and Training Project with funding from the International Program of the U.S. Forest Service and private donors. The project is focused on studying the winter ecology of Kirtland's Warbler while providing training for college students from the College of the Bahamas. The project has already had unprecedented success in finding and studying the species on Eleuthera, and students from the project have also been involved in research on the breeding grounds in Michigan.[1,3–11]

CONSERVATION NEEDS

- Continue management to maximize the amount of available jack pine habitat managed for Kirtland's Warbler over the long-term to further increase population.
- Continue cowbird trapping within the breeding range and fund research to investigate sustainable methods for decreasing cowbird pop-

ulations within the breeding range through habitat management.

- Develop a conservation plan for the wintering range of the species.
- Invest in further research into the species' winter range limits, habitat requirements, and ecology.

References

1. Mayfield, H.F. 1992. Kirtland's Warbler (*Dendroica kirtlandii*). In *The Birds of North America*, No. 19. (A. Poole, P. Stettenheim, and F. Gill, eds.). The Academy of Natural Sciences., Philadelphia, PA, and the American Ornithologists' Union, Washington, DC.

2. Chipley, R.M., G.H. Fenwick, M.J. Parr, and D.N. Pashley. 2003. *The American Bird Conservancy Guide to the 500 Most Important Bird Areas in the United States*. Random House, New York, NY.

3. U.S. Fish and Wildlife Service. 2003. *Seney National Wildlife Refuge Satellite Refuges*. http://midwest .fws.gov/seney/Satelits.htm (accessed 27 January 2004).

4. BirdLife International. 2000. *Threatened Birds of the World*. Lynx Editions and BirdLife International, Barcelona, Spain, and Cambridge, UK.

5. U. S. Fish and Wildlife Service. No date. *Kirtland's Warbler Population Graph*. http://midwest.fws .gov/endangered/birds/Kirtland/Kwpop02.htm (accessed 22 January 2004).

6. Michigan Department of Natural Resources. 2006. *Kirtland's Warbler Population Continues to Grow*. http://www.michigan.gov/dnr/0,1607,7-153—10371_ 10402-148280—,00.html (accessed 14 November 2006).

7. Currie, D., J. Wunderle, D. Ewert, and E. Carey. 2003. The Most Elusive Bird in the Bahamas? *World Birdwatch* 25 (4): 13–15.

8. World Wildlife Fund. 2001. *Bahamian Pine Forests (NT0301)*. http://www.worldwildlife.org/wild world/profiles/terrestrial/nt/nt0301_full.html (accessed 27 January 2004).

9. The Nature Conservancy. 2003. *Fire Management Assessment of the Caribbean Pine (Pinus caribea) Forest Ecosystems on Andros and Abaco Islands, Bahamas*. The Nature Conservancy, Arlington, VA.

10. Bahamas National Trust. 2003. *Bahamas National Trust*. http://www.bahamasnationaltrust.com/index .html (accessed 27 January 2004).

11. The Nature Conservancy. 2004. *Andros Island*. http://nature.org/wherewework/caribbean/bahamas/ work/art8286.html (accessed 27 January 2004).

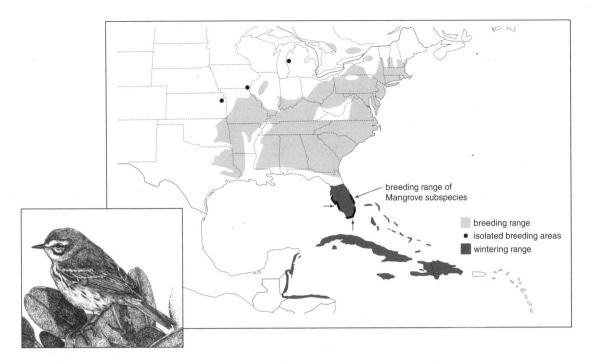

breeding range of
Mangrove subspecies

☐ breeding range
● isolated breeding areas
■ wintering range

PRAIRIE WARBLER (*Dendroica discolor*)

The buzzy, chromatically ascending song of the Prairie Warbler is a familiar sound of pine barren habitat and shrubby second growth across the eastern U.S. where it breeds. It winters almost exclusively in the Greater Antilles and southern Florida.

STATUS AND DISTRIBUTION

The Prairie Warbler breeding range is almost completely restricted to the eastern U.S. from southern New England west to Indiana and Missouri and south to Texas and the Gulf Coast states. Isolated populations occur in Ontario, Michigan, Iowa, and Kansas. A specialized mangrove-inhabiting subspecies (*D.d. paludicola*) breeds in coastal southern Florida. Breeding density maps produced from Breeding Bird Survey data indicate highest densities across a fairly widespread region from southern New Jersey south to Georgia and Alabama and north along the west side of the Appalachians through Tennessee and Kentucky to Ohio and West Virginia. The southeast U.S. was estimated to support 96% of the global population.

Among many important breeding areas for the species are the New Jersey Pinelands Biosphere Reserve, Virginia's Appomattox-Buckingham State Forest, North Carolina's Sandhills East Important Bird Area, including the Fort Bragg military instal-

lation, Georgia's Oconee National Forest, Tennessee's Arnold Air Force Base, and Kentucky's Fort Campbell.

In winter, birds migrate to southern Florida, the Bahamas and Greater Antilles, and more rarely to the central Caribbean coast of Central America from the Mexican state of Quintana Roo south to Honduras. A number of parks and protected areas exist across parts of the winter range and likely provide important wintering habitat for the species, though few data are available on occurrence (much less density) of the species at these locations. These include the Dominican Republic's Jaragua National Park, Cuba's Guanahacabibes Peninsula Biosphere Reserve and Ciénaga de Zapata Biosphere Reserve, Bahama's Abaco National Park, and Florida's Everglades National Park and Loxahatchee National Wildlife Refuge.

Breeding Bird Survey analysis shows a significant decrease of approximately 54% (2.0% per year) from 1966 to 2005 rangewide. The species' total population was estimated at 1,400,000 individuals in 2004.[1–12]

ECOLOGY

On the breeding range it occurs in natural pine and oak barrens, dune shrubs, and early successional shrub-scrub habitat, including regenerating clearcuts, abandoned agricultural land, and power-line right-of-ways. In some areas it uses Christmas tree plantations and regenerating strip-mine sites. Florida subspecies inhabits coastal mangroves. Nests typically built within 3–9 feet above ground in thick shrub or tree. The female lays 3–5 eggs.

On the wintering grounds it also uses shrubby, second-growth habitat generally at lower elevations. These habitats may include open pine forests, dry forests, coastal scrub, regenerating forests with thick understory, mangroves, and shade coffee plantations. Birds are thought to be territorial on wintering grounds but this has not been well-studied.[1]

THREATS

The greatest threat to the species on the breeding grounds is continued loss of natural shrub-scrub and early-successional habitat as the proportion of landscape in an early-successional state continues to decline across much of the East. This decline in amount of shrub-scrub habitat is attributable to a variety of factors, including the maturation of second-growth habitat after widespread farmland abandonment across the region as well as loss of habitat to development in some areas. The Florida mangrove-breeding subspecies is threatened by continuing loss and degradation of mangroves.

On the wintering grounds the species inhabits a fairly wide range of habitats but, in general, habitat loss has been severe across many habitats of south Florida and the Greater Antilles of the Caribbean. For example, Hispaniolan Dry Forest habitat is estimated to have declined by more than 50% and Cuban Dry Forest habitat by more than 90%. These habitats harbor many endemic plant and animal species and provide habitat for wintering migrants like Prairie Warbler. Forest habitats have been lost across the Caribbean from clearing for charcoal production and agriculture. Mangrove habitats have been destroyed in many areas for tourism development and for development of commercial shrimp farms. In many areas mangroves are being negatively impacted by sedimentation and pollution. An evaluation of conservation priorities for the Neotropics placed the Greater Antilles in the second-highest category (of five) of concern—"immediate action needed in all ecosystems to stem widespread declines."[1,3,9,13–17]

CONSERVATION ACTION

Partners in Flight Bird Conservation Plans that have been completed for eastern U.S. physiographic regions have identified Prairie Warbler and its associated suite of shrub-scrub bird species as a high priority and have provided recommendations for management, research, and monitoring. Healthy, stable bird populations will require forest harvest planning schemes that incorporate ecological needs at a broad landscape scale that provides a mosaic of appropriate age-class habitat, including early-successional habitat. Developing such planning schemes is not simple because while harvested forests can provide shrub-scrub habitat within a few years after clearing, it may take decades or even hundreds of years for forests to reach stages that provide habitat for birds that require mature forests.

The New Jersey Pinelands Commission, with a staff of 59, oversees implementation of the New Jersey Pinelands Comprehensive Management Plan that, through incentives and regulations, protects the pine barren habitats within the 1.1 million acre area. Over 300,000 acres within the Pinelands are publicly owned, most within New Jersey State Forests. On the remaining privately owned land, development is steered away from areas of high conservation value through various means, including through the government's purchase of development rights from private landowners.

Pronatura, a nongovernmental organization in the Dominican Republic, is working with the Nature Conservancy to develop and implement effective management and protection infrastructure for Jaragua National Park. Three guard stations and two docks were built, boundaries of the park were marked, and meetings to discuss ecotourism were initiated with local communities and government officials.

World Wildlife Fund Canada has provided grants to promote sustainable development activities by villagers living in and near the Ciénaga de Zapata Biosphere Reserve and to support national park staff working to halt poaching and habitat loss in the area.

With funding ($8 million Canadian) from the Canadian International Development Agency, the Jamaican Forestry Department has been engaged since 1992 in the Trees for Tomorrow Project. The Project has trained forestry department employees, allowed the demarcation and marking of park boundaries, instituted forest management plans, developed an environmental education program, and upgraded reforestation infrastructure. All of these activities are expected to decrease loss of habitat and encroachment into national parks.

Cuban ornithologists have initiated monitoring of the resident and migrant birds at Cuba's Guanahacabibes Peninsula Biosphere Reserve to evaluate different land management strategies that will be implemented in the area.[4,8,18–21]

CONSERVATION NEEDS

- Preserve remaining acreage of natural shrub-scrub habitat including barrens and shrub dune habitat.
- Slow or halt deforestation of wintering habitat for Prairie Warbler and restore habitat where possible.
- Increase acreage of shrub-scrub forest habitat within the breeding range of Prairie Warbler that is managed to attain conditions beneficial to the species within the context of large, landscape-level habitat management plans.
- Compare early successional habitats resulting from natural disturbances vs. forestry and other management practices, with regard to suitability for Prairie Warblers and other high-priority species.
- Develop management guidelines/policy for utility right-of-ways and other shrub habitats maintained in early-successional states.
- Develop baseline inventory of Prairie Warbler breeding and wintering populations.

References

1. Nolan, V., Jr., E.D. Ketterson, and C.A. Buerkle. 1999. Prairie Warbler (*Dendroica discolor*). In *The Birds of North America*, No. 455 (A. Poole and F. Gill, eds.). The Academy of Natural Sciences, Philadelphia, PA, and the American Ornithologists' Union, Washington, DC.

2. Sauer, J. R., J. E. Hines, and J. Fallon. 2005. *The North American Breeding Bird Survey, Results and Analysis 1966–2005*, Version 6.2.2006. USGS Patuxent Wildlife Research Center, Laurel, MD.

3. Rosenberg, K.V., and J.V. Wells. 2000. Global Perspectives in Neotropical Migratory Bird Conservation in the Northeast: Long-term Responsibility Versus Immediate Concern. Pages 32–43 in *Strategies for Bird Conservation: The Partners in Flight Planning Process*. Proceedings of the 3rd Partners in Flight Workshop, 1995 October 1–5, Cape May, NJ (R. Bonney, D.N. Pashley, and R.J. Niles, eds.). Proceedings RMRS-P-16, U.S. Department of Agriculture, Forest Service, Rocky Mountain Reserach Station, Ogden, UT.

4. New Jersey Pinelands Commission. 2003. *The Pinelands National Reserve*. http://www.state.nj.us/pine lands/pnrpc.htm (accessed 21 July 2003).

5. Virginia Department of Forestry. 2003. *Appomattox-Buckingham State Forest*. http://www.vdof.org/stfor est/index-absf.shtml (accessed 21 July 2003).

6. Audubon North Carolina. No date. *North Carolina's Important Bird Areas*. http://www.ncaudubon .org/IBA1.htm (accessed 21 July 2003).

7. Igl, L.D. 2003. *Bird Checklists of the United States* (Version 12MAY03). Northern Prairie Wildlife Research Center Home Page, Jamestown, ND. http://www.npwrc.usgs.gov/resource/othrdata/chekbird/chek bird.htm (accessed 21 July 2003).

8. Parks in Peril. No date. *Where the Parks in Peril Program Works: Dominican Republic*. http://parksin peril .org/03g_dominicanrepublic.shtml (accessed 21 July 2003).

9. World Wildlife Fund. 2001. *Cuban Dry Forests (NT0213)*. http://www.worldwildlife.org/wildworld/pro files/terrestrial/nt/nt0213_full.html (accessed 21 July 2003).

10. United Nations Educational, Scientific, and Cultural Organization. 2002. *Man and the Biosphere Reserves Directory*. http://www2.unesco.org/mab/bios1-2 .htm (accessed 22 July 2003).

11. Bahamas National Trust. No date. *National Parks*. http://www.bahamas.gov.bs/BahamasWeb/Visiting TheBahamas.nsf/Subjects/National+Parks (accessed 21 July 2003).

12. Rich, T.D., C. Beardmore, H. Berlanga, P. Blancher, M. Bradstreet, G. Butcher, D. Demarest, E. Dunn, C. Hunter, E. Iñigo-Elias, J. Kennedy, A. Martell, A. Panjabi, D. Pashley, K. Rosenberg, C. Rustay, S. Wendt, and T. Will. 2004. *Partners in Flight North American Landbird Conservation Plan*. Cornell Lab of Ornithology, Ithaca, NY.

13. World Wildlife Fund. 2001. *Hispaniolan dry forests (NT0215)*. http://www.worldwildlife.org/wild world/profiles/terrestrial/nt/nt0215_full.html (accessed 21 July 2003).

14. World Wildlife Fund. 2001. *Jamaican dry forests (NT0218)*. http://www.worldwildlife.org/wildworld/pro files/terrestrial/nt/nt0218_full.html (accessed 21 July 2003).

15. World Wildlife Fund. 2001. *Bahamian dry forests (NT0203)*. http://www.worldwildlife.org/wild world/profiles/terrestrial/nt/nt0203_full.html (accessed 21 July 2003).

16. World Wildlife Fund. 2001. *Greater Antilles mangroves (NT1410)*. http://www.worldwildlife.org/wild world/profiles/terrestrial/nt/nt1410_full.html (accessed 21 July 2003).

17. Stotz, D.F., J.W. Fitzpatrick, T.A. Parker III, and D. K. Moskovits. 1996. *Neotropical Birds: Ecology and Conservation*. University of Chicago Press, Chicago, IL. 481 pp.

18. Rosenberg, K.V., and J.V. Wells. 2003. *Conservation Priorities for Terrestrial Birds in the Northeastern United States*. Proceedings of the 4th International Partners in Flight Symposium, Asilomar, CA, March 2001.

19. World Wildlife Fund-Canada. No date. *Conservation Programs-International*. http://www.wwfcanada.org/AboutWWF/WhatWeDo/ConservationPrograms/Conservation.asp (accessed 22 July 2003).

20. Jamaican Forestry Department. No date. *The Trees for Tomorrow Project*. http://www.forestry.gov.jm/tft_info.htm (accessed 22 July 2003).

21. Optics for the Tropics. 2002. *Migratory Birds and Forest Conservation in Western Cuba*. http://www.opticsforthetropics.org/projects4.shtml (accessed 22 July 2003).

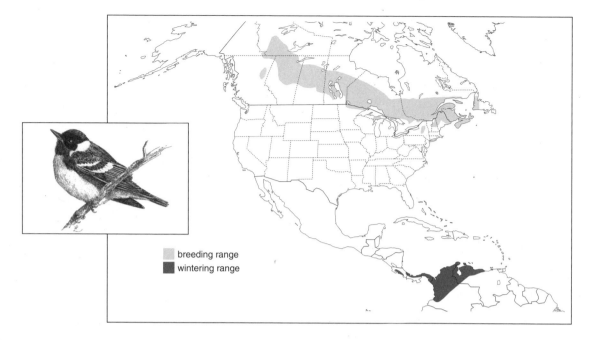

breeding range
wintering range

BAY-BREASTED WARBLER (*Dendroica castanea*)

A characteristic species of the vast boreal forests of Canada, the Bay-breasted Warbler shows great increases in abundance during spruce budworm outbreaks, but despite this it has shown significant declines in recent years. It winters in northern South America and southern Central America.

STATUS AND DISTRIBUTION

The Bay-breasted Warbler breeding range extends from southeastern Yukon and northeastern British Columbia across the boreal forest of Canada to the Maritime Provinces and southwestern Newfoundland and south through northern Minnesota, Michigan, and northern New England. A small, isolated population occurs in the Adirondack Mountains of New York. Breeding density maps produced from Breeding Bird Survey data indicate highest densities in New Brunswick and Quebec but there are no BBS routes through much of the northern boreal forest. Canada was estimated to support 97% of the global population and the northeastern U.S. the remaining 3%. Another analysis estimated that 82% of the global population occurred in Canada's boreal forest ecozone.

Although no systematic survey has been completed to identify sites that are of particular importance for breeding populations of Bay-breasted Warbler, many areas have large expanses of appropriate habitat within the species breeding range. These sites include New Brunswick's Fundy National Park, Québec's La Mauricie National Park, and Northwest Territories' Wood Buffalo National Park.

In winter, birds migrate to Central and South America, occurring in the lowlands on both coasts of Costa Rica and Panama south to northwestern Venezuela and western Colombia, where they are most common on Pacific Coast.

A number of parks and protected areas exist across parts of the winter range and likely provide important wintering habitat for the species, though few data are available on occurrence (much less density) of the species at these locations. In Panama, Darien National Park is one of the largest protected areas in that country that encompass habitat within the wintering range of Bay-breasted Warbler. In Colombia such areas include Farallones de Cali National Park and in Venezuela, Sierra Nevada National Park.

Breeding Bird Survey analysis shows a non-significant decrease of approximately 62% (2.5% per year) from 1966 to 2005 rangewide. The species' total population was estimated at 3,100,000 individuals in 2004.[1-10]

ECOLOGY

On the breeding range it occurs in mature and old spruce-fir forest, often near water and typically not at high elevations. During spruce budworm out-breaks, numbers of Bay-breasted Warblers can increase greatly because of the overabundance of food. Generally sings and forages at mid-canopy level of spruce and fir trees. It builds its nest 12–20 feet above ground on branch of spruce or fir tree, and lays 4–7 eggs.

On the wintering grounds it has not been well studied but it occurs in a range of forest and woodland habitats, including primary and second-growth woodland and woodland edges and shade coffee plantations generally in lowlands and foothill forests from 100 to 1,000 meters. It will readily take fruit and nectar when available, though generally it is otherwise an insectivore. In a study in Panama, birds typically foraged within mixed-species flocks of resident birds in the canopy with each flock containing 1–7 Bay-breasted Warblers. Apparently, it is quite variable in territoriality and density, adapting to food availability, with birds seemingly territorial when insect and fruit are at low availability but aggregating into flocks when fruit abundance is high.[1]

THREATS

The major issues impacting this species on the breeding grounds are all related to changes in management of forests for commercial timber production, especially a trend toward younger and more even-aged coniferous forests. In the Canadian portion of the range and in northern Maine, much of its habitat is within areas managed for forestry. An estimated 82% of the species' total world population occurs within Canada's boreal forest, so that any large changes in land use there will impact the species as a whole. Bay-breasted Warbler requires mature and old spruce-fir forests, and harvested forests take decades to regenerate and once again become suitable habitat for the species. Forest harvest levels have generally increased across most of the boreal zone of Canada. Though more than 90% of the Canadian boreal forest is publicly owned, almost a third is currently allocated to forestry companies for timber production amounting to tens of millions of acres that will be logged—primarily through clearcutting. For example, one logging license area of 375,000 acres in Quebec is scheduled to be harvested over the next twenty years. A 1995 forest-management plan for New Brunswick projected that mature spruce-fir forest will decline from 46% of land area

to 8% of land area in that province over the next 40 years. Forest harvesting plans need to be done at a broad landscape scale and will need to maintain large blocks of mature age-class spruce-fir forest to ensure continued, healthy populations of Bay-breasted Warblers. The broadscale application of pesticides to control spruce budworm infestations could have direct negative physiological effects on the birds and indirect effects by decreasing insect food supplies.

Other issues affecting boreal forest habitat include rapidly increasing development and prospecting for minerals, oil, and natural gas and, in some areas, the building of hydroelectric facilities.

On the wintering grounds, the lower-elevation foothill forests of southern Central America and the northern Andes where the species prefers to winter provide excellent conditions for growing various agricultural crops, including coffee as well as illicit coca plantations, and forests in this zone are full of commercially valuable trees. These foothill habitats are being lost and fragmented, perhaps faster than any other forest habitat in the Neotropics and already harbor large assemblages of endangered and threatened species.[1,4,11–16]

CONSERVATION ACTION

Partners in Flight Bird Conservation Plans that have been completed for eastern U.S. physiographic regions have identified Bay-breasted Warbler and its associated suite of mixed deciduous/coniferous forest bird species as a high priority and have provided recommendations for management, research, and monitoring.

In Canada a broad community of conservation organizations, industry, and First Nations have announced the Boreal Forest Conservation Framework—a new national conservation approach for Canada's boreal forest region. The Framework plan would protect the ecological integrity of the region while integrating sustainable forestry and other development activities. The Framework calls for the establishment of large, interconnected, protected areas covering at least half of the boreal region and application of leading-edge sustainable development practices on the lands that are developed. The Canadian Boreal Initiative and its partners are working to encourage the adoption of Framework principles by Canadian national and provincial government agencies and policy makers as a vision for the future of the vast, and largely publicly owned, boreal landscape.

A Canadian Senate subcommittee developed a comprehensive report in 1999 that recommended a set of actions needed to ensure the protection and sustainable use of Canada's boreal forests. Since then the Canadian Boreal Initiative has been advocating for adoption and implementation of these recommendations in addition to promoting the Framework and working with provincial governments to adopt the principles of the Framework on their lands. Some progress was reported in the establishment of protected areas, including the protection of 625,000 acres of boreal forest habitat in Quebec since 2000.

The Boreal Songbird Initiative has spearheaded work by a network of U.S. conservation groups to support the Boreal Forest Conservation Framework. This work has included outreach activities to increase awareness of the boreal wilderness and the threats it faces. For example, the National Wildlife Federation and National Audubon both have conducted letter-writing campaigns asking large retail catalog companies to use recycled paper and paper purchased from environmentally and socially responsible sources instead of using paper made from virgin boreal forest. The Natural Resources Defense Council has also designated the intact boreal forest in the Ontario–Manitoba border region as one of its twelve "BioGems" and is working to ensure that the conservation plans of local indigenous peoples are not threatened by hydropower and industrial development.

On the wintering grounds a number of government agencies and conservation groups are involved in efforts to protect and manage parks and other protected areas within the wintering range of Bay-breasted Warbler. The U.S. National Park Service Office of International Affairs conducted a training workshop for Venezuela's National Institute for Parks in 2002 to help in management of Venezuela's National Parks.

Panama's National Institute for Natural Renewable Resources, working with Panama's National Association for the Conservation of Nature, World Wildlife Fund, and the Nature Conservancy's Parks in Peril program has developed and implemented a management plan and hired rangers for Darien National Park. Plans for extending the Pan-American Highway through the region have been tabled at present.[11,12,16–21]

CONSERVATION NEEDS

- Develop broad, landscape-scale forest management plans for ensuring that large tracts of mature and old spruce-fir forest are available for Bay-breasted Warblers within the landscapes of the northeastern U.S. and Canada, especially the boreal forest region.
- Increase the number of protected areas through national and provincial parks in Canada's boreal forest.
- Implement the proposed protections near Lake Winnipeg to maintain the intact boreal forest in the Ontario–Manitoba border region.
- Implement the Boreal Forest Conservation Framework, which calls for protection of 50% of Canada's boreal region and ensures world-leading sustainable development practices in areas that are developed.
- Slow or halt deforestation of wintering habitat for Bay-breasted Warbler and restore habitat where possible.
- Develop baseline inventory of Bay-breasted Warbler breeding and wintering populations, habitat needs on breeding and wintering grounds, and factors responsible for continuing population declines.

References

1. Williams, J.M. 1996. Bay-breasted Warbler (*Dendroica castanea*). In *The Birds of North America*, No. 206 (A. Poole and F. Gill, eds.). The Academy of Natural Sciences, Philadelphia, PA, and the American Ornithologists' Union, Washington, D.C.

2. Sauer, J. R., J. E. Hines, and J. Fallon. 2005. *The North American Breeding Bird Survey, Results and Analysis 1966–2005*, Version 6.2.2006. USGS Patuxent Wildlife Research Center, Laurel, MD.

3. Rosenberg, K.V., and J.V. Wells. 2000. Global Perspectives in Neotropical Migratory Bird Conservation in the Northeast: Long-term Responsibility Versus Immediate Concern. Pages 32–43 in *Strategies for Bird Conservation: The Partners in Flight Planning Process*, Proceedings of the 3rd Partners in Flight Workshop; 1995 October 1–5, Cape May, NJ (R. Bonney, D.N. Pashley, and R.J. Niles, eds.). Proceedings RMRS-P-16, U.S. Department of Agriculture, Forest Service, Rocky Mountain Research Station, Ogden, UT.

4. Blancher, P. 2003. *Importance of Canada's Boreal Forest to Landbirds*. Canadian Boreal Initiative, Boreal

Songbird Initiative, Bird Studies Canada, Ottawa, ON, Seattle, WA, and Port Rowan, ON.

5. Parks Canada. 2003. *National Parks of Canada.* http://parkscanada.gc.ca/progs/np-pn/index_E.asp (accessed 25 June 2003).

6. Hilty, S.L., and W.L. Brown. 1986. *Birds of Colombia.* Princeton University Press, Princeton, NJ. 836 pp.

7. Hilty, S.L. 2003. *Birds of Venezuela,* 2nd ed. Princeton University Press, Princeton, NJ. 878 pp.

8. Panama Travel. No date. *Panama's National Parks.* http://www.panamatravel.com/natparks.htm (accessed 25 June 2003).

9. Unidad Administrativa Especial del Sistema de Parques Nacionales Naturales. No date. *Parques Nacionales de Colombia.* http://www.parquesnacionales.gov.co/areas.htm (accessed 23 June 2003).

10. Rich, T. D., C. Beardmore, H. Berlanga, P. Blancher, M. Bradstreet, G. Butcher, D. Demarest, E. Dunn, C. Hunter, E. Iñigo-Elias, J. Kennedy, A. Martell, A. Panjabi, D. Pashley, K. Rosenberg, C. Rustay, S. Wendt, and T. Will. 2004. *Partners in Flight North American Landbird Conservation Plan.* Cornell Lab of Ornithology, Ithaca, NY.

11. Sub-committee on Boreal Forest of the Standing Senate Committee on Agriculture and Forestry. 1999. *Competing Realities: The Boreal Forest at Risk.* Government of Canada, Ottawa, ON. http://www.parl.gc.ca/36/1/parlbus/commbus/senate/com-e/BORE-E/rep-e/rep09jun99-e.htm (accessed 24 June 2003).

12. Canadian Boreal Initiative. 2003. *The Boreal Forest at Risk: A Progress Report.* Canadian Boreal Initiative, Ottawa, ON.

13. Ricketts T.H., et. al. 1999. *Terrestrial Ecoregions of North America: A Conservation Assessment.* Island Press, Washington, DC. 485 pp.

14. Rosenberg, K.V., and T. P. Hodgman. 2000. *Partners in Flight Landbird Conservation Plan: Physiographic Area 28-Eastern Spruce-Hardwood Forest.* Partners in Flight and American Bird Conservancy, The Plains, VA. 48 pp.

15. Hagan, J. M. and S. L. Grove. 1995. *Selection Cutting, Old Growth, Birds, and Forest Structure.* 1995 Report #96002 of Manamet Center for Conservation Sciences, Manoment, MA. 36 pp.

16. Stotz, D.F., J.W. Fitzpatrick, T.A. Parker III, and D. K. Moskovits. 1996. *Neotropical Birds: Ecology and Conservation.* University of Chicago Press, Chicago, IL. 481 pp.

17. Boreal Songbird Initiative. 2006. http:www.borealbirds.org (accessed 20 January 2006).

18. Rosenberg, K.V., and J.V. Wells. 2003. *Conservation Priorities for Terrestrial Birds in the Northeastern United States.* Proceedings of the 4th International Partners in Flight Symposium, Asilomar, CA, March 2001.

19. National Park Service Office of International Affairs. No date. *Latin America and Caribbean.* http://www.nps.gov/oia/around/lac.htm (accessed 25 June 2003).

20. UNEP. 2001. *World Heritage Sites: Darien National Park, Panama.* Protected Areas Programme, UNEP World Conservation Monitoring Centre, Cambridge, UK. http://www.unep-wcmc.org/protected_areas/data/wh/darien.html (accessed 26 June 2003).

21. Parks in Peril. No date. *Parks in Peril: Panama.* http://parksinperil.org/03m_panama.shtml (accessed 26 June 2003).

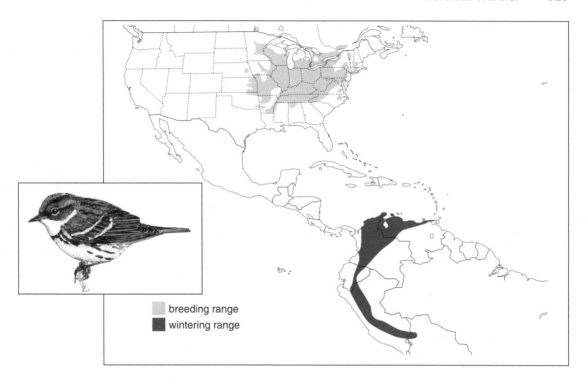

breeding range
wintering range

CERULEAN WARBLER (*Dendroica cerulea*)

One of the fastest declining songbirds in the U.S., the Cerulean Warbler breeds in mature forests of the eastern U.S. and winters in the Andes Mountains of South America.

STATUS AND DISTRIBUTION

The Cerulean Warbler breeding range is restricted to eastern North America from southern Ontario west to southeastern Minnesota south to Arkansas, western Alabama, and northern Mississippi. Within this range the species has a very patchy and discontinuous distribution with small isolated populations in southwestern Quebec, Vermont, Massachusetts, Connecticut, and Nebraska. Breeding density maps produced from Breeding Bird Survey data indicate highest densities in West Virginia, southern Ohio, eastern Kentucky, northcentral Tennessee, and northwestern Virginia.

Important breeding areas for the species include West Virginia's New River Gorge, Kanawha State Forest, and Guyandotte Mountain, each known to support a minimum of 50–100 pairs of Cerulean Warblers; Tennessee's Royal Blue Wildlife Management Area (430 pairs) and Edgar Evins State Park area (240 pairs); New York's Montezuma Wetlands Complex (325 pairs) and Allegany

State Park area (165 pairs); Illinois' Kaskaskia River Valley (300–1,000 pairs) and Shawnee National Forest area (200–500 pairs); Indiana's Jefferson Proving Ground (200 pairs); Kentucky's Daniel Boone National Forest (71 pairs); Ohio's Shawnee State Park and Forest (56 pairs); Michigan's Alleghan State Game Area vicinity (177 pairs); and Missouri's Eleven Point River (137 pairs) and Upper Current River (114 pairs). In Canada, important breeding areas include southern Ontario's Queen's University Biological Station that is estimated to host at least 200 pairs of Cerulean Warblers.

In winter, birds migrate to South America primarily inhabiting the foothills of the eastern slope of the Andes Mountains from Venezuela south to Peru. There are some records from lower elevations within this area and a few records from western slope of Andes in Ecuador and as far south as southeast Brazil.

A number of parks and protected areas exist across parts of the winter range and likely provide important wintering habitat for the species though few data are available on occurrence (much less density) of the species at these locations. In Ecuador, protected areas known to have hosted Cerulean Warblers include the Cayambe-Coca and Cotacachi-Cayapas Ecological Reserves, Podocarpus National Park, and Sumaco-Napo Galeras National Park. In Peru, areas known to host or have hosted Cerulean Warblers include Manu National Park, Codillera Azul National Park, Río Abiseo National Park, Yanachaga-Chemillen National Park, Apurimac Reserve, and the Tambopata-Candamo Reserve. In Colombia such areas include Los Katios National Park, Farallones de Cali National Park, and Yotoca Forest Reserve. In Venezuela, Henri Pittier National Park, El Tama National Park, Sierra Nevada National Park are among those where Cerulean Warblers have been documented.

Breeding Bird Survey analyses show a significant decrease of approximately 80% (4.3% per year) from 1966 to 2005 rangewide. The species' total population was estimated at 560,000 individuals in 2004.[1-9]

ECOLOGY

On the breeding range occurs in deciduous forests in both bottomlands or riparian areas but also along ridges and upland slopes. Throughout most of range occurs in relatively large blocks of mature forest with large, relatively old trees forming a rather dense, closed canopy but with occasional taller trees or openings in the forest. A study in Illinois found that Cerulean Warblers had strong preferences for feeding in certain tree species. In areas where the species is more abundant across the landscape and in southern Ontario, where the species is expanding its range, it also occupies relatively small forest fragments of second-growth forest. Generally sings, forages, and nests high in the forest canopy, making study of its life history quite challenging. Nests 15–60 feet from the ground on a limb of a deciduous tree, normally laying 3–4 eggs.

Little is known about the biology of the species during migration. One report of a significant concentration of Cerulean Warblers during migration exists for the Maya Mountains of southern Belize. This report raises the intriguing possibility that the species undergoes a leap-frog spring migration from South America to Central America in a single flight followed by another direct flight to the Gulf Coast of North America.

On the wintering grounds it has been little studied but an examination of specimen records and available site records showed that the species was typically found in a narrow elevation zone (600–1,300 meters) in the foothills of the eastern slope of the Andes Mountains within mature, humid, evergreen forest. Birds have also been found in shade coffee plantations within the same elevation zone and also in similar habitat on the Venezuelan tablelands or tepuis. Observations on the wintering grounds suggest that the birds typically forage within mixed-species flocks of resident birds but in low densities (no more than two birds in a flock), likely maintaining this density through territorial singing (a song very similar to that used on breeding grounds).[1,10-12]

THREATS

The greatest threat is loss and fragmentation of habitat on breeding and wintering grounds. Perhaps the most overriding current threat is from mountaintop removal mining within the areas of highest density for the species. For example, 246,000 acres had been lost or proposed for this practice in West Virginia by 2001. Mountaintop removal mining involves pushing the soil from the top of a mountain into the adjoining valley to reach horizontal coal seams hundreds of feet below the surface. Over 900 miles of stream filling had been authorized for this activity throughout the Appalachians by 2001.

On breeding grounds, the historic loss of habitat from clearing of large tracts of southeastern bottomland forest beginning in the 1800s was responsible for the extinction of Ivory-billed Woodpecker and Bachman's Warbler and for the decline of other species associated with this habitat, including the Cerulean Warbler. The loss of such habitat in the Mississippi Alluvial Valley was estimated at 50% and in the Lower Mississippi Valley more than 80%. Similarly, large amounts of bottomland forest habitat was converted to agriculture across the northeastern U.S. during the late 1800s and early 1900s but since that time the amount of forest has been increasing as farmland abandonment resulted in the regrowth of forested habitat. Unfortunately, habitat loss and fragmentation has increased in certain areas for development of homes, businesses, and the associated infrastructure (roads, utility corridors, etc.). Depending on how it is carried out, large-scale industrial forestry can be detrimental to Cerulean Warbler habitat or helpful in developing good habitat. In general, forestry practices that allow the growth of large, mature trees in large forest blocks with selective logging to create small forest gaps can be beneficial, while large-scale clearcuts and forests that are not allowed to grow large trees are not beneficial.

On the wintering grounds, the foothills of the Andes where the species prefers to winter provide excellent conditions for growing various agricultural crops, including coffee as well as illicit coca plantations, and forests in this zone are full of commercially valuable trees. Andean foothill habitats are being lost and fragmented faster than most other forest habitats in the Neotropics and harbor large assemblages of endangered and threatened species.[1,11,13–15]

CONSERVATION ACTION

Partners in Flight Bird Conservation Plans that have been completed for eastern U.S. physiographic regions have identified Cerulean Warbler and its associated suite of bottomland and upland forest bird species as a high priority and have provided recommendations for management, research, and monitoring. These suggestions have included specific goals for increasing the acreage of bottomland and upland forest in large blocks across the landscape. Within the Mississippi Alluvial Valley many projects to purchase or reforest lands are ongoing through many partner agencies and organizations, including the Lower Mississippi Valley Joint Venture, U.S. Fish and Wildlife Service Partners for Wildlife program, the National Resources Conservation Service Wetland Reserve Program, Ducks Unlimited, and the Nature Conservancy.

The species was petitioned for federal listing as a Threatened species in 2000 but no determination has yet been completed. The species has received heightened awareness in planning efforts on public lands, especially federally owned lands. Various land acquisition activities have taken place that have protected land supporting breeding Cerulean Warblers, though the overall acreage and impact have not yet been documented. In Tennessee nearly 12,000 acres of forest (now the John Tully Wildlife Management Area) in an area with a high concentration of Cerulean Warblers was purchased in 2002–2003 from the Anderson-Tully Company through the efforts of the Nature Conservancy and the Tennessee Wildlife Resources Agency with funding from a variety of

sources, including the USDA Forest Service's Forest Legacy program, Tennessee's Land Acquisition Fund and Wetland Acquisition Fund, and the North American Wetland Conservation Act. At the Montezuma Wetland Complex in upstate New York, the state Department of Environmental Conservation has acquired more than 1,200 acres of land, including forest tracts supporting Cerulean Warblers, since 1997.

Working in Ecuador's Podocarpus National Park, Fundacion Arcoiris has developed an outreach campaign in nearby communities that highlights the interconnectedness between people and birds. The project will help endemic species like the globally threatened White-breasted Parakeet and neotropical migrants like the Cerulean Warbler. In 2001, the Peruvian government established the country's second largest national park, known as Cordillera Azul National Park, protecting a 5.1-million-acre expanse of habitat used by wintering Cerulean Warblers and a host of rare resident species. The area's importance was identified through the efforts of the Chicago Field Museum's Environmental and Conservation program and the Peruvian Association for the Conservation of Nature. These organizations are assisting the newly formed Center for the Conservation, Investigation, and Management of Natural Areas to develop a management plan for the park and raise the funds necessary to implement the plan. Already rangers have been deployed along the park's western boundary to prevent or slow illegal logging within the park.[1,9,14–19]

CONSERVATION NEEDS

- Prevent surface mining on lands that support high-quality Cerulean Warbler habitat.
- Increase acreage of bottomland and upland forest habitats within the breeding range of Cerulean Warbler that is managed to attain conditions beneficial to the species.
- Develop a broad, landscape-scale interstate management plan and cooperative agreements for increasing the amount of optimum habitat for Cerulean Warblers available at all times on public and private lands.
- Slow or halt deforestation of stopover and wintering habitat for Cerulean Warbler and restore habitat where possible.
- Develop baseline inventory of Cerulean Warbler breeding and wintering populations.

- Develop a wintering ground conservation plan that specifically targets areas important for wintering Cerulean Warblers that are also areas of high biodiversity.

References

1. Hamel, P.B. 2000. Cerulean Warbler (*Dendroica cerulea*). In *The Birds of North America*, No. 511 (A. Poole and F. Gill, eds.). The Academy of Natural Sciences, Philadelphia, PA, and the American Ornithologists' Union, Washington, DC.

2. Sauer, J. R., J. E. Hines, and J. Fallon. 2005. *The North American Breeding Bird Survey, Results and Analysis 1966–2005*, Version 6.2.2006. USGS Patuxent Wildlife Research Center, Laurel, MD.

3. Rosenberg, K.V., S.E. Barker, and R.W. Rohrbaugh. 2000. *An Atlas of Cerulean Warbler Populations*. Final Report to USFWS: 1997–2000 Breeding Seasons. Cornell Lab of Ornithology, Ithaca, NY. 56 pp.

4. Ridgely, R.S., and P.J. Greenfield. 2001. *The Birds of Ecuador*, Volume 1: *Status, Distribution, and Taxonomy*. Cornell University Press, Ithaca, NY. 848 pp.

5. John Fitpatrick, personal communication (16 June 2003).

6. Clements, J.F., and N. Shany. 2001. *A Field Guide to the Birds of Peru*. Ibis Publishing Company, Temecula, CA. 283 pp.

7. Hilty, S.L., and W.L. Brown. 1986. *Birds of Columbia*. Princeton University Press, Princeton, NJ. 836 pp.

8. BirdLife International. 2006. *Neotropical Migrants in the Tropical Andes–Cerulean Warbler*, Dendroica cerulea. http://www.birdlife.org/action/science/species/neotrops/andes/species/cerulean_warbler.html?language=en (accessed 19 January 2006).

9. Rich, T. D., C. Beardmore, H. Berlanga, P. Blancher, M. Bradstreet, G. Butcher, D. Demarest, E. Dunn, C. Hunter, E. Iñigo-Elias, J. Kennedy, A. Martell, A. Panjabi, D. Pashley, K. Rosenberg, C. Rustay, S. Wendt, and T. Will. 2004. *Partners in Flight North American Landbird Conservation Plan*. Cornell Lab of Ornithology, Ithaca, NY.

10. Gabbe, A.P., S.K. Robinson, and J.D. Brawn. 2002. Tree-species Preferences of Foraging Insectivorous Birds: Implications for Floodplain Restoration. *Conservation Biology* 16:462–470.

11. Robbins, C.S., J.W. Fitzpatrick, and P.B. Hamel. 1992. A Warbler in Trouble: *Dendroica cerulea*. Pages 549–562 In *Ecology and Conservation of Neotropical Migrant Landbirds* (J.M. Hagan III and D.W. Johnston, eds). Smithsonian Institution Press, Washington, DC.

12. Parker, T.A., III. 1994. Habitat, Behavior, and Spring Migration of Cerulean Warbler in Belize. *American Birds* 48:70–75.

13. Cindy Tibbot, personal communication (29 June 2001, Northeast Partners in Flight meeting presentation).

14. Twedt, D.J., and C.R. Loesch. 1999. Forest Area and Distribution in the Mississippi Alluvial Valley: Implications for Breeding Bird Conservation. *Journal of Biogeography* 26:1215–1224.

15. Stotz, D.F., J.W. Fitzpatrick, T.A. Parker III, and D. K. Moskovits. 1996. *Neotropical Birds: Ecology and Conservation*. University of Chicago Press, Chicago, IL. 481 pp.

16. Mueller, A.J., D.J. Twedt, and C.R. Loesch. 2000. Development of Management Objectives for Breeding Birds in the Mississippi Alluvial Valley. Pages 12–17 in *Strategies for Bird Conservation: The Partners in Flight Planning Process*. Proceedings of the 3rd Partners in Flight Workshop, 1995 October 1–5, Cape May, NJ (R. Bonney, D.N. Pashley, and R.J. Niles, eds.). Proceedings RMRS-P-16, U.S. Department of Agriculture, Forest Service, Rocky Mountain Research Station, Ogden, UT.

17. Rosenberg, K.V., and J.V. Wells. 2003. *Conservation Priorities for Terrestrial Birds in the Northeastern United States*. Proceedings of the 4th International Partners in Flight Symposium, Asilomar, CA, March 2001.

18. The Nature Conservancy. 2004. *Ecuador: Podocarpus National Park*. http://nature.org/wherewework/northamerica/states/pennsylvania/files/podo_bird4pgr.pdf (accessed 23 January 2006).

19. The Field Museum. 2002. *Parque Nacional Cordillera Azul*. http://www.fmnh.org/cordilleraazul/parkstory.html (accessed 30 June 2003).

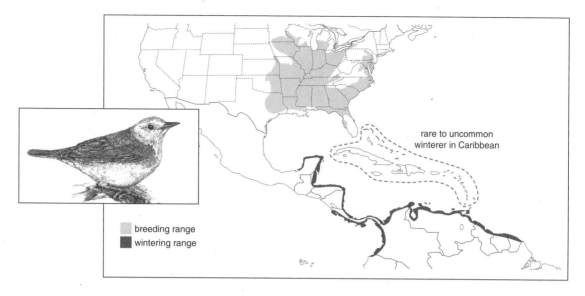

rare to uncommon
winterer in Caribbean

breeding range
wintering range

PROTHONOTARY WARBLER (*Protonotaria citrea*)

This large, golden warbler nests in holes in swamp forests of the eastern U.S. Its mangrove wintering habitat along the coasts of Central and South America is being rapidly lost and degraded.

STATUS AND DISTRIBUTION

Breeding range is restricted to the eastern U.S., barely making it as far north as extreme southern Ontario. Its U.S. range extends from New Jersey and eastern Pennsylvania (rarely farther north) west to southern Minnesota south to eastern Texas across the Gulf states to Florida. Within this range the species has a patchy distribution influenced by the availability of flooded forest habitat. Breeding density maps produced from Breeding Bird Survey data indicate highest densities in the Lower Mississippi Valley, especially in Louisiana and Mississippi, along the coastal plain from Virginia south to South Carolina, and in the Florida panhandle. The southeastern U.S. (south of Virginia and West Virginia) was estimated to support 96% of the global population.

Important breeding areas for the species include the Great Dismal Swamp Important Bird Area, over 100,000 acres of wilderness swamp forest habitat in North Carolina and Virginia that includes the Great Dismal Swamp National Wildlife Refuge (NWR), Tensas NWR in Louisiana, Congaree Swamp National Monument and Biosphere Reserve in South Carolina, White River NWR in Arkansas, and St. Marks NWR in Florida.

In winter, birds move south, with the wintering range extending from the Yucatan peninsula of Mexico south along the Caribbean coasts of Central America and South America to Venezuela. They also occur along the Pacific coasts of Costa Rica and Panama. They occur uncommonly in the Caribbean (including Trinidad and Tobago) and rarely in other parts of South America.

A number of parks and protected areas exist across parts of the winter range and likely provide important wintering habitat for the species, though few data are available on occurrence (much less density) of the species at these locations. In Mexico, the species is abundant within the Sian Ka'an Biosphere Reserve in the state of Quintana Roo. Other protected areas that encompass coastal mangrove habitat include Colombia's Ciénaga Grande de Santa Marta Fauna and Flora Sanctuary, Venezuela's Morrocoy National Park, Costa Rica's Golfo Dulce Forest Reserve, and Panama's Portobelo National Park.

Breeding Bird Survey analysis shows a significant decrease of approximately 39% (1.3% per year) from 1966 to 2005 rangewide. The species' total population was estimated at 1,800,000 individuals in 2004.[1-13]

ECOLOGY

On the breeding range it occurs in flooded forest or along water edges of lakes, ponds, and slow-moving rivers. Generally prefers mature forests larger than 250 acres with little understory and with permanent water. One of only two warbler species that breeds in cavities, this species uses cavities in trees and will use nest boxes. Nests are virtually always within 15 feet of standing water and typically 5–6 feet above ground. Birds lay 3–7 eggs and in the southern portion of breeding range regularly raise two broods per season. On the wintering grounds the species has not been well studied but shows strong preference for mangrove habitats, where birds are not territorial. Birds do occur in lower numbers in wooded habitats adjacent to coastal mangrove habitats.[1]

THREATS

On breeding grounds, the loss of habitat from clearing of large tracts of bottomland forest beginning in the 1800s was responsible for the extinction of Ivory-billed Woodpecker and Bachman's Warbler and for the decline of other species associated with this habitat including the Prothonotary Warbler. The loss of such habitat in the southeastern U.S. has been estimated at 90% and in the Lower Missippi Valley more at than 80%. In recent years the habitat loss within the Mississippi Alluvial Valley has halted and may have even begun to reverse.

Perhaps a greater threat is the continuing loss of mangrove wintering habitat for the species in Central and South America. For example, along Colombia's northwest coast, mangrove forest declined by 64% between 1956 and 1995 from development, highway construction, agriculture, and aquaculture. In Venezuela's Lake Maracaibo, the loss of mangrove habitat was estimated at 90% between 1960 and 1993. In some areas large expanses of mangroves have been removed for shrimp farming or salt production. Between 1964 and 1989 in Costa Rica's Gulf of Nicoya 1,582 acres of mangroves were lost to shrimp farms and 287 acres to salt production. Throughout the species' wintering range most mangrove habitats are lost or degraded by sedimentation and pollution from agricultural runoff and deforestation, changes in hydrology from road projects and developments, oil pollution, and cutting for fuel and charcoal production. In recent years there has been an increase in proposals for development of coastal tourism facilities that would destroy or degrade mangrove habitats. In general, mangrove habitat is underrepresented in parks and other protected areas throughout the wintering range. Several threatened bird species rely on these habitats, including the Mangrove Hummingbird, a species restricted to the Pacific coast of Costa Rica; the Yellow-billed Cotinga, occurring only on the Pacific coasts of Costa Rica and Panama; and the Sapphire-bellied Hummingbird, confined to the northern coast of Colombia. In addition, mangrove habitats support a host of other threatened animal species and marine species of economic importance.[1,11,14–21]

CONSERVATION ACTION

Partners in Flight Bird Conservation Plans that have been completed for southeastern U.S. physiographic regions have identified Prothonotary Warbler and its associated suite of bottomland forest bird species as a high priority and have provided recommendations for management, research, and monitoring.

These suggestions have included specific goals for increasing the acreage of bottomland forest in large blocks across the landscape. Within the Mississippi Alluvial Valley many projects to purchase or reforest lands are ongoing through many partner agencies and organizations, including the Mississippi Valley Joint Venture, U.S. Fish and Wildlife Service Partners for Wildlife program, the National Resources Conservation Service Wetland Reserve Program, Ducks Unlimited, and the Nature Conservancy. In many areas within the breeding range, nest box programs have been established that have increased local densities of breeding birds, though there is concern that birds breeding in nest boxes may have increased rates of nest predation.

On the wintering grounds there is an urgent need for increased awareness of communities and governments to the ecological importance of mangrove habitats and to increase acreage of mangroves within protected areas. Some limited work is being done to restore mangrove habitats in a few locations but few international conservation organizations seem to be working on the issue. The Pro-Ciénaga Project of the Colombian Ministry of the Environment has attempted to restore some of the hydrology of the Ciénaga Grande de Santa Marta Fauna and Flora Sanctuary where a large amount of mangrove forest was lost after road building. There are laws in Costa Rica and Venezuela that make it illegal to remove mangroves but these laws are not enforced.[1,13–15,20–22]

CONSERVATION NEEDS

- Increase acreage of bottomland and upland forest habitats within the breeding range of Prothonotary Warbler that is managed to attain conditions beneficial to the species.
- Slow or halt deforestation and degradation of wintering mangrove habitat for Prothonotary Warbler and restore habitat where possible.
- Develop baseline inventory of Prothonotary Warbler breeding and wintering populations.

References

1. Petit, L.J. 1999. Prothonotary Warbler (*Protonotaria citrea*). In *The Birds of North America*, No. 408 (A. Poole and F. Gill, eds.). The Academy of Natural Sciences, Philadelphia, PA, and the American Ornithologists' Union, Washington, DC.

2. Sauer, J. R., J. E. Hines, and J. Fallon. 2005. *The North American Breeding Bird Survey, Results and Analysis 1966–2005*, Version 6.2.2006. USGS Patuxent Wildlife Research Center, Laurel, MD.

3. Rosenberg, K.V., and J.V. Wells. 2000. Global Perspectives in Neotropical Migratory Bird Conservation in the Northeast: Long-term Responsibility Versus Immediate Concern. Pages 32–43 in *Strategies for Bird Conservation: The Partners in Flight Planning Process*; Proceedings of the 3rd Partners in Flight Workshop, 1995 October 1–5, Cape May, NJ (R. Bonney, D.N. Pashley, and R.J. Niles, eds.). Proceedings RMRS-P-16, U.S. Department of Agriculture, Forest Service, Rocky Mountain Research Station, Ogden, UT.

4. Audubon North Carolina. *North Carolina's Important Bird Areas*. http://www.ncaudubon.org/IBA1.htm (accessed 10 June 2003).

5. Igl, L.D. 2003. *Bird Checklists of the United States* (Version 12MAY03). Northern Prairie Wildlife Research Center Home Page, Jamestown, ND. http://www.npwrc.usgs.gov/resource/othrdata/chekbird/chekbird.htm (accessed 18 August 2003).

6. National Audubon Society. 2002. *South Carolina's Important Bird Areas Program*. http://www.audubon.org/bird/iba/sc.html (accessed 18 August 2003).

7. USFWS. No date. *White River National Wildlife Refuge*. http://whiteriver.fws.gov (accessed 18 August 2003).

8. CONABIO. 2002. *Áreas de Importancia para la Conservación de las Aves (AICAS)*. http://conabioweb.conabio.gob.mx/aicas/doctos/aicas.html (accessed 6 June 2003).

9. Unidad Administrativa Especial del Sistema de Parques Nacionales Naturales. No date. *Parques Nacionales de Colombia*. http://www.parquesnacionales.gov.co/areas.htm (accessed 23 June 2003).

10. Hilty, S.L. 2003. *Birds of Venezuela*, 2nd ed. Princeton University Press, Princeton, NJ. 878 pp.

11. Wege, D.C., and A.J. Long. 1995. *Key Areas for Threatened Birds in the Neotropics*. BirdLife International and Smithsonian Institution Press, Washington, DC. 311 pp.

12. UNEP-WCMC. 1986. *Portobelo National Park*. http://www.unep-wcmc.org/protected_areas/data/sample/0312q.htm (accessed 18 August 2003).

13. Rich, T.D., C. Beardmore, H. Berlanga, P. Blancher, M. Bradstreet, G. Butcher, D. Demarest, E. Dunn, C. Hunter, E. Iñigo-Elias, J. Kennedy, A. Martell, A. Panjabi, D. Pashley, K. Rosenberg, C. Rustay, S. Wendt, and T. Will. 2004. *Partners in Flight North American Landbird Conservation Plan*. Cornell Lab of Ornithology, Ithaca, NY.

14. Twedt, D.J., and C.R. Loesch. 1999. Forest Area and Distribution in the Mississippi Alluvial Valley: Implications for Breeding Bird Conservation. *Journal of Biogeography* 26:1215–1224.

15. Ellison, A.M., and E.J. Farnsworth. 1996. Anthropogenic Disturbance of Caribbean Mangrove Ecosystems: Past Impacts, Present Trends, and Future Predictions. *Biotropica* 28:549–565.

16. World Wildlife Fund. 2001. *Magdalena-Santa Marta Mangroves (NT1417)*. http://www.worldwildlife.org/wildworld/profiles/terrestrial/nt/nt1417_full.html (accessed 18 August 2003).

17. World Wildlife Fund. 2001. *Coastal Venezuelan Mangroves (NT1408)*. http://www.worldwildlife.org/wildworld/profiles/terrestrial/nt/nt1408_full.html (accessed 18 August 2003).

18. World Wildlife Fund. 2001. *Southern Dry Pacific Coast Mangroves (NT1434)*. http://www.worldwildlife.org/wildworld/profiles/terrestrial/nt/nt1434_full.html (accessed 18 August 2003).

19. World Wildlife Fund. 2001. *Moist Pacific Coast Mangroves (NT1423)*. http://www.worldwildlife.org/wildworld/profiles/terrestrial/nt/nt1423_full.html (accessed 18 August 2003).

20. Collar, N.J., L.P. Gonzaga, N. Krabbe, A. Madrono Nieto, L.G. Naranjo, T.A. Parker III, and D.C. Wege. 1992. *Threatened Birds of the Americas*. International Council for Bird Preservation, Cambridge, UK.

21. BirdLife International. 2000. *Threatened Birds of the World*. Lynx Editions and BirdLife International, Barcelona, Spain, and Cambridge, UK.

22. Mueller, A.J., D.J. Twedt, and C.R. Loesch. 2000. Development of Management Objectives for Breeding Birds in the Mississippi Alluvial Valley. Pages 12–17 in *Strategies for Bird Conservation: The Partners in Flight Planning Process*, Proceedings of the 3rd Partners in Flight Workshop, 1995 October 1–5, Cape May, NJ (R. Bonney, D.N. Pashley, and R.J. Niles, eds.). Proceedings RMRS-P-16, U.S. Department of Agriculture, Forest Service, Rocky Mountain Research Station, Ogden, UT.

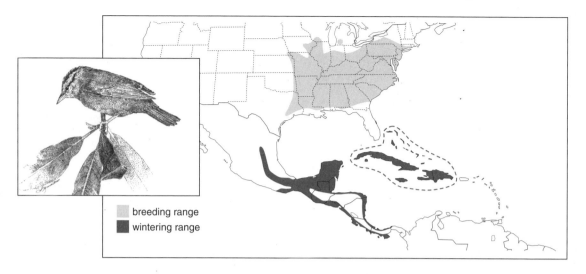

breeding range
wintering range

WORM-EATING WARBLER (*Helmitheros vermivorum*)

The trilling song of the Worm-eating Warbler drifts from the hillsides of deciduous forests of the eastern U.S. during the summer breeding season, where in some areas its song can be easily confused with similar sounding species like the Chipping Sparrow and the Dark-eyed Junco. The species is of conservation concern because of its relatively low breeding density and fragmented breeding range.

STATUS AND DISTRIBUTION

The Worm-eating Warbler breeding range is restricted to the eastern U.S. from southern Massachusetts west to southern Wisconsin and south to extreme eastern Texas and the Gulf states to Georgia. In many areas populations are highly fragmented and disjunct. Breeding density maps produced from Breeding Bird Survey data indicate highest densities in the Appalachians from southern Pennsylvania to Tennessee.

Among many important breeding areas for the species are West Virginia's Guyandotte Mountain area and Monongahela National Forest; the National Park Service's Ozark National Scenic Riverway in Missouri; and Great Smoky Mountains National Park in Tennessee and North Carolina.

In winter, birds migrate to the Caribbean, Mexico, and Central America. They regularly winter along Atlantic slope of Veracruz, Mexico south to Panama and along Pacific slope from Oaxaca, Mexico south to Panama. In Caribbean, they winter largely in the Bahamas and Greater Antilles. Although rather limited, Christmas Bird Count data indicate that higher densities occur in the Caribbean than in Mexico and Central America.

A number of parks and protected areas exist across parts of the winter range and likely provide important wintering habitat for the species, though few data are available on occurrence (much less density) of the species at these locations. In the Dominican Republic, sites that still have intact habitat that likely harbor wintering Worm-eating Warblers include Sierra de Bahoruco National Park and the Madre de las Aguas Conservation Area. In Jamaica, the Blue and John Crow Mountains National Park is known to support Worm-eating Warblers. In Mexico, the species is known to occur within the Sian Ka'an Biosphere Reserve in the state of Quintana Roo and the Calakmul Biosphere Reserve in the state of Campeche. In Guatemala, the Maya Biosphere Reserve likely supports the species. In Belize, the Rio Bravo Conservation and Management Area adjoins the Calakmul and Maya Biosphere Reserves and certainly must support Worm-eating Warblers.

Breeding Bird Survey analysis shows a nonsignificant increase of approximately 35% (1.1% per year) from 1966 to 2005 rangewide. The species' total population was estimated at 750,000 individuals in 2004.[1–11]

ECOLOGY

On the breeding range it occurs in deciduous and mixed forests with thick understory vegetation typically on moderate to steep hillsides and in perched wetlands (so-called "pocosin" wetlands), but in the coastal belt from New Jersey to Virginia it occurs also in flat bottomland forests. Throughout range it prefers relatively large blocks of mature forest and shows high levels of nest predation and cowbird parasitism in landscapes with fragmented forests. Results from BBIRD project suggest that self-sustaining populations occur only in areas where there is greater than 50% forest cover within a 100-km radius. Nests are built on the ground and are well concealed and birds lay 3–6 eggs.

On the wintering grounds it has been little-studied but occurs in a variety of forest habitats, including montane and lowland forests and primary and secondary forest and shade coffee plantations. In Central America, it is thought to prefer mature evergreen forest. Birds are territorial on wintering grounds, apparently maintaining spacing through calling but not through song, and likely associating with resident flocks.[1,4,5]

THREATS

The greatest threat is loss, fragmentation, and degradation of habitat on breeding and wintering grounds. Perhaps the most overriding current threat on the breeding grounds is from mountaintop removal mining within the areas of highest density for the species. For example, 246,000 acres had been lost or proposed for this practice in West Virginia by 2001. Mountaintop removal mining involves pushing the soil from the top of a mountain into the adjoining valley to reach horizontal coal seams hundreds of feet below the surface. Over 900 miles of stream filling had been authorized for this activity throughout the Appalachians by 2001.

Since the early 1900s the amount of forest in the northeastern U.S. has increased as farmland abandonment resulted in the regrowth of forested habitat. Unfortunately, habitat loss and fragmentation has also increased in certain areas for development of houses, businesses, and the associated infrastructure (roads, utility corridors, etc.). In areas of high fragmentation the species is prone to high rates of Brown-headed Cowbird parasitism and nest predation. Forestry practices that eliminate understory and fragment forests are a problem in many regions.

Another threat in much of the eastern U.S. is the widespread loss of understory habitat as a result of excessive browsing by overabundant white-tailed deer populations. This problem is made worse by the decreasing numbers of hunters and the lack of any large natural predators to control deer abundance.

On the wintering grounds, there has been extensive loss of primary forest wintering habitat. For example, in the Caribbean wintering range, 98.5% of forest has been lost in Haiti, 90% in Dominican Republic, 80–85% in Cuba, and 75% in Jamaica. These habitats have been identified as among those of highest global conservation concern because of the great loss of habitat and the many endemic animal and plants species that also occur in these habitats. Similarly, the lowland and mountain foothill forests of southern Mexico and Central America are being widely converted to agricultural uses. In many areas the cutting of forests has continued and occurs even within the borders of National Parks and other protected areas. Lack of resources to monitor and patrol parks and political difficulty of enforcing park regulations has hampered conservation efforts in many parks within the wintering range of the species.[1,4,6,12–14]

CONSERVATION ACTION

Partners in Flight Bird Conservation Plans that have been completed for eastern U.S. physiographic regions have identified the Worm-eating Warbler and its associated suite of forest bird species as a high priority and have provided recommendations for management, research, and monitoring. These suggestions have included specific goals for increasing the acreage of upland forest in large blocks across the landscape and recommendations for adoption of forestry management practices that maintain understory habitat.

On the wintering grounds a number of government agencies and conservation groups are involved in efforts to protect and manage parks and other protected areas within the wintering range of the Worm-eating Warbler. Within the Dominican Republic's Madre de las Aguas Conservation Area, Fundación Moscoso Puello, and the Nature Conservancy are developing plans for hiring and training park rangers, planting trees, and training local people in sustainable agriculture and foresty practices. In Jamaica, the Jamaican Conservation Development Trust and the Nature Conservancy are working to protect the forests in the Blue and

John Crow Mountains National Park by posting and securing park boundaries, hiring and training park rangers, providing them with guard stations, two-way radios, and vehicles, and monitoring short- and long-term changes in the park's plant and animal species.

At Mexico's Sian Ka'an Biosphere Reserve, organizations like the Amigos de Sian Ka'an, Pronatura Peninsula de Yucatan, and the Nature Conservancy (TNC) have helped to develop sustainable development projects, including ecotourism, to limit forest loss within the Reserve. These groups recently announced the purchase of an important buffer strip between the Reserve and the increasing development pressures from Cancún. Houston Audubon Society has provided funds to train local guides in birdwatching.

At Mexico's Calakmul Biosphere Reserve, the Friends of Calakmul have been using the jaguar as a flagship species to try to protect 600,000 acres in the buffer zone of the park from deforestation. They signed an agreement in 2001 with a local *ejido* (a community land cooperative) to purchase a conservation agreement for the 64,000 acres owned by the cooperative that reimburses the community in return for agreeing not to log the land.

Similarly, at the Maya Biosphere Reserve in Guatemala, the Nature Conservancy, working with the Guatemalan government and Defensores de la Naturaleza, entered into an agreement to cooperatively manage the Sierra del Lacandon National Park within the Reserve and helped purchase 22,500 acres of additional habitat in the park.

The Programme for Belize and TNC have built educational and research facilities and ranger posts at the Rio Bravo Conservation and Management Area in Belize and are experimenting with sustainable forestry management to prevent long-term loss of forest habitats within the area.[7,9,10,13,15–19]

CONSERVATION NEEDS

- Increase acreage of forest habitats within the breeding range of Worm-eating Warbler that is managed to attain conditions beneficial to the species. Specifically, maximize the number of blocks of unfragmented forest greater than 25,000 acres and decrease the number of forest openings (including roads) and human structures that facilitate cowbird parasitism.
- Slow or halt deforestation of wintering habitat for Worm-eating Warbler and restore habitat where possible.
- Develop baseline inventory of Worm-eating Warbler breeding and wintering populations.
- Increase the amount and distribution of protected areas that harbor the Worm-eating Warbler throughout the wintering range, particularly in the Caribbean.
- Conduct outreach and education efforts, particularly within winter range, to highlight the importance of habitat protection by local residents.

References

1. Hanner, L.A., and S.R. Patton. 1998. Worm-eating Warbler (*Helmitheros vermivorus*). In *The Birds of North America*, No. 367 (A. Poole and F. Gill, eds.). The Academy of Natural Sciences, Philadelphia, PA, and the American Ornithologists' Union, Washington, DC.

2. Sauer, J.R., J. E. Hines, and J. Fallon. 2005. *The North American Breeding Bird Survey, Results and Analysis 1966–2005*, Version 6.2.2006. USGS Patuxent Wildlife Research Center, Laurel, MD.

3. Igl, L. D. 2003. *Bird Checklists of the United States* (Version 12MAY03). Northern Prairie Wildlife Research Center Home Page, Jamestown, ND. http://www.npwrc.usgs.gov/resource/othrdata/chekbird/chekbird.htm (accessed 21 July 2003).

4. National Audubon Society. 2002. *West Virginia's Important Bird Areas Program*. http://www.audubon.org/bird/iba/wv.html (accessed 17 July 2003).

5. University of Montana. 2003. *BBIRD Species Accounts: Worm-eating Warbler*. http://pica.wru.umt.edu/BBIRD/speciesaccounts.html (accessed 14 August 2003).

6. World Wildlife Fund. 2001. *Hispaniolan Moist forests (NT0127)*. http://www.worldwildlife.org/wildworld/profiles/terrestrial/nt/nt0127_full.html (accessed 16 July 2003).

7. The Nature Conservancy. 2003. *Dominican Republic - Places We Work*. http://nature.org/wherewework/caribbean/dominicanrepublic/work/ (accessed 16 July 2003).

8. CONABIO. 2002. *Áreas de Importancia para la Conservación de las Aves (AICAS)*. http://conabioweb.conabio.gob.mx/aicas/doctos/aicas.html (accessed 18 June 2003).

9. The Nature Conservancy. 2002. *Rio Bravo Conservation and Management Area*. http://nature.org/where

wework/centralamerica/belize/work/art8860.html (accessed 19 June 2003).

10. Programme for Belize. 2003. *The Programme for Belize and The Rio Bravo Conservation and Management Area.* http://www.pfbelize.org/about.html (accessed 19 June 2003).

11. Rich, T.D., C. Beardmore, H. Berlanga, P. Blancher, M. Bradstreet, G. Butcher, D. Demarest, E. Dunn, C. Hunter, E. Iñigo-Elias, J. Kennedy, A. Martell, A. Panjabi, D. Pashley, K. Rosenberg, C. Rustay, S. Wendt, and T. Will. 2004. *Partners in Flight North American Landbird Conservation Plan.* Cornell Lab of Ornithology, Ithaca, NY.

12. Cindy Tibbot, personal communication (29 June 2001, Northeast Partners in Flight meeting presentation).

13. Rosenberg, K.V., and J.V. Wells. 2003. *Conservation Priorities for Terrestrial Birds in the Northeastern United States.* Proceedings of the 4th International Partners in Flight Symposium, Asilomar, CA, March 2001.

14. Stotz, D.F., J.W. Fitzpatrick, T.A. Parker III, and D. K. Moskovits. 1996. *Neotropical Birds: Ecology and Conservation.* University of Chicago Press, Chicago, IL. 481 pp.

15. The Nature Conservancy. 2003. *Blue and John Crow Mountains.* http://nature.org/wherewework/caribbean/jamaica/work/art8665.html (accessed 16 July 2003).

16. The Nature Conservancy. 2002. *Conservationists Buy Pez Maya Property on Yucatan Peninsula.* http:nature.org/wherewework/northamerica/mexico/press/press609.html (accessed 19 June 2003).

17. Houston Audubon. 2001. *The Sian Ka'an Partnership.* http://www.houstonaudubon.org/siankaan.html (accessed 19 June 2003).

18. Friends of Calakmul. No date. *Calakmul Biosphere Reserve.* http://www.calakmul.org/ (accessed 19 June 2003).

19. The Nature Conservancy. 2002. *Maya Biosphere Reserve.* http://nature.org/wherewework/centralamerica/guatemala/work/art8858.html (accessed 19 June 2003).

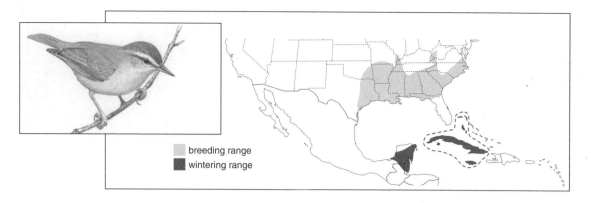

breeding range
wintering range

SWAINSON'S WARBLER (*Limnothlypis swainsonii*)

A rather secretive and little-studied bird of southeastern forests, the Swainson's Warbler has increased in recent years but has a relatively small estimated total population size compared to other songbirds in North America.

STATUS AND DISTRIBUTION

The Swainson's Warbler breeding range is restricted to the southeastern U.S. from southern Virginia westward to southern Missouri and eastern Oklahoma south to eastern Texas and the Gulf states to northern Florida. Within this range the species has a very patchy and discontinuous distribution. Breeding density maps produced from the rather limited amount of Breeding Bird Survey data available for the species indicate highest densities in eastern Texas and Louisiana.

Important breeding areas for the species include the Great Dismal Swamp Important Bird Area in North Carolina and Virginia that includes the Great Dismal Swamp National Wildlife Refuge (NWR), Tensas NWR in Louisiana, Big Thicket National Preserve in Texas, and Hatchie NWR in Tennessee.

In winter, birds move south to the Caribbean, including Cuba, Jamaica, the Caymans, and the Bahamas, and to the Yucatan Peninsula of Mexico, Belize, and northern Guatemala. The Sierra de Ticúl-Punto Put Important Bird Area that spans the borders of the Mexican states of Yucatan, Quintana Roo, and Campeche supports wintering populations of Swainson's Warbler. In Jamaica, the Blue and John Crow Mountains National Park is an important wintering area for the species and may support as many as 17,000–25,000 individuals. In Cuba, the highest numbers of wintering

Swainson's Warblers netted during the period 1991–1994 were within the provinces of Matanzas and Ciego de Avila.

Breeding Bird Survey analysis shows a significant increase of approximately 91% (6.4% per year) from 1966 to 2005 rangewide. The species' total population was estimated at 84,000 individuals in 2004.[1–7]

ECOLOGY

On the breeding range it occurs in two very different primary habitat types, both characterized by thick shrubby understory. Throughout most of breeding range it primarily occupies floodplain forests with dense understory but little ground cover. This habitat type occurs in regenerating logged areas and in natural gaps in older forests. Within the southern Appalachian mountains, the species uses habitats with thick rhododendron and mountain laurel thickets and mature deciduous forest habitats with dense understories of spicebush and greenbrier. It nests low to the ground (<10 feet) in thickets, laying 2–5 eggs. On the wintering grounds it has been little studied but a comparison of body conditions of birds captured in dry limestone forests versus second-growth scrub habitats in Jamaica suggested that dry limestone forests may provide higher quality habitat. Birds have also been found wintering in mangroves, montane habitat, and lowland riparian habitats.[1,8–10]

THREATS

On breeding grounds, the loss of habitat from clearing of large tracts of bottomland forest beginning in the 1800s was responsible for the extinction of Ivory-billed Woodpecker and Bachman's Warbler and for the decline of other species associated with this habitat, including the Swainson's Warbler. The loss of such habitat in the Mississippi Alluvial Valley was estimated at 50% and in the Lower Missippi Valley at more than 80%. In recent years the habitat loss within the Mississippi Alluvial Valley has halted and may have even begun to reverse, though the remaining large forest fragments tend to be wetter and may be unsuitable or less suitable for Swainson's Warblers. Loss or fragmentation of breeding and wintering habitats currently supporting Swainson's Warblers continues in many parts of the species' range.[1,11]

CONSERVATION ACTION

Partners in Flight Bird Conservation Plans that have been completed for southeastern U.S. physiographic regions have identified Swainson's Warbler and its associated suite of bottomland and upland forest bird species as a high priority and have provided recommendations for management, research, and monitoring. These suggestions have included specific goals for increasing the acreage of bottomland forest in large blocks across the landscape. Within the Mississippi Alluvial Valley many projects to purchase or reforest lands are ongoing through many partner agencies and organizations, including the Mississippi Valley Joint Venture, U.S. Fish and Wildlife Service Partners for Wildlife program, the National Resources Conservation Service Wetland Reserve Program, Ducks Unlimited, and the Nature Conservancy.

In Jamaica, the Jamaican Conservation Development Trust and the Nature Conservancy are working to protect the forests in the Blue and John Crow Mountains National Park by posting and securing park boundaries, hiring and training park rangers and providing them with guard stations, two-way radios, and vehicles, and monitoring short- and long-term changes in the park's plant and animal species. The Conservancy and its partners are also working with residents of local communities to introduce more environmentally compatible business ventures.

The Sierra de Ticúl-Punto Put Important Bird Area is within the project boundaries for Mexico's MesoAmerican Biological Corridor Project, a multifaceted $20 million conservation project largely funded by the Global Environmental Facility of the World Bank. The project, which is managed by Mexico's CONABIO, focuses on slowing or halting deforestation within the area through incentives, regulations, and grant programs.[12-15]

CONSERVATION NEEDS

- Increase acreage of bottomland and upland forest habitats within the breeding range of Swainson's Warbler that is managed to attain conditions beneficial to the species.
- Slow or halt deforestation of wintering habitat for Swainson's Warbler and restore habitat where possible.
- Develop baseline inventory of Swainson's Warbler breeding and wintering populations.

References

1. Brown, R.E., and J.G. Dickson. 1994. Swainson's Warbler (*Limnothlypis swainsonii*). In *The Birds of North America*, No. 126 (A. Poole and F. Gill, eds.). The Academy of Natural Sciences, Philadelphia, PA, and the American Ornithologists' Union, Washington, DC.

2. Sauer, J. R., J. E. Hines, and J. Fallon. 2005. *The North American Breeding Bird Survey, Results and Analysis 1966–2005*, Version 6.2.2006. USGS Patuxent Wildlife Research Center, Laurel, MD.

3. Audubon North Carolina. *North Carolina's Important Bird Areas*. http://www.ncaudubon.org/IBA1.htm (accessed 10 June 2003).

4. CONABIO. 2002. *Áreas de Importancia para la Conservación de las Aves (AICAS)*. http://conabioweb .conabio.gob.mx/aicas/doctos/aicas.html (accessed 6 June 2003).

5. Graves, G.R. 1996. Censusing Wintering Populations of Swainson's Warblers: Surveys in the Blue Mountains of Jamaica. *Wilson Bulletin* 108:94–103.

6. Kirkconnell, A., G.E. Wallace, and O.H. Garrido. 1996. Notes on the Status and Behavior of the Swainson's Warbler in Cuba. *Wilson Bulletin* 108: 175–178.

7. Rich, T.D., C. Beardmore, H. Berlanga, P. Blancher, M. Bradstreet, G. Butcher, D. Demarest, E. Dunn, C. Hunter, E. Iñigo-Elias, J. Kennedy, A. Martell, A. Panjabi, D. Pashley, K. Rosenberg, C. Rustay, S. Wendt, and T. Will. 2004. *Partners in Flight North American Landbird Conservation Plan*. Cornell Lab of Ornithology, Ithaca, NY.

8. Graves, G.R. 2002. Habitat Characteristics in the Core Breeding Range of the Swainson's Warbler. *Wilson Bulletin* 114:210–220.

9. Strong, A.M., and T.W. Sherry. 2001. Body Con-

dition of Swainson's Warblers Wintering in Jamaica and the Conservation Value of Caribbean Dry Forests. *Wilson Bulletin* 113:410–418.

10. Graves, G.R. 2001. Factors Governing the Distribution of Swainson's Warbler Along a Hydrological Gradient in Great Dismal Swamp. *Auk* 118:650–664.

11. Twedt, D.J., and C.R. Loesch. 1999. Forest Area and Distribution in the Mississippi Alluvial Valley: Implications for Breeding Bird Conservation. *Journal of Biogeography* 26:1215–1224.

12. Hunter, W.C., L. Peoples, and J. Callazo. 2001. *South Atlantic Coastal Plain Partners in Flight Bird Conservation Plan.* U.S. Fish and Wildlife Service, Atlanta, GA.

13. Mueller, A.J., D.J. Twedt, and C.R. Loesch. 2000. Development of Management Objectives for Breeding Birds in the Mississippi Alluvial Valley. Pages 12–17 in *Strategies for Bird Conservation: The Partners in Flight Planning Process.* Proceedings of the 3rd Partners in Flight Workshop; 1995 October 1–5; Cape May, NJ (R. Bonney, D.N. Pashley, and R.J. Niles, eds.). Proceedings RMRS-P-16, U.S. Department of Agriculture, Forest Service, Rocky Mountain Research Station, Ogden, UT.

14. The Nature Conservancy. 2003. *Blue and John Crow Mountains.* http://nature.org/wherewework/caribbean/jamaica/work/art8665.html (accessed 16 July 2003).

15. Comisión Nacional de Áreas Naturales Protegidas. No date. *Corredor Biológico Mesoamericano.* http://www.conanp.gob.mx/dcei/cbmm/ (accessed 6 January 2006).

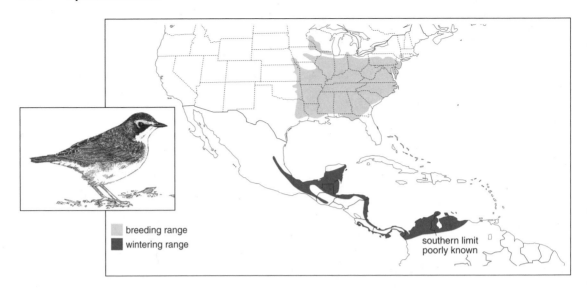

breeding range
wintering range

southern limit
poorly known

KENTUCKY WARBLER (*Oporornis formosus*)

A secretive bird of thick, shrubby forest understory, the Kentucky Warbler song is a familiar summer sound of the southeast U.S. The species has shown significant declines in recent decades making it a bird of a conservation concern.

STATUS AND DISTRIBUTION

The Kentucky Warbler breeding range is restricted to the eastern U.S. from southern New Jersey west to southern Wisconsin and south to eastern Texas and the Gulf states to northwestern Florida. A disjunct population occurs in southeastern New York's Hudson Valley. Breeding density maps produced from Breeding Bird Survey data indicate highest densities over a relatively broad region within the Mississippi and Ohio River drainages from Louisiana, Mississippi, and Alabama north to Ohio and western West Virginia.

Among many important breeding areas for the species are West Virginia's Guyandotte Mountain area, Louisiana's Tensas National Wildlife Refuge (NWR) and Bogue Chitto NWR, the Big Thicket National Preserve in Texas, Hatchie NWR in Tennessee, and Wapanocca NWR in Alabama.

In winter, birds migrate to Central America with apparently small numbers in the Caribbean and northern South America. They are restricted to eastern Mexico and the Atlantic slope north of Costa Rica but also occur on the Pacific slope of Costa Rica and Panama. They also occur in northern Colombia and northwestern Venezuela but

status there uncertain. They are primarily thought to inhabit lowland and foothill forests but sometimes are also found in higher elevation moist forests.

A number of parks and protected areas exist across parts of the winter range and likely provide important wintering habitat for the species, though few data are available on occurrence of the species at these locations. In Mexico, the species is abundant within the Sian Ka'an Biosphere Reserve in the state of Quintana Roo and is known to occur in the Calakmul Biosphere Reserve in the state of Campeche. In Guatemala, the Maya Biosphere Reserve supports high densities of the species. In Belize, the Rio Bravo Conservation and Management Area adjoins the Calakmul and Maya Biosphere Reserves and certainly must support Kentucky Warblers. In Panama, Darien National Park and Portobelo National Park are among the protected areas that encompass habitat within the wintering range of Kentucky Warbler.

Breeding Bird Survey analysis shows a significant decrease of approximately 29% (0.9% per year) from 1966 to 2005 rangewide. The species' total population was estimated at 1,100,000 individuals in 2004.[1-8]

ECOLOGY

On the breeding range occurs in deciduous forests with thick understory vegetation typically in bottomlands or riparian areas. Throughout most of range it prefers relatively large blocks of mature forest. Nests are built on the ground and are well concealed and birds lay 3–6 eggs.

On the wintering grounds it has been little studied but is usually found in the thick understory of lowland and foothill forests. Birds apparently can use forests with relatively young trees growing after being logged and forests of mature trees but more research is needed to understand differences in habitat quality. Birds are territorial on wintering grounds, apparently maintaining spacing through call notes but not through song, and likely associating with resident flocks.[1]

THREATS

The greatest threat is loss and fragmentation of habitat on breeding and wintering grounds. On breeding grounds, the historic loss of habitat from clearing of large tracts of southeastern bottomland forest for agriculture beginning in the 1800s was responsible for the extinction of Ivory-billed Woodpecker and Bachman's Warbler and undoubtedly caused declines in Kentucky Warbler populations. The loss of such habitat in the Mississippi Alluvial Valley was estimated at 50%. Unfortunately, habitat loss and fragmentation has increased in certain areas for development of homes, businesses, and the associated infrastructure (roads, utility corridors, etc.). In areas of high fragmentation the species is prone to high rates of Brown-headed Cowbird parasitism and nest predation.

Forestry practices that eliminate understory and fragment forests are a problem in many regions. A study of nesting success in a managed forest in Illinois showed that birds had higher reproductive output in mature large forest blocks more than one kilometer from agricultural edges than in second-growth forest or mature forest near agricultural edges.

On the wintering grounds, the lowland and mountain foothill forests of Central America and northern South America where Kentucky Warblers winter are being widely converted to agricultural uses. Birds will use second-growth forest though abundance is generally higher in undisturbed, mature forest.[1,9–11]

CONSERVATION ACTION

Partners in Flight Bird Conservation Plans that have been completed for eastern U.S. physio-

graphic regions have identified the Kentucky Warbler and its associated suite of bottomland forest bird species as a high priority and have provided recommendations for management, research, and monitoring. These suggestions have included specific goals for increasing the acreage of bottomland and upland forest in large blocks across the landscape and recommendations for adoption of forestry management practices that maintain understory habitat.

Within the Mississippi Alluvial Valley many projects to purchase or reforest lands are ongoing through many partner agencies and organizations, including the Lower Mississippi Valley Joint Venture, U.S. Fish and Wildlife Service Partners for Wildlife program, the National Resources Conservation Service Wetland Reserve Program, Ducks Unlimited, and the Nature Conservancy.

The species has received heightened awareness in planning efforts on public lands, especially federally owned lands, but there is no available assessment of the acreage of Kentucky Warbler habitat currently under public ownership and managed for wildlife conservation.

At Mexico's Sian Ka'an Biosphere Reserve, organizations like the Amigos de Sian Ka'an, Pronatura Peninsula Yucatan, and the Nature Conservancy have helped to develop sustainable development projects, including ecotourism, to limit forest loss within the Reserve. These groups recently announced the purchase of an important buffer strip between the Reserve and the increasing development pressures from Cancún. Houston Audubon Society has provided funds to train local guides in birdwatching.

At Mexico's Calakmul Biosphere Reserve, the Friends of Calakmul have been using the jaguar as a flagship species to try to protect 600,000 acres in the buffer zone of the park from deforestation. They signed an agreement in 2001 with a local *ejido* (a community land cooperative) to purchase a conservation agreement for the 64,000 acres owned by the cooperative that reimburses the community in return for agreeing not to log the land.

Similarly, at the Maya Biosphere Reserve in Guatemala, the Nature Conservancy working with the Guatemalan government and Defensores de la Naturaleza entered into an agreement to cooperatively manage the Sierra del Lacandon National Park within the Reserve and helped purchase 22,500 acres of additional habitat in the park. The Peregrine Fund has carried out a series of research, management and outreach activities at the Biosphere Reserve.

The Programme for Belize and the Nature Conservatory have built educational and research facilities and ranger posts at the Rio Bravo Conservation and Management Area in Belize and are experimenting with sustainable forestry management to prevent long-term loss of forest habitats within the area.[1,4-6,8,9,12-17]

CONSERVATION NEEDS

- Increase acreage of bottomland forest habitats within the breeding range of the Kentucky Warbler that is managed to attain conditions beneficial to the species.
- Slow or halt deforestation of wintering habitat for the Kentucky Warbler and restore habitat where possible.
- Develop baseline inventory of Kentucky Warbler breeding and wintering populations.
- Increase amount and distribution of protected areas that harbor the Kentucky Warbler throughout the wintering range.
- Conduct outreach and education efforts, particularly within winter range, to highlight the importance of habitat protection by local residents.

References

1. McDonald, M.V. 1998. Kentucky Warbler (*Oporornis formosus*). In *The Birds of North America*, No. 324 (A. Poole and F. Gill, eds.). The Academy of Natural Sciences, Philadelphia, PA, and the American Ornithologists' Union, Washington, DC.

2. Sauer, J. R., J. E. Hines, and J. Fallon. 2005. *The North American Breeding Bird Survey, Results and Analysis 1966–2005*, Version 6.2.2006. USGS Patuxent Wildlife Research Center, Laurel, MD.

3. CONABIO. 2002. *Áreas de Importancia para la Conservación de las Aves (AICAS)*. http://conabioweb.conabio.gob.mx/aicas/doctos/aicas.html (accessed 18 June 2003).

4. The Peregrine Fund. No date. *The Maya Project*. http://www.peregrinefund.org/maya_project/ (accessed 18 June 2003).

5. The Nature Conservancy. 2002. *Rio Bravo Conservation and Management Area*. http://nature.org/wherewework/centralamerica/belize/work/art8860.html (accessed 19 June 2003).

6. Programme for Belize. 2003. *The Programme for Belize and the Rio Bravo Conservation and Management Area*. http://www.pfbelize.org/about.html (accessed 19 June 2003).

7. Panama Travel. No date. *Panama's National Parks*. http://www.panamatravel.com/natparks.htm (accessed 19 June 2003).

8. Rich, T.D., C. Beardmore, H. Berlanga, P. Blancher, M. Bradstreet, G. Butcher, D. Demarest, E. Dunn, C. Hunter, E. Iñigo-Elias, J. Kennedy, A. Martell, A. Panjabi, D. Pashley, K. Rosenberg, C. Rustay, S. Wendt, and T. Will. 2004. *Partners in Flight North American Conservation Plan*. Cornell Lab of Ornithology, Ithaca, NY.

9. Twedt, D.J., and C.R. Loesch. 1999. Forest Area and Distribution in the Mississippi Alluvial Valley: Implications for Breeding Bird Conservation. *Journal of Biogeography* 26:1215–1224.

10. Morse, S.F., and S.K. Robinson. 1998. Nesting Success of a Neotropical Migrant in a Multiple-use, Forested Landscape. *Conservation Biology* 13:327–337.

11. Stotz, D.F., J.W. Fitzpatrick, T.A. Parker III, and D. K. Moskovits. 1996. *Neotropical Birds: Ecology and Conservation*. University of Chicago Press, Chicago, IL. 481 pp.

12. Mueller, A.J., D.J. Twedt, and C.R. Loesch. 2000. Development of Management Objectives for Breeding Birds in the Mississippi Alluvial Valley. Pages 12–17 in *Strategies for Bird Conservation: The Partners in Flight Planning Process*. Proceedings of the 3rd Partners in Flight Workshop, 1995 October 1–5, Cape May, NJ (R. Bonney, D.N. Pashley, and R.J. Niles, eds.). Proceedings RMRS-P-16, U.S. Department of Agriculture, Forest Service, Rocky Mountain Research Station, Ogden, UT.

13. Rosenberg, K.V., and J.V. Wells. 2005. Conservation Priorities for Terrestrial Birds In The Northeastern United States. In *Bird Conservation Implementation and Integration in the Americas*. Proceedings of the Third International Partners in Flight Conference 2002. (C.J. Ralph and T. D. Rich, eds.). USDA Forest Service, GTR-PSW-191, Albany, CA.

14. The Nature Conservancy. 2002. *Conservationists Buy Pez Maya Property on Yucatan Peninsula*. http:natture.org/wherewework/northamerica/mexico/press/press609.html (accessed 19 June 2003).

15. Houston Audubon. 2001. *The Sian Ka'an Partnership*. http://www.houstonaudubon.org/siankaan.html (accessed 19 June 2003).

16. Friends of Calakmul. No date. *Calakmul Biosphere Reserve*. http://www.calakmul.org/ (accessed 19 June 2003).

17. The Nature Conservancy. 2002. *Maya Biosphere Reserve*. http://nature.org/wherewework/centralamerica/guatemala/work/art8858.html (accessed 19 June 2003).

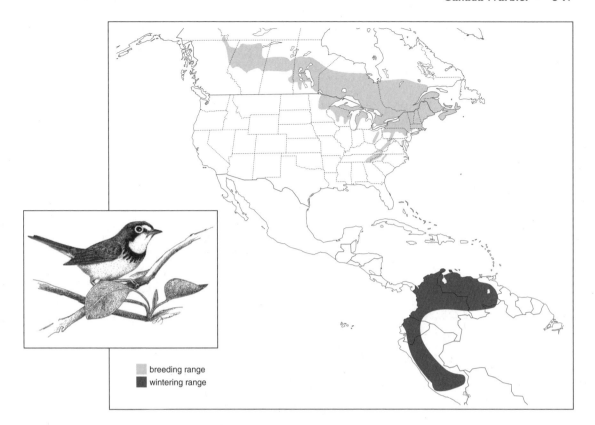

breeding range
wintering range

CANADA WARBLER (*Wilsonia canadensis*)

A favorite among birders for its loud song and strikingly contrasting plumage, the Canada Warbler has consistently declined over the last forty years. As its name suggests, the bulk of the population breeds in Canada, primarily in the boreal forest region.

STATUS AND DISTRIBUTION

The Canada Warbler breeding range extends from extreme northeastern British Columbia across Canada to the Maritime Provinces (but not Newfoundland) and south through Minnesota, Wisconsin, Michigan, and the northeast U.S. and at upper elevations south through the Appalachian Mountains to Georgia. Isolated populations occur in Illinois, Indiana, and Ohio. Breeding density maps produced from Breeding Bird Survey data indicate high densities in northwestern Maine and southwestern New Brunswick. It is estimated that Canada supports 79% of the global population and the northeast U.S. 16%. Another analysis estimated that 64% of the global population occurred in Canada's boreal forest ecozone.

Although no systematic survey has been completed to identify sites that are of particular importance for breeding populations of Canada Warbler, there are many areas that have large expanses of habitat and at which the species is known to occur. These sites include Maine's Moosehorn National Wildlife Refuge, New Brunswick's Kouchibouguac National Park, Nova Scotia's Kejimkujik National Park, Ontario's Algonquin Provincial Park, and New York's Adirondack Park.

In winter, birds migrate to South America in the Andean region and the eastern slope of the Andes from Venezuela south to Peru, with a few records from Amazonian Venezuela and Brazil, but the extent of winter range is generally poorly known. They are thought to be most abundant in eastern Colombia and the foothills of the eastern slope of the Andes of southern Ecuador and Peru.

A number of parks and protected areas exist across parts of the winter range and likely provide important wintering habitat for the species, though few data are available on occurrence of the species at these locations. In Colombia such areas include Chingaza National Natural Park, Sumapaz

National Park, Tatamá National Park, and El Cocuy National Park. In Ecuador, protected areas that encompass foothill forest habitat on the eastern slope of the Andes include the Cayambe-Coca Ecological Reserve, Podocarpus National Park, Sangay National Park, and Sumaco-Galeras National Park. In Peru, areas with similar habitat include Manu National Park, Codillera Azul National Park, Río Abiseo National Park, Yanachaga-Chemillen National Park, Apurimac Reserve, and the Tambopata-Candamo Reserve.

Breeding Bird Survey analysis shows a significant decrease of approximately 55% (2.1% per year) from 1966 to 2005 rangewide. The species' total population was estimated at 1,400,000 individuals in 2004.[1-10]

ECOLOGY

Has not been well studied, but on the breeding range this species occurs in mixed coniferous–deciduous forests with thick understory vegetation, often near water, especially bogs and swampy woods. In more southerly portions of the range it occurs only at higher elevations and is often associated with rhododendron thickets. Will readily breed in regenerating second-growth woodlands in the northern portion of the range. Generally sings and forages within 5–20 feet from ground in dense vegetation. Nests on or near the ground within dense vegetation, laying 2–6 eggs.

On the wintering grounds it has been little studied but occurs in thick undergrowth within range of general habitat types including primary forest, second-growth woodland, and shade coffee plantations, generally in submontane and foothill forests from 1,000 to 2,100 meters in elevation. Observations on migration and on the wintering grounds suggest that the birds typically forage within mixed-species flocks of resident birds but in low densities (no more than two birds per flock).[1]

THREATS

The major issues impacting this species on the breeding grounds include large increases in commercial timber production, effects of acid rain and deer overbrowse on forest habitats, and, in some areas, loss and fragmentation of habitat from development. The species is thought to have in-creased following abandonment of agricultural lands and subsequent regrowth of forests in the eastern U.S. in the first half of the 20th century but as forests matured, less optimum habitat was available and numbers declined. In addition, throughout the northeast U.S., much of the forested wetland habitats preferred by Canada Warblers were drained and developed after 1950.

In the Canadian portion of the range and in northern Maine, much of the Canada Warbler habitat is within areas managed for forestry. An estimated 64% of the species total world population occurs within Canada's boreal forest so that any large changes in land use through that area will significantly impact the species as a whole. Forest harvest levels have generally increased across most of the boreal zone of Canada. Though more than 90% of the Canadian boreal forest is publicly owned, almost a third of the boreal forest is currently allocated to forestry companies for timber production amounting to tens of millions of acres that will be logged during this century. For example, one logging license area of 375,000 acres in Quebec is scheduled to be harvested over the next twenty years. Clearcutting has been used in over 80% of forest harvest operations in Canada. In addition, forestry companies make increasingly widespread use of herbicides—in Ontario and Quebec approximately 250,000 acres were sprayed in 1996—with unknown effects on habitat conditions for wildlife. Canada Warblers can occupy second-growth woodlands following logging but healthy, stable bird populations will require forest harvest planning schemes that incorporate ecological needs. Such plans need to be done at a broad landscape scale that provides a mosaic of appropriate age-class forests and retains blocks of habitat that support source populations of birds.

Other issues affecting boreal forest habitat include rapidly increasing development and prospecting for minerals, oil, and natural gas and, in some areas, the building of hydroelectric facilities.

On the wintering grounds, the lower-elevation forests of the Andes where the species prefers to winter provide excellent conditions for growing various agricultural crops, including coffee as well as illicit coca plantations, and forests in this zone are full of commercially valuable trees. Andean foothill habitats are being lost and fragmented faster than most other forest habitats in the Neotropics and already harbor large assemblages of endangered and threatened species.[1,5,10-16]

CONSERVATION ACTION

Partners in Flight Bird Conservation Plans that have been completed for eastern U.S. physiographic regions have identified the Canada Warbler and a suite of associated mixed deciduous/coniferous forest bird species as a high priority and have provided recommendations for management, research, and monitoring. The Vermont Institute of Natural Science published a report and other materials that provide guidelines for managing habitat on the breeding grounds for Canada Warbler.

A diverse array of conservation groups, government agencies, and forest industry companies have been working together in various ways toward the conservation and sustainable use of large expanses of northern forests from New York's Adirondack region through Maine. For example, the Forest Society of Maine's West Branch Project protected 329,000 acres of forest in northwestern Maine largely through a conservation easement. The easement allows continued · sustainable forestry but was the first large-scale easement in Maine that included easement terms requiring that biological diversity be addressed. The Nature Conservancy and Great Northern Paper, with funding from the Open Space Institute, developed an agreement to protect 240,000 acres of forest adjacent to Baxter State Park in Maine. A conservation easement will allow sustainable forestry on 200,000 acres while the remaining acreage will remain a wilderness preserve. A conservation easement protecting 762,192 acres in northern Maine from development but allowing sustainable forestry was entered into by the New England Forestry Foundation and Pingree Associates. Other projects are underway targeting hundreds of thousands of additional acres across the region for protection and large amounts of funding for these acquisitions have come from various government programs, including the Forest Legacy Program.

In Canada a broad community of conservation organizations, industry, and First Nations have announced the Boreal Forest Conservation Framework—a new national conservation approach for Canada's boreal forest region. The Framework plan would protect the ecological integrity of the region while integrating sustainable forestry and other development activities. The Framework calls for the establishment of large, interconnected, protected areas covering at least half of the boreal region and application of lead-ing-edge sustainable development practices on the lands that are developed. The Canadian Boreal Initiative and its partners are working to encourage the adoption of Framework principles by Canadian national and provincial government agencies and policy makers as a vision for the future of the vast, and largely publicly owned, boreal landscape.

A Canadian Senate subcommittee developed a comprehensive report in 1999 that recommended a set of actions needed to ensure the protection and sustainable use of Canada's boreal forests. Since then the Canadian Boreal Initiative has been advocating for adoption and implementation of these recommendations in addition to promoting the Framework and working with provincial governments to adopt the principles of the Framework on their lands. Some progress was reported in the establishment of protected areas, including the protection of 625,000 acres of boreal forest habitat in Québec since 2000.

The Boreal Songbird Initiative has spearheaded work by a network of U.S. conservation groups to support the Boreal Forest Conservation Framework. This work has included outreach activities to increase awareness of the boreal wilderness and the threats it faces. For example, the National Wildlife Federation and National Audubon both have conducted letter-writing campaigns asking large retail catalog companies to use recycled paper and paper purchased from environmentally and socially responsible sources instead of using paper made from virgin boreal forest. The Natural Resources Defense Council has also designated the intact boreal forest in the Ontario–Manitoba border region as one of its twelve "BioGems" and is working to ensure that the conservation plans of local indigenous peoples are not threatened by hydropower and industrial development.

On the wintering grounds there are also many groups involved in conservation activities. For example, Fundacion Arcoiris has developed an outreach campaign in communities near Ecuador's Podocarpus National Park that highlights the interconnectedness between people and birds. The project will help endemic species like the globally threatened White-breasted Parakeet and neotropical migrants like the Canada Warbler. In 2001, the Peruvian government established the country's second largest national park, known as Cordillera Azul National Park, protecting a 5.1-million-acre expanse of habitat used by wintering Canada Warblers and a host of rare resident species. The area's importance was identified through the efforts of the Chicago Field Museum's Environmental and Conservation program and the Peruvian Association for the Conservation of Nature. These organizations are assisting the newly formed Center for the Conservation, Investigation, and Management of Natural Areas to develop a management plan for the park and raise the funds necessary to implement the plan. Already rangers have been deployed along the park's western boundary to prevent or slow illegal logging within the park.[13,16–25]

CONSERVATION NEEDS

- Develop broad, landscape-scale forest management plans for ensuring that large tracts of appropriate habitat are available for Canada Warblers within the landscapes of Canada and the northeast U.S., especially within the boreal forest region.
- Increase the number of protected areas through national and provincial parks in Canada's boreal forest.
- Implement the proposed protections near Lake Winnipeg to maintain the intact boreal forest in the Ontario–Manitoba border region.
- Implement the Boreal Forest Conservation Framework that calls for protection of 50% of Canada's boreal region and ensures world-leading sustainable development practices in areas that are developed.
- Slow or halt deforestation of wintering habitat for Canada Warbler and restore habitat where possible.
- Develop baseline inventory of Canada Warbler breeding and wintering populations, habitat needs on breeding and wintering grounds, and factors responsible for continuing population declines.
- Increase the number of protected areas within the species wintering range and increase support for management and on-the-ground enforcement of regulations within existing protected areas.

References

1. Conway, C.J. 1999. Canada Warber (*Wilsonia canadensis*). In *The Birds of North America*, No. 421 (A. Poole and F. Gill, eds.). The Birds of North America, Inc., Philadelphia, PA.

2. Sauer, J. R., J. E. Hines, and J. Fallon. 2005. *The North American Breeding Bird Survey, Results and Analysis 1966–2005*, Version 6.2.2006. USGS Patuxent Wildlife Research Center, Laurel, MD.

3. Rosenberg, K.V., and J.V. Wells. 2000. Global Perspectives in Neotropical Migratory Bird Conservation in the Northeast: Long-term Responsibility Versus Immediate Concern. Pages 32–43 in *Strategies for Bird Conservation: The Partners in Flight Planning Process*, Proceedings of the 3rd Partners in Flight Workshop, 1995 October 1–5, Cape May, NJ (R. Bonney, D.N. Pashley, and R.J. Niles, eds.). Proceedings RMRS-P-16, U.S. Department of Agriculture, Forest Service, Rocky Mountain Research Station, Ogden, UT.

4. Rosenberg, K.V., and J.V. Wells. 1995. *Importance of Geographic Areas to Neotropical Migrant Birds in the Northeast*. Final report to U.S. Fish and Wildlife Service, Region-5, Hadley, MA.

5. Blancher, P. 2003. *Importance of Canada's Boreal Forest to Landbirds*. Canadian Boreal Initiative, Boreal Songbird Initiative, Bird Studies Canada, Ottawa, ON, Seattle, WA, and Port Rowan, ON.

6. Unidad Administrativa Especial del Sistema de Parques Nacionales Naturales. No date. *Parques Nacionales de Colombia*. http://www.parquesnacionales.gov.co/areas.htm (accessed 23 June 2003).

7. Ridgely, R.S., and P.J. Greenfield. 2001. *The Birds of Ecuador*, Volume 1: *Status, Distribution, and Taxonomy*. Cornell University Press, Ithaca, NY. 848 pp.

8. John Fitpatrick, personal communication (16 June 2003).

9. Clements, J.F., and N. Shany. 2001. *A Field Guide to the Birds of Peru*. Ibis Publishing Company, Temecula, CA. 283 pp.

10. Rich, T. D., C. Beardmore, H. Berlanga, P. Blancher, M. Bradstreet, G. Butcher, D. Demarest, E. Dunn, C. Hunter, E. Iñigo-Elias, J. Kennedy, A. Martell, A. Panjabi, D. Pashley, K. Rosenberg, C. Rustay, S. Wendt, and T. Will. 2004. *Partners in Flight North American Landbird Conservation Plan*. Cornell Lab of Ornithology, Ithaca, NY.

11. Ricketts T.H., et al. 1999. *Terrestrial Ecoregions of North America: A Conservation Assessment*. Island Press, Washington, DC. 485 pp.

12. Sub-committee on Boreal Forest of the Standing Senate Committee on Agriculture and Forestry. 1999. *Competing Realities: The Boreal Forest at Risk*. Government of Canada, Ottawa. http://www.parl.gc.ca/36/1/parlbus/commbus/senate/com-e/BORE-E/rep-e/rep09jun99-e.htm (accessed 24 June 2003).

13. Canadian Boreal Initiative. 2003. *The Boreal Forest at Risk: A Progress Report*. Canadian Boreal Initiative, Ottawa, ON.

14. Hagan, J.M. and S. L. Grove. 1995. *Selection cutting, old growth, birds, and forest structure*. 1995 Report # 96002 of Manamet Center for Conservation Sciences, Manoment, MA. 36 pp.

15. Hagan, J. M., P. S. McKinley, A. L. Meehan, and S. L. Grove. 1997. Diversity and Abundance of Landbirds in a Northeastern Industrial Forest. *Journal of Wildlife Management* 61:718–735.

16. Rosenberg, K.V., and J.V. Wells. 2005. Conservation Priorities for Terrestrial Birds in the Northeastern United States. In *Bird Conservation Implementation and Integration in the Americas*. Proceedings of the Third International Partners in Flight Conference 2002 (C.J. Ralph and T. D. Rich, eds.). USDA Forest Service, GTR-PSW-191, Albany, CA.

17. Vermont Institute of Natural Sciences. 2006. *Canada Warbler Population Status, Habitat Use, and Stewardship Guidelines for Northeastern Forests*. http://www.vinsweb.org/cbd/CAWAresearch.html (accessed 24 January 2006).

18. Clark. J. 2003. *West Branch Crusade*. Down East—Talk of Maine. http:www.downeast.com/talk.html (accessed 24 June 2003).

19. The Nature Conservancy. 2002. *Katahdin Forest, Maine*. http://nature.org/success/katahdin.html (accessed 24 June 2003).

20. New England Forestry Foundation. 2003. *The Pingree Firest Easement: A Summary*. http:www.newengland forestry.org/projects/pingreeeasement.asp (accessed 24 June 2003).

21. Northern Forest Alliance. 2003. *Funding the Future of the Northern Forest*. http://www.northernforestalliance.org (accessed 23 June 2003).

22. Canadian Parks and Wilderness Society. 2005. Canadian Parks and Wilderness Society website. http//:www.cpaws.org.

23. Boreal Songbird Initiative. 2005. Boreal Songbird Initiative website. http://www.borealbirds.org.

24. The Nature Conservancy. 2004. *Ecuador: Podocarpus National Park*. http://nature.org/wherewework/northamerica/states/pennsylvania/files/podo_bird4pgr.pdf (accessed 23 January 2006).

25. The Field Museum. 2002. *Parque Nacional Cordillera Azul*. http://www.fmnh.org/cordilleraazul/park story.html (accessed 30 June 2003).

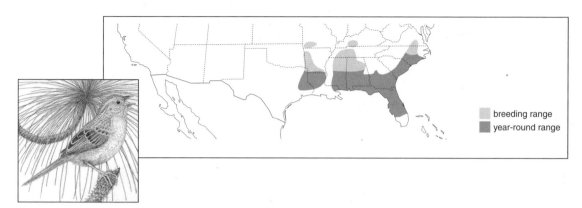

breeding range
year-round range

BACHMAN'S SPARROW (*Aimophila aestivalis*)

The Bachman's Sparrow's pure, whistled song was a familiar sound within the millions of acres of mature pine forest that once blanketed much of the southeastern U.S. This and other species of the native pine ecosystems like the Red-cockaded Woodpecker and Brown-headed Nuthatch have shown major declines.

STATUS AND DISTRIBUTION

The species' current breeding range extends from southern Missouri and southern Tennessee to North Carolina and south through the Gulf states from Texas east to Florida. An isolated population persists in southern Kentucky and northern Tennessee and an extension of the North Carolina range extends into a small area of southeastern Virginia. The species once bred north into Illinois, Indiana, Ohio, and southwestern Pennsylvania and west to Oklahoma. Breeding density maps produced from Breeding Bird Survey data indicate highest densities in central and northern Florida, southern Georgia, southern South Carolina, the Gulf Coasts of Alabama and Mississippi, and southeastern Louisiana.

Important sites for the species include Florida's Apalachicola National Forest, Osceola National Forest, Withlacoochee State Forest, and the Fred C. Babcock-Cecil M. Webb Wildlife Management Area; Louisiana's Fort Polk; Texas's Angelina National Forest; Mississippi Sandhill Crane National Wildlife Refuge in Mississippi; Georgia's Fort Stewart; Frances Marion National Forest; and North Carolina's Sandhills East Important Bird Area, including Fort Bragg and Weymouth Woods State Park.

Breeding Bird Survey analysis shows a non-significant decrease of approximately 52% (1.9% per year) from 1966 to 2005 rangewide. An analysis of Christmas Bird Count data shows a significant decrease of 1.0% per year from 1959 to 1988. The species' total population was estimated at 250,000 individuals in 2004.[1-6]

ECOLOGY

Occurs only in pine forests in the southeastern U.S. in areas with mature trees, little hardwood understory, and grassy ground cover. Such habitat is associated in much of the range with pine ecosystems that have fires at 1- to 5-year intervals. Throughout much of the range it occurs in longleaf/slash pine and loblolly/shortleaf pine habitats. In some areas it will occur in shrubby areas along powerlines and roadways and in clearcuts, though clearcuts are usually suitable for only a few years because of regrowth of habitat.

Females lay 3–4 eggs in a nest built on the ground among thick grass and often partly concealed by grass tufts. Eggs are incubated only by the female for 12–14 days. Both adults feed young, which fledge in about 9–10 days. Usually raise at least two broods, sometimes three, per season. Feeds on seeds, especially grass seeds and insects, especially in summer.[1]

THREATS

Greatest threat is loss, fragmentation, and degradation of mature pine forest habitat. Pine ecosystems once occupied an estimated 60–90 million acres of the southeast U.S. but have been reduced to less than 3 million acres and are continuing to decline from loss of native pine forests on private lands. Only about 3% (90,000 acres) of remaining forest is considered to still be in natural condition. Forestry practices that have been and remain a threat to the species include the conversion of longleaf pine forests to pine plantations of various species. This practice began in earnest in the 1940s so that by 1993 there were an estimated 15 million acres in plantations in the southeast U.S. Fire suppression in pine savanna habitats continues to be a threat as the fires are seen as negative events by the general public. This makes it difficult to carry out the crucial controlled fires needed to ensure the survival of the pine ecosystems upon which this and a host of other species depend, including Red-cockaded Woodpecker and Brown-headed Nuthatch.[1,7,8]

CONSERVATION ACTION

Bachman's Sparrow has benefited from the many positive management actions aimed initially at improving habitat conditions for the federally Endangered Red-cockaded Woodpecker. The more widespread adoption of prescribed burns and the mechanical removal of encroaching hardwoods to maintain healthy pine forests on public lands in particular has greatly benefited the species.

A variety of activities have been targeted at private lands. The Nature Conservancy has purchased a number of parcels of pine forest with Bachman's Sparrow populations, including a 150-acre-tract of longleaf pine in 2003 for addition to the Frances Marion National Forest in South Carolina and 1,160 acres of mature pine forest in 2000 in Virginia to create the 2,695-acre Piney Grove Preserve. As another example of how Bachman's Sparrow has benefited from work targeting the Red-cockaded Woodpecker, the U.S. Fish and Wildlife Service (USFWS) began implementing a private lands conservation strategy for the woodpecker in 1992. As of 2003, the USFWS had entered into various agreements with 139 private landowners, resulting in protection of 347,439 acres of southern pine forest habitat.

Partners in Flight Bird Conservation Plans that have been completed for southeastern U.S. physiographic regions have identified Bachman's Sparrow and its associated suite of southern pine forest bird species as a high priority and have provided recommendations for management, research, and monitoring. For example, the South Atlantic Coastal Plain plan recommended increasing the acreage of longleaf pine from 1.5 million acres to 2.2 million acres by 2025.[1,8–13]

CONSERVATION NEEDS

- Develop a rangewide conservation plan for Bachman's Sparrow that helps coordinate conservation work across the states that currently support the species.
- Increase amount of acreage undergoing prescribed burning programs in the proper season on both public and private lands.
- Incorporate Bachman's Sparrow habitat objectives into public land management where the species occurs on public lands.
- Provide incentives for private landowners to manage their lands to the benefit of Bachman's Sparrow and other native pine forest species.
- Purchase land or conservation easements on private lands in areas that still support healthy populations of Bachman's Sparrow and other native pine forest species.
- Increase monitoring and life-history research for the species.

References

1. Dunning, J.B. 1993. Bachman's Sparrow (*Aimophila aestivalis*). In *The Birds of North America*, No. 38 (A. Poole, P. Stettenheim, and F. Gill, eds.). The Academy of Natural Sciences, Philadelphia, PA, and the American Ornithologists' Union, Washington, DC.

2 Sauer, J. R., J. E. Hines, and J. Fallon. 2005. *The North American Breeding Bird Survey, Results and Analysis 1966–2005*, Version 6.2.2006. USGS Patuxent Wildlife Research Center, Laurel, MD.

3. Pranty, B. 2003. *The Important Bird Areas of Florida: 2000–2002*. http://www.audubon.org/bird/iba/florida/ (accessed 27 January 2004).

4. Audubon North Carolina. No date. *Sandhills East*. http://www.ncaudubon.org/IBAs/Coast/sandhills _east.htm (accessed 27 January 2004).

5. Chipley, R.M., G.H. Fenwick, M.J. Parr, and D.N. Pashley. 2003. *The American Bird Conservancy Guide to the 500 Most Important Bird Areas in the United States*. Random House, New York, NY.

6. Rich, T. D., C. Beardmore, H. Berlanga, P. Blancher, M. Bradstreet, G. Butcher, D. Demarest, E. Dunn, C. Hunter, E. Iñigo-Elias, J. Kennedy, A. Martell, A. Panjabi, D. Pashley, K. Rosenberg, C. Rustay, S. Wendt, and T. Will. 2004. *Partners in Flight North Amer-*

ican Landbird Conservation Plan. Cornell Lab of Ornithology, Ithaca, NY.

7. Ricketts, T.H., E. Dinerstein, D.M. Olson, C.J. Loucks, et al. 1999. *Terrestrial Ecoregions of North America: A Conservation Assessment.* Island Press, Washington, DC. 485 pp.

8. Jackson, J.A. 1994. Red-cockaded Woodpecker (*Picoides borealis*). In *The Birds of North America*, No. 85 (A. Poole and F. Gill, eds.). The Academy of Natural Sciences, Philadelphia, PA, and the American Ornithologists' Union, Washington, DC.

9. The Nature Conservancy. 1997. *Species Management Abstract: Bachman's Sparrow* (Aimophila aestivalis). http:www.conserveonline.org/2001/03/m/bmns (accessed 15 December 2004).

10. The Nature Conservancy. 2003. *Conservancy Acquires Strategic Tract as Addition to Frances Marion National Forest.* http://nature.org/wherewework/northamerica/states/southcarolina/press/press1276.html (accessed 18 January 2004).

11. The Nature Conservancy. 2000. *Nature Conservancy Adds 1,160 Acres to Red-cockaded Woodpecker Preserve.* http://nature.org/wherewework/northamerica/states/virginia/press/press130.html (accessed 15 January 2004).

12. U.S. Fish and Wildlife Service. 2003. *Recovery Plan for the Red-cockaded Woodpecker* (Picoides borealis), 2nd Rev. U.S. Fish and Wildlife Service, Atlanta, GA. 296 pp.

13. Hunter, W.C., L. Peoples, and J. Callazo. 2001. *South Atlantic Coastal Plain Partners in Flight Bird Conservation Plan.* U.S. Fish and Wildlife Service, Atlanta, GA.

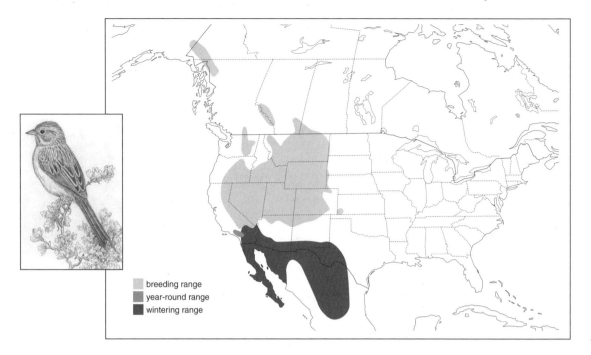

breeding range
year-round range
wintering range

BREWER'S SPARROW (*Spizella breweri*)

Less charismatic then the Greater Sage-Grouse with which it shares its breeding range, the Brewer's Sparrow has been described as the most abundant bird of the sagebrush sea and its song is one of the most memorable features of this habitat.

STATUS AND DISTRIBUTION

Breeding range extends from extreme southeastern British Columbia, southern Manitoba and Alberta south to eastern California and east to northern New Mexico. A small isolated population occurs in southwestern Oklahoma. A disjunct population described by some authors as a separate species, the Timberline Sparrow, breeds in southwestern Yukon and adjacent regions of southeast Alaska. Winter range extends from southern California east through southern Arizona and New Mexico and south to central Mexico and through Baja California and Sonora.

Breeding density maps produced from Breeding Bird Survey data indicate highest densities in southeastern Oregon, northern Nevada, southeastern Idaho, southwestern Wyoming, northeastern Utah, and northwestern Colorado. Important breeding sites for the species include Oregon's Malheur National Wildlife Refuge (NWR), which has one of the highest Breeding Bird Survey

counts for Brewer's Sparrow, Nevada's Ruby Lake NWR and Franklin Lake (15,400 acres-mostly private ownership), and Idaho's Grays Lake NWR.

Wintering density maps produced from Christmas Bird Count data indicate highest winter densities in the United States in southern Arizona and extreme southwestern New Mexico. Important wintering areas for the species in the U.S. include New Mexico's Gray Ranch and Arizona's Cabeza Prieta NWR and Organ Pipe Cactus National Monument. Important wintering areas in Mexico include the Gran Desierto de Altar Biosphere Reserve in Sonora and the Janos-Nuevo Casas Grandes Important Bird Area in Chihuahua.

Breeding Bird Survey analysis shows a significant decrease of approximately 62% (2.5% per year) from 1966 to 2005 rangewide. The total population size was estimated at 16,000,000 individuals in 2004.[1-7]

ECOLOGY

It is a species of shrub habitat, usually dominated by sagebrush (*Artemisia* spp.), but in some parts of the breeding range it also uses habitats dominated by other shrub species and habitats of other types. Northerly breeding populations occur in high-elevation shrub habitat above the timberline or in mountain valleys. In wintering range huge flocks occur with other sparrows in dry desert shrub habitat Nests are built in bush (usually sagebrush) within a few inches of the ground. Females lay 3–4 eggs, which hatch in 10–12 days. Young fledge at 6–9 days.[1,5]

THREATS

The greatest threat continues to be loss and degradation of native habitat largely through conversion to cropland, overgrazing on rangeland, spread of invasive plant species, such as cheat grass, changes in fire frequency and severity, road development, and mineral and oil extraction activities. Millions of acres of sagebrush have been destroyed for agricultural uses and on millions more sagebrush has been systematically removed. Less than 10% of the 84 million acres of the Great Basin Shrub Steppe ecoregion remains as intact habitat. Oil and gas well construction may be increasing in the region. A 1996 report estimated that 6,000–11,000 new oil and gas wells would be developed in southwestern Wyoming in the ensuing 20 years.

Types of sagebrush-dominated ecosystems vary greatly across the western U.S. There are differences in which species of sagebrush is dominant, aridity, the impacts of fire, and the role of native herbivores. For those whose experience with sagebrush is limited to its mention in movies or tv shows of the Old West this variability can be astounding. It has also led to confusion and unintentional land management mistakes in some regions.

In sagebrush ecosystems used for grazing, burning is sometimes practiced to increase grass cover and eliminate sagebrush. In such ecosystems, invasive grasses and other plants often invade after fires and outcompete native species. In many areas introduced cheatgrass (*Bromus tectorum*) has invaded, outcompeted, and eventually replaced sagebrush habitat. After cheatgrass becomes established fire frequency generally increases to the detriment of most sagebrush habitat. In other regions, fires are suppressed, allowing an increase in pinyon pines and other conifers.[1,7–9]

CONSERVATION ACTION

Partners in Flight Bird Conservation Plans that have been completed for western U.S. states with-

in the breeding range of Brewer's Sparrow have identified the species and its associated suite of sagebrush bird species as a high priority and have provided recommendations for management, research, and monitoring. In 1999 the Western Working Group of Partners in Flight published "Birds in a Sagebrush Sea," an outreach and management manual to guide land managers and landowners interested in managing sagebrush habitats for birds of conservation concern, including Brewer's Sparrow.

Declines in another sagebrush obligate species, the Greater Sage-Grouse, have prompted a flurry of concern, research, and conservation planning for sagebrush habitat. Clearly, Brewer's Sparrow should benefit from many of these activities that attempt to slow or reverse the loss and degradation of sagebrush habitats. The Bureau of Land Management (BLM), which manages over 50% of the remaining sagebrush habitat in the U.S., is in the final stages of completing a Final National Greater Sage-Grouse Habitat Conservation Strategy that should provide recommendations for habitat management that will also benefit Brewer's Sparrow.

While much of the activity so far has centered on the development of plans with extensive community involvement, in a few areas some specific conservation action has taken place. For example, at the Department of Defense's Yakima Training Center, sagebrush restoration activities are ongoing, including the planting of 300,000 sagebrush seedlings annually. The Nature Conservancy purchased the Crooked Creek Ranch in 2001—a 2500-acre Idaho ranch with 70,000 acres of public land grazing allotments—to protect and manage a large Greater Sage-Grouse population, but which should also provide benefits to Brewer's Sparrows. In Idaho, research is being carried out on BLM lands to assess whether burned areas can be restored through the planting of sagebrush seedlings and reduction in grazing pressure. A bill introduced but not passed in the U.S. Congress in 2003 would have reimbursed ranchers who wished to voluntarily give up their public land grazing permits and would have resulted in the retiring of grazing permits on about 7.8 million acres.

Within the species wintering range a coalition of groups, including Pronatura Noreste, World Wildlife Fund, and the Nature Conservancy, has targeted the Chihuahuan Desert ecoregion for conservation and in 2002 the group completed a detailed conservation assessment for the region. The assessment includes a portfolio of sites that require protection to meet minimum requirements for conserving the highest priorities species and ecological communities. In 2000, Pronatura Noreste and the Nature Conservancy purchased a 7,000-acre ranch in Mexico's Cuatro Ciénegas Valley that includes desert grasslands.[1,6–23]

CONSERVATION NEEDS

- Incorporate Brewer's Sparrow habitat objectives into all BLM lease allotments within the range of the species and ensure that objectives are being reached in allotments with existing habitat objectives.
- Continue purchase of conservation easements on private lands that support sagebrush habitat.
- Increase monitoring and life-history research for the species.

References

1. Rotenberry, J.T., M. A. Patten, and K. L. Preston. 1999. Brewer's Sparrow (*Spizella breweri*). In *The Birds of North America*, No. 390 (A. Poole and F. Gill, eds.). The Birds of North America, Inc., Philadelphia, PA.

2. Sauer, J. R., J. E. Hines, and J. Fallon. 2005. *The North American Breeding Bird Survey, Results and Analysis 1966–2005*, Version 6.2.2006. USGS Patuxent Wildlife Research Center, Laurel, MD.

3. Chipley, R.M., G.H. Fenwick, M.J. Parr, and D.N. Pashley. 2003. *The American Bird Conservancy Guide to the 500 Most Important Bird Areas in the United States*. Random House, New York, NY.

4. CONABIO. 2002. *Áreas de Importancia para la Conservación de las Aves (AICAS)*. http://conabioweb.conabio.gob.mx/aicas/doctos/aicas.html (accessed 18 June 2003).

5. Dieni, J.S., W.H. Howe, S.L. Jones, P. Manzano-Fischer, and C.P. Melcher. 2003. New Information on Wintering Birds of Northwestern Chihuahua. *American Birds*. The 103rd Christmas Bird Count.

6. Sauer, J. R., S. Schwartz, and B. Hoover. 1996. The Christmas Bird Count Home Page, Version 95.1. Patuxent Wildlife Research Center, Laurel, MD.

7. Rich, T. D., C. Beardmore, H. Berlanga, P. Blancher, M. Bradstreet, G. Butcher, D. Demarest, E. Dunn, C. Hunter, E. Iñigo-Elias, J. Kennedy, A. Martell, A. Panjabi, D. Pashley, K. Rosenberg, C. Rustay, S. Wendt, and T. Will. 2004. *Partners in Flight North American Landbird Conservation Plan*. Cornell Lab of Ornithology, Ithaca, NY.

8. Ricketts, T.H., E. Dinerstein, D.M. Olson, C.J. Loucks, et al. 1999. *Terrestrial Ecoregions of North America: A Conservation Assessment*. Island Press, Washington, DC. 485 pp.

9. Paige, C., and S. A. Ritter. 1999. *Birds in a Sagebrush Sea: Managing Sagebrush Habitats for Bird Communities*. Partners in Flight Western Working Group, Boise, ID.

10. Connelly, J.W., M.A. Schroeder, A.R. Sands, and C.E. Braun. 2000. Guidelines to Manage Sage Grouse Populations and Their Habitats. *Wildlife Society Bulletin* 28:967–985.

11. Nevada Partners in Flight Working Group. 1999. *Nevada Partners in Flight Bird Conservation Plan*. Reno, NV.

12. Montana Partners in Flight. 2000. *Partners in Flight Draft Bird Conservation Plan Montana*. American Bird Conservancy, Kalispell, MT.

13. Ritter, S. 2000. *Idaho Bird Conservation Plan*. Partners in Flight, Hamilton, MT.

14. Nicholoff, S. H., compiler. 2003. *Wyoming Bird Conservation Plan*, Version 2.0. Wyoming Partners in Flight. Wyoming Game and Fish Department, Lander, WY.

15. Parrish, J.R., F. P. Howe, and R. E. Norvell. 2002. *Utah Partners in Flight Avian Conservation Strategy*, Version 2.0. Utah Partners in Flight Program, Utah Division of Wildlife Resources, 1594 West North Temple, Salt Lake City, UT 84116, UDWR Publication Number 02-27. i–xiv + 302 pp.

16. Beidleman, C.A. 2000. *Partners in Flight Land Bird Conservation Plan Colorado*, Estes Park, CO.

17. Bureau of Land Management. No date. *Draft BLM Sage-Grouse Habitat Conservation Strategy*. http://www.blm.gov/nhp/spotlight/sage_grouse/draft_sage_grouse_strategy.pdf (accessed 20 February 2004).

18. Miller, M. 2003. *The Crooked Creek Project: A Cooperative Project for Sage Grouse Management*. http://nature.org/wherewework/northamerica/states/idaho/science/art8546.html (accessed 20 February 2004).

19. Yakima Training Center. No date. *Management of Sage Grouse on the Yakima Training Center*. Yakima, WA. 1 pp.

20. Idaho National Engineering and Environmental Laboratory, Environmental Surveillance Education and Research Program. No date. *Natural and Assisted Recovery of Sagebrush in Idaho's Big Desert: Effects of Seeding Treatments on Successional Trajectories of Sagebrush Com-

munities. http://www.stoller-eser.com/TinCup/Report .htm (accessed 20 February 2004).

21. National Public Lands Grazing Campaign. No date. *Voluntary Grazing Permit Buyout Legislation Introduced!* http://www.publiclandsranching.org/ (accessed 24 February 2004).

22. Pronatura Noreste. 2002. *Ecoregional Conservation Assessment of the Chihuahuan Desert.* www.conserve .online.

23. The Nature Conservancy. 2004. *Chihuahuan Desert.* http://nature.org/wherewework/northamerica/ mexico/work/art8620.html (accessed 29 January 2004).

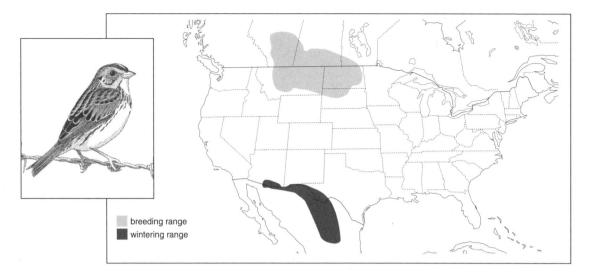

breeding range
wintering range

BAIRD'S SPARROW (*Ammodramus bairdii*)

The Baird's Sparrow's musical song is a characteristic sound of grasslands of the Northern Great Plains but this species has shown great declines like many other grassland birds.

STATUS AND DISTRIBUTION

The species' restricted breeding range extends from southeastern Alberta across southern Saskatchewan to the southwestern corner of Manitoba then south to northern South Dakota and the eastern two-thirds of Montana. A very small disjunct population occurs in western Minnesota. The range is known to have contracted in Minnesota and Manitoba. Breeding density maps produced from Breeding Bird Survey data indicate highest densities in North Dakota, northeastern Montana, and southern Saskatchewan. Important breeding sites for the species include North Dakota's Lostwood National Wildlife Refuge (NWR) and Little Missouri National Grassland and Montana's Bowdoin NWR and Medicine Lake NWR Complex.

The species also has a restricted wintering range, extending from the southeastern corner of Arizona southeast through the Chihuahuan Desert through the Mexican state of Chihuahua, and the southwestern border region of Texas south to northeast Durango and northern Zacatecas. Among many important wintering sites known for Baird's Sparrow are Arizona's Las Cienegas National Conservation Area, the Sistema de Islas Sierra Madre Occidental Important Bird Area

(IBA) in Sonora, Mexico, and the Janos-Nuevo Casas Grandes IBA in Chihuahua, Mexico.

Breeding Bird Survey analysis shows a significant decrease of approximately 78% (3.9% per year) from 1966 to 2005 rangewide. The species' total population was estimated at 1,200,000 individuals in 2004.[1–7]

ECOLOGY

During the breeding season, it is a species of the mixed-grass and fescue prairie intermixed with low shrubs and other vegetation. It is not found in areas that are heavily grazed or in cropland but in some areas it does occur in hayfields. Originally, its native habitat was likely maintained through regular fires and bison grazing in a large landscape matrix with areas rotating in suitability as they burned or were grazed then grew thicker and unsuitable over time. In some drier areas, habitat can remain suitable without burning or grazing for as many as 25 years. Females lay 4–5 eggs in a nest built on the ground among thick grass and sometimes partly concealed by grass tufts. Eggs are incubated by the female for 11–12 days. Both adults feed young, which fledge in 8–11 days. Young leave the parent's territory and presumably are self-sufficient within about 19 days after fledging. Normally this bird raises only one brood each year. Although variable across the species' range, in some areas nests are parasitized by Brown-headed Cowbirds. Nest losses are primarily from predators and ranged from 37% to 69% in three studies. The species wintering ecology and habitat requirements are poorly known but it is found in grasslands with few shrubs and sometimes in areas that are lightly to moderately grazed.[1,8]

THREATS

As in most grassland ecosystems, the greatest current threat continues to be loss and degradation of native habitat largely through conversion to cropland, overgrazing on rangeland, mineral and oil extraction activities, and fire suppression. Loss of northern mixed-grass prairie has been estimated at 36–69% and virtually no unaltered habitat persists in much of the breeding range. In some parts of the region there are only tiny fragments of native prairie still in existence. Although much conversion of prairie habitat was historical, large amounts continue to be lost today. From 1982 to 1997, 1.1 million acres of native prairie were lost in South Dakota alone. The recently enacted Farm Bill has provided incentives for further conversion of native prairie to cropland (especially for wheat production) and has worked against the smaller conservation provisions of the bill that encourage farmers to set aside acreage for conservation. The virtual extinction of bison in the area has also changed the dynamics of plant succession so that mixed-grass prairie ecosystems must be maintained through fire and carefully managed cattle grazing. Invasion of exotic plants species like leafy spurge is a continuing threat as well. Desert grasslands where the species winters have been extensively altered through agricultural conversion, grazing, urban development, invasive plants, and extensive encroachment by shrubs. There are few protected areas within the entire Chihuahuan Desert ecoregion.[1,9–11]

CONSERVATION ACTION

A rangewide status assessment and conservation plan was published in 1995. There is currently no management program focused on maintaining or increasing Baird's Sparrow populations, but some broad grassland restoration work has benefited the species. Habitat management, especially through rotational grazing and prescribed burns has been effective in maintaining and increasing number of birds in areas where populations are relatively large and unfragmented. For example, at Lostwood NWR prescribed burns and light grazing of grass-

lands aimed at restoring the native habitat have maintained Baird's Sparrow populations.

Montana Partners for Fish and Wildlife is working to secure perpetual grassland easements in the Upper Missouri Coteau, where Baird's Sparrows are found, with the hope of restoring 300,000 acres of grasslands on private and tribal lands. The group has spent $3.4 million over 13 years on projects with over 230 private landowners to protect, restore, or enhance wetland and grassland habitat primarily for increasing waterfowl production, but often also benefiting Baird's Sparrow and other grassland species.

The Prairie Pothole Joint Venture initiated the Chase Lake Prairie Project to conserve and restore habitat in a 5.5-million-acre block surrounding the Chase Lake NWR in North Dakota. The project area includes one of the largest intact pieces of native prairie in the state. Through the project the U.S. Fish and Wildlife Service has protected 12,890 acres of wetlands and grasslands through easements on private land and over 8,600 acres of habitat have been directly acquired. Rotational grazing systems have been implemented on over 35,000 acres of grasslands as well.

The South Dakota Department of Game, Fish, and Parks (SDGFP) has partnered with the U.S. Fish and Wildlife Service and Ducks Unlimited to protect grasslands and wetlands in the Missouri Coteau region of that state. In 2002 SDGFP purchased 2,116 acres, most of it prairie grassland, to establish the Chip Allen Wildlife Management Area. An additional 6,764 acres of grasslands are expected to be protected in the region through conservation easements.

Within the species' wintering range a coalition of groups, including Pronatura Noreste, World Wildlife Fund, and the Nature Conservancy, has targeted the Chihuahuan Desert ecoregion for conservation and in 2002 the group completed a detailed conservation assessment for the region. The assessment includes a portfolio of sites that require protection to meet minimum requirements for conserving the highest priorities species and ecological communities. In 2000, Pronatura Noreste and the Nature Conservancy purchased a 7,000-acre ranch in Mexico's Cuatro Ciénegas Valley that includes desert grasslands.[1,10–18]

CONSERVATION NEEDS

- Implement a rangewide conservation plan for Baird's Sparrow that helps coordinate conservation work across the states and provinces that currently support the species.

- Incorporate Baird's Sparrow habitat objectives into public land management where the species occurs on public lands.
- Provide incentives for private landowners to manage their lands to the benefit of Baird's Sparrow and other native grassland species.
- Purchase land or conservation easements on private lands in areas that still support healthy populations of Baird's Sparrow and other native grassland species in both the breeding and wintering range.
- Increase monitoring and life-history research for the species including on the wintering grounds and during migration.

References

1. Green, M.T., P.E. Lowther, S.L. Jones, S.K. Davis, and B.C. Dale. 2002. Baird's Sparrow (*Ammodramus bairdii*). In *The Birds of North America*, No. 638 (A. Poole and F. Gill, eds.). The Birds of North America, Inc., Philadelphia, PA.

2. Sauer, J.R., J. E. Hines, and J. Fallon. 2005. *The North American Breeding Bird Survey, Results and Analysis 1966–2005*, Version 6.2.2006. USGS Patuxent Wildlife Research Center, Laurel, MD.

3. National Audubon Society. 2001. *North Dakota's Important Bird Areas Program*. http://www.audubon.org/bird/iba/nd.html (accessed 22 January 2004).

4. Medicine Lake NWR. 2001. *Bird List for the Medicine Lake National Wildlife Refuge Complex*. http://medicinelake.fws.gov/Wildlife/bird_list.htm (accessed 22 January 2004).

5. Chipley, R.M., G.H. Fenwick, M.J. Parr, and D.N. Pashley. 2003. *The American Bird Conservancy Guide to the 500 Most Important Bird Areas in the United States*. Random House, New York, NY.

6. CONABIO. 2002. *Áreas de Importancia para la Conservación de las Aves (AICAS)*. http://conabioweb.conabio.gob.mx/aicas/doctos/aicas.html (accessed 21 January 2004).

7. Rich, T. D., C. Beardmore, H. Berlanga, P. Blancher, M. Bradstreet, G. Butcher, D. Demarest, E. Dunn, C. Hunter, E. Iñigo-Elias, J. Kennedy, A. Martell, A. Panjabi, D. Pashley, K. Rosenberg, C. Rustay, S. Wendt, and T. Will. 2004. *Partners in Flight North American Landbird Conservation Plan*. Cornell Lab of Ornithology, Ithaca, NY.

8. Dechant, J. A., M. L. Sondreal, D. H. Johnson, L. D. Igl, C. M. Goldade, M. P. Nenneman, and B. R. Euliss. 2003. *Effects of Management Practices on Grassland Birds: Baird's Sparrow*. Northern Prairie Wildlife Research Center, Jamestown, ND. Northern Prairie Wildlife Research Center Online. http://www.npwrc.usgs.gov/resource/literatr/grasbird/bais/bais.htm (Version 12AUG2004).

9. Ricketts, T.H., E. Dinerstein, D.M. Olson, C.J. Loucks, et al. 1999. *Terrestrial Ecoregions of North America: A Conservation Assessment*. Island Press, Washington, DC. 485 pp.

10. Delta Waterfowl Foundation. 2003. *The Great American Plowout Threatens Duck Production*. http://www.deltawaterfowl.org/home/archive/2003/030818_plowout.html (accessed 28 January 2004).

11. World Wildlife Fund. 2001. *Chihuahuan Desert (NA1303)*. http://www.worldwildlife.org/wildworld/profiles/terrestrial/na/na1303_full.html (accessed 28 January 2004).

12. Jones, S. L., and M. T. Green. 1998. *Baird's Sparrow Status Assessment and Conservation Plan*. Administrative Report. U.S. Fish and Wildlife Service, Denver, CO. http://mountain-prairie.fws.gov/bairdssparrow/planfinl.htm (accessed 24 January 2006).

13. Greatplains.org. 2001. *Shorebird Management Manual*, Chapter 2: *Interior Region*. http://www.greatplains.org/resource/1998/multspec/casehist.htm (accessed 22 January 2004).

14. Montana Partners for Fish and Wildlife. No date. *Upper Missouri Coteau Focus Area, Conservation Strategies*. http://montanapartners.fws.gov/mt3f2.htm (accessed 22 January 2004).

15. U. S. Fish and Wildlife Service. *Chase Lake Prairie Project*. http://chaselake.fws.gov/clpp.htm (accessed 22 January 2004).

16. Outdoor News Network. No date. *Wetland and Grassland Conservation Project Approved*. http://www.outdoorcentral.com/mc/pr/03/11/07d2.asp (accessed 22 January 2004).

17. Pronatura, the Nature Conservancy, and the World Wildlife Fund. 2004. *Ecoregional Conservation Assessment of the Chihuahuan Desert*, 2nd ed. www.conserveonline.org.

18. The Nature Conservancy. 2004. *Chihuahuan Desert*. http://nature.org/wherewework/northamerica/mexico/work/art8620.html (accessed 29 January 2004).

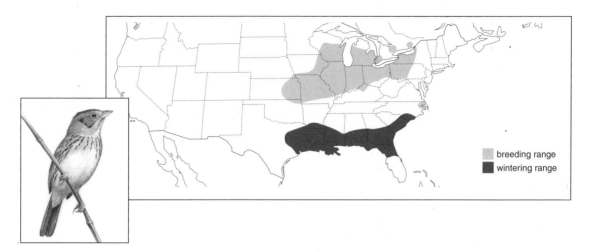

breeding range
wintering range

HENSLOW'S SPARROW (*Ammodramus henslowii*)

The Henslow's Sparrow's simple, insect-like song was once a common summer sound across the expanses of tallgrass prairie of the midwest U.S. and coastal grasslands of the eastern U.S. Now the population has been greatly reduced from the virtual elimination of the native tallgrass prairie and coastal grasslands combined with the similar massive loss of its southeastern U.S. pine-savanna wintering habitat.

STATUS AND DISTRIBUTION

The species' current breeding range extends from southeastern Minnesota east to western New York (small numbers in extreme southern Ontario) south through Pennsylvania to western West Virginia and west to the northeastern corner of Oklahoma. Small isolated populations occur in Delaware and North Carolina. Historically bred as far east as New Hampshire, Massachusetts, Connecticut, Rhode Island, and New Jersey. Breeding density maps produced from Breeding Bird Survey data indicate highest densities on the Oklahoma–Kansas border and in a small area in western Missouri. Important breeding sites for the species include Big Oaks National Wildlife Refuge (NWR) in Indiana (775 singing males in 2002), Fort Riley Military Reservation in Kansas (3,000 singing males estimated in 1997), the Nature Conservancy's Tallgrass Prairie Preserve in Oklahoma (3,000 singing males estimated in 1996), and Fort Campbell in Kentucky and Tennessee (small area sampled had 150 singing males in late 1990s). Former strip mine sites now planted with grasses sup-

port as many as 2,000 pairs in southwestern Illinois and hundreds of pairs in western Pennsylvania. At the receding eastern edge of the range in New York, Important Bird Areas supporting the species included the Perch River Grasslands (80+ pairs in 1997) and the Fort Drum Grasslands (30–40 pairs). In northeastern North Carolina an estimated 100–200 pairs occur at two Voice of America antenna fields.

The species' wintering range extends from eastern Texas across the Gulf states and north along the coastal plain to North Carolina. Among many important wintering sites known for Henslow's Sparrow are Mississippi Sandhill Crane NWR in Mississippi (hundreds of individuals), Louisiana's Fort Polk (500–1000 birds), Texas's Angelina National Forest, Sam Houston National Forest, Katy Prairie, and Sea Rim State Park, Florida's Apalachicola National Forest, North Carolina's Croatan National Forest, and South Carolina's ACE Basin.

Breeding Bird Survey analysis shows a significant decrease of approximately 95% (7.9% per year) from 1966 to 2005 rangewide. The species' total population was estimated at 79,000 individuals in 2004.[1-9]

ECOLOGY

During the breeding season it was originally a species of midwestern tallgrass prairie and eastern coastal grasslands, but now occurs in many human-created grasslands, including hayfields, reclaimed strip mines, capped landfills, and around airports. The species prefers grassland habitat that is rather thick and with a substantial ground-level layer of dead grass and dried vegetation but not with a substantial component of shrubs or other nongrasses. Originally native habitat was likely maintained through regular fires, bison grazing in some areas, and possibly from outbreaks of the now-extinct Rocky Mountain grasshopper, in a large landscape matrix with areas rotating in suitability as they burned or were grazed then grew thicker and unsuitable over time. Many of the human-created grassland habitats are managed in ways that mimic such a disturbance regime.

Females lay 3–5 eggs in a nest built very close to the ground among thick grass and often partly concealed by grass tufts. Eggs are incubated only by the female for 10–11 days. Both adults feed young, which fledge in about 9 days. These birds usually raise at least two broods, sometimes three, per season. They feed mostly on insects in summer but in winter and during migration also eat small seeds, especially grass seeds. The species' wintering ecology and habitat requirements are poorly known but it is found in fire-maintained pine savannas (longleaf pine in much of wintering range) with a grassy understory. A study in Mississippi found that the species preferred sites that had been burned within previous five years.[1]

THREATS

There is no doubt that this species suffered massive population declines as a result of the near elimination of most native grasslands in most of range. For example, 88–99% of the midwestern tallgrass prairie was estimated to have been lost since 1850. In some areas the loss has been even more severe. Less than 1% of original habitat in a forest/grassland ecozone extending from Illinois south to Texas is considered intact. Remnants of tallgrass prairie habitat in southern Iowa and northern Missouri are restricted to 20 sites, each less than 20 acres in size. Native grasslands of the eastern U.S. have been reduced to a few small, widely separated blocks. Fortunately for the survival of Henslow's Sparrow, it was able to adapt to using pastures and hayfields that were created across parts of range, especially in the eastern U.S. As agricultural grasslands in the east have been lost to development or forest succession following farm abandonment, the species status has gone from common to rare or even extirpated. Henslow's Sparrow has also

adapted to using grasslands created on formerly forested coal strip mines in Pennsylvania, southern Ohio, southwestern Indiana, and Kentucky. Large populations have developed on some of these areas but sites will likely need to be managed through mowing and burning to maintain populations. The Flint Hills of Kansas is one of the few areas supporting large numbers of Henslow's Sparrow and the area has not been extensively plowed for row-crops but cattle overgrazing and loss of habitat to housing developments is an increasing problem. The virtual extinction of bison in the area has also changed the dynamics of plant succession so that maintenance of prairie ecosystems must be maintained through fire and carefully managed cattle grazing.

The Gulf coastal prairies and pine savannas where the species winters have also been lost or degraded over vast regions. The Gulf coastal prairies were eliminated from Louisiana and only 1% of this habitat in Texas is now considered pristine. Similarly, longleaf pine ecosystems once occupied an estimated 60–90 million acres of the southeast U.S. but have been reduced to less than 3 million acres and are continuing to decline from loss of longleaf forests on private lands. Only about 3% (90,000 acres) of the remaining forest is considered to still be in natural condition. Forestry practices that have been and remain a threat to the species include the conversion of longleaf pine forests to pine plantations of various species, a practice that began in earnest in the 1940s so that by 1993 there were an estimated 15 million acres in plantations in the southeast U.S.

Fire suppression in pine savanna habitats continues to be a threat as the fires are seen as negative events by the general public, often making it difficult to carry out the crucial controlled fires needed to ensure the survival of the pine ecosystems upon which this and a host of other species depend, including Red-cockaded Woodpecker, Brown-headed Nuthatch, and Bachman's Sparrow.[1,10–14]

CONSERVATION ACTION

There has been no rangewide conservation plan or management program focused on maintaining or increasing Henslow's Sparrow populations but some broad grassland restoration work has benefited the species. In many areas, the Conservation Reserve Program (CRP) provisions of the

Farm Bill, which pays farmers to plant grasses and leave the enrolled acres untilled for at least 10 years, have provided habitat for Henslow's Sparrow and other grassland species. A number of grassland bird species (but not all), including Henslow's Sparrow, showed an increasing national trend after the start of the CRP, suggesting that the program is providing habitat and partially offsetting continuing loss of grassland habitat. The acreage enrolled in the CRP is amazingly large—approximately 34 million acres as of 2000—but because the loss of grassland habitat during the time period that CRP has been active was about 26 million acres, the net gain in grassland habitat was 8 million acres. Many CRP sites are also too small to attract Henslow's Sparrow or are planted with grasses inappropriate for grassland birds. Still, the CRP has clearly provided very large amounts of habitat in some areas to the benefit of the species.

Habitat management, especially through rotational grazing and prescribed burns, has been effective in maintaining and increasing numbers of Henslow's Sparrow. As in most grassland species, it is important to maintain a steady acreage of prime habitat within a preserve or region rather than burn too high a proportion of land in any one year because of the effect on species extinction risk. The Nature Conservancy is using such measures to manage habitat on its Tallgrass Prairie Preserve in Oklahoma. At Big Oaks NWR in Indiana, habitat management has increased the number of birds in recent years. In many areas, conservation work focused on Greater Prairie-Chicken is undoubtedly beneficial to Henslow's Sparrow as well. For example, in Missouri the Nature Conservancy has acquired several parcels of grassland habitat and are managing for the benefit of Greater Prairie-Chickens and various habitat enhancement projects were supported with approximately $200,000 in grants in 2001. In Iowa, the Kellerton Grasslands Bird Conservation Area was established in 2000 with the goal of establishing a 2,000-acre publicly owned prairie preserve within a 10,000-acre block that contains another 2,000 acres of privately owned grasslands.

On parts of its wintering range, Henslow's Sparrow has certainly been the recipient of some positive management actions aimed at improving habitat conditions for the federally Endangered Red-cockaded Woodpecker. The use of prescribed burns to maintain healthy pine forests on public lands, in particular, is likely to have benefited the species.

Partners in Flight Bird Conservation Plans that have been completed for eastern U.S. physiographic regions have identified Henslow's Sparrow and its associated suite of grassland bird species as a high priority and have provided recommendations for management, research, and monitoring. In PIF plans for the Midwest, an explicit objective to develop Bird Conservation Areas around which habitat restoration would take place to increase and maintain larger blocks of grassland habitat has been described.[1,4,12–25]

CONSERVATION NEEDS

- Develop a rangewide conservation plan for Henslow's Sparrow that helps coordinate conservation work across the states that currently support the species.
- Incorporate Henslow's Sparrow habitat objectives into public land management where the species occurs on public lands.
- Provide incentives for private landowners to manage their lands to the benefit of Henslow's Sparrow and other native grassland species.
- Purchase land or conservation easements on private lands in areas that still support healthy populations of Henslow's Sparrow and other native grassland species.
- Increase monitoring and life-history research for the species especially on the wintering grounds and during migration.

References

1. Herkert, J.R., P.D. Vickery, and D.E. Kroodsma. 2002. Henslow's Sparrow (*Ammodramus henslowii*). In *The Birds of North America*, No. 672 (A. Poole and F. Gill, eds.). The Birds of North America, Inc., Philadelphia, PA.

2. Sauer, J. R., J. E. Hines, and J. Fallon. 2005. *The North American Breeding Bird Survey, Results and Analysis 1966–2005*, Version 6.2.2006. USGS Patuxent Wildlife Research Center, Laurel, MD.

3. U.S. Fish and Wildlife Service. 1998. *Endangered and Threatened Wildlife and Plants: 90-day Finding for a Petition to List the Henslow's Sparrow as Threatened.* http://www.epa.gov/fedrgstr/EPA-SPECIES/1998/September/Day-09/e24122.htm (accessed 23 January 2004).

4. Chipley, R.M., G.H. Fenwick, M.J. Parr, and D.N. Pashley. 2003. *The American Bird Conservancy*

Guide to the 500 Most Important Bird Areas in the United States. Random House, New York, NY.

5. Burhans, D.E. 2001. *Conservation Assessment for Henslow's Sparrow (Ammodramus henslowii)*. USDA Forest Service, Eastern Region, North Central Research Station, University of Missouri, Columbia, MO.

6. Bajema, R.A., T. L. DeVault, P. E. Scott, and S. L. Lima. 2001. Reclaimed Coal Mine Grasslands and their Significance for Henslow's Sparrows in the American Midwest. *The Auk*: 118(2): 422–431.

7. Wells, J.V. 1998. *Important Bird Areas in New York State*. National Audubon Society, Albany, NY. 243 pp.

8. Pruitt, L. 1996. *Henslow's Sparrow Status Assessment*. USFWS, Fort Snelling, MN.

9. Rich, T. D., C. Beardmore, H. Berlanga, P. Blancher, M. Bradstreet, G. Butcher, D. Demarest, E. Dunn, C. Hunter, E. Iñigo-Elias, J. Kennedy, A. Martell, A. Panjabi, D. Pashley, K. Rosenberg, C. Rustay, S. Wendt, and T. Will. 2004. *Partners in Flight North American Landbird Conservation Plan*. Cornell Lab of Ornithology, Ithaca, NY.

10. Ricketts, T.H., E. Dinerstein, D.M. Olson, C.J. Loucks, et al. 1999. *Terrestrial Ecoregions of North America: A Conservation Assessment*. Island Press, Washington, DC. 485 pp.

11. Gauthier, D.A., A. Lafon, T. Tombs, J. Hoth, and E. Wilken. 2003. *Grasslands: Toward a North American Conservation Strategy*. Canadian Plains Research Center, University of Regina, Regina, SK, and Commission for Environmental Cooperation, Montreal, QC, Canada. 99 pp.

12. Vickery, P.D., P.B. Tubaro, J. M. Cardoso da Silva, B.G. Peterjohn, J.R. Herkert, and R.B. Cavalcanti. 1999. Conservation of Grassland Birds in the Western Hemisphere. Pages 2–26 in *Ecology and Conservation of Grassland Birds of the Western Hemisphere* (P.D. Vickery and J.R. Herkert, eds.). Studies in Avian Biology No. 19, Cooper Ornithological Society, Camarillo, CA.

13. Wells, J. V., and K. V. Rosenberg. 1999. Grassland Bird Conservation in Northeastern North America. *Studies in Avian Biology* 19:72–80.

14. Jackson, J.A. 1994. Red-cockaded Woodpecker (*Picoides borealis*). In *The Birds of North America*, No. 85 (A. Poole and F. Gill, eds.). The Academy of Natural Sciences, Philadelphia, PA, and the American Ornithologists' Union, Washington, D.C.

15. Vickery, P.D., and J. R. Herkert. 2001. Recent Advances in Grassland Bird Research: Where Do We Go from Here? *The Auk*: 118(1): 11–15.

16. Herkert, J. R. 2003. *Effects of Management Practices on Grassland Birds: Henslow's Sparrow*. Northern Prairie Wildlife Research Center, Jamestown, ND. Jamestown, ND: Northern Prairie Wildlife Research Center Home Page. http://www.npwrc.usgs.gov/resource/literatr/grasbird/hesp/hesp.htm (Version 12DEC2003).

17. Sample, D.W., and M.J. Mossman. 1997. *Managing Habitat for Grassland Birds: A Guide for Wisconsin*. Wisconsin Department of Natural Resources, Madison, WI.

18. Wells, J.V. 1997. Population Viability Analysis for Maine Grasshopper Sparrows. Pages 153–170 in *Grasslands of Northeastern North America* (P.D. Vickery and P. W. Dunwiddie, eds.). Massachusetts Audubon Society, Lincoln, MA.

19. Iowa Department of Natural Resources. 2002. *The Reintroduction of Prairie Chickens to Iowa*. http://www.iowadnr.com/wildlife/files/FMAmay2000.html (accessed 27 August 2003).

20. Missouri Department of Conservation. 2002. *Greater Prairie Chicken*. http://www.conservation.state.mo.us/nathis/birds/chickens/

21. Rosenberg, K.V., and J.V. Wells. 2000. Global Perspectives in Neotropical Migratory Bird Conservation in the Northeast: Long-term Responsibility Versus Immediate Concern. Pages 32–43 in *Strategies for Bird Conservation: The Partners in Flight Planning Process*. Proceedings of the 3rd Partners in Flight Workshop, 1995 October 1–5, Cape May, NJ (R. Bonney, D.N. Pashley, and R.J. Niles, eds.). Proceedings RMRS-P-16, U.S. Department of Agriculture, Forest Service, Rocky Mountain Research Station, Ogden, UT.

22. Rosenberg, K.V., and J.V. Wells. 2004. *Conservation Priorities for Terrestrial Birds in the Northeastern United States*. Proceedings of the 4th International Partners in Flight Symposium, Asilomar, CA, March 2001.

23. Fitzgerald, J.A., J.R. Herkert, and J.D. Brawn. 2000. *Partners in Flight Bird Conservation Plan for the Prairie Peninsula*. American Bird Conservancy, The Plains, VA.

24. Fitzgerald, J.A., B. Busby, M. Howery, R. Klataske, D. Reinking, and D. Pashley. 2000. *Partners in Flight Bird Conservation Plan for the Osage Plains*. American Bird Conservancy, The Plains, VA.

25. Hunter, W.C., L. Peoples, and J. Callazo. 2001. *South Atlantic Coastal Plain Partners in Flight Bird Conservation Plan*. U.S. Fish and Wildlife Service, Atlanta, GA.

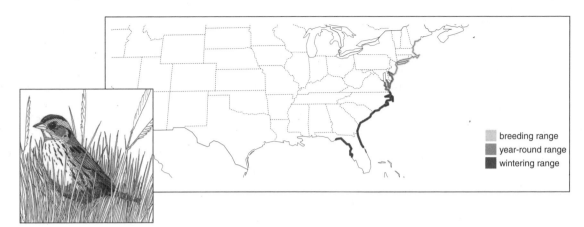

breeding range
year-round range
wintering range

SALTMARSH SHARP-TAILED SPARROW
(*Ammodramus caudacutus*)

This highly specialized sparrow inhabits only the narrow fringe of saltmarsh habitat along the Atlantic and Gulf Coasts, where its weak song is often impossible to hear over the constant ocean breeze.

STATUS AND DISTRIBUTION

The species' restricted breeding range extends as a narrow strip within saltmarshes along Atlantic coast from southern Maine to Virginia. Until relatively recently the Saltmarsh Sharp-tailed Sparrow was considered a subspecies with its closest relative the Nelson's Sharp-tailed Sparrow under the name Sharp-tailed Sparrow. The two species were thought to overlap in only a small section of the southern Maine coast, but recent research has shown that the zone of overlap between the two species is three times larger than previously documented. Important breeding sites for Saltmarsh Sharp-tailed Sparrow include Connecticut's East River Marsh, Hammonasset State Park, and Great Island, Maryland's Fishing Bay Wildlife Management Area, New Jersey's Forsythe National Wildlife Refuge (NWR), and Massachusett's Monomoy NWR and Duxbury/Plymouth Bays Complex Important Bird Area (IBA), which supports 5% of the state's population of the species. Important sites on New York's Long Island include the West Hempstead Bay/Jones Beach West IBA, Captree Island vicinity IBA, Moriches Bay IBA, and the Shinnecock Bay IBA.

The species' wintering range extends along the coast from Delaware (occasionally further north) south to northern Florida. Smaller numbers winter along the Gulf coast of northern Florida. Among many important wintering sites known for Saltmarsh Sharp-tailed Sparrow are Georgia's Cumberland Island National Seashore, the ACE Basin in South Carolina, Delaware's Coastal Zone IBA, and North Carolina's Cedar Island Marshes IBA and Lea/Hutaff Islands IBA.

The species is detected on too few Breeding Bird Survey routes for detection of any trends but is estimated to have declined by more than 50% over the last 100 years because of the extensive draining of wetlands prior to establishment of wetland regulations. The species' total population was estimated at 250,000 individuals in 2004.[1-8]

ECOLOGY

During both the breeding and wintering seasons, it is a species of the tidal saltmarsh dominated by cordgrass and saltmeadow grass. Populations of the species have been shown to decline in saltmarshes where tidal flow is blocked or restricted because of resultant habitat changes. Males mate with many females, often with many males competing to mate with a single female. The female lays 3–5 eggs in a nest built a few centimeters above ground in thick grass. Eggs are incubated only by the female for 11–12 days. Only the female feeds young, which fledge in 8–11 days. Young are self-sufficient within 15–20 days after fledging. Usually these birds raise two broods per season. Nest losses are primarily from nest flooding during high-tide events. The species' biology in the migratory and wintering season has been little studied.[1]

THREATS

Loss of habitat from drainage and filling of wetlands for agriculture and development was once a major problem but has stabilized in recent decades. More than 50% of wetlands in the continental U.S. have been lost since the 1700s. For example, New York is estimated to have lost 1.5 million acres of wetland habitats between 1780 and 1980, representing 60% of the state's original wetlands. Maryland has lost over 1.2 million acres of wetlands, New Jersey over 580,000 acres, and Connecticut nearly 500,000 acres. Many estuarine systems within the range of Saltmarsh Sharp-tailed Sparrow are showing degraded environmental conditions. For example, the percentage of the Delaware Estuary that tested above EPA ecological limits for metal contaminants increased from 5% to 22% from 1990–93 to 1997. Similarly, the percentage of the Chesapeake Bay that tested above EPA ecological limits for organic contaminants increased from 2% to 34% from 1990–93 to 1997. Interestingly, a study of mercury levels in blood samples of Saltmarsh Sharp-tailed Sparrows and Nelson's Sharp-tailed Sparrows from Maine showed higher levels than other insectivorous species sampled using similar techniques in Maine. Saltmarsh Sharp-tailed Sparrow blood mercury levels were higher than those of Nelson's Sharp-tailed Sparrow. Clearly, any activities that result in loss or degradation of habitat, including through alteration of water levels, destruction of buffer habitat, spraying of pesticides, ditching, accumulation of contaminants, or spread of invasive species like phragmites, are continuing threats to the species. Sea level rise with global warming may become the most pervasive and difficult threat to the species and loss of saltmarsh habitat to sea level rise has already become a problem in some areas of the northeastern U.S.[1,4,9–15]

CONSERVATION ACTION

Partners in Flight Bird Conservation Plans that have been completed for eastern U.S. physiographic regions have identified Saltmarsh Sharp-tailed Sparrow and its associated suite of saltmarsh bird species as a high priority and have provided recommendations for management, research, and monitoring. Ideally, all sites where the species currently occurs would be managed to maintain proper habitat and tidal flow for the species. At National Wildlife Refuges and state-owned Wildlife Management Areas this could involve changes in timing of management of water levels and tidal flow to maintain sufficient high marsh habitat.

The Coastal America Partnership, a coalition of federal agencies, state and local governments, and private organizations, identifies and implements local wetland restoration and protection projects throughout the U.S. The Partnership had initiated more than 500 projects impacting hundreds of thousands of acres of wetland habitat as of 2002. In 2003, for example, the coalition awarded funds for the creation of 570 acres of tidal wetland at Poplar Island in Chesapeake Bay. NOAA's Community–based Restoration Program and the U.S. Fish and Wildlife Service's Partners for Wildlife program have contributed funding to many saltmarsh restoration projects within the breeding range of Saltmarsh Sharp-tailed Sparrow. Ducks Unlimited (DU) has spearheaded a host of initiatives along the Atlantic coast to restore saltmarshes. For example, DU and USFWS partnered with Suffolk County Vector Control and the New York State Department of Environmental Conservation to restore hundreds of acres of saltmarsh on Long Island. Similar partnership initiatives with other state and federal agencies and private organizations are underway across the species range.

The North Carolina Coastal Federation is a private organization working to protect coastal ecosystems in that state. The group has initiated a number of projects, such as the $1.2 million acquisition of nearly 2,000 acres along the North River, including 821 acres of coastal marsh.

A jointly sponsored research project between the University of Connecticut and Audubon Connecticut, to study breeding ecology of Saltmarsh Sharp-tailed Sparrows, with funding provided by the EPA, Connecticut Department of Environmental Protection, and Connecticut Sea Grant, began field work in 2002. This project will provide information that is critical to the species' management.[1,13,15–18]

CONSERVATION NEEDS

- Slow production of global warming pollution.
- Develop a rangewide conservation plan for Saltmarsh Sharp-tailed Sparrow that helps co-

ordinate conservation work across the states that currently support the species.

- Incorporate Saltmarsh Sharp-tailed Sparrow habitat objectives into public land management where the species occurs on public lands.
- Increase monitoring and life-history research for the species, especially on the wintering grounds and during migration.
- Continue research into how different types of saltmarsh restoration may impact the species.

References

1. Greenlaw, J.S. and J. D. Rising 1994. Sharp-tailed Sparrow (*Ammodramus caudacutus*). In *The Birds of North America*, No. 112 (A. Poole and F. Gill, eds.). Philadelphia: The Academy of Natural Sciences, Philadelphia, PA, and the American Ornithologists' Union, Washington, DC.

2. Hodgman, T. P., W. G. Shriver, and P. D. Vickery. 2002. Redefining Range Overlap Between the Sharp-tailed Sparrows of Coastal New England. *The Wilson Bulletin*, 114(1): 38–43.

3. Chipley, R.M., G.H. Fenwick, M.J. Parr, and D.N. Pashley. 2003. *The American Bird Conservancy Guide to the 500 Most Important Bird Areas in the United States*. Random House, New York, NY.

4. National Audubon Society. 2002. *Saltmarsh Sharp-tailed Sparrow*. http://audubon2.org/webapp/watchlist/viewSpecies.jsp?id=196 (accessed 26 January 2004).

5. Audubon North Carolina. *North Carolina's Important Bird Areas*. http://www.ncaudubon.org/IBA1.htm (accessed 3 September 2003).

6. Elphick, C. 2004. Personal communication.

7. Wells, J.V. 1998. *Important Bird Areas in New York State*. National Audubon Society, Albany, NY. 243 pp.

8. Rich, T. D., C. Beardmore, H. Berlanga, P. Blancher, M. Bradstreet, G. Butcher, D. Demarest, E. Dunn, C. Hunter, E. Iñigo-Elias, J. Kennedy, A. Martell, A. Panjabi, D. Pashley, K. Rosenberg, C. Rustay, S. Wendt, and T. Will. 2004. *Partners in Flight North American Landbird Conservation Plan*. Cornell Lab of Ornithology, Ithaca, NY.

9. Stein, B.A., L.S. Kutner, and J.S. Adams. 2000. *Precious Heritage: The Status of Biodiversity in the United States*. Oxford University Press, New York, NY. 399 pp.

10. Dahl, T.E. 1990. *Wetlands Losses in the United States 1780's to 1980's*. U.S. Department of the Interior, Fish and Wildlife Service, Washington, DC. Northern Prairie Wildlife Research Center Home Page, Jamestown, ND. http://www.npwrc.usgs.gov/resource/othrdata/wetloss/wetloss.htm (Version 16JUL97).

11. U.S. EPA. 2002. *Mid-Atlantic Integrated Assessment 1997–98 Summary Report*, EPA/620/R-02/003. U.S. Environmental Protection Agency, Atlantic Ecology Division, Narragansett, RI. 115 pp.

12. DiQuinzio, D.A, P.W.C. Paton, and W. R. Eddleman. 2001. Nesting Ecology of Saltmarsh Sharp-tailed Sparrows in a Tidally Restricted Salt Marsh. *Wetlands* 22:179–185.

13. Rosenberg, K.V., and J.V. Wells. 2003. *Conservation Priorities for Terrestrial Birds in the Northeastern United States*. Proceedings of the 4th International Partners in Flight Symposium, Asilomar, CA, March 2001.

14. Shriver, W. G., D. Evers, and T. Hodgman. 2002. *Mercury Exposure Profile for Sharp-tailed Sparrows Breeding in Coastal Maine Salt Marshes*. Report BRI 2002 – 11 submitted to the Maine Department of Environmental Protection. BioDiversity Research Institute, Falmouth, ME.

15. Hunter, W.C., L. Peoples, and J. A. Collazo. 2001. *South Atlantic Plain Partners in Flight Bird Conservation Plan*. American Bird Conservancy, The Plains, VA. 158 pp.

16. Coastal America. 2002. *Coastal America: A Partnership for Action*. http://www.coastalamerica.gov (accessed 3 September 2003).

17. North Carolina Coastal Federation. No date. *Restoration and Protection of Key Coastal Habitats*. http://www.nccoast.org/skrestore.htm (accessed 3 September 2003).

18. National Audubon Society. 2004. *Connecticut's WatchList Birds*. http://www.audubon.org/bird/watchlist/bs-bc-connecticut.html (accessed 26 January 2004).

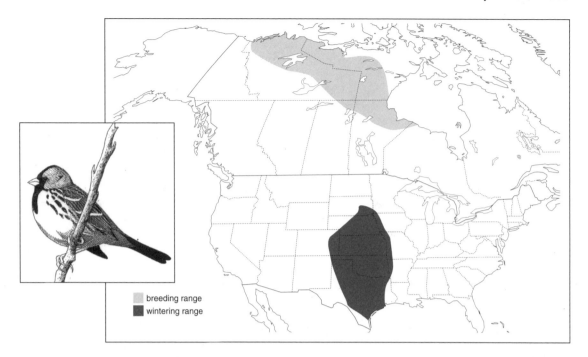

breeding range
wintering range

HARRIS'S SPARROW (*Zonotrichia querula*)

The only songbird whose global breeding range is restricted to Canada, the Harris's Sparrow also has an unusual wintering range, occurring only in a rather narrow corridor within the midwest U.S.

STATUS AND DISTRIBUTION

The Harris's Sparrow northern tundra-forest breeding range extends from northwestern Northwest Territories east across northeastern Saskatchewan and northern Manitoba to western Nunavut and south to the northwestern corner of Ontario. There is no available information about densities of the species across the breeding range. The species' entire population breeds within Canada with the bulk of the range within Northwest Territories and Nunavut. Important breeding areas for the species include the Thelon Wildlife Sanctuary in Nunavut and Northwest Territories, Tuktuk Nogait National Park in Northwest Territories, Queen Maud Gulf Migratory Bird Sanctuary in Nunavut, and the Caribou River Provincial Park and Wapusk National Park, both in Manitoba.

In winter, birds migrate to the midwest U.S. from South Dakota and southwestern Minnesota south to Texas. Wintering density maps produced from Christmas Bird Count data indicate highest densities in Kansas, central Oklahoma, and north-

central Texas. Important wintering areas for the species include Kansas's Flint Hills National Wildlife Refuge (NWR), Cheyenne Bottoms Wildlife Area and Preserve and Konza Prairie Research Natural Area, Oklahoma's Salt Plains NWR, and, in Texas, the Attwater Prairie Chicken NWR and Big Thicket National Preserve.

There are no Breeding Bird Survey data available for this species. An analysis of Christmas Bird Count data showed a significant decrease of 1.8% per year from 1965/66 to 2002/03. The species' total population was estimated at 3,700,000 individuals in 2004.[1-6]

ECOLOGY

On the breeding range it occurs in the forest–tundra transition zone where there is a mix of trees, shrubs, and tundra vegetation. It avoids areas with no trees or with thick tree cover. Females lay 3–5 eggs in an open cup nest built on the ground under low shrubs. Eggs are incubated only by females for about 12–14 days. Both adults feed young, which fledge in 8–10 days. Adults continue to feed young for as many as 14 days after fledging. On the wintering grounds it occurs in shrubby areas along rivers and streams and in shelterbelts and hedgerows. It is not territorial in winter but older birds dominate younger ones in feeding flocks.[1]

THREATS

The greatest potential threat on the breeding grounds is from habitat loss and degradation from increased development for oil and gas industry and mining. For example, an 800-mile natural gas pipeline has been proposed to be built through the Mackenzie Valley of the Northwest Territories in part to speed the development of the Alberta Oil Sands, the world's second largest oil and gas deposit in the world. The influx of workers and development of roads and other infrastructure will likely increase accessibility of more areas for further industrial development activities.

On the wintering grounds the greatest threat is probably loss, fragmentation, and degradation of shrub-scrub habitats across the midwest U.S. as the bulk of habitat in Canadian breeding range has not been greatly altered, though mining operations have impacted some breeding areas. Shrubby habitats within the Tallgrass Prairie ecoregion and parts of the Osage Plains and other ecoregions of the midwest U.S. were historically thought to be maintained by periodic fires and were often along stream corridors or within wet areas. More than 99% of the original savanna/woodland within which these shrub-scrub habitats existed has been lost in the Midwest since European settlement. Many other bird species of these habitats have also shown significant declines, including Northern Bobwhite, Brown Thrasher, Bell's Vireo, and Field Sparrow. These habitats have been lost and fragmented due to conversion to cropland and rangeland, suppression of fires, loss of and change in water flow from dams and irrigation, urban development, and increases in invasive plant species.[1,5,7,9,10,13-16]

CONSERVATION ACTION

In Canada a broad community of conservation organizations, industry, and First Nations have announced the Boreal Forest Conservation Framework—a new national conservation approach for Canada's boreal forest region. The Framework plan would protect the ecological integrity of the region while integrating sustainable forestry and other development activities. The Framework calls for the establishment of large, interconnected, protected areas covering at least half of the boreal region and application of leading-edge sustainable development practices on the lands that are developed. The Canadian Boreal Initiative and its partners are working to encourage the adoption of Framework principles by Canadian national and provincial government agencies and policy makers as a vision for the future of the vast, and largely publicly owned, boreal landscape. The Boreal Songbird Initiative has spearheaded work by a network of U.S. conservation groups to support the Boreal Forest Conservation Framework. This work has included outreach activities to increase awareness of the boreal wilderness and the threats it faces.

Since the 1990s a number of initiatives have been finalized to establish protected areas in northern Canada, including Tuktuk National Park and Wapusk National Park which were both established in 1996. Negotiations are continuing to add 250,000 additional acres to Tuktuk NP. These parks and the already established Thelon Wildlife Sanctuary are now cooperatively managed with representatives of indigenous communities so that subsistence hunting and fishing rights are maintained for the original inhabitants. Other protected areas have been proposed, including a national park at Ukkusiksalik (Wagner Bay) in Nunavut that would encompass more than 5.8 million acres. The Queen Maud Gulf Migratory Bird Sanctuary was designated as a RAMSAR wetland of international significance in 1982 because it supports virtually the entire global breeding population of Ross' Goose and large numbers of Brant. A 1995 report of the Canadian Wildlife Service recommended that the sanctuary be decreased in size by 10% (about 1.6 million acres) to allow mineral development. Consultations with regional groups on the sanctuary boundaries and management are continuing through the Nunavut Land Claim Agreement. Many conservation groups, including Ducks Unlimited Canada, Nature Canada, Sierra Club of Canada, Canadian Parks and Wilderness Society, and World Wildlife Fund, are urging the Canadian government to ensure the completion of the Northwest Territories Protected Areas Strategy before plans for the 800-mile Mackenzie pipeline project are considered.

In the wintering range, Partners in Flight Bird Conservation Plans in the midwest U.S. have identified the suite of shrub-scrub habitat bird species as a high priority and have provided recommendations for management, research, monitoring, and outreach. A variety of conservation efforts for Black-capped Vireo and Golden-cheeked Warbler may provide some benefits to Harris's Sparrow, including management efforts at several sites focused on improving habitat conditions through prescribed burns. Some work has also focused on protecting remaining habitat patches from conversion to housing developments or agricultural uses. For example, Balcones Canyonlands NWR near Austin, Texas was created in 1992 with the goal of acquiring and protecting 46,000 acres of nesting habitat for Black-capped Vireo and Golden-cheeked Warbler. About 16,000 acres had been acquired from willing sellers as of 2003. Similarly, the Bexar Land Trust received a grant in 2004 to purchase 150-acres of land adjacent to a private 500-acre ranch in Kendall County, Texas, that is managing habitat for Black-capped Vireo and Golden-cheeked Warbler under a Safe Harbor Agreement.[1,7-19]

CONSERVATION NEEDS

- Continue efforts to establish representative protected areas with the breeding range of Harris's Sparrow.
- Upgrade protections against mineral development within Queen Maud Gulf Bird Sanctuary.
- Implement the protected area strategy for the Northwest Territories before consideration of further large-scale industrial development in the region like the proposed 800-mile Mackenzie pipeline project.
- Implement the Boreal Forest Conservation Framework that calls for protection of 50% of Canada's boreal region and ensures world-leading sustainable development practices in areas that are developed.
- Increase acreage of healthy riparian and shrub-scrub habitat within the wintering range of Harris's Sparrow that is managed to attain conditions beneficial to the species.
- Decrease acreage of lowland riparian habitat within the wintering range of Harris's Sparrow that is degraded by cattle grazing and invasive plant species and lack of regular flooding regimes.
- Develop baseline inventory of Harris's Sparrow breeding and wintering populations.

References

1. Norment, C.J., and S.A. Shackleton. 1993. Harris' Sparrow (Zonotrichia querula). In The Birds of North America, No. 64 (A. Poole and F. Gill, eds.). The Academy of Natural Sciences, Philadelphia, PA, and The American Ornithologists' Union, Washington, D.C.

2. Sauer, J.R., S. Schwartz, and B. Hoover. 1996. The Christmas Bird Count Home Page, Version 95.1. Patuxent Wildlife Research Center, Laurel, MD.

3. Rich, T. D., C. Beardmore, H. Berlanga, P. Blancher, M. Bradstreet, G. Butcher, D. Demarest, E. Dunn, C. Hunter, E. Iñigo-Elias, J. Kennedy, A. Martell, A. Panjabi, D. Pashley, K. Rosenberg, C. Rustay, S. Wendt, and T. Will. 2004. Partners in Flight North American Landbird Conservation Plan. Cornell Lab of Ornithology, Ithaca, NY.

4. Chipley, R.M., G.H. Fenwick, M.J. Parr, and D.N. Pashley. 2003. The American Bird Conservancy Guide to the 500 Most Important Bird Areas in the United States. Random House, New York, NY.

5. Ricketts, T.H., E. Dinerstein, D.M. Olson, C.J. Loucks, et al. 1999. Terrestrial Ecoregions of North America: A Conservation Assessment. Island Press, Washington, DC. 485 pp.

6. Niven, D. K., J. R. Sauer, G. S. Butcher, and W. A. Link. Christmas Bird Count Provides Insights into Population Change in Land Birds That Breed in the Boreal Forest. The 104th Christmas Bird Count (American Birds 58):10–20.

7. Fitzgerald, J.A., and D.N. Pashley. 2000. Partners in Flight Bird Conservation Plan for the Dissected Till Plains. American Bird Conservancy, The Plains, VA.

8. Fitzgerald, J.A., B. Busby, M. Howery, R. Klataske, D. Reinking, and D. Pashley. 2000. Partners in Flight Bird Conservation Plan for the Osage Plains. American Bird Conservancy, The Plains, VA.

9. Wetlands International. 2003. A Directory of Wetlands of International Importance. http://www.wetlands.org/RDB/Ramsar_Dir/Canada?CA012D02.htm (accessed 20 May 2004).

10. Canadian Boreal Initiative. 2003. The Boreal Forest at Risk: A Progress Report. Canadian Boreal Initiative, Ottawa, ON.

11. Boreal Songbird Initiative. 2006. http:www.borealbirds.org (accessed 20 January 2006).

12. New Parks North. 2004. New Parks North. http://www.newparksnorth.org/ (accessed 20 May 2004).

13. Northwest Territories Protected Areas Strategy Advisory Committee. 1999. Northwest Territories Pro-

tected Areas Strategy. Department of Resources, Wildlife, and Economic Development, Government of the Northwest Territories, Yellowknife, NT.

14. Mackenzie WILD. 2006. *Sign on to the Mackenzie WILD Declaration*. http://www.mackenziewild.ca/ (accessed 27 January 2006).

15. World Wildlife Fund Canada. 2005. *Conservation Initiatives: Mackenzie Valley*. http://www.wwf .ca/AboutWWF/WhatWeDo/Initiatives/Initiatives .asp?project=mackenzievalley (accessed 27 January 2006).

16. World Wildlife Fund. 2002. *First Key Natural Area Protected in Advance of Mackenzie Pipeline Development*. http://www.panda.org/about_wwf/where_we_work/ arctic/news/index.cfm?uNewsID=14942 (accessed 27 January 2006)

17. Texas Parks and Wildlife Department. 20 May 2003. *Black-capped Vireo Trends—Kerr WMA*. http:// www.tpwd.state.tx.us/wma/find_a_wma/list/wildlife _management/kerr_wma/bcv_trends.phtml (accessed 20 January 2004).

18. U.S. Fish and Wildlife Service. No date. *Wildlife—Balcones Canyonlands NWR*. http://southwest .fws.gov/refuges/texas/balcones/wildlife.html (accessed 20 January 2004).

19. Land Trust Alliance. 2004. *Grant Benefits the Black-capped Vireo in Texas*. http://www.lta.org/regionlta/ s_sw.htm (accessed 22 January 2004).

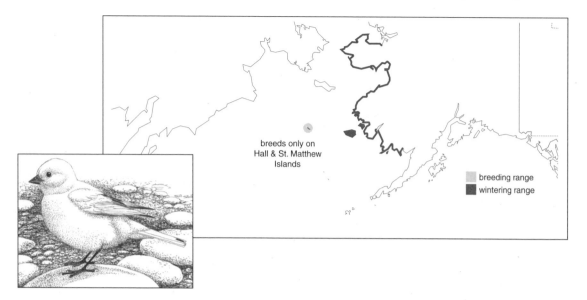

breeds only on
Hall & St. Matthew
Islands

breeding range
wintering range

McKAY'S BUNTING (*Plectrophenax hyperboreus*)

One of the most restricted range species of North American birds and as a consequence also one of the least numerous. It is the only bird species endemic to Alaska and is virtually unstudied.

STATUS AND DISTRIBUTION

McKay's Bunting breeds only on the small Bering Sea islands of Hall and St. Matthew. Occasional possible breeding records have been reported for St. Lawrence and St. Paul islands but have never been confirmed. In winter it migrates to the Bering Sea coast of western Alaska with most of the population thought to winter between Seward and Alaska peninsulas. Birds are occasionally found north and south of this area with exceptional records as far south as British Columbia, Washington, and Oregon. Primary wintering areas for McKay's Bunting include the Yukon-Kuskokwim Delta in the Yukon Delta National Wildlife Refuge (NWR), and Togiak NWR. This species can also be found wintering in the Seward Peninsula Important Bird Area.

No surveys have been conducted for the species so there is no trend information available. The species' total population had been estimated to be no more than 6,000 individuals and likely closer to 2,800 individuals but a 2003 survey was said to have increased the estimate to 30,000 individuals.[1-5]

ECOLOGY

The most common upland bird on St. Mathew and Hall islands where it breeds in crevices in cliffs, rock scree, drift wood, and occasionally vole holes. The female lays 3–5 eggs, commonly 4, and may occasionally interbreed with the closely related Snow Bunting. In winter, birds often flock with Snow Buntings occurring along coastal beaches and marshes.[1,4,5]

THREATS

Species is generally thought to be secure but its limited breeding range and small numbers make it continually susceptible to introduced mammals (especially rats), disease, or, though more unlikely, unexpected weather events, or sudden widespread habitat change. Reindeer were introduced to St. Matthew in 1944 by the U.S. Coast Guard as a backup food source for men stationed at a small Coast Guard station that was subsequently abandoned. The reindeer increased exponentially to over 6,000 individuals by 1963 and ate all the vegetation and eventually died out by the 1980s. It is unknown whether the habitat changes on the island had any effect on McKay's Bunting populations. The island has been proposed as a location to build a staging facility for Bering Sea offshore oil exploration. In fact, in 1983 the island was transferred by the Reagan Administration to a native corporation in exchange for land interests on mainland Alaska. The native corporation was going to lease the island to oil and gas companies to build staging facilities. The National Audubon Society challenged the transfer in court based on the Alaska National Interest Lands Conservation Act and won the challenge, thereby causing the island to remain as part of the U.S. Fish and Wildlife Service's Bering Sea Unit of the Alaska Maritime National Wildlife Refuge. Any development of facilities on the island with resulting regular transportation to and from the island would increase the risks of accidental introduction of rats, which could become major nest predators of McKay's Bunting and devastate the population. The island is seldom visited because of its remoteness but commercial Bering Sea eco-cruises do sometimes stop briefly. In the wintering range, oil and gas development and other industrial development in key wintering areas is a potential threat. Accumulation of persistent organic pollutants in both breeding and wintering areas could be an increasing threat. Habitat change caused by global warming may become the most pervasive and difficult threat to the species.[1,3-7]

CONSERVATION ACTION

St. Matthew and Hall islands were designated as part of the Bering Sea Bird Reservation in 1909 and are now part of the Bering Sea Unit of the U.S. Fish and Wildlife Service's Alaska Maritime National Wildlife Refuge. The National Audubon Society succeeded in preventing the loss of the island as a protected area and the development of oil exploration staging facilities during the 1980s. Continued diligence may be required to prevent similar attempts to use the island for commercial purposes. The USFWS monitors the island to pre-vent the establishment of any populations of accidentally introduced mammals.[1,4,7]

CONSERVATION NEEDS

- Slow production of global warming pollution.
- Implement regular surveys of McKay's Bunting populations.
- Implement some baseline research into the species' breeding biology.

References

1. Lyon, B., and R. Montgomerie. 1995. Snow Bunting and McKay's Bunting (*Plectrophenax nivalis* and *Plectrophenax hyperboreus*). In *The Birds of North America*, Nos. 198–199 (A. Poole and F. Gill, eds.). The Academy of Natural Sciences, Philadelphia, PA, and the American Ornithologists' Union, Washington, DC.

2. Chipley, R.M., G.H. Fenwick, M.J. Parr, and D.N. Pashley. 2003. *The American Bird Conservancy Guide to the 500 Most Important Bird Areas in the United States*. Random House, New York, NY.

3. Matsuoka, S. 2005. Personal communication.

4. Winker, K., D.D. Gibson, A.L. Sowls, B.E. Lawhead, P.D. Martin, E.P. Hoberg, and D. Causey. 2002. The Birds of St. Matthew Island, Bering Sea. *Wilson Bulletin* 114:491–509.

5. Rogers, J. 2005. Identifying McKay's Bunting. *Birding* 37(6):618–626.

6. Rozell, N. 2003. Island Proved No Paradise for Reindeer. *Anchorage Daily News*. http://www.adn.com/life/story/4430739p-4420683c.html (accessed 11 February 2004).

7. Institute of the North. 1999. *ANILCA Case Summaries*. Alaska Pacific University. http://www.institutenorth.org/LegalProgram/ANILCA_cases.htm (accessed 11 February 2004).

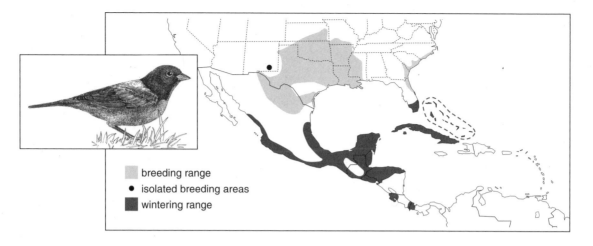

- breeding range
- ● isolated breeding areas
- wintering range

PAINTED BUNTING (*Passerina ciris*)

The gaudy, dramatically colorful plumage of the male Painted Bunting has made it not only a favorite of birdwatchers but, sadly, also a favorite of the caged-bird trade. In its Mexican, Central American, and Cuban wintering range the species is captured in the thousands for sale and export.

STATUS AND DISTRIBUTION

The Painted Bunting breeding range is split into two distinct areas. The species has a limited eastern range occurring along the coastal plain from North Carolina south to northeastern Florida. The western range is much larger, extending from Kansas and southern Missouri south through Mississippi, Louisiana, and Texas and into the Mexican states of Chihuahua, Coahuila, and Nuevo León. Some evidence suggests that eastern and western populations may be genetically distinct. Breeding density maps produced from Breeding Bird Survey data indicate highest densities in southern and central Texas and southcentral Oklahoma, though there are no Breeding Bird Survey data from the Mexican portion of the breeding range.

Among many important breeding areas for the species in its western breeding range are Oklahoma's Wichita Mountains National Wildlife Refuge (NWR) and, in Texas, Aransas NWR, Balcones Canyonlands NWR, Attwater Prairie Chicken NWR, Laguna Atascosa NWR, and the King Ranch. Important breeding areas in the eastern breeding range include Cumberland Island National Seashore and, in South Carolina, the ACE Basin region, including ACE Basin NWR and Bear Island and Donnelley Wildlife Management Areas.

In winter, birds migrate to southern Florida, the Bahamas, and Cuba, and to Mexico and Central America, occurring rarely south to Panama. A number of parks and protected areas exist across parts of the winter range and likely provide important wintering habitat for the species, though few data are available on occurrence (much less density) of the species at these locations. These include Mexico's Marismas Nacionales Important Bird Area (IBA) in Nayarit, Coalcomán-Pómaro IBA in Michoacán, and Centro de Veracruz IBA in Veracruz and Cuba's Guanahacabibes Peninsula Biosphere Reserve and Ciénaga de Zapata Biosphere Reserve.

Breeding Bird Survey analysis shows a significant decrease of approximately 46% (1.6% per year) from 1966 to 2005 rangewide. The species' total population was estimated at 4,500,000 individuals in 2004.[1–7]

ECOLOGY

On the breeding range it occurs in shrub-scrub habitat, including riparian areas and forest edges, abandoned agricultural land, power line right-of-ways, dune shrubs, and early successional shrub-scrub habitat. Nests are typically built within 3–6 feet above ground in thick shrub or a tree. The females lays 3–4 eggs that hatch in 11–12 days. Young fledge in 8–9 days. On the wintering grounds this bird also uses shrubby, second-growth habitat, generally at lower elevations. Birds occur singly or in small flocks on the wintering grounds.[1]

THREATS

The greatest threat to the species on the breeding grounds is continued loss of natural shrub-scrub and early-successional habitat as proportion of landscape in an early-successional state continues to decline across most of the range, but especially for the east coast population. This decline in amount of shrub-scrub habitat is attributable to a variety of factors, including the maturation of second-growth habitat after widespread farmland abandonment across the region as well as loss of habitat to development in some areas.

On the wintering grounds the species continues to be widely trapped for the wild bird cage trade in large numbers. This and wintering habitat loss and degradation are the biggest threats. In Mexico, a minimum of tens of thousands of birds have been trapped annually but the numbers are not officially tracked. In Cuba, the trapping of wild birds is officially banned but the ban is ignored and large numbers of birds, including Painted Buntings, are taken. A Cornell Lab of Ornithology researcher counted over 700 male Painted Buntings in an informal survey of four bird traders in Cuba in spring 2004.

The species inhabits a fairly wide range of habitats but, in general, loss has been severe across many habitats of south Florida and the Greater Antilles of the Caribbean. For example, Cuban Dry Forest habitat is estimated to have declined by more than 90%. These habitats harbor many endemic plant and animal species and provide habitat for wintering migrants like Painted Bunting. Forest habitats have been lost across the Caribbean from clearing for charcoal production and agriculture.[1,3,8,11]

CONSERVATION ACTION

Partners in Flight Bird Conservation Plans that have been completed for the Southeastern Coastal Plain and the Osage Plains regions have identified Painted Bunting and its associated suite of shrub-scrub bird species as a high priority and have provided recommendations for management, research, and monitoring. The restoration and protection of maritime scrub habitats has been identified as a priority within the Southeastern

Coastal Plain bird conservation plan. A cooperative program entitled the Southeastern Atlantic Painted Bunting Conservation Initiative (SAPABUCI) was formed in 2001 to address the research and management needs of Painted Bunting populations in North Carolina, South Carolina, Georgia, and Florida.

In 2004 a USFWS proposal to add the species to Appendix 3 of CITES was not adopted. Such a designation would not have prohibited international trade in the species but would have required that all trapping and trade be carefully monitored to assess whether trade was impacting populations of the species.

World Wildlife Fund Canada has provided grants to promote sustainable development activities by villagers living in and near Cuba's Ciénaga de Zapata Biosphere Reserve and to support national park staff working to halt poaching and habitat loss in the area. Cuban ornithologists have initiated monitoring of the resident and migrant birds at Cuba's Guanahacabibes Peninsula Biosphere Reserve to evaluate different land management strategies that will be implemented in the area.[1,6,8–11]

CONSERVATION NEEDS

- Preserve remaining acreage of natural shrub-scrub habitat, including barrens and shrub dune habitat.
- Halt trapping of species for cage bird trade, especially birds from smaller eastern population, and monitor trade if it continues.
- Convince countries receiving large numbers of Painted Buntings in pet trade to support the CITES Appendix III designation.
- Slow or halt deforestation of wintering habitat for Painted Bunting and restore habitat where possible.
- Increase acreage of shrub-scrub forest habitat within the breeding range of Painted Bunting that is managed to attain conditions beneficial to the species within the context of large, landscape level habitat management plans, especially on public lands.
- Develop management guidelines/policy for utility right-of-ways and other shrub habitats maintained in early-successional states.
- Develop baseline inventory of Painted Bunting breeding and wintering populations.
- Study genetic differences between eastern and

western Painted Bunting populations to clarify their taxonomic status.

References

1. Lowther, P.E., S.M. Lanyon, and C.W. Thompson. 1999. Painted Bunting (*Passerina ciris*). In *The Birds of North America*, No. 398 (A. Poole and F. Gill, eds.). The Birds of North America, Inc., Philadelphia, PA.

2. Sauer, J.R., J. E. Hines, and J. Fallon. 2005. *The North American Breeding Bird Survey, Results and Analysis 1966–2005*, Version 6.2.2006. USGS Patuxent Wildlife Research Center, Laurel, MD.

3. Chipley, R.M., G.H. Fenwick, M.J. Parr, and D.N. Pashley. 2003. *The American Bird Conservancy Guide to the 500 Most Important Bird Areas in the United States*. Random House, New York, NY.

4. Audubon North Carolina. No date. *North Carolina's Important Bird Areas*. http://www.ncaudubon .org/IBA1.htm (accessed April 2004).

5. CONABIO. 2002. *Áreas de Importancia para la Conservación de las Aves (AICAS)*. http://conabioweb .conabio.gob.mx/aicas/doctos/aicas.html (accessed April 2004).

6. Rich, T. D., C. Beardmore, H. Berlanga, P. Blancher, M. Bradstreet, G. Butcher, D. Demarest, E. Dunn, C. Hunter, E. Iñigo-Elias, J. Kennedy, A. Martell, A. Panjabi, D. Pashley, K. Rosenberg, C. Rustay, S. Wendt, and T. Will. 2004. *Partners in Flight North American Landbird Conservation Plan*. Cornell Lab of Ornithology, Ithaca, NY.

7. United Nations Educational, Scientific, and Cultural Organization. 2002. *Man and the Biosphere Reserves Directory*. http://www2.unesco.org/mab/bios1-2 .htm (accessed 22 July 2003).

8. World Wildlife Fund. 2001. *Cuban Dry Forests (NT0213)*. http://www.worldwildlife.org/wildworld/ profiles/terrestrial/nt/nt0213_full.html (accessed 21 July 2003).

9. World Wildlife Fund-Canada. No date. *Conservation Programs-International*. http://www.wwfcanada .org/AboutWWF/WhatWeDo/ConservationPrograms/ Conservation.asp (accessed 22 July 2003).

10. Optics for the Tropics. 2002. *Migratory Birds and Forest Conservation in Western Cuba*. http://www.optics forthetropics.org/projects4.shtml (accessed 22 July 2003).

11. Iñigo-Elias, E.E., K. V. Rosenberg, and J.V. Wells. 2002. The Danger of Beauty. *Birdscope* 16:1, 14.

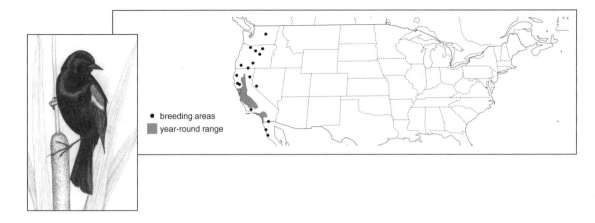

- breeding areas
- year-round range

TRICOLORED BLACKBIRD (*Agelaius tricolor*)

Perhaps a better name for this species would be California Blackbird as virtually its entire population occurs in that state. Tricolored Blackbird is very similar in appearance to its closest relative, the Red-winged Blackbird, but is quite different behaviorally; the Tricolored Blackbird is North America's most colonial passerine. Habitat loss in its restricted range has raised it to a species of national conservation concern.

STATUS AND DISTRIBUTION

The Tricolored Blackbird occurs year-round in the Central Valley and coastal regions of central and southern California. Small numbers have bred at isolated locations in Oregon, Nevada, and Washington and in northern Baja California. Breeding density maps produced from Breeding Bird Survey data indicate highest densities in the Central Valley of California. More than 99% of the species' population is estimated to breed within California.

Important breeding sites include East Park Reservoir (up to 10,000 birds), Grasslands Ecological Area (50,000 breeding birds in some years), Kern National Wildlife Refuge (thousands of breeders), the Lake Success Area Important Bird Area (IBA) (thousands of breeders), Mendota Wildlife Area IBA (25,000 birds in 2001 on private farmland), Sacramento Valley Wetlands IBA (130,000 breeding birds in 2004), and Yolo Bypass Area IBA (15,000 birds in 1999).

Work in the 1970s found that the species was greatly reduced from numbers reported in the 1930s. Intensive surveys showed a decline of approximately 50% between 1994 and 2000. The species' total population is estimated to be between 150,000 and 200,000.[1–7]

ECOLOGY

Breeds primarily in cattail marshes and in agricultural fields near water in dense colonies that historically contained up to 200,000 nests. Increasingly, birds have been found to use a variety of other habitats as well, including blackberry thickets. Builds an open-cup nest among plant stems usually quite close to surface of water or ground. Males defend a small territory and may mate with 1–4 females, who build their nests within his territory. Females lay 3–4 eggs that are incubated only by the female for 11–12 days. Young are fed by both parents and fledge in 11–14 days. Nesting locations may not be used every year depending on habitat conditions, and individuals may even move from one site to another to raise a second brood within the same season. As the breeding season progresses, birds seem to move generally south to north within the Central Valley for subsequent nesting attempts. Nest success is often very low in some breeding colonies because of predation from a diverse array of predators, including Black-crowned Night-Herons, Common Ravens, and coyotes. Nests in agricultural fields are often lost when field is mowed or plowed. During the nonbreeding season this species forms large flocks, sometimes with Red-winged and Brewer's blackbirds and European Starlings, and roosts in marshes near foraging sites.[1,8]

THREATS

The greatest historical threat to the species has been the loss of wetland breeding habitat, although market hunting into the 1930s and poisoning until the 1960s also took a heavy toll on Tricolored Blackbird populations. Massive loss of habitat has occurred within the species' range in California with most habitat in the Central Valley lost or degraded for agricultural production of fruits and vegetables for supplying supermarkets across the U.S. California has lost 91% of its wetland habitats and in the Central Valley, the most important breeding area for the species, only 6% of the original marshland remains. The species is adaptable enough that nesting colonies are now often established in agricultural grasslands but such locations are often ecological traps as mowing and haying operations will destroy virtually all nests and young. Colonies containing more than 50,000 nests were destroyed by such activity in the 1990s. Spraying of pesticides and herbicides is thought to have caused the loss of several breeding colonies.[1,6,7]

CONSERVATION ACTION

A group of government and nongovernmental organizations and private individuals is working together specifically on Tricolored Blackbird conservation and management, to reverse the population trend of this species. Habitat restoration and enhancement efforts for Tricolored Blackbird require close attention to three primary factors that determine colony site selection: suitable nesting habitat structure, proximity to water, and proximity to foraging areas.

Hundreds of conservation groups and agencies from the local to the national level have been struggling to protect and restore wetland habitat within California in the face of continuing rapid loss and degradation of habitat for agriculture and development. For example, the Central Valley Habitat Joint Venture, a coalition of conservation organizations, has proposed to restore 20,000 acres of wetlands and had purchased 10,000 acres by 2001. The U.S. Fish and Wildlife Service (USFWS) and the California Department of Fish and Game (CDFG) have purchased many important sites within the species' range and are working together to better manage those lands for Tricolored Blackbirds and associated wetland and grassland species. Within the Sacramento Valley Wetlands IBA, the USFWS manages 24,000 acres of wildlife refuges and CDFG 9,000 acres within wildlife management areas. At the local level, groups like the Sierra-Los Tulares Land Trust and Wildlands Conservancy are spearheading conservation activities within their regions of interest. These are just a few examples of the massive efforts many groups have put into conservation of wetlands within the breeding range of the species.

To maintain populations of the species, the California Department of Fish and Game and the U.S. Fish and Wildlife Service sometimes negotiate with agricultural landowners to compensate them for an agreement to delay harvesting of grasslands where Tricolored Blackbirds have established breeding colonies. In 1993 and 1994 such action allowed 37,000 and 44,000 young to survive that would otherwise have died from agricultural operations. Similarly, in 2000 a farmer delayed mowing of 56 acres of grasslands, allowing 20,000 young to fledge. Because the species nests in such dense colonies, such actions make major contributions to the species' long-term survival.

The Conservation Reserve Enhancement Program for the Central Valley of California paid farmers to convert cropland to native habitat for 10 to 15 years. Although it has not been evaluated in this context, sites enrolled in the program may provide habitat for the species in some areas.[1,7,9–14]

CONSERVATION NEEDS

- Ensure that management of locations currently supporting Tricolored Blackbird continues to maintain water levels and habitat conditions beneficial to the species.
- Increase acreage of wetland habitat on public and private lands within the range of Tricolored Blackbird that is managed to attain conditions beneficial to the species.
- Provide incentives for private landowners to maintain Tricolored Blackbird colonies on their properties.
- Develop outreach materials to inform landowners of the status of the species and what role they can play on its conservation.
- Decrease acreage of wetland habitat degraded by erosion, pollution, invasive species, pesticides, and other factors.
- Continue rangewide surveys designed to assess overall population status and trends.

- Improve survey methods for more accurate population surveys.
- Increase the number of protected areas supporting breeding populations of the species.

References

1. Beedy, E.C., and W. J. Hamilton. 1999. Tricolored Blackbird (*Agelaius tricolor*). In *The Birds of North America*, No. 423 (A. Poole and F. Gill, eds.). The Birds of North America, Inc., Philadelphia, PA.

2. Sauer, J. R., J. E. Hines, and J. Fallon. 2003. *The North American Breeding Bird Survey, Results and Analysis 1966–2002*, Version 2003.1, USGS Patuxent Wildlife Research Center, Laurel, MD.

3. Chipley, R.M., G.H. Fenwick, M.J. Parr, and D.N. Pashley. 2003. *The American Bird Conservancy Guide to the 500 Most Important Bird Areas in the United States.* Random House, New York, NY.

4. Rich, T. D., C. Beardmore, H. Berlanga, P. Blancher, M. Bradstreet, G. Butcher, D. Demarest, E. Dunn, C. Hunter, E. Iñigo-Elias, J. Kennedy, A. Martell, A. Panjabi, D. Pashley, K. Rosenberg, C. Rustay, S. Wendt, and T. Will. 2004. *Partners in Flight North American Landbird Conservation Plan.* Cornell Lab of Ornithology, Ithaca, NY.

5. Cooper, D. 2001. Important bird areas of California. Unpublished manuscript available from Audubon California, 6042 Monte Vista St., Los Angeles, CA 90042.

6. Hamilton, W.J., III. 2000. *Tricolored Blackbird 2000 Breeding Season Census and Survey—Observations and Recommendations.* Report prepared for the U.S. Fish and Wildlife Service, Portland, OR.

7. Hamilton, B. 2004. Management Implications of the 2004 Central Valley Tricolored Blackbird Survey. *Central Valley Bird Club Bulletin.* 7(2–3): 32–46.

8. Hamilton, W.J., III. 1998. Tricolored Blackbird Itinerant Breeding in California. *The Condor* 100: 218–226.

9. Hamilton, W.J., III. 2003. Current policies and programs affecting Tricolor Blackbird (*Agelaius tricolor*) restoration. In *California Riparian Systems: Processes and Floodplain Management, Ecology, and Restoration* (P.M. Faber, ed.). 2001 Riparian Habitat and Floodplains Conference Proceedings, RHJV, Sacramento, CA.

10. Ricketts, T.H., E. Dinerstein, D.M. Olson, C.J. Loucks, et al. 1999. *Terrestrial Ecoregions of North America: A Conservation Assessment.* Island Press, Washington, DC. 485 pp.

11. Stein, B.A., L.S. Kutner, and J.S. Adams. 2000. *Precious Heritage: The Status of Biodiversity in the United States.* Oxford University Press, New York, NY. 399 pp.

12. California Department of Fish and Game, Coastal Conservancy, and U. S. Fish and Wildlife Service. No date. *South Bay Salt Pond Restoration Project.* http://www.southbayrestoration.org/Project_Description.html (accessed 26 January 2004).

13. U. S. Fish and Wildlife Service. 2000. *Farmer, Wildlife Agencies Unite to Save Colony of Tricolored Blackbirds.* http://pacific.fws.gov/news/2000/2000-107.htm (accessed 26 January 2004).

14. U.S. Department of Agriculture. No date. *Conservation Reserve Program—California Enhancement Program.* http://www.fsa.usda.gov/pas/publications/facts/html/crepca01.htm (accessed 9 February 2004).

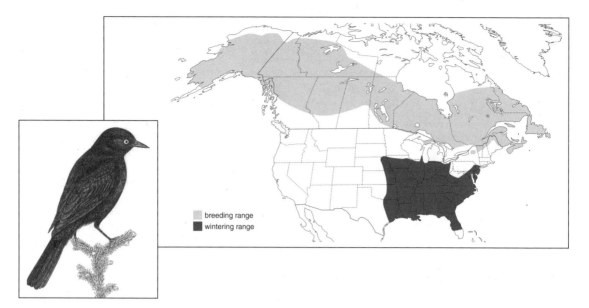

breeding range
wintering range

RUSTY BLACKBIRD (*Euphagus carolinus*)

The northernmost breeding blackbird, the Rusty Blackbird also has the dubious distinction of showing one of the steepest declines of any North American bird. It is also one of the least-studied blackbird species.

STATUS AND DISTRIBUTION

The Rusty Blackbird breeding range extends from Alaska across the boreal forest of Canada to Labrador and Newfoundland and south through northern Minnesota, Michigan, New York, and northern New England. Except for small numbers in northern New England and New York, Canada and Alaska support nearly the entire breeding population of the Rusty Blackbird. An estimated 85% of the global population breeds in the boreal forests of Canada and Alaska.

Although no systematic survey has been completed to identify sites that are of particular importance for breeding populations of Rusty Blackbird there are many areas that have large expanses of appropriate habitat within the species' breeding range. These include Canada's Wood Buffalo National Park in Alberta and the Northwest Territories, Manitoba's Wapusk National Park, Ontario's Pukaskwa National Park, and Québec's La Mauricie National Park. Important protected areas in Alaska include the Yukon Delta National Wildlife Refuge (NWR), Innolo NWR, and Togiak NWR.

In winter, birds migrate to the eastern U.S., wintering primarily from eastern Nebraska east to southeastern Pennsylvania and southern New Jersey south to the Gulf states and the northern half of Florida. Very small numbers winter irregularly north of this area to southern Canada and coastal Alaska. Wintering density maps produced from Christmas Bird Count data show highest densities in North Carolina, South Carolina, Georgia, Alabama, Tennessee, and Kentucky.

A number of parks and protected areas exist across parts of the winter range and likely provide important wintering habitat for the species. These include Arkansas' White River and Cache River NWRs, Kentucky's Clarks River NWR and Land Between the Lakes National Recreation Area, Missouri's Mingo NWR, North Carolina's Pocosin Lakes NWR, South Carolina's ACE Basin NWR, and the Tennessee National Wildlife Refuge.

Breeding Bird Survey analysis shows a significant decrease of approximately 99% (12.5% per year) from 1966 to 2005 rangewide. Analysis of Christmas Bird Count data shows a significant decrease of 7.7% per year from 1959 to 1988. Analysis of the Québec checklist database and several other datasources all corroborate a decline of approximately 90% over the last 30 years. The species' total population was estimated at 2,000,000 individuals in 2004.[1–7]

ECOLOGY

On the breeding range this bird occurs near bogs, ponds, lakes, and streams within coniferous forest. It builds a nest near water from ground level to as high as 18 feet. Nests are usually placed within thick vegetation and on side branches of a tree or shrub. Females lay 3–5 eggs but produce only a single clutch each year.

On the wintering grounds in the southeastern U.S. the species is found in wet forests and swamps, including bottomland hardwoods and cypress swamps. Birds sometimes feed in agricultural areas and forage in small single-species flocks, though they sometimes roost in large mixed-species blackbird flocks.[1,6]

THREATS

Despite the fact that the Rusty Blackbird has suffered one of the steepest declines of any surviving North American bird, it has received little research attention. The reasons behind the steep decline of Rusty Blackbird populations are still largely unknown, but a number of issues have been identified that are likely major contributors to the decline. In the eastern portion of the breeding range, acidification of wetlands from acid precipitation as a result of industrial air pollution in the eastern U.S. may have decreased availability of calcium-rich invertebrates crucial to egg production and chick rearing. In the western part of the breeding range there is increasing evidence that wetland habitats are drying and shrinking as a result of global warming.

In addition, there has been much habitat loss within the species' breeding range. Habitat loss and degradation from development for oil and gas industry and mining is increasing. For example, an 800-mile natural gas pipeline has been proposed to be built through the Mackenzie Valley of the Northwest Territories in part to speed the development of the Alberta Oil Sands, the world's second largest oil and gas deposit in the world. The influx of workers and development of roads and other infrastructure will likely increase accessibility of more areas for further industrial development activities. More than 2.2 million acres of boreal wetlands in Canada have been lost due to hydroelectric projects alone. Much wetland habitat has also been lost along the southern edge of the breeding range as habitat is converted to agriculture.

Much of the Rusty Blackbird breeding range is within areas managed for forestry and other types of industrial resource development. Though more than 90% of the Canadian boreal forest is publicly owned, almost a third of the boreal is currently allocated to forestry companies for timber production, amounting to tens of millions of acres that will be logged during this century. Clearcutting has been used in over 80% of forest harvest operations in Canada.

Wintering habitat in the southeastern U.S. has been greatly reduced. For example, 80% of the bottomland hardwood habitat in the Lower Mississippi Valley has been lost since historical times and 25% of forested wetland habitat in the southeastern U.S. was lost between the 1950s and 1980s.

Massive mixed-species wintering blackbird flocks have been regularly sprayed with avicides in the southeastern U.S. to kill large numbers because they are considered an agricultural pest. These flocks are typically made up largely of more common species, including Brown-headed Cowbird, Red-winged Blackbird, and Common Grackle, but there is no estimate available of the number of Rusty Blackbirds killed through these control efforts.[1,6,8–13]

CONSERVATION ACTION

In Canada a broad community of conservation organizations, industry, and First Nations have announced the Boreal Forest Conservation Framework—a new national conservation approach for Canada's boreal forest region. The Framework plan would protect the ecological integrity of the region while integrating sustainable forestry and other development activities. The Framework calls for the establishment of large, interconnected, protected areas covering at least half of the boreal region and application of cutting-edge sustainable development practices on the lands that are developed. The Canadian Boreal Initiative and its partners are working to encourage the adoption of Framework principles by Canadian national and provincial government agencies and policy makers as a vision for the future of the vast, and largely publicly owned, boreal landscape.

A Canadian Senate subcommittee developed a comprehensive report in 1999 that recommended a set of actions needed to ensure the protection and sustainable use of Canada's boreal forests. Since then the Canadian Boreal Initiative has been advocating for adoption and implementation of these recommendations in addition to promoting the Framework and working with provincial governments to adopt the principles of the Framework on their lands. Some progress was reported in the establishment of protected areas, including the protection of 625,000 acres of boreal forest habitat in Québec since 2000. Many conservation groups, including Ducks Unlimited Canada, Nature Canada, Sierra Club of Canada, Canadian Parks and Wilderness Society, and World Wildlife Fund, are urging the Canadian government to ensure the completion of the Northwest Territories Protected Areas Strategy before plans for the 800-mile Mackenzie pipeline project are considered.

The Boreal Songbird Initiative has spearheaded work by a network of U.S. conservation groups to support the Boreal Forest Conservation Framework. This work has included outreach activities to increase awareness of the boreal wilderness and the threats it faces. For example, the National Wildlife Federation and National Audubon both have conducted letter-writing campaigns asking large retail catalog companies to use recycled paper and paper purchased from environmentally and socially responsible sources instead of using paper made from virgin boreal forest. The Natural Resources Defense Council has also designated the intact boreal forest in the Ontario–Manitoba border region as one of its twelve "BioGems" and is working to ensure that the conservation plans of local indigenous peoples are not threatened by hydropower and industrial development.

The U.S. Environmental Protection Agency's Acid Rain Program has worked toward reducing sulfur dioxide and nitrogen oxide emissions from industrial sources especially coal-fired power generating facilities, the primary contributor to acid rain. By 1996 emissions from U.S. sources had decline by about 27% compared to 1980 levels. Similarly, Environment Canada's Eastern Canada Acid Rain Program had resulted in a 58% reduction in emissions by 1999 compared to 1980 levels. Unfortunately, further research has also shown that eastern Canadian wetland ecosystems are more sensitive to acid rain than first thought and further reductions in emissions are necessary to preserve these wetland systems. In 1998 various Canadian government agencies signed the Canada-wide Acid Rain Strategy for Post-2000 to reduce emissions to levels that would not harm Canadian ecosystems.

Partners in Flight Bird Conservation Plans that have been completed for southeastern U.S. physiographic regions have identified the suite of bottomland forest bird species as a high priority and have provided recommendations for management, research, and monitoring. These suggestions have included specific goals for increasing the acreage of bottomland forest in large blocks across the landscape. Within the Mississippi Alluvial Valley many projects to purchase or reforest lands are ongoing through many partner agencies and organizations, including the Mississippi Valley Joint Venture, U.S. Fish and Wildlife Service Partners for Wildlife Program, the National Resources Conservation Service Wetland Reserve Program, Ducks Unlimited, and the Nature Conservancy.[8–10,12,14–20]

CONSERVATION NEEDS

- Slow production of global warming pollution.
- Decrease rates of acid deposition from air pollution, especially from sources impacting eastern portion of breeding range of Rusty Blackbird.
- Implement the protected area strategy for the Northwest Territories before consideration of further large-scale industrial development in the region like the proposed 800-mile Mackenzie pipeline project.
- Implement the proposed protections near Lake Winnipeg to maintain the intact boreal forest in the Ontario–Manitoba border region.
- Implement the Boreal Forest Conservation Framework that calls for protection of 50% of Canada's boreal region and ensures world-leading sustainable development practices in areas that are developed.
- Within the breeding range of Rusty Blackbird implement broad, landscape-scale forest management plans that maintain boreal wetlands and the forests bordering them.
- Increase the number of protected areas through national and provincial parks in Canada's boreal forest.
- Slow or halt deforestation of wintering habitat for Rusty Blackbird and restore habitat where possible.
- Develop baseline inventory of Rusty Blackbird breeding and wintering populations and identify high-density breeding areas and source populations.

- Focus research on factors responsible for continuing population declines and habitat needs on breeding and wintering grounds.
- Study impact of blackbird poisoning programs on Rusty Blackbird populations.

References

1. Avery, M.L. 1995. Rusty Blackbird (*Euphagus carolinus*) In *The Birds of North America*, No. 200 (A. Poole and F. Gill, eds.). The Academy of Natural Sciences, Philadelphia, PA, and the American Ornithologists' Union, Washington, DC.

2. Sauer, J. R., J. E. Hines, and J. Fallon. 2005. *The North American Breeding Bird Survey, Results and Analysis 1966–2005*, Version 6.2.2006. USGS Patuxent Wildlife Research Center, Laurel, MD.

3. Blancher, P., and J.V. Wells. 2005. *The Boreal Forest Region: North America's Bird Nursery.* Canadian Boreal Initiative, Boreal Songbird Initiative, Bird Studies Canada, Ottawa, Seattle, and Port Rowan, ON. 10 pp.

4. Parks Canada. 2003. *National Parks of Canada.* http://parkscanada.gc.ca/progs/np-pn/index_E.asp (accessed 25 June 2003).

5. Sauer, J. R., S. Schwartz, and B. Hoover. 1996. *The Christmas Bird Count Home Page*, Version 95.1. Patuxent Wildlife Research Center, Laurel, MD.

6. Greenberg, R., and S. Droege. 1999. On the Decline of the Rusty Blackbird and the Use of Ornithological Literature to Document Long-term Population Trends. *Conservation Biology* 13:553–559.

7. Rich, T. D., C. Beardmore, H. Berlanga, P. Blancher, M. Bradstreet, G. Butcher, D. Demarest, E. Dunn, C. Hunter, E. Iñigo-Elias, J. Kennedy, A. Martell, A. Panjabi, D. Pashley, K. Rosenberg, C. Rustay, S. Wendt, and T. Will. 2004. *Partners in Flight North American Landbird Conservation Plan.* Cornell Lab of Ornithology, Ithaca, NY.

8. Sub-committee on Boreal Forest of the Standing Senate Committee on Agriculture and Forestry. 1999. *Competing Realities: The Boreal Forest at Risk.* Government of Canada, Ottawa. http://www.parl.gc.ca/36/1/parlbus/commbus/senate/com-e/BORE-E/rep-e/rep09jun99-e.htm (accessed 24 June 2003).

9. Canadian Boreal Initiative. 2003. *The Boreal Forest at Risk: A Progress Report.* Canadian Boreal Initiative, Ottawa, ON.

10. Boreal Songbird Initiative. 2006. http:www.borealbirds.org (accessed 20 January 2006).

11. Ricketts, T.H., E. Dinerstein, D.M. Olson, C.J. Loucks, et al. 1999. *Terrestrial Ecoregions of North America: A Conservation Assessment.* Island Press, Washington, DC. 485 pp.

12. Twedt, D.J., and C.R. Loesch. 1999. Forest Area and Distribution in the Mississippi Alluvial Valley: Implications for Breeding Bird Conservation. *Journal of Biogeography* 26:1215–1224.

13. Stein, B.A., L.S. Kutner, and J.S. Adams. 2000. *Precious Heritage: The Status of Biodiversity in the United States.* Oxford University Press, New York, NY. 399 pp.

14. Northwest Territories Protected Areas Strategy Advisory Committee. 1999. *Northwest Territories Protected Areas Strategy.* Department of Resources, Wildlife, and Economic Development, Government of the Northwest Territories, Yellowknife, NT.

15. Mackenzie WILD. 2006. *Sign on to the Mackenzie WILD Declaration.* http://www.mackenziewild.ca/ (accessed 27 January 2006).

16. World Wildlife Fund Canada. 2005. *Conservation Initiatives: Mackenzie Valley.* http://www.wwf.ca/AboutWWF/WhatWeDo/Initiatives/Initiatives.asp?project=mackenzievalley (accessed 27 January 2006).

17. World Wildlife Fund. 2002. *First Key Natural Area Protected in Advance of Mackenzie Pipeline Development.* http://www.panda.org/about_wwf/where_we_work/arctic/news/index.cfm?uNewsID=14942 (accessed 27 January 2006).

18. Environmental Protection Agency. 2002. *Acid Rain.* http://www.epa.gov/airmarkets/acidrain/ (accessed 14 July 2003).

19. Environment Canada. 2003. *Acid Rain—What Is Being Done?* http://www.ec.gc.ca/acidrain/done-canada.html (accessed 14 July 2003).

20. Mueller, A.J., D.J. Twedt, and C.R. Loesch. 2000. Development of Management Objectives for Breeding Birds in the Mississippi Alluvial Valley. Pages 12–17 in *Strategies for Bird Conservation: The Partners in Flight Planning Process.* Proceedings of the 3rd Partners in Flight Workshop, 1995 October 1–5, Cape May, NJ (R. Bonney, D.N. Pashley, and R.J. Niles, eds.). Proceedings RMRS-P-16, U.S. Department of Agriculture, Forest Service, Rocky Mountain Research Station, Ogden, UT.

Appendix I
North American Birds of Conservation
Concern Listed by Different Agencies and Organizations

Key

Audubon WatchList (2002)
Red: Species in this category are declining rapidly, have very small populations or limited ranges, and face major conservation threats. These typically are species of global conservation concern.
Yellow: This category includes those species that are also declining but at a slower rate than those in the red category. These typically are species of national conservation concern.

American Bird Conservancy Green List (2003)
hcc: Highest Continental Concern. Species suffer from multiple problems and include many of the birds listed under the Endangered Species Act.
rdlp: Species with Restricted Distributions or Low Population Size. This category covers species for which populations may be stable and threats apparently limited, but are limited in number or range.
madht: Moderately Abundant Species with Declines or High Threats. This category includes birds that are still found in relatively high numbers, but are declining at an alarming rate.

BirdLife Internationa/IUCN Redlist (2004/2006)
CR: Critically Endangered. A taxon is Critically Endangered when the best available evidence indicates that it is facing an extremely high risk of extinction in the wild.
EN: Endangered. A taxon is Endangered when the best available evidence indicates that it is facing a very high risk of extinction in the wild.
VU: Vulnerable. A taxon is Vulnerable when the best available evidence indicates that it is facing a high risk of extinction in the wild.
NT: Near Threatened. A taxon is Near Threatened when it has been evaluated against the criteria and does not qualify for Critically Endangered, Endangered, or Vulnerable now, but is close to qualifying for or is likely to qualify for a threatened category in the near future.

Partners in Flight: All Birds (Watch List 2000)
ex h: Extremely High Priority
mod h: Moderately High Priority
mod: Moderate Priority

Partners in Flight: Landbirds (Watch List 2004)
mcc: Multiple causes for concern across entire range
dht: Moderately abundant or widespread with declines or high threats
rdlp: Restricted distribution or low population size
adss: Additional Stewardship Species

U.S. Shorebird Conservation Plan (2001)
5: Highly imperiled. All species listed as threatened or endangered nationally, plus all species with significant population declines and either low populations or some other high-risk factor.
4: Species of High Concern. Populations of these species are known or thought to be declining, and have some other known or potential threat as well.
3: Species of Moderate Concern. Populations of these species are (a) declining with moderate threats or distributions; (b) stable with known or potential threats and moderate to restricted distributions; (c) relatively small; (d) relatively restricted; or (e) declining but with no other known threats.
2: Species of Low Concern. Populations of these species are (a) stable with moderate threats and distribution; (b) increasing but with known or potential threats and moderate to restricted distributions; or (c) of moderate size.

Waterbird Conservation for the Americas (2002)
Imperiled (Highly Imperiled): This includes all species with significant population declines and either low populations or some other high-risk factor.
High Concern: Species that are not Highly Imperiled. Populations of these species are known or thought to be declining, and have some other known or potential threat as well.
Moderate Concern: Species that are not Highly Imperiled or High Concern. Populations of these species are (a) declining with moderate threats or distributions; (b) stable with known or potential threats and moderate to restricted distributions; or (c) relatively small with relatively restricted distributions.
Low Concern: Species that are not Highly Imperiled, High Concern, or Moderate Concern. Populations of these species are (a) stable with moder-

ate threats and distributions; (b) increasing buth with known or potential threats and moderate to restricted distributions; or (c) of moderate size with known or potential threats and moderate to restricted distributions.

USFWS Birds of Conservation Concern (2002)

National: "Recognized at the national level. These species should be viewed as a barometer of the status of continental bird populations, providing an 'early warning' of birds that may decline to levels requiring ESA protection unless additional conservation measures are taken."

USFWS: Recognized within one of the seven regions administered by the USFWS.

BCR: "Recognized within one of 37 basic ecological units (bird conservation regions, or BCRs) within which all-bird conservation efforts will be planned and evaluated through NABCI."

USFWS Threatened and Endangered Species List

E: Endangered. A species is considered endangered when it is in danger of extinction throughout all or a significant portion of its range.

T: Threatened. A species is considered threatened when it is likely to become endangered within the foreseeable future throughout all or a significant portion of its range.

Canada Species at Risk

Extp: Extirpated. A species that no longer exists in the wild in Canada, but exists elsewhere.

E: Endangered. A species that is facing imminent extirpation or extinction.

T: Threatened. A species that is likely to become endangered if nothing is done to reverse the factors leading to its extirpation or extinction.

SC: Special Concern. A species that may become threatened or endangered because of a combination of biological characteristics and identified threats.

North American Birds and Their Listing Status

Species/Family	Scientific Name	Audubon WatchList	ABC Green List	BirdLife Intntl 2004	BirdLife Intntl 2006	PIF: All Birds	PIF: Land-bird	Shore-bird Plan	Water-bird Plan	USFWS Cons. Concern	USFWS Threatened & Endangered	Canada Species at Risk
Ducks, Geese, and Swans (Anatidae)												
Black-bellied Whistling-Duck	Dendrocygna autumnalis											
Fulvous Whistling-Duck	Dendrocygna bicolor											
Bean Goose	Anser fabalis											
Pink-footed Goose	Anser brachyrhynchus											
Greater White-fronted Goose	Anser albifrons											
Lesser White-fronted Goose	Anser erythropus											
Emperor Goose	Chen canagica	Red	rdlp	NT	NT	ex h						
Snow Goose	Chen caerulescens											
Ross's Goose	Chen rossii											
Brant	Branta bernicla	Yellow	madht			mod						
Barnacle Goose	Branta leucopsis											
Cackling Goose	Branta hutchinsii				LC							
Canada Goose	Branta canadensis											
Mute Swan	Cygnus olor											
Trumpeter Swan	Cygnus buccinator	Yellow				mod h						
Tundra Swan	Cygnus columbianus											
Whooper Swan	Cygnus cygnus											
Muscovy Duck	Cairina moschata											
Wood Duck	Aix sponsa											
Gadwall	Anas strepera											
Falcated Duck	Anas falcata				NT							
Eurasian Wigeon	Anas penelope											
American Wigeon	Anas americana											
American Black Duck	Anas rubripes	Yellow	madht			mod h						
Mallard	Anas platyrhynchos											
Mottled Duck	Anas fulvigula	Yellow	rdlp			mod h						
Spot-billed Duck	Anas poecilorhyncha											
Blue-winged Teal	Anas discors											
Cinnamon Teal	Anas cyanoptera											
Northern Shoveler	Anas clypeata											

Species/Family	Scientific Name	Audubon WatchList	ABC Green List	BirdLife Intntl 2004	BirdLife Intntl 2006	PIF: All Birds	PIF: Land-bird	Shore-bird Plan	Water-bird Plan	USFWS Cons. Concern	USFWS Threatened & Endangered	Canada Species at Risk
White-cheeked Pintail	Anas bahamensis											
Northern Pintail	Anas acuta											
Garganey	Anas querquedula											
Baikal Teal	Anas formosa											
Green-winged Teal	Anas crecca											
Canvasback	Aythya valisineria											
Redhead	Aythya americana											
Common Pochard	Aythya ferina											
Ring-necked Duck	Aythya collaris											
Tufted Duck	Aythya fuligula											
Greater Scaup	Aythya marila											
Lesser Scaup	Aythya affinis											
Steller's Eider	Polysticta stelleri	Red	hcc			ex h					T	
Spectacled Eider	Somateria fischeri	Red	hcc			ex h					T (AK breeding pop)	
King Eider	Somateria spectabilis											
Common Eider	Somateria mollissima											
Harlequin Duck	Histrionicus histrionicus		rdlp									SC (Eastern population)
Labrador Duck	Camptorhynchus labradorius			EX	EX							EXTINCT
Surf Scoter	Melanitta perspicillata											
White-winged Scoter	Melanitta fusca											
Black Scoter	Melanitta nigra		madht									
Long-tailed Duck	Clangula hyemalis											
Bufflehead	Bucephala albeola											
Common Goldeneye	Bucephala clangula											
Barrow's Goldeneye	Bucephala islandica											SC (Eastern population)
Smew	Mergellus albellus											
Hooded Merganser	Lophodytes cucullatus											
Common Merganser	Mergus merganser											
Red-breasted Merganser	Mergus serrator											

Masked Duck	*Nomonyx dominicus*								USFWS
Ruddy Duck	*Oxyura jamaicensis*								USFWS
Curassows and Guans (Cracidae)									
Plain Chachalaca	*Ortalis vetula*					mod h			
Partridges, Grouse, Turkeys, and Old World Quail (Phasianidae)									
Chukar	*Alectoris chukar*								
Himalayan Snowcock	*Tetraogallus himalayensis*								
Gray Partridge	*Perdix perdix*								
Ring-necked Pheasant	*Phasianus colchicus*								
Ruffed Grouse	*Bonasa umbellus*								
Greater Sage-Grouse	*Centrocercus urophasianus*	Yellow	madht	NT	NT	mod	dht	National	Extrp (*phaios* subspecies), E (*urophasianus* subspecies)
Gunnison Sage-Grouse	*Centrocercus minimus*	Red	hcc	EN	EN	mod	mcc	National	
Spruce Grouse	*Falcipennis canadensis*						adss		
Willow Ptarmigan	*Lagopus lagopus*						adss		
Rock Ptarmigan	*Lagopus muta*						adss		
White-tailed Ptarmigan	*Lagopus leucura*								
Blue Grouse	*Dendragapus obscurus*	Yellow	madht				dht		
Sharp-tailed Grouse	*Tympanuchus phasianellus*						adss		
Greater Prairie-Chicken	*Tympanuchus cupido*	Red	madht	VU	VU	ex h	dht		E (Attwater's)
Lesser Prairie-Chicken	*Tympanuchus pallidicinctus*	Red	hcc	VU	VU	ex h	mcc	National	Extrp
Wild Turkey	*Meleagris gallopavo*								
New World Quail (Odontophoridae)									
Mountain Quail	*Oreortyx pictus*	Yellow	rdlp			mod h	rdlp		
Scaled Quail	*Callipepla squamata*		madht			mod	dht		
California Quail	*Callipepla californica*					mod			
Gambel's Quail	*Callipepla gambelii*						adss		
Northern Bobwhite	*Colinus virginianus*			NT	NT				
Montezuma Quail	*Cyrtonyx montezumae*	Yellow	rdlp			mod h	rdlp		E (Merriam's)
Loons (Gaviidae)									
Red-throated Loon	*Gavia stellata*							BCR	

Species/Family	Scientific Name	Audubon WatchList	ABC Green List	BirdLife Intntl 2004	BirdLife Intntl 2006	PIF: All Birds	PIF: Land-bird	Shore-bird Plan	Water-bird Plan	USFWS Cons. Concern	USFWS Threatened & Endangered	Canada Species at Risk
Arctic Loon	Gavia arctica											
Pacific Loon	Gavia pacifica											
Common Loon	Gavia immer											
Yellow-billed Loon	Gavia adamsii	Red	rdlp							National		
Grebes (Podicipedidae)												
Least Grebe	Tachybaptus dominicus											
Pied-billed Grebe	Podilymbus podiceps											
Horned Grebe	Podiceps auritus		madht									
Red-necked Grebe	Podiceps grisegena											
Eared Grebe	Podiceps nigricollis								Moderate			
Western Grebe	Aechmophorus occidentalis								Moderate			
Clark's Grebe	Aechmophorus clarkii		rdlp						Low			
Albatrosses (Diomedeidae)												
Yellow-nosed Albatross	Thalassarche chlororhynchos			EN	EN							
Shy Albatross	Thalassarche cauta			NT	NT							
Black-browed Albatross	Thalassarche melanophris			EN	EN							
Wandering Albatross	Diomedea exulans			VU	VU							
Laysan Albatross	Phoebastria immutabilis	Yellow	rdlp	VU	VU	mod h			High	BCR		
Black-footed Albatross	Phoebastria nigripes	Red	rdlp	EN	EN	mod h			Imperiled	National		
Short-tailed Albatross	Phoebastria albatrus	Red	hcc	VU	VU	ex h			High		E	T
Shearwaters and Petrels (Procellariidae)												
Northern Fulmar	Fulmarus glacialis								Moderate			
Great-winged Petrel	Pterodroma macroptera											
Herald Petrel	Pterodroma arminjoniana			VU					High	BCR		
Murphy's Petrel	Pterodroma ultima			NT	VU							
Mottled Petrel	Pterodroma inexpectata			NT	NT							
Bermuda Petrel	Pterodroma cahow	Red	hcc	EN	EN	ex h			High			
Black-capped Petrel	Pterodroma hasitata	Red	hcc	EN	EN	ex h			Imperiled	National		
Galapagos/Hawaiian ("Dark-rumped") Petrel	Pterodroma phaeopygia/sandwichensis			CR/VU	CR/VU				Imperiled			

Common Name	Scientific Name			NT/CR	NT/CR				
Fea's/Zino's Petrel	Pterodroma feae/madeira								
Cook's Petrel	Pterodroma cookii			EN	EN				T
Stejneger's Petrel	Pterodroma longirostris			VU	VU				
Bulwer's Petrel	Bulweria bulwerii						Moderate		
Streaked Shearwater	Calonectris leucomelas		rdlp						
Cory's Shearwater	Calonectris diomedea						Moderate		
Cape Verde Shearwater	Calonectris edwardsii			NT	NT				
Pink-footed Shearwater	Puffinus creatopus	Red	hcc	VU	VU		High		
Flesh-footed Shearwater	Puffinus carneipes		rdlp				Low		
Greater Shearwater	Puffinus gravis		madht				High		
Wedge-tailed Shearwater	Puffinus pacificus						Low		
Buller's Shearwater	Puffinus bulleri	Yellow	rdlp	VU	VU				
Sooty Shearwater	Puffinus griseus			NT	NT		Moderate		
Short-tailed Shearwater	Puffinus tenuirostris								
Manx Shearwater	Puffinus puffinus		rdlp				Moderate		
Black-vented Shearwater	Puffinus opisthomelas	Red	rdlp	NT	NT	mod h	High		
Audubon's Shearwater	Puffinus lherminieri		madht				Imperiled	USFWS	
Little Shearwater	Puffinus assimilis								
Storm-Petrels (Hydrobatidae)									
Wilson's Storm-Petrel	Oceanites oceanicus								
White-faced Storm-Petrel	Pelagodroma marina								
Black-bellied Storm-Petrel	Fregetta tropica								
European Storm-Petrel	Hydrobates pelagicus								
Fork-tailed Storm-Petrel	Oceanodroma furcata								
Leach's Storm-Petrel	Oceanodroma leucorhoa	Yellow					Low		
Ashy Storm-Petrel	Oceanodroma homochroa	Red	hcc	EN	EN	mod h	Imperiled	National	
Band-rumped Storm-Petrel	Oceanodroma castro		madht				Imperiled	National	
Wedge-rumped Storm-Petrel	Oceanodroma tethys						Low		
Black Storm-Petrel	Oceanodroma melania	Yellow	rdlp			mod	High		
Least Storm-Petrel	Oceanodroma microsoma		rdlp			ex h	High		
Tropicbirds (Phaethontidae)									
White-tailed Tropicbird	Phaethon lepturus						High	USFWS	
Red-billed Tropicbird	Phaethon aethereus						High	USFWS	
Red-tailed Tropicbird	Phaethon rubricauda						Moderate		
Boobies and Gannets (Sulidae)									

Species/Family	Scientific Name	Audubon WatchList	ABC Green List	BirdLife Intntl 2004	BirdLife Intntl 2006	PIF: All Birds	PIF: Land-bird	Shore-bird Plan	Water-bird Plan	USFWS Cons. Concern	USFWS Threatened & Endangered	Canada Species at Risk
Masked Booby	*Sula dactylatra*								High	USFWS		
Blue-footed Booby	*Sula nebouxii*								High			
Brown Booby	*Sula leucogaster*								High	USFWS		
Red-footed Booby	*Sula sula*								High	USFWS		
Northern Gannet	*Morus bassanus*											
Pelicans (Pelecanidae)												
American White Pelican	*Pelecanus erythrorhynchos*								Moderate	BCR		
Brown Pelican	*Pelecanus occidentalis*								Moderate		E (all US except Atlantic Coast, FL, AL)	
Cormorants (Phalacrocoracidae)												
Brandt's Cormorant	*Phalacrocorax penicillatus*		madht						High			
Neotropic Cormorant	*Phalacrocorax brasilianus*								Moderate			
Double-crested Cormorant	*Phalacrocorax auritus*											
Great Cormorant	*Phalacrocorax carbo*								Moderate			
Red-faced Cormorant	*Phalacrocorax urile*	Red	rdlp						High			
Pelagic Cormorant	*Phalacrocorax pelagicus*		madht						High			
Darters (Anhingidae)												
Anhinga	*Anhinga anhinga*								Moderate			
Frigatebirds (Fregatidae)												
Magnificent Frigatebird	*Fregata magnificens*		rdlp						High			
Great Frigatebird	*Fregata minor*								Moderate			
Lesser Frigatebird	*Fregata ariel*											
Bitterns, Herons, and Allies (Ardeidae)												
American Bittern	*Botaurus lentiginosus*											
Yellow Bittern	*Ixobrychus sinensis*											
Least Bittern	*Ixobrychus exilis*											T
Great Blue Heron	*Ardea herodias*											SC (fannini subspecies)
Great Egret	*Ardea alba*											

Common Name	Scientific Name									
Chinese Egret	*Egretta eulophotes*									
Little Egret	*Egretta garzetta*									
Western Reef-Heron	*Egretta gularis*									
Snowy Egret	*Egretta thula*							High		
Little Blue Heron	*Egretta caerulea*		madht					High	National	
Tricolored Heron	*Egretta tricolor*							High		
Reddish Egret	*Egretta rufescens*	Yellow	rdlp			mod h		Moderate	National	
Cattle Egret	*Bubulcus ibis*									
Chinese Pond-Heron	*Ardeola bacchus*									
Green Heron	*Butorides virescens*							Low		
Black-crowned Night-Heron	*Nycticorax nycticorax*							Moderate		
Yellow-crowned Night-Heron	*Nyctanassa violacea*							Moderate		
Ibises and Spoonbills (Threskiornithidae)										
White Ibis	*Eudocimus albus*							Moderate	BCR	
Scarlet Ibis	*Eudocimus ruber*									
Glossy Ibis	*Plegadis falcinellus*							Low		
White-faced Ibis	*Plegadis chihi*							Low		
Roseate Spoonbill	*Platalea ajaja*							Moderate		
Storks (Ciconiidae)										
Jabiru	*Jabiru mycteria*							High		
Wood Stork	*Mycteria americana*							High		E (AL, FL, GA, SC)
New World Vultures (Cathartidae)										
Black Vulture	*Coragyps atratus*									
Turkey Vulture	*Cathartes aura*									
California Condor	*Gymnogyps californianus*	Red	hcc	CR	CR	ex h	mcc			E
Flamingos (Phoenicopteridae)										
Greater Flamingo	*Phoenicopterus ruber*					mod		Low		
Hawks, Kites, Eagles, and Allies (Accipitridae)										
Osprey	*Pandion haliaetus*									
Hook-billed Kite	*Chondrohierax uncinatus*									
Swallow-tailed Kite	*Elanoides forficatus*		madht			ex h	dht		National	
White-tailed Kite	*Elanus leucurus*									
Snail Kite	*Rostrhamus sociabilis*					ex h		High		E (Everglade)

Species/Family	Scientific Name	Audubon WatchList	ABC Green List	BirdLife Intntl 2004	BirdLife Intntl 2006	PIF: All Birds	PIF: Land-bird	Shore-bird Plan	Water-bird Plan	USFWS Cons. Concern	USFWS Threatened & Endangered	Canada Species at Risk
Mississippi Kite	Ictinia mississippiensis						adss			BCR		
Bald Eagle	Haliaeetus leucocephalus						adss				T	
White-tailed Eagle	Haliaeetus albicilla			NT	NT							
Steller's Sea-Eagle	Haliaeetus pelagicus			VU	VU							
Northern Harrier	Circus cyaneus									National		
Sharp-shinned Hawk	Accipiter striatus											
Cooper's Hawk	Accipiter cooperii											
Northern Goshawk	Accipiter gentilis									BCR		T (laingi subspecies)
Crane Hawk	Geranospiza caerulescens											
Gray Hawk	Buteo nitidus									USFWS		
Common Black-Hawk	Buteogallus anthracinus									USFWS		
Harris's Hawk	Parabuteo unicinctus	Yellow								BCR		
Roadside Hawk	Buteo magnirostris											
Red-shouldered Hawk	Buteo lineatus						adss					SC
Broad-winged Hawk	Buteo platypterus											
Short-tailed Hawk	Buteo brachyurus					ex h				USFWS		
Swainson's Hawk	Buteo swainsoni	Yellow	madht				dht			National		
White-tailed Hawk	Buteo albicaudatus									USFWS		
Zone-tailed Hawk	Buteo albonotatus											
Red-tailed Hawk	Buteo jamaicensis											
Ferruginous Hawk	Buteo regalis	Yellow		NT	NT		adss			National		
Rough-legged Hawk	Buteo lagopus											SC
Golden Eagle	Aquila chrysaetos									USFWS		
Caracaras and Falcons (Falconidae)												
Collared Forest-Falcon	Micrastur semitorquatus											
Crested Caracara	Caracara cheriway										T (Audubon's)	
Eurasian Kestrel	Falco tinnunculus											
American Kestrel	Falco sparverius											
Merlin	Falco columbarius									BCR		
Eurasian Hobby	Falco subbuteo											

Common Name	Scientific Name											
Aplomado Falcon	*Falco femoralis*											
Gyrfalcon	*Falco rusticolus*						ass					
Peregrine Falcon	*Falco peregrinus*						ass			National		T (*anatum* subspecies), SC (*pealei* subspecies, *tundrius* subspecies)
Prairie Falcon	*Falco mexicanus*									National		
Rails, Gallinules, and Coots (Rallidae)												
Yellow Rail	*Coturnicops noveboracensis*	Yellow	hcc			mod h				National		SC
Black Rail	*Laterallus jamaicensis*	Red	hcc	NT	NT					National		
Corn Crake	*Crex crex*			NT	NT	ex h				National		
Clapper Rail	*Rallus longirostris*										E (California, Light-footed, and Yuma)	
King Rail	*Rallus elegans*		hcc									E
Virginia Rail	*Rallus limicola*											
Sora	*Porzana carolina*											
Paint-billed Crake	*Neocrex erythrops*											
Spotted Rail	*Pardirallus maculatus*											
Purple Gallinule	*Porphyrio martinica*											
Common Moorhen	*Gallinula chloropus*											
Eurasian Coot	*Fulica atra*											
American Coot	*Fulica americana*											
Limpkins (Aramidae)												
Limpkin	*Aramus guarauna*									National		
Cranes (Gruidae)												
Sandhill Crane	*Grus canadensis*										E (Mississippi)	
Common Crane	*Grus grus*											
Whooping Crane	*Grus americana*	Red	hcc	EN	EN	ex h					E	E
Thick-knees (Burhinidae)												
Double-striped Thick-knee	*Burhinus bistriatus*											
Lapwings and Plovers (Charadriidae)												
Northern Lapwing	*Vanellus vanellus*											

Species/Family	Scientific Name	Audubon WatchList	ABC Green List	BirdLife Intntl 2004	BirdLife Intntl 2006	PIF: All Birds	PIF: Landbird	Shore-bird Plan	Water-bird Plan	USFWS Cons. Concern	USFWS Threatened & Endangered	Canada Species at Risk
Black-bellied Plover	Pluvialis squatarola							3a				
European Golden-Plover	Pluvialis apricaria											
American Golden-Plover	Pluvialis dominica	Yellow	madht					4a,b		National		
Pacific Golden-Plover	Pluvialis fulva	Yellow	rdllp					4b		National		
Lesser Sand-Plover	Charadrius mongolus											
Greater Sand-Plover	Charadrius leschenaultii											
Collared Plover	Charadrius collaris											
Snowy Plover	Charadrius alexandrinus	Red	hcc			ex h		5a		National	T (Western)	
Wilson's Plover	Charadrius wilsonia	Yellow	rdllp			mod h		4b		National		
Common Ringed Plover	Charadrius hiaticula											
Semipalmated Plover	Charadrius semipalmatus							2a				
Piping Plover	Charadrius melodus	Red	hcc	VU	VU	ex h		5a			E (Great Lakes water-shed in States of IL, IN, MI, MN, NY, OH, PA, and WI and Canada (Ont.)), T everywhere else	E (circumcinctus sub-species, melodus subspecies)
Little Ringed Plover	Charadrius dubius											
Killdeer	Charadrius vociferus							3a				
Mountain Plover	Charadrius montanus	Red	hcc	VU	VU	ex h		5a		National		E
Eurasian Dotterel	Charadrius morinellus											
Oystercatchers (Haematopodidae)												
Eurasian Oystercatcher	Haematopus ostralegus											
American Oystercatcher	Haematopus palliatus	Yellow	rdllp			mod h		4b		National		
Black Oystercatcher	Haematopus bachmani	Yellow	rdllp			mod h		4a,b		National		
Stilts and Avocets (Recurvirostridae)												
Black-winged Stilt	Himantopus himantopus											
Black-necked Stilt	Himantopus mexicanus							2a				
American Avocet	Recurvirostra americana		madht					3b		BCR		
Jacanas (Jacanidae)												

Northern Jacana	*Jacana spinosa*								
Sandpipers, Phalaropes, and Allies (Scolopacidae)									
Common Greenshank	*Tringa nebularia*								
Greater Yellowlegs	*Tringa melanoleuca*						3b	BCR	
Lesser Yellowlegs	*Tringa flavipes*		madht				2a		
Marsh Sandpiper	*Tringa stagnatilis*								
Common Redshank	*Tringa totanus*								
Spotted Redshank	*Tringa erythropus*								
Wood Sandpiper	*Tringa glareola*								
Green Sandpiper	*Tringa ochropus*								
Solitary Sandpiper	*Tringa solitaria*		madht				4b	National	
Willet	*Tringa semipalmata*						3c	BCR	
Wandering Tattler	*Tringa incana*						3b		
Gray-tailed Tattler	*Tringa brevipes*								
Common Sandpiper	*Actitis hypoleucos*								
Spotted Sandpiper	*Actitis macularius*						2a		
Terek Sandpiper	*Xenus cinereus*								
Upland Sandpiper	*Bartramia longicauda*		madht				2b	National	
Little Curlew	*Numenius minutus*								
Eskimo Curlew	*Numenius borealis*	Red	hcc	CR	CR	ex h	5a		E
Whimbrel	*Numenius phaeopus*	Yellow	madht				4a	National	E
Bristle-thighed Curlew	*Numenius tahitiensis*	Red	rdlp	VU	VU	mod	4b	National	
Far Eastern Curlew	*Numenius madagascariensis*					mod	4b	National	
Slender-billed Curlew	*Numenius tenuirostris*			CR	CR				
Eurasian Curlew	*Numenius arquata*								
Long-billed Curlew	*Numenius americanus*	Red	hcc	NT	NT	mod	5a	National	SC
Black-tailed Godwit	*Limosa limosa*			NT	NT				
Hudsonian Godwit	*Limosa haemastica*	Yellow	rdlp			mod h	4b	National	
Bar-tailed Godwit	*Limosa lapponica*	Yellow	rdlp			mod	4b	National	
Marbled Godwit	*Limosa fedoa*	Yellow	madht			mod h	4a,b	National	
Ruddy Turnstone	*Arenaria interpres*						4a,b		
Black Turnstone	*Arenaria melanocephala*	Yellow	rdlp			ex h	4b	National	
Surfbird	*Aphriza virgata*	Yellow	rdlp			mod	4a,b	National	

Species/Family	Scientific Name	Audubon WatchList	ABC Green List	BirdLife Intnl 2004	BirdLife Intnl 2006	PIF: All Birds	PIF: Land-bird	Shore-bird Plan	Water-bird Plan	USFWS Cons. Concern	USFWS Threatened & Endangered	Canada Species at Risk
Great Knot	Calidris tenuirostris											
Red Knot	Calidris canutus	Yellow	rdlp			mod		4a		National		
Sanderling	Calidris alba		madht					4a		BCR		
Semipalmated Sandpiper	Calidris pusilla		madht					3a		USFWS		
Western Sandpiper	Calidris mauri		madht					3b				
Red-necked Stint	Calidris ruficollis											
Little Stint	Calidris minuta											
Temminck's Stint	Calidris temminckii											
Long-toed Stint	Calidris subminuta											
Least Sandpiper	Calidris minutilla							3e				
White-rumped Sandpiper	Calidris fuscicollis							2a		BCR		
Baird's Sandpiper	Calidris bairdii							2a				
Pectoral Sandpiper	Calidris melanotos							2a				
Sharp-tailed Sandpiper	Calidris acuminata											
Purple Sandpiper	Calidris maritima	Yellow						2b		USFWS		
Rock Sandpiper	Calidris ptilocnemis	Yellow				mod		3b		National		
Dunlin	Calidris alpina		madht					3a		USFWS		
Curlew Sandpiper	Calidris ferruginea											
Stilt Sandpiper	Calidris himantopus		madht					3b		National		
Spoon-billed Sandpiper	Eurynorhynchus pygmeus											
Broad-billed Sandpiper	Limicola falcinellus											
Buff-breasted Sandpiper	Tryngites subruficollis	Red	rdlp	NT	NT	mod h		4a,b		National		
Ruff	Philomachus pugnax											
Short-billed Dowitcher	Limnodromus griseus	Yellow	madht			mod		4a		National		
Long-billed Dowitcher	Limnodromus scolopaceus							2b				
Jack Snipe	Lymnocryptes minimus											
Wilson's Snipe	Gallinago delicata		madht					3e				
Common Snipe	Gallinago gallinago											
Pin-tailed Snipe	Gallinago stenura											
Eurasian Woodcock	Scolopax rusticola											
American Woodcock	Scolopax minor	Yellow	madht			mod h		4a				

Common Name	Scientific Name	Yellow	madht		mod h	4a		National
Wilson's Phalarope	*Phalaropus tricolor*							
Red-necked Phalarope	*Phalaropus lobatus*					3a		
Red Phalarope	*Phalaropus fulicarius*		madht			3a		
Pratincoles (Glareolidae)								
Oriental Pratincole	*Glareola maldivarum*							
Skuas, Gulls, Terns, and Skimmers (Laridae)								
Great Skua	*Stercorarius skua*						Moderate	
South Polar Skua	*Stercorarius maccormicki*						Moderate	
Pomarine Jaeger	*Stercorarius pomarinus*						Low	
Parasitic Jaeger	*Stercorarius parasiticus*						Low	
Long-tailed Jaeger	*Stercorarius longicaudus*						Low	
Laughing Gull	*Larus atricilla*							
Franklin's Gull	*Larus pipixcan*						Moderate	
Little Gull	*Larus minutus*						High	
Black-headed Gull	*Larus ridibundus*						Moderate	
Bonaparte's Gull	*Larus philadelphia*						Moderate	
Heermann's Gull	*Larus heermanni*	Red	rdlp	NT	mod		Moderate	
Gray-hooded Gull	*Larus cirrocephalus*			NT				
Belcher's Gull	*Larus belcheri*							
Black-tailed Gull	*Larus crassirostris*							
Mew Gull	*Larus canus*							
Ring-billed Gull	*Larus delawarensis*							
California Gull	*Larus californicus*						Moderate	
Herring Gull	*Larus argentatus*						Low	
Yellow-legged Gull	*Larus cachinnans*							
Thayer's Gull	*Larus thayeri*						Moderate	
Iceland Gull	*Larus glaucoides*						Low	
Lesser Black-backed Gull	*Larus fuscus*						Moderate	
Slaty-backed Gull	*Larus schistisagus*							
Yellow-footed Gull	*Larus livens*	Yellow	rdlp		mod h		Moderate	
Western Gull	*Larus occidentalis*						Low	
Glaucous-winged Gull	*Larus glaucescens*						Low	
Glaucous Gull	*Larus hyperboreus*							
Great Black-backed Gull	*Larus marinus*							

Species/Family	Scientific Name	Audubon WatchList	ABC Green List	BirdLife Intntl 2004	BirdLife Intntl 2006	PIF: All Birds	PIF: Land-bird	Shore-bird Plan	Water-bird Plan	USFWS Cons. Concern	USFWS Threatened & Endangered	Canada Species at Risk
Kelp Gull	*Larus dominicanus*											
Sabine's Gull	*Xema sabini*								Low			
Black-legged Kittiwake	*Rissa tridactyla*											
Red-legged Kittiwake	*Rissa brevirostris*	Red	rdlp	VU	VU				High	National		
Ross's Gull	*Rhodostethia rosea*								High			T
Ivory Gull	*Pagophila eburnea*								Moderate			SC
Gull-billed Tern	*Gelochelidon nilotica*		madht						High	National		
Caspian Tern	*Hydroprogne caspia*			.					Low	BCR		
Royal Tern	*Thalasseus maximus*								Moderate			
Elegant Tern	*Thalasseus elegans*	Red	rdlp	NT	NT				Moderate	USFWS		
Sandwich Tern	*Thalasseus sandvicensis*											
Roseate Tern	*Sterna dougallii*		madht						High		E (U.S.A. (Atlantic Coast south to NC), Canada (Newf., N.S, Que.), Bermuda), T elsewhere (Western Hemisphere and adjacent oceans, incl. U.S.A. (FL, PR, VI)), where not listed as endangered	E
Common Tern	*Sterna hirundo*								Low	National		
Arctic Tern	*Sterna paradisaea*								High	USFWS		
Forster's Tern	*Sterna forsteri*								Moderate			
Least Tern	*Sternula antillarum*		madht						High	National	E (AR, CO, IA, IL, IN, KS, KY, LA_Miss. R. and tribs. N of Baton Rouge,	

Common Name	Scientific Name								MS_Miss. R., MO, MT, ND, NE, NM, OK, SD, TN, TX_except within 50 miles of coast); California Least Tern Endangered everywhere
Aleutian Tern	*Onychoprion aleuticus*		rdlp				High	National	
Bridled Tern	*Onychoprion anaethetus*		rdlp				High		
Sooty Tern	*Onychoprion fuscatus*						Moderate		
Large-billed Tern	*Phaetusa simplex*								
White-winged Tern	*Chlidonias leucopterus*								
Whiskered Tern	*Chlidonias hybrida*								
Black Tern	*Chlidonias niger*						Moderate	USFWS	
Brown Noddy	*Anous stolidus*								
Black Noddy	*Anous minutus*						Moderate		
Black Skimmer	*Rynchops niger*		madht				High	National	
Auks, Murres, and Puffins (Alcidae)									
Dovekie	*Alle alle*						Moderate		
Common Murre	*Uria aalge*						Moderate		
Thick-billed Murre	*Uria lomvia*						Moderate		
Razorbill	*Alca torda*		madht				Moderate	National	
Great Auk	*Pinguinus impennis*				EX	EX			EXTINCT
Black Guillemot	*Cepphus grylle*								.
Pigeon Guillemot	*Cepphus columba*		madht				Moderate		
Long-billed Murrelet	*Brachyramphus perdix*				NT	NT			
Marbled Murrelet	*Brachyramphus marmoratus*	Red	hcc	mod	EN	EN	High	National	T (CA, OR, WA)
Kittlitz's Murrelet	*Brachyramphus brevirostris*	Red	rdlp		CR	CR	High	National	
Xantus's Murrelet	*Synthliboramphus hypoleucus*	Red		mod h	VU	VU	High	National	
Craveri's Murrelet	*Synthliboramphus craveri*	Red	hcc	mod h	VU	VU	High		

Species/Family	Scientific Name	Audubon WatchList	ABC Green List	BirdLife Intntl 2004	BirdLife Intntl 2006	PIF: All Birds	PIF: Land-bird	Shore-bird Plan	Water-bird Plan	USFWS Cons. Concern	USFWS Threatened & Endangered	Canada Species at Risk
Ancient Murrelet	*Synthliboramphus antiquus*		rdlp						High	BCR		SC
Cassin's Auklet	*Ptychoramphus aleuticus*								Moderate	BCR		
Parakeet Auklet	*Aethia psittacula*								Low			
Least Auklet	*Aethia pusilla*								Moderate			
Whiskered Auklet	*Aethia pygmaea*	Yellow	rdlp			mod			Moderate	National		
Crested Auklet	*Aethia cristatella*								Moderate			
Rhinoceros Auklet	*Cerorhinca monocerata*								Low			
Atlantic Puffin	*Fratercula arctica*											
Horned Puffin	*Fratercula corniculata*								Moderate			
Tufted Puffin	*Fratercula cirrhata*								Low			
Pigeons and Doves (Columbidae)												
Rock Pigeon	*Columba livia*											
Scaly-naped Pigeon	*Patagioenas squamosa*											
White-crowned Pigeon	*Patagioenas leucocephala*	Yellow	madht	NT	NT	mod	dht			USFWS		
Red-billed Pigeon	*Patagioenas flavirostris*					mod				USFWS		
Band-tailed Pigeon	*Patagioenas fasciata*	Yellow	madht				dht					
Oriental Turtle-Dove	*Streptopelia orientalis*											
Eurasian Collared-Dove	*Streptopelia decaocto*											
Spotted Dove	*Streptopelia chinensis*											
White-winged Dove	*Zenaida asiatica*											
Zenaida Dove	*Zenaida aurita*											
Mourning Dove	*Zenaida macroura*											
Passenger Pigeon	*Ectopistes migratorius*		EX	EX								EXTINCT
Inca Dove	*Columbina inca*											
Common Ground-Dove	*Columbina passerina*									BCR		
Ruddy Ground-Dove	*Columbina talpacoti*											
White-tipped Dove	*Leptotila verreauxi*											
Key West Quail-Dove	*Geotrygon chrysia*									USFWS		
Ruddy Quail-Dove	*Geotrygon montana*											
Lories, Parakeets, Macaws, and Parrots (Psittacidae)												

Common Name	Scientific Name			EX	EX				
Budgerigar	*Melopsittacus undulatus*								
Monk Parakeet	*Myiopsitta monachus*								
Carolina Parakeet	*Conuropsis carolinensis*								
Green Parakeet	*Aratinga holochlora*	Red				ex h	mcc		
Thick-billed Parrot	*Rhynchopsitta pachyrhyncha*	Red	hcc	EN	EN	ex h	mcc		E
White-winged Parakeet	*Brotogeris versicolurus*								
Yellow-chevroned Parakeet	*Brotogeris chiriri*								
Red-crowned Parrot	*Amazona viridigenalis*	Red		EN	EN	ex h			
Cuckoos, Roadrunners, and Anis (Cuculidae)									
Common Cuckoo	*Cuculus canorus*								
Oriental Cuckoo	*Cuculus optatus*								
Black-billed Cuckoo	*Coccyzus erythropthalmus*							National	
Yellow-billed Cuckoo	*Coccyzus americanus*							National	
Mangrove Cuckoo	*Coccyzus minor*		madht				dht	USFWS	
Greater Roadrunner	*Geococcyx californianus*								
Smooth-billed Ani	*Crotophaga ani*							USFWS	
Groove-billed Ani	*Crotophaga sulcirostris*								
Barn Owls (Tytonidae)									
Barn Owl	*Tyto alba*								E (eastern population), SC (western population)
Typical Owls (Strigidae)									
Flammulated Owl	*Otus flammeolus*	Yellow	rdlp			mod h	rdlp	National	SC
Oriental Scops-Owl	*Otus sunia*								
Western Screech-Owl	*Megascops kennicottii*								E (*macfarlanei* subspecies), SC (*kennicottii* subspecies)
Eastern Screech-Owl	*Megascops asio*								
Whiskered Screech-Owl	*Megascops trichopsis*	Yellow				mod h		USFWS	
Great Horned Owl	*Bubo virginianus*								
Snowy Owl	*Bubo scandiacus*						adss		
Northern Hawk Owl	*Surnia ulula*								

Species/Family	Scientific Name	Audubon WatchList	ABC Green List	BirdLife Intnl 2004	BirdLife Intnl 2006	PIF: All Birds	PIF: Land-bird	Shore-bird Plan	Water-bird Plan	USFWS Cons. Concern	USFWS Threatened & Endangered	Canada Species at Risk
Northern Pygmy-Owl	Glaucidium gnoma											
Ferruginous Pygmy-Owl	Glaucidium brasilianum									USFWS	E (Cactus)	
Elf Owl	Micrathene whitneyi	Yellow	rdlp			mod h	rdlp			USFWS		
Burrowing Owl	Athene cunicularia									National		E
Mottled Owl	Ciccaba virgata											
Spotted Owl	Strix occidentalis	Red	rdlp	NT	NT	ex h	rdlp			BCR	T (Northern and Mexican)	E (caurina subspecies)
Barred Owl	Strix varia											
Great Gray Owl	Strix nebulosa											
Long-eared Owl	Asio otus									BCR		
Stygian Owl	Asio stygius											
Short-eared Owl	Asio flammeus	Yellow	madht			mod	dht			National		SC
Boreal Owl	Aegolius funereus											
Northern Saw-whet Owl	Aegolius acadicus									BCR		
Goatsuckers (Caprimulgidae)												
Lesser Nighthawk	Chordeiles acutipennis											
Common Nighthawk	Chordeiles minor											
Antillean Nighthawk	Chordeiles gundlachii	Yellow	rdlp				rdlp					
Common Pauraque	Nyctidromus albicollis											
Common Poorwill	Phalaenoptilus nuttallii											
Chuck-will's-widow	Caprimulgus carolinensis					mod	adss			National		
Buff-collared Nightjar	Caprimulgus ridgwayi					mod						
Whip-poor-will	Caprimulgus vociferus									National		
Gray Nightjar	Caprimulgus indicus											
Swifts (Apodidae)												
Black Swift	Cypseloides niger	Yellow	rdlp				rdlp			National		
White-collared Swift	Streptoprocne zonaris											
Chimney Swift	Chaetura pelagica											
Vaux's Swift	Chaetura vauxi											
White-throated Needletail	Hirundapus caudacutus											
Common Swift	Apus apus											

Fork-tailed Swift	*Apus pacificus*							
White-throated Swift	*Aeronautes saxatalis*	Yellow	madht				dht	
Antillean Palm-Swift	*Tachornis phoenicobia*							
Hummingbirds (Trochilidae)								
Green Violet-ear	*Colibri thalassinus*							
Green-breasted Mango	*Anthracothorax prevostii*							
Broad-billed Hummingbird	*Cynanthus latirostris*					mod		USFWS
White-eared Hummingbird	*Hylocharis leucotis*					mod		
Xantus's Hummingbird	*Hylocharis xantusii*		hcc					
Berylline Hummingbird	*Amazilia beryllina*							
Buff-bellied Hummingbird	*Amazilia yucatanensis*	Yellow				mod h		USFWS
Cinnamon Hummingbird	*Amazilia rutila*							
Violet-crowned Hummingbird	*Amazilia violiceps*							
Blue-throated Hummingbird	*Lampornis clemenciae*					mod		
Magnificent Hummingbird	*Eugenes fulgens*							
Plain-capped Starthroat	*Heliomaster constantii*							
Bahama Woodstar	*Calliphlox evelynae*							
Lucifer Hummingbird	*Calothorax lucifer*	Yellow				mod h	adss	USFWS
Ruby-throated Hummingbird	*Archilochus colubris*							
Black-chinned Hummingbird	*Archilochus alexandri*							
Anna's Hummingbird	*Calypte anna*							
Costa's Hummingbird	*Calypte costae*	Yellow	rdlp				rdlp	
Calliope Hummingbird	*Stellula calliope*	Yellow	rdlp				rdlp	
Bumblebee Hummingbird	*Atthis heloisa*							
Broad-tailed Hummingbird	*Selasphorus platycercus*							
Rufous Hummingbird	*Selasphorus rufus*	Yellow	madht			mod h	dht	National
Allen's Hummingbird	*Selasphorus sasin*	Yellow	rdlp			mod	rdlp	
Trogons (Trogonidae)								
Elegant Trogon	*Trogon elegans*		madht			mod	dht	USFWS
Eared Quetzal	*Euptilotis neoxenus*			NT	NT	ex h		
Hoopoes (Upupidae)								
Eurasian Hoopoe	*Upupa epops*							
Kingfishers (Alcedinidae)								
Ringed Kingfisher	*Ceryle torquattus*							
Belted Kingfisher	*Ceryle alcyon*							

Species/Family	Scientific Name	Audubon WatchList	ABC Green List	BirdLife Intntl 2004	BirdLife Intntl 2006	PIF: All Birds	PIF: Land-bird	Shore-bird Plan	Water-bird Plan	USFWS Cons. Concern	USFWS Threatened & Endangered	Canada Species at Risk
Green Kingfisher	*Chloroceryle americana*											
Woodpeckers and Allies (Picidae)												
Eurasian Wryneck	*Jynx torquilla*											
Lewis's Woodpecker	*Melanerpes lewis*	Yellow	rdlp			mod h	rdlp			National		SC
Red-headed Woodpecker	*Melanerpes erythrocephalus*	Yellow	madht	NT	NT	mod	dht			National		SC
Acorn Woodpecker	*Melanerpes formicivorus*											
Gila Woodpecker	*Melanerpes uropygialis*									BCR		
Golden-fronted Woodpecker	*Melanerpes aurifrons*											
Red-bellied Woodpecker	*Melanerpes carolinus*						adss					
Williamson's Sapsucker	*Sphyrapicus thyroideus*						adss			National		E
Yellow-bellied Sapsucker	*Sphyrapicus varius*						adss			BCR		
Red-naped Sapsucker	*Sphyrapicus nuchalis*						adss			National		
Red-breasted Sapsucker	*Sphyrapicus ruber*						adss					
Great Spotted Woodpecker	*Dendrocopos major*											
Ladder-backed Woodpecker	*Picoides scalaris*									BCR		
Nuttall's Woodpecker	*Picoides nuttallii*	Red	rdlp				rdlp					
Downy Woodpecker	*Picoides pubescens*											
Hairy Woodpecker	*Picoides villosus*											
Arizona Woodpecker	*Picoides arizonae*	Red	rdlp			ex h	rdlp			USFWS		
Red-cockaded Woodpecker	*Picoides borealis*	Red	hcc	VU	VU	ex h	mcc				E	
White-headed Woodpecker	*Picoides albolarvatus*	Yellow	rdlp			mod h	rdlp			National		E
American Three-toed Woodpecker	*Picoides dorsalis*				LC							
Black-backed Woodpecker	*Picoides arcticus*					.	adss					
Northern Flicker	*Colaptes auratus*											
Gilded Flicker	*Colaptes chrysoides*	Yellow				mod				USFWS		
Pileated Woodpecker	*Dryocopus pileatus*											
Ivory-billed Woodpecker	*Campephilus principalis*	Red	hcc	CR	CR	ex h	mcc				E	
Tyrant Flycatchers (Tyrannidae)												
Northern Beardless-Tyrannulet	*Camptostoma imberbe*									USFWS		
Greenish Elaenia	*Myiopagis viridicata*											
Caribbean Elaenia	*Elaenia martinica*											

Common Name	Scientific Name			NT	NT			National	
Tufted Flycatcher	Mitrephanes phaeocercus								
Olive-sided Flycatcher	Contopus cooperi	Yellow	madht				dht	USFWS	
Greater Pewee	Contopus pertinax					mod h			
Western Wood-Pewee	Contopus sordidulus								
Eastern Wood-Pewee	Contopus virens								
Cuban Pewee	Contopus caribaeus								
Yellow-bellied Flycatcher	Empidonax flaviventris						adss		
Acadian Flycatcher	Empidonax virescens						adss	USFWS	E
Alder Flycatcher	Empidonax alnorum						adss		
Willow Flycatcher	Empidonax traillii	Yellow	madht				dht		E (southwestern)
Least Flycatcher	Empidonax minimus								
Hammond's Flycatcher	Empidonax hammondii								
Gray Flycatcher	Empidonax wrightii						adss		
Dusky Flycatcher	Empidonax oberholseri						adss		
Pacific-slope Flycatcher	Empidonax difficilis						adss		
Cordilleran Flycatcher	Empidonax occidentalis								
Buff-breasted Flycatcher	Empidonax fulvifrons					mod h		USFWS	
Black Phoebe	Sayornis nigricans								
Eastern Phoebe	Sayornis phoebe								
Say's Phoebe	Sayornis saya								
Vermilion Flycatcher	Pyrocephalus rubinus								
Dusky-capped Flycatcher	Myiarchus tuberculifer								
Ash-throated Flycatcher	Myiarchus cinerascens								
Nutting's Flycatcher	Myiarchus nuttingi								
Great Crested Flycatcher	Myiarchus crinitus								
Brown-crested Flycatcher	Myiarchus tyrannulus								
La Sagra's Flycatcher	Myiarchus sagrae								
Great Kiskadee	Pitangus sulphuratus								
Social Flycatcher	Myiozetetes similis								
Sulphur-bellied Flycatcher	Myiodynastes luteiventris								
Piratic Flycatcher	Legatus leucophaius								
Variegated Flycatcher	Empidonomus varius								
Tropical Kingbird	Tyrannus melancholicus								
Couch's Kingbird	Tyrannus couchii								

Species/Family	Scientific Name	Audubon WatchList	ABC Green List	BirdLife Intntl 2004	BirdLife Intntl 2006	PIF: All Birds	PIF: Land-bird	Shore-bird Plan	Water-bird Plan	USFWS Cons. Concern	USFWS Threatened & Endangered	Canada Species at Risk
Cassin's Kingbird	Tyrannus vociferans											
Thick-billed Kingbird	Tyrannus crassirostris	Yellow	rdlp			mod h	rdlp					
Western Kingbird	Tyrannus verticalis											
Eastern Kingbird	Tyrannus tyrannus											
Gray Kingbird	Tyrannus dominicensis					mod						
Scissor-tailed Flycatcher	Tyrannus forficatus									National		
Fork-tailed Flycatcher	Tyrannus savana											
(placement uncertain) ((Incertae sedis))												
Rose-throated Becard	Pachyramphus aglaiae									USFWS		
Masked Tityra	Tityra semifasciata											
Shrikes (Laniidae)												
Brown Shrike	Lanius cristatus											
Loggerhead Shrike	Lanius ludovicianus									National	E (San Clemente)	E (migrans subspecies), T (excubitorides subspecies)
Northern Shrike	Lanius excubitor						adss					
Vireos (Vireonidae)												
White-eyed Vireo	Vireo griseus						adss					
Thick-billed Vireo	Vireo crassirostris											
Bell's Vireo	Vireo bellii	Red	madht	NT	NT	ex h	dht			National	E (Least)	
Black-capped Vireo	Vireo atricapilla	Red	hcc	VU	VU	ex h	mcc				E	
Gray Vireo	Vireo vicinior	Yellow	rdlp			mod	rdlp			National		
Yellow-throated Vireo	Vireo flavifrons					mod	adss					
Plumbeous Vireo	Vireo plumbeus											
Cassin's Vireo	Vireo cassinii											
Blue-headed Vireo	Vireo solitarius						adss					
Hutton's Vireo	Vireo huttoni											
Warbling Vireo	Vireo gilvus											
Philadelphia Vireo	Vireo philadelphicus						adss					
Red-eyed Vireo	Vireo olivaceus											

Common Name	Scientific Name										
Yellow-green Vireo	*Vireo flavoviridis*										
Black-whiskered Vireo	*Vireo altiloquus*										
Yucatan Vireo	*Vireo magister*										
Jays and Crows (Corvidae)											
Gray Jay	*Perisoreus canadensis*						adss				
Steller's Jay	*Cyanocitta stelleri*						adss				
Blue Jay	*Cyanocitta cristata*										
Green Jay	*Cyanocorax yncas*										
Brown Jay	*Cyanocorax morio*										
Florida Scrub-Jay	*Aphelocoma coerulescens*	Red	hcc	VU	VU	ex h	mcc			T	
Island Scrub-Jay	*Aphelocoma insularis*	Red	hcc	NT	NT	ex h	mcc		National		
Western Scrub-Jay	*Aphelocoma californica*						adss				
Mexican Jay	*Aphelocoma ultramarina*										
Pinyon Jay	*Gymnorhinus cyanocephalus*	Yellow	madht	VU	VU		dht	BCR			
Clark's Nutcracker	*Nucifraga columbiana*						adss				
Black-billed Magpie	*Pica hudsonia*										
Yellow-billed Magpie	*Pica nuttalli*	Yellow	rdlp				rdlp				
Eurasian Jackdaw	*Corvus monedula*										
American Crow	*Corvus brachyrhynchos*										
Northwestern Crow	*Corvus caurinus*										
Tamaulipas Crow	*Corvus imparatus*	Yellow									
Fish Crow	*Corvus ossifragus*										
Chihuahuan Raven	*Corvus cryptoleucus*										
Common Raven	*Corvus corax*										
Larks (Alaudidae)											
Sky Lark	*Alauda arvensis*										
Horned Lark	*Eremophila alpestris*								National		E (strigata subspecies)
Swallows (Hirundinidae)											
Purple Martin	*Progne subis*										
Cuban Martin	*Progne cryptoleuca*										
Gray-breasted Martin	*Progne chalybea*										
Southern Martin	*Progne elegans*										
Brown-chested Martin	*Progne tapera*										
Tree Swallow	*Tachycineta bicolor*										

Species/Family	Scientific Name	Audubon WatchList	ABC Green List	BirdLife Intntl 2004	BirdLife Intntl 2006	PIF: All Birds	PIF: Land-bird	Shore-bird Plan	Water-bird Plan	USFWS Cons. Concern	USFWS Threatened & Endangered	Canada Species at Risk
Mangrove Swallow	*Tachycineta albilinea*											
Violet-green Swallow	*Tachycineta thalassina*											
Bahama Swallow	*Tachycineta cyaneoviridis*			VU	VU							
Northern Rough-winged Swallow	*Stelgidopteryx serripennis*											
Bank Swallow	*Riparia riparia*											
Cliff Swallow	*Petrochelidon pyrrhonota*											
Cave Swallow	*Petrochelidon fulva*											
Barn Swallow	*Hirundo rustica*											
Common House-Martin	*Delichon urbicum*											
Chickadees and Titmice (Paridae)												
Carolina Chickadee	*Poecile carolinensis*											
Black-capped Chickadee	*Poecile atricapillus*									BCR		
Mountain Chickadee	*Poecile gambeli*											
Mexican Chickadee	*Poecile sclateri*					mod						
Chestnut-backed Chickadee	*Poecile rufescens*						adss					
Boreal Chickadee	*Poecile hudsonica*						adss					
Gray-headed Chickadee	*Poecile cincta*											
Bridled Titmouse	*Baeolophus wollweberi*					mod						
Oak Titmouse	*Baeolophus inornatus*	Yellow	madht			mod h	dht					
Juniper Titmouse	*Baeolophus ridgwayi*											
Tufted Titmouse	*Baeolophus bicolor*											
Black-crested Titmouse	*Baeolophus atricristatus*						adss					
Verdin (Remizidae)												
Verdin	*Auriparus flaviceps*						adss			BCR		
Bushtits (Aegithalidae)												
Bushtit	*Psaltriparus minimus*											
Nuthatches (Sittidae)												
Red-breasted Nuthatch	*Sitta canadensis*											
White-breasted Nuthatch	*Sitta carolinensis*											
Pygmy Nuthatch	*Sitta pygmaea*									BCR		
Brown-headed Nuthatch	*Sitta pusilla*	Yellow	madht			mod h	dht			National		
Creepers (Certhiidae)												

Common Name	Scientific Name						
Brown Creeper	*Certhia americana*						
Wrens (Troglodytidae)							
Cactus Wren	*Campylorhynchus brunneicapillus*				adss	BCR	
Rock Wren	*Salpinctes obsoletus*						
Canyon Wren	*Catherpes mexicanus*						
Carolina Wren	*Thryothorus ludovicianus*				adss		
Bewick's Wren	*Thryomanes bewickii*					National	
House Wren	*Troglodytes aedon*						
Winter Wren	*Troglodytes troglodytes*				adss		
Sedge Wren	*Cistothorus platensis*					National	
Marsh Wren	*Cistothorus palustris*					BCR	
Dippers (Cinclidae)							
American Dipper	*Cinclus mexicanus*						
Bulbuls (Pycnonotidae)							
Red-whiskered Bulbul	*Pycnonotus jocosus*						
Kinglets (Regulidae)							
Golden-crowned Kinglet	*Regulus satrapa*						
Ruby-crowned Kinglet	*Regulus calendula*						
Old World Warblers and Gnatcatchers (Sylviidae)							
Middendorff's Grasshopper-Warbler	*Locustella ochotensis*						
Lanceolated Warbler	*Locustella lanceolata*						
Willow Warbler	*Phylloscopus trochilus*						
Wood Warbler	*Phylloscopus sibilatrix*						
Dusky Warbler	*Phylloscopus fuscatus*						
Yellow-browed Warbler	*Phylloscopus inornatus*						
Arctic Warbler	*Phylloscopus borealis*					USFWS	
Lesser Whitethroat	*Sylvia curruca*						
Blue-gray Gnatcatcher	*Polioptila caerulea*						
California Gnatcatcher	*Polioptila californica*	Red	rdlp	ex h	rdlp		T (coastal)
Black-tailed Gnatcatcher	*Polioptila melanura*				adss		
Black-capped Gnatcatcher	*Polioptila nigriceps*	Yellow	rdlp	mod h	rdlp		
Old World Flycatchers (Muscicapidae)							
Narcissus Flycatcher	*Ficedula narcissima*						

Species/Family	Scientific Name	Audubon WatchList	ABC Green List	BirdLife Intntl 2004	BirdLife Intntl 2006	PIF: All Birds	PIF: Land-bird	Shore-bird Plan	Water-bird Plan	USFWS Cons. Concern	USFWS Threatened & Endangered	Canada Species at Risk
Mugimaki Flycatcher	*Ficedula mugimaki*											
Red-breasted Flycatcher	*Ficedula parva*											
Dark-sided Flycatcher	*Muscicapa sibirica*											
Gray-streaked Flycatcher	*Muscicapa griseisticta*											
Asian Brown Flycatcher	*Muscicapa dauurica*											
Spotted Flycatcher	*Muscicapa striata*											
Thrushes (Turdidae)												
Siberian Rubythroat	*Luscinia calliope*											
Bluethroat	*Luscinia svecica*											
Siberian Blue Robin	*Luscinia cyane*											
Red-flanked Bluetail	*Tarsiger cyanurus*											
Northern Wheatear	*Oenanthe oenanthe*											
Stonechat	*Saxicola torquatus*											
Eastern Bluebird	*Sialia sialis*											
Western Bluebird	*Sialia mexicana*											
Mountain Bluebird	*Sialia currucoides*						adss					
Townsend's Solitaire	*Myadestes townsendi*											
Orange-billed Nightingale-Thrush	*Catharus aurantiirostris*											
Black-headed Nightingale-Thrush	*Catharus mexicanus*											
Veery	*Catharus fuscescens*											
Gray-cheeked Thrush	*Catharus minimus*											
Bicknell's Thrush	*Catharus bicknelli*	Red	hcc	VU	VU	ex h	mcc			National		SC
Swainson's Thrush	*Catharus ustulatus*											
Hermit Thrush	*Catharus guttatus*											
Wood Thrush	*Hylocichla mustelina*	Yellow	madht			mod h	dht			National		
Eurasian Blackbird	*Turdus merula*											
Eyebrowed Thrush	*Turdus obscurus*											
Dusky Thrush	*Turdus naumanni*											
Fieldfare	*Turdus pilaris*											
Redwing	*Turdus iliacus*											
Clay-colored Robin	*Turdus grayi*											
White-throated Robin	*Turdus assimilis*											

Common Name	Scientific Name							
Rufous-backed Robin	*Turdus rufopalliatus*				mod			
American Robin	*Turdus migratorius*							
Varied Thrush	*Ixoreus naevius*					adss		
Aztec Thrush	*Ridgwayia pinicola*							
Babblers (Timaliidae)								
Wrentit	*Chamaea fasciata*	Yellow	rdlp			rdlp		
Mockingbirds and Thrashers (Mimidae)								
Gray Catbird	*Dumetella carolinensis*							
Northern Mockingbird	*Mimus polyglottos*							
Bahama Mockingbird	*Mimus gundlachii*							
Sage Thrasher	*Oreoscoptes montanus*					adss		E
Brown Thrasher	*Toxostoma rufum*					adss		
Long-billed Thrasher	*Toxostoma longirostre*				ex h			
Bendire's Thrasher	*Toxostoma bendirei*	Red	rdlp	VU	ex h	rdlp	National	
Curve-billed Thrasher	*Toxostoma curvirostre*	Yellow		VU		adss	BCR	
California Thrasher	*Toxostoma redivivum*	Yellow	rdlp		mod h	rdlp		
Crissal Thrasher	*Toxostoma crissale*	Yellow				adss	National	
Le Conte's Thrasher	*Toxostoma lecontei*	Yellow	rdlp		mod h	rdlp	National	
Blue Mockingbird	*Melanotis caerulescens*							
Starlings (Sturnidae)								
European Starling	*Sturnus vulgaris*							
Accentors (Prunellidae)								
Siberian Accentor	*Prunella montanella*							
Wagtails and Pipits (Motacillidae)								
Eastern Yellow Wagtail	*Motacilla tschutschensis*							
Citrine Wagtail	*Motacilla citreola*							
Gray Wagtail	*Motacilla cinerea*							
White Wagtail	*Motacilla alba*							
Tree Pipit	*Anthus trivialis*							
Olive-backed Pipit	*Anthus hodgsoni*							
Pechora Pipit	*Anthus gustavi*							
Red-throated Pipit	*Anthus cervinus*							
American Pipit	*Anthus rubescens*							
Sprague's Pipit	*Anthus spragueii*	Red	madht	VU	mod h	dht	National	T

Species/Family	Scientific Name	Audubon WatchList	ABC Green List	BirdLife Intntl 2004	BirdLife Intntl 2006	PIF: All Birds	PIF: Land-bird	Shore-bird Plan	Water-bird Plan	USFWS Cons. Concern	USFWS Threatened & Endangered	Canada Species at Risk
Waxwings (Bombycillidae)												
Bohemian Waxwing	*Bombycilla garrulus*						adss					
Cedar Waxwing	*Bombycilla cedrorum*											
Silky-flycatchers (Ptilogonatidae)												
Gray Silky-flycatcher	*Ptilogonys cinereus*											
Phainopepla	*Phainopepla nitens*						adss					
Olive Warbler (Peucedramidae)												
Olive Warbler	*Peucedramus taeniatus*					mod h				USFWS		
Wood-Warblers (Parulidae)												
Bachman's Warbler	*Vermivora bachmanii*	Red	hcc	CR	CR	ex h	mcc				E	
Blue-winged Warbler	*Vermivora pinus*	Yellow	rdlp			mod	rdlp			USFWS		
Golden-winged Warbler	*Vermivora chrysoptera*	Red	hcc	NT	NT	ex h	mcc			National		
Tennessee Warbler	*Vermivora peregrina*						adss					
Orange-crowned Warbler	*Vermivora celata*											
Nashville Warbler	*Vermivora ruficapilla*						adss					
Virginia's Warbler	*Vermivora virginiae*	Yellow	rdlp			mod h	rdlp			USFWS		
Colima Warbler	*Vermivora crissalis*	Red	hcc	NT	NT	ex h	mcc			USFWS		
Lucy's Warbler	*Vermivora luciae*	Yellow	rdlp			mod h	rdlp			USFWS		
Crescent-chested Warbler	*Parula superciliosa*									BCR		
Northern Parula	*Parula americana*									BCR		
Tropical Parula	*Parula pitiayumi*									USFWS		
Yellow Warbler	*Dendroica petechia*									USFWS		
Chestnut-sided Warbler	*Dendroica pensylvanica*						adss			BCR		
Magnolia Warbler	*Dendroica magnolia*						adss					
Cape May Warbler	*Dendroica tigrina*						adss			USFWS		
Black-throated Blue Warbler	*Dendroica caerulescens*					mod h				USFWS		
Yellow-rumped Warbler	*Dendroica coronata*											
Black-throated Gray Warbler	*Dendroica nigrescens*						adss			USFWS		
Golden-cheeked Warbler	*Dendroica chrysoparia*	Red	hcc	EN	EN	ex h	mcc			USFWS	E	
Black-throated Green Warbler	*Dendroica virens*						adss			BCR		
Townsend's Warbler	*Dendroica townsendi*											
Hermit Warbler	*Dendroica occidentalis*	Yellow	rdlp			mod h	rdlp					

Common Name	Scientific Name								
Blackburnian Warbler	Dendroica fusca					adss			
Yellow-throated Warbler	Dendroica dominica					adss	BCR		
Grace's Warbler	Dendroica graciae	Yellow	madht			dht	National		
Pine Warbler	Dendroica pinus					adss			
Kirtland's Warbler	Dendroica kirtlandii	Red	hcc	VU	ex h	mcc		E	E
Prairie Warbler	Dendroica discolor	Yellow	madht		mod	dht	National		
Palm Warbler	Dendroica palmarum					adss			
Bay-breasted Warbler	Dendroica castanea	Yellow	madht		mod	dht	USFWS		
Blackpoll Warbler	Dendroica striata						USFWS		
Cerulean Warbler	Dendroica cerulea	Red	madht	VU	ex h	dht	National		SC
Black-and-white Warbler	Mniotilta varia								
American Redstart	Setophaga ruticilla								
Prothonotary Warbler	Protonotaria citrea	Yellow	madht		mod h	dht	National	E	
Worm-eating Warbler	Helmitheros vermivorum	Yellow	madht		mod h	dht	National		
Swainson's Warbler	Limnothlypis swainsonii	Red	rdlp		ex h	rdlp	National		
Ovenbird	Seiurus aurocapilla								
Northern Waterthrush	Seiurus noveboracensis						USFWS		
Louisiana Waterthrush	Seiurus motacilla					adss	USFWS		SC
Kentucky Warbler	Oporornis formosus	Yellow	madht		mod	dht	National		
Connecticut Warbler	Oporornis agilis					adss	USFWS		
Mourning Warbler	Oporornis philadelphia					adss			
MacGillivray's Warbler	Oporornis tolmiei								
Common Yellowthroat	Geothlypis trichas						BCR		
Gray-crowned Yellowthroat	Geothlypis poliocephala								
Hooded Warbler	Wilsonia citrina					adss			T
Wilson's Warbler	Wilsonia pusilla								
Canada Warbler	Wilsonia canadensis	Yellow	madht			dht	National		
Red-faced Warbler	Cardellina rubrifrons	Yellow	rdlp		mod h	rdlp	USFWS		
Painted Redstart	Myioborus pictus								
Slate-throated Redstart	Myioborus miniatus								
Fan-tailed Warbler	Euthlypis lachrymosa								
Golden-crowned Warbler	Basileuterus culicivorus								
Rufous-capped Warbler	Basileuterus rufifrons								

Species/Family	Scientific Name	Audubon WatchList	ABC Green List	BirdLife Intntl 2004	BirdLife Intntl 2006	PIF: All Birds	PIF: Land-bird	Shore-bird Plan	Water-bird Plan	USFWS Cons. Concern	USFWS Threatened & Endangered	Canada Species at Risk
Yellow-breasted Chat	*Icteria virens*											E (*auricollis* subspecies/ British Columbia population), SC (*virens* subspecies)
Bananaquits (Coerebidae)												
Bananaquit	*Coereba flaveola*											
Tanagers (Thraupidae)												
Hepatic Tanager	*Piranga flava*											
Summer Tanager	*Piranga rubra*											
Scarlet Tanager	*Piranga olivacea*											
Western Tanager	*Piranga ludoviciana*											
Flame-colored Tanager	*Piranga bidentata*											
Western Spindalis	*Spindalis zena*											
Emberizids (Emberizidae)												
White-collared Seedeater	*Sporophila torqueola*											
Yellow-faced Grassquit	*Tiaris olivaceus*											
Black-faced Grassquit	*Tiaris bicolor*											
Olive Sparrow	*Arremonops rufivirgatus*					mod						
Green-tailed Towhee	*Pipilo chlorurus*					mod h	adss					
Spotted Towhee	*Pipilo maculatus*					ex h	rdlp			BCR		
Eastern Towhee	*Pipilo erythrophthalmus*			NT		mod	adss					
Canyon Towhee	*Pipilo fuscus*		hcc		NT	ex h	adss					
California Towhee	*Pipilo crissalis*					mod	adss				T (Inyo)	
Abert's Towhee	*Pipilo aberti*	Yellow	rdlp			mod h	rdlp					
Rufous-winged Sparrow	*Aimophila carpalis*	Red	rdlp			ex h	rdlp			National		
Cassin's Sparrow	*Aimophila cassinii*					mod	adss			National		
Bachman's Sparrow	*Aimophila aestivalis*	Red	hcc	NT		ex h	mcc			National		
Botteri's Sparrow	*Aimophila botterii*	Yellow				mod				USFWS		
Rufous-crowned Sparrow	*Aimophila ruficeps*									BCR		
Five-striped Sparrow	*Aimophila quinquestriata*	Red	rdlp		.	ex h	rdlp					

Common Name	Scientific Name									
American Tree Sparrow	*Spizella arborea*						adss			
Chipping Sparrow	*Spizella passerina*									
Clay-colored Sparrow	*Spizella pallida*									
Brewer's Sparrow	*Spizella breweri*	Yellow	madht	NT	NT	mod	dht	National		
Field Sparrow	*Spizella pusilla*			EN	EN			BCR		
Worthen's Sparrow	*Spizella wortheni*									
Black-chinned Sparrow	*Spizella atrogularis*	Yellow	rdlp			mod h	rdlp	National		
Vesper Sparrow	*Pooecetes gramineus*							BCR		
Lark Sparrow	*Chondestes grammacus*									
Black-throated Sparrow	*Amphispiza bilineata*						adss			
Sage Sparrow	*Amphispiza belli*					mod	adss	USFWS	T (San Clemente)	
Lark Bunting	*Calamospiza melanocorys*					mod	adss	USFWS		
Savannah Sparrow	*Passerculus sandwichensis*						adss	National	E (Florida)	SC (*princeps* subspecies)
Grasshopper Sparrow	*Ammodramus savannarum*						adss	National		
Baird's Sparrow	*Ammodramus bairdii*	Red	madht			ex h	dht	National		
Henslow's Sparrow	*Ammodramus henslowii*	Red	hcc	NT	NT	ex h	mcc	National		E
Le Conte's Sparrow	*Ammodramus leconteii*							National		
Nelson's Sharp-tailed Sparrow	*Ammodramus nelsoni*	Red	rdlp			ex h	rdlp	National		
Saltmarsh Sharp-tailed Sparrow	*Ammodramus caudacutus*	Red	hcc	VU	VU	ex h	mcc	National		
Seaside Sparrow	*Ammodramus maritimus*	Yellow	rdlp			mod h	rdlp	National	E (Cape Sable)	
Fox Sparrow	*Passerella iliaca*						adss			
Song Sparrow	*Melospiza melodia*							BCR		
Lincoln's Sparrow	*Melospiza lincolnii*						adss			
Swamp Sparrow	*Melospiza georgiana*						adss			
White-throated Sparrow	*Zonotrichia albicollis*						adss			
Harris's Sparrow	*Zonotrichia querula*	Yellow	madht			mod h	dht	National		
White-crowned Sparrow	*Zonotrichia leucophrys*									
Golden-crowned Sparrow	*Zonotrichia atricapilla*						adss			
Dark-eyed Junco	*Junco hyemalis*									
Yellow-eyed Junco	*Junco phaeonotus*									
McCown's Longspur	*Calcarius mccownii*	Red	rdlp			ex h	rdlp	National		

Species/Family	Scientific Name	Audubon WatchList	ABC Green List	BirdLife Intntl 2004	BirdLife Intntl 2006	PIF: All Birds	PIF: Land-bird	Shore-bird Plan	Water-bird Plan	USFWS Cons. Concern	USFWS Threatened & Endangered	Canada Species at Risk
Lapland Longspur	Calcarius lapponicus						adss					
Smith's Longspur	Calcarius pictus		rdlp			ex h	rdlp			National		
Chestnut-collared Longspur	Calcarius ornatus			NT	NT	mod	adss			National		
Pine Bunting	Emberiza leucocephalos											
Little Bunting	Emberiza pusilla											
Rustic Bunting	Emberiza rustica											
Yellow-throated Bunting	Emberiza elegans											
Yellow-breasted Bunting	Emberiza aureola											
Gray Bunting	Emberiza variabilis											
Pallas's Bunting	Emberiza pallasi											
Reed Bunting	Emberiza schoeniclus											
Snow Bunting	Plectrophenax nivalis						adss					
McKay's Bunting	Plectrophenax hyperboreus	Red	rdlp	NT	NT	mod h	rdlp			National		
Cardinals, Saltators, and Allies (Cardinalidae)												
Crimson-collared Grosbeak	Rhodothraupis celaeno											
Northern Cardinal	Cardinalis cardinalis											
Pyrrhuloxia	Cardinalis sinuatus					adss	adss			BCR		
Yellow Grosbeak	Pheucticus chrysopeplus											
Rose-breasted Grosbeak	Pheucticus ludovicianus											
Black-headed Grosbeak	Pheucticus melanocephalus											
Blue Bunting	Cyanocompsa parellina											
Blue Grosbeak	Passerina caerulea											
Lazuli Bunting	Passerina amoena											
Indigo Bunting	Passerina cyanea						adss					
Varied Bunting	Passerina versicolor		madht			mod	dht			USFWS		
Painted Bunting	Passerina ciris	Yellow	madht	NT	NT	mod h	dht			National		
Dickcissel	Spiza americana	Yellow	madht			mod h	dht			National		
Blackbirds (Icteridae)												
Bobolink	Dolichonyx oryzivorus					mod				USFWS		
Red-winged Blackbird	Agelaius phoeniceus											

Common Name	Scientific Name	Color	hcc		EN	h	mcc			National		
Tricolored Blackbird	*Agelaius tricolor*	Yellow										
Tawny-shouldered Blackbird	*Agelaius humeralis*											
Eastern Meadowlark	*Sturnella magna*											
Western Meadowlark	*Sturnella neglecta*											
Yellow-headed Blackbird	*Xanthocephalus xanthocephalus*						adss					
Rusty Blackbird	*Euphagus carolinus*	Yellow	madht				dht			USFWS		
Brewer's Blackbird	*Euphagus cyanocephalus*											
Common Grackle	*Quiscalus quiscula*											
Boat-tailed Grackle	*Quiscalus major*											
Great-tailed Grackle	*Quiscalus mexicanus*											
Shiny Cowbird	*Molothrus bonariensis*											
Bronzed Cowbird	*Molothrus aeneus*											
Brown-headed Cowbird	*Molothrus ater*											
Black-vented Oriole	*Icterus wagleri*											
Orchard Oriole	*Icterus spurius*										BCR		
Hooded Oriole	*Icterus cucullatus*										USFWS		
Streak-backed Oriole	*Icterus pustulatus*											
Bullock's Oriole	*Icterus bullockii*											
Spot-breasted Oriole	*Icterus pectoralis*											
Altamira Oriole	*Icterus gularis*					mod h					USFWS		
Audubon's Oriole	*Icterus graduacauda*	Red	rdlp			ex h	rdlp			USFWS		
Baltimore Oriole	*Icterus galbula*										BCR		
Scott's Oriole	*Icterus parisorum*						adss					
Fringilline and Cardueline Finches and Allies (Fringillidae)											
Common Chaffinch	*Fringilla coelebs*											
Brambling	*Fringilla montifringilla*											
Gray-crowned Rosy-Finch	*Leucosticte tephrocotis*											
Black Rosy-Finch	*Leucosticte atrata*	Yellow	rdlp				rdlp					
Brown-capped Rosy-Finch	*Leucosticte australis*	Red	rdlp				rdlp					
Pine Grosbeak	*Pinicola enucleator*						adss					
Common Rosefinch	*Carpodacus erythrinus*											
Purple Finch	*Carpodacus purpureus*											
Cassin's Finch	*Carpodacus cassinii*			NT	NT							
House Finch	*Carpodacus mexicanus*						adss					

Species/Family	Scientific Name	Audubon WatchList	ABC Green List	BirdLife Intntl 2004	BirdLife Intntl 2006	PIF: All Birds	PIF: Land-bird	Shore-bird Plan	Water-bird Plan	USFWS Cons. Concern	USFWS Threatened & Endangered	Canada Species at Risk
Red Crossbill	Loxia curvirostra									BCR		E (perna subspecies)
White-winged Crossbill	Loxia leucoptera						adss					
Common Redpoll	Carduelis flammea											
Hoary Redpoll	Carduelis hornemanni						adss					
Eurasian Siskin	Carduelis spinus											
Pine Siskin	Carduelis pinus											
Lesser Goldfinch	Carduelis psaltria											
Lawrence's Goldfinch	Carduelis lawrencei	Red	rdlp			ex h	rdlp			National		
American Goldfinch	Carduelis tristis											
Oriental Greenfinch	Carduelis sinica											
Eurasian Bullfinch	Pyrrhula pyrrhula											
Evening Grosbeak	Coccothraustes vespertinus											
Hawfinch	Coccothraustes coccothraustes											
Old World Sparrows (Passeridae)												
House Sparrow	Passer domesticus											
Eurasian Tree Sparrow	Passer montanus											

Appendix II
Hawaiian Birds of Conservation Concern and Extinct Species

Key

USFWS-Endangered: Officially listed by the U.S. Fish and Wildlife Service as Endangered under the Endangered Species Act.

USFWS-Threatened: Officially listed by the U.S. Fish and Wildlife Service as Threatened under the Endangered Species Act.

IUCN Red List-Critical: Listed by the International Union for the Conservation of Nature (IUCN) and BirdLife International as a species meeting criteria for being in critical danger of extinction.

IUCN Red List-Vulnerable: Listed by the International Union for the Conservation of Nature (IUCN) and BirdLife International as a species meeting criteria that make it vulnerable to extinction.

IUCN Red List-Near Threatened: Listed by the International Union for the Conservation of Nature (IUCN) and BirdLife International as a species nearly meeting criteria that make it vulnerable to extinction.

NAWCP-High Concern: Listed by the North American Waterbird Conservation Plan as a species of High Conservation Concern.

USSCP-High Concern: Listed by the U.S. Shorebird Conservation Plan as a species of High Conservation Concern.

Hawaiian Birds and Extinct Species

Common Name	Scientific Name	Occurrence	Status	Population Size
Hawaiian Goose (Nene)	Branta sandvicensis	Hawaiian Islands	USFWS-Endangered	960–1,000
Hawaiian Duck	Anas wyvilliana	Hawaiian Islands	USFWS-Endangered	2,500
Laysan Duck	Anas laysanensis	Laysan	USFWS-Endangered	375
Laysan Albatross	Phoebastria immutabilis	Northwestern Hawaiian Islands	NAWCP-High Concern	1,100,000
Black-footed Albatross	Phoebastria nigripes	Northwestern Hawaiian Islands	IUCN Red List-Vulnerable	148,000
Hawaiian Petrel	Pterodroma sandwichensis	Hawaiian Islands	USFWS-Endangered	2,000
Christmas Shearwater	Puffinus nativitatis	Northwestern Hawaiian Islands	NAWCP-High Concern	5,000–6,600
Newell's (Townsend's) Shearwater	Puffinus (auricularis) newelli	Hawaiian Islands	USFWS-Threatened	29,200
Tristham's Storm-Petrel	Oceanodroma tristami	Northwestern Hawaiian Islands	IUCN Red List-Near Threatened	<10,000
Hawaiian Hawk	Buteo solitarius	Hawaii	USFWS-Endangered	1,600–2,700
Laysan Rail	Porzana palmeri	Laysan	Extinct	0
Hawaiian Rail	Porzana sandwichensis	Hawaii	Extinct	0
Hawaiian Moorhen	Gallinula chloropus sandvicensis	Hawaiian Islands	USFWS-Endangered	<1,000
Hawaiian Coot	Fulica alai	Hawaiian Islands	USFWS-Endangered	2,000–4,000
Pacific Golden-Plover	Pluvialis fulva	Hawaiian Islands	USSCP-High Concern	16,000
Hawaiian Black-necked Stilt	Himantopus mexicanus knudseni	Hawaiian Islands	USFWS-Endangered	1,200–1,600
Bristle-thinged Curlew	Numenius tahitiensis	Northwestern Hawaiian Islands	USSCP-High Concern	10,000
Blue-gray Noddy	Procelsterna cerulea	Hawaiian Islands	NAWCP-High Concern	Unknown
Kauai Oo	Moho braccatus	Kauai	Extinct	0
Oahu Oo	Moho apicalis	Oahu	Extinct	0
Bishop's Oo	Moho bishopi	Molokai	Extinct	0
Hawaii Oo	Moho nobilis	Hawaii	Extinct	0
Kioea	Chaetoptila angustipluma	Hawaii	Extinct	0
Hawaiian Crow	Corvus hawaiiensis	Hawaii	USFWS-Endangered	50–60 in captivity
Elepaio	Chasiempis sandwichensis	Hawaiian Islands	IUCN Red List-Vulnerable	237,000
Millerbird	Acrocephalus familiaris	Nihoa	USFWS-Endangered	31–731
Kamao	Myadestes myadestinus	Kauai	Extinct	0
Amaui	Myadestes oahensis	Oahu	Extinct	0
Olomao	Myadestes lanaiensis	Maui, Lanai, Molokai	Extinct	0
Omao	Myadestes obscurus	Hawaii	IUCN Red List-Vulnerable	170,000
Puaiohi	Myadestes palmeri	Kauai	USFWS-Endangered	200–300
Laysan Finch	Telespiza cantans	Laysan	USFWS-Endangered	5,000–20,000
Nihoa Finch	Telespiza ultima	Nihoa	USFWS-Endangered	946–6,686
Ou	Psittirostra psittacea	Hawaiian Islands	Extinct	0
Lanai Hookbill	Dysmorodrepanis munroi	Lanai	Extinct	0
Palila	Loxioides bailleui	Hawaii	USFWS-Endangered	1,584–5,685
Lesser Koa-Finch	Rhodacanthis flaviceps	Hawaii	Extinct	0
Greater Koa-Finch	Rhodacanthis palmeri	Hawaii	Extinct	0
Kona Grosbeak	Chloridops kona	Hawaii	Extinct	0
Maui Parrotbill	Pseudonestor xanthophrys	Maui	USFWS-Endangered	500
Hawaii Amakihi	Hemignathus virens	Hawaii	Apparently secure	>800,000
Oahu Amakihi	Hemignathus flavus	Oahu	IUCN Red List-Vulnerable	20,000–60,000
Kauai Amakihi	Hemignathus kauaiensis	Kauai	IUCN Red List-Vulnerable	15,000–20,000
Anianiau	Hemignathus parvus	Kauai	IUCN Red List-Vulnerable	15,000–20,000
Greater Amakihi	Hemignathus sagittirostris	Hawaii	Extinct	0
Lesser Akialoa	Hemignathus obscurus	Hawaiian Islands	Extinct	0
Greater Akialoa	Hemignathus ellisianus	Kauai, Oahu, Lanai	Extinct	0
Nukupuu	Hemignathus lucidus	Hawaiian Islands	Extinct	0
Akiapolaau	Hemignathus munroi	Hawaii	USFWS-Endangered	1,163

Hawaiian Birds and Extinct Species (*cont.*)

Common Name	Scientific Name	Occurrence	Status	Population Size
Akikiki	*Oreomystis bairdi*	Kauai	IUCN Red List-Critical	800–1000
Hawaii Creeper	*Oreomystis mana*	Hawaii	USFWS-Endangered	2,500–10,000
Oahu Alauahio	*Paroreomyza maculata*	Oahu	Extinct	0
Kakawahie	*Paroreomyza flammea*	Molokai	Extinct	0
Maui Alauahio	*Paroreomyza montana*	Maui, Lanai	IUCN Red List-Vulnerable	35,000
Akekee	*Loxops caeruleirostris*	Kauai	USFWS-Endangered	5,066
Akepa	*Loxops coccineus*	Hawaiian Islands	USFWS-Endangered	14,000
Ula-ai-hawane	*Ciridops anna*	Hawaii	Extinct	0
Iiwi	*Vestiaria coccinea*	Hawaiian Islands	IUCN Red List-Near Threatened	350,000
Hawaii Mamo	*Drepanis pacifica*	Hawaii	Extinct	0
Black Mamo	*Drepanis funerea*	Molokai	Extinct	0
Akohekohe	*Palmeria dolei*	Maui, Molokai	IUCN Red List-Vulnerable	3,800
Apapane	*Himatione sanguinea*	Hawaiian Islands	Apparently secure	1,300,000
Poo-uli	*Melamprosops phaeosoma*	Maui	Extinct	0

Appendix III
Mexican Government Official List of Endangered, Threatened, and Special Concern Bird Species

Key

Extirpated: This species has disappeared from the wild in Mexico.

Endangered: In danger of extinction. The range or population size of this species has decreased dramatically, due to habitat destruction and degradation, unsustainable use, disease, or predation, among other causes.

Threatened: This species is in danger of disappearing in the short or medium term if the factors affecting its viability continue, such as habitat degradation or direct loss of population size.

Special Concern: This species could become threatened and there is a need to bring about its recovery and conservation.

Mexican Government Official List of Endangered, Threatened, and Special Concern Bird Species

English Common Name	Scientific Name	Subspecies	Mexican Common Name	Category
Great Tinamou	*Tinamus major*		tinamú mayor	Special Concern
Little Tinamou	*Crypturellus soui*		tinamú menor	Special Concern
Slaty-breasted Tinamou	*Crypturellus boucardi*		tinamú jamuey	Special Concern
Least Grebe	*Tachybaptus dominicus*		zambullidor menor	Special Concern
Laysan Albatross	*Phoebastria immutabilis*		albatros de Laysan	Threatened
Black-footed Albatross	*Phoebastria nigripes*		albatros pata negra	Threatened
Townsend's Shearwater	*Puffinus auricularis*	auricularis	pardela de Revillagigedo	Endangered
Black-vented Shearwater	*Puffinus opisthomelas*		pardela mexicana	Endangered
Leach's Storm-Petrel	*Oceanodroma leucorhoa*	willetti	paíño de Leach de Coronados	Endangered
Leach's Storm-Petrel	*Oceanodroma leucorhoa*	chapmani	paíño de Leach de San Benito	Threatened
Leach's Storm-Petrel	*Oceanodroma leucorhoa*	socorrensis	paíño de Leach de Socorro	Endangered
Ashy Storm-Petrel	*Oceanodroma homochroa*		paíño cenizo	Threatened
Black Storm-Petrel	*Oceanodroma melania*		paíño negro	Threatened
Guadalupe Storm-Petrel	*Oceanodroma macrodactyla*		paíño de Guadalupe	Extirpated
Least Storm-Petrel	*Oceanodroma microsoma*		paíño mínimo	Threatened
Red-billed Tropicbird	*Phaethon aethereus*		rabijunco pico rojo	Threatened
American Bittern	*Botaurus lentiginosus*		avetoro del Eje Neovolcánico	Threatened
Bare-throated Tiger-Heron	*Tigrisoma mexicanum*		garza-tigre mexicana	Special Concern
Great Blue Heron	*Ardea herodias*	santilucae	garza morena	Special Concern
Reddish Egret	*Egretta rufescens*		garceta rojiza	Special Concern
Agami Heron	*Agamia agami*		garza agami	Special Concern
Yellow-crowned Night-Heron	*Nyctanassa violacea*	gravirostris	pedrete corona clara de Socorro	Threatened
Jabiru	*Jabiru mycteria*		cigüeña jabirú	Endangered
Wood Stork	*Mycteria americana*		cigüeña americana	Special Concern
California Condor	*Gymnogyps californianus*		cóndor californiano	Extirpated
King Vulture	*Sarcoramphus papa*		zopilote rey	Endangered
Greater Flamingo	*Phoenicopterus ruber*		flamenco americano	Threatened
Brant	*Branta bernicla*	nigricans	ganso de collar	Threatened
Trumpeter Swan	*Cygnus buccinator*		cisne trompetero	Extirpated
Tundra Swan	*Cygnus columbianus*		cisne de tundra	Endangered
Muscovy Duck	*Cairina moschata*		pato real	Endangered
Mallard	*Anas platyrhynchos*	diazi	pato mexicano	Threatened
Mottled Duck	*Anas fulvigula*		pato tejano	Threatened
Masked Duck	*Nomonyx dominicus*		pato enmascarado	Threatened
Gray-headed Kite	*Leptodon cayanensis*		gavilán cabeza gris	Special Concern
Hook-billed Kite	*Chondrohierax uncinatus*		gavilán pico gancho	Special Concern
Swallow-tailed Kite	*Elanoides forficatus*		milano tijereta	Special Concern
Snail Kite	*Rostrhamus sociabilis*		gavilán caracolero	Special Concern
Double-toothed Kite	*Harpagus bidentatus*		gavilán bidentado	Special Concern
Mississippi Kite	*Ictinia mississippiensis*		milano de Mississipi	Special Concern
Plumbeous Kite	*Ictinia plumbea*		milano plomizo	Threatened
Bald Eagle	*Haliaeetus leucocephalus*		águila cabeza blanca	Endangered
Black-collared Hawk	*Busarellus nigricollis*		aguililla canela	Special Concern
Sharp-shinned Hawk	*Accipiter striatus*		gavilán pecho rufo	Special Concern
Cooper's Hawk	*Accipiter cooperii*		gavilán de Cooper	Special Concern
Bicolored Hawk	*Accipiter bicolor*		gavilán bicolor	Threatened
Northern Goshawk	*Accipiter gentilis*		gavilán azor	Threatened
Crane Hawk	*Geranospiza caerulescens*		gavilán zancón	Threatened
White Hawk	*Leucopternis albicollis*		aguililla blanca	Special Concern
Common Black-Hawk	*Buteogallus anthracinus*		aguililla-negra menor	Special Concern
Mangrove Black-Hawk	*Buteogallus subtilis*		aguililla-negra de manglar	Threatened
Great Black-Hawk	*Buteogallus urubitinga*		aguililla-negra mayor	Special Concern
Harris's Hawk	*Parabuteo unicinctus*		aguililla rojinegra	Special Concern
Solitary Eagle	*Harpyhaliaetus solitarius*		águila solitaria	Endangered
Red-shouldered Hawk	*Buteo lineatus*		aguililla pecho rojo	Special Concern
Broad-winged Hawk	*Buteo platypterus*		aguililla ala ancha	Special Concern
Swainson's Hawk	*Buteo swainsoni*		aguililla de Swainson	Special Concern
White-tailed Hawk	*Buteo albicaudatus*		aguililla cola blanca	Special Concern
Zone-tailed Hawk	*Buteo albonotatus*		aguililla aura	Special Concern

English Common Name	Scientific Name	Subspecies	Mexican Common Name	Category
Red-tailed Hawk	*Buteo jamaicensis*	fumosus	aguililla cola roja de Tres Marías	Special Concern
Red-tailed Hawk	*Buteo jamaicensis*	socorroensis	aguililla cola roja de Socorro	Endangered
Ferruginous Hawk	*Buteo regalis*		aguililla real	Special Concern
Rough-legged Hawk	*Buteo lagopus*		aguililla ártica	Special Concern
Crested Eagle	*Morphnus guianensis*		águila crestada	Endangered
Harpy Eagle	*Harpia harpyja*		águila arpía	Endangered
Golden Eagle	*Aquila chrysaetos*		águila real	Threatened
Black-and-white Hawk-Eagle	*Spizastur melanoleucus*		águila blanquinegra	Endangered
Black Hawk-Eagle	*Spizaetus tyrannus*		águila tirana	Endangered
Ornate Hawk-Eagle	*Spizaetus ornatus*		águila elegante	Endangered
Barred Forest-Falcon	*Micrastur ruficollis*		halcón-selvático barrado	Special Concern
Collared Forest-Falcon	*Micrastur semitorquatus*		halcón-selvático de collar	Special Concern
Red-throated Caracara	*Ibycter americanus*		caracara comecacao	Extirpated
Crested Caracara	*Caracara cheriway*	lutosus	caracara quebranta-huesos de Guadalupe	Extirpated
Aplomado Falcon	*Falco femoralis*		halcón fajado	Threatened
Aplomado Falcon	*Falco femoralis*	septentrionalis	halcón fajado	Special Concern
Orange-breasted Falcon	*Falco deiroleucus*		halcón pecho rufo	Endangered
Peregrine Falcon	*Falco peregrinus*		halcón peregrino	Special Concern
Prairie Falcon	*Falco mexicanus*		halcón mexicano	Threatened
White-bellied Chachalaca	*Ortalis leucogastra*		chachalaca vientre blanco	Special Concern
Crested Guan	*Penelope purpurascens*		pava cojolita	Threatened
Highland Guan	*Penelopina nigra*		pajuil	Threatened
Horned Guan	*Oreophasis derbianus*		pavón o guan cornudo	Endangered
Great Curassow	*Crax rubra*		hocofaisán	Threatened
Great Curassow	*Crax rubra*	griscomi	hocofaisán	Endangered
Wild Turkey	*Meleagris gallopavo*		guajolote norteño	Special Concern
Ocellated Turkey	*Meleagris ocellata*		guajolote ocelado	Threatened
Bearded Wood-Partridge	*Dendrortyx barbatus*		codorniz-coluda veracruzana	Endangered
Long-tailed Wood-Partridge	*Dendrortyx macroura*		codorniz-coluda neovolcánica	Special Concern
Buffy-crowned Wood-Partridge	*Dendrortyx leucophrys*		codorniz-coluda centroamericana	Threatened
Northern Bobwhite	*Colinus virginianus*	ridgwayi	codorniz cotuí	Endangered
Spotted Wood-Quail	*Odontophorus guttatus*		codorniz bolonchaco	Special Concern
Singing Quail	*Dactylortyx thoracicus*		codorniz silbadora	Special Concern
Montezuma Quail	*Cyrtonyx montezumae*		codorniz Moctezuma	Special Concern
Montezuma Quail	*Cyrtonyx montezumae*	sallaei	codorniz Moctezuma pacífica	Threatened
Ocellated Quail	*Cyrtonyx ocellatus*		codorniz ocelada	Threatened
Yellow Rail	*Coturnicops noveboracensis*	goldmani	polluela amarilla	Endangered
Black Rail	*Laterallus jamaicensis*	coturniculus	polluela negra	Endangered
Clapper Rail	*Rallus longirostris*		rascón picudo	Special Concern
Clapper Rail	*Rallus longirostris*	levipes	rascón picudo californiano	Endangered
Clapper Rail	*Rallus longirostris*	yumanensis	rascón picudo de Arizona	Threatened
King Rail	*Rallus elegans*		rascón real	Special Concern
King Rail	*Rallus elegans*	tenuirostris	rascón real	Endangered
Virginia Rail	*Rallus limicola*		rascón limícola	Special Concern
Rufous-necked Wood-Rail	*Aramides axillaris*		rascón cuello rufo	Threatened
Uniform Crake	*Amaurolimnas concolor*		rascón café	Threatened
Yellow-breasted Crake	*Porzana flaviventer*		polluela pecho amarillo	Special Concern
Sungrebe	*Heliornis fulica*		pájaro cantil	Special Concern
Sunbittern	*Eurypyga helias*		ave sol	Endangered
Sandhill Crane	*Grus canadensis*		grulla gris	Special Concern
Whooping Crane	*Grus americana*		grulla blanca	Endangered
Piping Plover	*Charadrius melodus*		chorlo chiflador	Endangered
Mountain Plover	*Charadrius montanus*		chorlo llanero	Threatened
Eskimo Curlew	*Numenius borealis*		zarapito boreal	Endangered
Heermann's Gull	*Larus heermanni*		gaviota ploma	Special Concern
Yellow-footed Gull	*Larus livens*		gaviota pata amarilla	Special Concern
Elegant Tern	*Thalasseus elegans*		charrán elegante	Special Concern
Roseate Tern	*Sterna dougallii*		charrán rosado	Special Concern
Least Tern	*Sterna antillarum*	browni	charrán mínimo de Guerrero	Endangered
Least Tern	*Sternula antillarum*		charrán mínimo	Special Concern
Bridled Tern	*Onychoprion anaethetus*	nelsoni	charrán embridado guerrerense	Special Concern
Xantus's Murrelet	*Synthliboramphus hypoleucus*		mérgulo de Xantus	Endangered

English Common Name	Scientific Name	Subspecies	Mexican Common Name	Category
Craveri's Murrelet	*Synthliboramphus craveri*		mérgulo de Craveri	Threatened
Cassin's Auklet	*Ptychoramphus aleuticus*	aleuticus	alcuela oscura	Threatened
Pale-vented Pigeon	*Patagioenas cayennensis*	pallidicrissa	paloma colorada	Special Concern
Scaled Pigeon	*Patagioenas speciosa*		paloma escamosa	Special Concern
White-crowned Pigeon	*Patagioenas leucocephala*		paloma corona blanca	Threatened
Band-tailed Pigeon	*Patagioenas fasciata*	vioscae	paloma de collar de La Laguna	Special Concern
Short-billed Pigeon	*Patagioenas nigrirostris*		paloma triste	Special Concern
Zenaida Dove	*Zenaida aurita*		paloma aurita	Special Concern
Socorro Dove	*Zenaida graysoni*		paloma de Socorro	Extirpated
Passenger Pigeon	*Ectopistes migratorius*		paloma viajera	Extirpated
Common Ground-Dove	*Columbina passerina*	socorroensis	tórtola coquita de Socorro	Threatened
Maroon-chested Ground-Dove	*Claravis mondetoura*		tórtola pecho morado	Threatened
White-tipped Dove	*Leptotila verreauxi*	capitalis	paloma arroyera de Tres Marías	Special Concern
White-faced Quail-Dove	*Geotrygon albifacies*		paloma-perdiz cara blanca	Threatened
Tuxtla Quail-Dove	*Geotrygon carrikeri*		paloma-perdiz tuxtleña	Endangered
Green Parakeet	*Aratinga holochlora*		perico mexicano	Threatened
Green Parakeet	*Aratinga holochlora*	brevipes	perico de Socorro	Threatened
Green Parakeet	*Aratinga holochlora*	brewsteri	perico del noroeste	Endangered
Pacific Parakeet	*Aratinga strenua*		perico centroamericano	Threatened
Olive-throated Parakeet	*Aratinga nana*		perico pecho sucio	Special Concern
Orange-fronted Parakeet	*Aratinga canicularis*		perico frente naranja	Special Concern
Military Macaw	*Ara militaris*		guacamaya verde	Endangered
Scarlet Macaw	*Ara macao*		guacamaya roja	Endangered
Thick-billed Parrot	*Rhynchopsitta pachyrhyncha*		cotorra-serrana occidental	Endangered
Maroon-fronted Parrot	*Rhynchopsitta terrisi*		cotorra-serrana oriental	Threatened
Barred Parakeet	*Bolborhynchus lineola*		perico barrado	Threatened
Mexican Parrotlet	*Forpus cyanopygius*		perico catarina	Special Concern
Mexican Parrotlet	*Forpus cyanopygius*	insularis	perico catarina de las Islas Marías	Threatened
Orange-chinned Parakeet	*Brotogeris jugularis*		perico ala amarilla	Threatened
Brown-hooded Parrot	*Pionopsitta haematotis*		loro cabeza oscura	Threatened
White-crowned Parrot	*Pionus senilis*		loro corona blanca	Threatened
Yellow-lored Parrot	*Amazona xantholora*		loro yucateco	Special Concern
Red-crowned Parrot	*Amazona viridigenalis*		loro tamaulipeco	Endangered
Lilac-crowned Parrot	*Amazona finschi*		loro corona lila	Threatened
Mealy Parrot	*Amazona farinosa*		loro corona azul	Threatened
Yellow-headed Parrot	*Amazona oratrix*		loro cabeza amarilla	Endangered
Yellow-headed Parrot	*Amazona oratrix*	tresmariae	loro cabeza amarilla de las Islas Tres Marías	Threatened
Yellow-naped Parrot	*Amazona auropalliata*		loro nuca amarilla	Endangered
Greater Ani	*Crotophaga major*		garrapatero mayor	Extirpated
Smooth-billed Ani	*Crotophaga ani*		garrapatero pico liso	Threatened
Groove-billed Ani	*Crotophaga sulcirostris*	pallidula	garrapatero pijuy de Los Cabos	Extirpated
Eastern Screech-Owl	*Megascops asio*		tecolote oriental	Special Concern
Balsas (Western) Screech-Owl	*Megascops seductus*		tecolote del Balsas	Special Concern
Pacific (Western) Screech-Owl	*Megascops cooperi*		tecolote de Cooper	Special Concern
Bearded (Bridled) Screech-Owl	*Megascops barbarus*		tecolote barbudo	Threatened
Crested Owl	*Lophostrix cristata*		búho cuerno blanco	Threatened
Spectacled Owl	*Pulsatrix perspicillata*		búho de anteojos	Threatened
Great Horned Owl	*Bubo virginianus*	mayensis	búho cornudo	Threatened
Northern Pygmy-Owl	*Glaucidium gnoma*	hoskinsii	tecolote serrano	Special Concern
Central American Pygmy-Owl	*Glaucidium griseiceps*		tecolote mesoamericano	Special Concern
Tamaulipas Pygmy-Owl	*Glaucidium sanchezi*		tecolote tamaulipeco	Endangered
Colima Pygmy-Owl	*Glaucidium palmarum*	griscomi	tecolote del Balsas	Special Concern
Elf Owl	*Micrathene whitneyi*	graysoni	tecolote enano	Extirpated
Burrowing Owl	*Athene cunicularia*	rostrata	tecolote llanero de Isla Clarión	Endangered
Black-and-white Owl	*Ciccaba nigrolineata*		búho blanquinegro	Threatened
Spotted Owl	*Strix occidentalis*		búho manchado	Threatened
Barred Owl	*Strix varia*		búho listado	Special Concern
Fulvous Owl	*Strix fulvescens*		búho leonado	Threatened
Stygian Owl	*Asio stygius*		búho cara oscura	Special Concern
Short-eared Owl	*Asio flammeus*		búho cuerno corto	Special Concern
Striped Owl	*Pseudoscops clamator*		búho cara clara	Threatened

English Common Name	Scientific Name	Subspecies	Mexican Common Name	Category
Unspotted Saw-whet Owl	*Aegolius ridgwayi*		tecolote canelo	Threatened
Eared Poorwill	*Nyctiphrynus mcleodii*		tapacamino prío	Special Concern
Great Potoo	*Nyctibius grandis*		bienparado mayor	Threatened
White-fronted Swift	*Cypseloides storeri*		vencejo frente blanca	Special Concern
White-naped Swift	*Streptoprocne semicollaris*		vencejo nuca blanca	Special Concern
Lesser Swallow-tailed Swift	*Panyptila cayennensis*		vencejo-tijereta menor	Special Concern
Great Swallow-tailed Swift	*Panyptila sanctihieronymi*		vencejo-tijereta mayor	Special Concern
Little Hermit	*Pygmornis longuemareus*		ermitaño enano	Special Concern
Long-tailed Sabrewing	*Campylopterus excellens*		fandanguero cola larga	Special Concern
Rufous Sabrewing	*Campylopterus rufus*		fandanguero rojizo	Special Concern
Emerald-chinned Hummingbird	*Abeillia abeillei*		colibrí pico corto	Special Concern
Short-crested (Rufous-crested) Coquette	*Lophornis brachylophus*		coqueta cresta corta	Endangered
Black-crested Coquette	*Lophornis helenae*		coqueta cresta negra	Special Concern
Broad-billed Hummingbird	*Cynanthus latirostris*	lawrencei	colibrí pico ancho de Tres Marías	Special Concern
Mexican Woodnymph	*Thalurania ridgwayi*		ninfa mexicana	Special Concern
Cinnamon Hummingbird	*Amazilia rutila*	graysoni	colibrí canela de Tres Marías	Special Concern
Green-fronted Hummingbird	*Amazilia viridifrons*		colibrí frente verde	Threatened
Blue-capped Hummingbird	*Eupherusa cyanophrys*		colibrí oaxaqueño	Threatened
White-tailed Hummingbird	*Eupherusa poliocerca*		colibrí cola blanca	Threatened
Green-throated Mountain-gem	*Lampornis viridipallens*		colibrí garganta verde	Special Concern
Garnet-throated Hummingbird	*Lamprolaima rhami*		colibrí ala castaña	Threatened
Purple-crowned Fairy	*Heliothryx barroti*		hada enmascarada	Special Concern
Long-billed Starthroat	*Heliomaster longirostris*		colibrí pico largo	Special Concern
Slender Sheartail	*Doricha enicura*		colibrí tijereta	Special Concern
Mexican Sheartail	*Doricha eliza*		colibrí cola hendida	Endangered
Sparkling-tailed Hummingbird	*Tilmatura dupontii*		colibrí cola pinta	Threatened
Wine-throated Hummingbird	*Atthis ellioti*		zumbador magenta	Threatened
Collared Trogon	*Trogon collaris*		trogón de collar	Special Concern
Slaty-tailed Trogon	*Trogon massena*		trogón cola oscura	Threatened
Eared Quetzal	*Euptilotis neoxenus*		trogón orejón	Threatened
Resplendent Quetzal	*Pharomachrus mocinno*		quetzal mesoamericano	Endangered
Tody Motmot	*Hylomanes momotula*		momoto enano	Threatened
Blue-throated Motmot	*Aspatha gularis*		momoto garganta azul	Threatened
Keel-billed Motmot	*Electron carinatum*		momoto pico quilla	Endangered
White-necked Puffbird	*Notharchus macrorhynchos*		buco de collar	Threatened
White-whiskered Puffbird	*Malacoptila panamensis*		buco barbón	Threatened
Rufous-tailed Jacamar	*Galbula ruficauda*		jacamar cola rufa	Threatened
Emerald Toucanet	*Aulacorhynchus prasinus*		tucaneta verde, tucanete esmeralda	Special Concern
Emerald Toucanet	*Aulacorhynchus prasinus*	warneri	tucaneta verde de Los Tuxtlas Veracruz	Threatened
Collared Aracari	*Pteroglossus torquatus*		arasari de collar	Special Concern
Keel-billed Toucan	*Ramphastos sulfuratus*		tucán pico canoa, tucán pecho azufrado	Threatened
Acorn Woodpecker	*Melanerpes formicivorus*	angustifrons	carpintero bellotero de La Laguna	Special Concern
Strickland's Woodpecker	*Picoides stricklandi*		carpintero de Strickland	Special Concern
Northern Flicker	*Colaptes auratus*	rufipileus	carpintero de pechera de Guadalupe	Extirpated
Chestnut-colored Woodpecker	*Celeus castaneus*		carpintero castaño	Special Concern
Pale-billed Woodpecker	*Campephilus guatemalensis*		carpintero pico plata	Special Concern
Imperial Woodpecker	*Campephilus imperialis*		carpintero imperial	Extirpated
Buff-throated Foliage-gleaner	*Automolus ochrolaemus*		breñero garganta pálida	Special Concern
Ruddy Foliage-gleaner	*Automolus rubiginosus*		breñero rojizo	Threatened
Plain Xenops	*Xenops minutus*		picolezna liso	Special Concern
Tawny-throated Leaftosser	*Sclerurus mexicanus*		hojarasquero pecho rufo	Special Concern
Scaly-throated Leaftosser	*Sclerurus guatemalensis*		hojarasquero oscuro	Special Concern
Tawny-winged Woodcreeper	*Dendrocincla anabatina*		trepatroncos sepia	Special Concern
Wedge-billed Woodcreeper	*Glyphorynchus spirurus*		trepatroncos pico cuña	Special Concern
Strong-billed Woodcreeper	*Xiphocolaptes promeropirhynchus*	omiltemensis	trepatroncos gigante de Omiltemi	Endangered
Northern Barred-Woodcreeper	*Dendrocolaptes sanctithomae*		trepatroncos barrado	Special Concern
Black-banded Woodcreeper	*Dendrocolaptes picumnus*		trepatroncos vientre barrado	Threatened
Spotted Woodcreeper	*Xiphorhynchus erythropygius*		trepatroncos manchado	Threatened
Great Antshrike	*Taraba major*		batará mayor	Special Concern
Russet Antshrike	*Thamnistes anabatinus*		batará café	Special Concern
Plain Antvireo	*Dysithamnus mentalis*		hormiguero sencillo	Special Concern
Slaty Antwren	*Myrmotherula schisticolor*		hormiguero apizarrado	Special Concern

English Common Name	Scientific Name	Subspecies	Mexican Common Name	Category
Dot-winged Antwren	*Microrhopias quixensis*		hormiguero ala punteada	Special Concern
Scaled Antpitta	*Grallaria guatimalensis*		hormiguero-cholino escamoso	Threatened
Yellow-bellied Tyrannulet	*Ornithion semiflavum*		mosquero ceja blanca	Special Concern
Stub-tailed Spadebill	*Platyrinchus cancrominus*		mosquero pico chato	Special Concern
Royal Flycatcher	*Onychorhynchus coronatus*		mosquero real	Endangered
Ruddy-tailed Flycatcher	*Terenotriccus erythrurus*		mosquero cola castaña	Special Concern
Belted Flycatcher	*Xenotriccus callizonus*		mosquero fajado	Threatened
Pileated Flycatcher	*Xenotriccus mexicanus*		mosquero del Balsas	Special Concern
Western Wood-Pewee	*Contopus sordidulus*	peninsulae	pibí de La Laguna	Special Concern
Pacific-slope Flycatcher	*Empidonax difficilis*	cineritius	mosquero de La Laguna	Special Concern
Bright-rumped Attila	*Attila spadiceus*	cozumelae	atila de Cozumel	Special Concern
Flammulated Flycatcher	*Deltarhynchus flammulatus*		papamoscas jaspeado	Special Concern
Speckled Mourner	*Laniocera rufescens*		plañidera jaspeada	Special Concern
Gray-collared Becard	*Pachyramphus major*	uropygialis	mosquero-cabezón mexicano	Special Concern
Lovely Cotinga	*Cotinga amabilis*		cotinga azuleja	Threatened
White-collared Manakin	*Manacus candei*		manaquín cuello blanco	Special Concern
Long-tailed Manakin	*Chiroxiphia linearis*		manaquín cola larga	Special Concern
White-eyed Vireo	*Vireo griseus*	perquisitor	vireo ojo blanco veracruzano	Threatened
Mangrove Vireo	*Vireo pallens*		vireo manglero	Special Concern
Cozumel Vireo	*Vireo bairdi*		vireo de Cozumel	Special Concern
Bell's Vireo	*Vireo bellii*	pusillus	vireo de Bell californiano	Threatened
Black-capped Vireo	*Vireo atricapilla*		vireo gorra negra	Endangered
Dwarf Vireo	*Vireo nelsoni*		vireo enano	Special Concern
Blue-headed Vireo	*Vireo solitarius*	lucasanus	vireo anteojillo de La Laguna	Special Concern
Hutton's Vireo	*Vireo huttoni*	cognatus	vireo reyezuelo de La Laguna	Special Concern
Warbling Vireo	*Vireo gilvus*	victoriae	vireo gorjeador de La Laguna	Special Concern
Tawny-crowned Greenlet	*Hylophilus ochraceiceps*		verdillo ocre	Special Concern
Rufous-browed Peppershrike	*Cyclarhis gujanensis*	insularis	vireón ceja rufa de Cozumel	Special Concern
Tufted Jay	*Cyanocorax dickeyi*		chara pinta	Endangered
Purplish-backed Jay	*Cyanocorax beecheii*		chara de Beechy	Threatened
Azure-hooded Jay	*Cyanolyca cucullata*		chara gorro azul	Threatened
Black-throated Jay	*Cyanolyca pumilo*		chara de niebla	Threatened
Dwarf Jay	*Cyanolyca nana*		chara enana	Endangered
White-throated Jay	*Cyanolyca mirabilis*		chara garganta blanca	Endangered
Unicolored Jay	*Aphelocoma unicolor*		chara unicolor	Threatened
Clark's Nutcracker	*Nucifraga columbiana*		cascanueces	Endangered
Sinaloa Martin	*Progne sinaloae*		golondrina sinaloense	Special Concern
Black-capped Swallow	*Notiochelidon pileata*		golondrina gorra negra	Special Concern
Oak Titmouse	*Baeolophus inornatus*	cineraceus	carbonero sencillo de La Laguna	Special Concern
Bushtit	*Psaltriparus minimus*	grindae	sastrecillo de La Laguna	Special Concern
Red-breasted Nuthatch	*Sitta canadensis*		sita de Guadalupe	Extirpated
White-breasted Nuthatch	*Sitta carolinensis*	lagunae	sita pecho blanco de La Laguna	Special Concern
Giant Wren	*Campylorhynchus chiapensis*		matraca chiapaneca	Special Concern
Rufous-naped Wren	*Campylorhynchus rufinucha*	rufinucha	matraca nuca rufa del sureste	Threatened
Yucatan Wren	*Campylorhynchus yucatanicus*		matraca yucateca	Endangered
Rock Wren	*Salpinctes obsoletus*	guadeloupensis	chivirín saltarroca de Guadalupe	Endangered
Rock Wren	*Salpinctes obsoletus*	tenuirostris	chivirín saltarroca de San Benito	Threatened
Rock Wren	*Salpinctes obsoletus*	exsul	chivirín saltarroca de San Benedicto	Extirpated
Sumichrast's Wren	*Hylorchilus sumichrasti*		chivirín de Sumichrast	Threatened
Nava's Wren	*Hylorchilus navai*		chivirín de Nava	Endangered
Happy Wren	*Thryothorus felix*	lawrencei	chivirín feliz de Tres Marías	Special Concern
Bewick's Wren	*Thryomanes bewickii*	brevicauda	chivirín cola oscura de Guadalupe	Extirpated
Socorro Wren	*Troglodytes sissonii*		chivirín de Socorro	Endangered
House Wren	*Troglodytes aedon*	beani	chivirín saltapared de Cozumel	Special Concern
Clarion Wren	*Troglodytes tanneri*		chivirín de Clarión	Endangered
American Dipper	*Cinclus mexicanus*		mirlo-acuático norteamericano	Special Concern
Ruby-crowned Kinglet	*Regulus calendula*	obscurus	reyezuelo de rojo de Guadalupe	Endangered
California Gnatcatcher	*Polioptila californica*	atwoodi	perlita californiana	Threatened
Tropical Gnatcatcher	*Polioptila plumbea*		perlita tropical	Special Concern
Townsend's Solitaire	*Myadestes townsendi*		clarín norteño	Special Concern
Brown-backed Solitaire	*Myadestes occidentalis*		clarín jilguero	Special Concern
Slate-colored Solitaire	*Myadestes unicolor*		clarín unicolor	Threatened

English Common Name	Scientific Name	Subspecies	Mexican Common Name	Category
Ruddy-capped Nightingale-Thrush	*Catharus frantzii*		zorzal de Frantzius	Threatened
Black-headed Nightingale-Thrush	*Catharus mexicanus*		zorzal corona negra	Special Concern
Spotted Nightingale-Thrush	*Catharus dryas*		zorzal pecho amarillo	Threatened
Black Robin	*Turdus infuscatus*		mirlo negro	Threatened
Mountain Robin	*Turdus plebejus*		mirlo plebeyo	Special Concern
Rufous-backed Robin	*Turdus rufopalliatus*	graysoni	mirlo dorso rufo de las Islas Marías	Special Concern
American Robin	*Turdus migratorius*	confinis	mirlo primavera de La Laguna	Special Concern
Aztec Thrush	*Ridgwayia pinicola*		mirlo pinto	Special Concern
Socorro Mockingbird	*Mimus graysoni*		centzontle de Socorro	Endangered
Cozumel Thrasher	*Toxostoma guttatum*		cuitlacoche de Cozumel	Endangered
Blue Mockingbird	*Melanotis caerulescens*	longirostris	mulato azul	Special Concern
Colima Warbler	*Vermivora crissalis*		chipe crisal	Special Concern
Tropical Parula	*Parula pitiayumi*	insularis	parula de las Islas Marías	Endangered
Tropical Parula	*Parula pitiayumi*	graysoni	parula de Socorro	Special Concern
Yellow-rumped Warbler	*Dendroica coronata*	goldmani	chipe coronado guatemalteco	Threatened
Golden-cheeked Warbler	*Dendroica chrysoparia*		chipe mejilla dorada	Threatened
Swainson's Warbler	*Limnothlypis swainsonii*		chipe corona café	Special Concern
MacGillivray's Warbler	*Oporornis tolmiei*		chipe de Potosí	Threatened
Belding's Yellowthroat	*Geothlypis beldingi*		mascarita peninsular	Endangered
Altamira Yellowthroat	*Geothlypis flavovelata*		mascarita de Altamira	Threatened
Black-polled Yellowthroat	*Geothlypis speciosa*		mascarita transvolcánica	Endangered
Pink-headed Warbler	*Ergaticus versicolor*		chipe rosado	Endangered
Red-breasted Chat	*Granatellus venustus*	francescae	granatelo de las Islas Marías	Special Concern
Common Bush-Tanager	*Chlorospingus ophthalmicus*	wetmorei	chinchinero de Los Tuxtlas	Special Concern
Gray-headed Tanager	*Eucometis penicillata*		tángara cabeza gris	Special Concern
Black-throated Shrike-Tanager	*Lanio aurantius*		tángara garganta negra	Special Concern
Olive-backed Euphonia	*Euphonia goüldi*		eufonia olivácea	Special Concern
White-vented Euphonia	*Euphonia minuta*		eufonia vientre blanco	Special Concern
Azure-rumped Tanager	*Tangara cabanisi*		tángara chiapaneca	Endangered
Shining Honeycreeper	*Cyanerpes lucidus*		mielero brillante	Special Concern
Blue Seedeater	*Amaurospiza concolor*		semillero azulgris	Special Concern
Slaty Finch	*Haplospiza rustica*		semillero pizarra	Special Concern
Chestnut-capped Brush-Finch	*Buarremon brunneinucha*	apertus	atlapetes gorra castaña de Los Tuxtlas	Special Concern
Prevost's Ground-Sparrow	*Melozone biarcuata*		rascador patilludo	Special Concern
White-eared Ground-Sparrow	*Melozone leucotis*		rascador oreja blanca	Special Concern
Eastern Towhee	*Pipilo erythrophthalmus*	consobrinus	toquí pinto de Guadalupe	Extirpated
Eastern Towhee	*Pipilo erythrophthalmus*	socorrensis	toquí pinto de Socorro	Endangered
Eastern Towhee	*Pipilo erythrophthalmus*	magnirostris	toquí pinto de La Laguna	Special Concern
Cinnamon-tailed Sparrow	*Aimophila sumichrasti*		zacatonero istmeño	Endangered
Rufous-crowned Sparrow	*Aimophila ruficeps*	sanctorum	zacatonero rojizo de Todos Santos	Extirpated
Oaxaca Sparrow	*Aimophila notosticta*		zacatonero oaxaqueño	Special Concern
Savannah Sparrow	*Passerculus sandwichensis*	beldingi	gorrión sabanero	Threatened
Savannah Sparrow	*Passerculus sandwichensis*	rostratus	gorrión sabanero	Special Concern
Worthen's Sparrow	*Spizella wortheni*		gorrión de Worthen	Threatened
Black-throated Sparrow	*Amphispiza bilineata*	carmenae	zacatonero garganta negra	Threatened
Black-throated Sparrow	*Amphispiza bilineata*	tortugae	zacatonero garganta negra de Tortuga	Threatened
Savannah Sparrow	*Passerculus sandwichensis*	sanctorum	gorrión sabanero de San Benito	Threatened
Sierra Madre Sparrow	*Xenospiza baileyi*		gorrión serrano	Endangered
Song Sparrow	*Melospiza melodia*	coronatorum	gorrión cantor de Coronados	Endangered
Dark-eyed Junco	*Junco hyemalis*	insularis	junco ojo oscuro	Endangered
Yellow-eyed Junco	*Junco phaeonotus*	bairdi	junco ojo de lumbre de La Laguna	Special Concern
Yellow-eyed Junco	*Junco phaeonotus*	alticola	junco ojo de lumbre del Tacaná	Special Concern
Northern Cardinal	*Cardinalis cardinalis*	mariae	cardenal rojo de Tres Marías	Special Concern
Rose-bellied Bunting	*Passerina rositae*		colorín azulrosa	Threatened
Slender-billed Grackle	*Quiscalus palustris*		zanate de Lerma	Extirpated
Bar-winged Oriole	*Icterus maculialatus*		bolsero guatemalteco	Special Concern
Orchard Oriole	*Icterus spurius*	fuertesi	bolsero castaño del noreste	Special Concern
Streak-backed Oriole	*Icterus pustulatus*	graysoni	bolsero dorso rayado de las Islas Marías	Special Concern
Chestnut-headed Oropendola	*Psarocolius wagleri*		oropéndola cabeza castaña	Special Concern
Montezuma Oropendola	*Psarocolius montezuma*		oropéndola Moctezuma	Special Concern
House Finch	*Carpodacus mexicanus*	clementis	pinzón de San Clemente	Endangered
House Finch	*Carpodacus mexicanus*	mcgregori	pinzón del Mar de Cortez	Extirpated
House Finch	*Carpodacus mexicanus*	amplus	pinzón de Guadalupe	Endangered
Pine Siskin	*Carduelis pinus*	perplexus	jilguero pinero de Chiapas	Special Concern
Black-capped Siskin	*Carduelis atriceps*		jilguero corona negra	Special Concern

Appendix IV
Agencies and Organizations Involved in Bird Conservation

GOVERNMENT AGENCIES

US Bureau of Land Management
1849 C Street NW
Washington, DC 20240
www.blm.gov

US Department of Commerce
1401 Constitution Avenue, NW
Washington, DC 20230
202-482-2000
www.commerce.gov

US Department of Defense
Directorate for Public Inquiry and Analysis
Office of the Secretary of Defense (Public Affairs)
Room 3A750–The Pentagon
1400 Defense Pentagon
Washington, DC 20301-1400
703-545-6700
www.defenselink.mil

US Department of Transportation
400 7th Street SW, Washington DC 20590
202-366-4000
www.dot.gov

US Environmental Protection Agency
Ariel Rios Building
1200 Pennsylvania Avenue NW
Washington, DC 20460
202-272-0167
www.epa.gov

US Federal Aviation Association (Under DOT)
800 Independence Avenue SW
Washington, DC 20591
866-TELL-FAA (866-835-5322)
www.faa.gov

US Fish & Wildlife Service
Division of Public Affairs
1849 C Street NW,
Room 3359
Washington, DC 20240-0001
202-208-4131
800-344-WILD
www.fws.gov

US Forest Service
1400 Independence Avenue SW
Washington, DC 20250-0003
202-205-8333
www.fs.fed.us

US National Oceanic and Atmospheric Administration
14th Street & Constitution Avenue NW
Room 6217
Washington, DC 20230
202-482-6090
www.noaa.gov

US Natural Resources Conservation Service
Attn: Conservation Communications Staff
PO Box 2890
Washington, DC 20013

USDA, NRCS, Office of the Chief
14th and Independence Avenue SW,
Room 5105-A
Washington, DC 20250
202-720-7246
www.nrcs.usda.gov

Environment Canada
70 Crémazie Street,
Gatineau, Quebec K1A 0H3
819-997-2800 or 1-800-668-6767
www.ec.gc.ca

SEMARNAP, Environment, Natural Resources, and Fisheries Ministry of Mexico
http://www.semarnap.gob.mx/

NORTH AMERICAN NONPROFIT ORGANIZATIONS

American Birding Association
4945 N 30th Street, Suite 200
Colorado Springs, CO 80919
member@aba.org;
800-850-2473 or 719-578-9703 / fax 719-578-1480
www.americanbirding.org

American Bird Conservancy
PO Box 249
The Plains, VA 20198
540-253-5780
www.abcbirds.org

Bird Conservation Alliance
www.birdconservationalliance.org

Bird Conservation Network
5225 Old Orchard Road, Suite 37
Skokie, IL 60077
847-965-1150
www.bcnbirds.org

BirdPAC
719 G Street SE, Suite 1
Washington, DC 20003
202-549-1032
www.birdpac.org

Bird Studies Canada
PO Box 160
Port Rowan, ON N0E 1M0
1-888-448-BIRD
www.bsc-eoc.org

Boreal Songbird Initiative
1904 Third Avenue, Suite 305
Seattle, WA 98101
206-956-9040
www.borealbirds.org

Canadian Boreal Initiative
249 McLeod Street
Ottawa, ON
Canada K2P 1A1
613-230-4739
www.borealcanada.ca

Canadian Parks and Wilderness Society
National Office
250 City Centre Avenue, Suite 506
Ottawa, ON K1R 6K7
613-569-7226 or 800-333-WILD (9453)

Connecticut Audubon Society
2325 Burr Street
Fairfield, CT 06824
203-259-6305
www.ctaudubon.org

Cornell Lab of Ornithology
159 Sapsucker Woods Road
Ithaca, NY 14850
800-843-BIRD (1-800-843-2473)
www.birds.cornell.edu

Defenders of Wildlife
Membership Services
1130 17th Street NW
Washington, DC 20036
800-385-9712
www.defenders.org

Ducks Unlimited, Inc.
One Waterfowl Way
Memphis, TN 38120
800-45DUCKS or 901-758-3825
www.ducks.org

Ducks Unlimited Canada
PO Box 1160
Stonewall, MB
R0C 2Z0
800-665-DUCK (3825)
www.ducks.ca

Environmental Defense Fund
257 Park Avenue South
New York, NY 10010
212-505-2100
www.environmentaldefense.org

Forest Ethics
One Haight Street
San Francisco, CA 94102
415-863-4563
www.forestethics.org

Great Lakes Bird Conservation
www.uwgb.edu/birds/greatlakes

Hawk Mountain Sanctuary
1700 Hawk Mountain Road
Kempton, PA 19529
610-756-6961
www.hawkmountain.org

HawkWatch International
1800 South West Temple, #226
Salt Lake City, UT 84115
801-484-6808
www.hawkwatch.org

Institute for Bird Populations
PO Box 1346
11435 S.R.#1, Suite 23
Point Reyes Station, CA 94956
www.birdpop.org

International Association of Fish and Wildlife Agencies
444 North Capitol Street NW
Suite 725
Washington, DC 20001
202-624-7890
info@iafwa.org
www.iafwa.org

Land Trust Alliance
1331 H Street NW, Suite 400
Washington DC 20005-4734
202-638-4725
lta@lta.org
www.lta.org

Manomet Center for Conservation Science
81 Stage Road, P.O. Box 1770
Manomet, MA 02345
508-224-6521
www.manomet.org

Massachusetts Audubon Society
208 South Great Road
Lincoln, MA 01773
781-259-9500
800-AUDUBON

National Audubon Society
700 Broadway
New York, NY 10003
212-979-3000
www.audubon.org

National Fish and Wildlife Foundation
1120 Connecticut Avenue NW,
   Suite 900
Washington, DC 20036
202-857-0166
www.nfwf.org

National Wildlife Federation
11100 Wildlife Center Drive
Reston, VA 20190-5362
800-822-9919
www.nwf.org

The Nature Conservancy
4245 North Fairfax Drive, Suite 100
Arlington, VA 22203-1606
703-841-5300
http://nature.org

Nature Canada
85 Albert Street, Suite 900
Ottawa, ON K1P 6A4
613-562-3447 or 800-267-4088
www.cnf.ca

Natural Resources Defense Council
40 West 20th Street
New York, NY 10011
212-727-2700
www.nrdc.org

New Hampshire Audubon
3 Silk Farm Road
Concord, NH 03301
603-224-9909
asnh@nhaudubon.org
www.nhaudubon.org

New Jersey Audubon Society
9 Hardscrabble Road
PO Box 126
Bernardsville, NJ 07924
908-204-8998
hq@njaudubon.org
www.njaudubon.org

Ornithological Society of North America
www.osnabirds.org

The Peregrine Fund
5668 West Flying Hawk Lane
Boise, ID 83709
208-362-3716
www.peregrinefund.org

Rainforest Action Network
221 Pine Street, 5th Floor
San Francisco, CA 94104
415-398-4404
www.ran.org

Rhode Island Audubon Society
Audubon Society of RI Headquarters
12 Sanderson Road
Smithfield, RI 02917

Rhode Island Audubon Society (*cont.*)
401-949-5454
audubon@asri.org
www.asri.org

Sierra Club
National Headquarters
85 Second Street, 2nd Floor
San Francisco, CA 94105
415-977-5500
www.sierraclub.org

Sutton Avian Research Center
PO Box 2007
Bartlesville, OK 74005
918-336-7778
www.suttoncenter.org

Vermont Institute of Natural Science
2723 Church Hill Road
Woodstock, VT 05091
802.457.2779
www.vinsweb.org

Western Hemisphere Reserve Shorebird Network
Manomet Center for Conservation Sciences
PO Box 1770, 81 Stage Point Road,
Manomet, MA 02345
508-224-6521
www.manomet.org/WHSRN

The Wildlife Conservation Society
2300 Southern Boulevard
Bronx, NY 10460
718-220-5100
www.wcs.org

INTERNATIONAL PROGRAMS

Asociación Armonía
PO Box 3566
Santa Cruz de la Sierra
Bolivia
+591-3-3568808
http://freespace.virgin.net/susan.armitage/
ARMONIA.HTM

Aves Argentinas—Asociación Ornitológica del Plata
25 de Mayo 749 2°6 (C1002ABO), Buenos Aires,
Argentina

(+54)11-4312-1015 / 2284 / 8958
www.avesargentinas.org.ar

Avina
PO Box 0832-0390 WTC
Panama City, Panama
+[507] 208 9430
www.avina.com

The Bahamas National Trust
PO Box N-4105
Nassau, Bahamas
242-393-1317
http://www.bahamas.gov.bs/bahamasweb/
visitingthebahamas.nsf/subjects/
national+trust

Belize Audubon Society
PO Box 1001, Belize City, Belize
501-223-4985
www.belizeaudubon.org

BirdLife International
Wellbrook Court
Girton Road
Cambridge CB3 0NA, UK
+44 (0)1223 277 318
www.birdlife.org

Birds Without Borders/Aves Sin Fronteras
Zoological Society of Milwaukee
10005 West Blue Mound Road
Milwaukee, WI 53226
414-258-2333
www.zoosociety.org/Conservation/
BWB-ASF/

CIPAMEX
Apartado Postal 77-297,
Lomas de Sotelo, CP 11201,
México, DF
www.iztacala.unam.mx/cipamex/

CONABIO
Avenida Liga Periferico
Insurgentes Sur No. 4903
Col. Parques del Pedregal, Delegacion Tlalpan
14010 Mexico, DF
5528-91-00
www.conabio.gob.mx

Conservation International
1919 M Street NW, Suite 600
Washington, DC 20036
202-912-1000 or 800-406-2306
www.conservation.org/xp/CIWEB/

Greenpeace International
Ottho Heldringstraat 5
1066 AZ Amsterdam
The Netherlands
+31 20 7182000
www.greenpeace.org/international

Guyra Paraguay
Cnel. Franco Nº 381 c/ Leandro Prieto
Asunción, Paraguay
(59521) 227-777 / 229-097
www.guyra.org.py/index1.htm

IUCN (International Union for Conservation of Nature and Natural Resources)
Rue Mauverney 28
Gland 1196
Switzerland
+41 (22) 999-0000
www.iucn.org

Jocotoco Foundation (Ecuador)
John Guarnaccia, US Coordinator
Jocotoco Foundation
1407 Finntown Road
Waldoboro, ME 04572 USA
207-832-7852
www.fjocotoco.org

ProAves Colombia
Carrera 20 Nº 36-61
Bogotá DC, Colombia
(57-1) 3403229 / 3403261 / 2455134
www.proaves.org

SalvaNATURA
33 Avenida Sur No. 640
Colonia Flor Blanca
San Salvador, El Salvador, CA
503-279-1515
www.salvanatura.org

Wetlands International
Postbus 47
6700 AA Wageningen
The Netherlands

+31 (0)317 478854
www.wetlands.org

World Land Trust
Blyth House, Bridge Street
Halesworth, Suffolk
IP19 8AB, UK
+44 (0)1986 874422
www.worldlandtrust.org

World Parks
2806 P Street NW,
Washington, DC 20007
202-333-1044
www.worldparks.org

World Wildlife Fund
U.S. Headquarters
1250 Twenty-Fourth Street NW
PO Box 97180
Washington, DC 20090-7180
202-293-4800
www.worldwildlife.org

BIRD OBSERVATORIES
(complete list at http://www.pwrc.usgs.gov/BBL/
manual/birdobs.htm)

Alaska Bird Observatory
418 Wedgewood Drive
Fairbanks, AK 99701
www.alaskabird.org

Braddock Bay Bird Observatory
PO Box 12876
Rochester, NY 14612
585-234-3525
www.bbbo.org

Cape May Bird Observatory
The Northwood Center
701 East Lake Drive
PO Box 3
Cape May Point, NJ 08212
609-884-2736

Gulf Coast Bird Observatory
103 West Highway 332
Lake Jackson, TX 77566
979-480-0999
www.gcbo.org

Lesser Slave Lake Bird Observatory
Boreal Center for Bird Conservation
PO Box 1076
Slave Lake, AB
Canada TOG2A0
780-849-8240
www.lslbo.org
www.borealbirdcentre.ca

Long Point Bird Observatory
Bird Studies Canada
P.O. Box 160
Port Rowan, ON
Canada N0EIM0
1-888-448-BIRD
www.bsc-eoc.org/lpbo/lpbirdo.html

Point Reyes Bird Observatory
4990 Shoreline Highway
Stinson Beach, CA 94970

415-868-1221
www.prbo.org

Powdermill Avian Research Center
Powdermill Nature Reserve
1847 Route 381
Rector, PA 15677
724-593-7521
www.powdermill.org

Rocky Mountain Bird Observatory
230 Cherry Street
Fort Collins, CO 80521
970-482-1707
www.rmbo.org

Whitefish Point Bird Observatory
16914 North Whitefish Point Road
Paradise, MI 49768-9612
906-492-3596
www.wpbo.org

ILLUSTRATION CREDITS

Emperor Goose (*Chen canagica*) — Mimi Hoppe Wolf
Brant (*Branta bernicla*) — Louise Zemaitis/Swallowtail Studio
Trumpeter Swan (*Cygnus buccinator*) — Shawneen Finnegan
American Black Duck (*Anas rubripes*) — Louise Zemaitis/Swallowtail Studio
Mottled Duck (*Anas fulvigula*) — Louise Zemaitis/Swallowtail Studio
Steller's Eider (*Polysticta stelleri*) — John Sill
Spectacled Eider (*Somateria fischeri*) — Louise Zemaitis/Swallowtail Studio
Greater Sage-Grouse (*Centrocercus urophasianus*) — Mimi Hoppe Wolf
Gunnison Sage-Grouse (*Centrocercus minimus*) — Louise Zemaitis/Swallowtail Studio
"Blue Grouse" (*Dendragapus obscurus*) — Louise Zemaitis/Swallowtail Studio
Greater Prairie-Chicken (*Tympanuchus cupido*) — Mimi Hoppe Wolf
Lesser Prairie-Chicken (*Tympanuchus pallidicinctus*) — John Sill
Montezuma Quail (*Cyrtonyx montezumae*) — Georges Dremeaux
Yellow-billed Loon (*Gavia adamsii*) — Michael O'Brien/Swallowtail Studio
Laysan Albatross (*Phoebastria immutabilis*) — John Sill
Black-footed Albatross (*Phoebastria nigripes*) — Georges Dremeaux
Short-tailed Albatross (*Phoebastria albatrus*) — John Sill
Bermuda Petrel (*Pterodroma cahow*) — Georges Dremeaux
Black-capped Petrel (*Pterodroma hasitata*) — John Sill
Pink-footed Shearwater (*Puffinus creatopus*) — John Sill
Black-vented Shearwater (*Puffinus opisthomelas*) — Shawneen Finnegan
Ashy Storm-Petrel (*Oceanodroma homochroa*) — John Sill
Black Storm-Petrel (*Oceanodroma melania*) — John Sill
Least Storm-Petrel (*Oceanodroma microsoma*) — John Sill
Red-faced Cormorant (*Phalacrocorax urile*) — John Sill
California Condor (*Gymnogyps californianus*) — Mimi Hoppe Wolf
Ferruginous Hawk (*Buteo regalis*) — Louise Zemaitis/Swallowtail Studio
Yellow Rail (*Coturnicops noveboracensis*) — John Sill
Black Rail (*Laterallus jamaicensis*) — Georges Dremeaux
Whooping Crane (*Grus americana*) — Mimi Hoppe Wolf
American Golden-Plover (*Pluvialis dominica*) — Georges Dremeaux
Pacific Golden-Plover (*Pluvialis fulva*) — John Sill
Snowy Plover (*Charadrius alexandrinus*) — Shawneen Finnegan
Piping Plover (*Charadrius melodus*) — Shawneen Finnegan
Mountain Plover (*Charadrius montanus*) — Georges Dremeaux
Eskimo Curlew (*Numenius borealis*) — John Sill
Whimbrel (*Numenius phaeopus*) — John Sill
Bristle-thighed Curlew (*Numenius tahitiensis*) — Shawneen Finnegan
Long-billed Curlew (*Numenius americanus*) — Louise Zemaitis/Swallowtail Studio
Marbled Godwit (*Limosa fedoa*) — Louise Zemaitis/Swallowtail Studio
Surfbird (*Aphriza virgata*) — Louise Zemaitis/Swallowtail Studio
Red Knot (*Calidris canutus*) — Louise Zemaitis/Swallowtail Studio
Buff-breasted Sandpiper (*Tryngites subruficollis*) — Michael O'Brien/Swallowtail Studio
Short-billed Dowitcher (*Limnodromus griseus*) — Michael O'Brien/Swallowtail Studio
American Woodcock (*Scolopax minor*) — Georges Dremeaux
Wilson's Phalarope (*Phalaropus tricolor*) — Georges Dremeaux
Heermann's Gull (*Larus heermanni*) — Shawneen Finnegan
Red-legged Kittiwake (*Rissa brevirostris*) — John Sill
Elegant Tern (*Thalasseus elegans*) — Shawneen Finnegan
Marbled Murrelet (*Brachyramphus marmoratus*) — Shawneen Finnegan

Kittlitz's Murrelet (*Brachyramphus brevirostris*) — Shawneen Finnegan
Xantus's Murrelet (*Synthliboramphus hypoleucus*) — John Sill
Craveri's Murrelet (*Synthliboramphus craveri*) — Shawneen Finnegan
White-crowned Pigeon (*Patagioenas leucocephala*) — Louise Zemaitis/Swallowtail Studio
Green Parakeet (*Aratinga holochlora*) — Mimi Hoppe Wolf
Thick-billed Parrot (*Rhynchopsitta pachyrhyncha*) — Mimi Hoppe Wolf
Red-crowned Parrot (*Amazona viridigenalis*) — Mimi Hoppe Wolf
Spotted Owl (*Strix occidentalis*) — Louise Zemaitis/Swallowtail Studio
Rufous Hummingbird (*Selasphorus rufus*) — Louise Zemaitis/Swallowtail Studio
Red-headed Woodpecker (*Melanerpes erythrocephalus*) — Louise Zemaitis/Swallowtail Studio
Red-cockaded Woodpecker (*Picoides borealis*) — Mimi Hoppe Wolf
Ivory-billed Woodpecker (*Campephilus principalis*) — Dan Lane
Olive-sided Flycatcher (*Contopus cooperi*) — Sophie Webb
Bell's Vireo (*Vireo bellii*) — Mimi Hoppe Wolf
Black-capped Vireo (*Vireo atricapillus*) — Mimi Hoppe Wolf
Gray Vireo (*Vireo vicinior*) — Mimi Hoppe Wolf
Florida Scrub-Jay (*Aphelocoma coerulescens*) — John Fitzpatrick
Island Scrub-Jay (*Aphelocoma insularis*) — Mimi Hoppe Wolf
Pinyon Jay (*Gymnorhinus cyanocephalus*) — Mimi Hoppe Wolf
Brown-headed Nuthatch (*Sitta pusilla*) — Mimi Hoppe Wolf
California Gnatcatcher (*Polioptila californica*) — Mimi Hoppe Wolf
Bicknell's Thrush (*Catharus bicknelli*) — Shawneen Finnegan
Bendire's Thrasher (*Toxostoma bendirei*) — Mimi Hoppe Wolf
Sprague's Pipit (*Anthus spragueii*) — Mimi Hoppe Wolf
Bachman's Warbler (*Vermivora bachmanii*) — Dan Lane
Golden-winged Warbler (*Vermivora chrysoptera*) — John Sill
Virginia's Warbler (*Vermivora virginiae*) — Louise Zemaitis/Swallowtail Studio
Colima Warbler (*Vermivora crissalis*) — Mimi Hoppe Wolf
Lucy's Warbler (*Vermivora luciae*) — Louise Zemaitis/Swallowtail Studio
Golden-cheeked Warbler (*Dendroica chrysoparia*) — Louise Zemaitis/Swallowtail Studio
Grace's Warbler (*Dendroica graciae*) — Louise Zemaitis/Swallowtail Studio
Kirtland's Warbler (*Dendroica kirtlandii*) — Mimi Hoppe Wolf
Prairie Warbler (*Dendroica discolor*) — Louise Zemaitis/Swallowtail Studio
Bay-breasted Warbler (*Dendroica castanea*) — Louise Zemaitis/Swallowtail Studio
Cerulean Warbler (*Dendroica cerulea*) — Louise Zemaitis/Swallowtail Studio
Prothonotary Warbler (*Protonotaria citrea*) — Louise Zemaitis/Swallowtail Studio
Worm-eating Warbler (*Helmitheros vermivorum*) — Louise Zemaitis/Swallowtail Studio
Swainson's Warbler (*Limnothlypis swainsonii*) — John Sill
Kentucky Warbler (*Oporornis formosus*) — Louise Zemaitis/Swallowtail Studio
Canada Warbler (*Wilsonia canadensis*) — Louise Zemaitis/Swallowtail Studio
Bachman's Sparrow (*Aimophila aestivalis*) — Mimi Hoppe Wolf
Brewer's Sparrow (*Spizella breweri*) — Mimi Hoppe Wolf
Baird's Sparrow (*Ammodramus bairdii*) — Michael O'Brien/Swallowtail Studio
Henslow's Sparrow (*Ammodramus henslowii*) — John Sill
Saltmarsh Sharp-tailed Sparrow (*Ammodramus caudacutus*) — Michael O'Brien/Swallowtail Studio
Harris's Sparrow (*Zonotrichia querula*) — Michael O'Brien/Swallowtail Studio
McKay's Bunting (*Plectrophenax hyperboreus*) — Mimi Hoppe Wolf
Painted Bunting (*Passerina ciris*) — Louise Zemaitis/Swallowtail Studio
Tricolored Blackbird (*Agelaius tricolor*) — Mimi Hoppe Wolf
Rusty Blackbird (*Euphagus carolinus*) — Mimi Hoppe Wolf

Index